I0810684

MAGNIFICENT
Trees of Indiana

MAGNIFICENT
Trees of Indiana

Carroll D. Ritter

Purdue University Press | West Lafayette, Indiana

Copyright 2022 by Purdue University. All rights reserved.
Printed in the United States of America.

Cataloging-in-Publication data is on file with the Library of Congress.
Hardback ISBN: 978-1-61249-741-9
ePDF ISBN: 978-1-61249-743-3

Cover image: Towering oaks at Jeremy Keith Oakley Preserve, Lawrence County

Unless otherwise indicated, all photographs are reproduced courtesy of Carroll D. Ritter.

This book is dedicated to my father, who taught me about trees very early in life.

It is further dedicated to my wonderful wife, who traveled around the state with me, supplied many suggestions, and helped to edit the writing.

Lastly, to my talented and supportive sons, who are always there for me, and my grandchildren, who will inherit my love for trees.

Contents

Preface

Trees have always been a passion for me. Their beauty, character, and importance to humankind are worth highest consideration and admiration from all of us. With inspiration from reading many historical accounts of Indiana's great natural heritage, an idea for this broad-based book was created with its emphasis on photography, education, history, use, and protection. It is not intended to be a field guide or duplicate other tree books, rather a fresh approach of looking at Indiana through the lens of its great trees—Past to Present. This one tree book, perhaps your first, just may cover exactly the range to begin your understanding of what Indiana's trees have meant in the past and what they still do for us today.

Acknowledgments

While most of the photos were taken by the author, several are featured by good friend and professional photographer Gary Potts. His creativity and skills were invaluable in rendering the finest possible images for both of us. Of exceptional help in finding the champion trees were the Big Trees Register and the coordinator of the database, Janet Eger, IDNR district forester. Another primary resource was the Trees, Inc. booklet on specimens in Vigo County with Mary Beth Eberwein from Terre Haute most gracious in assisting. At Evansville, Shawn Dickerson, city forester, knew every tree in the county, it seemed, and had photos of many on his computer organized in specific folders. For Owen and Monroe counties, Ralph Unversaw, IDNR district forester, led us to several champions or unique forms. On the NSA Crane base in Martin County, Trent Osmon, base forester, was of assistance, leading the visit to the famous Constitution Grove. At Camp Atterbury, IDNR forester Will Capello guided us to two great trees. Jeremy Beavin, naturalist at Charlestown State Park, showed us the hidden yellow buckeye. John Taylor and Dave LeBlanc of Ball State University were gracious in taking time to tour the historic Ginn Woods. With the Nature Conservancy, good friend and Blue River field office director Allen Pursell was on board to show some remarkable specimens. Division of Nature Preserves regional ecologists Ryan Keller and Jason Larson were very helpful in advising about locations for unique species. Nature Preserves director Ron Hellmich was also very helpful with information. Mike Spalding, IDNR forester, located mysterious yellowwoods for us. Long-time friend John Bacone, former director of the Division of Nature Preserves, went along to several significant locations, as did Cliff Chapman of the Central Indiana Land Trust. Good times were relived. Then we met up with an extraordinary person, Dave Coppert, of Columbus. He has a passion for documenting trees in the Muscatatuck National Wildlife Refuge near Seymour. Dave has found three new state champions there and documented over 250 other trees by GPS and with dimensions. In Lawrence County, John Stambaugh, consultant forester, was very helpful making contacts, giving advice on content, proof-reading, and all-around assistance. For editing and nomenclature, author and good friend Kay Yatskievych was an invaluable help. There were many more wonderful people throughout this process who helped with information and guidance.

Of course, meeting folks who owned some of these big old trees and admired them was a special treat. Generous permission to photograph and talk personally was very rewarding. The absolute love and dedication for their tree was most humbling and inspiring. One gentleman related that he had to stay inside and could not bear watching the arborist cutting down a magnificent old linden tree, despite it being dead and hollow. Others related the many special occasions held by their family under their special tree.

The many donors and supporters for funding of this book are also highly appreciated and without them, this venture would not be possible.

DONORS

The Seib Family
Woodcrest Farm
John P. Stambaugh
G. Michael Schopmeyer, Attorney, Kahn. Dees, Donovan & Kahn, LLP—Evansville
Koetter Woodworking
Jess Gwinn
Indiana Chapter, The Nature Conservancy
Thomas Insurance
Graber and Sons Cabinets
Keith Dunlap
Steve Grubbs
Indiana Chapter, The American Chestnut Foundation
Mininger Carpentry
John Bacone
Good Sports
Mike and Crystal Fidler
JA Benefits
B2B Businesses
Andis Logging, Inc.
Walker Family Trust
Evan, Jessica, Rhettman, and Everest Smith
Trees, Inc., Terre Haute
Salem High School Science Club
Bedford Federal Savings Bank
With gratitude to Lynton Keith Caldwell
In memory of Rudy Savich
River Bend Farm

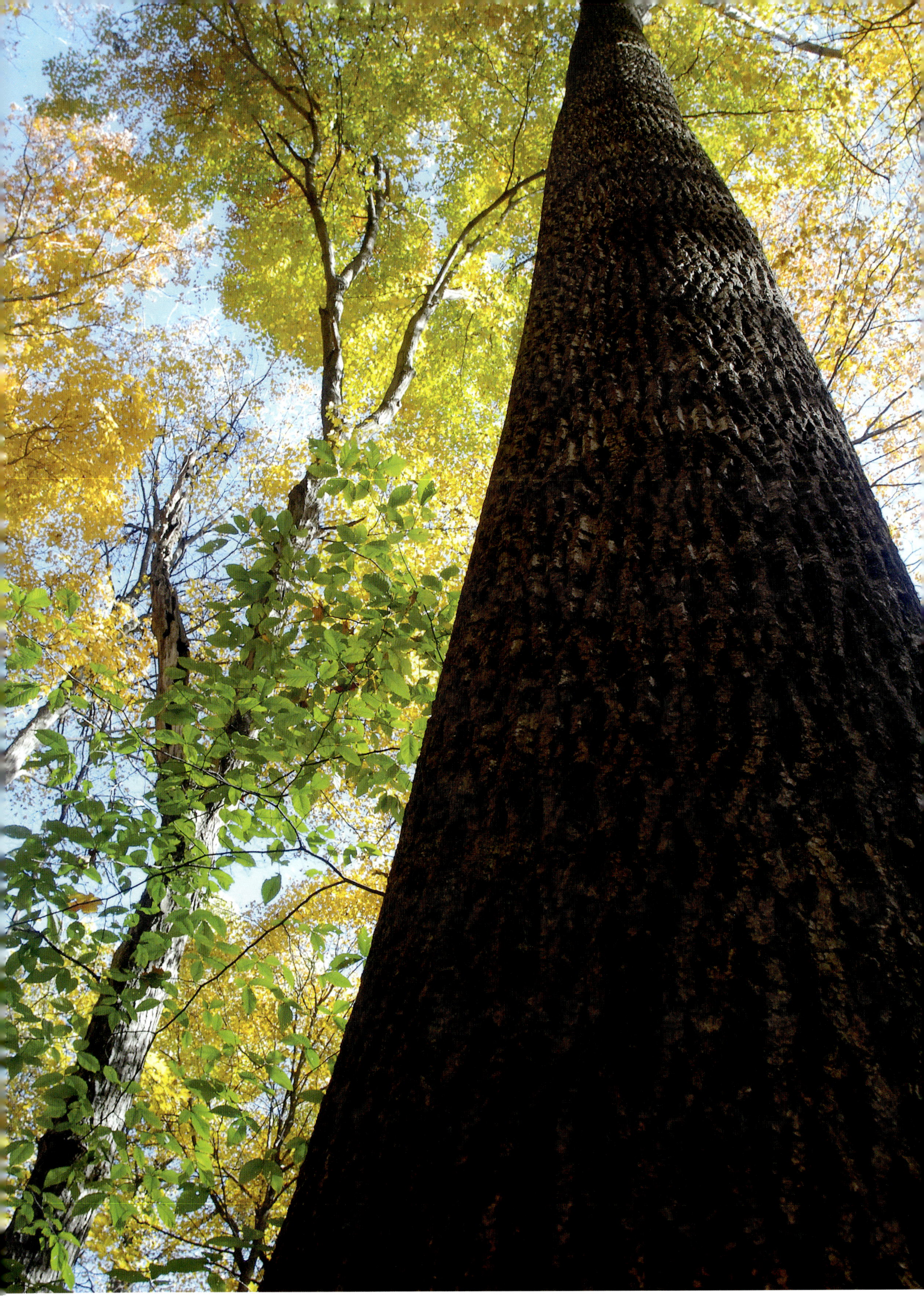

CHAPTER ONE

Past to Present

In the late 1700s and early 1800s when settlers were first entering Indiana, the original woodlands were described as the "finest broadleaved hardwood forests anywhere in the world." Included were many trees that stood 100 to 150 feet tall and 4 to 6 feet in diameter. Sycamores 150 to 200 feet tall and 25 to 30 feet in diameter were common. These observations given by naturalist Robert Ridgway in his "Notes on the Vegetation of the Lower Wabash Valley" (1872) indicate an extraordinary array of magnificent timber not yet cut. His writings during the 1870s–1890 described the stands of timber in that region as "an exceedingly heavy virgin forest, some of the heaviest hardwood forest I have ever seen . . . covering almost the entire floodplain on the Indiana side." Black walnut, highly valuable today, rose to 120 feet, clear of limbs to 60 feet, with a diameter of 7 feet. He gave similar staggering figures about splendid sweet gum, tulip, oaks, pecan, white ash, and others. He later reflected on the great changes that had already happened by the end of the nineteenth century.

Left page: Indiana's state tree is magnificent in all seasons

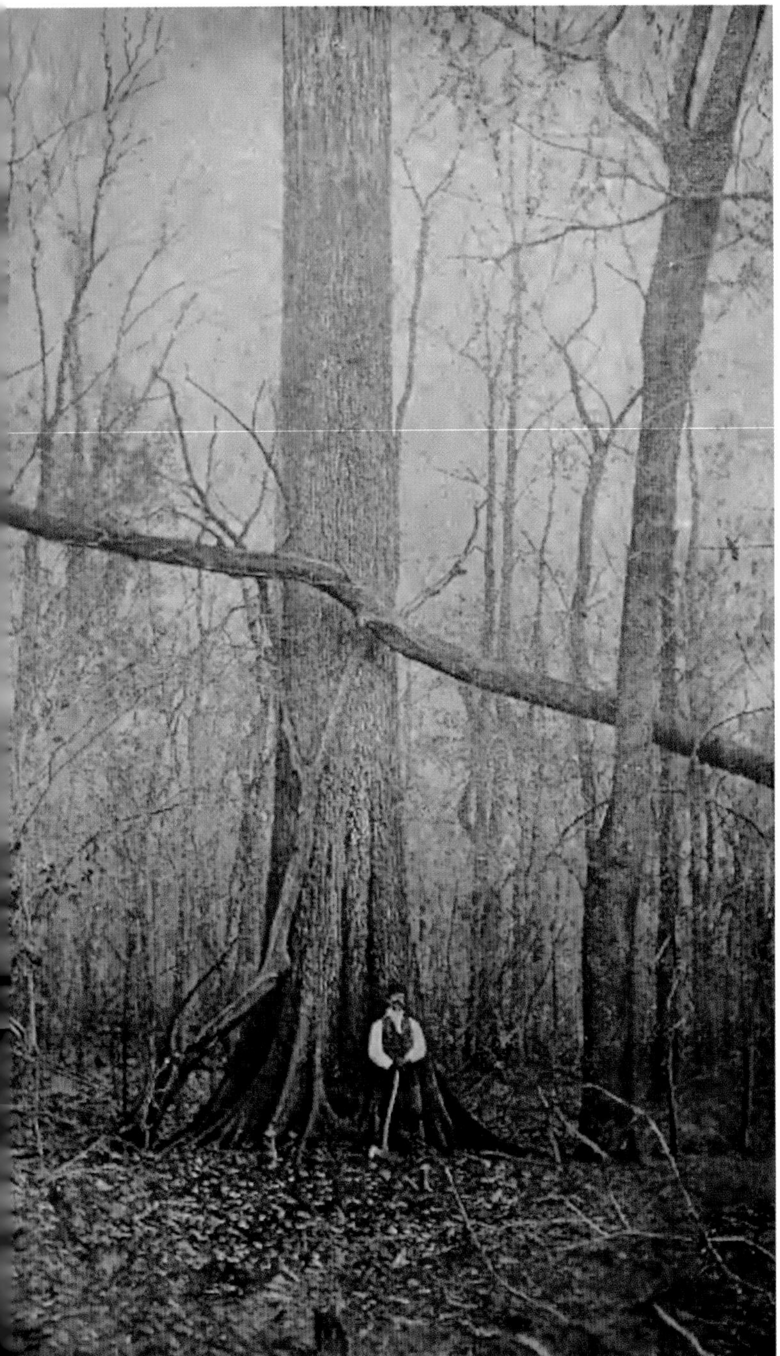

Original Robert Ridgway photo, period 1880–1890
Courtesy of the Indiana Academy of Science

Ridgway (1850–1929) was born in Mount Carmel, Illinois, just across the Wabash River from Gibson County, Indiana. The family later moved to Wheatland, Indiana, east of Vincennes. His interest in nature developed into mastery of trees, shrubs, and birds. Such was his stature in ornithology that he became curator of birds at the Smithsonian in 1886 and retained that title until his death. We remember him as one of the most remarkable naturalists in Indiana history and one whose writings and photographs carry us back to the grandeur of the lower Wabash region, where many trees were awe-inspiring champions.

Ridgway also authored other fascinating papers reflecting on trees and accompanying vegetation. In 1919 he corresponded with Charles C. Deam, Indiana's state forester, reflecting on the original observations he had made in the Wabash areas and the changes over time. A selection of photographs was sent to Deam, who treasured them until his own passing in 1953.

Other exceptional insights into Indiana's early landscape are provided in the journals of William Rector, early surveyor and later one of the first residents of Perry County. His 1805 notes along the line from Clark's Grant, near New Albany, followed a buffalo trail to the Vincennes Tract. As trees were marked along the way, the records indicate sizes and species. Looking at these old notes gives a sense of enchantment, almost allowing you to relive the experiences. It is of interest to see "a beech, 22," "a white oak 18," and so on. Most of the trees on the sheets I inspected also included black oak, tulip, hickory, and even dogwood. Along with these are notations of springs, creeks, and early cabins, such as that of Samuel Hay, along the Little Blue River. Further noted on early surveys were areas of downed timber from windstorms and tornadoes, openings, and barrens. Some evidence also existed of the presence of native people, who lived closely with the land.

Rector's notes were not alone; many journals of early Indiana surveys across the state used denotations of trees as waypoints, markers, and boundary corners. W. B. Crankshaw's PhD research at Purdue University in 1964 included data on more than 60,000 trees that the General Land Office (GLO) surveyors selected as bearing or witness trees to mark section corners during the original survey of land now comprising southern Indiana.

In this wilderness an important event occurred, which needs its own section. It is exceptionally important because it lays out the basis for all new settlements and land ownerships in the Northwest Territory and westward. The location is only a few miles south of one of our remaining old-growth forests at Pioneer Mothers Memorial Forest. A visit there first can prepare you for what it might have been like at this next famous location.

PIVOT POINT (INITIAL POINT), ORANGE COUNTY

A wooden post was driven into the ground on September 1, 1805. Set by Ebenezer Buckingham, Jr., U.S. deputy surveyor, this significant spot is one of the most important locations in Indiana. Then located in wilderness lands of Indiana Territory, it marks the beginning of all land surveys in the state and westward. It was referenced to corners of the Vincennes Tract and also bounded by Indian treaty lines still in existence at that time. There was extensive untamed country to negotiate, especially to arrive at one point in the middle of nowhere. Hills, hollows, cliffs, and creeks had to be crossed. Wild animals were all around, including bears, panthers (probably the cougar), snakes, and insects. Today we cannot conceive of trudging through such wilderness and with risk at every turn. Most likely there were a few settlers in the Indiana Territory, along with occasional Indian encampments, as this was still part of their hunting grounds. The point itself is at the intersection of the Base Line and the 2nd Principal Meridian, both surveyed from then existing survey markers. This new concept of land surveys followed from the Northwest Ordinance of 1787 and eliminated the faults of the metes and bounds method of describing property, which used rocks, trees, or other land features to describe ownership. Our survey system was now to be determined by townships and ranges, those being north-south or east-west of established base lines and meridians.

Today this historical point is still visited by many who recognize its tremendous importance. The location is 6.5 miles south of Paoli, off Highway 37. A sign marks the turnoff. The U.S. Forest Service maintains the site, with a trail downhill to the exact area and a flagged bearing tree nearby as a reference.

A stone post replaced the original wooden one in 1866. Even today there are fairly large trees here, but imagine huge beech, oak, and tuliptrees of the past that must have been in the area. It certainly might be of interest to know what tree was used for making this original famous post! Also noted in records was that the crew did not think

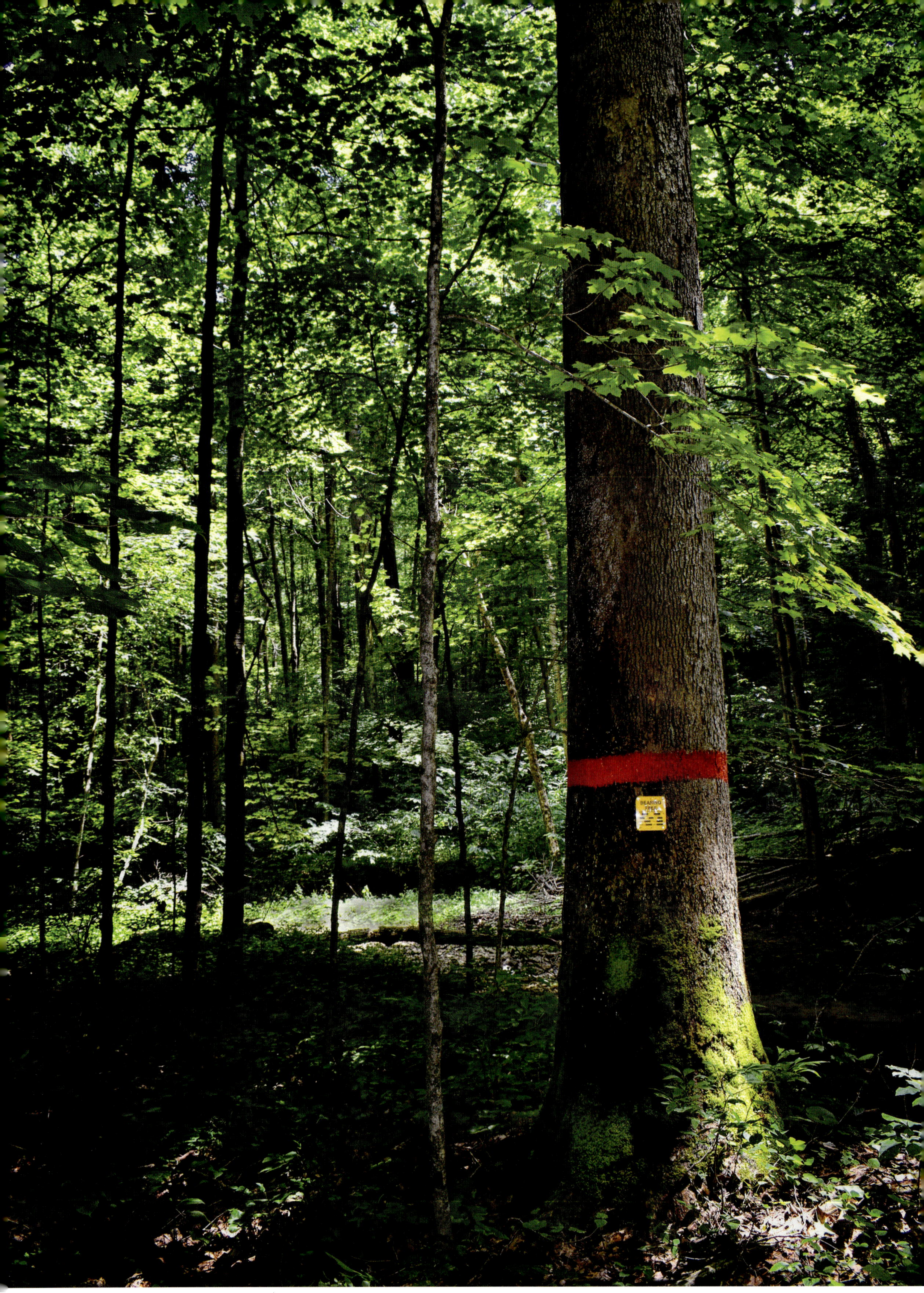
BEARING

much about this as anything so significant then—another day in the wild woods setting points and running lines. Buckingham reportedly traveled only a short distance north as he and the crew left, crossing another significant feature—the Buffalo Trace, a primitive road created by bison, but widely used by early settlers moving into the deep woods of southern Indiana and on westward. The wilds were indeed that as three of the crew were later to die further west in today's Pike and Gibson counties. Thomas Shay was killed by a "panther" and his colleague George Tate severely mauled. David Sanford died of malaria, while Ziba Foote drowned in a swamp.[1] Both Sanford and Foote were young men, age 20 at their deaths. Ziba was with a crew surveying across the pond (swamp) and sank when the depth became more than they had expected. His remains were taken for burial in a grave nearby, wrapped in bark, which served as shroud and coffin.[2]

MOVING IN

Today, about 21 percent of Indiana is in forest cover, compared to an estimated 87 percent 200 years ago. The remaining early landscape featured prairies and wetlands, mostly in the north. In the south, even the great expanse of forest was patchy in areas of karst terrain. This physiographic area is now named the Mitchell Plateau (shown on Map 1). With rapid surface drainage, exposed bedrock, and shallow soils, the mixed deciduous forest often yielded to extensive barrens and glades. Harrison County was estimated to have some 21,500 acres of barrens, and Washington County around 11,750 acres.[3] Fire doubtless contributed to maintaining these openings, whether natural or by native people. All of these features have been significantly altered over the course of settlement and urbanization.

As pioneers established homesteads in the territory and then the state, they began to cut the timber for building homes and to clear land for farming. Trees were piled, burned, and wasted, as there was limited transportation and little market destination then. As primitive road improvements were made, much of the remaining old-growth forest was then harvested for sale to local markets or loaded on flatboats to be shipped down the Ohio and Mississippi rivers.

The amount of forest markedly declined to alarming proportions by the 1920s and fears were raised that we could lose most of what had been a seemingly endless supply of timber. The federal Swamp Act of 1850 had encouraged settlers to move in and drain swamps and bogs, resulting in the beginning of the destruction of many major wetlands across the northern part of Indiana and surrounding states. The very special nature of places like the Limberlost was changing. Gene Stratton Porter's remarkable essays, books, and reflections document the great variety of living things of the 1800s. Today the original 13,000-acre wetland is gone but a nicely restored remnant of 440 acres exists as the Loblolly Nature Preserve.

NEW DIRECTIONS

The beginning of state forestry and planning for the future began in 1909 with Charles C. Deam, Indiana's first state forester. In his time the state forest system emphasized wise-use management and continuity of forest resources. In 1921, Deam wrote and lobbied for the passage of the Forest Classification Act, which established methods to keep the state's private forests intact through reduction in the tax rate for landowners.

The situation was dire in the 1930s with the Great Depression, Dust Bowl, and abandonment of land. Left with little cover, hillsides and almost any slope were mercilessly attacked by rain, resulting in large-scale erosion and millions of cubic yards of soils washed away.

The arrival of the federal Civilian Conservation Corps (CCC) program, and then land purchases for the newly created Hoosier National Forest provided relief efforts through new conservation strategies including planting

Left page: Bearing Tree, Pivot Point

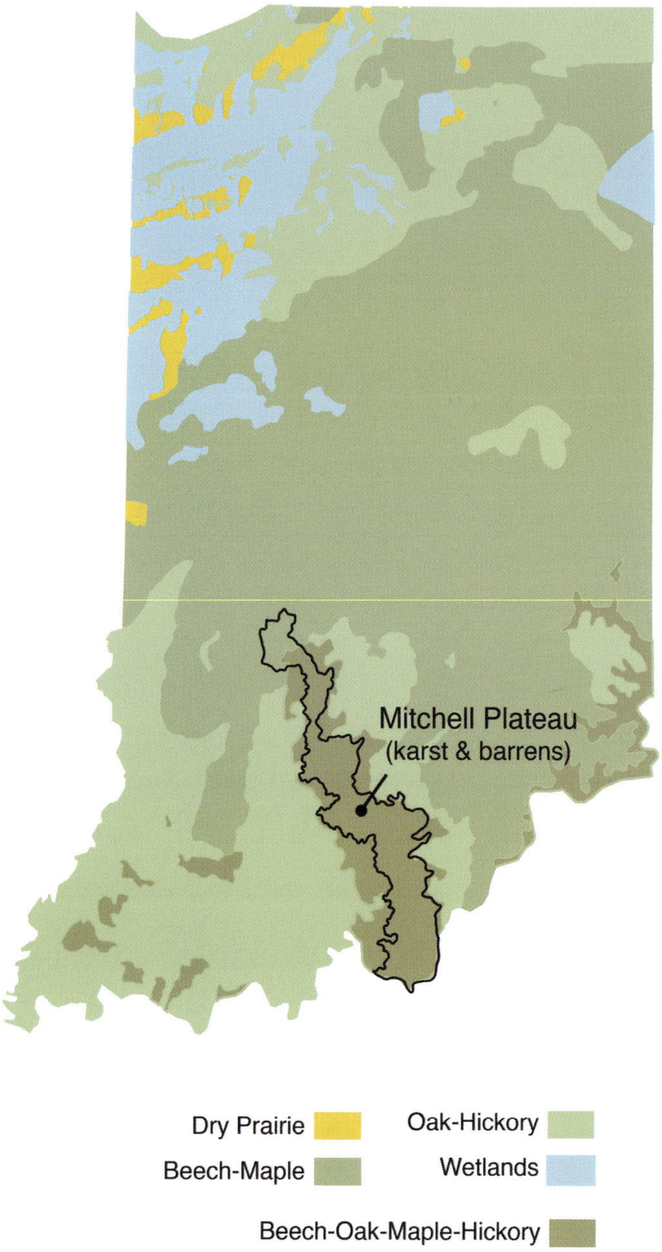

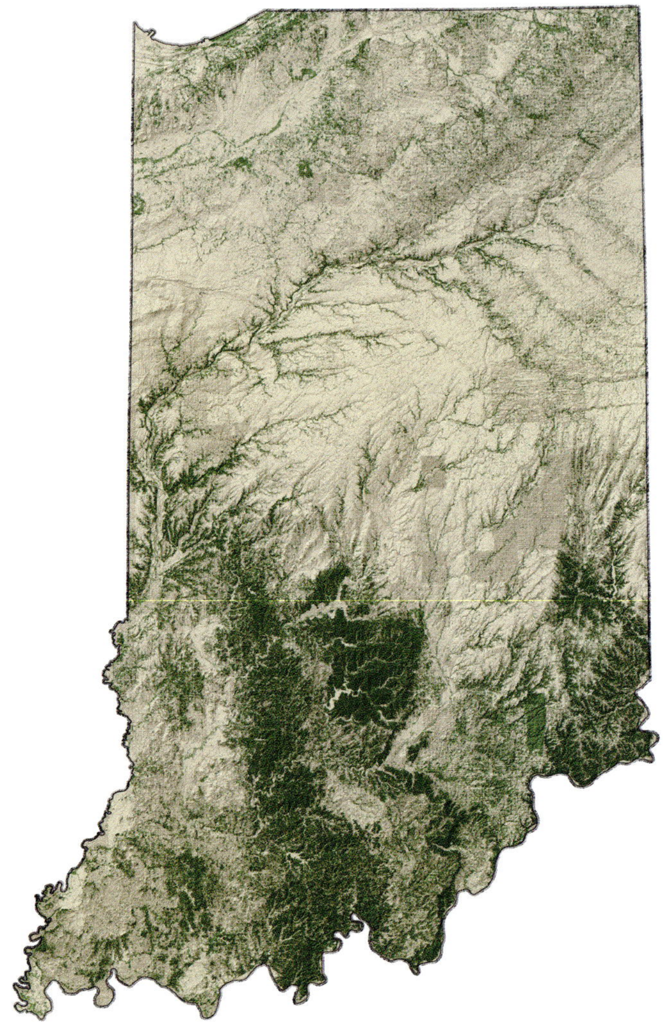

Map 1. Circa 1800 presettlement vegetation of Indiana, with forest types
Courtesy of P. David Polly, Dept. of Earth and Atmospheric Sciences, Indiana University, based on data from Lindsey et al. (1965): Lindsey, A. A., W. B. Crankshaw, and S. A. Qadir. 1965. Soil relations and distribution map of the vegetation of presettlement Indiana. Botanical Gazette, 126: 155–163.

Map 2. Present Indiana forest land cover
Courtesy of Dale Gormanson, U.S. Forest Service, fs.fed.us

millions of white, red, shortleaf, and longleaf pines. Though not native, these trees were able to tolerate poor conditions and grow quickly, thus holding soils that were left. To remove dead stands and allow natural regeneration is part of the ongoing management of selected units within the Hoosier National Forest. Progression to today has resulted in better science, public involvement, and a much-improved restoration of forestlands. Responsible foresters and loggers follow a plan for each harvest area that delineates proper care for the land during and after cutting. This is known as best management practices and addresses skid trails, roads, and log yards. Care is to be taken to minimize erosion, protect stream banks and water quality, and remove all trash.

Sustainability and environmental responsibility are now emphasized worldwide. The Forest Stewardship Council (FSC) is a nonprofit organization devoted to encouraging the responsible management of the world's forests. FSC sets high standards that ensure forestry is practiced in an environmentally responsible, socially beneficial, and economically viable way. Indiana landowners can join the Indiana Classified Forest Certified Group, which provides certification through the Forest Stewardship Council.

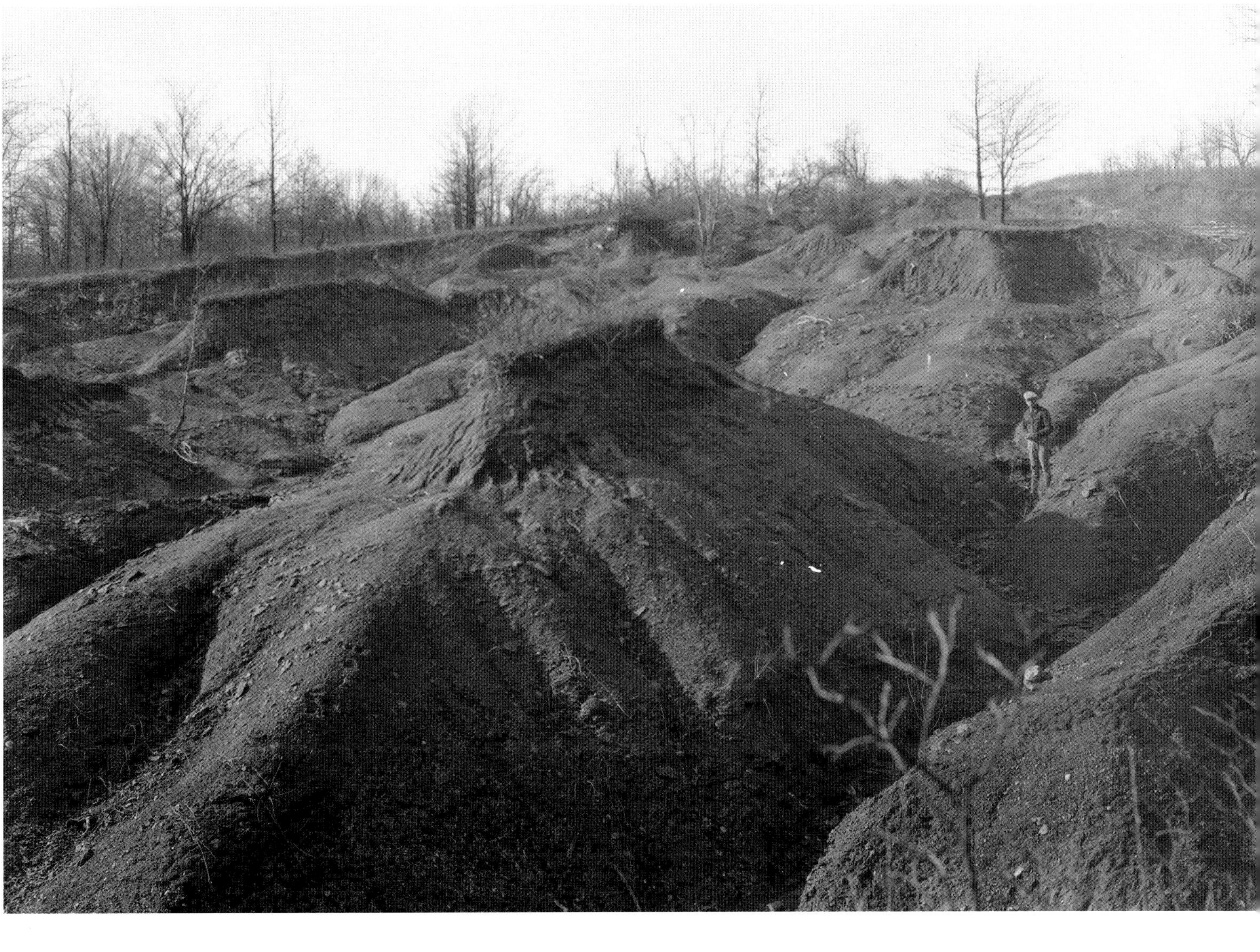

Monumental erosion in the 1930s
Courtesy of Indiana Dept. of Natural Resources

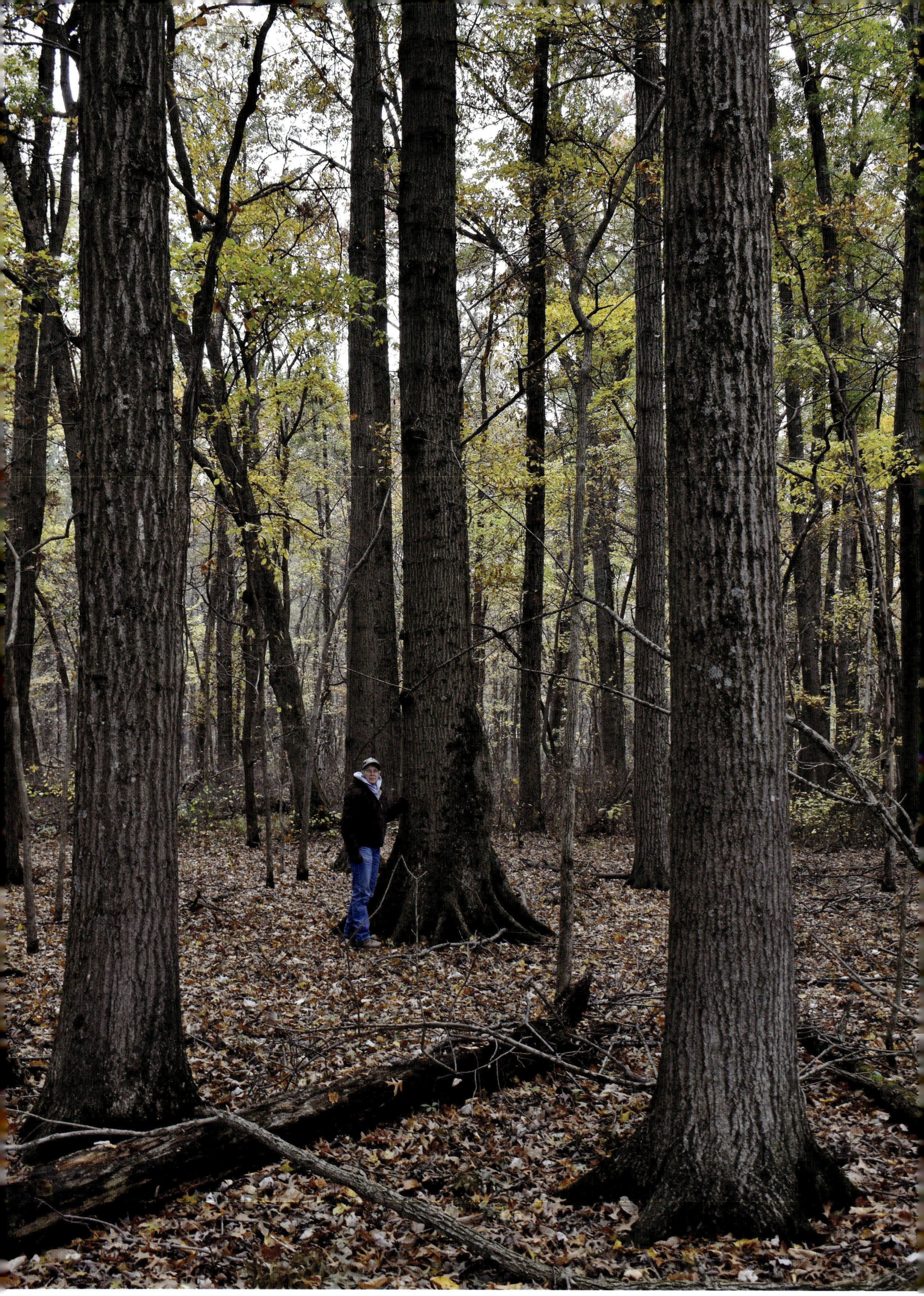

CHAPTER TWO

Landscapes of Indiana and Their Relationships to Forests

THE ANCIENT TIMES

Varying landforms through major events of geologic time have shaped the current physiography and resultant vegetation patterns of the state. Some 250–300 million years ago the continental landmass we know as North America was part of a supercontinent known as Pangaea. The position of Indiana on that landmass would have been close to the equator, prior to the continent's breakup and rotation into our present-day location. In this time period the temperatures and rainfall favored what we might call forests, but with plants more resembling tropical trees, different from but loosely equating to palms or other living cycads of today. The swamps in which these "trees" and other vegetation grew were later in geologic time covered by sediments, heating and compressing the plant material and forming coal. Some coal seams and sandstones contain visible impressions of these plants and cycads. A remarkable revelation occurred as I stood within an old forest in Daviess County. This current woods (see photo) of aged

Left page: Janet Eger, district forester in 1000 Acre Woods, a present-day forest on top of old coal forests below

standing trees, fallen logs, and decaying mats of vegetation was directly on top of ancient forests in those Carboniferous swamps. The trees of millions of years ago lay right below the forest of today. Further, not only was there one swamp with those ancient cycads, but another one below it and then another perhaps, all now in layered seams of coal. Communications with Dr. Maria Mastalerz of the Indiana Geological Survey established that the spot upon which I had stood most likely was only 150 feet above the Seelyville Coal member, which was my hidden ancient forest.

CURRENT PHYSIOGRAPHY

In *The Natural Regions of Indiana* (Homoya et al., 1985) the state is divided into twelve natural regions that reflect the diversity of geology, soils, flora, and fauna. Great variety is found from north to south with much of that due to glacial periods, which flattened the northern half. In northwest Indiana, remnant kettle lakes, dunes, swales, and moraines created their niche vegetative types, including tree species. There are many extraordinary, protected places with prairie, wetlands, sand savannas, and glacial deposits. Of particular interest today are locations like Tefft Savanna with its black oak community and Moraine Nature Preserve with ravines, uplands, and kettles. Residing here are old-growth remnants of oak-hickory type along with beech-maple.

Central and northeast Indiana also have great variety with soils above glacial till as a major constituent over limestone bedrock. Upon this expanse, which today is mostly farmland, originally lay a most grand beech-maple landscape along with oak, hickory, walnut, tulip, ash, and elm. Here must have been forest as far as one could imagine, ready for clearing as settlement encroached from the east and south. Today that grandeur only persists in a few areas saved from the axe. The Indiana Division of Nature Preserves, Indiana Chapter of the Nature Conservancy, Acres, Inc., Merry Lea Educational Center, Ball State University, Purdue University, conservancies, and land trusts have been invaluable in saving and restoring several of this section of Indiana's special places, numbering some sixty properties.

The unglaciated southern portion of Indiana obviously renders a different character than that of terrain shaped by ice and its deposits. Below the terminus of the last advance of the Wisconsin glaciation sheet we find a landscape of hills, valleys, ancient river bottoms with outwash, and karst. The composition of bedrock and exposures shows vast thicknesses of sandstone, limestone, and shale. The soils derived from source material and enriched by organic matter over long periods of time have helped create the growing conditions for trees. Species preferences are sometimes very obvious for aspect, soil depth, moisture, and spacing. An example is finding big old walnut trees in rich, deep soils, while chestnut oak resides on rocky hillsides, often with a southern aspect.

Prior to the new work of Homoya et al. in 1985, Lindsey (*Natural Areas of Indiana and Their Preservation*, 1969) offered three regions, which he called the southwestern lowlands, south central oak and mixed woods, and southeastern till plain beech-maple divisions. Today we classify these as part of the Interior Low Plateau. Forests in southern Indiana are more extensive, with species quite varied. While northern Indiana has tree types including tamarack, birch, willow, pin-cherry, and quaking aspen, southern Indiana also has particular species from southern and Appalachian regions. These include cypress, magnolia, laurels, Virginia pine, sugarberry, sourwood, yellow buckeye, and some of the oaks.

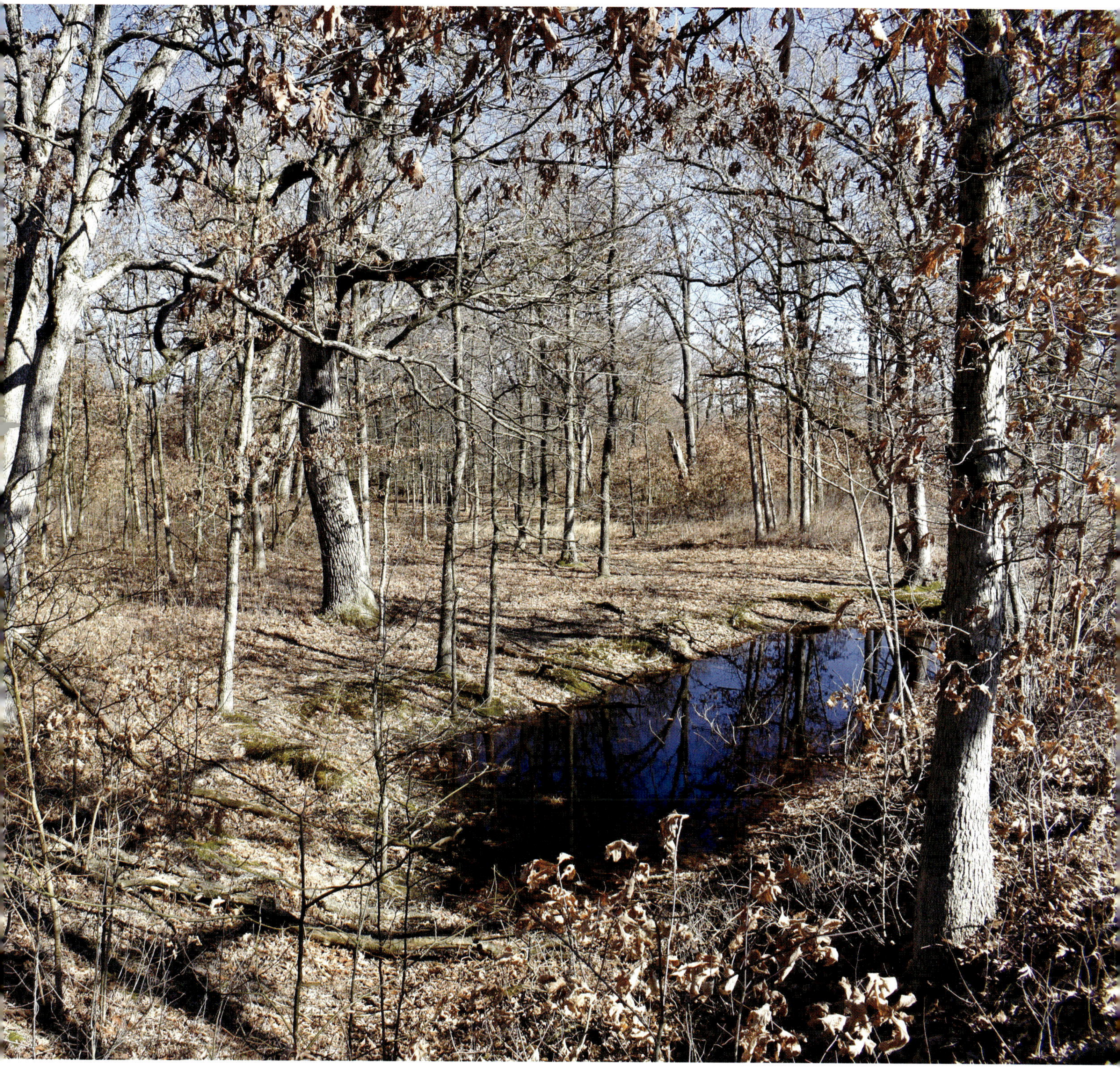

Tefft Savanna, Jasper County

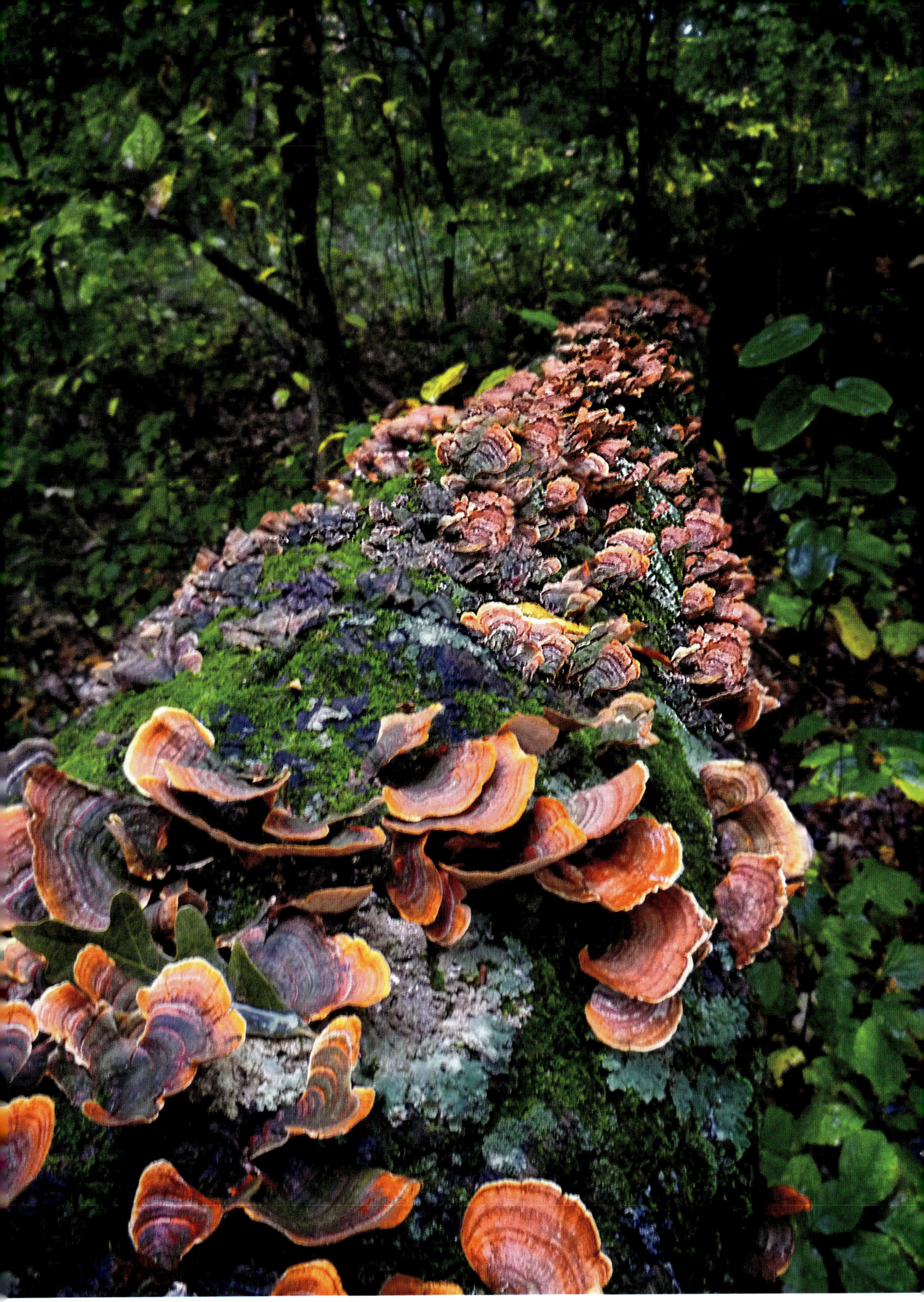

CHAPTER THREE

The Forest as a Living Community

BIOLOGICAL INTERRELATIONSHIPS

The state has a remarkable diversity of living organisms that include not only tree species but also other surrounding cast members. There are ground plants, tree-dwelling plant life on trunks, limbs, leaves, fungi, bacteria, a myriad of small rodents, and mammals that coexist with or depend upon the tree for life. Some are so specific in their dependence upon the tree/shrub community that they are obligates, totally tied to the precise tree species.

Looking at the forest as a whole, or even fencerow trees side by side, one contemplates the very thoughts posed by Peter Wohlleben in *The Hidden Life of Trees,* believing that there is cooperation and even communication by trees for the mutual benefits of growth, survival, and defense. Research is being done at Purdue's School of Agriculture in the investigation of microbiomes, a direct application investigating interrelationships of multiple intersecting factors to determine how these work together. This study involves soils, bacteria, fungi, nutrients, water,

Left page: Fungi decomposing an old log

and O_2/CO_2 exchanges. As forests change over time in response to environmental and physical factors, diversity will remain critical to forest health and productivity. When there is one major alteration, such as maple replacing oak, entire community shifts may arise, from large to small. Examples might include types of soil microbes, soil nutrient depletion, production of food for wildlife, and types of wildlife found. Indiana's species composition may also change over time due to climate factors and moisture. Infestations of invasive plants and insects such as emerald ash borer, gypsy moth, Asian longhorned beetle, and perhaps the nefarious spotted lanternfly can also dramatically impact forest composition and diversity, even to the point of replacing it.

CLIMATE CHANGE AND CARBON STORAGE

As we move further into this 21st century, long-term changes will become short-term urgencies. The tremendous progress humankind has made over the past few centuries has also brought into focus concerns that had sometimes been disregarded, the few voices of warning often muted. Many great conservationists did take notice and made a great impact. In forestry, Gifford Pinchot, Theodore Roosevelt, and Franklin D. Roosevelt are often recalled. Indiana's Charles Deam and Alton Lindsey were also important.

What has always been realized is that trees are invaluable in the functioning of the earth's biodiversity and its huge role in climate influence. The standard course in high school biology does recite that trees provide oxygen, wildlife habitat, erosion control, products, and beauty. There is much more depth of science now to understand the effects of deforestation, reforestation, and proforestation. Atmospheric changes do occur from burning fossil fuels, clearing and burning large swaths of tropical forests, and even from naturally caused forest fires. The release of carbon through these processes in combination with that resulting from melting permafrost and methane creates atmospheric dynamics still being researched. While it is well understood that trees store carbon from photosynthesis, new studies contrast the storage capacities of young regenerating forests recovering from harvest to intact forests in an existing old-growth setting or those in a progenerative stage, delaying harvest for a longer rotation period. This fosters the increase of mature components of the forest as it develops. Variations of research studies may seem to differ in their conclusions about which forest age sequesters more carbon, but the consensus will still conclude that forest cover, whether old growth or recovering young age class, is extraordinarily important for the planet's future. As research continues, new strategies will arise to cope with changes. Genetic tools may also help us maintain the diversity and productivity of our Hoosier forests. The Purdue Climate Change Research Center is on the forefront of studying the long-term effects of a warming climate on Indiana's future.

CHAPTER FOUR

Big Trees and Champions

OBJECTIVES

One major goal for this book was to visit as many state record champion trees as possible within the time frame available. Some of the originals on the last register were no longer standing. The champion pawpaw was dead, the mockernut cut down, the catalpa fallen, the dogwood gone, along with others. Since I was also recording many other features of interest for other sections of this book, seventy-four species were selected. Most are or were state champions; others are fine examples of their species and were also impressive. The latter were chosen if the prior champion was no longer alive or easily accessible. It is noted that there may be changes and new additions in the next Big Tree Register.

There are specific requirements for a tree to receive the designation of a state champion. First is the circumference of the tree at the specific height of 4½ feet above the ground. Next, one measures the height by an acceptable method. The last dimension considered is the crown's spread or how far the limbs extend. For anyone finding an extraordinary specimen, first check the current record for that species on the Big Tree Register, then consult the IDNR website for information on how to calculate the above measurements and submit.

Folks do ask about the age of their tree. It is indeed a natural curiosity. There are three basic ways one might be able to tell. First, if it has been cut down from necessity, tree rings can be counted.

But if it is standing, perhaps a record of when it was planted, or an old photo with a date might help. Third, a coring can be done with an increment borer; a little core sample is removed and rings counted. Only a few arborists or forest researchers are equipped with this tool or recommend it be done. Age estimation is possible just by measuring the circumference of the tree. Dr. Lindsey Purcell at Purdue has a chart of various trees and growth factors, which can be used. There are many variables affecting a particular tree's growth rate, but this generalized table is an interesting approach. See www.purduelandscapereport.org/article/how-old-is-my-tree.

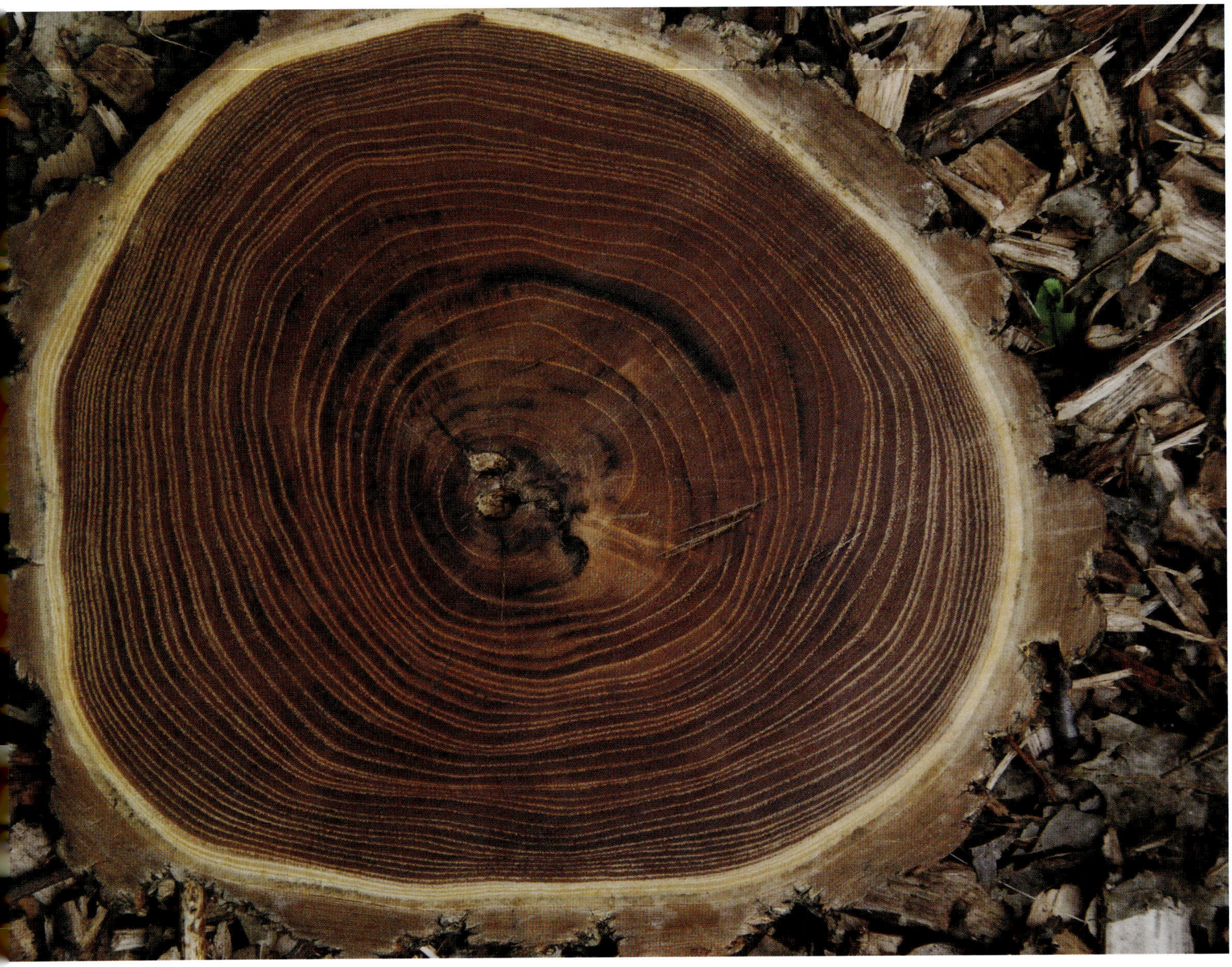

Tree rings allow an easy way to date the tree

THE PROCESS

Step one was to take the list on the registry and select which trees to photograph. The registry or other records determined locations, landowner names, and contact information if available. Missing a contact did not happen very often, and indeed so many folks were very helpful and happy to permit a picture. On the other hand, a phone call ahead did work out many times, but the news was sad—the tree had blown down, died, or was not even there anymore. It is to be expected—the old giants had already been there for 200+ years, so it was their time to go. Once the selections were in order, trips across the state were made, often involving hundreds of miles in a day, and an accumulation of over 1,900 miles by the end of the project. The book could almost be called "From Savannas to Swamps" or "Big Oaks to Big Cypress," crossing eco-regions, river systems, urban settings, parks, and even private yards. Not surprisingly, some very large trees were found in old cemeteries. These trees were often very distinguished, and their history was intriguing. Other great ones were found in city parks like Deming Park in Terre Haute and Wesselman Woods in Evansville. Celery Bog, operated by West Lafayette Parks and Recreation, had an interesting woods and great educational facility. Historic sites like Tippecanoe Battlefield displayed many massive oaks. State parks such as Turkey Run and Spring Mill are well known for very old and large patriarchs.

The visits to so many different places were a memorable experience. Hoosier hospitality was alive and well as I was cordially received and often privileged to hear great stories about the history and importance of these trees.

TREE ESSAYS

Following are essays about the trees visited, reflections on them, characteristics, and uses. Lengthy identification keys are avoided to keep the narrative enjoyable, yet descriptive. There are many field guides (included in the Bibliography) for further exploration, and these are also excellent for your library. These guides will also show smaller details and maps of distribution for the species. The BONAP (Biota of North America Program) website will also add a valuable source to your investigations.

It must be said that the eloquence of Donald Culross Peattie inspired much thought of how to write the essays. His book *A Natural History of Trees of Eastern and Central North America* was a primary source. Another valuable resource on identification and wildlife uses comes from *Native Trees of the Midwest* by Sally Weeks, Harmon P. Weeks Jr., and George Parker of Purdue. Charles C. Deam's *Trees of Indiana* is also a classic and has undergone multiple printings. *The Book of Trees for Positive Identification* by William Carey Grimm was also a much-used reference. Finally, for its complete coverage of all trees visited, old friend Marion T. Jackson's *101 Trees of Indiana,* a great field guide, was paramount to the success of writing this book.

Organization of the essays is primarily by alphabetical order, but trees within a genus are grouped together. This permits easy flow from one particular species to another in its genus, for those inclined to find this valuable.

AMERICAN BEECH

(Fagus grandifolia)

Truly a favorite: handsome, massive in old age, and beloved by creatures, the American beech is an icon of late succession. Patient, waiting for the opportune time under the shade of oaks, hickories, and other larger trees, the small gray sapling may eventually get an opening provided by wind damage to other trees, forest clearing, or harvest. It can then begin its long-awaited chance to grow upward to maturity.

While the beech is quite magnificent to some, it is not totally desired by foresters since it and companion maples will gradually displace the oak-hickory forest. As large specimens they would shade out reproduction of the other more desirable timber-producing trees. In a forest managed for high-quality timber, beech and maple may well be girdled and significantly reduced. The desirability of beech from an aesthetic standpoint and its value as a fine tree for wildlife do render it a valuable component of an overall forest system. On a moonlit night you may spot a raccoon or an owl in the hollow cavity, or in the olden days there could well have been a bear den in a large opening in the base of a 6-foot diameter tree.

The beech has played a huge role in both in Europe and America, for it contributed to so many uses. Beechnuts alone, as food for creatures and people, made the tree valuable. Audubon wrote about millions of passenger pigeons feasting on beechnuts as they migrated.[1] Alas, in pioneer days clearing the rich soils of Indiana for farms doomed any large beech forests. Scattered throughout the state now are still some individual specimens of great size, allowed to pursue happiness into old age. Our state champion in Vigo County is 5½ feet in diameter and 94 feet tall, but it is showing decline in its last years and may have perished by the time this book is being read. A replacement has been submitted. Many other striking beeches are found across the state, all commanding attention and admiration.

Characteristics

- Distinctive gray, smooth bark, graceful form, may be straight and then many-branched, some of those branches massive in their own right.
- Root structure flaring near base also intriguing and pleasing. Shallow root system but wide.
- May hollow out early in life but not noticeable until old age. Hollows provide habitat. Amazing that the outer live wood in a ring can support a huge old hollow tree.
- Susceptible to beech scale disease, canker, root rot, and newly observed beech leaf disease.
- Wood is heavy, strong, close-grained, difficult to split, doesn't hold up well when exposed to weather after being felled.

Uses

- Some cabinetry, flooring, woodcrafting.
- Good for wood stove fuel: warms you two or three times fighting it when sawing and splitting it.

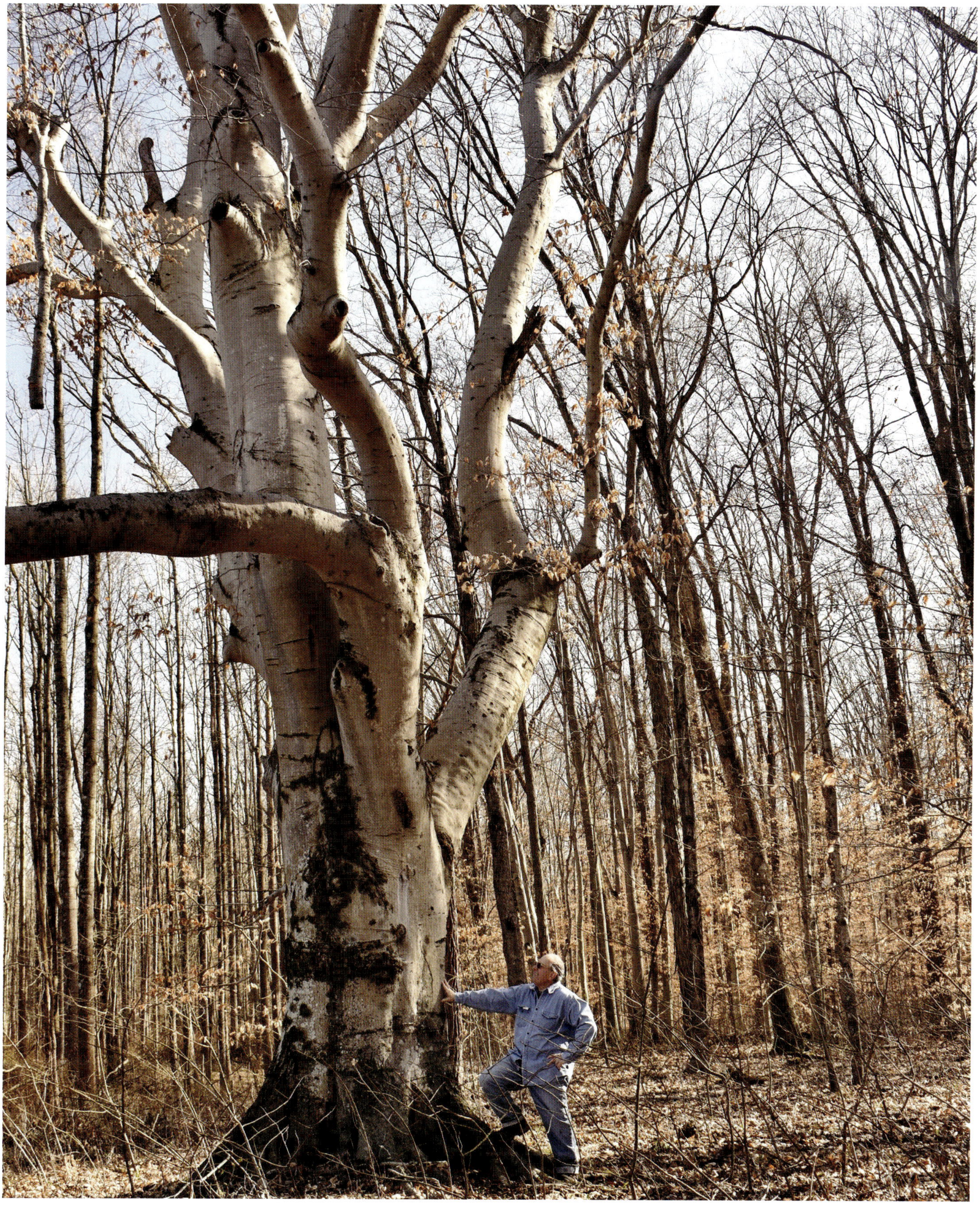

Grand old beech in Muscatatuck NWR/Dave Coppert

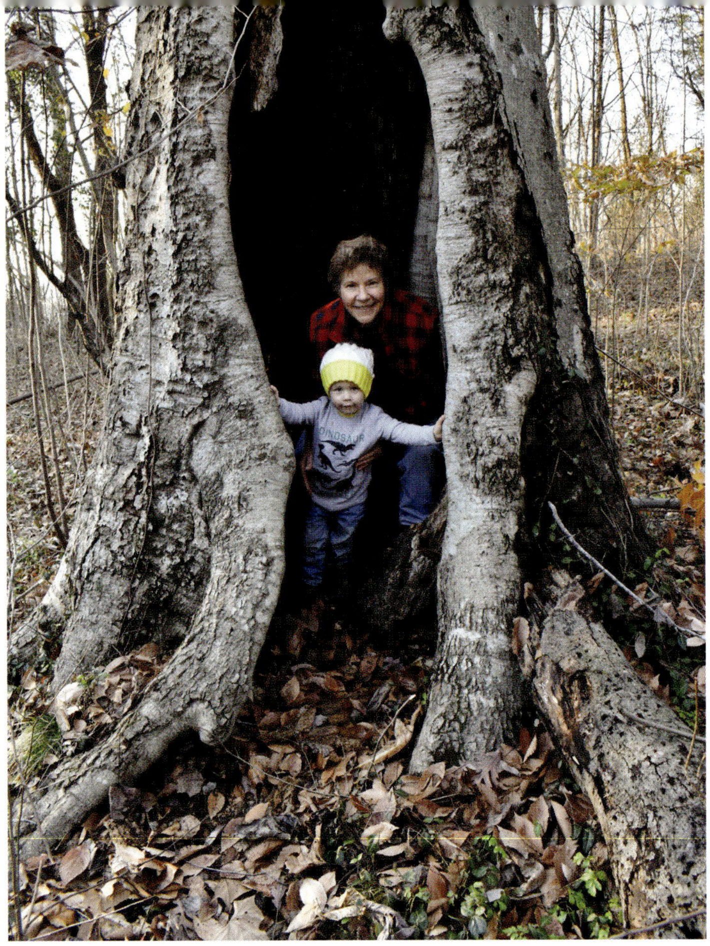

Right: Hollow, 200-year-old beech, Lawrence County

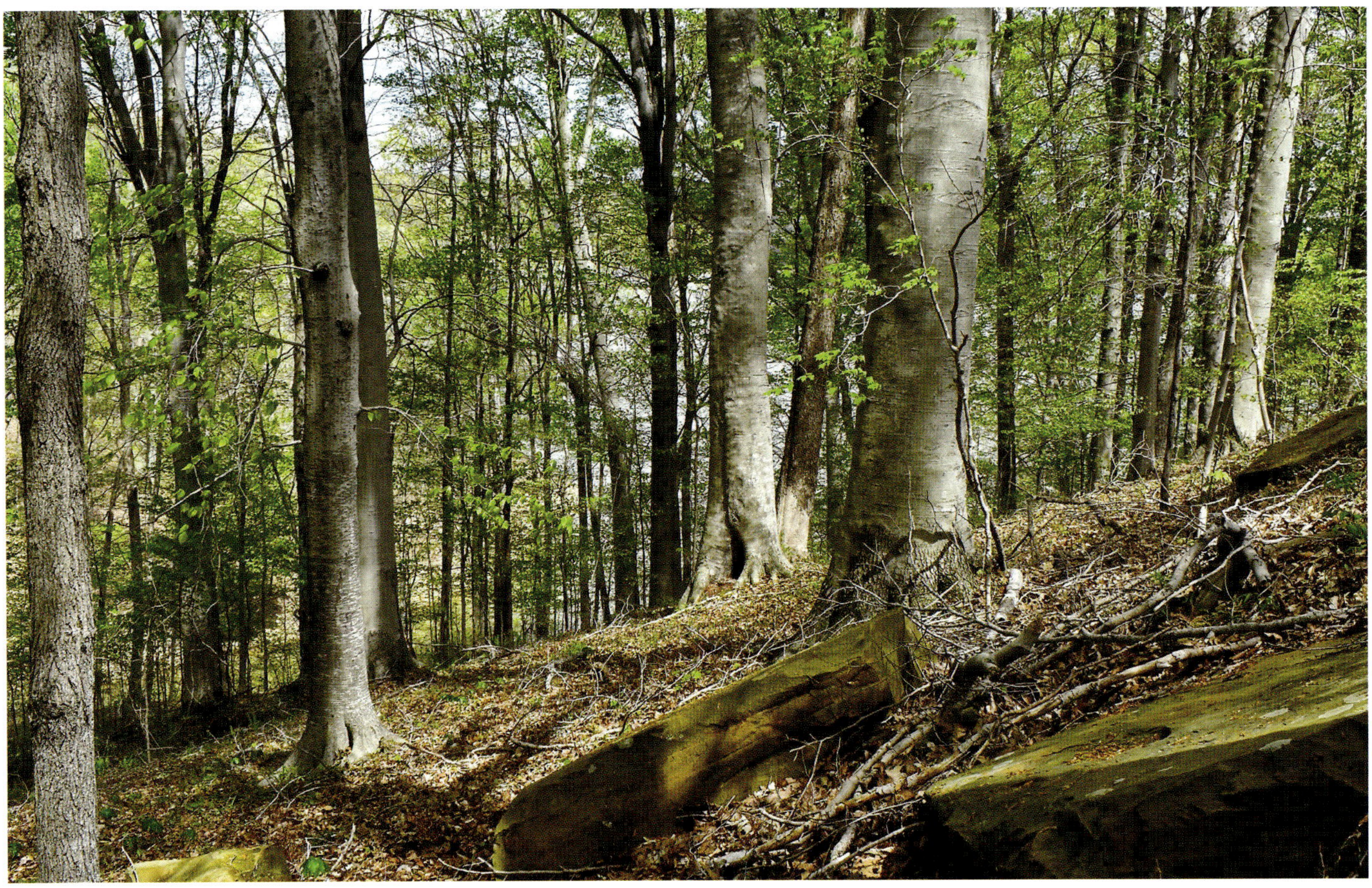

Above: Beech grove, Amy Weingartner Branigan Preserve, Sycamore Land Trust, Monroe Co.

Right page: Former champion beech, now deceased, Vigo County

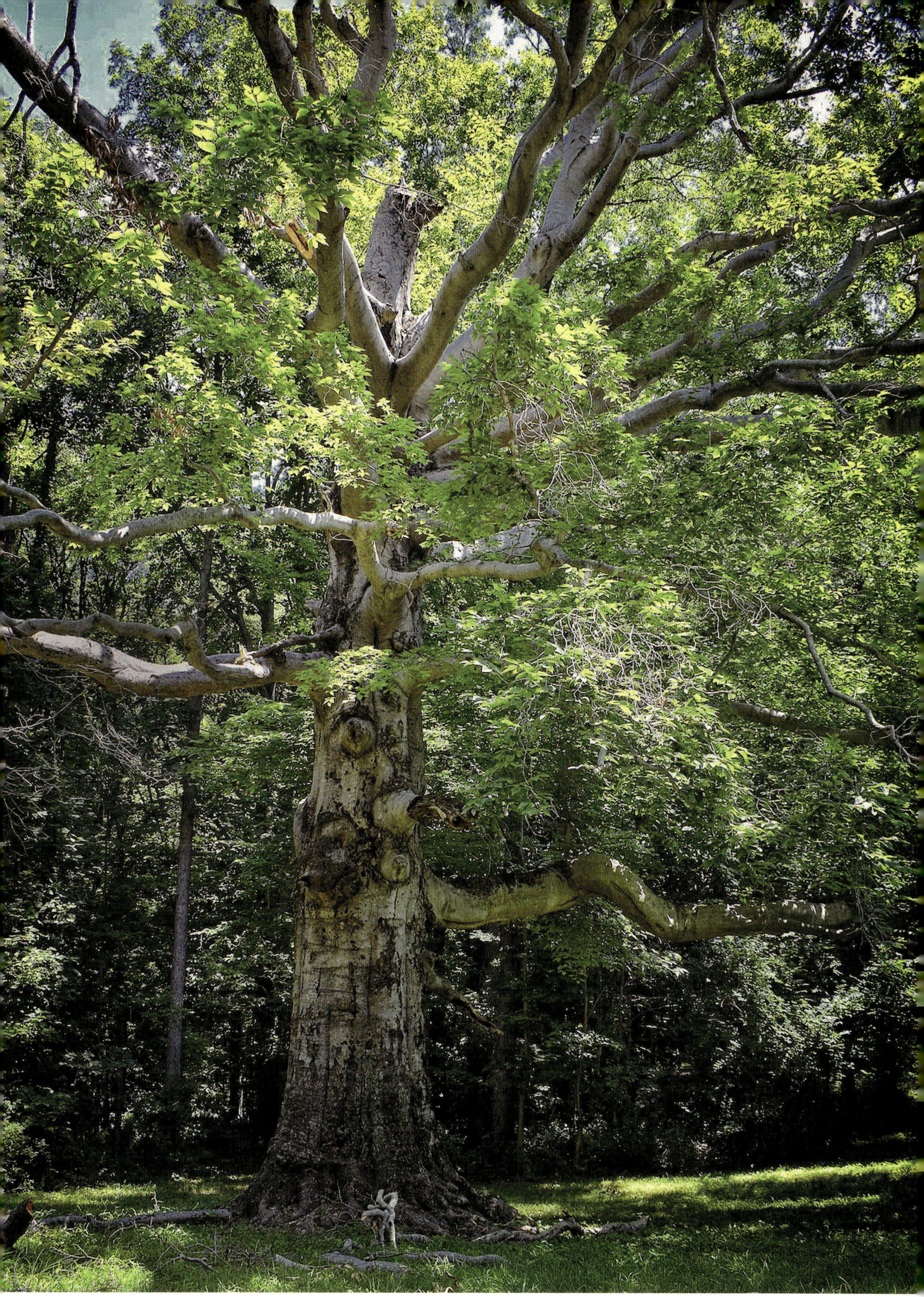

AMERICAN CHESTNUT

(Castanea dentata)

Unbelievably grand, important, irreplaceable. An American icon: one of the most significant trees in the history of our country. Gone in a few decades, mourned by all. The deadly *Cryphonectria parasitica,* a fungus first detected in New York in 1904, originated from Asia, but upon finding our American chestnut, rapidly attacked and devastated billions of trees. The pathogen enters the bark through any kind of wound or open pathway, spreads into the cambium, and kills the tissue, thus depriving the tree of nutrient flow.[2]

The predominance of the species was eastern, especially the Appalachians, thus when those trees were impacted, whole economies, uses, and dependencies were severely affected. The extraordinary qualities of the fine, straight, easily worked, lightweight, beautiful, and rot-resistant wood made it part of the way of life for rural communities. Nut production alone was another major contribution of chestnut trees for wild animals and livestock turned into the woods. Collecting nuts in the fall was often a family tradition and resulted in a famous phrase: "chestnuts roasted over an open fire."

Although the American chestnut's range was mostly in the east, stretching along the Appalachians, a tongue extended into Indiana. Only a few mature trees can be found today, although stump sprouts do occur.

Young chestnut trees may seem to do well for a while but eventually develop cankers from the blight and most often succumb early. They may reach bur-producing capacity, however. A few lucky trees have avoided the blight and reached a mature size. Such is the case with the state champion pictured near Roselawn in Newton County. This fine tree is in an unexpected location in a small woods along the highway. The owner is aware of the significance of a surviving American chestnut and pledges to protect it.

Other chestnut tree species such as Chinese and Japanese seem more resistant to the blight.

Research is being done in backcrossing Chinese with pure American to develop a higher capacity for blight resistance. This work is being carried out in Indiana by Purdue's Hardwood Tree Improvement and Regeneration Center and with members of the Indiana Chapter of the American Chestnut Foundation. Another technique now in research is gene sequencing and attempting to identify the chromosome pairs responsible for resistance, then using transgenic insertion. While the truly pure American chestnut forest is gone, a new-generation tree line may someday restore an almost true replication of the form and function of the previous era when chestnut was king.

Characteristics

- Originally a wonderful 100-foot-tall tree, now reduced to much less or even stump sprouts. State champion tree is 2 feet in diameter and 88 feet in height.
- Brown shallow furrowed bark with platy ridges.
- Leaf elongate to 6 or 8 inches, toothed. Leaf narrower than on Chinese chestnut, which has been broadly planted as a "replacement."
- Beautiful clusters of white flowers in June–July. Male and female flowers on the same tree.
- Bur develops in fall with 2–3 nuts. Nut may be bored and ruined by weevils—even observed in Chinese chestnuts.

Uses

- Historic uses for building lumber, flooring, barns, and fences.
- Nut production was an important food source for humans and animals.

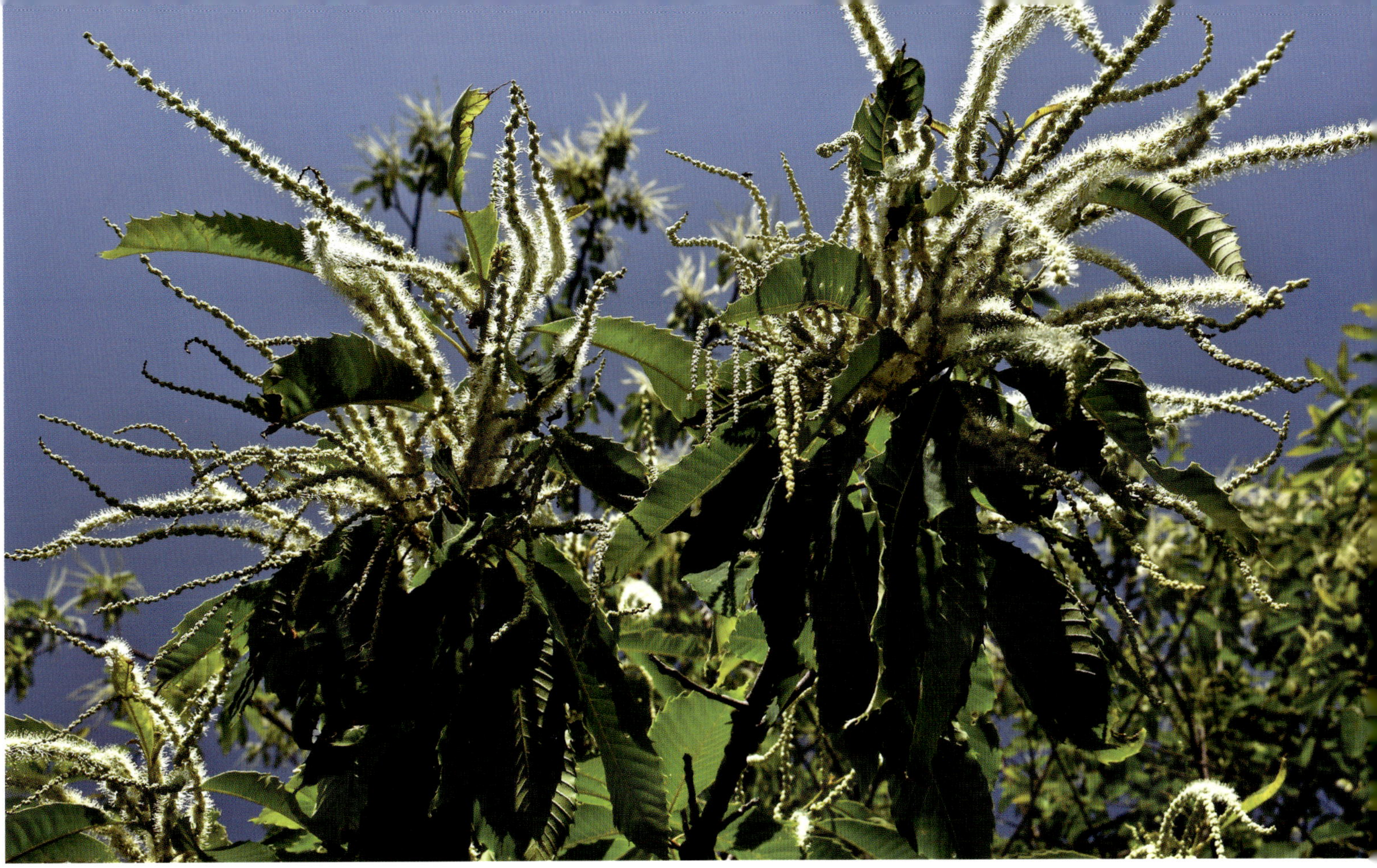

American chestnut in bloom

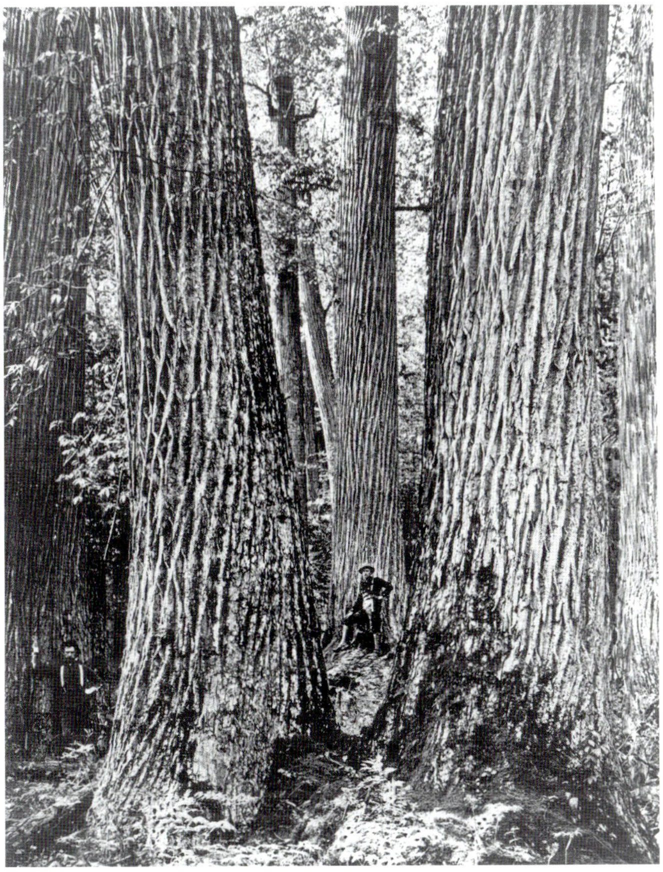

Chestnut giants, Great Smoky Mountains, western North Carolina, ca. 1910.
Courtesy of the Forest History Society

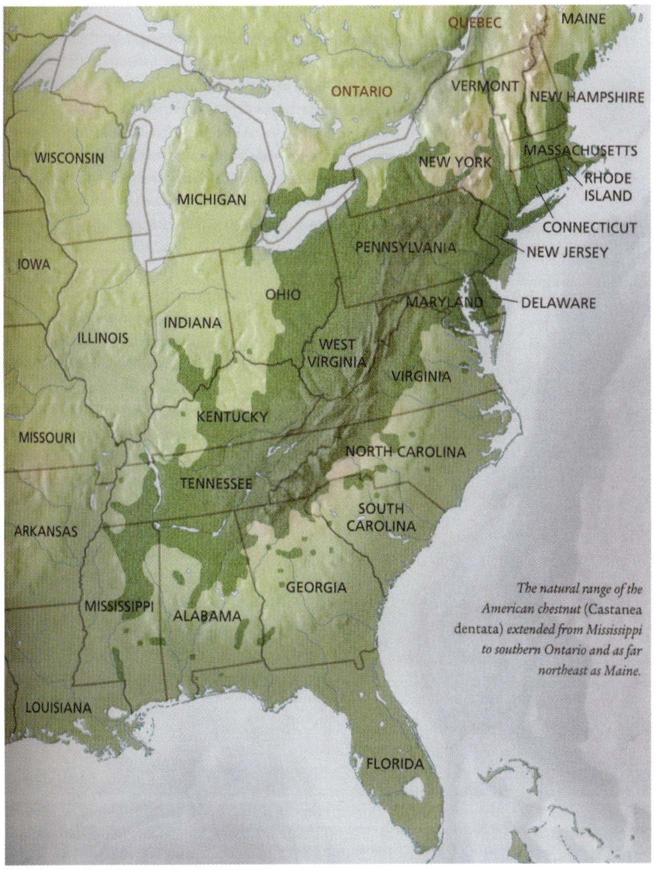

Historic range of American chestnut
Courtesy of the American Chestnut Foundation

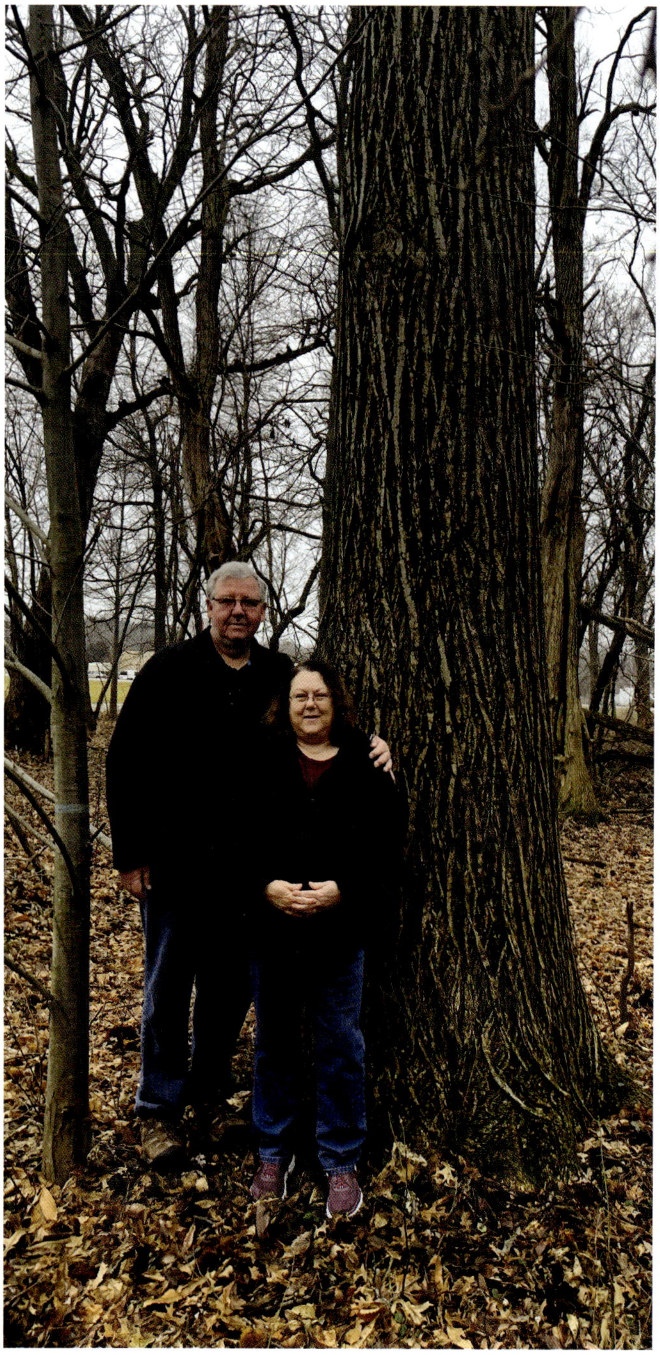

State champion American chestnut
with proud owners, Mr. and Mrs. John Morgin
Courtesy of Bruce Wakeland

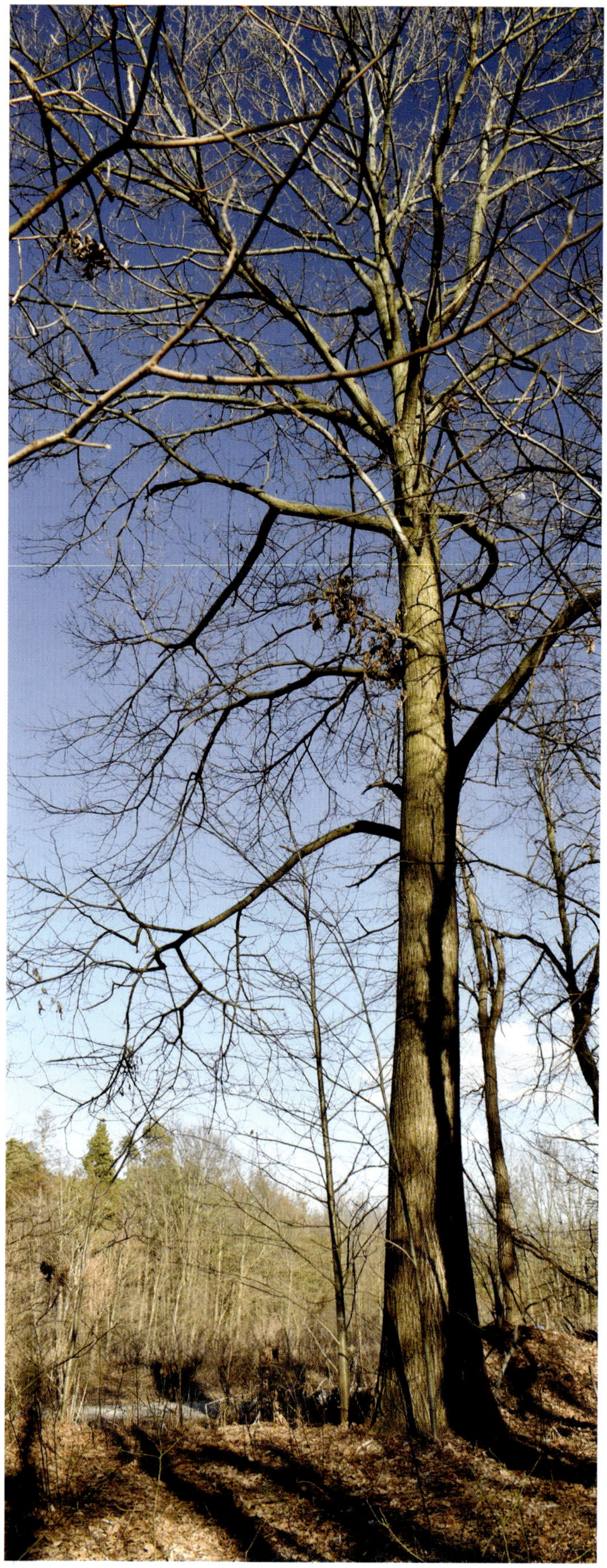

State champion American chestnut, Roselawn, IN

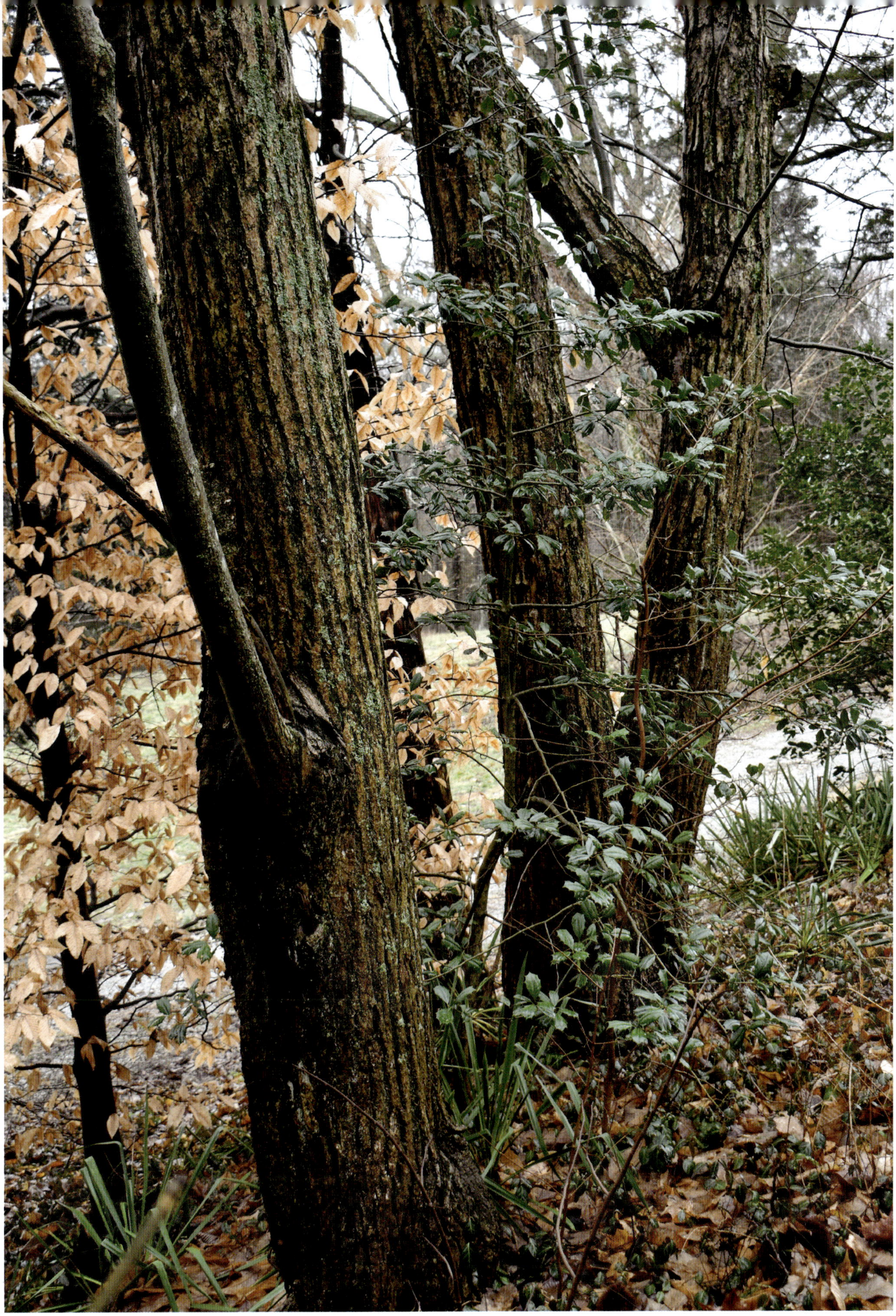

Chinese chestnut

BASSWOOD

(American Linden) (Tilia americana)

American linden (commonly called basswood) is a tree for everyone. From the strikingly handsome heart-shaped leaf, interesting textured bark, and the absolute heaven of fragrance produced by blooms in the spring, this might be a favorite to please most all of us. Some consider basswood honey a delicacy. We can appreciate those diligent little worker bees transporting that pollen back to the hive where it will not only feed the colony, but can be extracted for use by humans. It is of interest that hive frames are often constructed of this same tree's light but sturdy wood. Basswood's low density and softness make it quite useful for crates, boxes, sashes, drawer sides, and yesteryear's yardsticks. Peattie (1966) also describes its uses by Native Americans who stripped out the inner bark and rendered long stringy fibers to make rope or cords. The fiber could also be used to bind cattail mats together.

A very large basswood is handsome in appearance, contributes fine shade, and can be a desirable street tree. While enjoying the company of ashes and cottonwoods at low elevations, it also adapts well to many sites. In those rich bottomland soils it may reach over 100 feet in height and to 4–5 feet in diameter. Commonly you will observe many sprouts around the main tree, emanating from the roots. This is often a giveaway in identification, especially when paired with the asymmetrical heart-shaped leaf, which may reach 7 inches in length. Another noteworthy feature is the flamboyantly red bud, which stands out in the winter.

The new champion tree is located in Floyd County on private property very near Indian Creek and close to the Knobstone hill country. It was a truly impressive specimen close to 150 feet high and 5½ feet across. There were two very large trunks diverging just about head height, and the typical stump sprouts were present and growing well. The tree was obviously very old and in command of this favorable location overlooking the gurgling, happy sound of the meandering creek as it flowed southwestward toward its eventual mouth at the Ohio River.

Characteristics

- Check those root sprouts coming up alongside the main tree.
- Look for a heart-shaped leaf with asymmetrical base and finely toothed margin.
- Bark may be gray to dark color in old trees, some fissures in old age.
- Flowers bisexual (male and female parts in same flower). Long stalk and pendant flowers.
- Winter bud red with two scales.
- Rather soft wood.

Uses

- A very productive wood—as mentioned above, utensils, drawers, cabinets, carving.
- Basswood honey sold as a delicacy.
- Nice ornamental tree with good shade.
- Common for pulpwood use.

Right page, top left: State champion basswood, Floyd County

Top right: Basswood's stately character

Bottom: Splendid basswood near Potawatomi Inn, Pokagon State Park

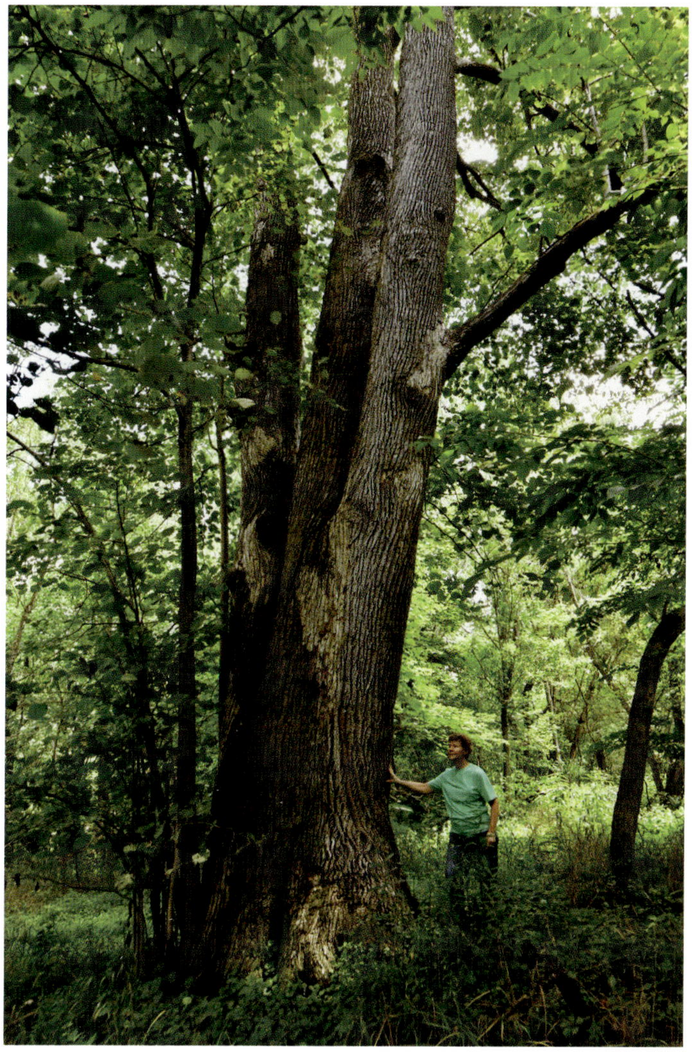
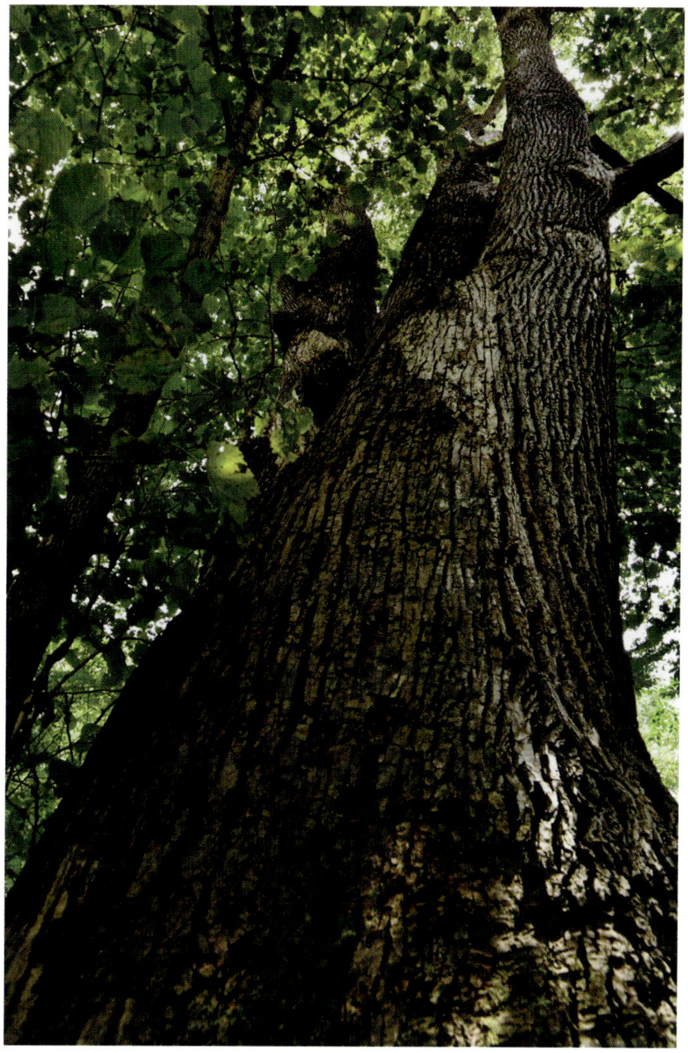
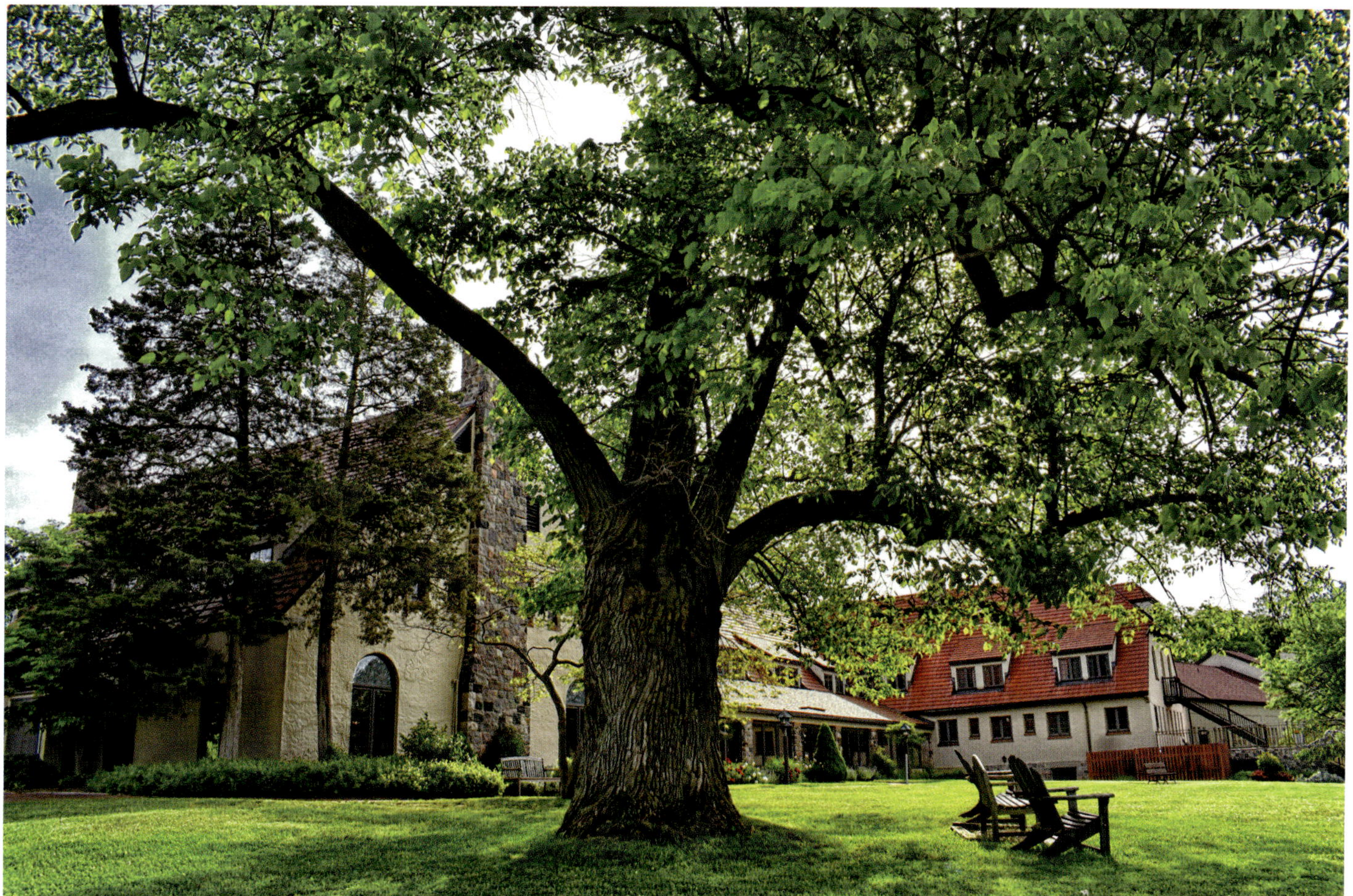

BLACK CHERRY

(Prunus serotina)

Cresting a hill in Owen County with Ralph Unversaw provided the first glimpse of what was obviously a huge tree. Arriving at the base, we felt dwarfed by its presence. This 6-foot diameter and 86-foot-tall beauty was the state champion black cherry.

We saw it in late summer, but a spring trip would be interesting to see the great amounts of delicate white blooms.

Due to its massive multiple branches, this specimen would not be highly valuable as far as a prime timber candidate. Fine-quality black cherry free of defects commands very good prices on the market. In days past cherry was plentiful, and in a closed forest grew straight and tall. The smooth-grained wood became valuable enough to occupy space on river barges traveling down the Mississippi to New Orleans in the early 1800s. It was later used in Pullman coaches, streetcars, fancy bars, and tycoons' elegant offices. In Appalachian mountain country, old-timers even infused their brandy with cherry juice. Although bitter by itself, it became more tolerable to consume or at least was not noticed as the amount of rum or brandy imbibed clouded one's perceptions. There were also accounts of black bears climbing cherry trees in search of bountiful crops of wild berries.

At one time cherry was second only to black walnut in cost for cabinet and furniture wood. Indeed, some of the highest quality and priciest antique furniture made in the 1800s is crafted of these two woods. Many of our best cupboards and chests display that aged reddish color that is warmly radiant, especially if it is a perfect 2-foot-wide cherry plank. Today, all the old prime cherry is long gone, so craftsmen glue up smaller widths to yield our cabinets and tables.

Indiana cherry is generally not of high quality due to attacks by borers and other insects. It also forms gum pockets in response to damage from these pests. Trees may grow crooked and show poor form on lateral limbs as well. Defoliation is common in the summer as the tent caterpillar makes its prodigious webs in the branches. Usually the tree can put forth another round of leaves to compensate for the temporary damage. Ground critters and deer may impact young trees of all species and cherry is no exception.

Characteristics

- Remarkably, a member of the rose family; also related to peach trees.
- Prefers sunlight and good soils, but will be limby in open fields.
- Alternate arrangement, long, slender, somewhat pinnate leaves, often with fungal spots.
- Bark scaly, black, sometimes identified as a "cornflakes" appearance.
- Fruits to ½ inch turn red-black, bitter. Seeds carried by birds for miles.
- May be of poor quality in Indiana if gummy or stunted, but could also be an outstanding specimen of up to 100 feet and 36 inches in diameter.

Uses

- Exceptional wood with beautiful color and grain producing high-quality cabinets and furniture.
- Important wildlife tree. Seeds spread far and wide.

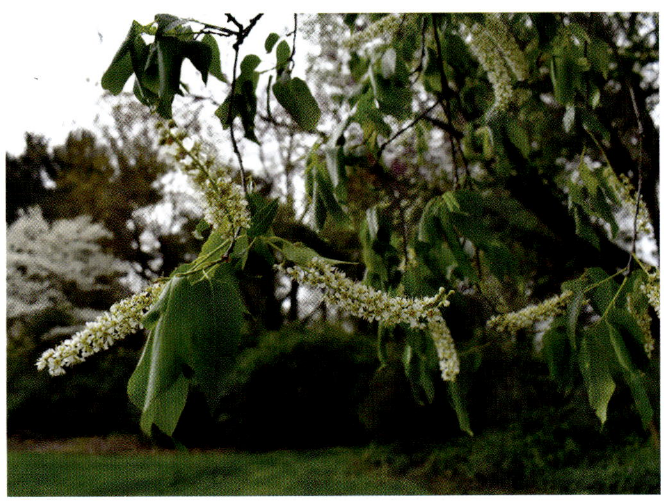

Black cherry blooms

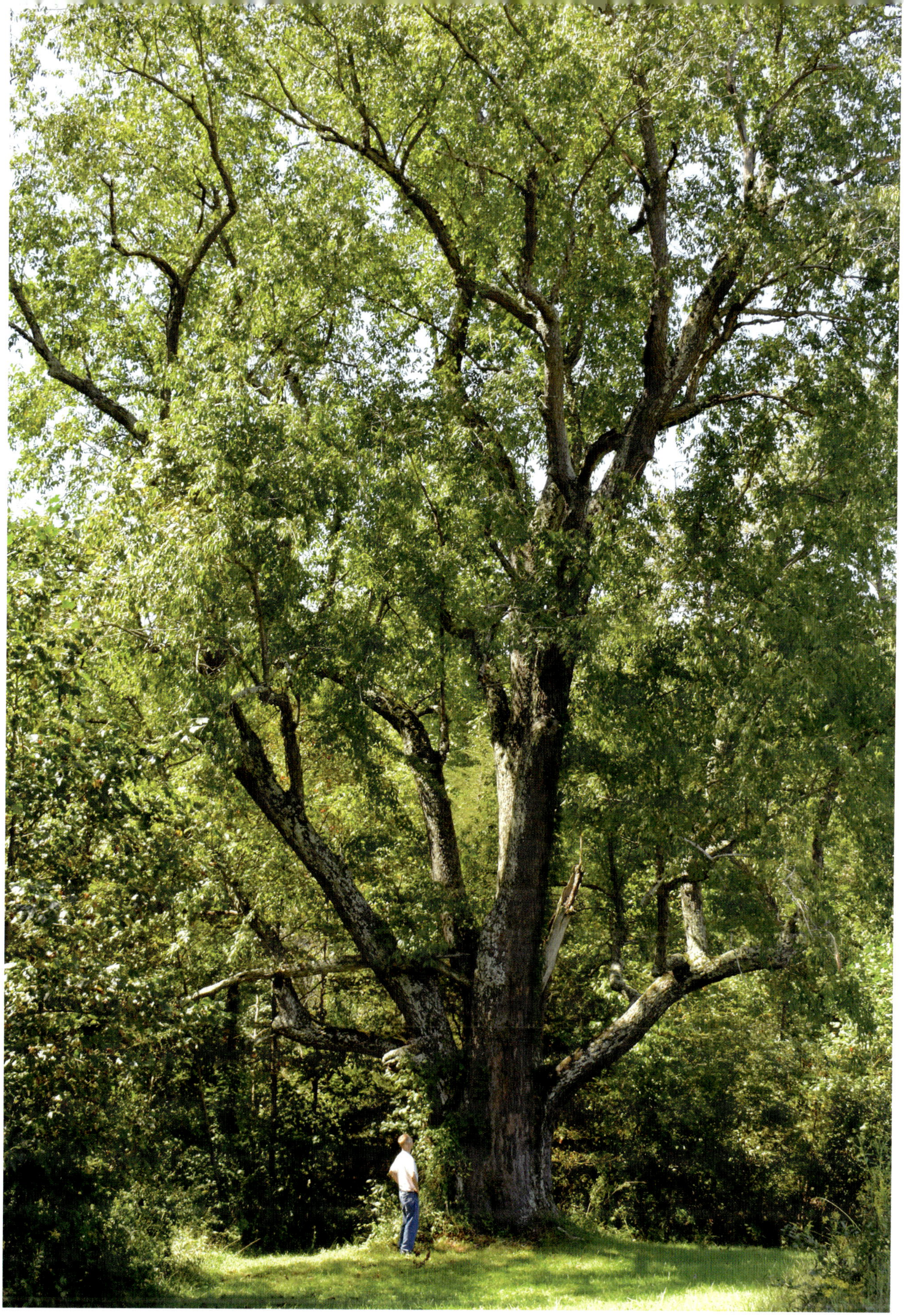

State champion black cherry, Owen County

BLACK GUM

(Nyssa sylvatica)

A most splendid tree commanded admiration and awe here in northern St. Joseph County. This one just didn't have the typical look of dark, almost black alligatored bark seen on smaller specimens down in southern Indiana. Nor was it forked. The proud owners at Red Hen Turf Farm near New Carlisle kindly provided access to the small woods where the tree was the obvious dominate of the whole area. With dimensions of almost 4 feet across and 96 feet tall, it dwarfed every other tree. The nominator of this record specimen, Mr. Ken Feltz, lives adjacent to the woods and meticulously cares for the property. Black gum can be found about everywhere except in areas with alkaline soils. It does seem more prevalent in the southern half of the state and the northern third, but it is not so common in central Indiana.

It has a long history in literature and song, as far back as Andrew Jackson's time in the War of 1812. Also called tupelo and sour gum, the tree had another reputation—hard, tough, and nearly impossible to split. Doubtless the very attempts to master it caused consternation; the warping, shrinking, difficulty in splitting, and lack of durable rot resistance relegated it to a lower-class wood. But its very stubbornness and toughness could be used to great advantage in handles, gunstocks, and in olden times for agricultural machinery and mining rollers that supported heavy steel cables attached to ore cars.

When hollows develop inside and old limbs decay, openings allow for occupation by opossums, raccoons, squirrels, and honeybee colonies. After cutting an old tree down, sections could be sawed into thick slices with open centers. These could house bees, hence the name "bee gums." Instead of a commercial hive as we think of today, the old hollowed-out piece was set upon a bottom plank, then a top board placed over it. With an opening provided, bees could come in and out. This approach was an ingenious way to use nature's provisions with no cost.

Leaves of the black gum are ovate, somewhat wavy, glossy dark green, and quite attractive. The bark texture seems to vary somewhat by site and geography but is mostly dark brown to black, rough, or alligator blocky. This can make identification tricky.

All else said and done about the black gum tree, we must end the essay with superlatives. Extraordinary, flaming burgundy fall color of this tree absolutely captures full attention. Whether in deep woods, along the edge, or on rocky ledges overlooking the Ohio River, the black gum shines radiantly. Along with black gum's companion sugar maple, sassafras, red maple, and some of the oaks, this combination is what makes Indiana postcard perfect in fall.

Characteristics

- Most often 60 feet in height but may reach to 100 feet in exceptional trees.
- Attractive in all seasons, even in bud and early leaf set. Exceptional in fall display.
- Blocky bark, straight trunk, but may die back earlier than other hardwoods.
- Wood is tough and hard to split, but portable sawmills can work it into dimensional sizes or cants.
- May have male and female flowers on the same tree, or on different trees.
- Adaptable to different soils, often found in rich bottomland forests.

Uses

- Historically for items that demanded really tough wear.
- Can still be used for flooring in high-use areas, crates, planks, and barrels.
- Ornamentally it lends great color. Transplanting may be difficult due to the long taproot.

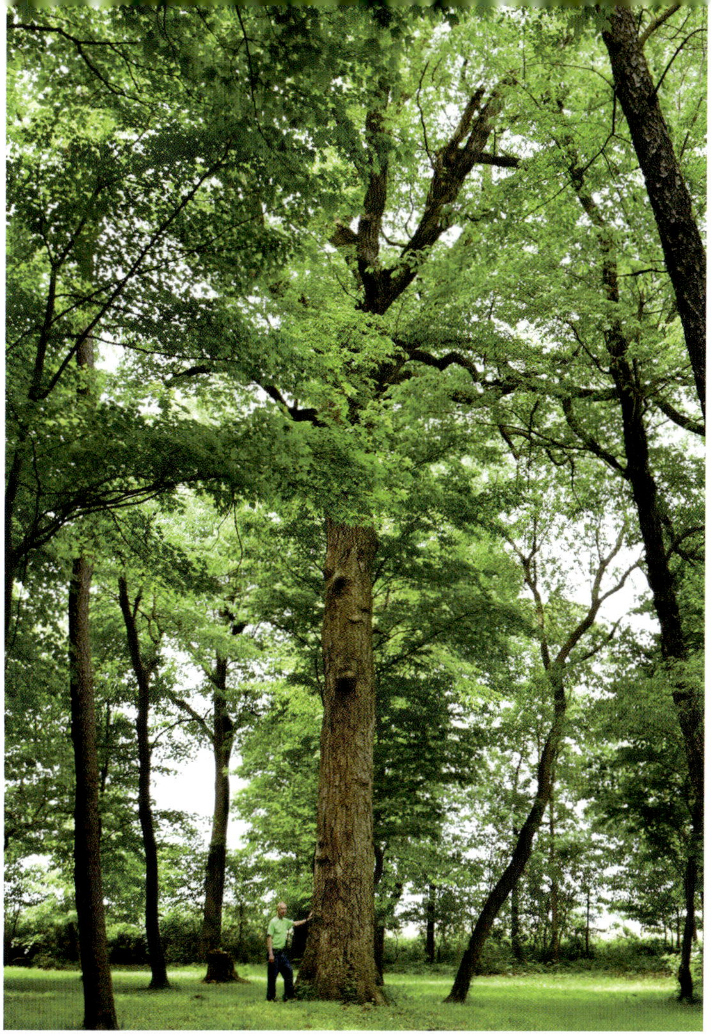

Left: Black gum state champion, St. Joseph County

Below: Superlative black gum fall color

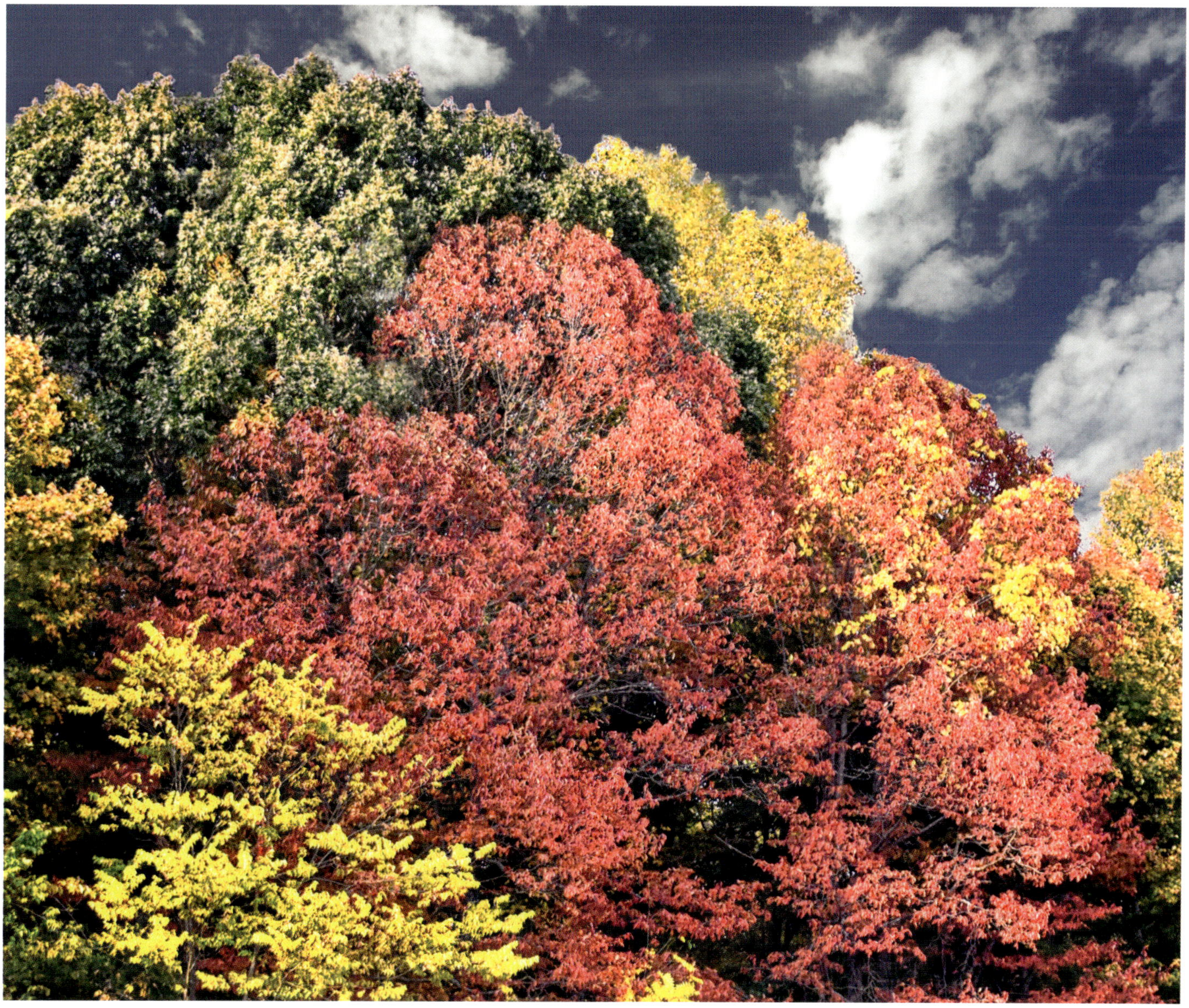

BLUE ASH

(*Fraxinus quadrangulata*)

The name of this tree comes from the presence of a soluble substance within the inner bark. A slick mucilaginous sap turns blue on exposure to air, hence the name. It was learned long ago that this inner bark could be immersed in pails of water, creating a bluish dye. That dye was then found useful for coloring yarn and clothing.

Blue ash can be a handsome tree, although when open grown, it is often shorter with many branches. If you can grab a branch, note the quadrangular shape of the twigs. That always identifies this particular ash. In a forest the tree may be much more impressive as to size. The tree is not as abundant overall as white ash and green ash. It does seem to tolerate dry conditions and last to a very old age. Look for blue ash on rocky hillsides where limestone is the principal surface rock.

A superb blue ash, which is the state record holder, was found at wonderful Deming Park in Terre Haute. At 15 feet in girth and 91 feet in height, this great beauty adorns a small rise in the landscape, commanding the park with its oversight. A huge side limb thrusts outward to gather as much light as possible for this giant. Ironically, this species seems more resistant to the ash borer, but time will tell if that remains true. Although on some of these big ash trees there is evidence of a little die-off in the top, perhaps it will be many more decades before these wonderful specimens decline and return to Mother Earth.

Characteristics

- Opposite leaves, 7–11 pointed leaflets.
- Gray, scaly bark, somewhat shaggy in very old trees.
- Coarse-grained, open-grained wood.
- Quadrangular twigs.
- Winged single-seed propeller permits wind carry.

Uses

- Handles, bats, trim, cabinetry.
- Good landscaping tree in the past.

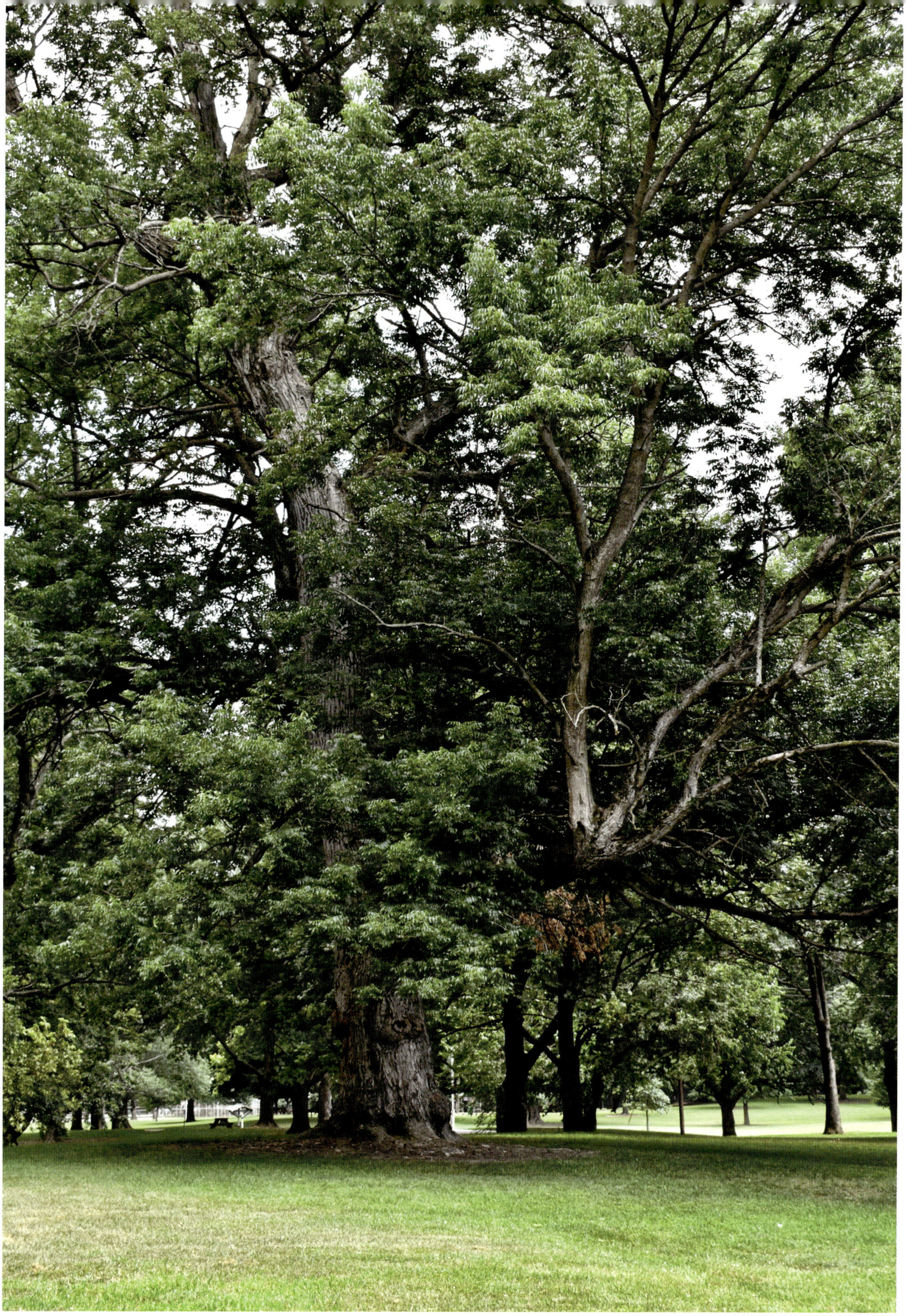

Blue ash state champion, Deming Park, Terre Haute

GREEN ASH

(Fraxinus pennsylvanica)

Ash trees come in many sizes, shapes, and colors. Well, by name, we do indeed see many "colors"—black, white, green, red, and blue. Those were assigned to the common names for several reasons, which Peattie so aptly describes. Black ash has shiny black winter buds; the foliage and heartwood are both moderately dark. White ash has light sapwood and the blondish hue that made it very desirable for furniture and those great baseball bats of yesteryear. Green ash is perhaps named for its darker green lustrous leaves and formerly was separated from a variation called red ash. Jackson (2004), in *101 Trees of Indiana*, recognizes these two as basically the same, with reddish cinnamon color inner bark and rust color on the hairs of buds.

Although the emerald ash borer has significantly affected most native ash trees, an extraordinary find was made on a visit to the Terre Haute Country Club. There it was, on the edge of the golf course, a magnificent green ash, and a survivor so far, radiant with its beauty and perfection as the best of the best. Listed as the state record, it is almost 19 feet around and 80 feet tall. As an inspiration for all who see it and are humbled, we will hope that it stands for many years in the future as a classic icon for what an ash can be.

Characteristics

- Ashes are opposite in their leaf arrangement, which helps identification from other species that are alternate. The old acronym MADBUCAT helps (maple, ash, dogwood, buckeye, and catalpa have common opposite arrangements).
- Green and white ash may be hard to distinguish and almost look alike. Green has somewhat more diamond-shaped interlacing ridges.
- Male and female flowers on separate trees.
- Often grows in wetter settings but may be somewhat shorter and have more limbs than white ash.
- Is one of the most cold-hardy ashes.
- The dead trees, like the other ashes, are often huge and become a danger in woods or towns, creating serious safety issues.

Uses

- Color and grain desirable for furniture.
- Hard and strong, used for many years in handles, bats, boat oars.
- Easy to split for great firewood.
- Used ornamentally, fairly tolerant of both wet and dry settings.
- Wildlife use of propeller-like seeds.

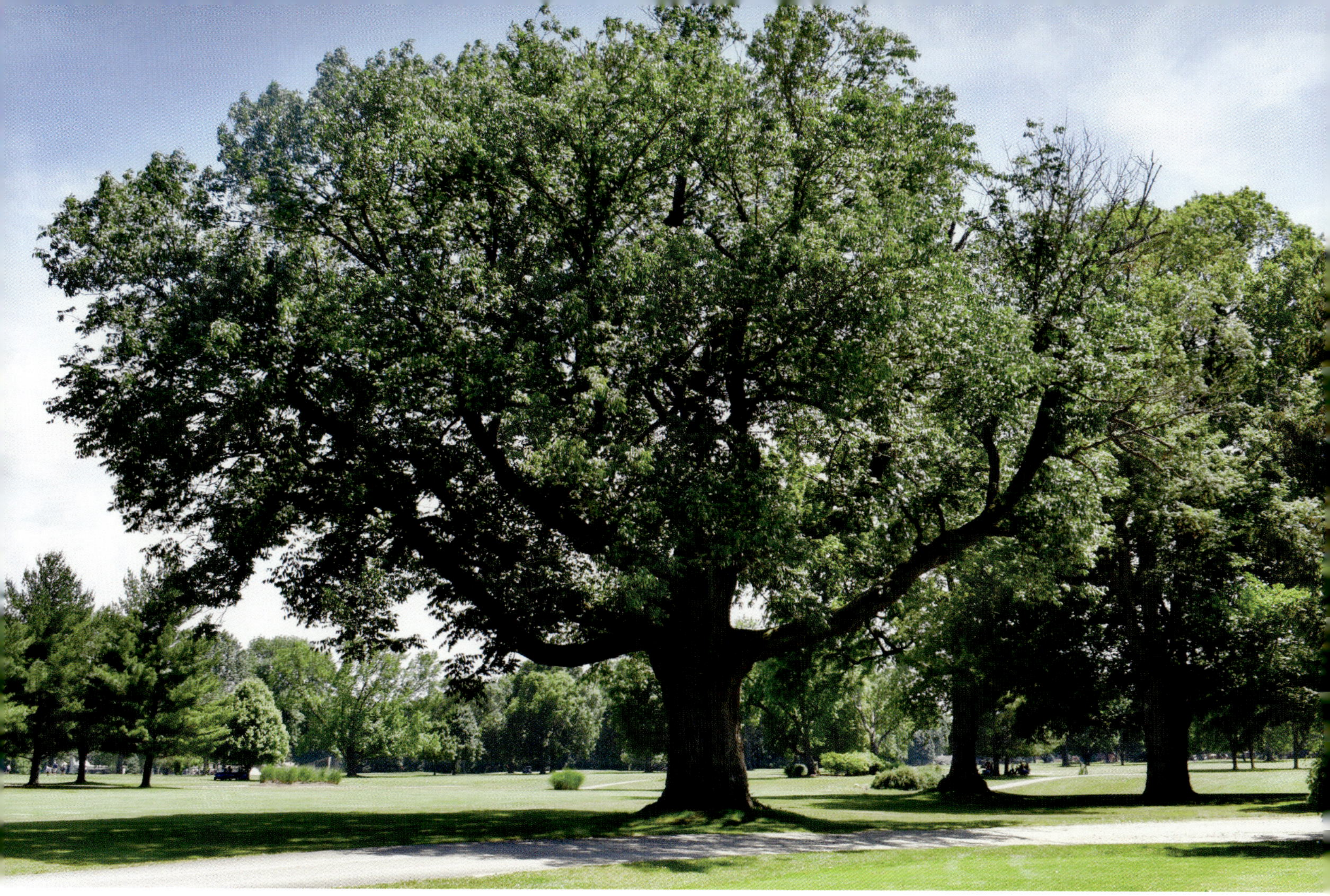

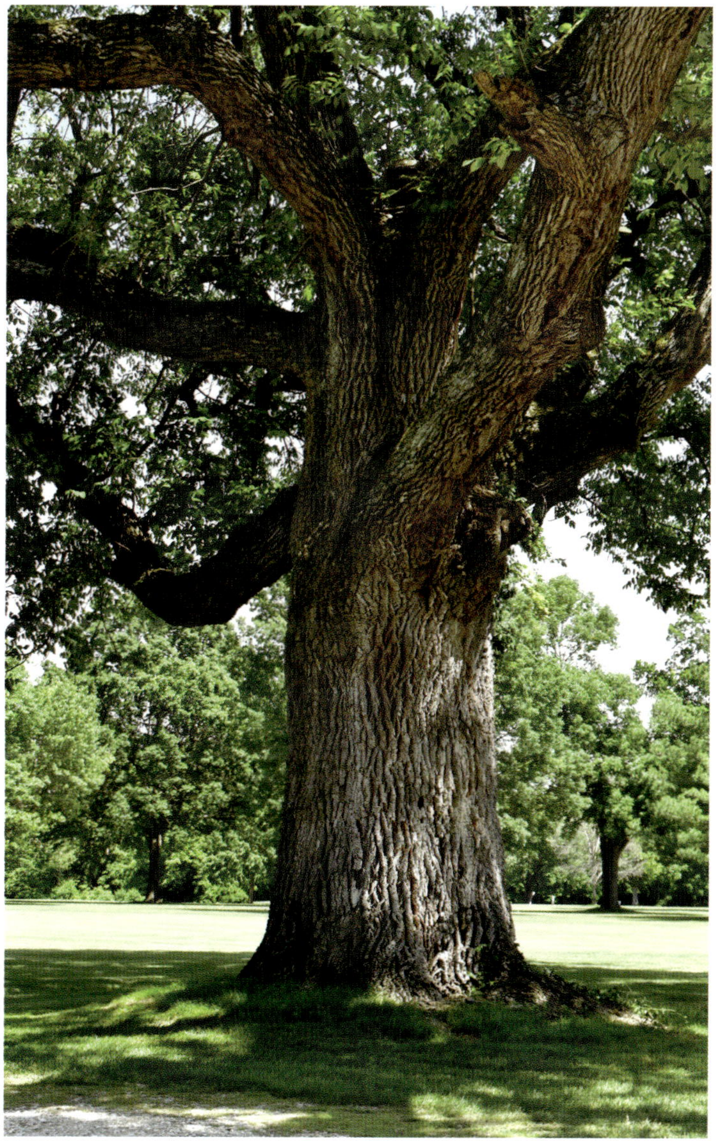

Above: Grand state champion green ash, Terre Haute

Left: Outstanding fissured bark of green ash

PUMPKIN ASH

(*Fraxinus profunda*)

This species does not yield a profusion of pumpkins as the name might suggest. In its river bottom domain, often surrounded by temporary floodwaters and long-lasting wet soggy soils, the base of the trunk actually becomes swollen, and with the orange color, was henceforth called "pumpkin" ash. It is sometimes companion to the bald cypress and swamp cottonwood lowlands and probably more abundant than the casual visitor realizes. Not commonly known to the general public, it is nevertheless a widely occurring species in both northern and southern regions of the Midwest. The southern variety has some slight differences in the leaf, being smoother than its northern brethren, which have somewhat woolly surfaces. The northern variety has twigs that are gray-brown, stout, and with dense, woolly hair.

Our search for the state champion pumpkin ash did not require wading in a flooded quagmire in the Blue River bottoms, but took us nearby to the upland property of Mr. Norman Pennington in Fredericksburg (Washington County). Indeed, this was a great tree, not merely from size, but also because of its regal punctuation to the scenic and well-manicured side yard. With a swing attached to a large limb for young and old to enjoy and a rock garden, the setting was picture-perfect. It was explained to us that many gatherings, meetings, and weddings had taken place at the base of this fine old giant. There was some dieback on the upper limbs, but the tree seemed in very good health at the time of our visit. Research did tell us that pumpkin ash is still susceptible to the emerald ash borer, as well as several other ash pests, so we will keep fingers crossed and wish many more remarkable years for the tree and its many admirers. In the meantime, keep your eyes out for this remarkable species on your next adventure in hip-waders to some mysterious southern Indiana swamp.

Characteristics

- Can be a very tall tree to 100 feet in height and 4 feet across.
- Light gray to tan bark, diamond fissures in old age.
- Long, compound, opposite-arrangement leaves up to 18 inches, with 7–9 leaflets.
- Stout twigs and limbs, round, open crown.
- Largest fruits of the ash group. Dioecious trees (separate male and female).

Uses

- Not a high-grade-value tree; used for crates, pallets, boxes, flooring, and firewood.
- Ornamentally handsome but subject to limb drop or wind damage. The site preference is definitely wet loam, but can occur in uplands, although more stressed there.
- Like most ash species, may be decimated by ash borer and other pests.

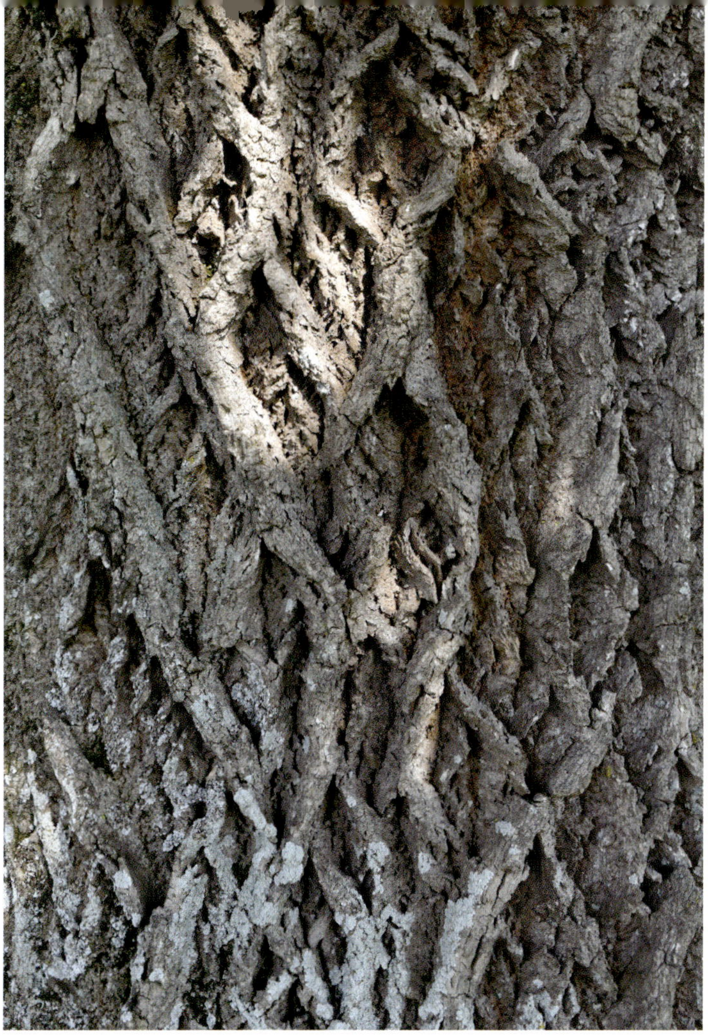

Left: Pumpkin ash shows attractive interwoven bark with slight orange color

Below: State champion pumpkin ash, Washington County

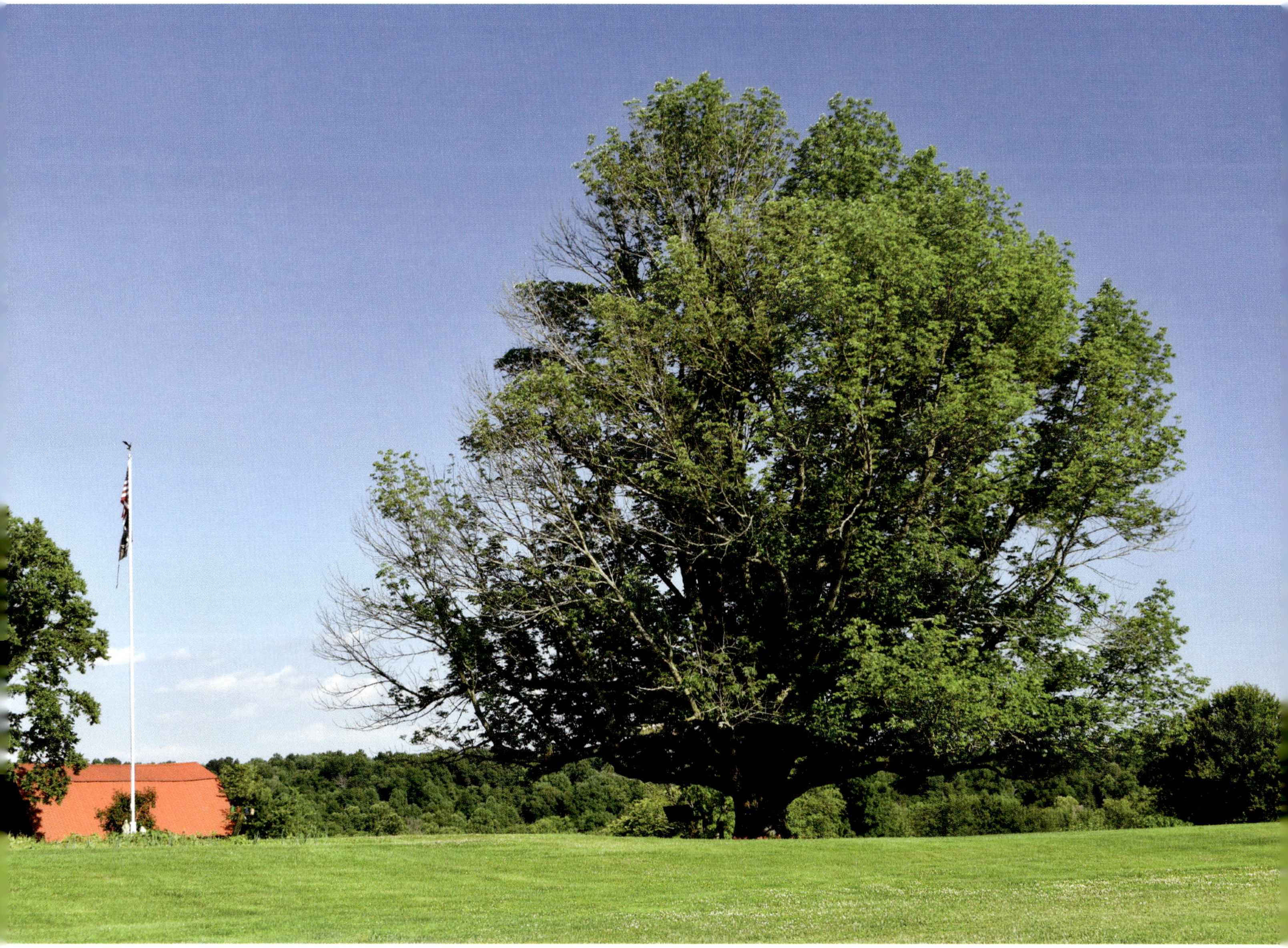

WHITE ASH

(*Fraxinus americana*)

One of the most desirable trees gracing the forests of the eastern United States, this member of the family of ashes stood out for its extraordinary usefulness and was indeed the "all-American tree."

In the forest, white ash is recognizable by its blocky gray-white bark as it rises with a clear trunk far above to the first limbs, then onward to heights of up to 100 feet or more, towering upward with strength and beauty. The crown is not overly broad in younger trees but widens as the tree ages. There is some degree of openness at the top such that summer's azure blue sky provides a fine painter's canvas as the backdrop. With trees planted in the open or along woods' edge, the great boughs develop lower, spread wide, and provide a respite of shade in the heat of summer. The ash loves rich loamy soils and if permitted the full sunlight it needs, grows fast. Historically, ash has truly been a national wood—light, strong, workable, and with subtle beauty in its sometimes wide grain. A remarkable number of uses are credited: handles, tools, boats, flooring, cabinetry, and of course those famous baseball bats. While the very old virgin specimens of up to 150 feet tall and 5 feet wide are long gone, second- and third-generation prodigies aptly filled the need until the current demise of this beloved tree.

Emerald ash borer, another one of a line of introduced pests, arrived from Asia in 2002. It began to move from southeast Michigan and now has infected thirty-five states with devastation.[3] Many ash species are affected, but white ash is the most heartbreaking loss. Tens of millions of trees have been destroyed and millions of dollars spent in treatment attempts, removal, and frantic research. To date the borer continues to spread and quarantine mandates have not stopped its march. Current research is on biological/chemical control methodologies with hopes that solutions can be found to halt the infestation. A goal is to assure that reproduction of young stock can once again generate a viable component of our hardwood forest ecosystem

Ash was planted extensively in yards and parks for its beauty, shade, and lack of limb litter. It lined city streets and became an institution in itself as a beloved icon. With the attack of the emerald ash borer, towns were faced with not only loss of beauty and shade, but with the hazards now created by dead trees and falling limbs. Removal became not only time-consuming, but an impact on the street and park budgets. Substitute species were pondered but none quite compare to the glorious white ash.

There are still several living old white ash trees occasionally found, and it is of interest to see if they will survive. We were lucky to find a fine example in Muscatatuck National Wildlife Refuge. It was a large specimen, tall and beautiful, at least for now.

Another great specimen was observed in a protected woods near Cortland in Jackson County. This grand tree spired upward to 95 feet and appeared to have leaf buds on it when we visited.

Characteristics

- Ash is opposite in leaf arrangement, compound, with 5–9 leaflets per leaf, each perhaps 3–5 inches in length, pointed tip, smooth or very finely toothed margins.
- Bark is variable, from chunky, blocky, to smoother with some ridging, diamond patterned.
- Seed is on a single propeller, in a cluster, wind dispersed in autumn.

Uses

- As mentioned above and of some wildlife food value.
- Severely affected by EAB; harvest has to occur quickly or wood stains black.
- Firewood from scavenged limbs and trees that are not merchantable.

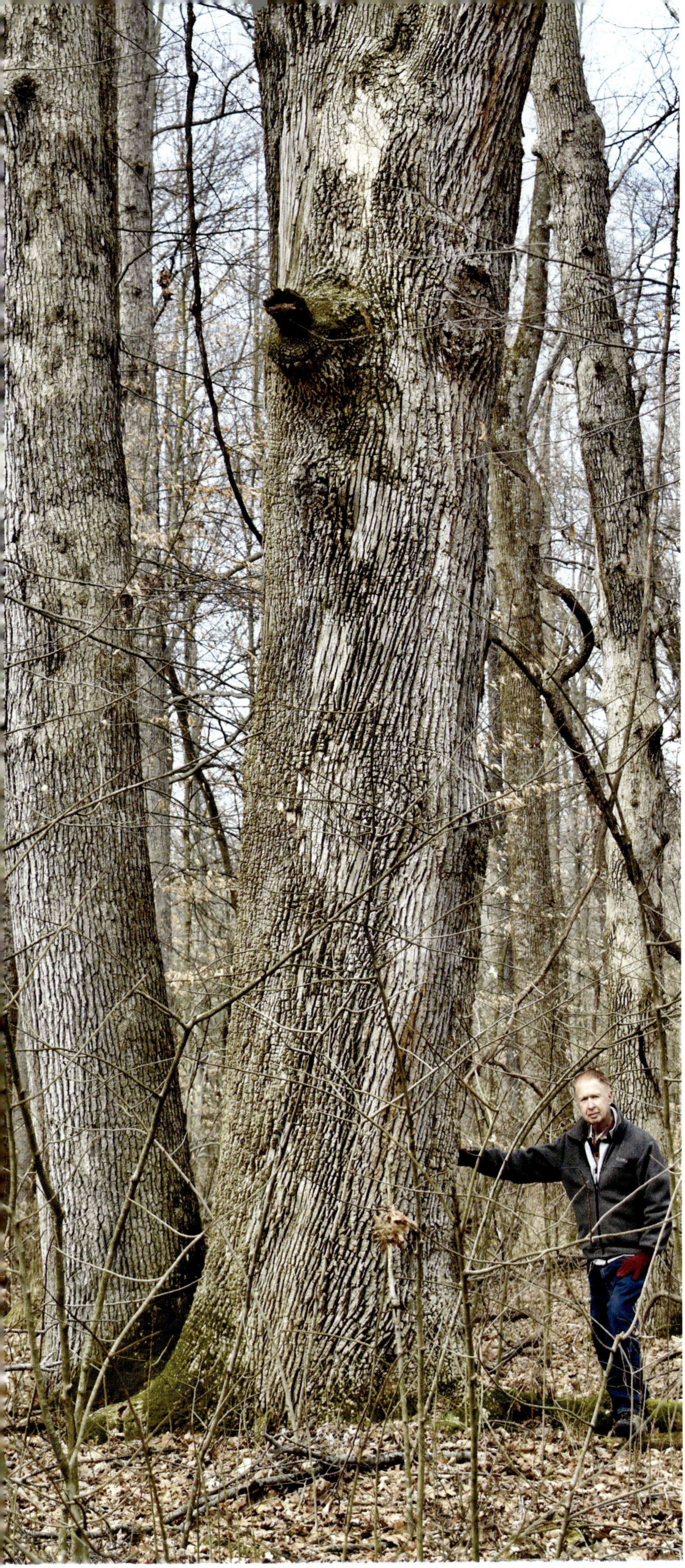

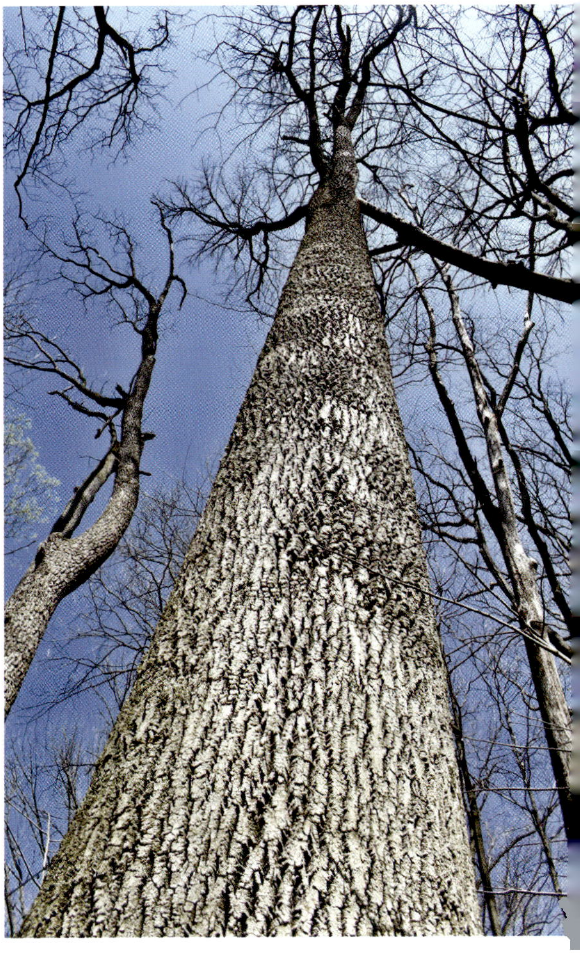

Above: Fine white ash, Keller Woods, Jackson County

Left: Huge white ash, Muscatatuck National Wildlife Refuge

RIVER BIRCH

(Betula nigra)

A very old river birch with great countenance clung to the banks of Guthrie Creek near Devil's Backbone in Lawrence County. It was the state champion in 1976 and had doubtless survived floods and many other events that would be interesting to know. A 2019 drive back to look for this old tree found it gone, perhaps losing its grip on the ever-changing creek bank.

The current champion was found in a nicely manicured subdivision of Avon, complete with a treehouse, obviously giving much pleasure to the children at the residence. It is 4 feet across and 74 feet tall. Another very nice specimen was previously in Riverside Cemetery in Seymour, distinguished and gracefully occupying a serene spot. Since storm damage had occurred and decay was present, workers had to remove it.

River birch is common along stream courses and wetlands throughout the state. It is often multistem but can reach an impressive diameter. The flaky, peeling bark is quite distinctive, varying from pinkish red to reddish-brown. In old trees the bark may become more firmly plate-like and blackish. To some, the tree is not particularly noteworthy since it often branches and rarely achieves that tall, spar-like straight trunk. But to others, the unique bark and stems are quite showy and add nice variety, especially in urban settings.

The river birch has other relatives with dainty, toothed leaves and interesting bark. These include gray birch, paper birch, cherry birch, and yellow birch. Gray and paper birches are found in northern Indiana, with cherry birch more in states east of Indiana. Yellow birch can be more common in northern Indiana but rare in southern Indiana. The sandstone cliffs of Yellow Birch Ravine in Crawford County host a few of these intriguing trees clinging onto ledges and steep hillsides that plunge into the pristine creek.

Not particularly sought after by lumbermen, the tree is content to occupy lowlands and stream sides, providing bank stabilization and erosion mitigation. The abundant catkin seeds distribute readily by winds or stream flows in May and June, traveling to the next suitable moist locale to readily sprout. River birch flourishes today in much of the Midwest, South, and East, serving as a touch of color, texture, and physical structure for our admiration.

Characteristics

- Alternate, toothed, single leaf.
- Flaky, colorful bark.
- Height to 80 feet, width to about that as well, often with diverging multistems.
- Likes wetter sites but adaptable to many environments.

Uses

- Historically, for rice cask hoops, woodenware, general uses.
- Today somewhat used for specialty woodcrafts and cabinets since the wood can be pretty.
- Although it adds interest to yards, it drops limbs, dies back, and is not typically long-lived.
- Not a particularly valuable wildlife tree; some seed use by birds; old dead trees used by woodpeckers.

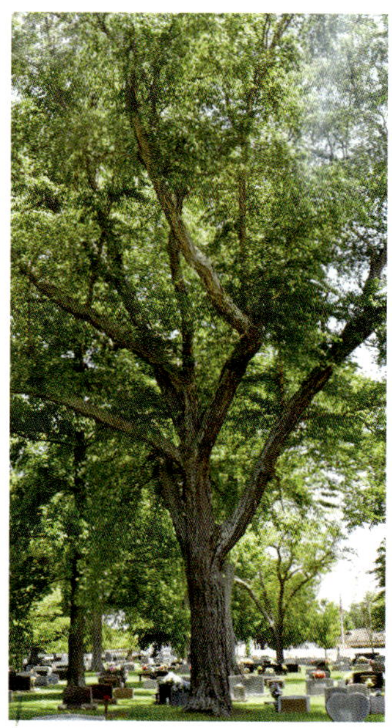

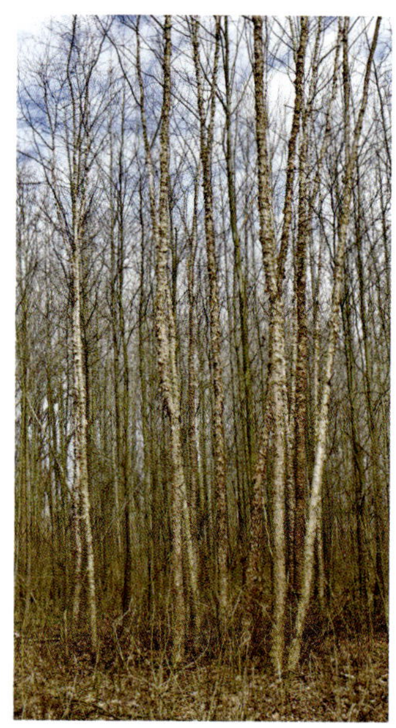

Stately river birch, Jackson County and river birch reclaiming wetland, Muscatatuck National Wildlife Refuge

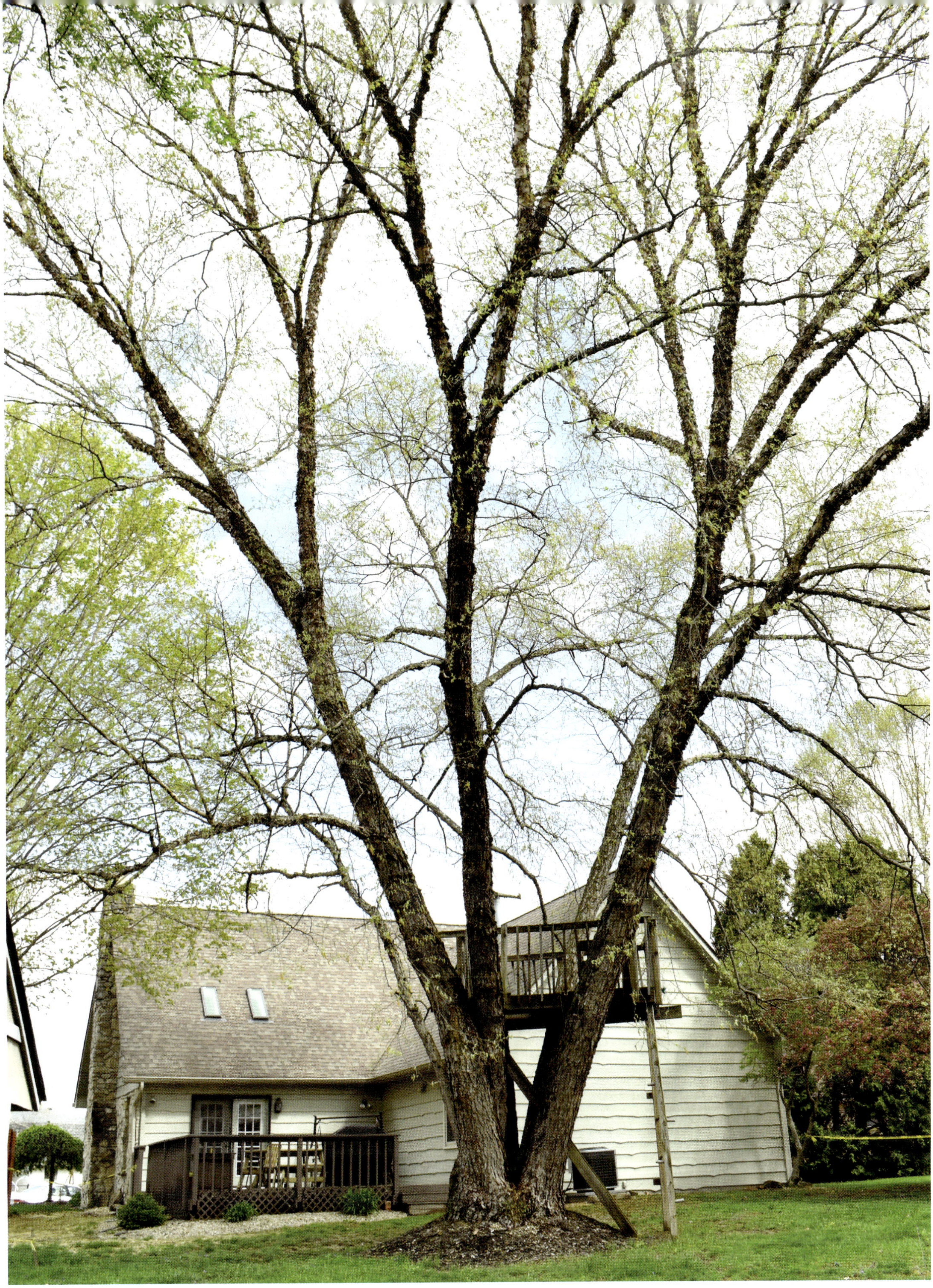

State champion river birch, Hendricks County

YELLOW BIRCH

(*Betula alleghaniensis*)

The tough climb up the steep hillside among huge sandstone blocks and boulders brought me to the rare tree being sought. Here, at Yellow Birch Ravine, the quest for yellow birch is not easy. The terrain is challenging. Trees have a difficult time growing on the slopes, with roots struggling to find footing among the myriad of rocks. Those unluckily perched on the brink of the cliff face certain demise if they do survive to adulthood. The companion trees here were beech, oaks, and hemlocks, the latter presenting a most marvelous green backdrop on lofty precipices.

The yellow birch found was a lucky old specimen, growing in the confinement of the cliff crevice in the honeycombed, sandstone walls. The struggles of this tree will never be known, but it somehow has attained over 3 feet in girth and 65 feet in height. The yellow-gray flaking bark was an identification key, along with those typical birch-shape leaves, most of which had fallen in early November. Far below, the pristine creek, teeming with minnows, carved its winding path through the bedrock. Abundant mosses and ferns adorned not only rock, but rich woodland as well.

Yellow Birch Ravine is a classic sandstone canyon-cliff setting in Crawford County. It has been known as an outstanding biological and geological area for many years.

Lindsey (1969) also mentions this special location. It is the only known location of the intersection of three species—mountain laurel, eastern hemlock, and yellow birch. An old quarry did destroy some of the original trees on the north side. There are several side ravines, alcoves, and waterfalls. After a heavy rain, gushing torrents of water pour over these, creating a most spectacular scene. The combinations of botany and geology justify this 441-acre area designated as a state nature preserve, with the name appropriate to the rare tree found here.

Yellow birch trees are also found more abundantly in northern Indiana bogs, and distribution occurs widely in the eastern United States. As with his yellowwood discovery, French botanist explorer André Michaux also found this new species in North America in 1803 (Peattie, 1966). Once the values of yellow birch were realized, it became a valuable lumber tree and remains the primary birch used for many products.

Even though the tree is common in the north and east, the special rarity of seeing a secluded yellow birch hidden away in a remote sandstone ravine in rural Crawford County made our day one of great natural rewards.

Characteristics

- Small to medium-sized tree in Indiana to 12 inches in diameter, 60 feet tall.
- Curly, peeling yellow-bronze bark, grayer with age.
- Male and female flowers on same tree.
- Prolific seeder in good years, low germination rate.

Uses

- Yellow birch lumber and veneer are used in making furniture, paneling, plywood, cabinets, boxes, woodenware, handles, and interior doors.
- It is one of the principal hardwoods used in the distillation of wood alcohol, acetate of lime, charcoal, tar, and oils.[4]
- Deer may extensively browse young birch. Catkins and seeds used by several birds.

Right page: Yellow birch at Yellow Birch Ravine, Crawford County

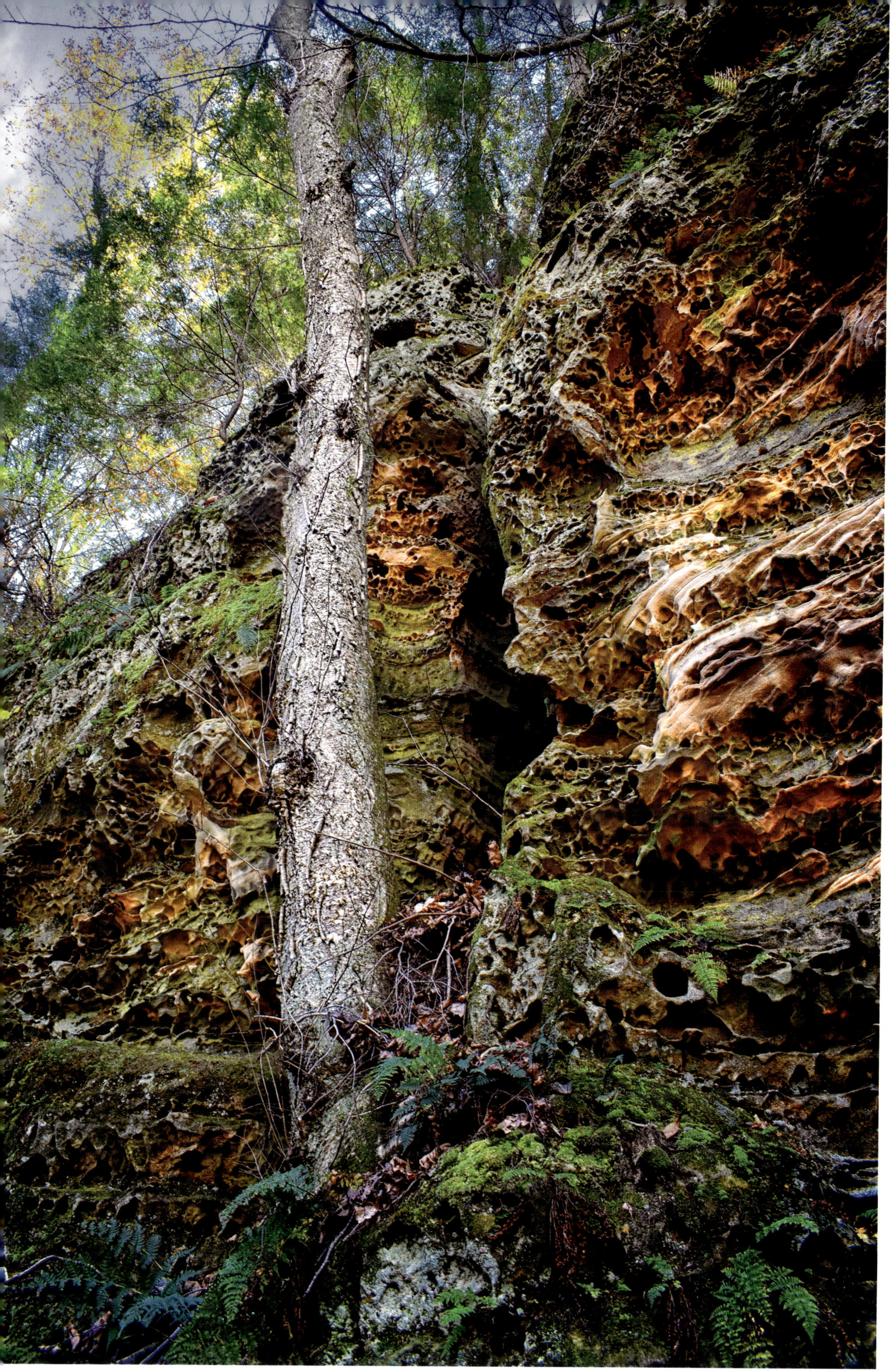

TWO BUCKEYES: YELLOW BUCKEYE AND OHIO BUCKEYE

(*Aesculus flava and Aesculus glabra*)

Two incredible trees in one incredible trip. Sometimes these tree adventures became a little more complicated than planned. The first stop was to be Charlestown State Park for the **yellow buckeye**, a rarely seen tree on the state "watch list." Naturalist Jeremy Beavin knew its approximate location and was eager to see the champion once again. There were two reasons he had to show us personally. The first was because it was in a restricted area, formerly part of the old Indiana Army Ammunition Plant. That amazing facility was the largest smokeless powder plant in the world during World War II. The Clark County historical records of this huge operation are intriguing.

The second reason was that the tree was just difficult to find among all the regrowth after the area was acquired by the state. Access was on old roadways, many of which were gated. We were able to enter one of those and drive far back through encroaching vegetation, stopping at one location that was thought to be close to the tree. After a short hike the group decided that this spot was not going to be productive. Jeremy drove on a little further. Visible out the right side was a tree in the far distance that had lost most of its leaves high up in the canopy. Since buckeyes do lose them early, perhaps a closer look was in order. We parked and began a hike on an almost totally overgrown roadway, unsure of what might be found in all that brush. Then, suddenly—there it was—a huge old tree! Found! A true champion, this yellow buckeye measured almost 6 feet in diameter and 70 feet in height. With dark gray, rough, scaly bark and massive gnarly side limbs, it was a spectacle to behold. How could it have been protected all these years when all other timber of size was long gone? Fortunately it was spared because yellow buckeye is not too common, and specimens of this integrity are rarely found.

Yellow buckeye's range in Indiana is primarily in the southeast corner and along the Ohio River bottoms and benches. It does occupy higher ground and some hillsides or ravines. But it prefers that rich soil type and can become a very handsome specimen, whether open and branched or a fairly tall individual to 70 feet. One notices two things right away about this wondrous tree—fairly large, compound, palmate leaves, almost like a hand beckoning one to come closer. Then, the product of its beautiful April yellow blooms is a thin-shelled capsule 2–3 inches in length. When this falls to the ground in late summer and the smooth husk is opened, two seeds fall out, each with that "buck's-eye" look. The leaves, young shoots, and seeds are poisonous to humans and cattle rarely dare consume them. Yellow buckeye is also called "sweet buckeye," which sounds odd because what eats it? The primary reason is that it doesn't have a stinking odor when bruised or its leaves are crushed. Its cousin, Ohio buckeye, does have that property, as described below, and its seeds are more toxic.

The second find of the trip, an **Ohio buckeye**, also a state champion, was north of Madison on private property in a remote part of Jefferson County very near the Switzerland County line. With a map and a dot on it to locate the tree, we drove across an overgrown field to the woods' edge. Walking down the forested hillside and crossing a creek brought us to the area where the tree was supposedly standing. A search was not proving productive at all, but as luck was with us this day, the owner arrived to bush hog the property's pathways. The three of us made our way back to the area of our original wandering. With surrounding beech trees of equal size, the buckeye was blending in so well that our guide had to find it again himself. There it was on the rocky hillside, not intuitively obvious to anyone but a tree ID buff. At 2½ feet in diameter and 110 feet in height, it did command utmost respect

Right page: Champion yellow buckeye, Clark County—a remarkable find

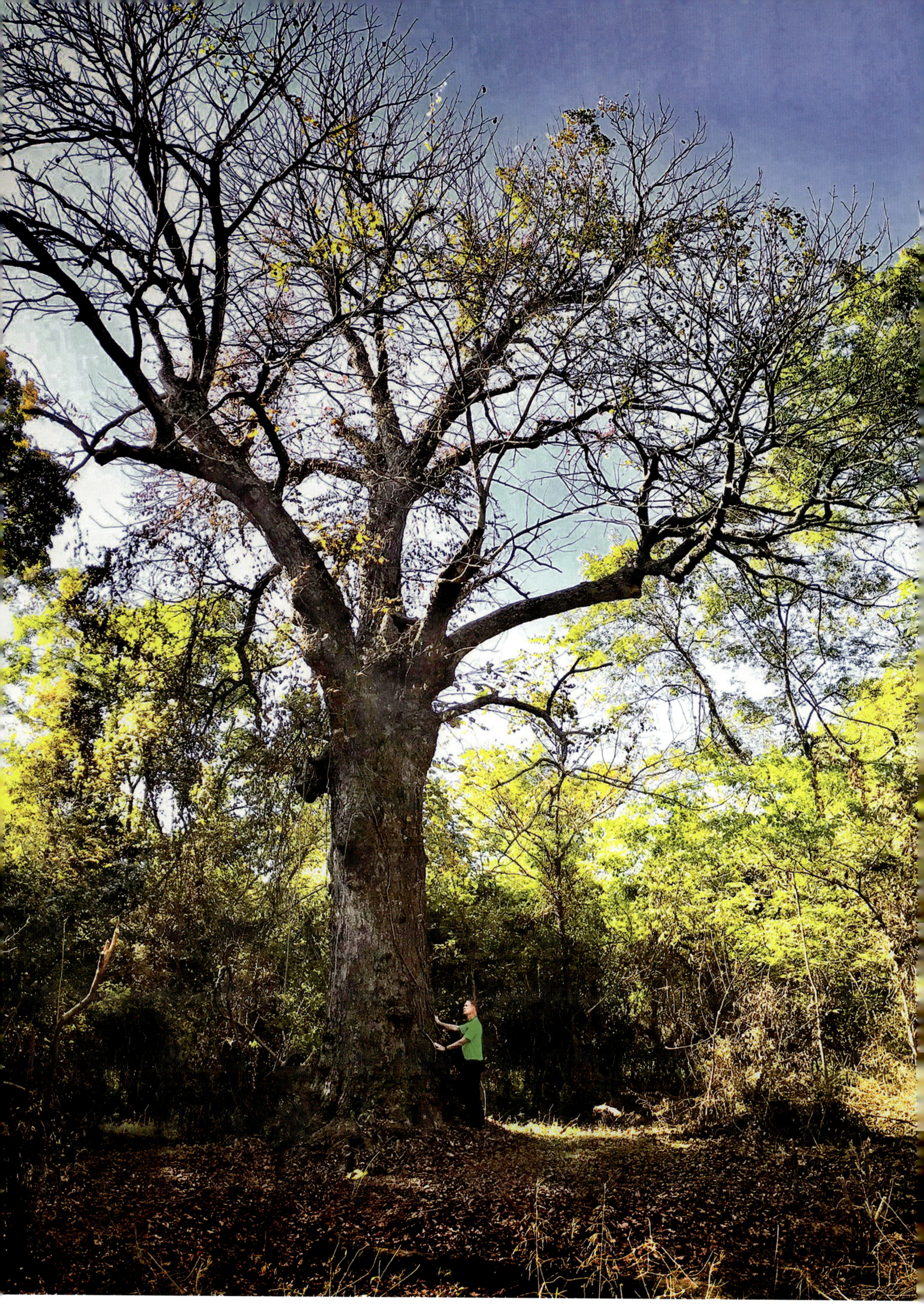

as a favored, protected tree, marked as a "save" from the last timber harvest in the forest. Even though the lifespan of buckeyes is not extremely long, may this one grace the hillside many more decades.

Ohio buckeye has a fascinating history all the way back to 1788 and the early territory of Ohio. Ever since, the term has been an identifier for those fine folks next door to Indiana. The ostentatious bloom of yellow-green flowers in the spring, right after the early emergence of green leaves, is delightful in every aspect. Even the large orange-red buds flash joy at their opening. The bark is gray-brown, often scaly, and on very old trees may become fissured. This species is not generally as large as yellow buckeye, in stature or in leaf size. It also produces those "buck-eyes," but in this case, the husked capsule is spiny, splits in three parts, and yields one to three shiny marble-sized prizes. Collect a few of those to put in your pocket for good luck.

There are so many positives about this tree that one may overlook that the name is also "Fetid Buckeye" or "Stinking Buckeye." A slight odor on approach may be noticed, but if one crushes flowers, twigs, or leaves, prepare for a pungent smell. Other than that, the species is a delight.

Characteristics

- Buckeyes are palmately compound, usually five leaves attached right onto the stem.
- They are also opposite branching.
- Generally they prefer moist, rich soils and lowlands, but are adaptable.
- Buckeye is often the very first tree to leaf out in the woods, grabbing attention before the other trees take on their own emergence.
- The flower is quite showy and the fruit or capsule produced contains those noted shiny seeds.

Uses

- Buckeye wood is not hard or durable, and it is not a prized timber tree.
- Its softness did allow some old uses for utensils, carving, and even making artificial limbs.
- The seeds are of visual interest to humans, but of little value to animals or us.
- The tree form and lack of edibility make it of low interest to wildlife.
- It can make an interesting ornamental tree for those wanting something a little different.

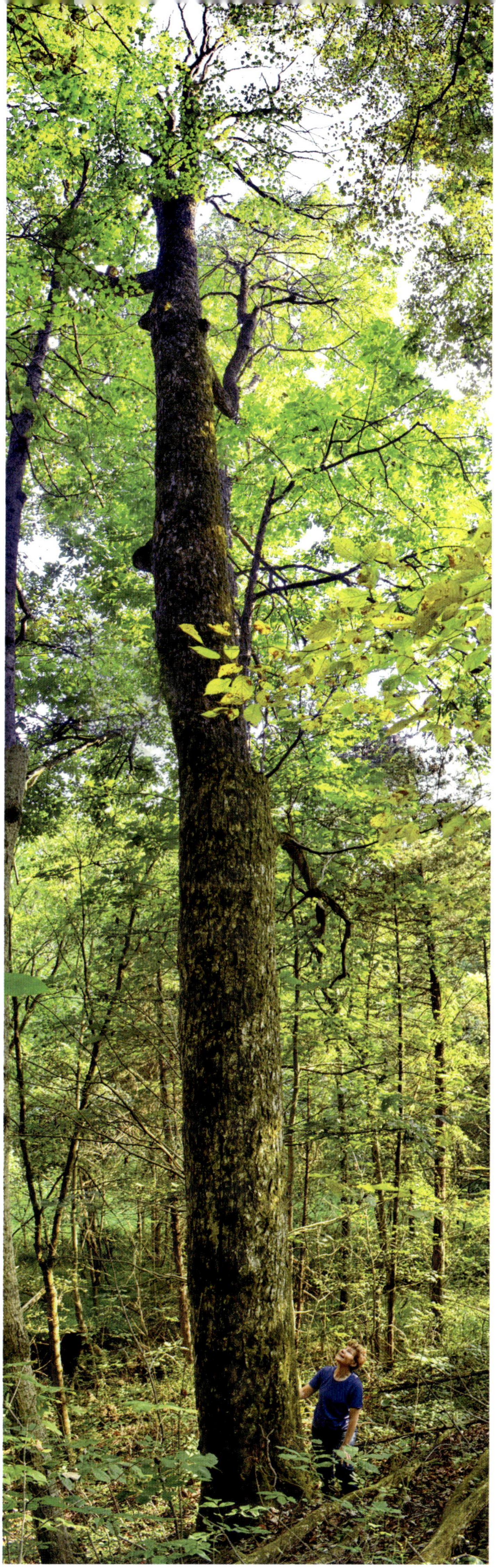

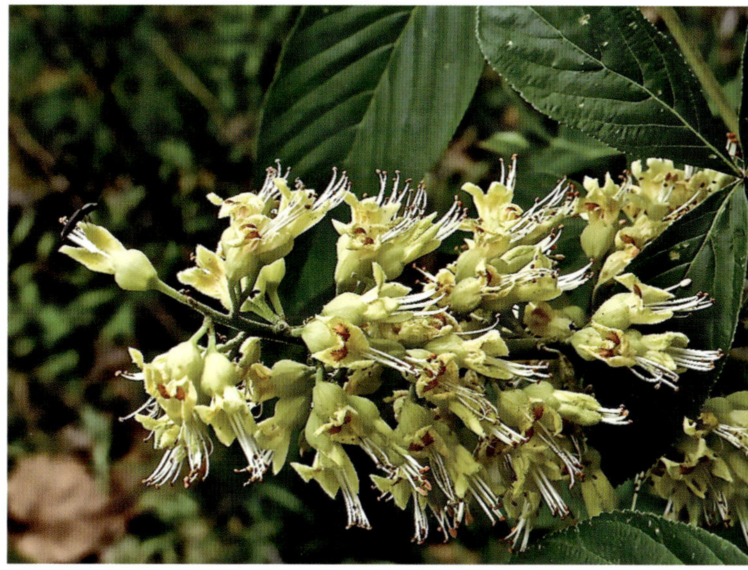

Above: Ohio buckeye showing beautiful spring blooms

Left: State champion Ohio buckeye, Jefferson County

BOXELDER

(Acer negundo)

Considered a wallflower and not often invited to prestigious gatherings, the neglected boxelder is not held in much esteem. Often of short stature, with limbs undecided where they want to go, and not yielding spectacular fall color like their kin, the other maples, they are relegated to the lowest rank. Also called ash-leaved maple, Manitoba maple, and sugar ash, the boxelder just does not seem to fit in anywhere. The leaf is odd, more like that of an elder, the bark between an ash and a maple, and the form does not entice a lumberman. Yet it has those winged propeller seeds just like a "normal" maple, an opposite leaf arrangement, and is 3-lobed. As seeds develop in the spring, they become a food source for the infamous boxelder bug. Great numbers of these insects may also be found on maples and even ash. When disturbed from their ravenous feeding, they exude a foul-smelling liquid repulsive to most other predators and not particularly pleasing to humans as well. Thus is the poor boxelder tree laden down with pejorative criticism.

Never minding its status here in the Midwest, the species actually becomes more appreciated in the Great Plains and southern Canada. The tree's form seems straighter, the canopy rather impressive, and sap is actually tapped for a moderate amount of sugar. The fast-growing nature of the species out there increases its worth as a much appreciated shade tree in the hot, dry seasons.

One of the specimens featured here is rather typical. It resided along the banks of Sugar Creek at Turkey Run State Park. The species seems to like those lowlands along stream corridors. Again, however, the boxelders along the trail were far overclassed by the huge sycamore and walnut trees. Such is the sad fate of the lowly ones, but today, this pictured tree was actually loved for what it was, a valuable piece of the natural world.

Characteristics

- Short in stature to perhaps 60 feet, with crown spread sometimes two-thirds that.
- Diameters vary from 1 to 3 feet.
- Opposite leaf arrangement as per maples in general.
- Three to five leaflets on the compound leaf, with the shape three-lobed.

Uses

- Soft wood of low economic value. Used for boxes, crates, pallets, and pulp.
- Some trees have inner wood of pinkish tint, making them interesting for woodworking novelties.

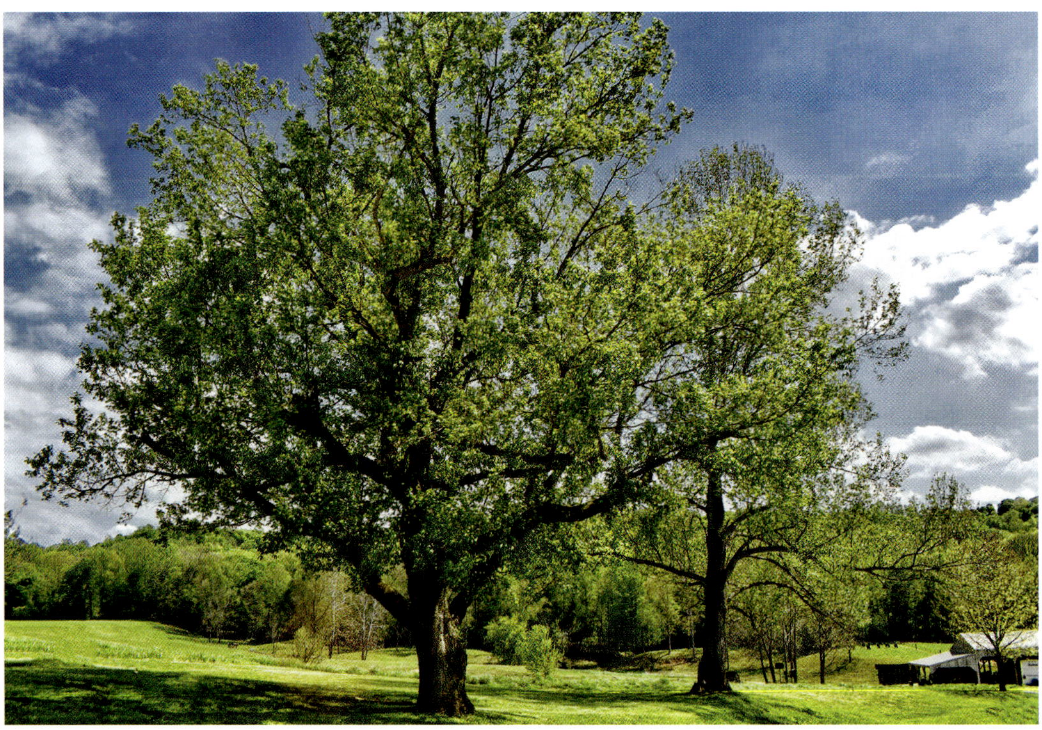

Boxelder can also be a fine yard tree, such as this one near Williams

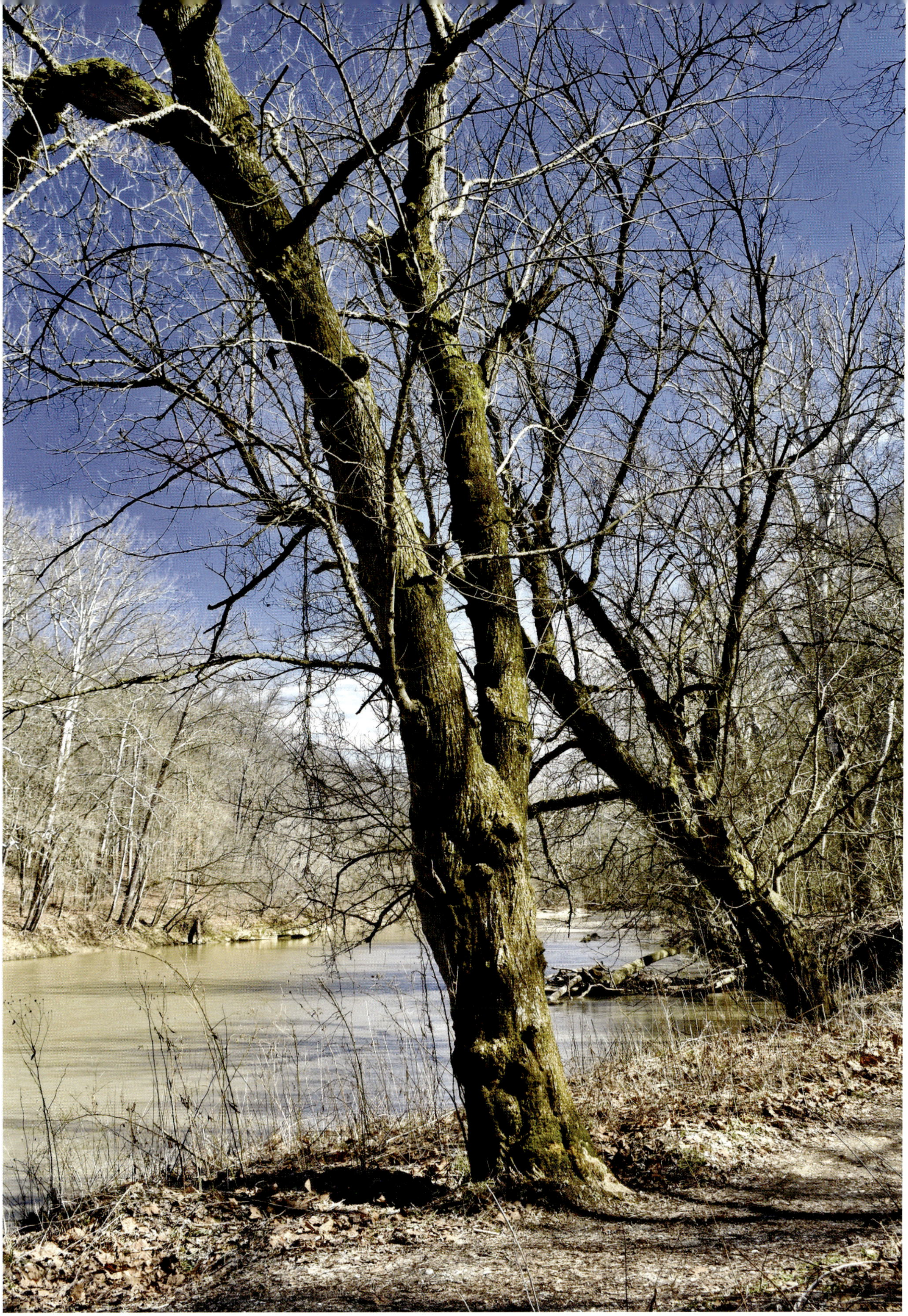

Boxelders along Sugar Creek, Turkey Run State Park

BLACK WALNUT

(Juglans nigra)

This truly is a species with great character, beauty, and exceptional qualities. A common Indiana tree often growing to large sizes, it prefers rich well-drained soils and may frequently be found on floodplains, but also in upland woods. It is highly valued if of veneer-grade quality, that character not frequently found. In a mature forest where the tree has grown straight and tall with no defects, it may command an extraordinary price like that of an Ohio prime specimen bringing $35,000. In the old days of Indiana, some of these massive walnuts must have been remarkable. Robert Ridgway and others cited sizes of this great tree in the 1800s.

To see the current state champion required a trip to Elkhart County where there was a beloved grand specimen well cared for by its owners. This must have been an open-grown tree since it had large branching limbs. The tree was cabled and hollow on one side; nonetheless it was a very wonderful old giant 6 feet across and 88 feet in height. The largest diameter black walnut in the country is actually in Oregon, over 8 feet across. Black walnut is found in Europe as well, with the world's tallest one in Belgium.[5]

There are other awe-inspiring walnut locations in Indiana for those who wish to reflect on what those great ones of the past must have looked like. An impressive grouping of large individuals can be found along the Sugar Creek trail at Turkey Run State Park. It was a privilege to see these same old giants as mentioned in Alton Lindsey's *Natural Areas of Indiana and Their Preservation* (1969). Shrader-Weaver Woods, mentioned in this book's Chapter 5 on old growth, has some large ones, and Pioneer Mothers Memorial Forest in Orange County has exceptional representatives as well. All of these locations have trails, and any admirer of big trees will not be disappointed.

The color and grain make it an exceptional wood and hand-hewn or very old factory production walnut furniture is always highly valued. A large antique walnut three-corner cupboard crafted with perfection in a small shop during the 1840s using basic tools might today be worth $4,000.

The spectacle of a full crop of walnuts borne on heavy-laden limbs in the fall is impressive. In good years, the fallen nuts cover the ground. They are a treat for both humans and squirrels. If one can beat the critters to the harvest, walnuts can be collected and taken to a local hulling operation that pays a nominal price. Just be careful in walking under the tree loaded with the heavy nuts!

Black walnut and butternut walnut are seriously threatened by several pests including thousand cankers disease. Although this has not yet spread in Indiana, a more recent report cites finding the fungus at one site and walnut twig beetle at another site.[6] Since the disease is caused by the combination of the two, it is hoped that quarantines in place will prevent or slow its introduction. Walnut trees are also affected by bunch disease and fusarium canker.[7] These too can be serious problems for one of our most important timber trees.

Characteristics

- Black walnut is a large tree that grows to over 100 feet high and 4 feet in diameter.
- The leaf stalks are up to 2 feet long, with 15–23 leaflets.
- Inner bark chocolate brown, outer bark dark chocolate, ridged.
- Roots contain juglone, an allelopathic compound that may inhibit growth of other nearby plants. The dye has been used in textiles and even in hair coloring.

Uses

- Fine furniture, flooring, cabinets, gunstocks, and woodworking specialties.
- Nuts desirable and of value. Nuts can be used to start new plantations.
- Has often been planted in yards, but not advisable if you want to stay upright on your feet after a heavy nut crop has fallen.

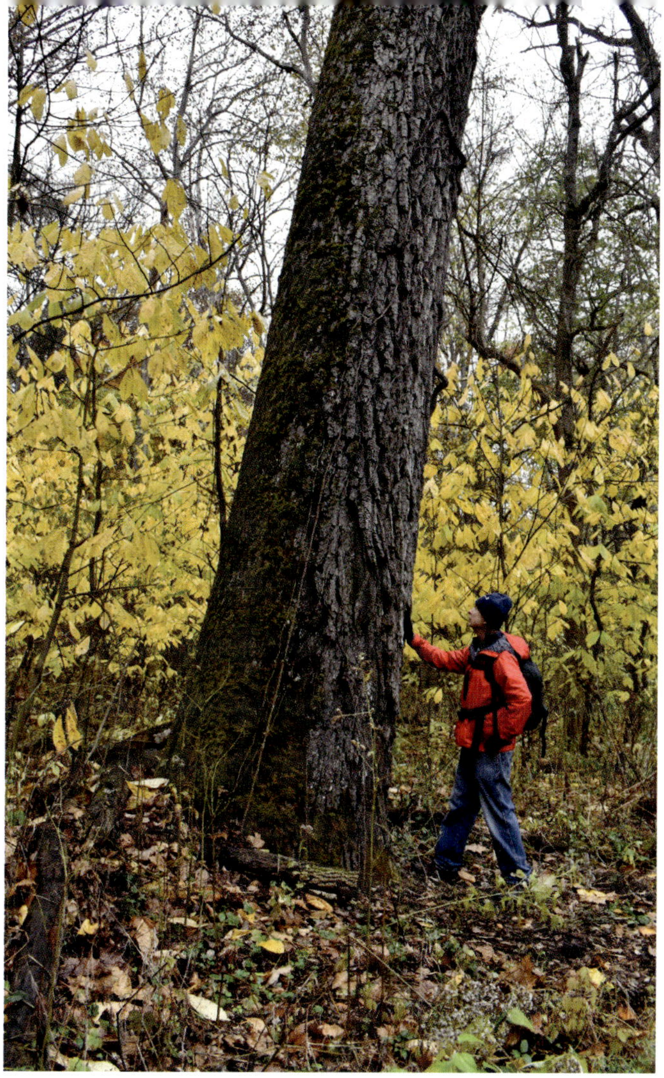

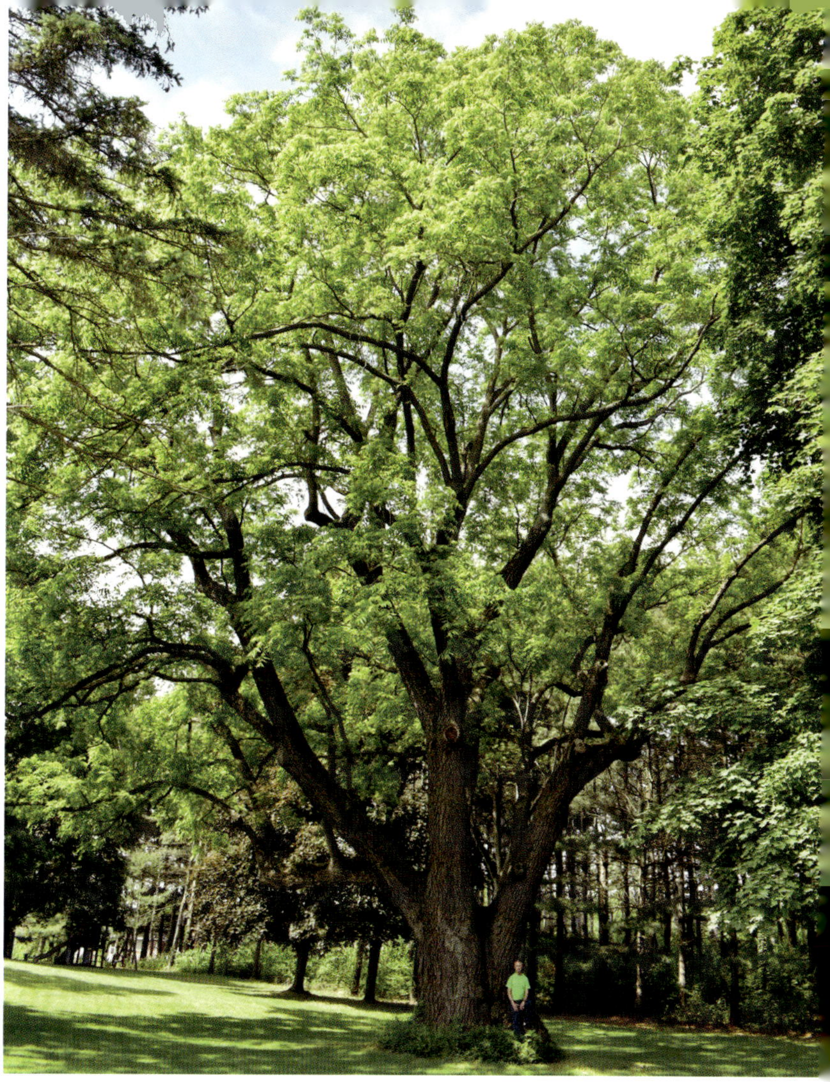

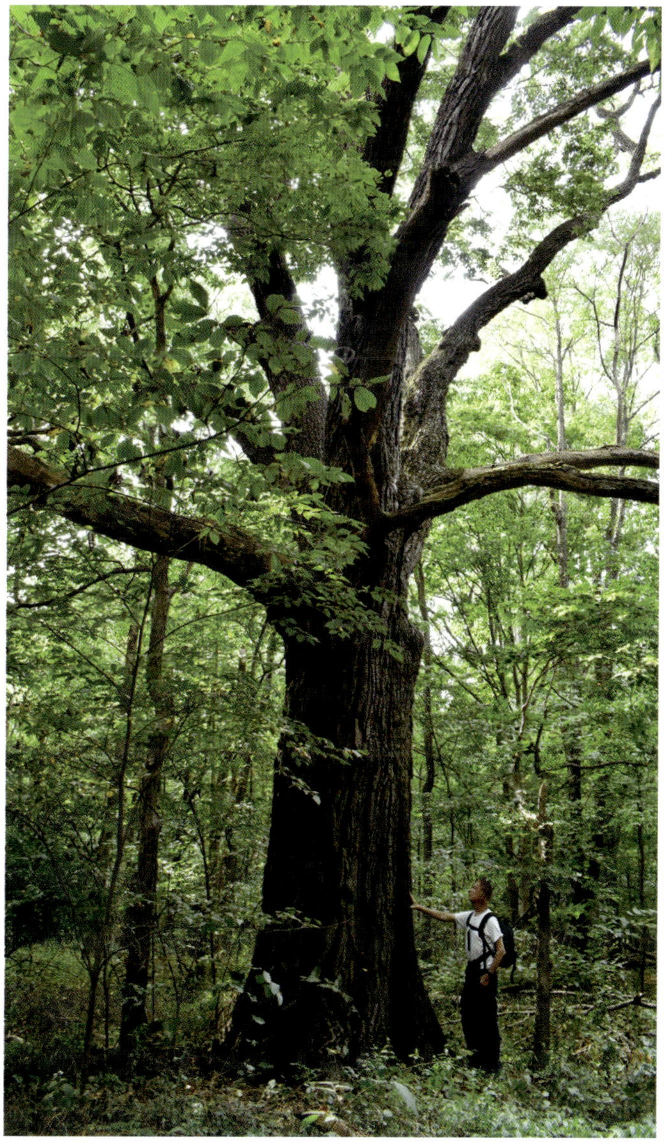

Above left: Old black walnut trees grace Sugar Creek at Turkey Run State Park

Above right: State champion black walnut, Elkhart County

Left: Patriarch black walnut, Shrader-Weaver Woods

BUTTERNUT

(Juglans cinerea)

The state champion butternut tree in Lawrence County was so unusual in part because this threatened species rarely grows large due to early infection with butternut canker. But here it was, 6.6 feet in diameter and 62 feet tall, still surviving and even bearing nuts. Standing alone in a yard, its exposure to strong wind and severe storms was in itself a threat to the integrity of the old, branched giant.

When butternut is found it already most likely has acquired the disease that causes cankers. Even a vigorous tree will likely succumb, although the eventuality may stretch its life out for 30 years. The fungus is prevalent throughout its range in the Midwest and northeast and apparently originated abroad. It may also attack black walnut, although serious problems with that species have not been observed. Purdue Extension's "Conservation and Management of Butternut Trees" is a fine guide to the description of the problems, outlook, research with hybrids, and suggestions for landowner retention of any butternut trees they may have.

Butternut wood's richness, grain, and color made it highly desirable for antique furniture, musical instruments, and office paneling. The dye from the nut was also used to color early homespun clothing, a tradition evidently coming from southern Indiana and Illinois. Some Confederate soldiers' uniforms were also reportedly dyed with butternut hulls, rendering them somewhat yellowish or tan-gray. A fine resource on this subject is adolphusconfederateuniforms.com/basics-of-confederate-uniforms.html

Characteristics

- Healthy trees grew originally to 100 feet, today not much more than half that.
- If butternut hybridizes with black walnut, the offspring may show stronger resistance to the canker and also produce nuts.
- Nut green like black walnut, but more elongated. The meat has a richer taste to both humans and squirrels.
- Bark lighter gray than black walnut, hence the name "white walnut" is sometimes used.
- Leaves alternate, singly compound, main stem up to 2 feet long with 11–17 smaller leaflets.

Uses

- Unique furniture, woodcarving, veneer—now scarce and expensive to find.
- Dyes, folk remedy medicines.
- Tasty walnut meats and really nice in warm chocolate chip walnut cookies.

Right page: Champion butternut, Lawrence County

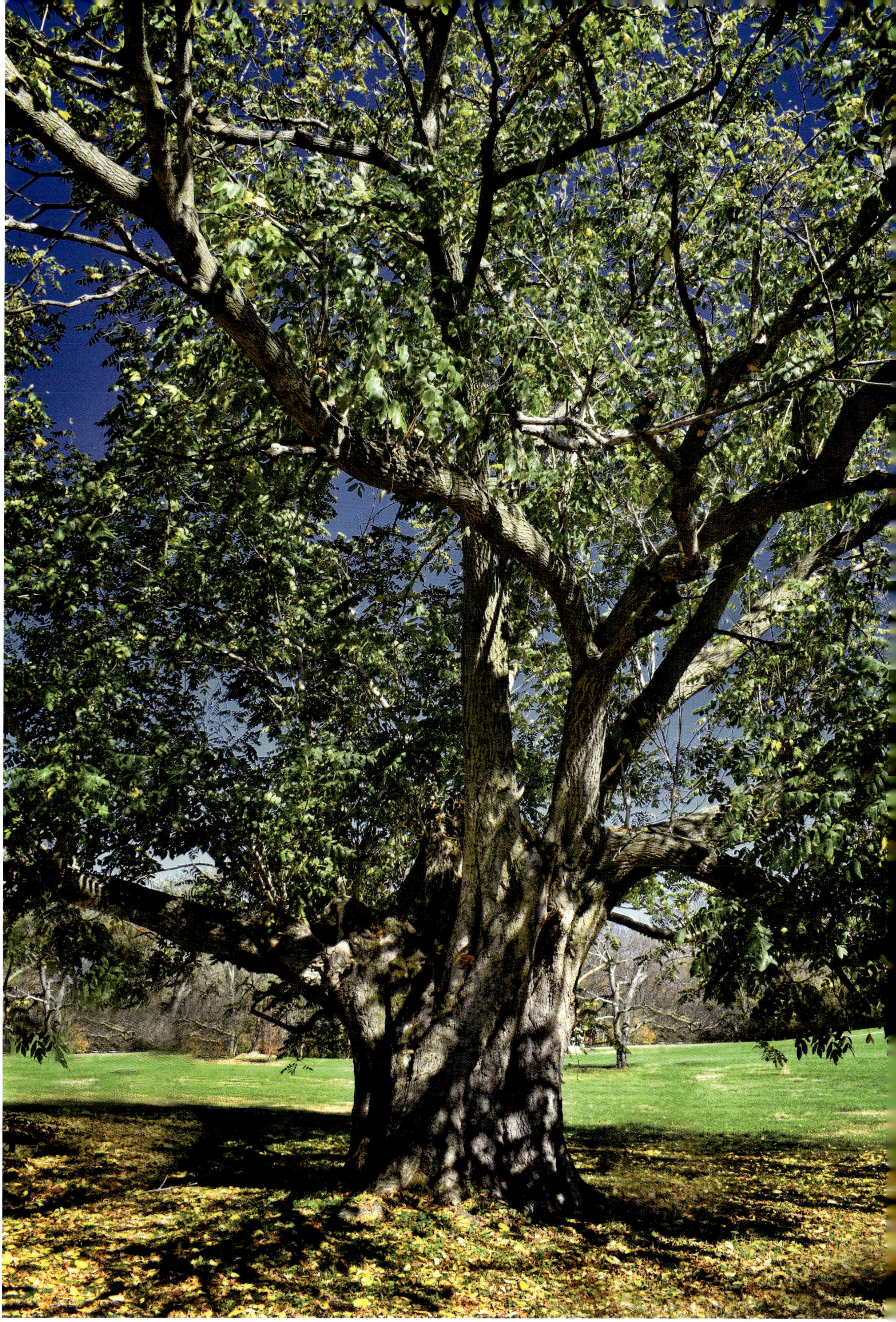

CANADA PLUM

(*Prunus nigra*)

In the everyday discussion of iconic Indiana hardwoods, the name plum usually does not arise. We typically think of plums, cherries, and peaches as delicious wonders of the orchard basket. But the genus *Prunus* contains not only those grafted, hybrid fruit trees, but also other native woodland trees such as the black cherry and Canada plum (also called Canadian plum). The range is expansive, from eastern Canada all the way across the upper Midwest and down into northern and central Indiana. While not a common occurrence here, several can indeed be found. The fruits are edible and the white or pink bloom is one of the larger ones in the genus. Related native species found in Indiana are American wild plum, a variety called wool-ly-leaf, Hortulan plum, and another *Prunus* grouped with plums but called pin-cherry or fire-cherry.

Visiting the woodlot in Owen County with friend and district forester Ralph Unversaw revealed several nice-sized Canada plums and a few deceased. The one pictured was measured and is indeed is the new state champion. On approaching the tree, one immediately notices the large peeling bark pieces and the mottled dark color on the trunk and limbs.

We definitely see something different growing here among the other "normal" hardwood trees. The Canada plum is generally not large, reaching 25–30 feet in height and perhaps a foot across. Upon visiting in mid-April, we saw the spectacular eruption of blooms. It was not only attractive to us, but also to hundreds of honeybees that had homed in on the wondrous blossoms.

Characteristics

- Small tree, often branched, mottled bark.
- Leaf 2–4 inches, toothed.
- Prolific producer of spring blooms with fruit set following.
- Red-orange fruits 1–1½ inches, fleshy, edible, single stone.

Uses

- Nice ornamental tree.
- The plums are very delicious and used for jams and jellies.

Right page, top: State champion Canada plum in full show

Immediate right: Champion Canada plum, Owen County

Far right: Canada plum blooms attract scores of bees

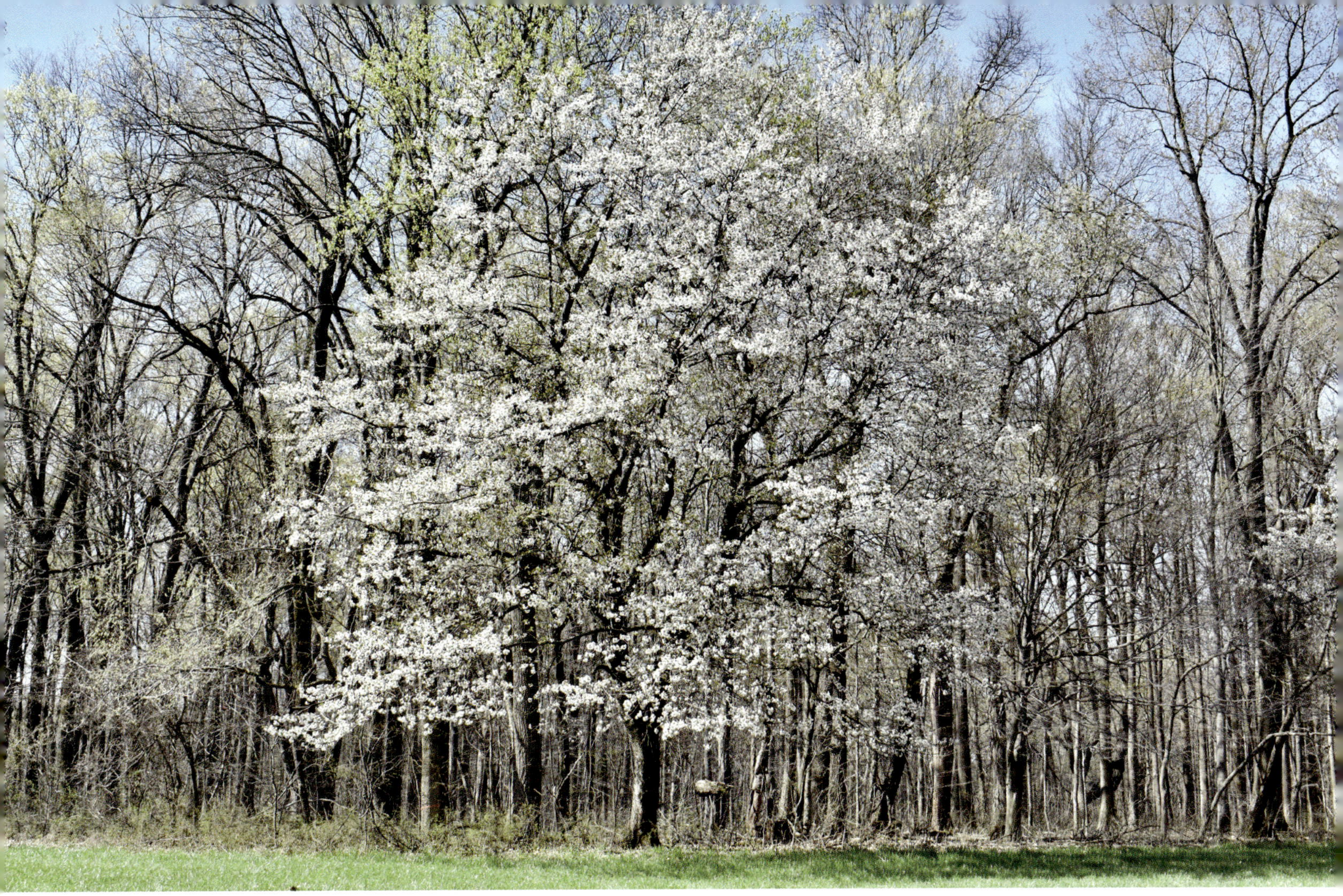

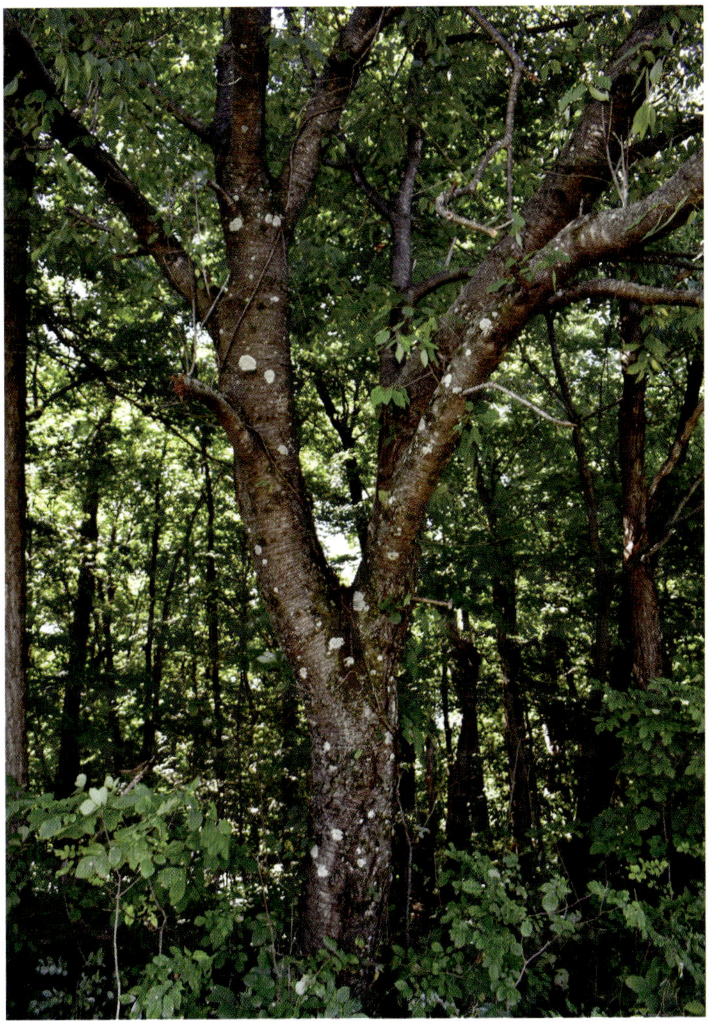

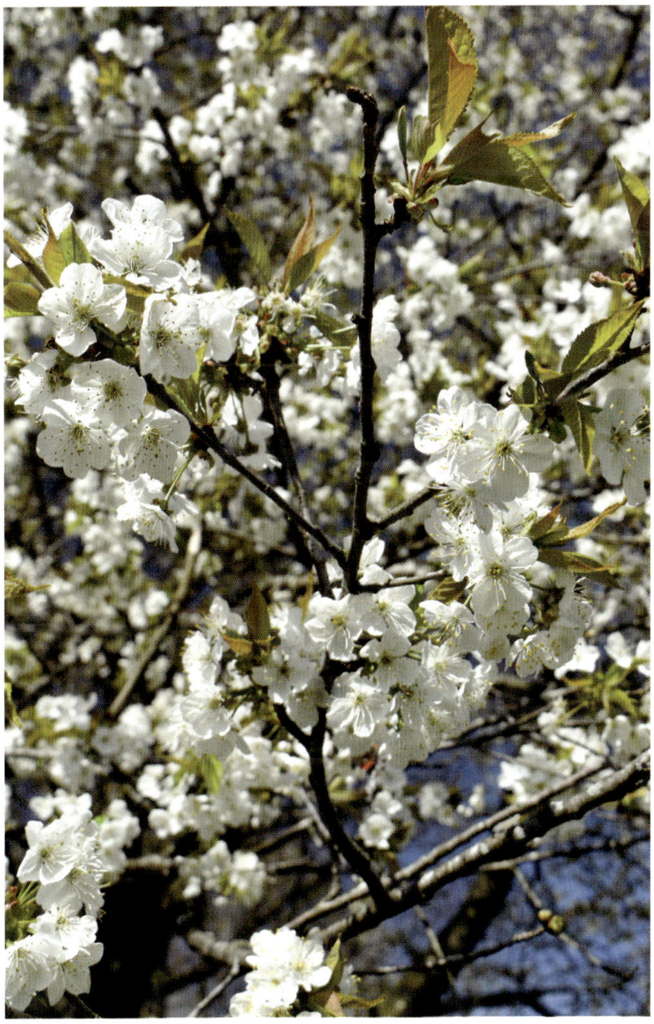

NORTHERN CATALPA
(*Catalpa speciosa*)

One of our most intriguing trees with its large heart-shaped leaves, fragrant white blossoms in late May, and long "bean-like" seed pods, the catalpa has been planted in residential yards and also incorporated into urban landscapes as part of tree plots or parks. The stem of the tree most often will begin branching out at 6 or 10 feet and as a mature specimen, will create quite a marvelous canopy. Allen Pursell of the Nature Conservancy pointed us to a great grouping of catalpas along a country road in Harrison County. They were indeed splendid and in fine linear arrangement along the Ohio River bottomlands. The nation's largest catalpa was located in Evansville until it succumbed in 2020. At 7.7 feet in diameter, 80 feet tall, and with a crown spread of 94 feet, this one was indeed a regal champion. Pure *Catalpa speciosa* is now a state threatened species.

Indiana has two species of catalpa: northern (*C. speciosa*), considered native, and southern (*C. bignonioides*), considered introduced from southern states. Both occur in Indiana and may actually hybridize. The name derives from the Muscogee Indian name for the tree, *kutuhlpa*, meaning "winged head."[8] This referred to the markings on the flower. The old name, *patalpha*, was another corrupted version; this term was locally used in the lower Wabash and White River valleys of southern Indiana.[9]

The larvae of the catalpa sphinx moth (*Ceratomia catalpae*) feed voraciously on the leaves and can be quite destructive. Anglers prize them as bait and in fishermen's nomenclature are commonly called "catalfie worms." A fine story about these was right here in Lawrence County. Seeking some glorious catalpas in bloom took us to the Mitchell property of Harry Russell, who was proud to show them off in a field with some fine horses nearby.

His wife, Mary Lee, recollected the two of them using these worms. "He has used them alive to put on a trotline or on a fishing pole line for years, as do many local fishermen. They are good for almost any kind of fish—bass, bluegill, catfish, or white perch. A few years ago his brother from Louisiana told us fish would still like them if frozen in Fruit-Fresh powder to keep their color, but not if they turned black. Not having any Fruit-Fresh, I tried shaking live worms in powdered lemonade mix, freezing them just enough for them to stop wiggling, then spreading them apart in a pan to finish freezing without them sticking together. He was right. Fish still love them and alive or frozen they have a tough enough skin to be hard for fish to steal from the hook. We use whole live ones, but sometimes cut a frozen one in half for bluegill."[10]

The wood of *C. speciosa* is rather soft and workable, fairly durable in ground contact, but limited in uses. Historically it was utilized for fence posts, crates, and some cheaper quality furniture. The long pods, regionally called "Indian beans," may be locally called "cigars." They are interesting but their accumulation on the ground can be quite messy in the fall. Communities often planted catalpas along sidewalks or in tree plats. Such was the case many years ago in Bedford where the author grew up. The trees are all gone now, but warmly remembered.

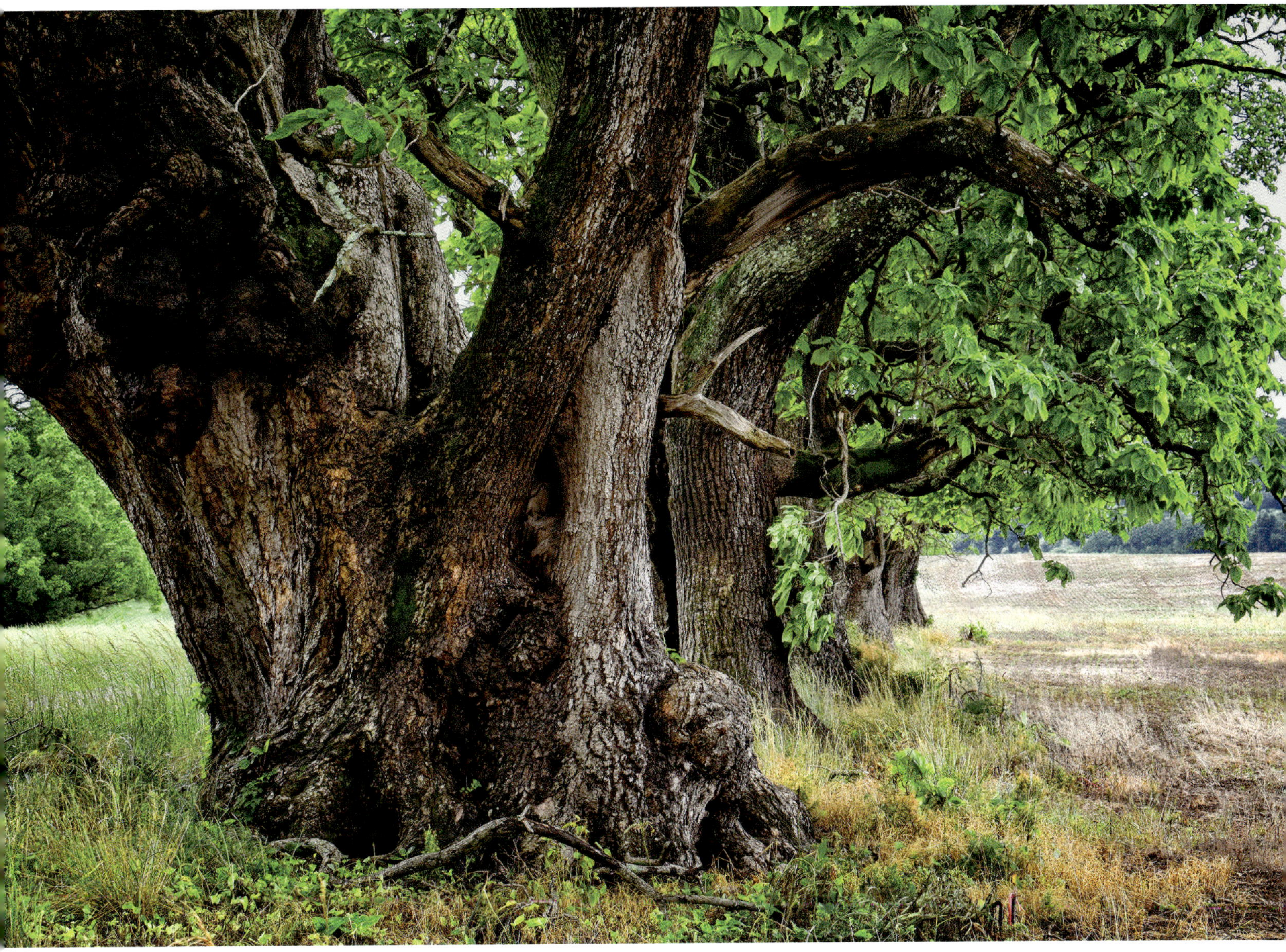

Harrison County catalpa grove

Characteristics

- Short tree to 60 feet, 2–3 feet in diameter; however, some reach huge widths to 6 feet in river bottoms.
- Bark brown and scaly with some fissures in old age.
- Attractive heart-shaped leaves to 1 foot in length, opposite in arrangement.
- Very showy white perfect flowers (male and female parts in the same flower) in June.
- Pods turn brown, split, and release wind-borne seeds after leaf drop.

Uses

- Light and easily worked wood, pretty grain, used as a specialty in woodworking.
- Old fence posts were fairly durable in contact with soil.
- Grown extensively for railroad ties in earlier times.
- Worms on the tree still occasionally used as fishing bait.

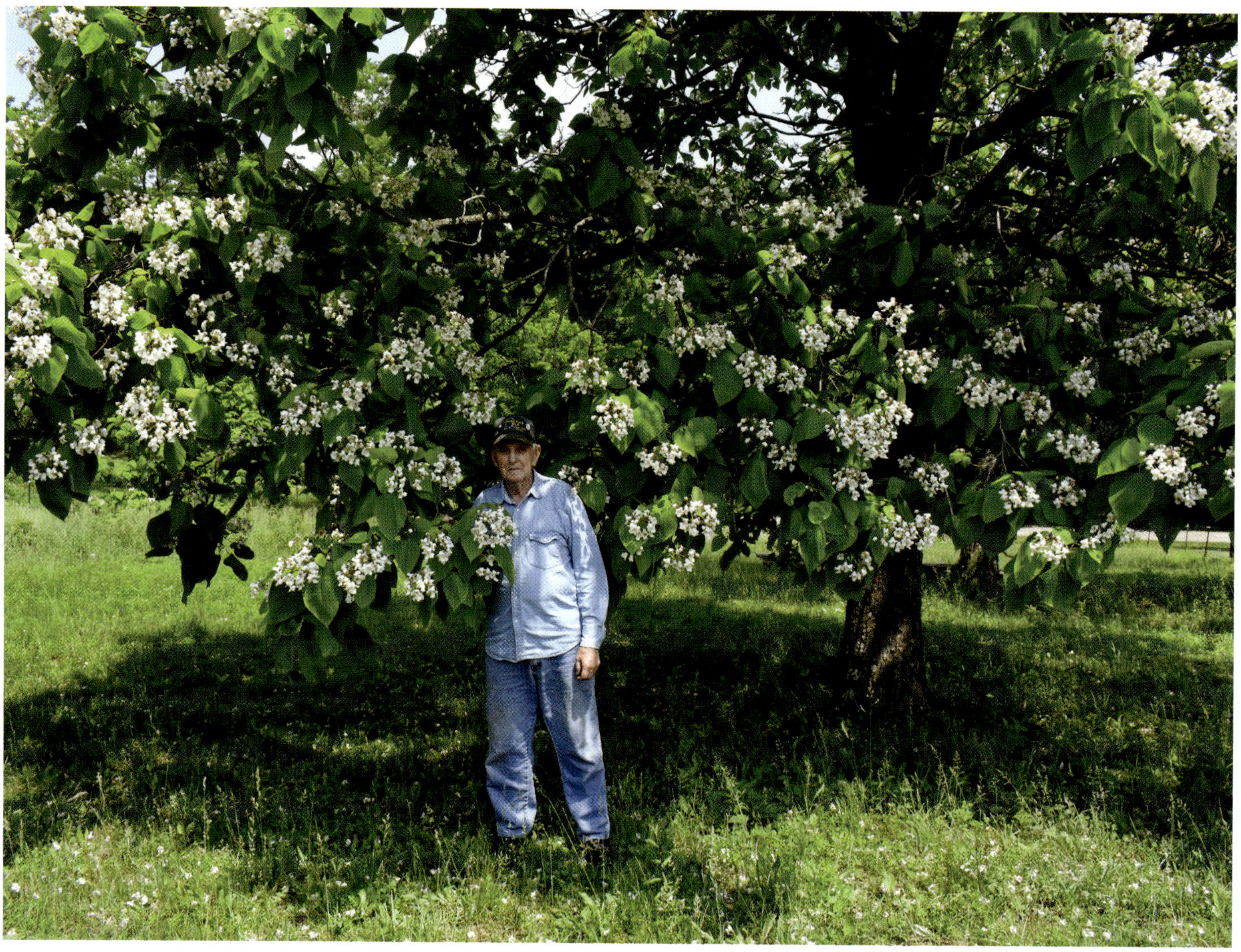

Harry Russell and his catalpa trees

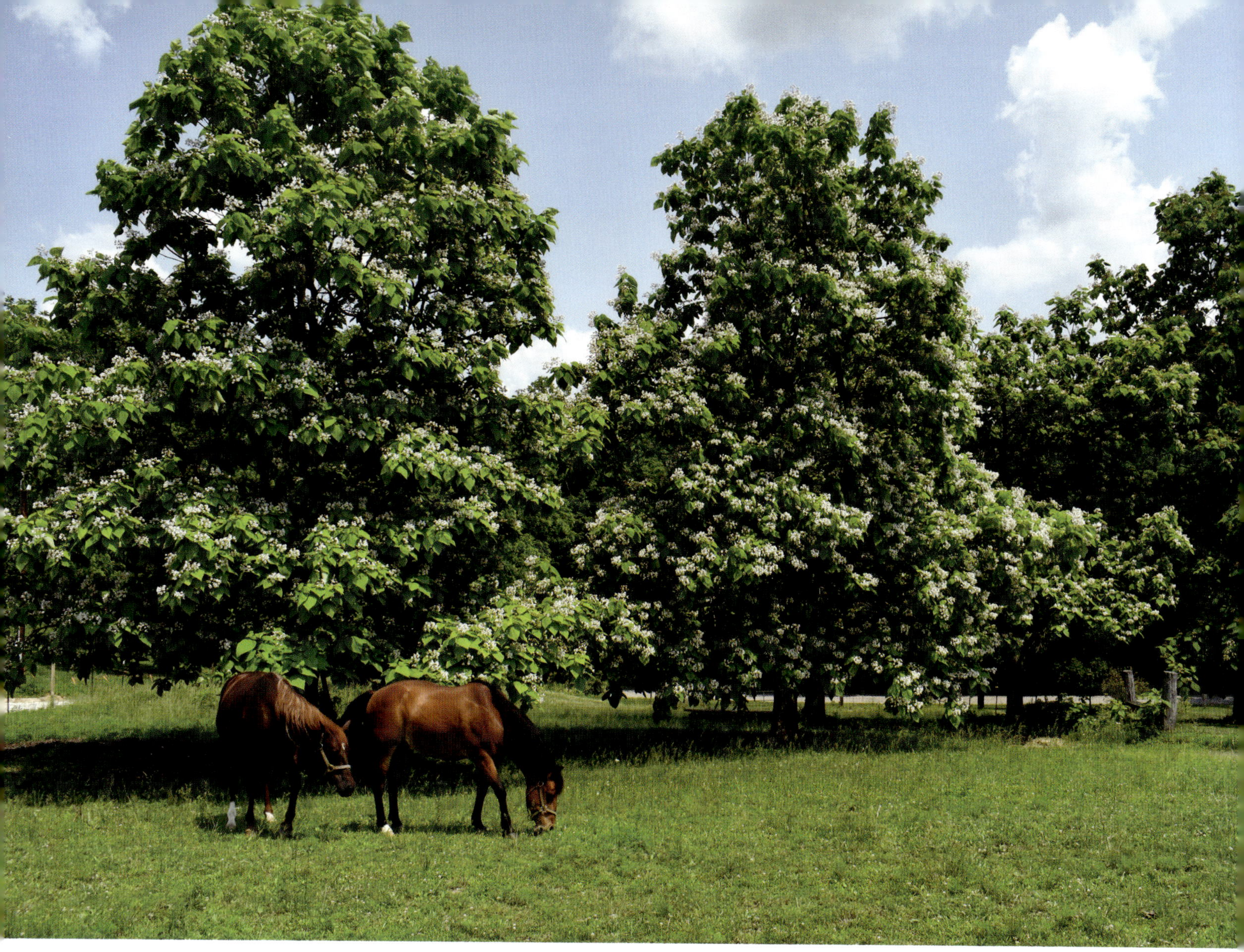

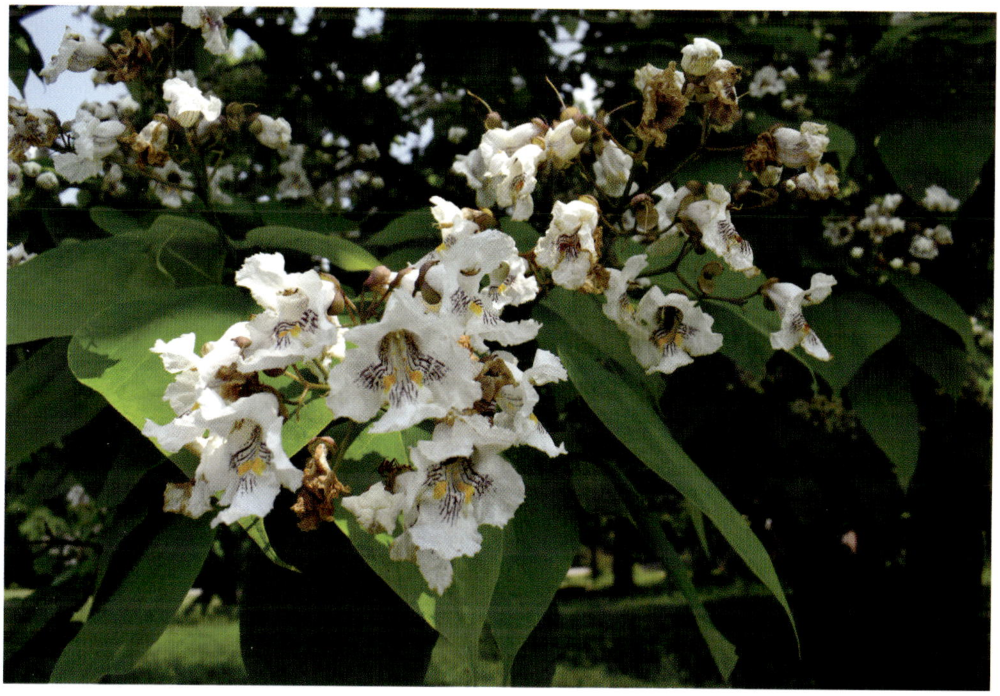

Above: Russell farm with beauty of horses and catalpa trees

Left: Exquisite blooms of catalpa

EASTERN COTTONWOOD

(Populus deltoides)

Mightily ascending with massive trunk, the crown is finally reached with a full spreading array of handsome limbs. On those are found the most interesting triangular leaves fluttering in the breeze on flat stalks. What respite a great cottonwood provides to both seeker and visitor during those hot dry days in summer. Just months before, in early spring, the phenomenal outburst of cottony seeds released and carried on the wind delivered potential prodigy far and wide. Through town and countryside, the cottonwood had announced itself in dainty white fluffs that delighted the eye.

Early occurrence of cottonwood found it scattered in limited locales and in less demand than the mighty oaks, hickories, and tuliptrees. Gracing riverbanks and stream bottoms, the majestic tree could reach heights of 150 feet and diameters of 10 feet. Many old specimens are forked close to the base and thus their overall size reflects multiple trunks joined by common included wood. Some great old patriarchs occur along bottomland benches near the confluence of the Wabash and Ohio rivers.

Once cottonwood was extensively cut for many uses, most of the huge trees disappeared from those majestic forests. Those that were left, however, grew on to large sizes and some remain today along Ohio River bottomlands. From the old cut stumps sprouts regrew quickly to begin replenishment as a new generation. Actually, it is one of the fastest growing trees, as much as 4–5 feet per year, and within 60 years the base may be as much as 4–6 feet across. But the payback for rapid maturity is also rapid decay within the heart of the tree, resulting in early demise of the giant. By the time the white oak is just reaching its prime, the cottonwood has seen its best days.

While the tree is not as dramatically showy as some of the glorious hardwoods with their leaves of many colors, fall triggers the development of a pleasing yellow and one by one the large leaf waves goodbye with its last flutter in autumn winds, dropping silently to the waiting earth below. The massive old deeply furrowed gray trunk and limbs now stand conspicuously alone. The waiting period is then set until spring's arrival and the onset of bright yellow male catkins and the carmine female flowers. Another cycle of life thus begins.

Characteristics

- Related to aspens in same *Populus* genus. Not related to our "tulip-poplar."
- Coarse-toothed leaf, large, flutters on flat stem.
- One of the fastest growing trees; may reach great heights and widths but not extremely long-lived.
- Fruits in long showy cottony cluster of seeds that drift in wind.
- Even after being cut, stump sprouts regenerate, some resulting in forked trunks.

Uses

- Poor, soft, lightweight wood with limited commercial value today. May end up in boxes, crates, pulpwood, and other general uses or as a curiosity wood in crafts.
- Should be left along stream corridors for its great bank stabilization.
- Western cottonwood is related and did have several uses for pioneer cabins, floors, and fences. The trees often signal water. Shade for livestock was also important.

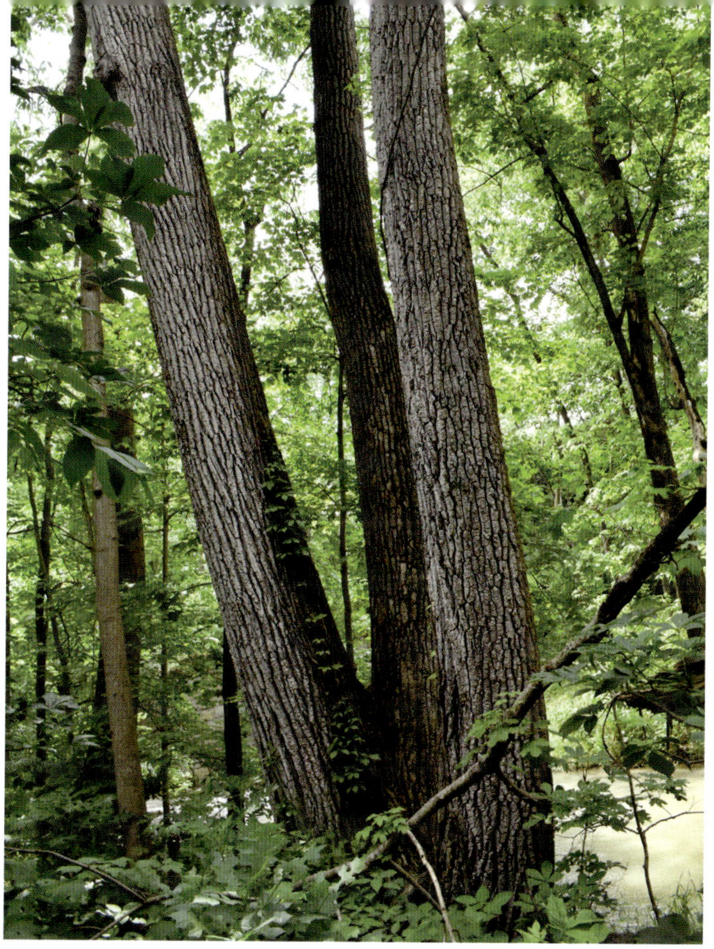

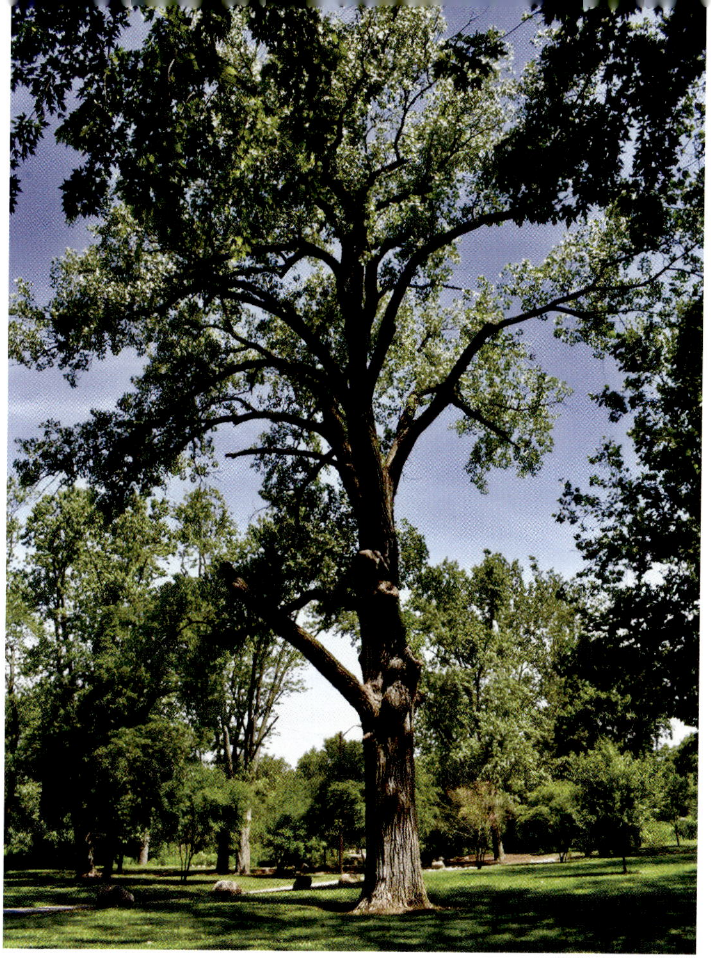

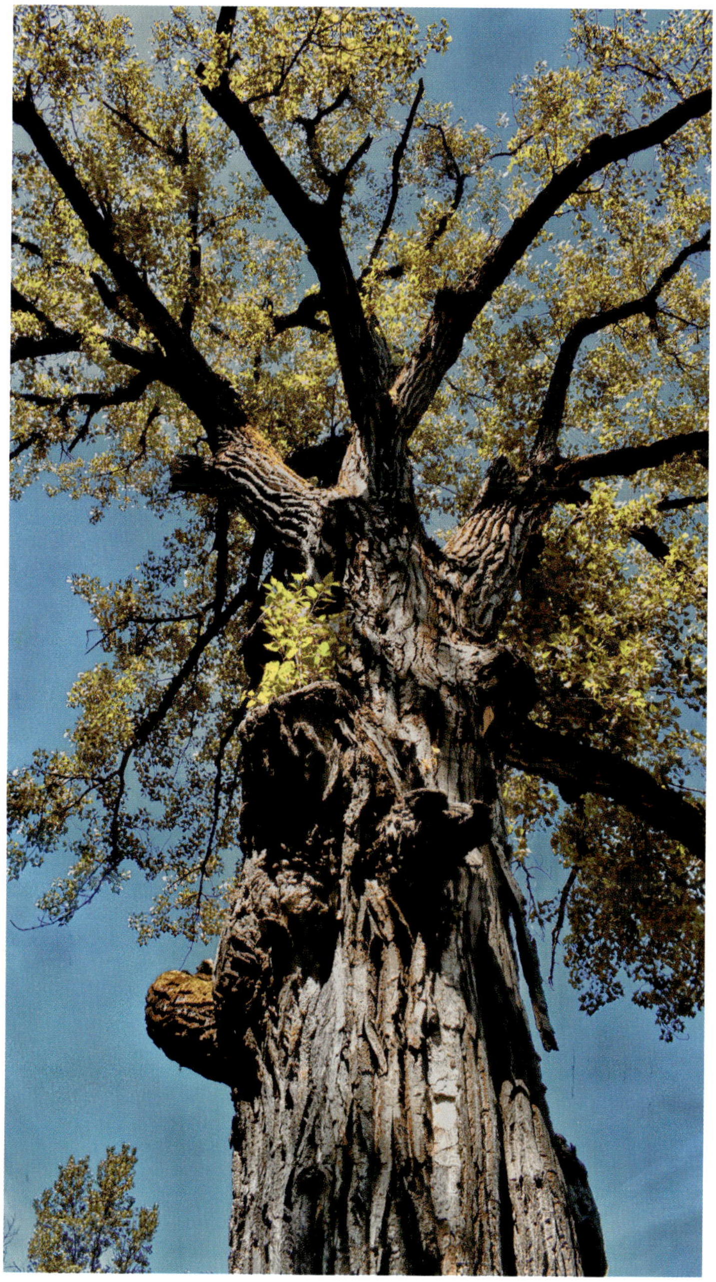

Above left: Fine cottonwoods along Metamora-Whitewater Canal

Above right: Large cottonwood, Province Park, Franklin

Left: Gnarly, furrowed bark of eastern cottonwood

SWAMP COTTONWOOD

(Populus heterophylla)

Finding an interesting or intriguing tree with Dave Coppert is always an adventure. He knows many species including large state record ones discovered on the 7,724-acre Muscatatuck National Wildlife Refuge in Jackson and Jennings counties. Seasonal flooding occurs across the area since it is low, thus access to some sections is not easy. But in the "drier" late summer we set out through briars and woods back to a choice spot where Dave had found a new state record swamp cottonwood, almost 2 feet across and 105 feet tall. The site was near standing water and swampy ground with crayfish castles among other wetland shrubs and trees that like these kinds of conditions. The only thing missing was a cottonmouth snake, or at least we didn't see it. Only Dave could find such a place and such a tree, as many people would have no idea what a swamp cottonwood even was. Later, Dave discovered an even larger one, 8 feet in circumference and 108 feet tall (pictured).

Swamp cottonwood has a large range from southern bayou country up through the Mississippi and Ohio valleys to northern Indiana. When found it is often just called "cottonwood" and not distinguished from the related eastern cottonwood. Swamp cottonwood became more important for use as the eastern cottonwood was becoming less available. It also has the names black cottonwood, downy poplar, and swamp poplar. This species can often tolerate much wetter conditions and standing water for a period of time. The lack of commercial value in Indiana and the site conditions allow swamp cottonwood to grow among swamp chestnut oak, swamp white oak, red maple, and black willow.

This tree is rarely cultivated or promoted and does not propagate from cuttings, but primarily from seeds. In natural settings, even after a harvest, the stump sprouts or new seedlings grow rapidly and regenerate the tree within a few years.

They are useful to the wildlife around them, being host trees to the viceroy, red-spotted purple, and tiger swallowtail butterflies, among others. Mammals also get nurture from swamp cottonwoods. Voles and beavers feed on the bark during winter, and white-tailed deer browse twigs and foliage as well. Many birds build nests high in the branches that provide great overviews of the wetland community.

The area with this champion tree held many secrets, lost in the rarely visited section of the property. Away from the mainstream of civilization, there were other old swamp cottonwoods, red maples, and willows, each holding special bonds as if they kept the magic of the place all to themselves. In the depth of stillness, the rattling of pileated woodpeckers brought a primeval feeling to the mysteries of life here.

Characteristics

- As described, loves wetlands and in preferred locations can reach 3 feet in diameter and 100 feet in height.
- The fairly thick 6–8 inch oval leaf is a little more heart-shaped and not as triangular at the base as its relative eastern cottonwood.
- The leaf's underside is woolly in younger trees. Prodigious cottony seeds drift away to a new location or coat the ground under the tree with a white cover.
- The stem is round, not flat, so there is less "flutter" than eastern cottonwood.

Uses

- Pulpwood, crates, boxes, miscellaneous other uses; in southern states used for excelsior.

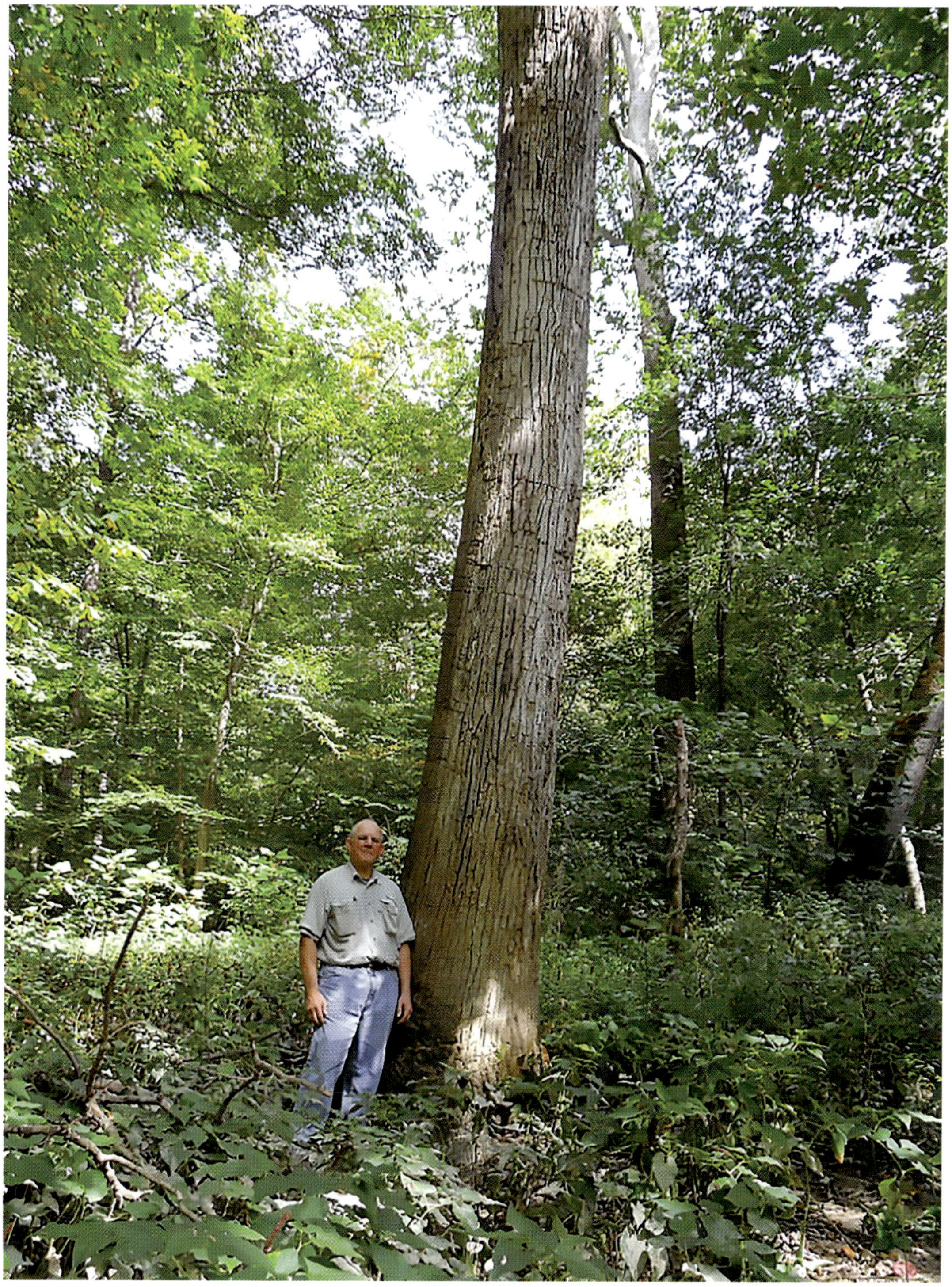

State champion swamp cottonwood, with Dave Coppert
Courtesy of Dave Coppert

DOGWOOD, REDBUD, AND SERVICEBERRY

(Cornus florida, Cercis canadensis, Amelanchier arborea)

This great trio covers those much-admired icons of spring. What better season to have these early signals that life and beauty begin anew after the passing of winter?

FLOWERING DOGWOOD

Several *Cornus* species occur across the country, many of which are tall shrubby plants. Our flowering dogwood reaches true tree size up to 35 feet. The champion tree in Evansville has died, but was 2½ feet in diameter, much greater than almost any dogwood you will ever see. The excitement of all the white blooms across the countryside or in yards certainly welcomes spring with joyful glee. The popular Dogwood Festival in Orleans keys around a spectacular display of trees in full bloom.

The fall berries are bright red, and along with colorful leaf display, once again proclaim its year-round beauty.

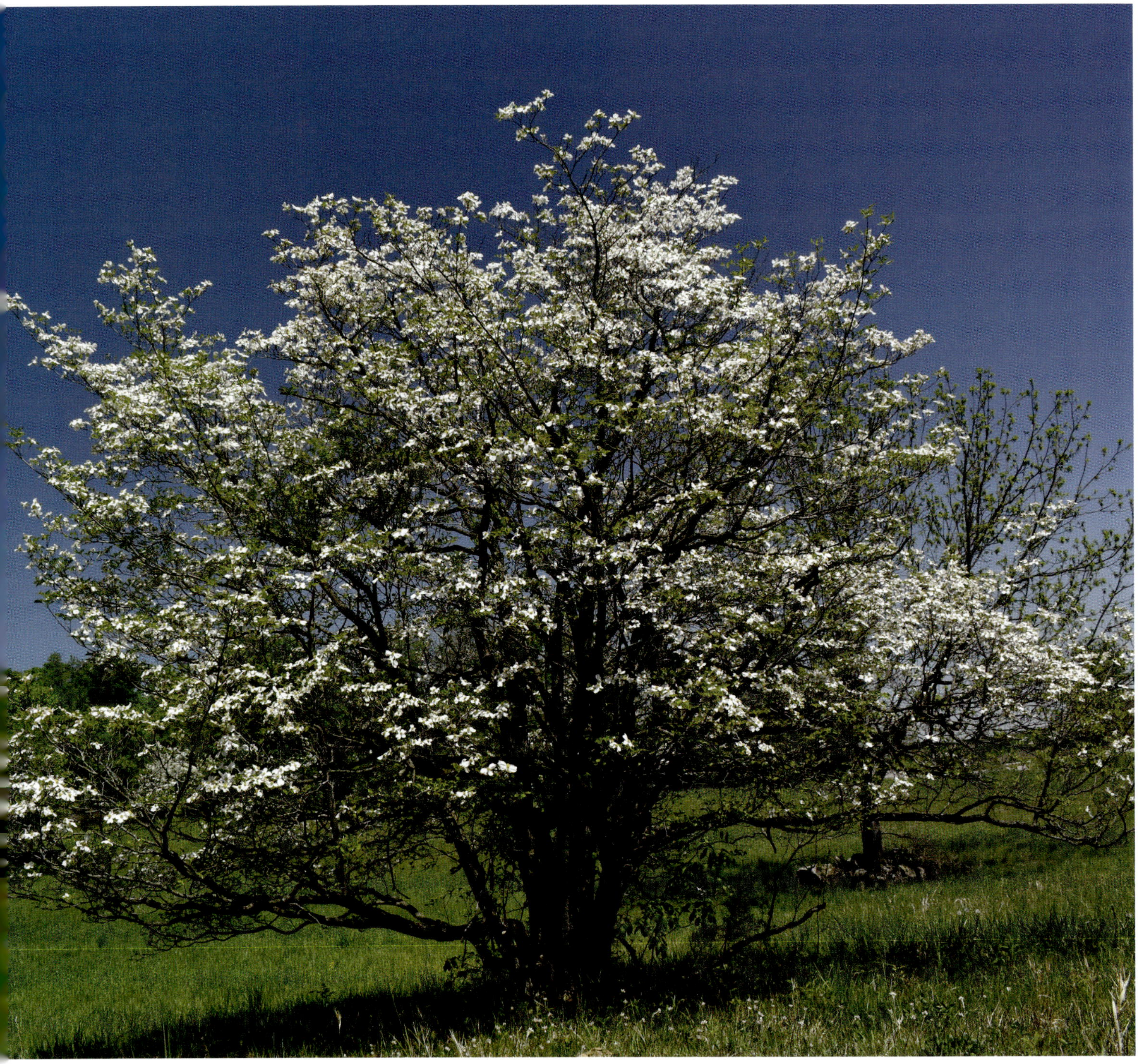

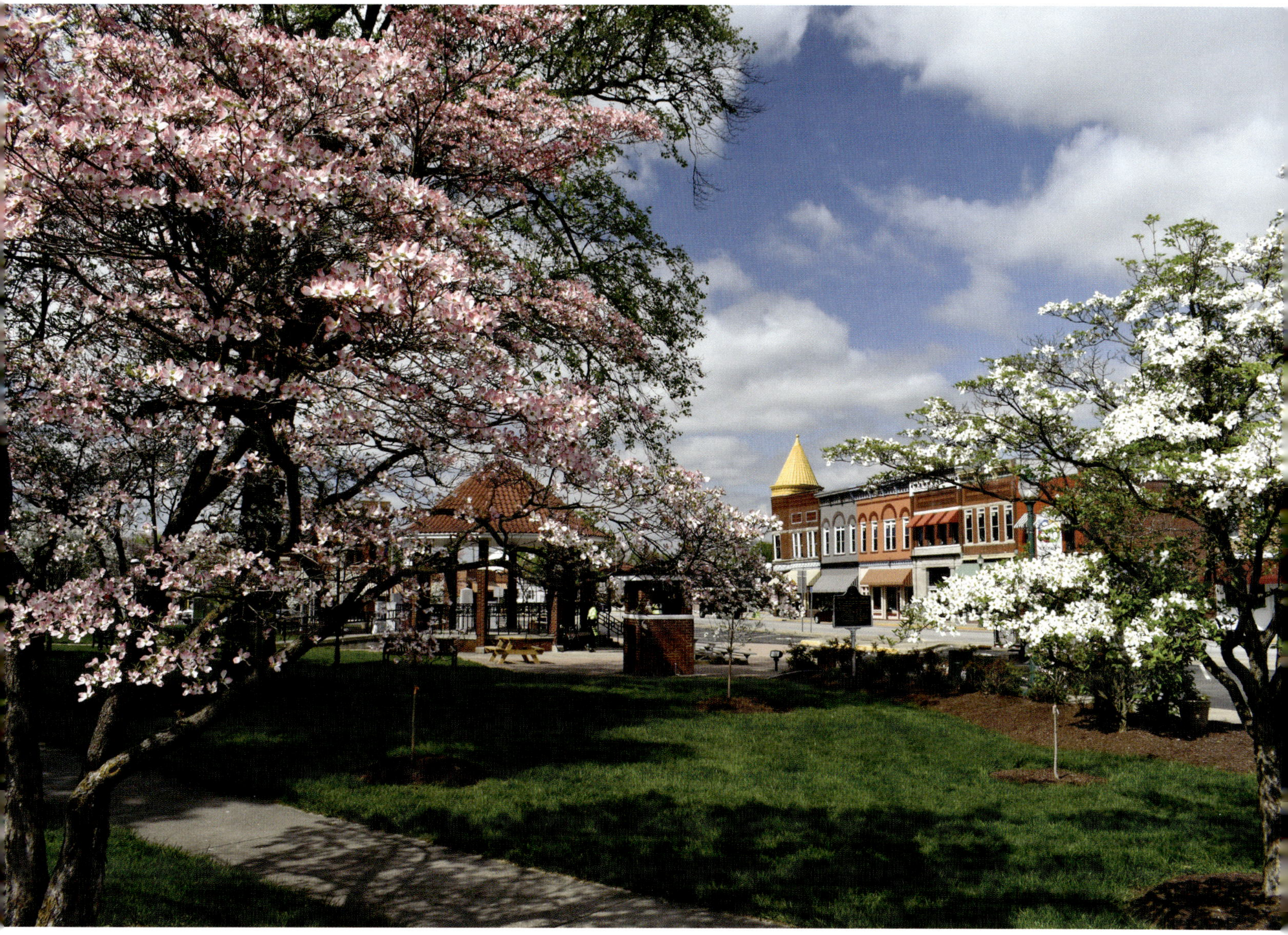

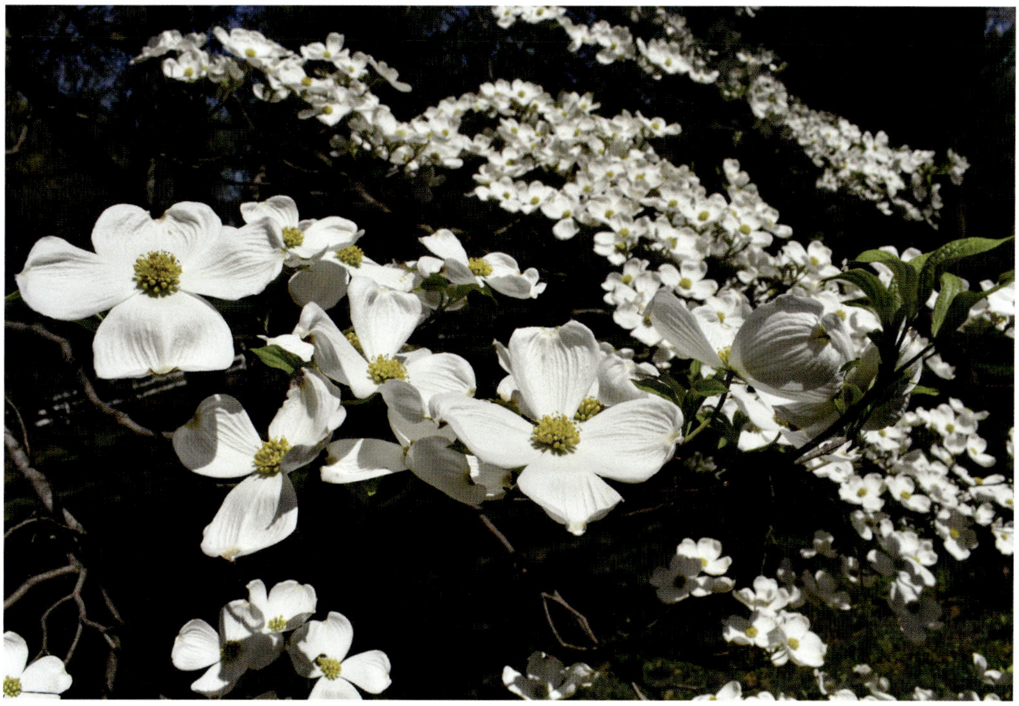

Above: Dogwood beauty in Orleans, Indiana

Left: The eloquent, iconic dogwood blooms

Left page: Dogwood in its stunning glory

EASTERN REDBUD

Not to be outdone, and in a perfect spring where both dogwood and redbud are in synchrony, the extravagance of pinkish red provides the one-two punch that makes the season just right. Redbud seeds prolifically from those bean-like pods and thus can be an opportunist wherever it finds a receptive, open landing spot. It is often planted for both pleasing form and, of course, gorgeous spring color. Fall leaves may show yellow, then brown quickly. They are also a pleasant heart shape.

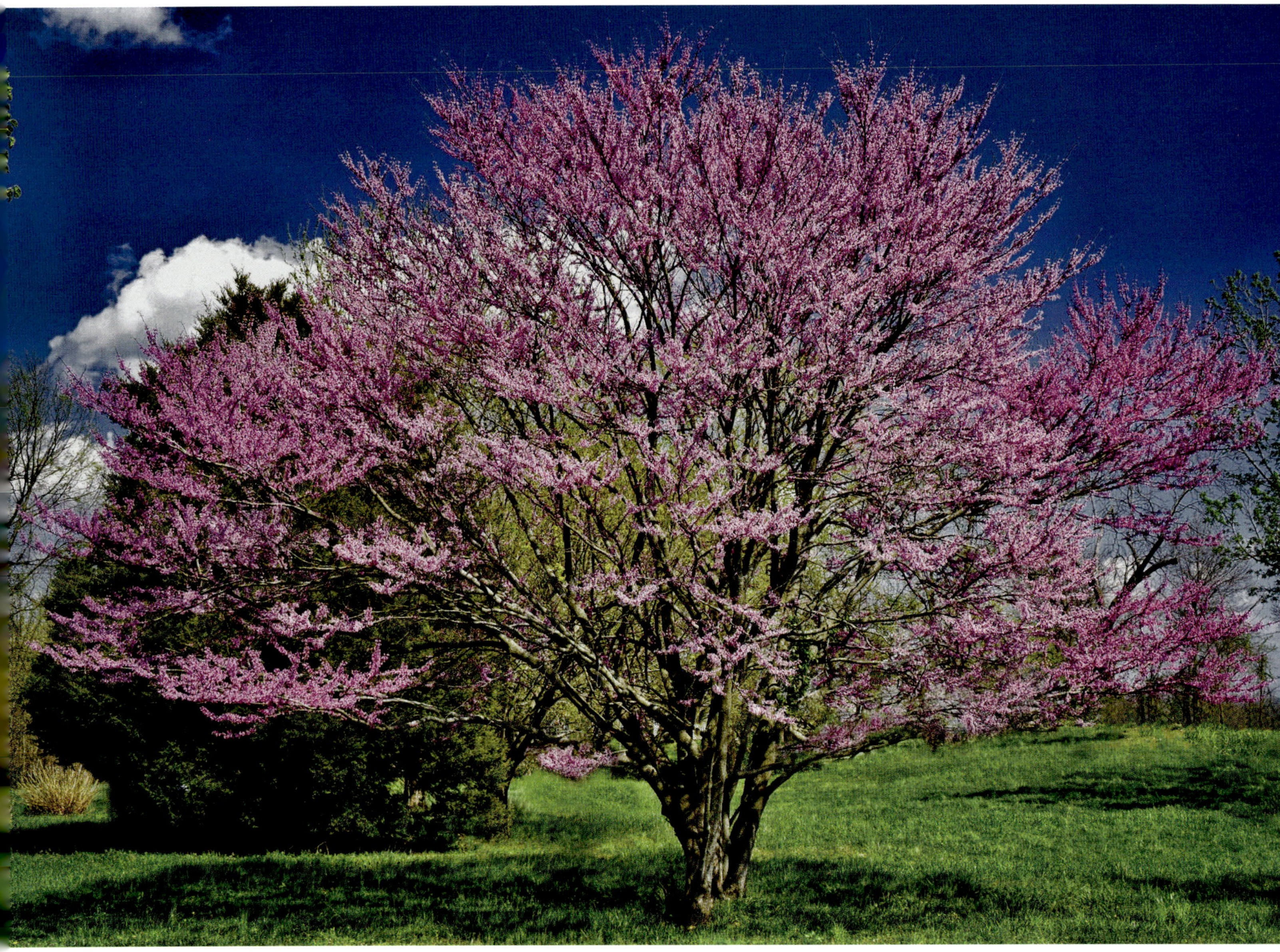

Redbud masterpiece

DOWNY SERVICEBERRY

Dainty, delicate, profuse white clusters of star-shaped flowers announce early that spring is starting. Found throughout the countryside, these trees add spots of delight to the open woods.

An old-timer's name for the tree was "sarvis," thought to be from its "service" to floral displays in pioneer churches. Another version of the name derives from the Roman *sorbus*, meaning fruit. The ripe berries have been used by both people and wildlife for a very long time. Berries can be put into muffins or pastries. They historically were also added to beef strips and tallow to make pemmican carried by Native Americans, fur traders, explorers, and pioneers. An amazing variety of birds feast on the fleshy berries. Many mammals also prize them, from small to as large as deer, elk, and even black bears. It would seem that there could not be enough of this desired delicacy to satisfy all the demand.

Other notes

- Flowering dogwood has an opposite leaf arrangement; redbud and serviceberry have an alternate arrangement.
- Dogwood's white bloom is actually the bract (sheath) surrounding the interior, less noticed actual "flower."
- The wood of dogwood and serviceberry is hard and did have historical uses for handles and other turned utensils. It is said that the Cree used serviceberry wood for arrows.
- All three are rather short-lived species.
- Dogwoods in certain parts of the United States suffer from mildew or anthracnose.
- All three are commercially sold in great quantities. They are also locally dug from the woods and transplanted.

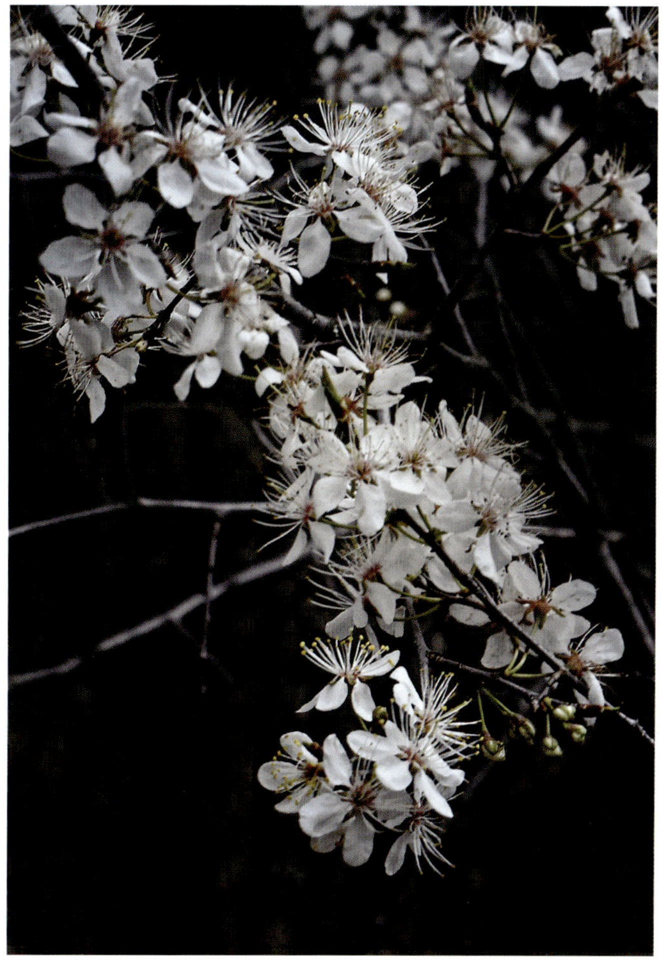

Common serviceberry, Lincoln Woods Nature Preserve

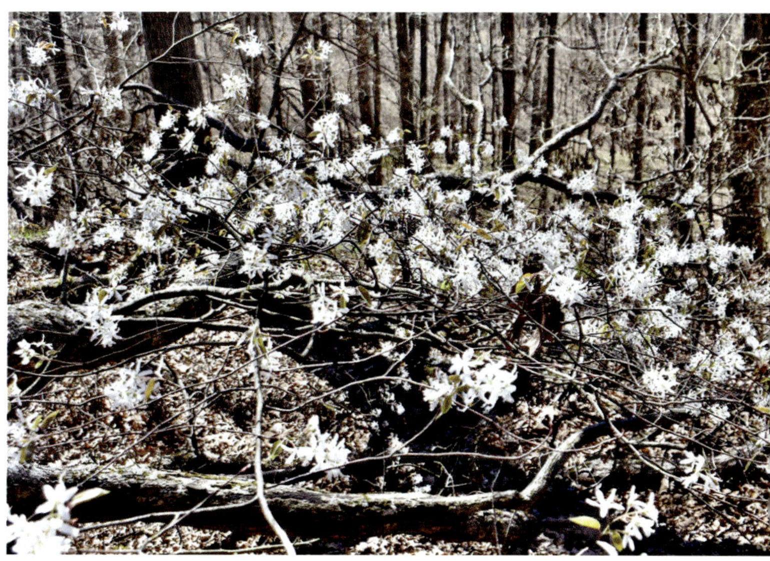

Delicate serviceberry blooms

AMERICAN ELM

(Ulmus americana)

Large, magnificent, spreading crowns depict our native elms. Graceful diverging limbs often bow toward the earth and move ever so slightly in an evening breeze. Elms have such grand history, importance, and regal deportment that can fill literature and historical essays to the brim with lore. Assemblages of Native Americans, whites, and combinations of the two groups meeting in treaty signings under a grand elm marked such spots in fame. The tree is a living monument, or if now long gone, served a place in recorded history. Such are those American elms so important in New England history—the William Penn Elm, the Whipping Post Elm, and then those scions chosen by George Washington for planting at Mount Vernon. Of course, we must mention the grand Constitution Elm at Corydon, our first state capital. In 1816, forty-three Indiana delegates met to draft the first state constitution. Since it was hot inside the log cabin where the meeting took place, they moved outside to work on the document under this grand elm tree. At the time, the elm was reported to be over 50 feet tall, 130 feet wide, and about 150 years old. The tree is now gone, but the stump is preserved.

American or "white elm" as it is also called was once one of the most important shade and ornamental trees in the eastern United States. By 1930, a pestilence arrived from Europe in logs carrying a beetle that transmitted the fungal Dutch elm disease, now infamous for its relentless attack on our beloved trees. Widely destroyed, the noble American elm is still found locally but rarely achieves the grandiose proportions of olden days. The past state champion in Parke County was 6½ feet in diameter but as of this writing it has succumbed. The photos shown here are of a 4-foot-diameter specimen in Lawrence County, exhibiting that lovely spreading canopy and majesty of presentation.

Characteristics

- Alternate leaf arrangement, fairly symmetrical leaf base.
- Bark rather gray, may become ridged in old age and peel outward. If a piece is cut and inspected, note the alternating layers of gray and red bands. This helps distinguish the tree from slippery elm.
- American elm is usually a taller tree than slippery elm and its canopy is often more aesthetic.
- Still ornamental where surviving. Otherwise, used for boxes, crates, handles, and miscellaneous furniture or woodworking.

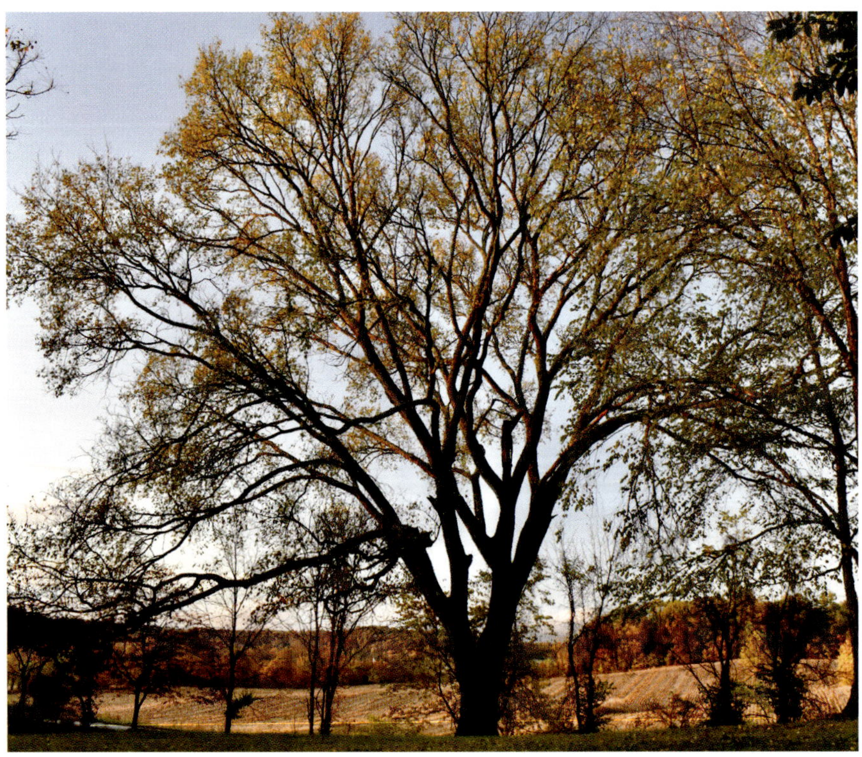

Right: Graceful form of American elm

Right page: Large American elm, Lawrence County

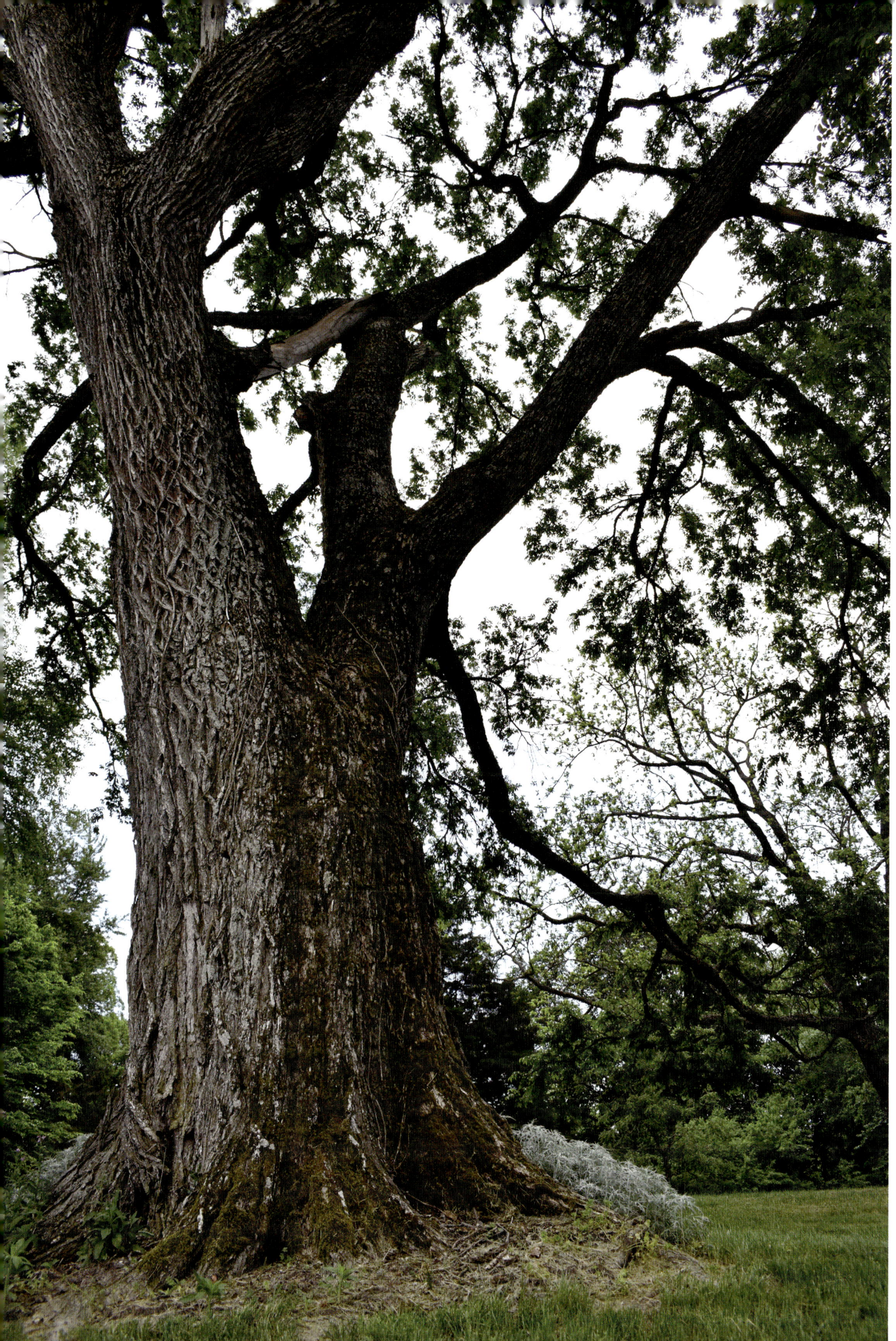

RED ELM (OR SLIPPERY ELM)

(*Ulmus rubra*)

Peattie (1966) writes about Prince Maximillian of Wied-Neuwied and his adventure to early New Harmony in 1832, where, among his many scientific observations, he recorded uses of the red or "slippery elm." If the bark is chewed it becomes a slimy gel, but with water becomes useful to "allay inflammation . . . and treats cholera" (pp. 250–251). The bark was stripped from the tree and powdered or saved as shavings for mushing into poultices later. Early physicians and apothecaries were never without it. Another more recent use has been to treat sore throat.

Red elm is also affected by bark beetles and other diseases, but to a somewhat lesser degree than American elm. Trees in my woods can be noticed as succumbing to disease when the flaky bark starts coming off and leaves the tree denuded. After a period of standing, it will then fall and give itself back to the earth to decay and enrich the soil.

The champion red elm today is a great specimen catching the eye on a meticulously kept area of Province Park in Franklin. The stately tree stands alone, obviously to show off its finery. It measures almost 6 feet across, 72 feet in height, and the crown spread average is 112 feet. A short distance away flows peaceful Young's Creek, lined with many wondrous planted weeping willows. Following the paved walking trail quickly takes one to the picnic and playground area of the park, which also contains many fine old trees.

Characteristics

- Red elm is a moderately large tree with a spreading crown.
- The leaves are rough, like sandpaper. They are doubly serrated.
- The fruits are wafer-like.
- Bark is dark brown, long ridges, shallow fissures.
- A knife can cut into the bark, removing a piece; notice that the bands are all reddish.

Uses

- Still has ornamental value where surviving. Some wildlife value.
- Has been used for boxes, crates, handles, and miscellaneous furniture or woodworking.
- Stringy fiber makes red elm a frustrating one to split, but many like its firewood.
- Red elm does have a beautiful color if processed on a portable sawmill and nice planks can be made.

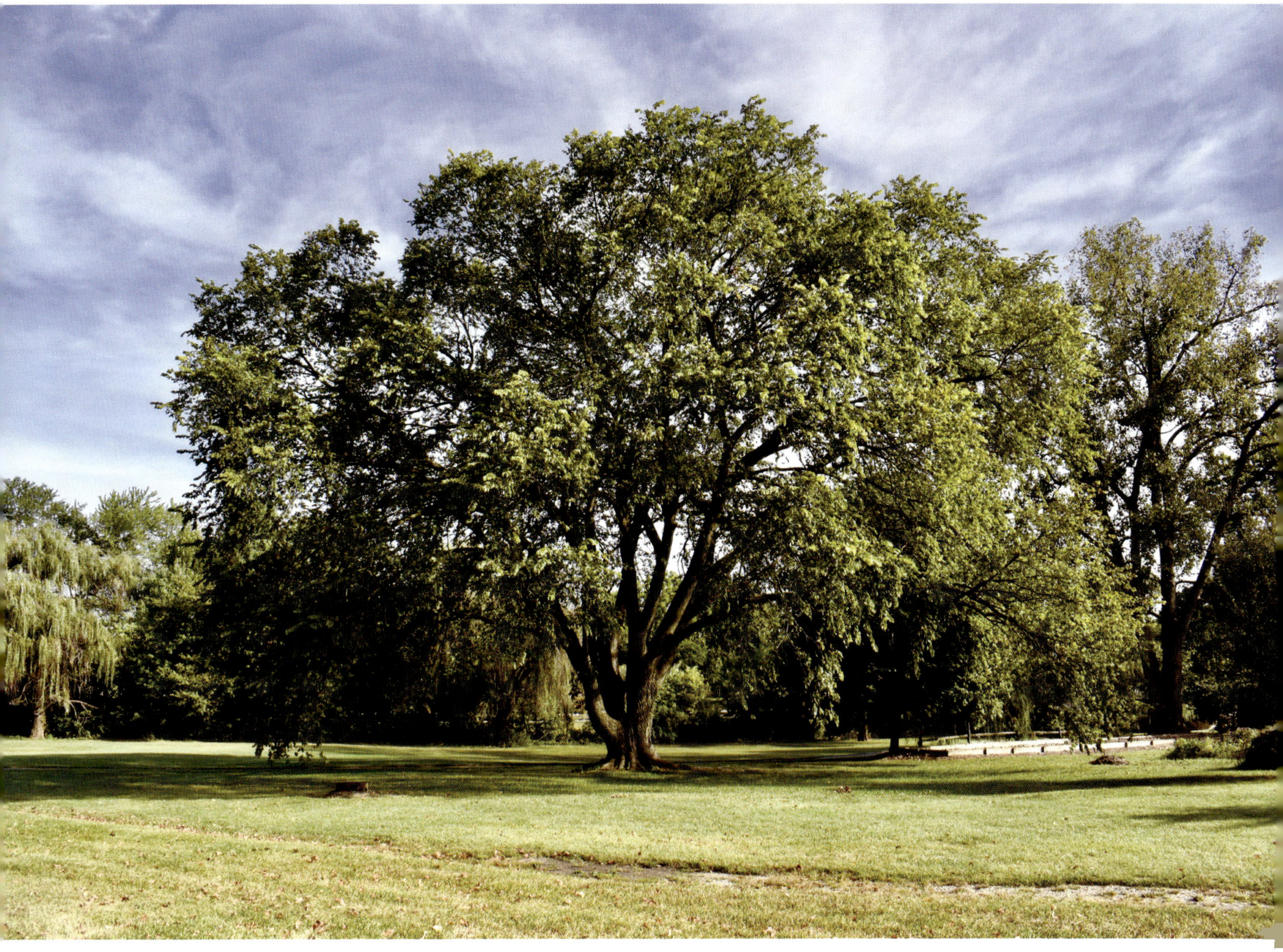

Red elm state champion, Franklin

TWO HACKBERRIES

(*Celtis occidentalis* and *Celtis laevigata*)

Imagine being called "Nettletree, Hoop Ash, or Hagberry" and relegated to a lowly position without fanfare, celebration, or admiration. Such were hackberry trees, even from the beginning of the colonies. It was surely a low-class tree with leaves that looked like stinging nettle, the wood not considered overly desirable, the "berries" certainly not fruit-like, and the leaf venation unusual. Even the bark is described as "warty" in appearance. But once understood, these trees became useful and more appreciated.

The northern hackberry (*occidentalis*) is found statewide in varying soil types and wetness sites, but prefers lowlands, moist areas, and riparian zones. The state champion tree, however, is in a yard within the city of Terre Haute and some distance from the Wabash lowlands. This old specimen is 6½ feet across and well over 100 feet in height. Another great find was one at the Pleasant Run golf course in Indianapolis. This stunning specimen was a dominant landmark that commanded attention. It was close to a cart pathway and could be appreciated by all those who walked or drove by.

Southern hackberry (*laevigata*) is generally more common in southern Indiana and once again prefers lowlands or even swamps. The 2015 state champion was in Posey County, measuring over 6 feet across, slightly surpassing one in Evansville, also a huge specimen. Both are now gone. Another one photographed (shown) is in a cemetery in Jackson County, obviously planted long ago with other trees of varying species selected for variety in that serene environment. Due to some damage, it may have to be removed, but will be fondly remembered.

Characteristics

- Tree height to 60–80 feet; diameter normally 2 feet, our champions 6 feet.
- Leaves to 6 inches, elongated, somewhat rough, more toothed on *occidentalis*.
- Leaf surface often showing white galls from insects.
- Canopy may have swooping branches, somewhat graceful, with upper twigs resembling "witches' brooms."

Uses

- Unglamorous history but useful for "any wood will do" tasks such as old cabin floors, boxes, crates, pallets.
- Might be an interesting wood for specialty cabinets, coffee tables.

Right page, top left: State champion northern hackberry, Vigo County

Top right: Superb northern hackberry, Pleasant Run Golf Course, Indianapolis

Bottom: Southern hackberry, Jackson County

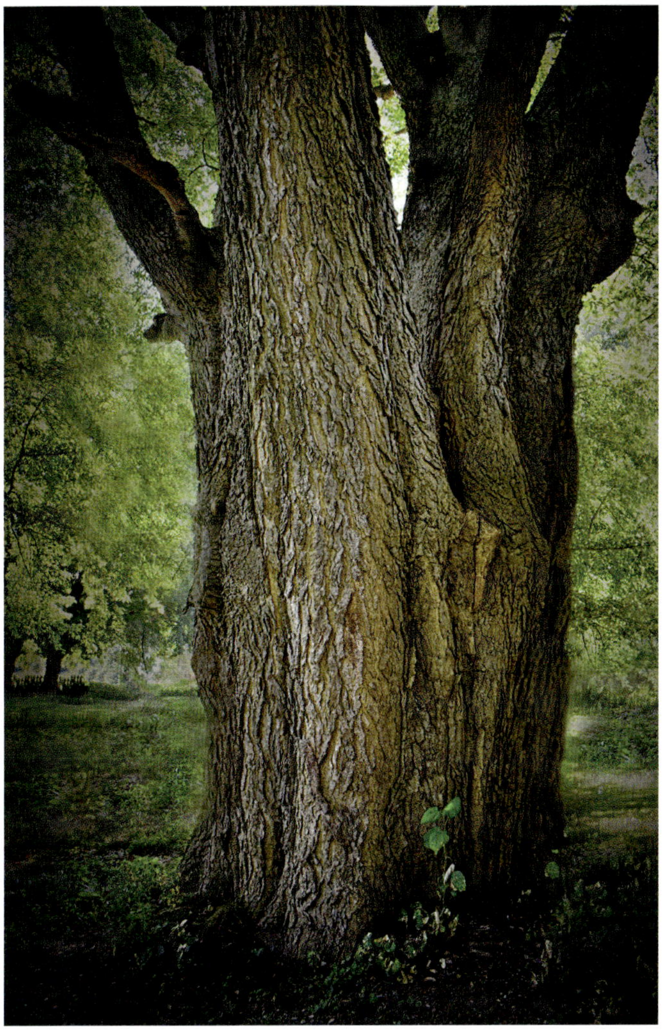

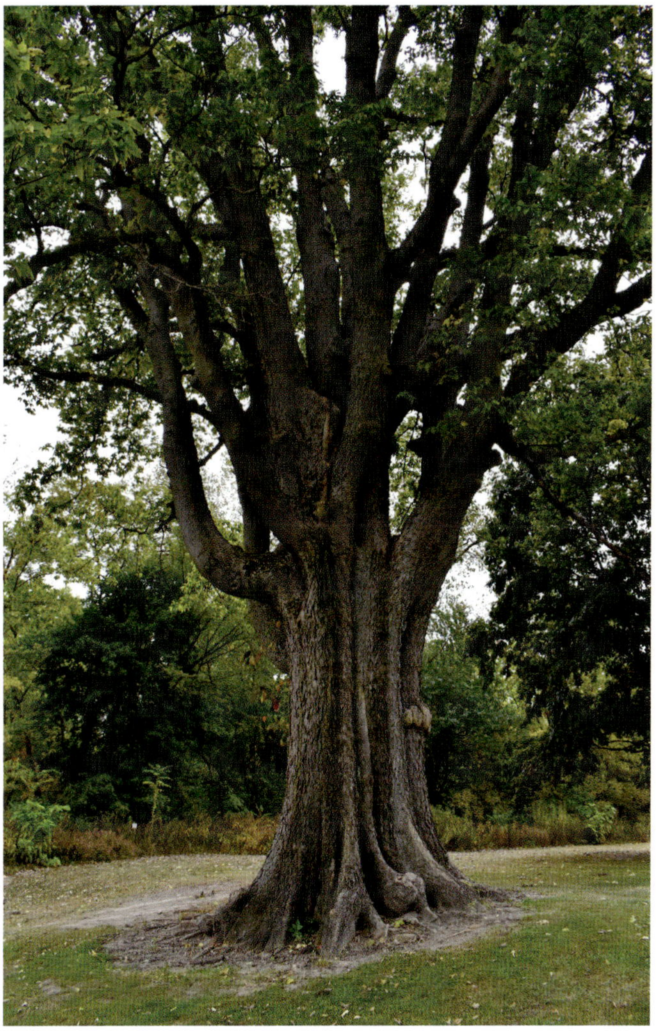

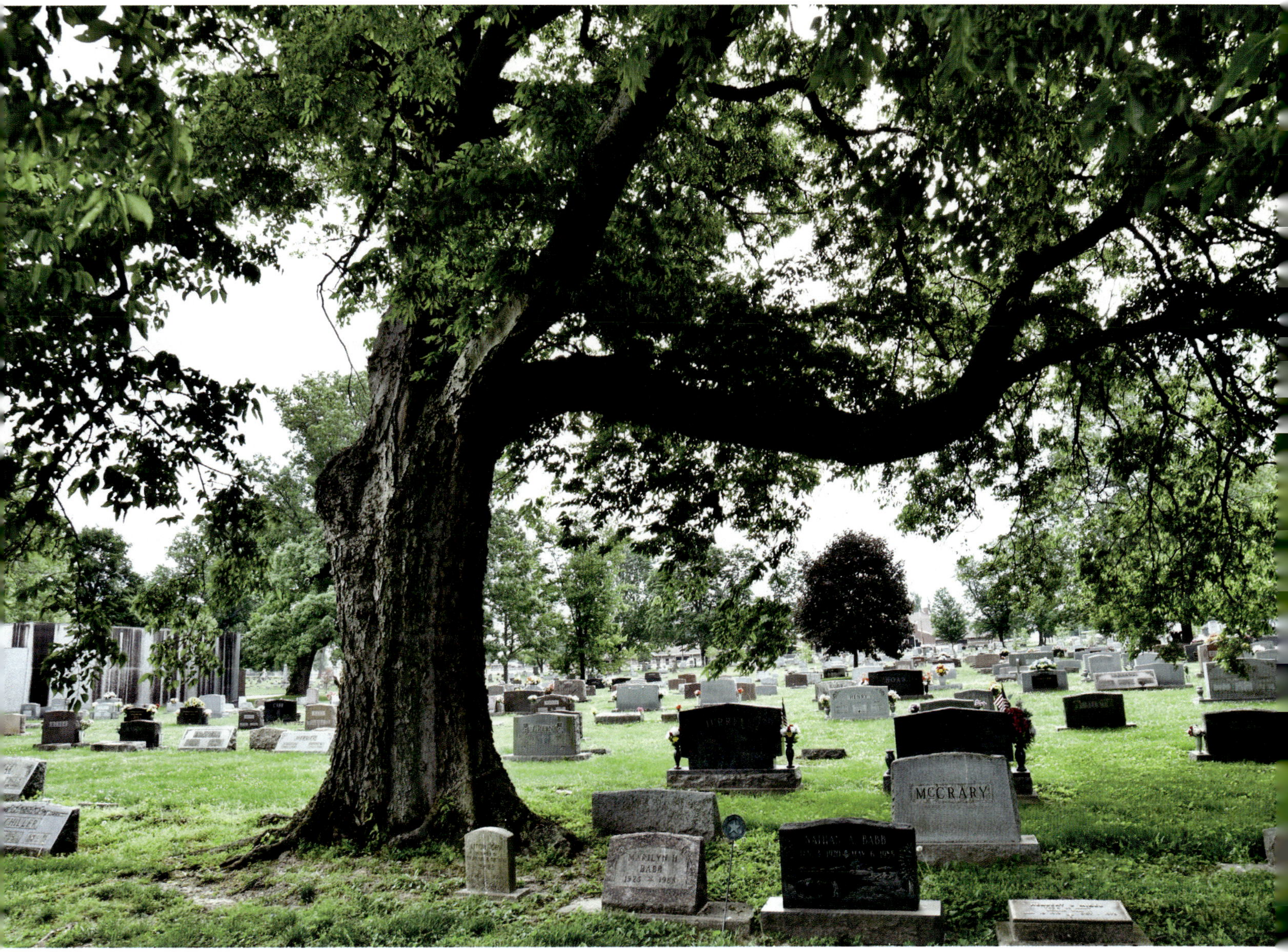
MCCRARY

BITTERNUT HICKORY

(*Carya cordiformis*)

Down in the hill country close to the Ohio River, forester and owner Mike Fenn guided us into a section of woods where, on the side of a ravine, rose upward a most impressive spire of a tree. Probably 100 years old and growing, this 155-foot tree required the viewer to look almost straight up.

The tree was grand; we didn't taste the nut. That is supposed to be the test of one's limit in accepting bitterness; well, maybe except that of an unripe persimmon. Nevertheless, the bitternut hickory is a respectable member of its genus and brings great honor to how it renders itself in fine cabinetry. The wood is close to that of pecan—rich, lustrous, creamy tan, somewhat similar to butternut.

Bitternut is a dominant hickory species west of the Mississippi in Iowa, Kansas, and Nebraska, but ranges across the Midwest into the east and north into Canada. In Indiana, it is found in many of our counties, although perhaps not a well-known household name like shagbark, pignut, and shellbark. The oil of the nut was extracted in olden times for such mundane purposes as lamp oil and for rheumatism treatment.

Since this is a relatively fast-growing hickory, any opening in the forest canopy allows for rapid development. In the spring the male flowers hang as pendants, up to 4 inches long, while the female flower on the same tree is small on a short spike. A giveaway for identification is that sulphur-yellow terminal bud, flat and pointy. The bark of this species doesn't have that old shaggy look, but rather is tight with very shallow ridges in a diamond-shaped pattern.

The small nut is rather thin, ridged, and splits into four parts to the midpoint. After they fall to the ground in profusion, footing can be quite challenging!

The fall color is a rich yellow, lending its own adornment to the other trees sharing the woodland.

Characteristics

- In good rich bottomland soils or rich humus uplands, can reach 3 feet in diameter and 100 feet high. Is an adaptable tree to many sites.
- Leaf is compound with 7–9 leaflets, pointed tips, fine sawtooth edges.
- Fruit, bark, and bud as described above give good identification clues.

Uses

- Typical hickory uses, perhaps not quite as strong, but good for trim, cabinetry, some rustic furniture.
- Not a great wildlife tree since the bitter kernel makes even the hungry squirrel grimace and turn away. At least the branches would be welcomed for birds resting or perching.
- Actually, this is a nice-looking tree and can be found as a planted specimen occasionally. But watch all those round ball-bearing nuts as you walk.

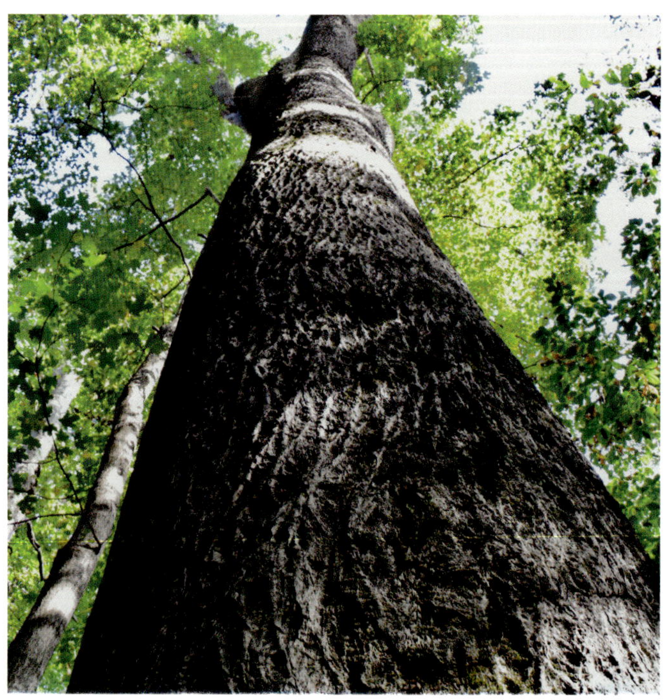

Bitternut state champion with tightbark diamond pattern

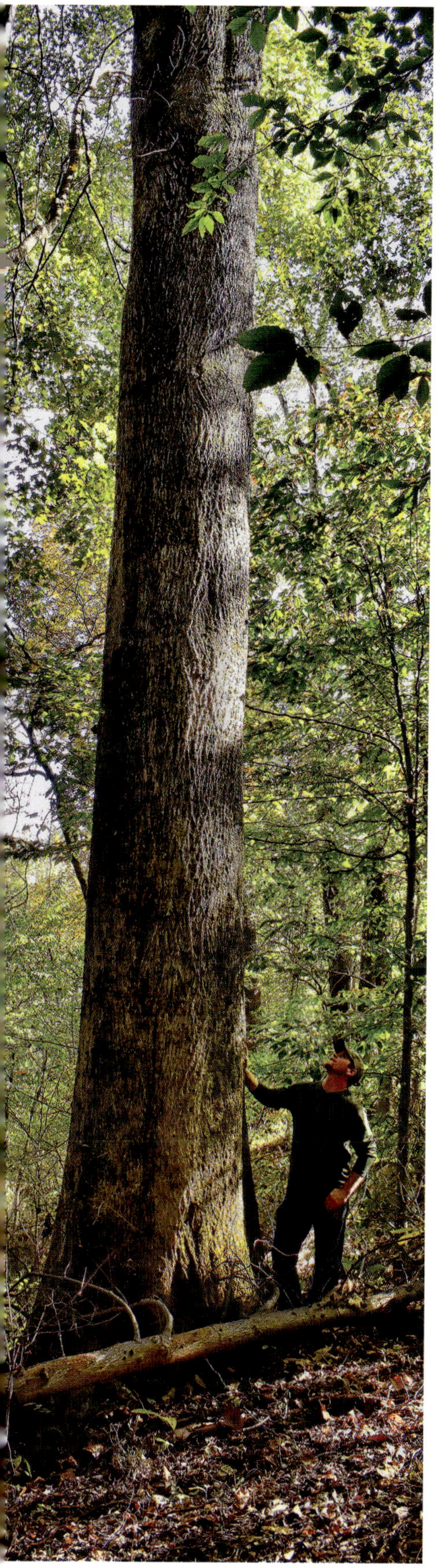

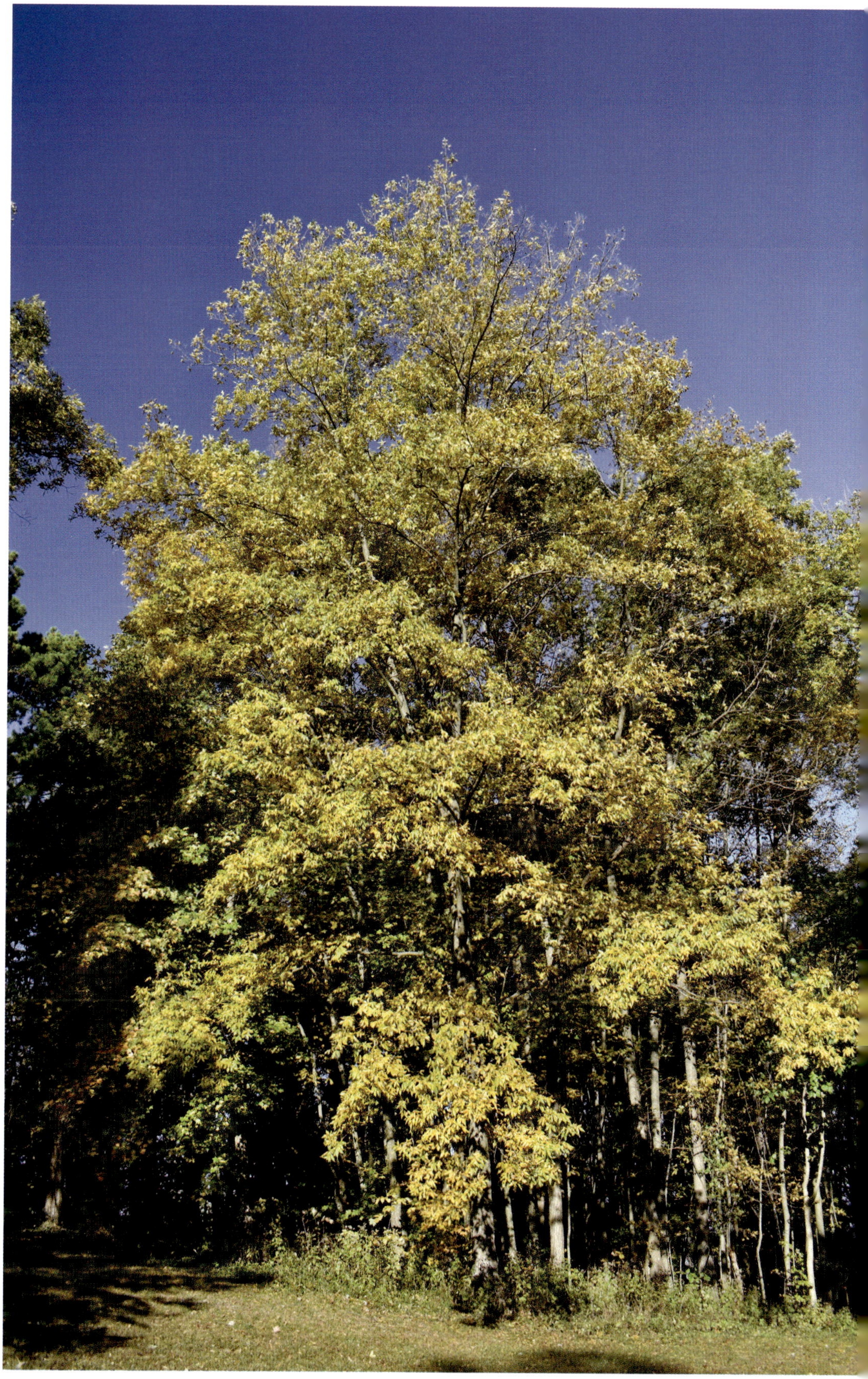

Left: Bitternut hickory champion with owner, Perry County. **Right:** Bitternut hickory in fall color.

PECAN

(Carya illinoiensis)

Largest of all the hickory species, this great tree of the Ohio River bottomlands may reach up to 150 feet in height, commanding great stature with other large trees populating the vast floodplains. Notes by Robert Ridgway from his 1871 records describe his findings, including height to 170 feet, trunk 85 feet clear, and circumference of 152 inches. He observed, "One of the most symmetrical and majestic of all our trees; the trunk clean, straight and long, and the head spreading and slightly drooping, usually elevated sixty to ninety feet from the ground."

Peattie, in *A Natural History of Trees of Eastern and Central North America*, speaks eloquently about the long history of the pecan. Evidently first encountered in 1541 by Hernando DeSoto's expedition in the lower Mississippi River region, what was then called "walnut" was not that at all, rather a new species with a delicious nut arousing much interest. Long before white settlers ventured westward into these remote interior regions, traders or fur trappers carried the nuts eastward. Then called "Illinois nuts" or "Mississippi nuts" (those names originally from Native American dialects), they were prized enough to find much favor with Thomas Jefferson, who subsequently sent some to George Washington for planting at Mount Vernon; those aged trees still exist today.

Later, in the very heartlands where the finest trees originally grew, the giant pecans were mercilessly cut down just to gather a year's bountiful crop of nuts to be marketed. The sad fate of the wondrous pecan tree reduced its abundance to such a degree that it became much more a rare specimen than a once overflowing presence in the rich Midwestern bottomlands.

The pecan tree is of course noted for that delicacy provided in the fall when the fine oval nut yields its delightful treasure. Most consumers of pecans have never seen the actual tree bearing this product. The range of this valuable species occurred from Texas, Oklahoma, Louisiana, Arkansas, Illinois, Indiana, Kentucky and into Tennessee. Most store-bought pecans do not come from Indiana, but are brought in from those fine southern farms where the tree is raised and pampered for prodigious production. Many states now benefit from those early prized nuts brought from original sites. Grafting and selective propagation have created numerous varieties. Georgia is the nation's largest supplier, accounting for about a third of U.S. pecan production. An average harvest in that state is about 88 million pounds—enough to make 176 million pecan pies.[11]

Indiana's pecan trees naturally occur in the southwestern part of the state, preferring those riparian lands of the Ohio, Wabash, and White River basins. They may be found scattered with other hickory species or with companion wetland oaks. Shawn Dickerson's new nomination for the state record occurs in Vanderburgh County, close to the river and to several other very stately pecans in the area. This tree is almost 5½ feet in diameter and 94 feet in height, the sole occupant in a farmed field, and only ½ mile away from the previous champion, now gone from storms. The photo shown here required cutting away brush around the base, but evidence is still seen of the voracious poison ivy growing up the trunk.

Characteristics

- Large spreading crown providing much shade.
- Fine clear trunk in a woodland, reaching over 100 feet high.
- Alternate compound leaves to 20 inches, with 9–17 lance-shaped leaflets.
- Handsome hairy orange-brown buds.
- Reddish-brown bark, scaling somewhat in maturity, with shallow, fissured ridge plates.

Uses

- Highly desired and marketable nuts to 2 inches in length.
- Obvious wildlife value.
- Prime boards from the bandsaw yield a fine beautiful "pecan" color for exceptional cabinetry.
- Pecan trees from grafts and hybrids are commonly planted for nut production and landscaping.

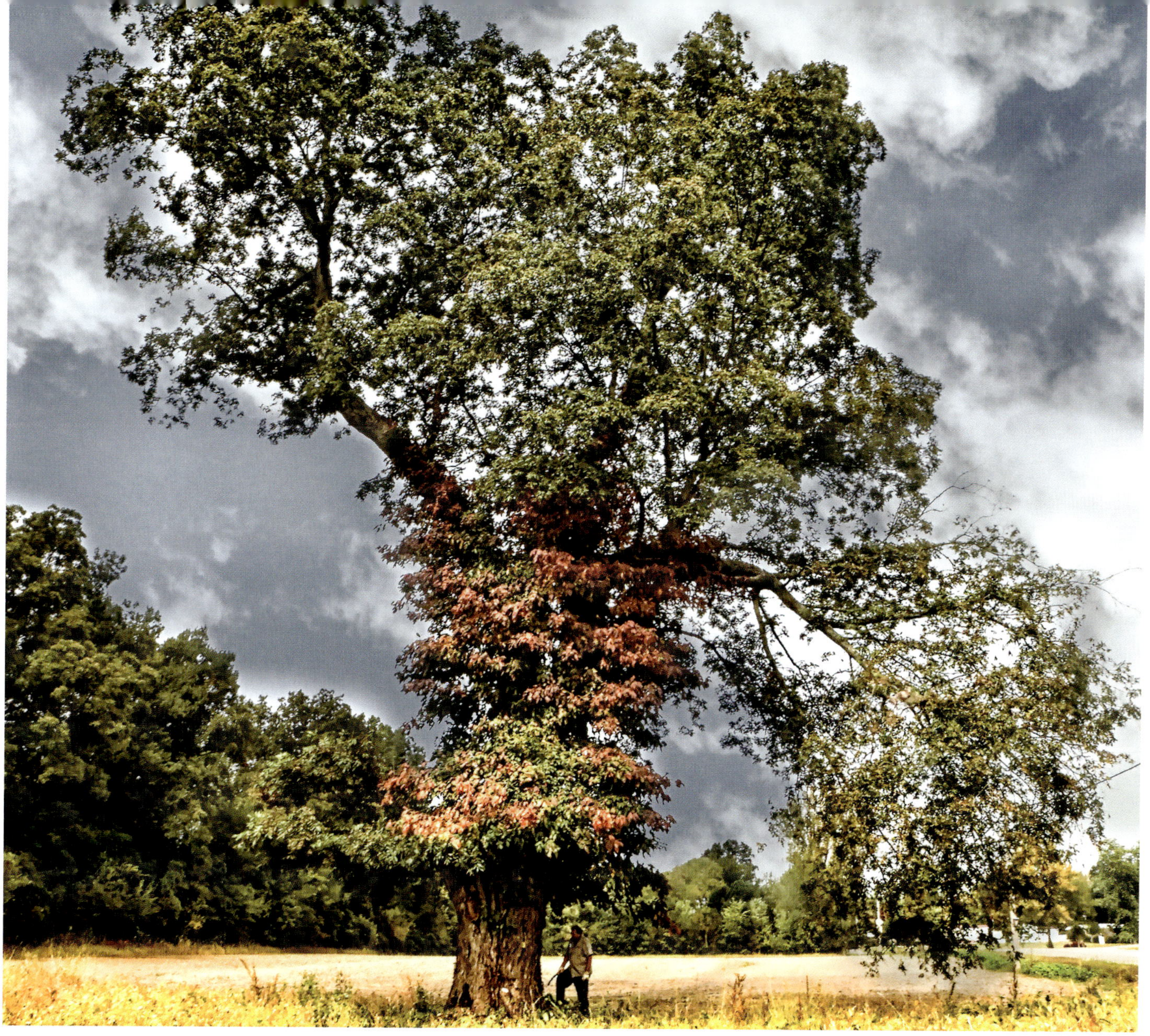

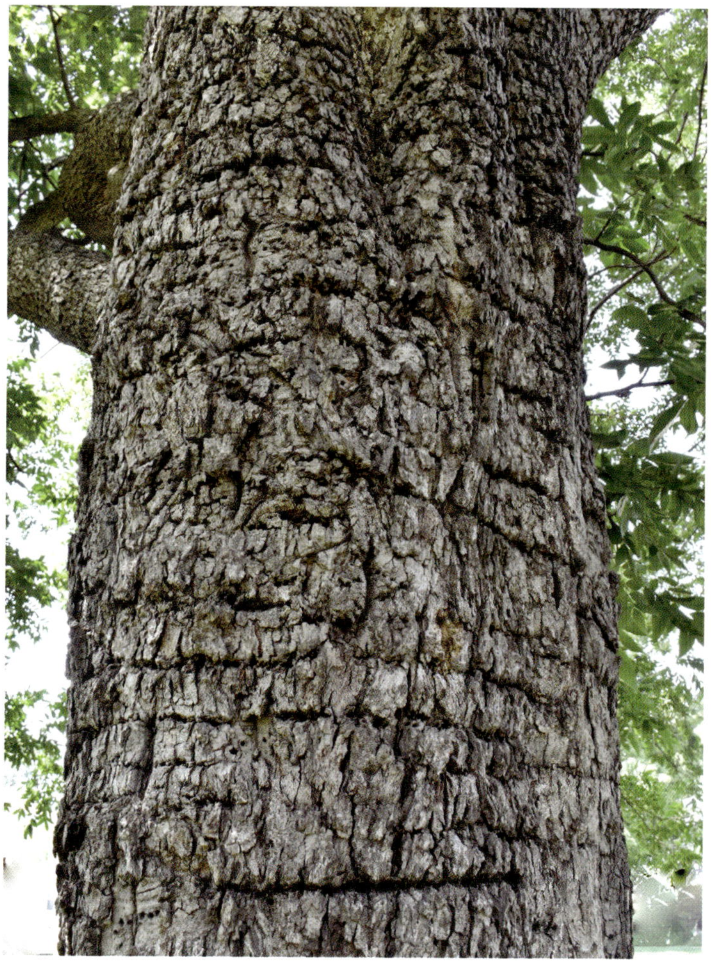

Above: Champion pecan, Vanderburgh County

Left: Pecan's intriguing bark pattern

PIGNUT HICKORY

(Carya glabra)

The daily routines of life sometimes diminish attention to little details that may go unnoticed. Such was the case on this fine spring day, entering the campus of the University of Southern Indiana and turning into the large parking lot. The road passes by an almost hidden trail leading off near a picnic table shelter. Most likely very few folks who commute daily and rush about know about this trail nor the fact that a state champion tree exists here. Fortunately, we were accompanied by our friend Shawn Dickerson, who had certified this tree.

We proceeded down a well-trodden nature trail through the woods. The blooms of toothwort and spring beauty graced the ground and welcomed our appreciation. The gently undulating path crossed two creek channels, with sandstone rocks and a small waterfall. Vibrant mosses carpeted the worn rocky surfaces. We reached a trail fork, the right side leading onward to the location of the state champion pignut hickory. Here, within sounds of the busy highway, stood an obviously aged giant of a tree. At almost 3½ feet in diameter and 116 feet tall, its presence could not be missed. Now with some decay, perhaps caused by a previous lightning strike years ago, the old guard of the woods was still fighting with all remaining vigor to continue for as long as possible.

In pioneer times, strips of hickory were peeled back to make broom ends and the hard stock used for the handle. The tree had the original name of "broom hickory." Pignut was later derived because the nut was too bitter for humans to care much about but seemed to find favor with the hogs scrounging around for whatever might be available. Between the pigs and squirrels, this hickory was desirable. Much more acclaim was given to pignut hickory for its extremely durable tolerance to rough use. The heavy, hard wood made old wagon wheel hubs very resistant to that grinding frictional wear to which they were subjected. Even in weaving, shuttles were made of this hickory. Flooring, cabinets, and tool handles have long been products of all the hickories.

Pignut is a slow-growing, long-lived tree, resistant to drought. It is often found in upland woods among the oaks. The species may even hybridize with other hickories, expressing slight variations in character. The bark of pignut is somewhat tight, with interlacing shallow ridges, dark gray in color, and sometimes grouped into the same description as red hickory. Not only is the bloom attractive in spring, but the fall color can be quite impressive with the yellow leaves radiantly reflecting splendor in late evening light.

Characteristics

- Alternate branching, singly compound leaves usually with 5 leaflets instead of 7, which some of the other hickories have.
- The nut is about 1½ inches long; when it matures, the husk splits partway open, and the nut may stay inside until removed by animals.
- Pignut may reach the 3-foot-diameter size, but more often is found to 24–30 inches.

Uses

- Historic uses cited above. May be used now for cabinetry, furniture, flooring, firewood, and cooking smokers.
- Good landscape tree for strength, longevity, and color.

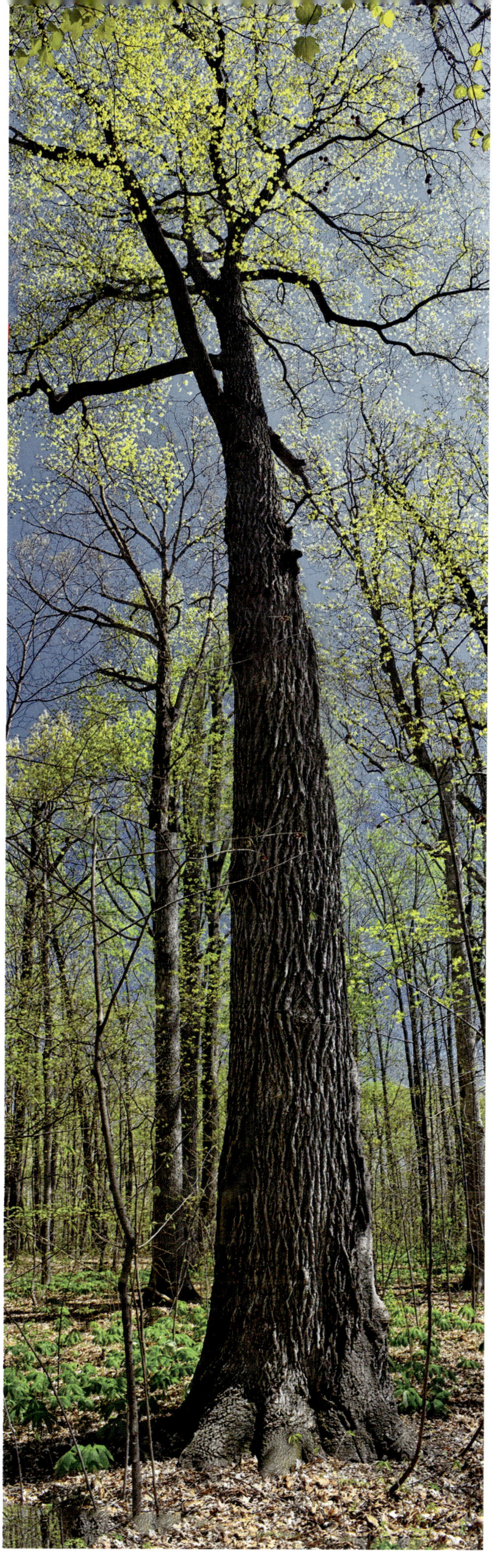

Champion pignut hickory,
Vanderburgh County

RED HICKORY

(*Carya ovalis*)

Tucked away in Burdette Park near Evansville is a tree unfamiliar to most people. This red hickory happens to be the state champion. The park staff directed us to its location across the road from cabin 11, and there is a sign indicating its status as the record tree. At 2½ feet in diameter and 116 feet high, it might be confused with pignut hickory, which is closely related and often shows similar bark patterns. In fact, some taxonomists just group red hickory with pignut in the species *glabra*. Another name for this tree is sweet pignut hickory. If a branch with leaves is found on the ground, red hickory usually has seven leaflets, whereas pignut usually has five. However, they may cross-hybridize, which adds another dimension to positive identification.

Red hickory is not overly noticed, but its range does include all of Indiana. Hemmer Woods in Gibson County also protects some of these trees. Even greater occurrence lies in the deeper South and Southeast of the United States. Many hickory species are susceptible to multiple pests including bark beetles, fungi, and caterpillars. Coupled with environmental factors, a condition known as hickory decline has occurred. A seemingly strong hickory may show the effects of these many problems. When harvested in a timber sale, often only a limited percentage of wood is of value, thus reducing its market price. The red hickory we observed here appeared in very good condition and hopefully will remain healthy for many more years.

The leaves of red hickory, among many others, serve as hosts for larvae of butterflies and moths. The beautiful Luna moth is noted as being one of those found on this tree. Another fascinating caterpillar that can be found on hickories is the hickory horned devil. It is one of the largest of all caterpillars, up to 5 inches in length. While a formidable-looking creature, it is harmless. The moth that lays the eggs is named the regal moth or royal walnut moth.

Characteristics

- Alternate leaves, singly compound, 7 leaflets.
- Similar to pignut hickory, but bark somewhat scalier.
- Thin husk splits fully apart and nut is sweeter. Enjoyed by turkey, mallards, deer, and rodents.
- Hard, heavy, wear-resistant wood may be somewhat darker reddish-brown than other hickories.

Uses

- Tool handles, cabinetry, baskets, good firewood.
- Desirable landscape tree with nice fall color.
- Attractive to wildlife.

Right page: Splendid champion red hickory, Vanderburgh County

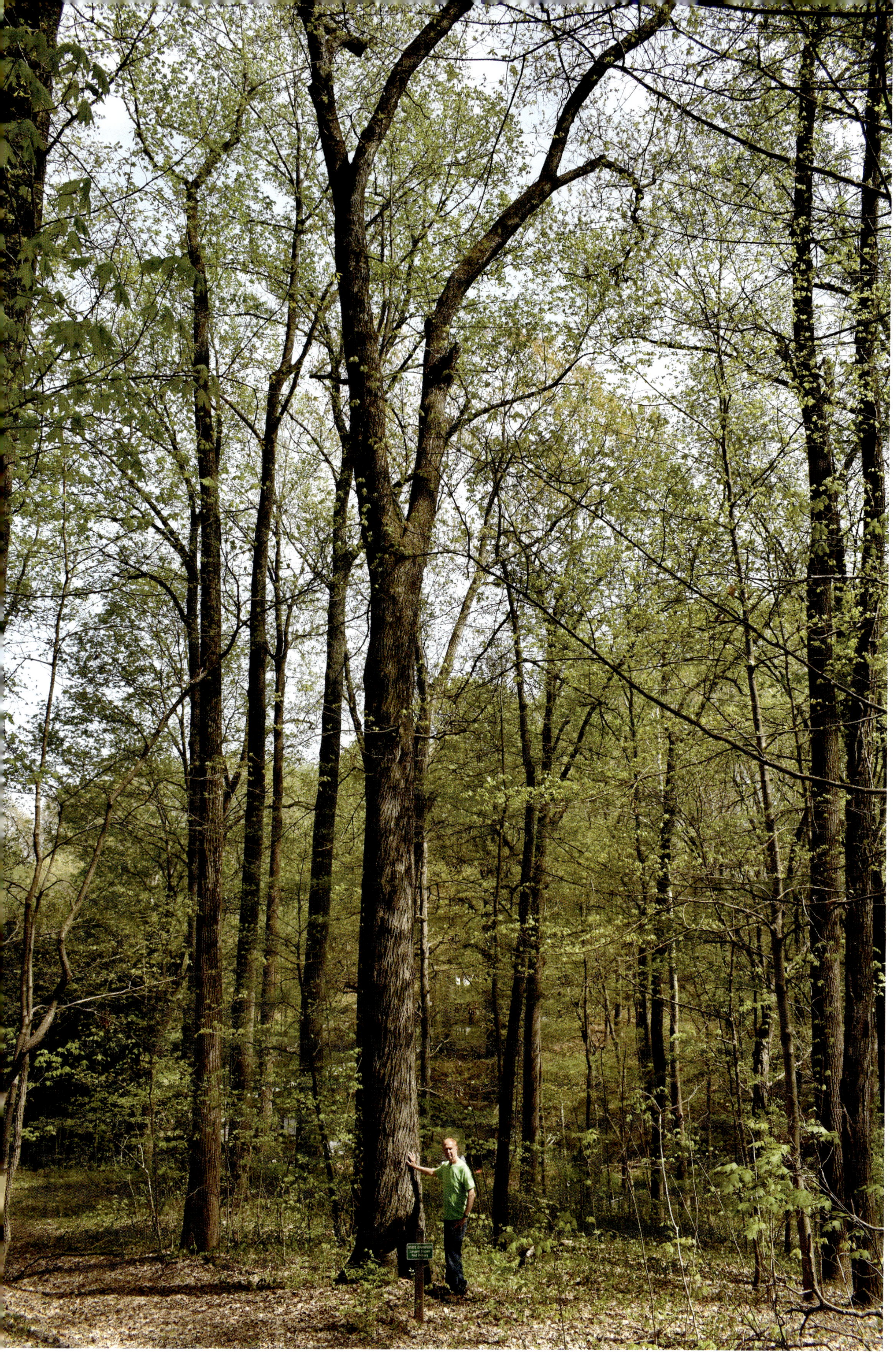
STATE CHAMPION

SHAGBARK HICKORY

(*Carya ovata*)

A fall romp of squirrels all around a large tree brought us over to inspect what was such an attraction. The tree was one of several in the vicinity, all bearing their annual production of a most pleasing delicacy—hickory nuts. In the branches were gray squirrels chatting away and cutting furiously on some of the hard morsels. Hickories are indeed some of our most important wildlife trees in the woods. In this book we do not attempt to cover all of them, but think of mockernut, red, sand, pignut, bitternut, and shellbark. The genus *Carya* is well represented in Indiana forests and is of much importance.

In olden days shagbark hickory symbolized the rugged and tough life of pioneers. Both hickory nuts and walnuts were cracked and considered a delicacy. Native Americans collected great volumes of these nuts and processed them by mashing, boiling, and straining the liquid, which was called "hickory milk."

The merit of hickory as a fuel is seldom surpassed, ranking it highly valuable to settlers for heating their drafty log cabins and in present times when it is often cut alongside oak as preferred firewood. Some old-timers will also fondly recall the smoke shack out back where a ham or other meats were hung and flavored by aromatic hickory smoke. Other early uses were for barrel hoops, log cabin door hinges, joinery in dowels for early furniture, and yellowish tint from the inner bark for homespun clothing. This wood is tough, strong, hard, and even today can throw sparks from a chainsaw trying to cut through it. Of course, we still remember the famous nickname of Andrew Jackson, "Old Hickory," the general who proved his mettle with the troops during the days of the Natchez Trace trek back into his beloved Tennessee and then became the seventh president of the United States.

The impressive state champion shagbark stands reverently overlooking Elkhorn Cemetery near Richmond. At a height of 100 feet and a diameter of 4½ feet, it and companion hickories nearby add a watchful colonnade over the immaculate grounds.

Characteristics

- Can reach over 100 feet in height and 4 feet in diameter. Unmistakable shaggy plate bark.
- Compound leaves to 1 foot long with 5–7 leaflets, turning golden yellow or brown in fall.
- Large nut to 1½ inches, thick husk, separates in four parts, sweet, edible kernels.
- Can hybridize with pecan and shellbark hickories.

Uses

- Baskets, fine cabinetry, hard handles.
- Great firewood, long-lasting charcoal fire, aroma highly desired in cooking.
- Valuable for wildlife food and edible by humans as well.

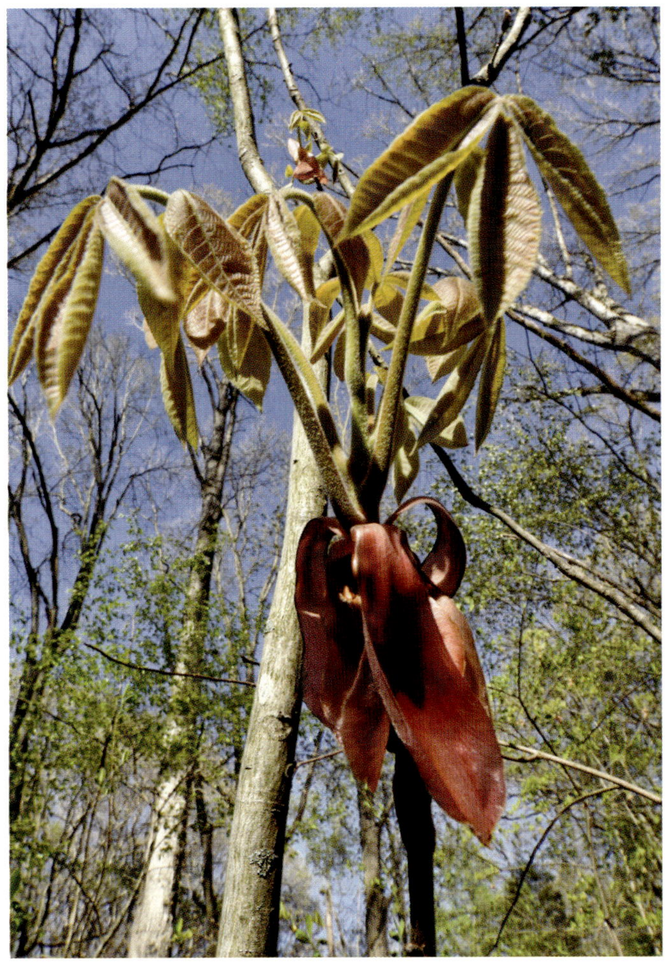

Shagbark hickory bloom

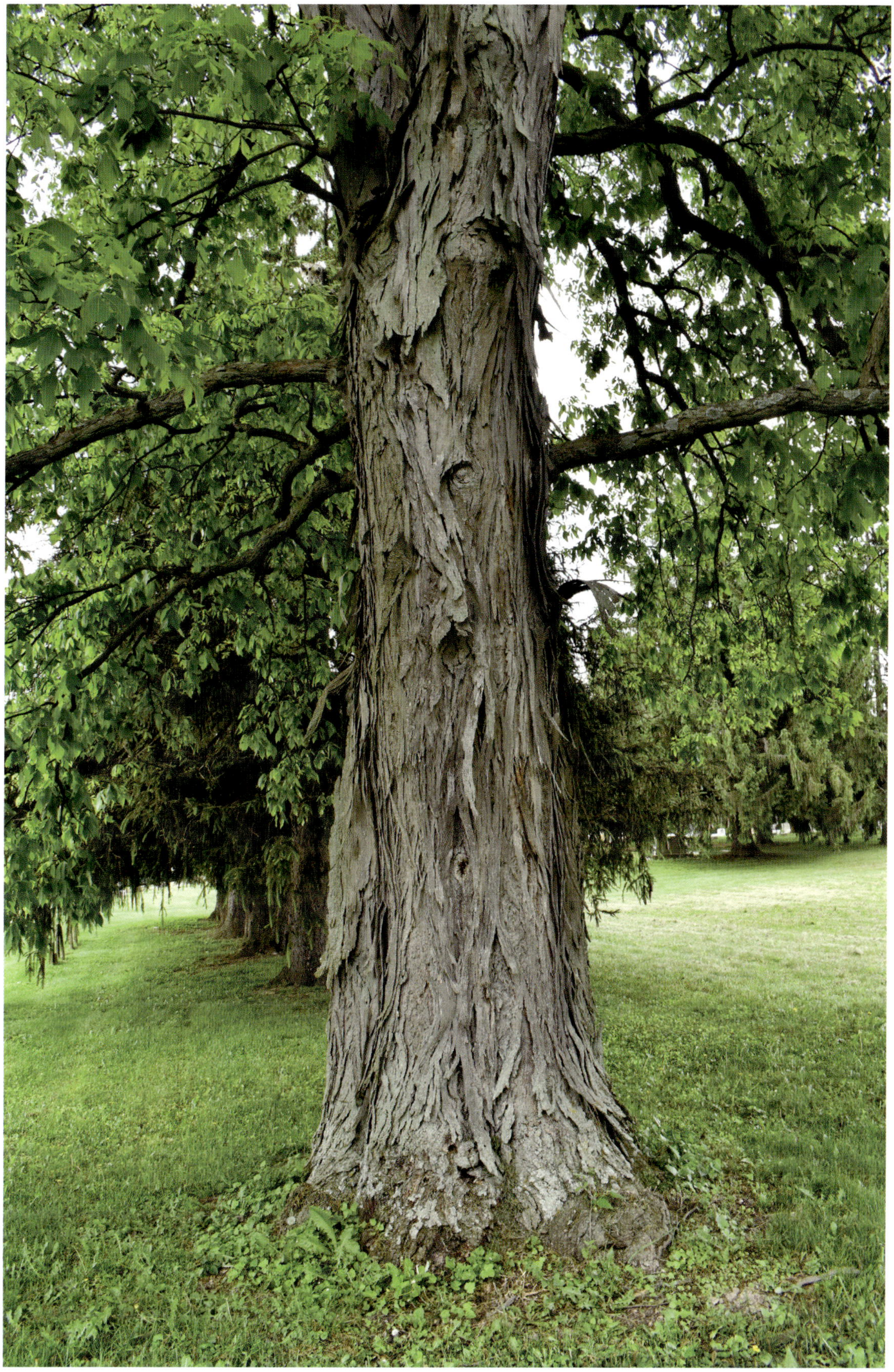

Champion shagbark hickory, Wayne County.

SHELLBARK HICKORY

(*Carya laciniosa*)

Not far from the mother woodcock carefully guarding her nest, on a rocky hillside with a limestone outcrop, stood a splendid example of a tree with the largest nuts of any hickory species. The only rivals were some pecan nuts we saw in southwestern Indiana. This shaggy specimen in Lawrence County stood with companion oaks and a Kentucky coffeetree. Against a clear blue sky, the gray unfurled bark struck a most wondrous effect. The landowner accompanied us on this fine day, showing us this shellbark and an old white oak he also admired. The abundant fall product of the tree was of great interest to the local squirrel community, we are sure, but the owner cordially invited us to come back next year and collect all the nuts we wanted as well.

Another adventurous trip over near Metamora in Franklin County was to see the state champion tree. It was a fine specimen to behold, some 4 feet across and 134 feet in height. A bonus for the location was that it was right off the old historic Metamora-Whitewater Canal at what is called Twin Locks. The canal was constructed in the late 1830s and 1840s to facilitate goods going to market. It lasted only a few years, but today portions are preserved as a tourist attraction. This huge old shellbark was most likely a young tree within view of the laborers trying to dig and move all the soil, roots, and rocks. The present owner of the tree, who has lived there seventy years, recalled stories about the workers and the weekly deaths from malaria.

Also known as kingnut and bottom hickory, this dweller of fine rich soils in alluvial bottomlands of major river drainages in Indiana and Illinois was large and abundant in early times of French settlement. American pioneers also noted these resplendent producers of fine nuts and superb timber among the great sycamores, tulip, and walnut. Needless to say, as with the others, large shellbarks were felled, used, and the land cleared for crops. Much less known today by the average onlooker, when occasionally found, it is most often taken as shagbark hickory. Subtle differences in twig, bud, leaf, and tightness of the bark strips may give it away. And then there are those 2–2½-inch, thick-hulled, delicious nuts, a final clue.

Characteristics

- Graceful, spreading crown, normally to 100 feet; state champion was 134 feet.
- Diameters often to 24–32 inches; state record specimen is almost 4 feet across.
- Long leaves with normally seven leaflets, alternate.
- Orange-brown twig. Bud may be slightly pubescent.
- Beautiful gray peeling bark.
- Nut hull 4–6 ribbed, thick.

Uses

- Hard, heavy, tough, strong wood makes great axe handles. In olden times used for hubs and spokes of wagons.
- Like its cousin, shagbark, makes great firewood, fine flooring, and cabinets.

Right page: State champion shellbark hickory, Franklin County

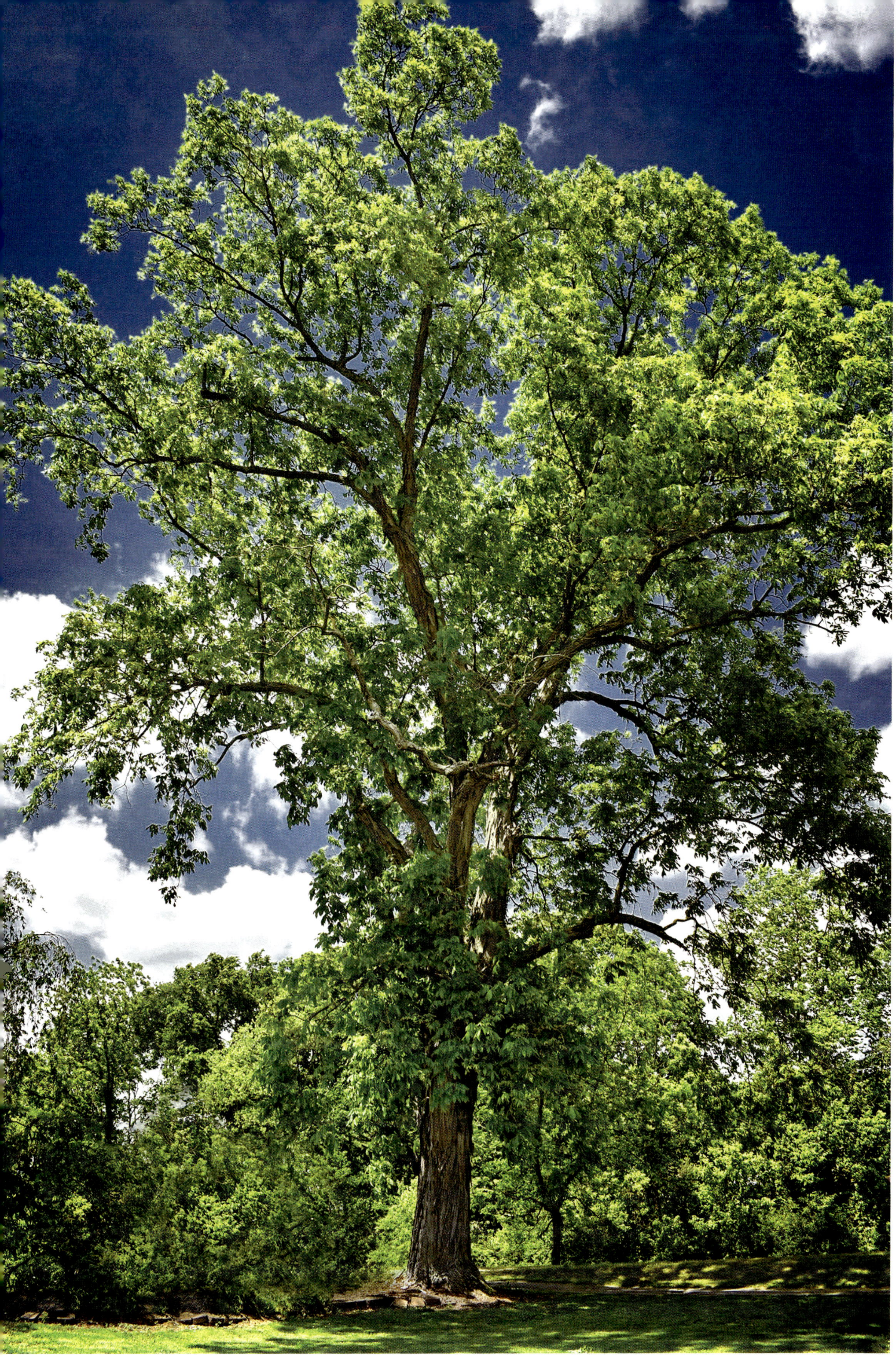

AMERICAN HORNBEAM AND EASTERN HOP-HORNBEAM

(*Carpinus caroliniana* and *Ostrya virginiana*)

These two trees are grouped together for three reasons: They are both in the birch family (Betulaceae), are rather small, and have hornbeam in the name. They both are locally called "ironwood." In fact, folks usually never refer to these trees by the book name. They even find it confusing to differentiate between the two. In the woods, both can be found in the same area—but they do not look alike at all if observing the bark.

American hornbeam is often called "blue beech," "water beech," "ironwood," or commonly "muscle wood." The latter seems to stick well with observers. Naturalists will often have children feel the "muscles" of the tree. The tree normally does not grow very large—perhaps to 30 feet, and the diameter to 4–6 inches. The fine-toothed leaves are smoother than those of *Ostrya*, and the petiole a little longer. The fruit pod is a feathery-looking paper-like sack in clusters. It contains one seed and ripens in the fall.

The past champion American hornbeam was in Crown Hill Cemetery, Indianapolis. Part of this distinguished tree has died and the remaining branched stems are only a remnant left of the original. A new candidate has been nominated in Jackson County. This hornbeam resides in the Muscatatuck National Wildlife Refuge, near Seymour. It was a great specimen, much larger than the norm. Tromping through in muck boots, Dave Coppert led us to his find in a low-elevation woods along a stream and close to grand beech trees, whose gray bark color looks much like hornbeam.

Eastern hop-hornbeam is quite a mouthful to pronounce, and when called that, blank stares arise. If called "ironwood," a smile of familiarity may arise. But then again, American hornbeam is also called ironwood by locals, so we must dig a little more as to how this hop-hornbeam tree is indeed different. The best way is to start with the bark. Hornbeam is smooth, gray, and muscular. Hop-hornbeam's bark is brown and shreddy. It can actually be rubbed off by hand.

Hop-hornbeam is in a different genus as well if you are into classification. The size of this species is about like the American hornbeam, generally to 30 feet. One last identifier is the fruit, seen in fall. Those clusters of ovate papery sacks are rounder. Each small sack contains one seed.

Most often hop-hornbeams are found in woodlands with fairly good soils along with other understory companions like pawpaw, spicebush, and American hornbeam. The champion hop-hornbeam is in Brookside Park, Indianapolis. The photo shown illustrates that it is indeed a little larger than normal. At almost a foot across and 50 feet in height, tall and slender, this is an exceptional tree. Few people passing by would never know what kind of tree this was and may get tongue-twisted saying "eastern hop-hornbeam." You are permitted just to say "ironwood" if you like.

For those who know little about these two trees and might relegate them to a status of no worth, it is best to remember that they, too, have roles in nature that play out in the life of the overall natural system. They add to the shade, soils, and foods for creatures in ways we must respect.

Characteristics

- Both are understory trees, found in similar wooded settings.
- Male flowers are catkins, pendant on twigs, like other members of the birch family.
- The bark is different (see above). The fruit pods are also distinct.
- The leaves look very similar, but hornbeam are usually smoother, teeth may be finer.
- Both are very tough, hard woods. No wonder they are called ironwood.
- Hornbeam not as long-lived as hop-hornbeam.

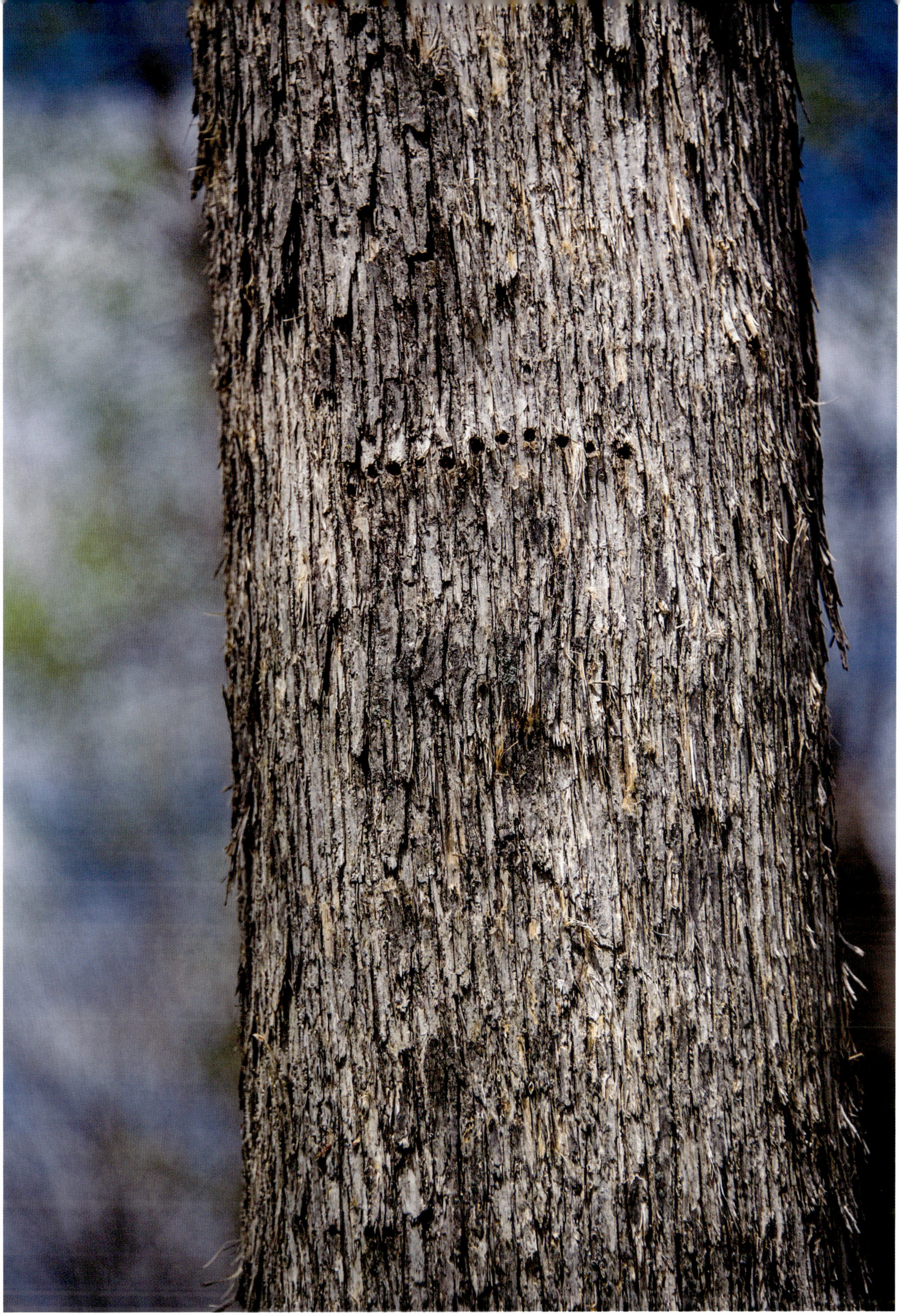

Shreddy bark pattern of *Ostrya,* with yellow-bellied sapsucker work displayed
Courtesy of Gary Potts

Uses

- Since these are small trees, small items are produced. Mallet heads, handles, and pry-bar wooden levers were used in olden days.
- Hornbeam was one of those very early woods used for bowls and dishes. Treenware, as the product of several hardwood species was called, now sells for very high prices in the antique collectors' markets.
- Wildlife uses are made of both trees—nesting and food sources.
- Landscape values are of interest. Both species have attributes of bark, form, and fall color, while remaining small in stature, and are shade tolerant. American hornbeam is easier to transplant than hop-hornbeam.

Right: The author and his wife with the state champion American hornbeam
Courtesy of Dave Coppert

Right page: State champion hop-hornbeam, Brookside Park, Indianapolis, with Tree-Centric Solutions arborist Jerome Delbridge
Courtesy of Gary Potts

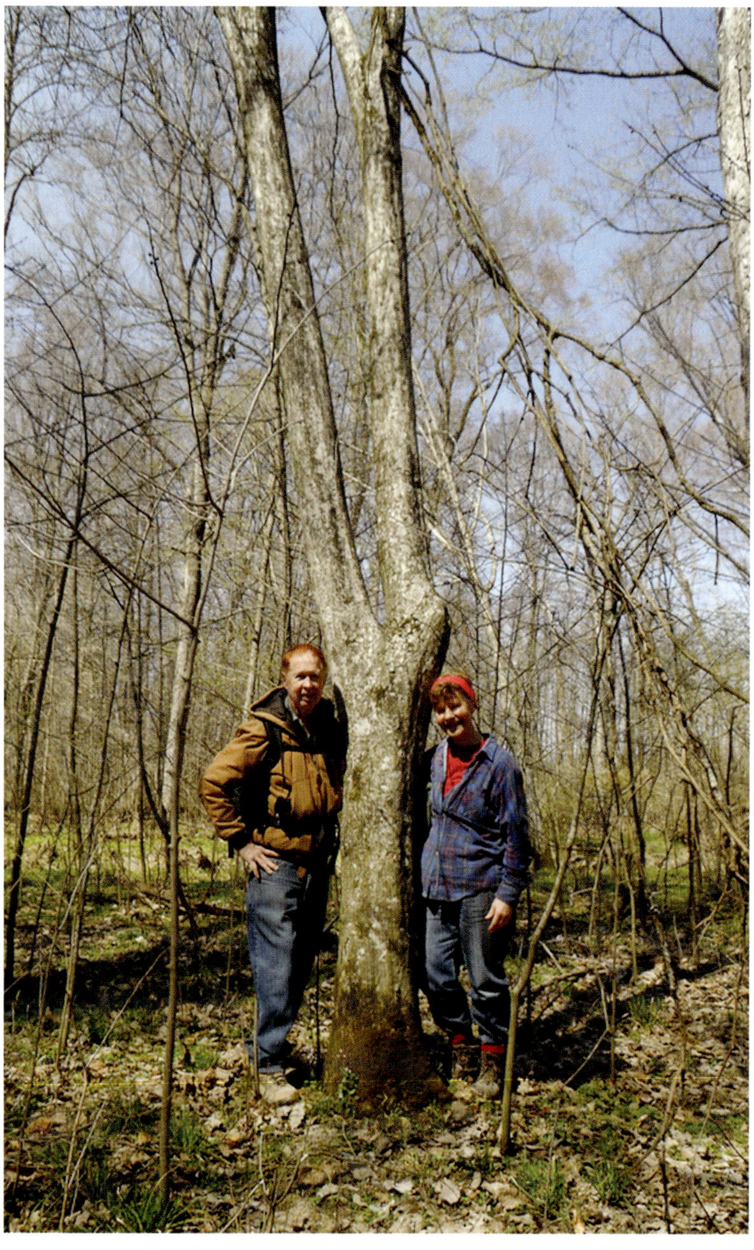

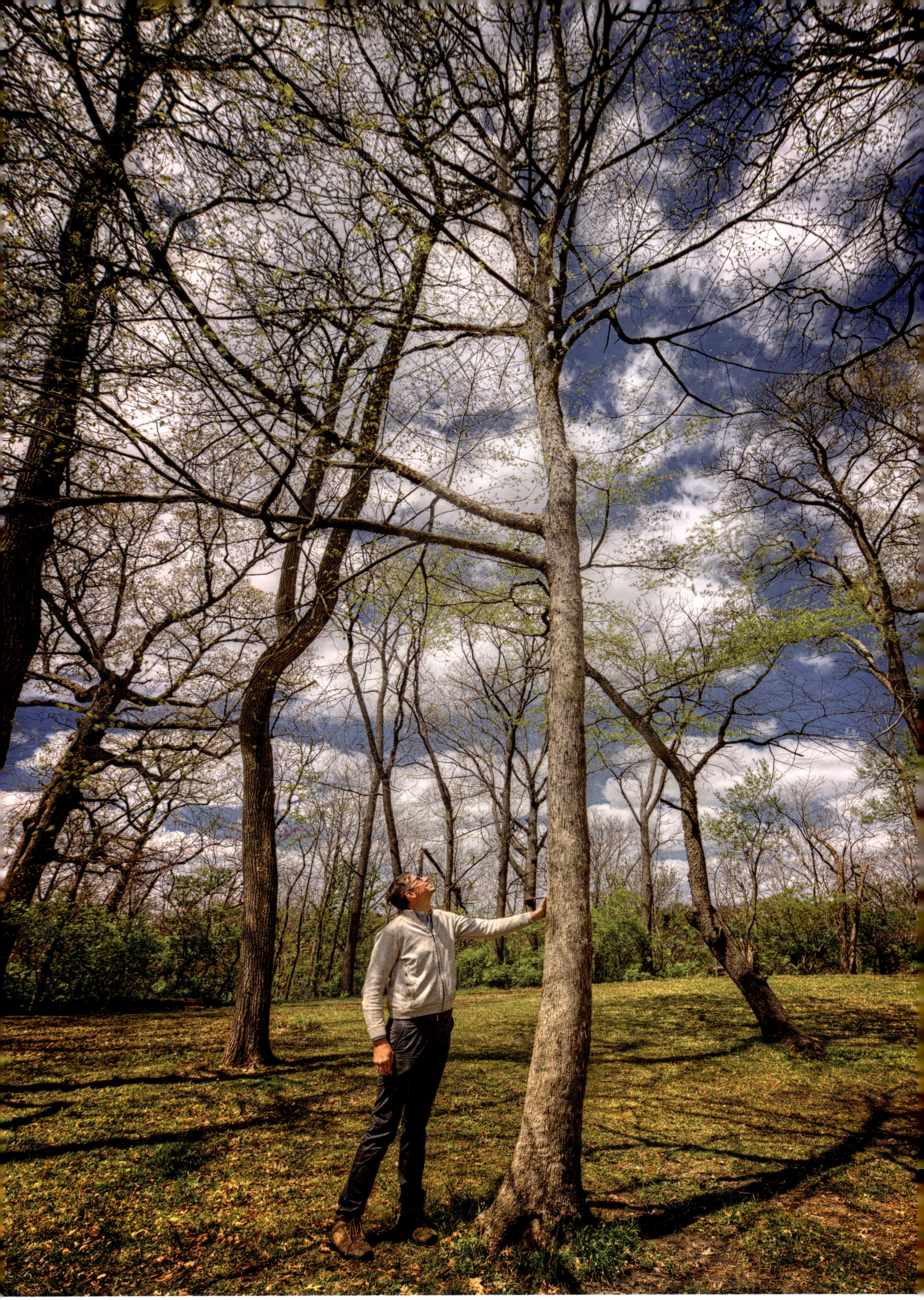

BLACK LOCUST

(Robinia pseudoacacia)

A profusion of white blooms signaling spring's arrival in the hillside grove of trees in Monroe County was an obvious attractor for hundreds of honeybees working diligently. The scent carried through the air near and far, wafting the sweet fragrance to both bee and human observers.

Here is a tree far underappreciated, despite its long history back to Jamestown. Often called honey locust due to its highly aromatic nature, the name is confusing, since another tree, sweet locust (*Gleditsia triacanthos*), is now accepted as honey locust. Therefore, black locust now is recognized as the correct nomenclature.

Of interest is the scientific name origin for the species. As often happens, a significant person is the basis for the name—perhaps the first discoverer of the plant, or some other notable (such as Charles Deam for our Indiana Deam oak). In the instance of *Robinia*, Peattie (1966) cites the Frenchman Jean Robin, herbalist to King Henry IV, as likely sending seeds from Louisiana, perhaps as early as 1601. The species *pseudoacacia* derives from the similar leaf appearance of the acacia subfamily, one member of which is the mimosa tree. Other members of this group are shrubby plants found in the southwestern United States. Black locust is a native to our area—the other acacias are not.

The exact original range of the species is not completely known, but it was thought to concentrate mostly in the Appalachians, perhaps coastal areas, and in the Ozark Plateau. The wood was so highly prized in early times that it has been planted almost everywhere, much to the chagrin of ecologists who now classify it as a nuisance plant. It is a fast grower in open areas ripe for succession and if left alone can overwhelm the other desired species of trees, native grasses, and flowers. Hence, habitat management plans often call for its total removal. Compounding the seed reproduction dispersal is the fact that it produces suckers that can rapidly march forward to colonize every available acre.

Originally reaching upward to 80 feet and with trunks 3–4 feet across, the trees' amazing hardness and strength were recognized as superlative qualities that were highly desired. Durability in the ground far surpassed that of almost every other species; it barely shrank upon drying, the beam strength was excellent, and the woodworking color was very pleasing. When burned as a fuel it rates above oak and hickory, which are often standards for heat output.

But sadly, most majestic old locusts have gone away, once again because of a ruinous insect, the locust borer beetle. Now the remaining occurrences across America are but poor quality, infected, and rarely able to grow into fine magnificent specimens. The previous state champion in Vigo County is in poor shape now and its lifespan is completed. Some very nice and fairly good-sized locusts are in Pine Hills State Nature Preserve. The prodigious amounts of these had found a receptive haven on previously cleared land and were growing fairly straight and tall. These were chosen to illustrate this essay.

Characteristics

- Compound leaves, smooth margins, may curl up in the evening. Pair of spiny thorns on the limb.
- Medium sized tree 60–80 feet.
- Gray bark in youth; black, fissured in old age.
- Inner bark and roots may be yellow to orange.
- Brown, long seed pods.
- Likes dry, sunny sites in old fields.

Uses

- Fence posts, railroad ties, mine timbers, woodworking if quality boards can be milled.
- Useful in reclamation areas needing fast growth. May then limit all other trees.
- Attracts pollinators.

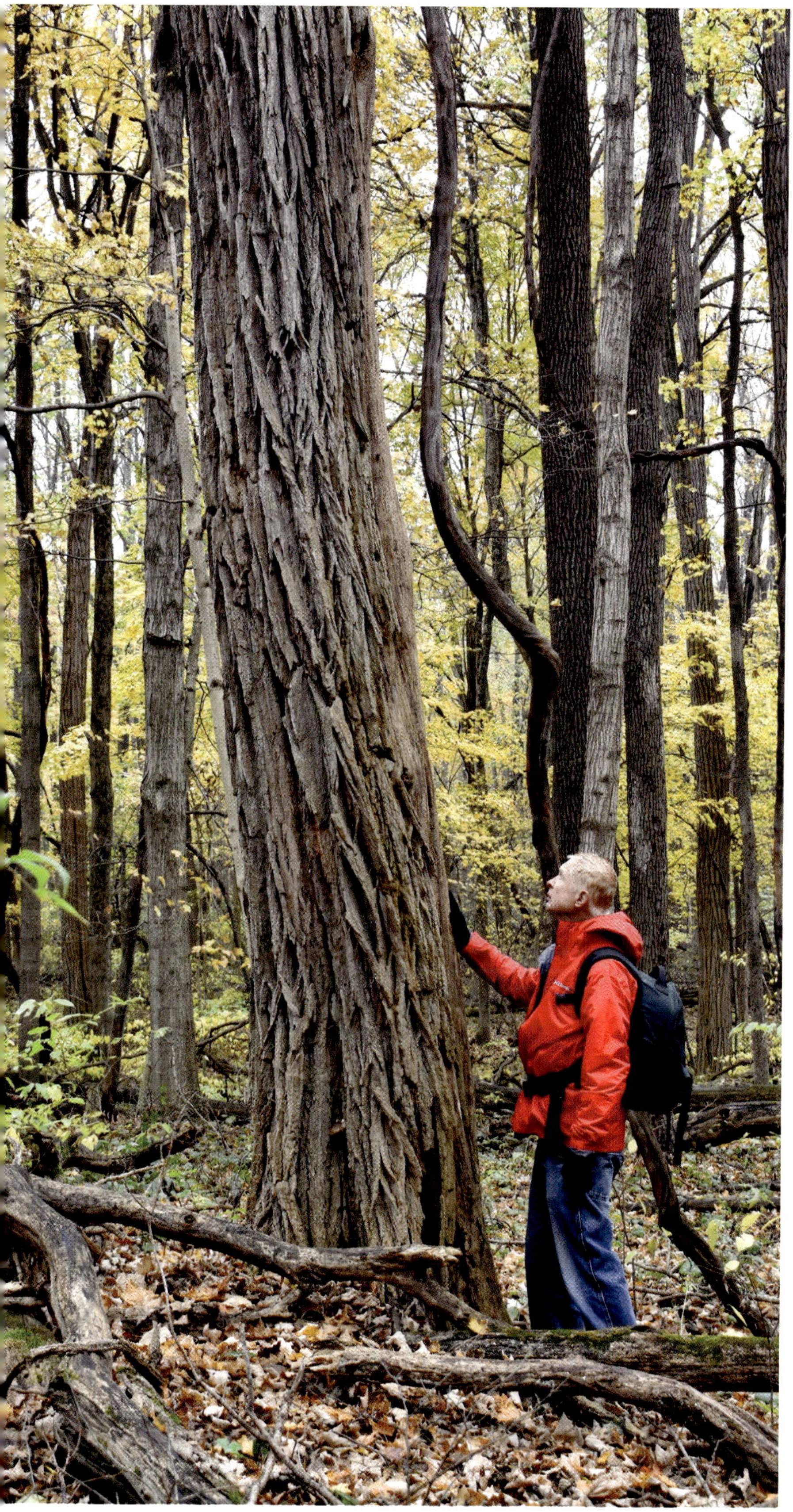

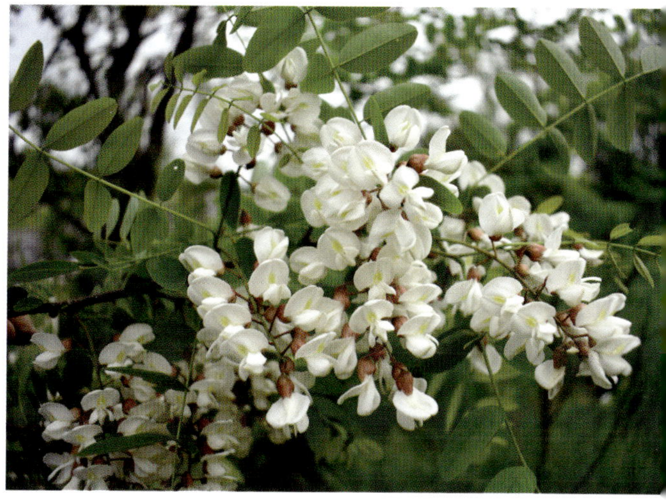

Above: Black locust blooms

Left: Black locust, Pine Hills Nature Preserve, Montgomery County

HONEYLOCUST

(Gleditsia triacanthos)

Among the jewels of Muscatatuck National Wildlife Refuge lay the thorns. A hot summer day was not a pleasant time to begin the hike back along an old road leading to this potential new state champion. Dave Coppert had discovered this large specimen on one of his many outings looking for new discoveries. The tree stood on the other side of a drainage ditch, making access somewhat more difficult through the brush. Once close to this old giant, great care was taken not to step on some of those nefarious 3-inch-long thorns. Protruding from the trunk and rising upwards, many of these deterrent three-pronged spikes challenged any living creature daring to even think about climbing. This specimen, 101 feet in height and 3 feet in diameter, is large for the species, so the find is significant.

Southern Indiana and Illinois are where honeylocusts are largest, with heights of up to 140 feet. It grows quickly but the lifespan is only 120 years.[12] If open-grown, the tree form is often branched low with perhaps two large stems diverging at 4–6 feet above the ground. On old trees the gray-brown bark seems to curl and peel, with some fissures. On young trees the honey-colored bark is much smoother, but those insidious thorns begin early and warn all creatures to stay away.

Although the flower itself is not particularly as fragrant as that of black locust, it is still a good pollinator-friendly tree. The female and male flowers are on separate trees. The "bean pod" produced by honeylocust is about 12–18 inches long, twisted and curled around. When ripe, the pulp within is rather rich and sweet, giving the name credence. Several seeds of size less than ½ inch occupy this leguminous pod and if consumed by animals, transported away, and redeposited, become the next generation of fast-growing progeny. If the pods remain on trees during winter, they may rattle in the wind or dance fancily upon their branches.

Characteristics

- Alternate branched, has both single and doubly compound leaves.
- Fairly rapid in growth but lifespan usually 100 years.
- Often forks or divides within the first few feet, especially if open-grown.
- The flat seedpods are curly, distinctive, and used in crafts.
- Likes bottomlands and is quick to take over open areas.
- Shows those wicked thorns early, deterring man and beast.

Uses

- Wood is hard, strong, and heavy; useful for fence posts and rough lumber.
- When prime specimens are cut on a bandsaw and finished, the beauty of the pinkish-red coloration shows up. Grain may be wide and open. Occasional dark spots show where ingrown thorns were.
- Wildlife values fleshy pods and seeds. Squirrel nests sometimes visible near top of tree.
- The tree is rather pretty, interesting, and grows fast. Those thorns make it formidable, however. A substitute is thornless honeylocust available in nurseries.

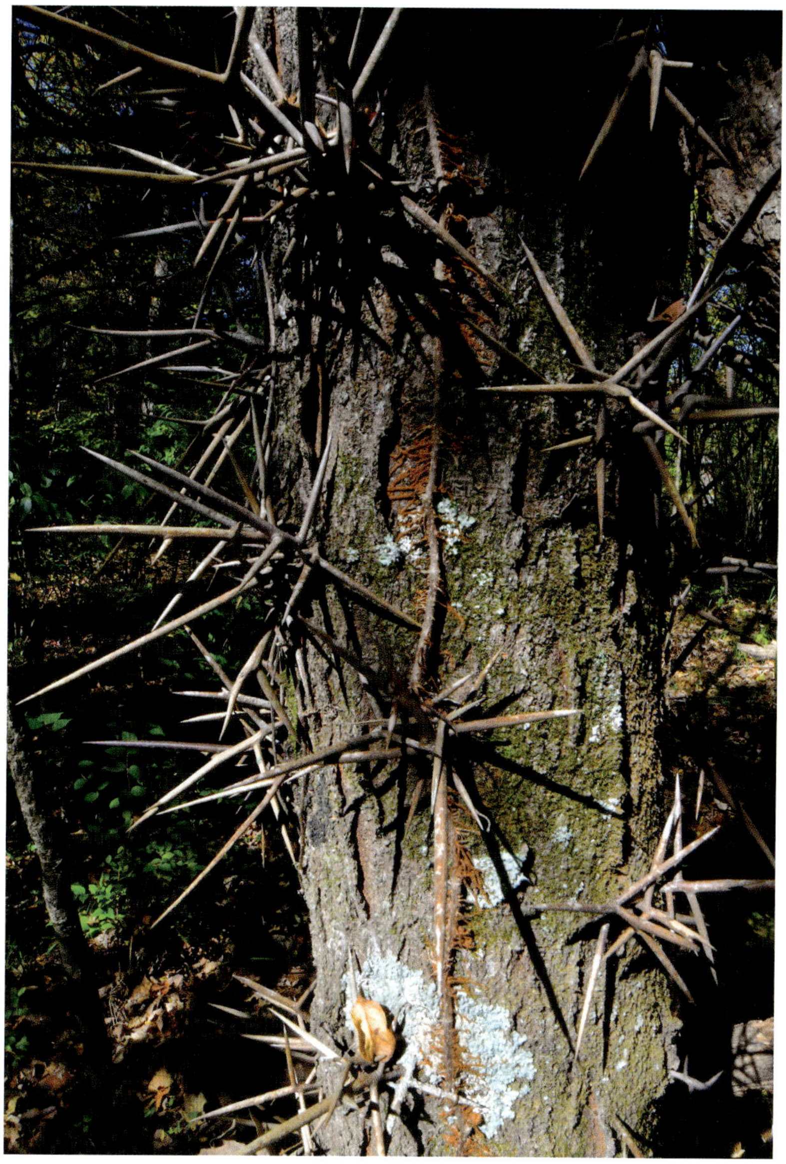

Honeylocust's formidable thorns

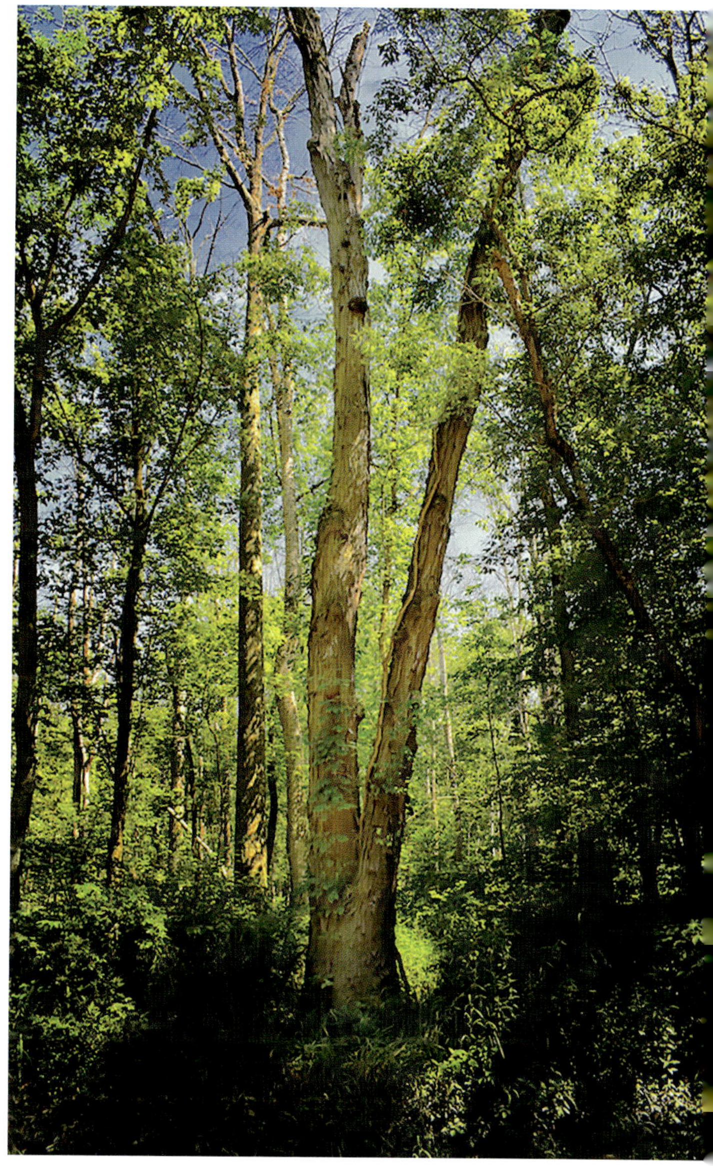

State champion honeylocust, Muscatatuck NWR

KENTUCKY COFFEETREE

(Gymnocladus dioicus)

As settlers and explorers came westward, they found species of plants that were new to them but were well known to Native Americans. Such is the Kentucky coffeetree, that unique species with the largest of all leaves of native trees (along with the devil's-walkingstick)—doubly compound with length 1–3 feet, 5–9 side branchlets, and 6–14 leaflets on each. The whole array thus forms a most incredible lacy green fan in the canopy.

Gymnocladus derives from the Greek "naked branch," referring to the remnant short stubby branches especially noticeable in winter.[13] While the early spring color of developing leaflets may be tinged with lime and pink, they then assume the darker green with lighter underside. On a perfect sunny blue-sky day in fall, the gorgeous yellow fronds far overhead render a most splendid scene. The display must be caught in the right timing because the leaflets turn brown soon and fall away to the ground below. Remaining bare for six months, one other defining characteristic still gives this tree away. Ashen-gray to tannish-brown, the large rough, flaky, curly bark draws attention in every season. The old bean pods, still clinging tightly to the forlorn branches, rattle away, oblivious to the onset of winter.

In early times the tree was evidently first encountered in Kentucky, or at least named from there. Later, this species would become Kentucky's state tree. The "beans" in long pods were tried as a coffee substitute in the backwoods where real coffee was a scarcity. These must be roasted first and not boiled straight into a pot. Otherwise, the alkaloid brew is highly toxic. Needless to say, once real coffee became plentiful, the rather disdainful taste of the "substitute" resulted in its discontinuation.

It has been postulated that the tree has earlier origins and lived during the time of mastodons and mammoths. The beasts' massive molars may have been able to break open that leathery, tough pod and assist in seed distribution.[14] In more recent times Native Americans traded the seeds, resulting in introduction of the tree to other parts of the continent. Not only were the seeds brewed, but also the pulp from the wood was used to treat insanity. A tea was also made from the leaves and used as a laxative. Further, they threw seeds and leaves into small bodies of water or pools to stupefy fish.[15]

Also a member of the pea family like the locusts, it is capable of making good fence posts that resist decay for many years. Kentucky coffeetree is often forked not far above the ground and is not considered a valuable timber tree, nor does it occur abundantly. But it does produce some very handsome brownish-red boards that can be turned into rather unique cabinetry or flooring.

Characteristics

- Alternate leaves, 1–3 feet in length and doubly compound
- Reaching 3 feet in diameter and usually less than 100 feet in height.
- May form colonies in rich woods.
- Handsome peeling gray bark, described as "curly," can expose salmon-colored inner bark.
- Brown seedpods may hang on during the winter on the female tree.

Uses

- Interesting wood for cabinets with a unique rosy salmon to light brown color. Illustrations on Purdue Extension's Hardwood Lumber and Veneer site show varying grain, described by Dan Cassens as a wild, coarse pattern undulating and weaving. This definitely catches the eye on fine boards.
- Often historically important as fence posts.
- Actually a pretty landscape tree and hardy.
- Of limited wildlife value.

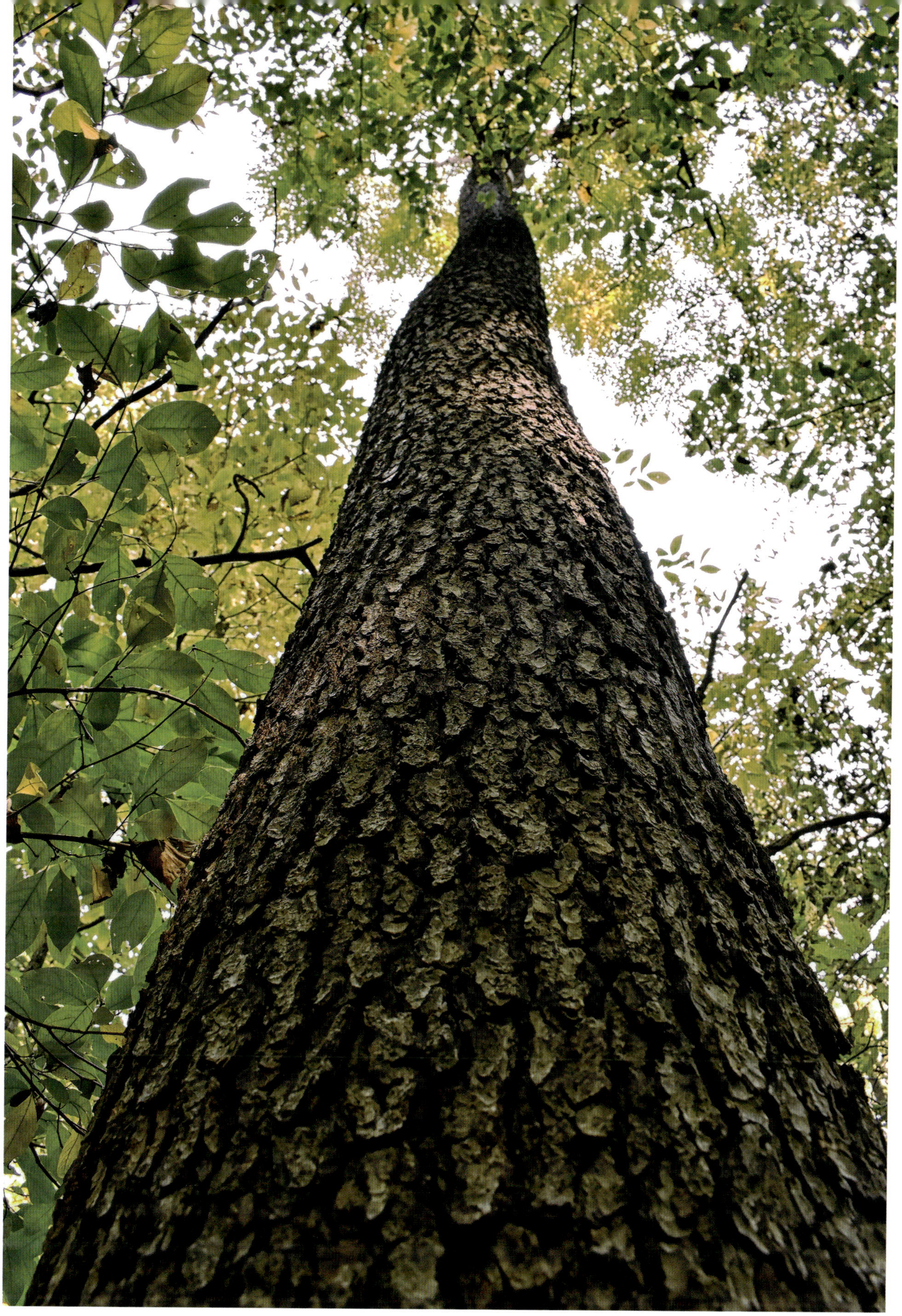

Large Kentucky coffeetree, Meltzer Woods, Shelby County

LARGE-TOOTHED ASPEN

(Populus grandidentata)

Some say the leaves tremble in the wind. Others say they flutter. Maybe they dance. While the greatest show of this charm is exhibited by the quaking aspen (*Populus tremuloides*), the large-toothed aspen is not far behind in this delightful character.

Also known as bigtooth aspen, it occurs in Indiana rather extensively and certainly adds excitement to the landscape. Few trees are as handsome year-round. Emergent greens appear in May as the leaf develops on its dainty stalk. Many other surrounding hardwoods are also in competition with their initial outburst of energy, putting on leaves and developing their flowers. Aspens are unisexual: male and female flowers on two separate trees. The prodigious and rambunctious product of the fruit produced in little capsules on pendant catkins are those cottony seeds, which release into even the gentlest of breezes willing to transport them far and wide.

The large-toothed aspen is found in many locales including sandy loam hills, siltstone-limestone ridges, and down in bottomlands. It is an opportunist seeking new occupancy of openings, often in reclaimed lands or abandoned sites. Postfire successional areas often see rapid growth of aspen if it has habituated that region in the past. The species also does produce clonal progeny through its root system, although not to the degree of quaking aspen. While largetooth aspen is found statewide, quaking aspen is mostly in the northern half. Its spectacular color show is much like the photo shown here of western aspen.

Aspens are largely passed by as far as importance in industry, although some fine specimens do yield delicate and figured grain or creamy white sapwood for paneling. Other uses capitalize on its softness and low density. When areas are cleared of aspen for planting other hardwoods, the sad trees are hauled off, destined for pulp mills, and then are at least cycled into some useful product to regain some of their pride.

The largest largetoothed aspen on the Big Tree Registry is in Indianapolis, ironically along a city street, a multistem specimen 4 feet in diameter and 69 feet high. Other aspens in the wild are present in Indiana, with many as clumps, but also some fine single-stem specimens, tall and straight.

Characteristics

- Large handsome, toothed leaf to 7 inches, borne singly and alternately on branch.
- Flattened petiole (stem) permits flapping and gleeful gyration in the wind.
- Attractive white-gray bark, becoming dark and fissured in old age.
- Leaf color pale yellow in fall, less intense than cousin *tremuloides*.
- Can be defoliated by the gypsy moth caterpillar and also threatened by ambrosia beetles.

Uses

- Planted as an ornamental, much like paper birch, for the white trunks.
- Can be felled by sharp incisors of the beaver, munched, and dragged in to construct lodges.
- Some minor woodcrafting, specialty items, panels, and often relegated to the pulp industry.

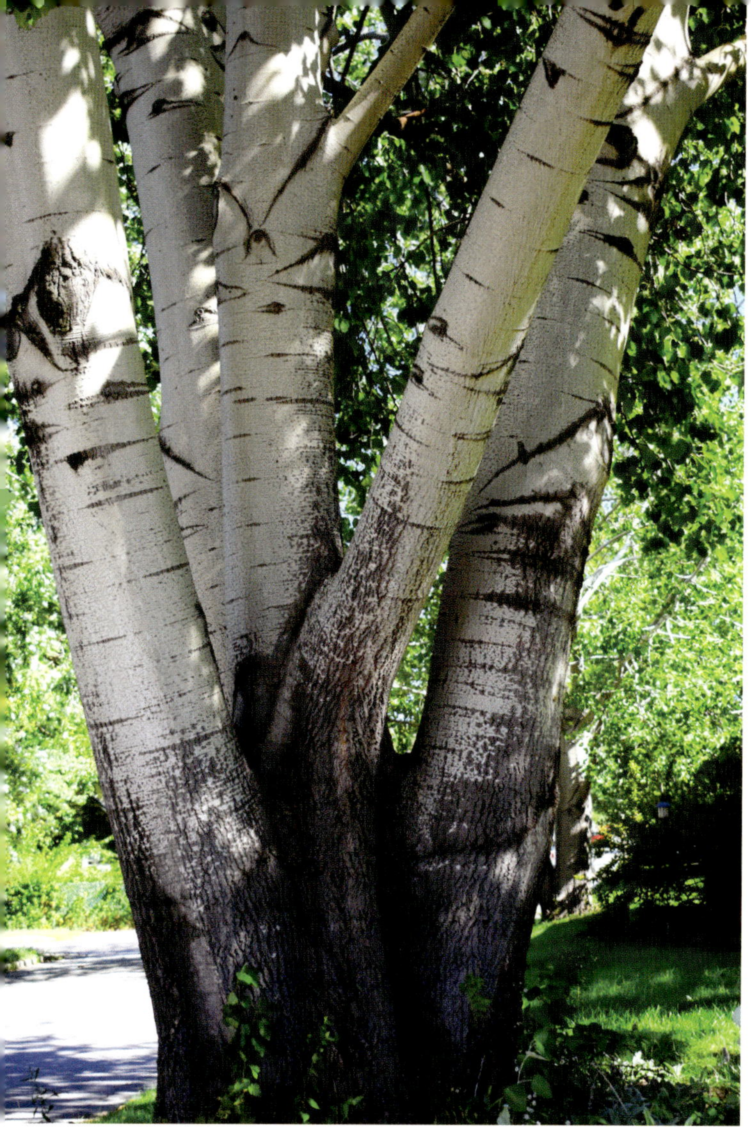

Left: State champion large-toothed aspen, Indianapolis

Bottom left: Large-toothed aspen clonal group, Lawrence County

Bottom right: Aspen fall colors

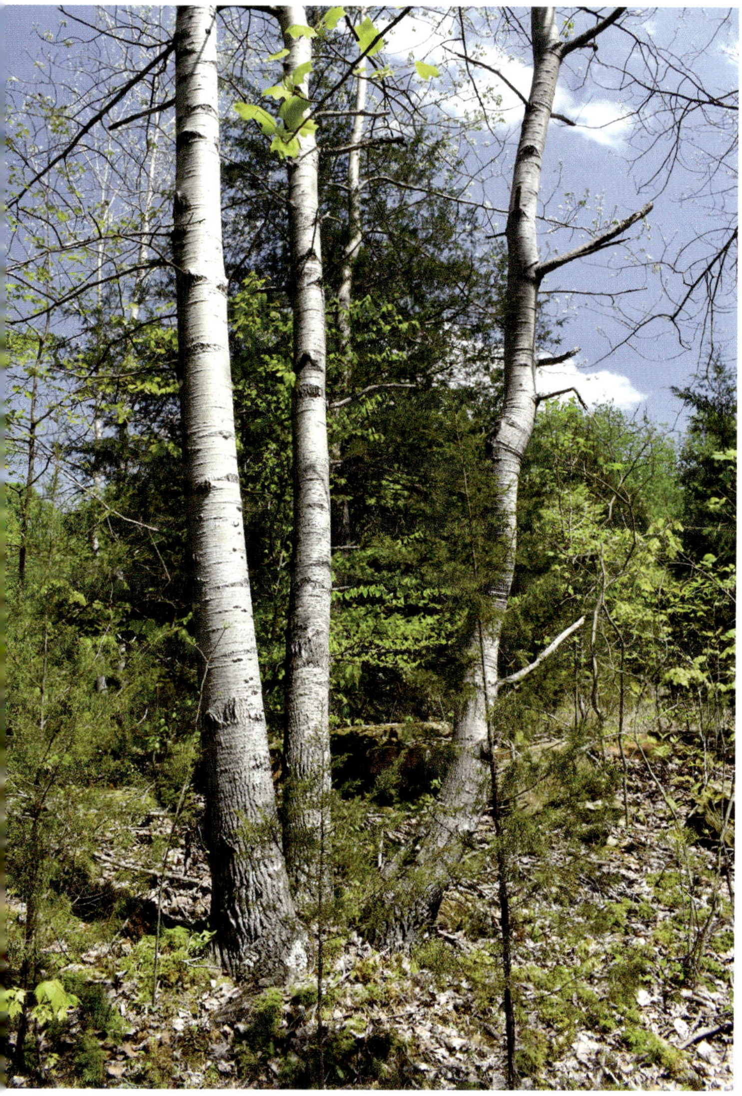

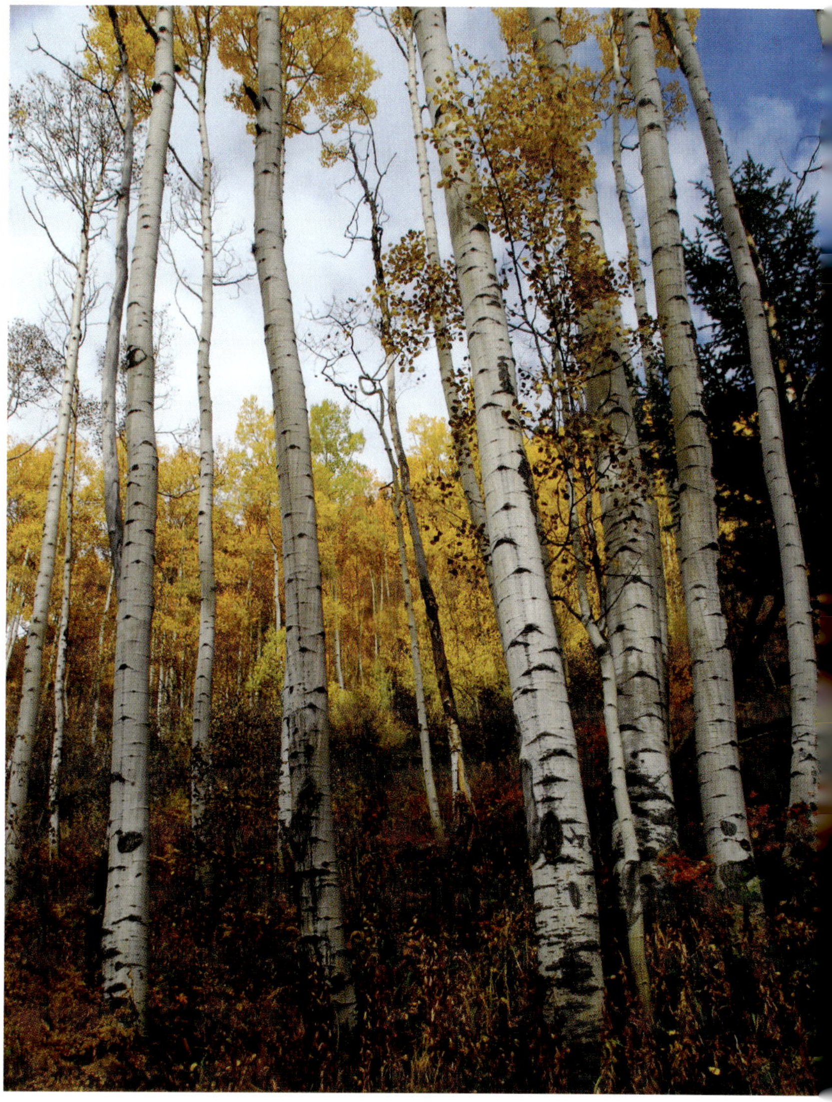

MAGNOLIAS

(*Magnolia tripetala* and *Magnolia acuminata*)

Hiking cross-country with no trail, up and down ravines and across spring-fed creeks, my wife and I finally arrived at the secluded natural area of cliffs where a native stand of umbrella magnolia lay untouched. Here, deep in the Hoosier National Forest not far from the wondrous Hemlock Cliffs Natural Area, was one of several natural locations for this rare tree. The typical range for *Magnolia tripetala* is from Pennsylvania down along the Appalachian country, and across to Tennessee, Kentucky, and even Arkansas. Its northerly limit reaches into one primary Indiana county—Crawford. There are several fascinating Appalachian-flora communities in Crawford and neighboring Perry County with *M. tripetala* interspersed among such goodies as sourwood, mountain laurel, deerberry, blueberry, rattlesnake plantain orchid, and rare clubmosses. As we sat alone in the precipitous cliff alcove, only the music of water dripping from the sandstone lip and occasional calls of birds punctuated the silence. Basking in the shafts of sunlight penetrating the forest canopy, the grove of young magnolias had established their territory and prepared to grow into maturity.

Their large 1½-foot-long leaves are only part of the show. The lustrous, creamy white flowers in mid-May are superlative and themselves quite large.

Subsequently, the long pod, which develops and ripens to a glorious red ovate cluster of many seeds, is also quite a remarkable sight. The smooth gray bark is most handsome, whether on the tall, straight stem or upon its diverging clustered forks. As a forest tree among many other taller species, it often achieves no greater height than 30 feet. There is nothing less than positive acclamation for such a tree and its attributes make it a desirable ornamental. Only nursery stock from sustainable locations (usually out east or south) should be bought; our rare native plants must be protected. Of note, the past champion tree in Oak Hill Cemetery, Evansville, was in such poor condition that a picture was not taken.

The cucumber tree, *Magnolia acuminata,* is also a rare anomaly in Indiana, limited to only a few locations including Washington and Jackson counties, but elusive there and known only to the botanically inclined. Cucumber magnolia is perhaps the hardiest of the genus, reaches a large size in the Appalachian Mountains, and has wood similar to its relative, the tuliptree. Unlike the large specimens in the North Carolina cove hardwood stands, this species does not reach a great size in our state. An Appalachian or southerner by nature, the long history back to its discovery in 1736 made it well known in its preferred range and useful in many capacities there. It has also been called Indian bitter, a very old reference to its supposed infusion of the green cone-fruit into whiskey. A small number of *M. acuminata* are found in Indian Bitters Nature Preserve in the Jackson-Washington State Forest. When we visited, they were small and a little difficult to find, but beginning to bud out into their typical erect greenish form.

The flower itself is not as spectacular as the umbrella tree and the bark is very different, being rougher, browner, and scaly. The state champion *acuminata* is in Lick Creek Cemetery near Connorsville, but not in good condition.

It should be noted that both *M. tripetala* and *M. acuminata* are on Indiana's list of state endangered species.

Characteristics

- Generally to 30 feet here in southern Indiana.
- Often associated with other Appalachian-type flora in hills, ridges, and cliff communities.
- Very large and distinguished leaves (especially *tripetala*), ovate, to 1-foot length.
- May be found in clustered groups or multistems.

Uses

- Mostly ornamental in Indiana, usually derived from nursery stock from growers out of state.
- An interesting component of biological diversity in our state in rare plant community types.
- We do not have an industry here that depends on *M. tripetala* and *M. acuminata* since they are rare, of small size, or planted in landscapes.

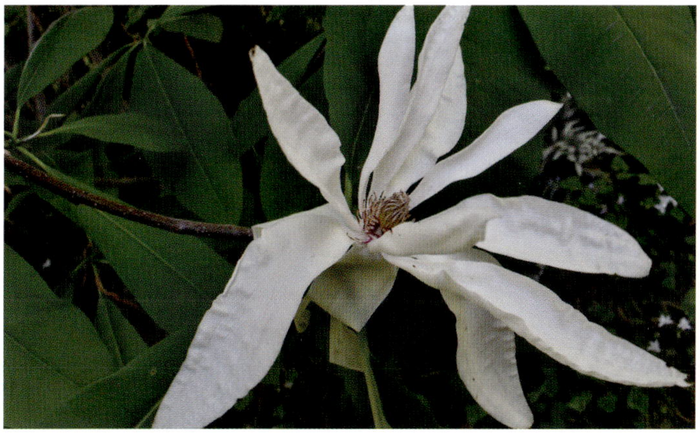

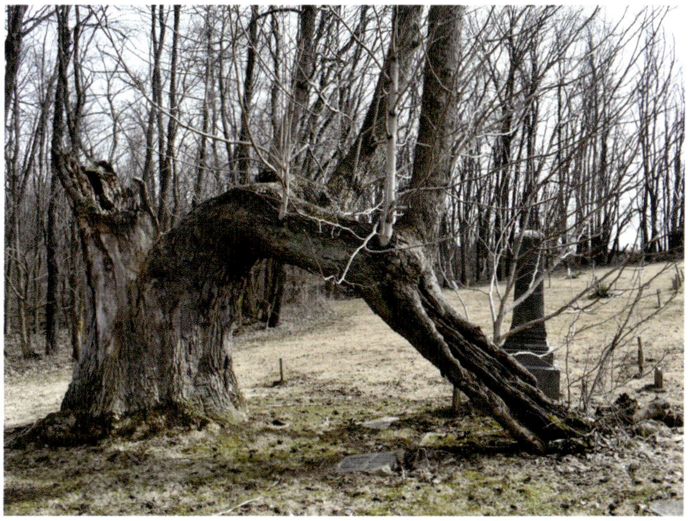

Top: *Magnolia tripetala* in gorgeous flower

Middle: Cucumber magnolia champion, Fayette County

Bottom left: *Magnolia tripetala*, native cove, Crawford County

Bottom right: *Magnolia acuminata* in early flower

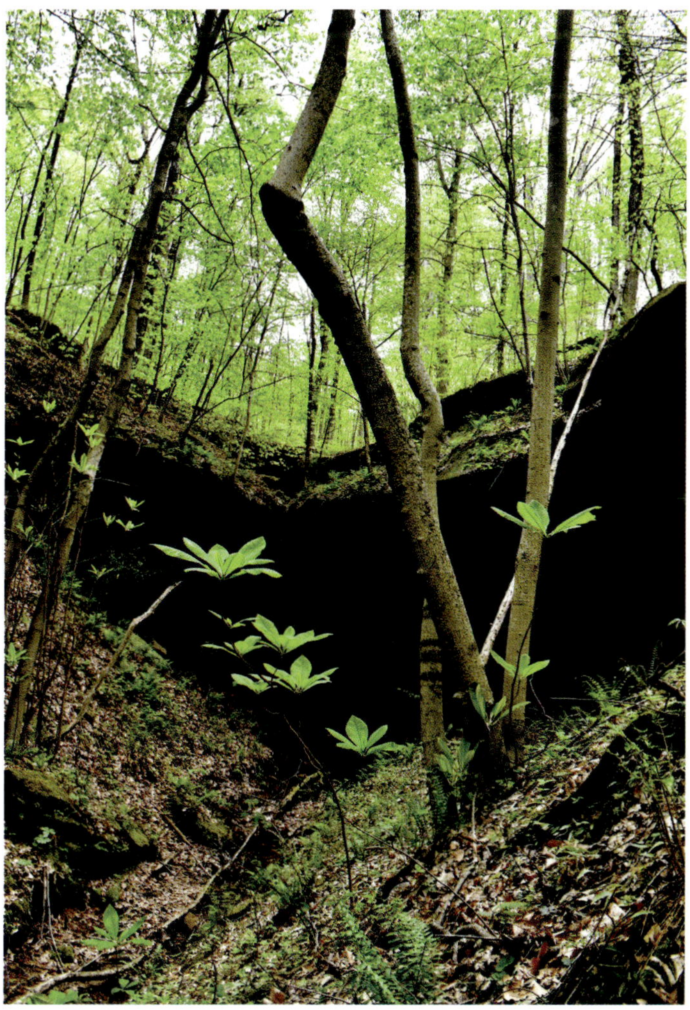

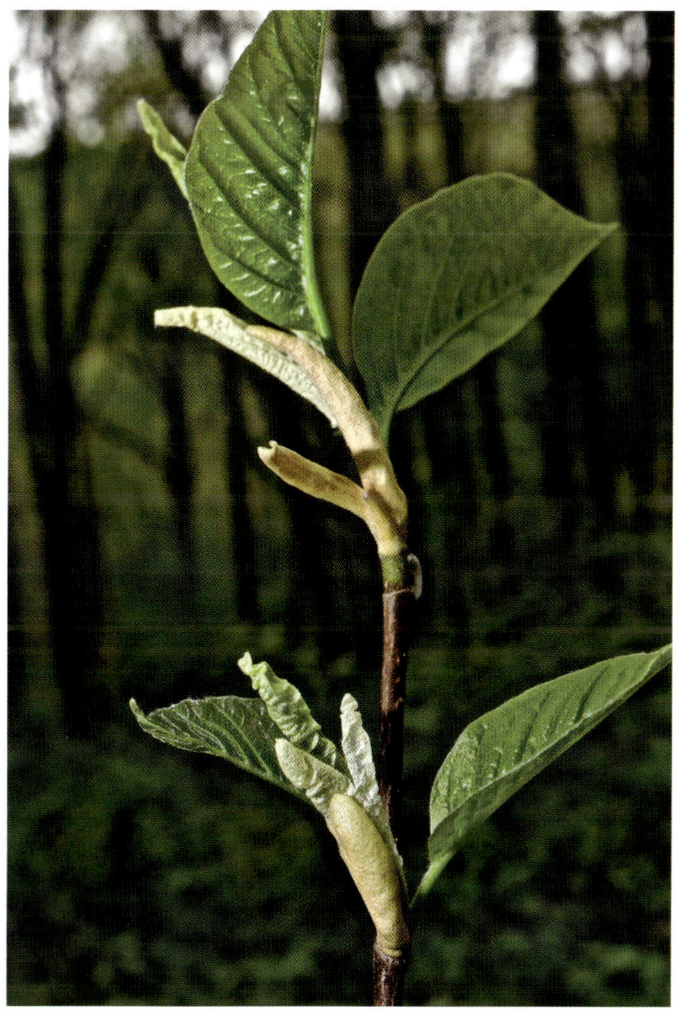

BLACK MAPLE

(*Acer nigrum*)

Of the many maples common to Hoosiers, one does not find black maple as an oft-mentioned household name. Much less well known but widely found across Indiana, it resembles sugar maple and is not distinguished from it except by those who know the tree a little better. Black maple grows to be as large as sugar maple and may in fact be tapped for syrup in the spring. Westward from Indiana toward Iowa the black maple is actually much more common and some contend that it yields even more and better sugar syrup.

One of the features that allow identification is the small leaf-like stipule at the base of the leafstalk. The stalk itself is about 3–5 inches long and stout. Marion Jackson (2004) describes the leaf as "goosefoot-shaped, hairy, with drooping edges" (p. 262). The top surface of the leaf is dark green and the underside more yellow-green and velvety, unlike the sugar maple. The bark may be darker than that of the sugar maple, especially in older age, perhaps with some furrows accentuating the surface. It is thought that black maple may hybridize with sugar maple, thus rendering a more difficult identification challenge.

Whether in lumber production or quality of fall color, black maple is a very desirable specimen. It has many attributes that deserve a little more attention by the casual botanist.

Our state record black maple is near Monrovia, in Morgan County, 4½ feet in diameter and 88 feet tall, although it has lost some upper structure and is not in very good condition. When all our old record-holding trees finally do fall, others may step up to become the new champions.

Characteristics

- Opposite leaf arrangement as per most maples. Leaf to 4–6 inches, often 3-lobed, drooped edges.
- Some trees show darker bark, with very old ones fissured and almost blackish.
- Same "helicopter" seeds as other maples, flying in the wind for dispersal in the fall.
- Likes stream valleys, rich soils, but also inhabits woodlands very well.

Uses

- Lumber grouped with other "hard" maples. Many uses such as cabinetry.
- Good maple syrup producer.
- Good ornamental color and form.

Right page: Champion black maple, Morgan County

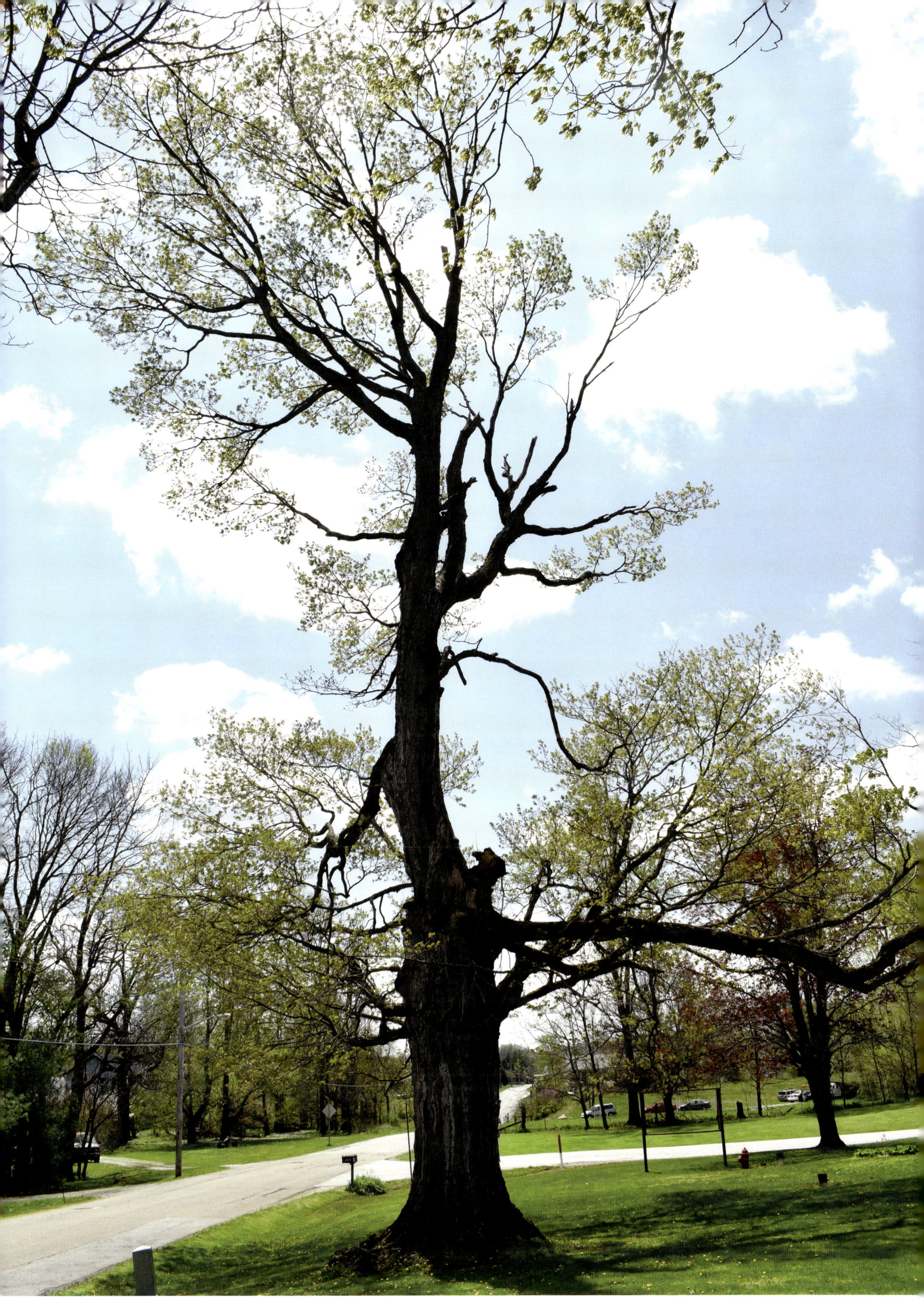

RED MAPLE

(Acer rubrum)

Not many trees can claim year-round punctuation of color. Throughout the seasons red maple has something to show—sometimes subtle, sometimes ostentatious. There may be tints of red on twigs in winter, reddish buds in early spring, and beautiful red female flowers. Red-hued propeller fruits form in late spring, and then gloriously red leaves in the fall. It seems to always have something boastful to say, "Just wait 'til the next act!"

Red maple is very widely distributed in the United States and Canada and occupies varying types of sites. The photo here shows it in a preferred location—wetlands. Whereas sugar maple would rather not inhabit places where its feet are always wet or submerged for a period, red maple relishes those mucky bottomland forests and grows in profusion.

Hundreds of these were observed, interspersed with swamp-loving oaks, cypress, and other tolerant shrubs in Twin Swamps Nature Preserve and along Hovey Lake in Posey County. Red maples were also mixed with sugar maple when I visited Prairie Creek Park in Vigo County. That fall day provided splendor exemplifying Indiana's remarkable autumn displays. Other prime locations for bottomland or floodplain forest environments are at Patoka National Wildlife Refuge and Muscatatuck National Wildlife Refuge.

Red maple is also at home on uplands and hillsides. It is quite diverse and adaptable, even seeming quite happy when planted in urban environments. The size of this species ranges up to 100 feet in height and over 6 feet in diameter. The largest one may occur in Calvert-Porter Woods in Montgomery County and is to be verified.

Red maple does have an interesting hand-shaped leaf, with a rather sharp angle in the interior lobe. The early blooms are distinctive, colorful, and provide a wondrous contrast with the gray flaky bark of the main tree or the smoother gray on the twig. While often grouped with "soft maple" in a timber harvest, the wood is not nearly as valued as that of sugar maple, which is classified as "hard maple." Syrup production is not important in red maple since the amount of sap produced is minimal. The tree does shine for ornamental use and is planted for its definite contribution of remarkable color throughout the seasons. It may be noted that there are actually three recognized varieties of *A. rubrum*, each with slight variations.

Characteristics

- Leaves simple, opposite in arrangement, V-notched, rounded at base.
- Young twigs reddish, older ones reddish-brown, with little white bumps called lenticels (these allow for gas exchange between the twig's internal tissue and the atmosphere).
- Tree may grow quite large with bark character changing from smooth-gray at youth to scaly, platy-gray in old age.
- Is a preferred host for red maple spanworm and maple looper moth, and their caterpillars feed on the foliage. Many other pests can be problems for these and other maple species.

Uses

- The wood is hard and heavy, but its strength is less than hard maple. Often used in cabinetry, some flooring, and furniture.
- This species provides those unique "curly maple" and "bird's-eye maple" grain patterns, which were prized in creating remarkable antique maple beds and tables.
- Red maple is a good tree for wildlife, as many use it for food or shelter. Old open-cavity trees provide nesting for owls and woodpeckers.
- Exceptional ornamental and widely appreciated.

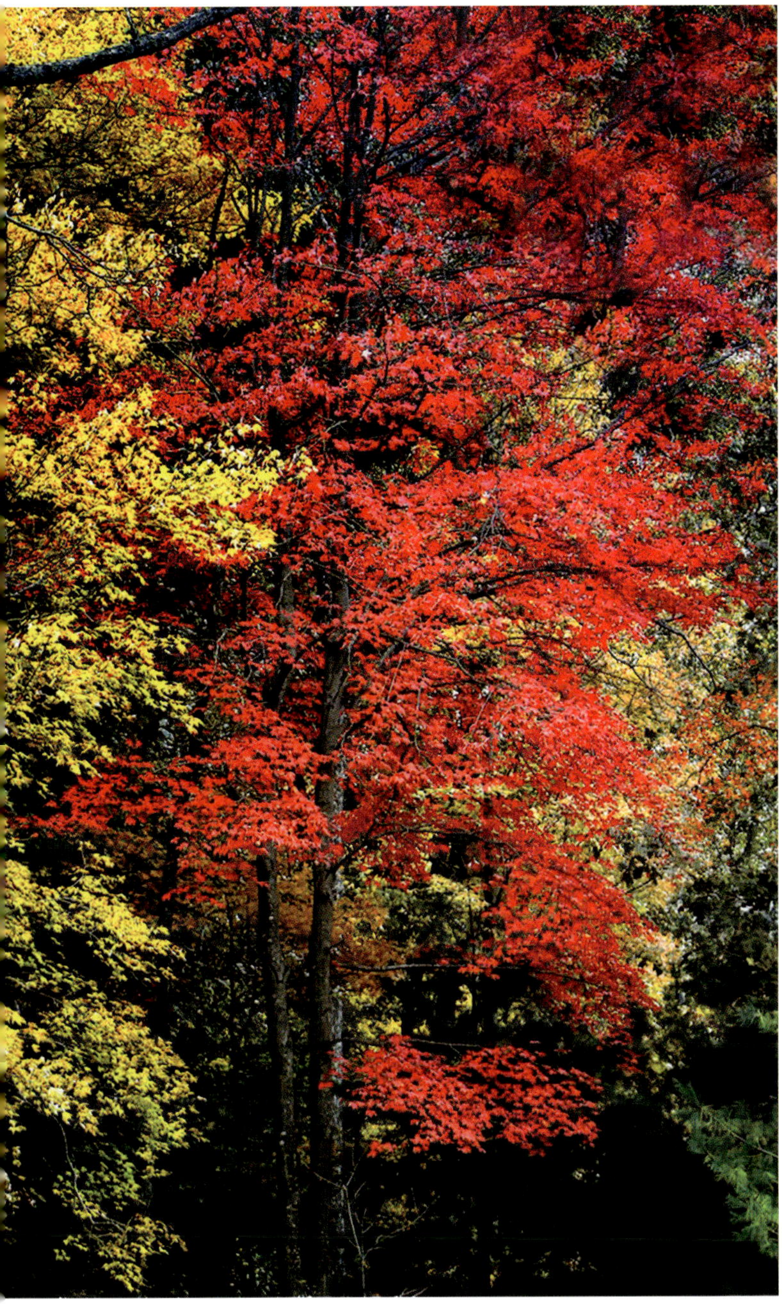

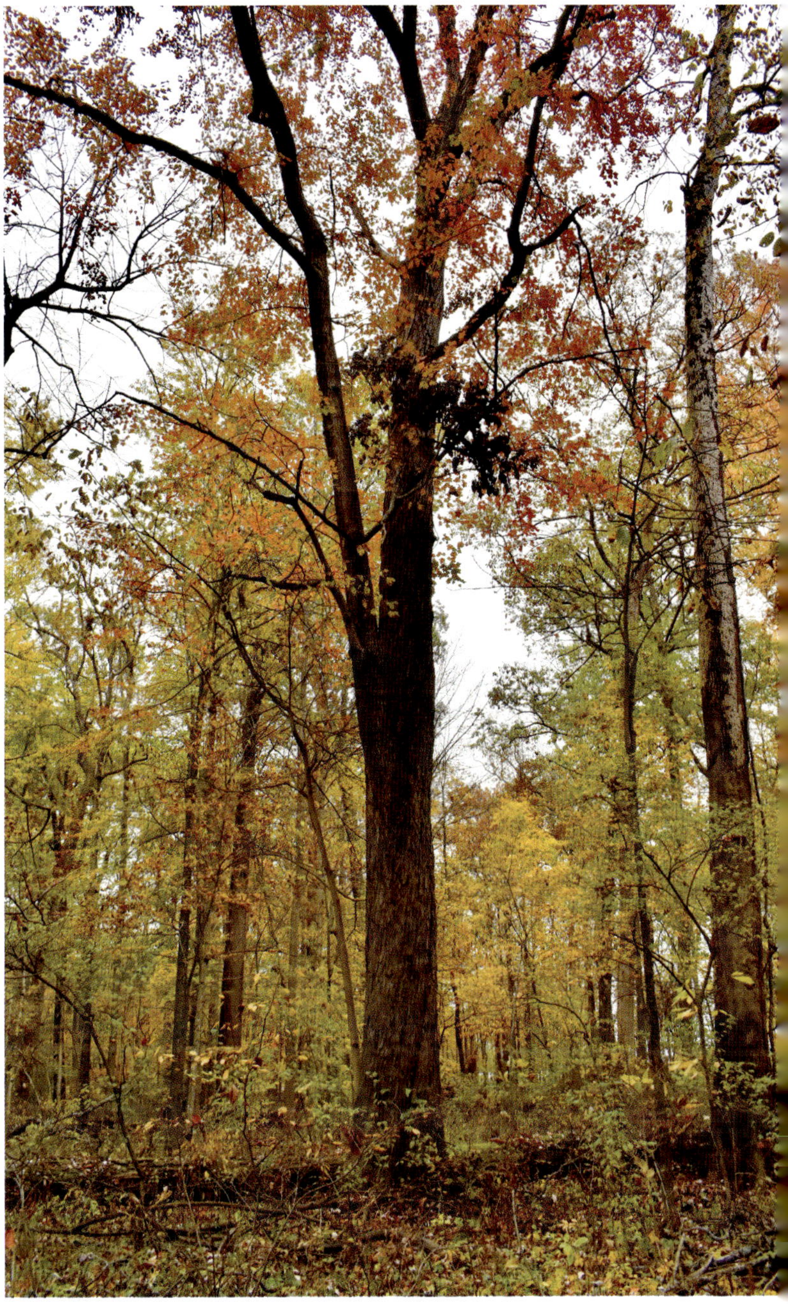

Left: Red maple's finest show, Jackson County. **Right:** Old red maple, Calvert-Porter Woods, Montgomery County.

SILVER MAPLE

(*Acer saccharinum*)

With grace and subtle beauty, the sweeping, diverging, and arching trunks of the silver maples lined the banks of the White River that summer day, providing shade for a few fishermen relaxing while keenly awaiting a bite on the submerged hooks. Not far from here stood the state champion tree, itself a most impressive 10 feet across, with massive branches themselves as large as trees in their own right. Often seen along streams in wetter areas, the silver maple also chooses to claim higher ground as well and makes itself adaptable to being planted in all geographic locations imaginable.

Although considered bland in color and mediocre in use, the very daintiness of the cut leaf, the artistic expressive bending of the boughs, and the size that it may attain draws to it many tributes by its human overseers. With pale green-white emergence of early leaves and the concomitant release of the early winged propeller fruits wafted in spring winds for great distances, the maple makes its announcement of being ready to run its annual race. Through summer storm and buffeting wind, the limbs bend and being brittle, may snap, often in small disruptions to the overall structure. On occasion, even massive side limbs yield and split off the trunk. All the while the leaves, being silver underneath, have turned around facing the observer, and now waving and twisting furiously, signal the power of the wind.

Fall brings a muted palette of color to the delicate lacy leaf with mostly yellow being expressed as the chlorophyll has disintegrated and the carotene compounds have now come forward into view. Not long in colorful display, the leaves turn brown on their flattened stalk and prepare for the soon-to-be descent to the ground where they will add new nutrients to the earth. Then, in winter, the gray scaly bark remains and on old trees shows a darker pattern while upper bare limbs yet retain their smoother gray distinction against the cold, petulant sky.

While silver maple has established itself over a large geographic area, the economic value is minimal, and it often finds use in low-quality furniture and pulpwood. The sweetness of syrup produced from this tree is remarkably as good as from sugar maple, but the amount of flow limits its suitability for large-scale tapping. Silver maple grows rapidly, which is a positive attribute, but landscape architects rarely recommend it due to the fragility of branches and tendency to crack, split, and drop limbs. Even with its several limitations, we admire many characteristics of this abundant tree and recognize its place in the natural world.

Characteristics

- Opposite leaf arrangement, deeply cut and lacy, dark green above, paler silver below.
- Height to over 100 feet with widths of up to 10 feet, branched widely.
- Natural habitat is floodplains, but adaptable to many locations.

Uses

- Not a valuable wood, so relegated to various low-grade products or mulch and pulp. Decays rapidly.
- Some ornamental planting, but branches snap and can become a maintenance issue.

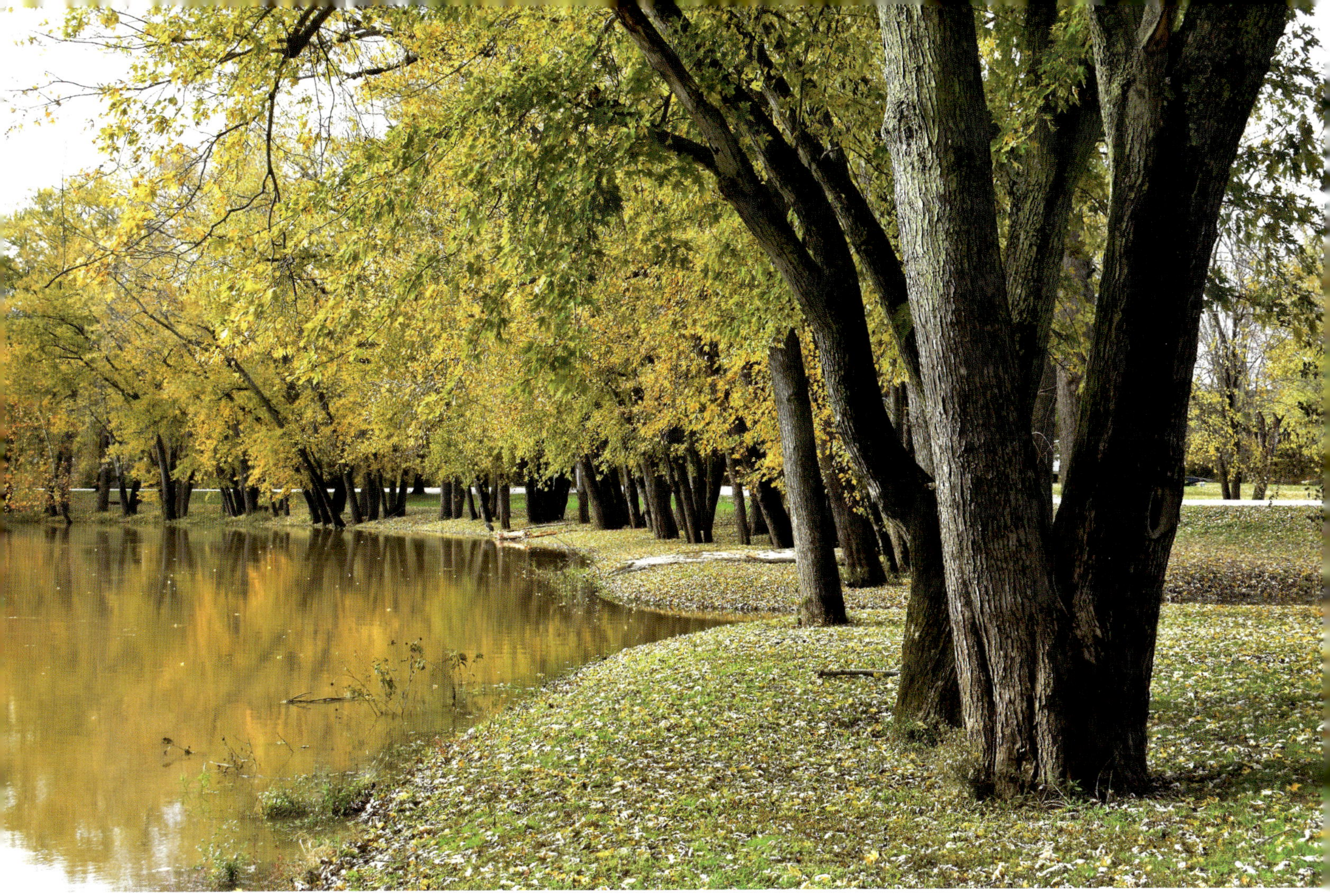

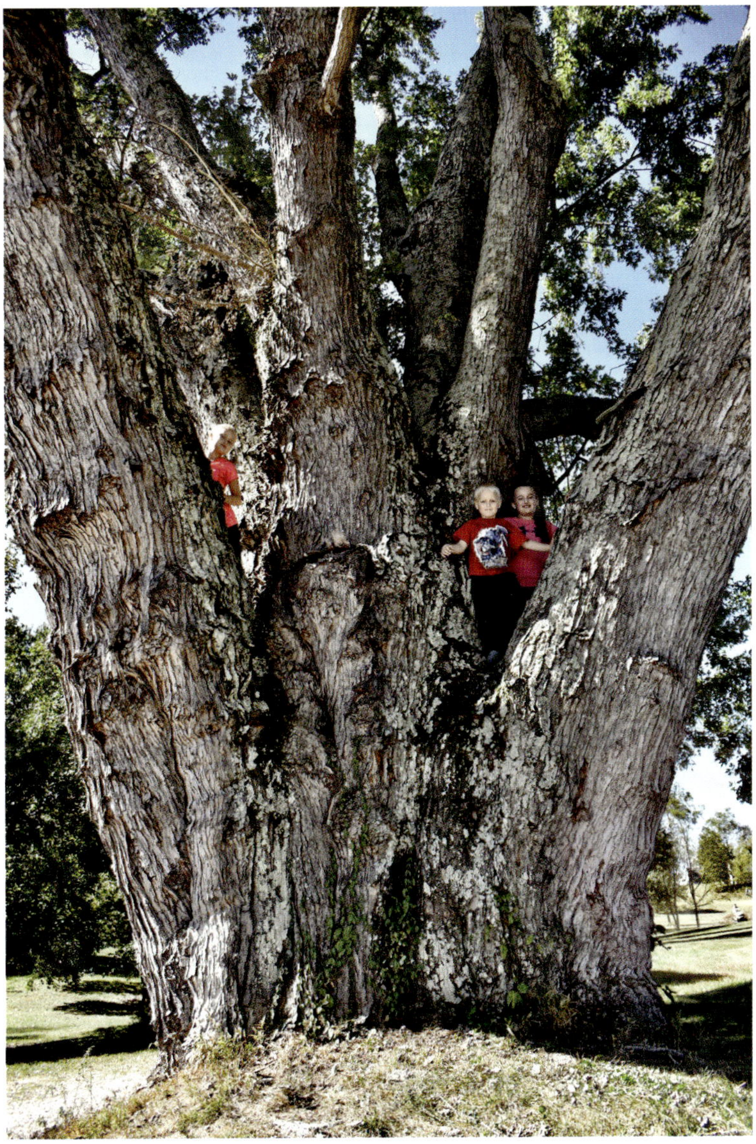

Above: Silver maples along White River near Williams

Left: State champion silver maple, Lawrence County

SUGAR MAPLE

(*Acer saccharum*)

Near the top of everyone's favorite tree list has to be the sugar maple. It captures respect in all seasons with attributes that please the painter's palette and the eye. Bare-limbed in winter, yet standing firm and noble, then bursting forth in spring with unfurling pale green leaf, marching onward into summer fullness with full verdant crown, and finalizing in blazing autumnal glory with passionate red, orange, and yellow, the sugar maple is indeed fit to be crowned with highest honors. Along with the notable American elm, it is adored as a street and park tree and ranks now even higher due to the decline of those great elms.

Come late winter, near springtime and with frosty foggy morning, the clank of pails rings in the woods with the tree's offering up of its sweetest treasure: rising sap that can be tapped and collected. Even Captain John Smith of colonial times mentioned this wondrous gift and its usage by the Native Americans of the time. Early colonists rapidly took to the trade and untold gallons of the delicacy have been produced ever since. Indiana alone has no doubt fond stories in almost every county of the "sugar shack," with boiling pans of sugar water, hickory fires underneath, and steam rising all through the night to collect that one gallon of syrup for every 40 gallons of sap water.

Notwithstanding all the above accolades for the sugar maple, the wood products from timbering the tree yield a long historical litany of honors. Hard maple, as the tree is called, produces solid flooring that still endures a hundred years later. Cabinetmakers use hard maple today in large quantities. The wood can be varnished in natural color or rendered with stains to mimic cherry, walnut, or other nuances to please any homemaker.

Premium prices are commanded for old antique furniture made of bird's-eye maple or curly maple, unusual variations in the wood grain.

The new state record tree shown here was decked out in its finest wardrobe on a stunning October day when the photo was taken. Located in a cemetery near Gosport, in Owen County, this 85-foot-tall and 5.6-foot-diameter beauty exemplified all glorious adjectives for what a treasured tree can be.

Characteristics

- Height to 100 feet with diameters of 3–4 feet in old trees.
- Gray-brown bark that is smooth in younger trees but becomes ridged and somewhat shaggy in very old specimens.
- Leaf simple, 5-lobed, opposite arrangement, 3–6 inches long and about as wide.
- Seeds are propellers, in pairs, travel by wind, great gutter-cloggers, prolific in reseeding.

Uses

- As mentioned above, exceedingly important throughout American history for beauty, syrup, and many uses of the wood, including a desirable firewood source.

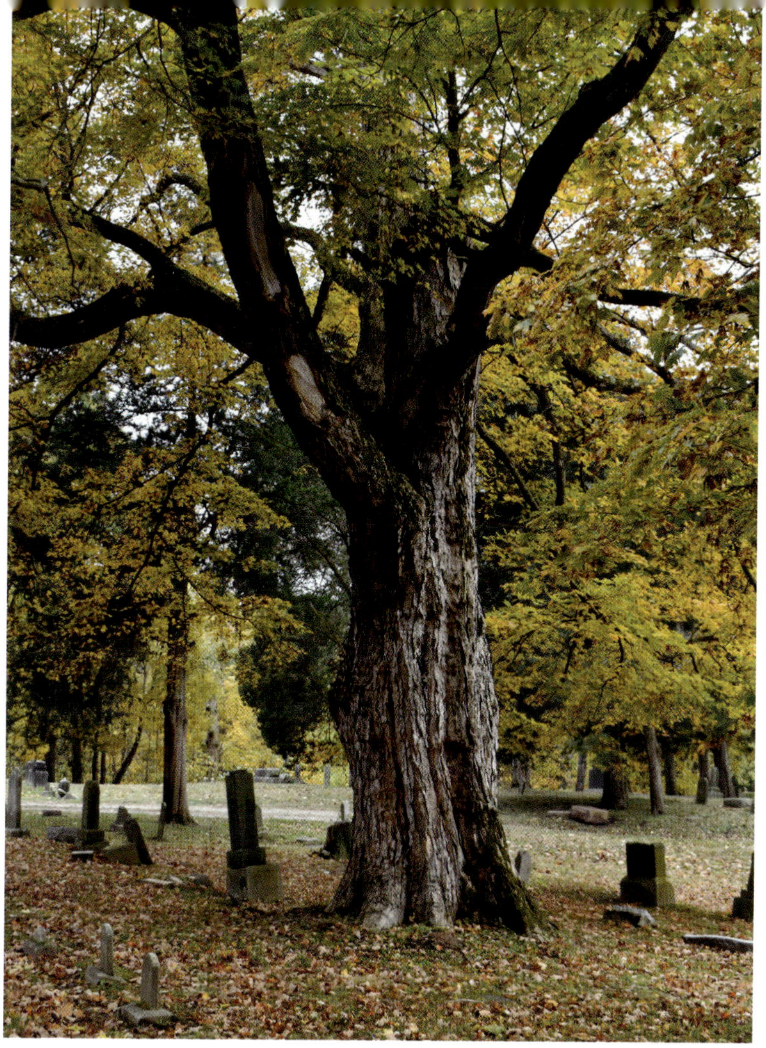

Left: Wise overseer of Sulphur Springs Cemetery, Vigo County

Below: State champion sugar maple, Owen County

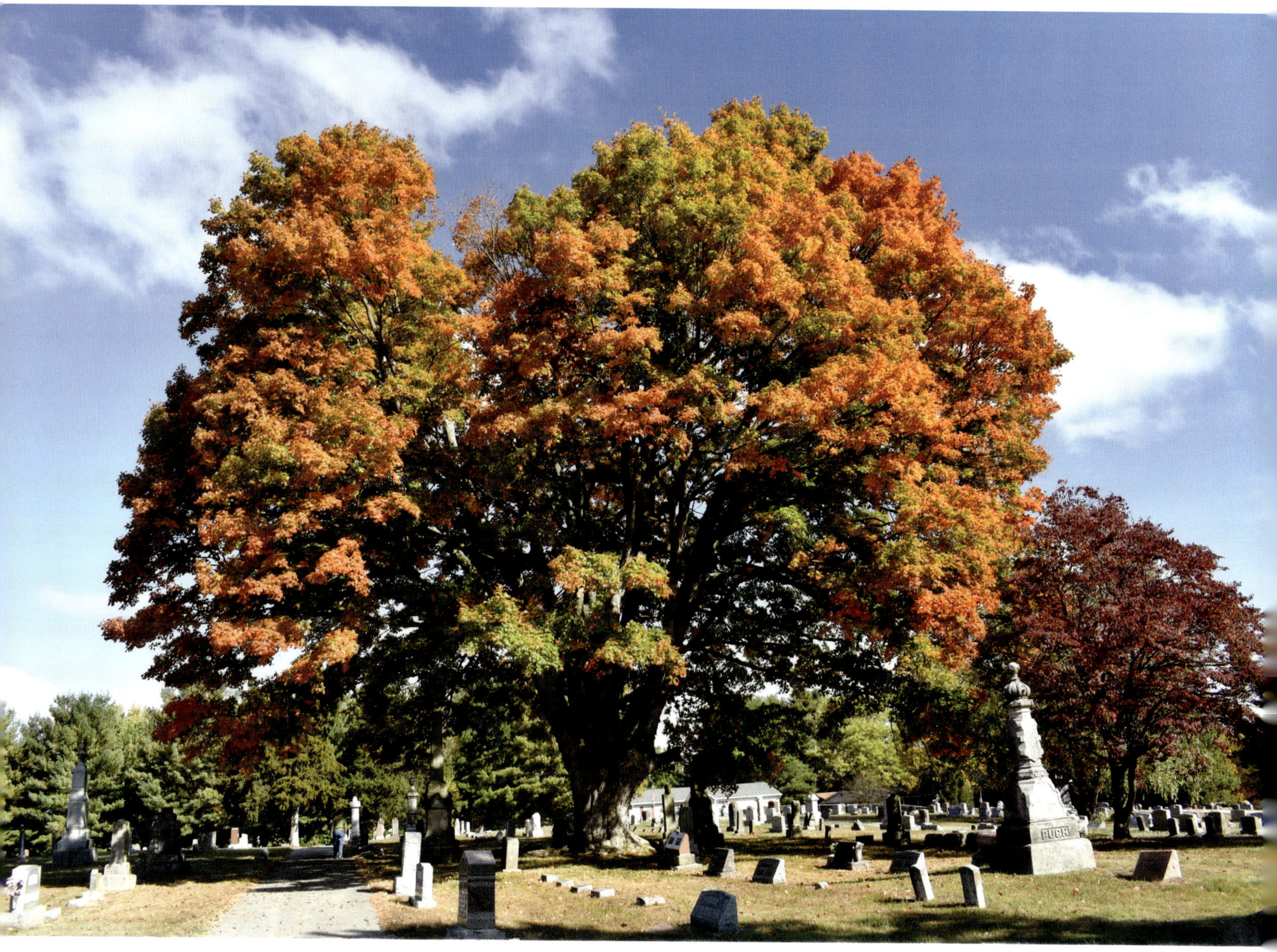

BARREN OAKS: POST OAK (*Quercus stellata*) AND BLACKJACK OAK (*Quercus marilandica*)

The heading "Barren Oaks" may imply that the trees themselves are leafless or produce no offspring. They are indeed normal and native. Barrens are the locations for these trees. Indiana has several very interesting plant communities that have developed in specific hydrologic, physiographic, or geologic settings. Among these are bogs, fens, swamps, glades, and barrens. The latter is indeed where we explored for unusual post and blackjack oaks. A barren can be thought of as rough, rocky, somewhat sparsely endowed with trees and interspersed with unusual plants adapted to dry sites. Sometimes limestone shelf rock and ledges dominate the area, and erosion may have taken its toll over millennia. Interspersed pockets of soils and vegetation occur frequently enough to permit plant growth and allow penetrating roots of post and blackjack oak to establish their footing. Often these trees, having a hardscrabble existence, do not achieve great height or fine form. However, they are fascinating survivors and occupy a niche that many other trees would find impossible to tolerate. They may have some rare or endangered friends at their feet, those being plants possibly adapted to dry sites, such as coneflowers, sunflowers, aster, compass plant, prairie dock, and others.

Three locations were visited to document these two oak species. One was in Harrison-Crawford State Forest, west of Corydon. At Post Oak–Cedar Nature Preserve, Division of Nature Preserves regional ecologist Ryan Keller discussed not only barrens and glades, but led us to some rather gnarly, scrubby-looking post oaks. On the rocky sandstone and limestone terrain here, mixed with some white oak, chinquapin oak, and cedar, the post oaks were doing well and their spring leaves were emergent and colorful.

The state champion post oak is in the city of Evansville near a busy corner. It is not a tall, straight tree by any means, but with huge limbs spreading out at about 12 feet, its massive 5-foot diameter and 76-foot height are remarkable. Post oak also inhabits wetlands and can be found in the depths of old bottomland forests among friends such as the overcup oak, swamp white, willow, and soft maples. In the old days, posts were indeed made of that same-name species, a good use for rather poor trees. As railroads marched across the land, trees that were available and not particularly valuable could be snatched from stunted groves of oaks. Such was the fate of post oak, only of value for low-grade crossties (Peattie, 1966).

The next site, Leavenworth Barrens, was one with both species, but we were enticed by a greater abundance of blackjack oak. This species is quite interesting with very dark, almost black bark and it retains many of the lower dead limbs. The clubby-shaped leaf makes identification fairly easy.

This species is rather uncommon in Indiana but does have a widespread distribution throughout the Midwest, albeit usually as a scraggly, unkempt, and unappreciated cast-off on few botanical bucket lists. Interestingly, while the above locations had mostly small- to medium-sized specimens on a particular landscape setting, both post and blackjack occur as large trees in more amenable soils. The largest blackjack oak is in Evansville. It is listed as 3 feet across and 118 feet in height, very atypical of the usual size.

Characteristics

- Both oaks often of height range to 30 feet and up to 2 feet across.
- **Post oak** is in the white oak group, with rounded sinuses and a "Maltese cross" shaped leaf.
- **Blackjack oak** has very dark bark, sometimes blocky or scaly, retains dead old lower limbs, and has a club-shaped leaf. It is in the red oak group, showing the bristle tip on leaf lobes.

Right page: Champion post oak, Evansville

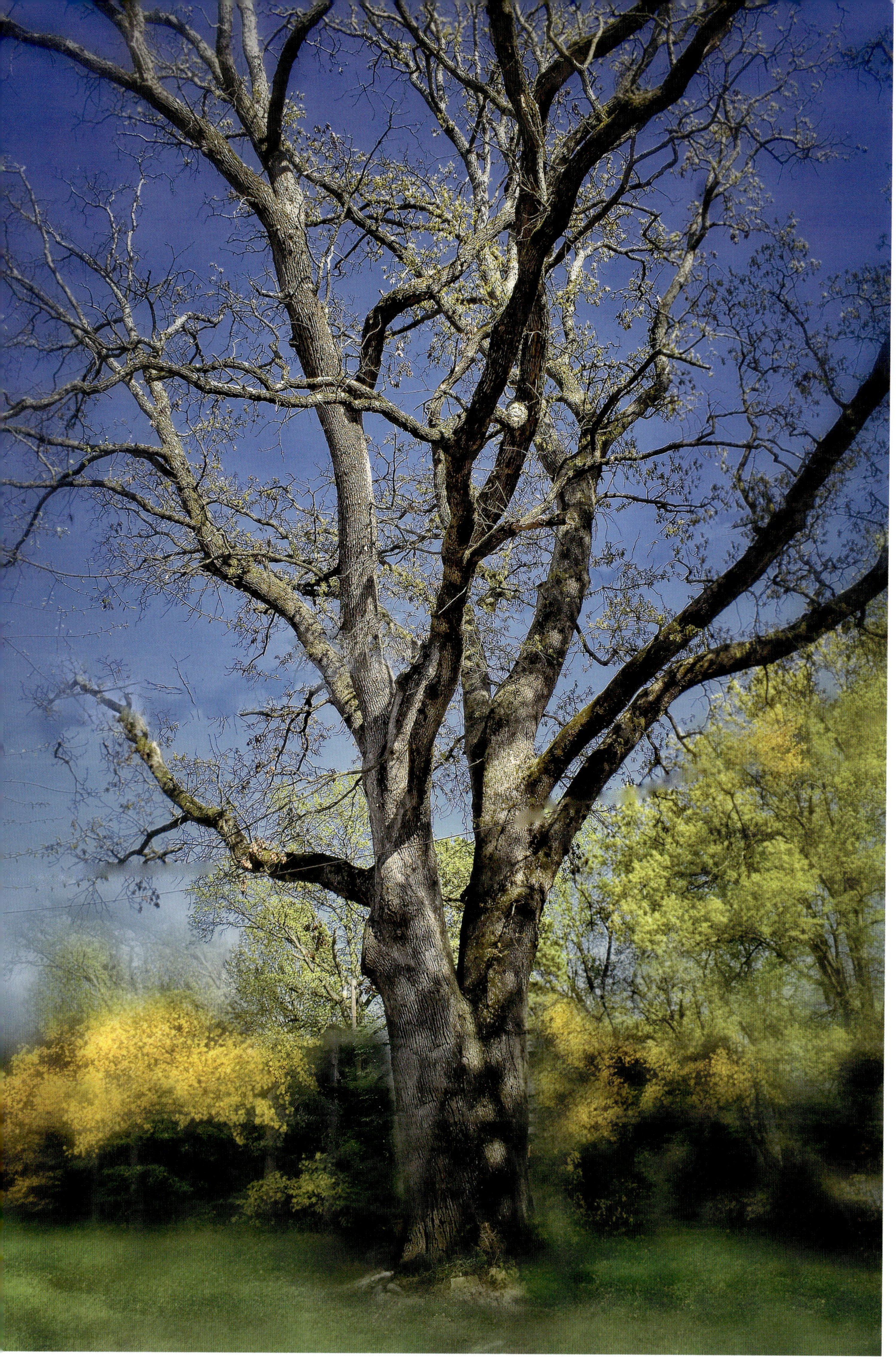

Uses

- **Post oak** is often a better tree in form and size, although still not highly valued. It was indeed used for posts in yesteryear, for some general lumber, and for fuel.
- **Blackjack oak** is mostly a scrub tree and its form and size lend poorly to much use. Perhaps we can say it holds the soil somewhat in those forsaken hillsides of rocky outcrops.
- It does produce acorns for wildlife and offers some menial shade on hot parched days. Otherwise, it may just be good firewood.

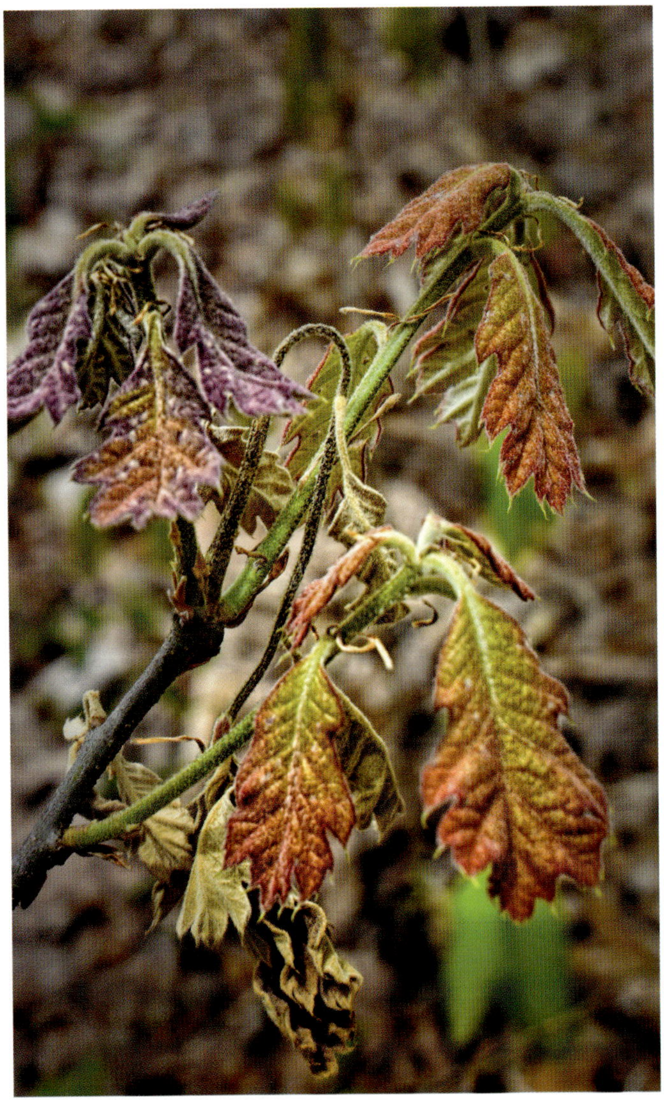

Post oak spring leaf emergence

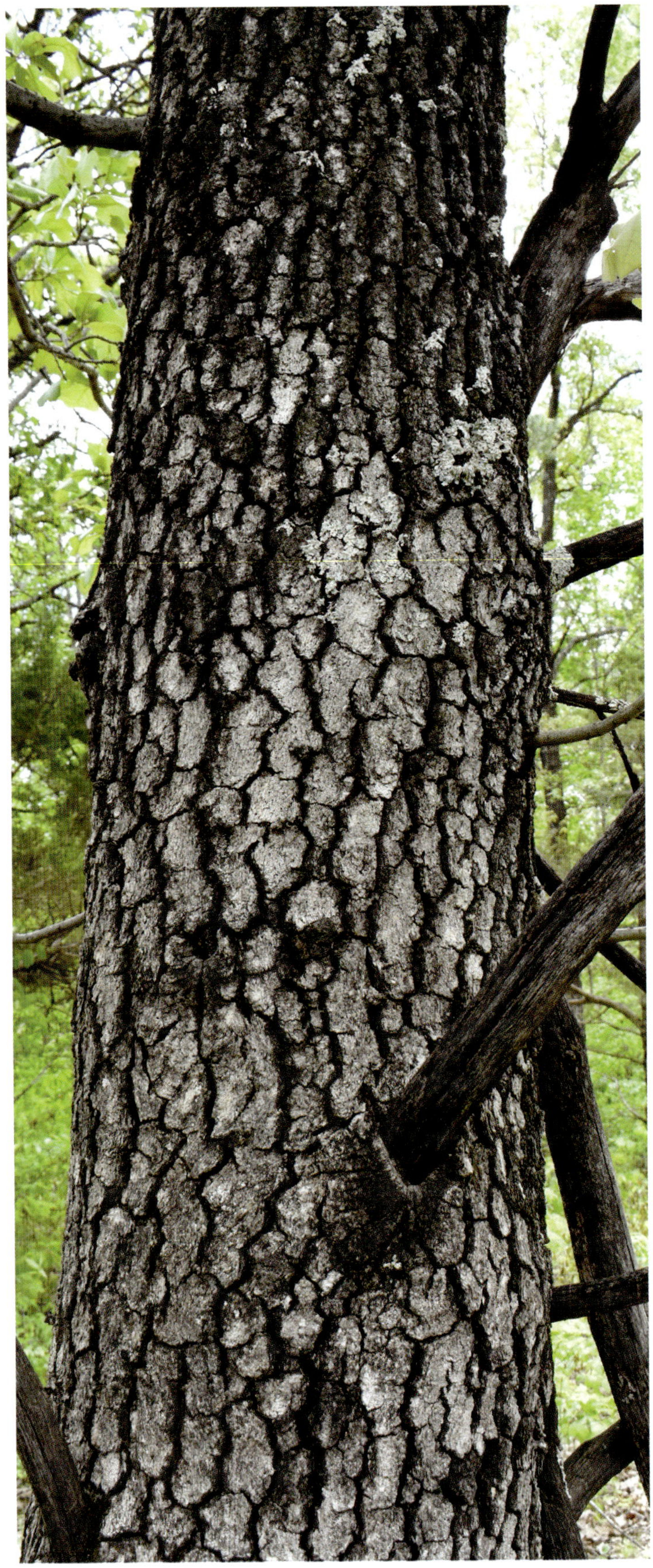

Above: Blackjack oak, Leavenworth Barrens, Crawford County

Right page: Black oak grove (see entry on page 112)

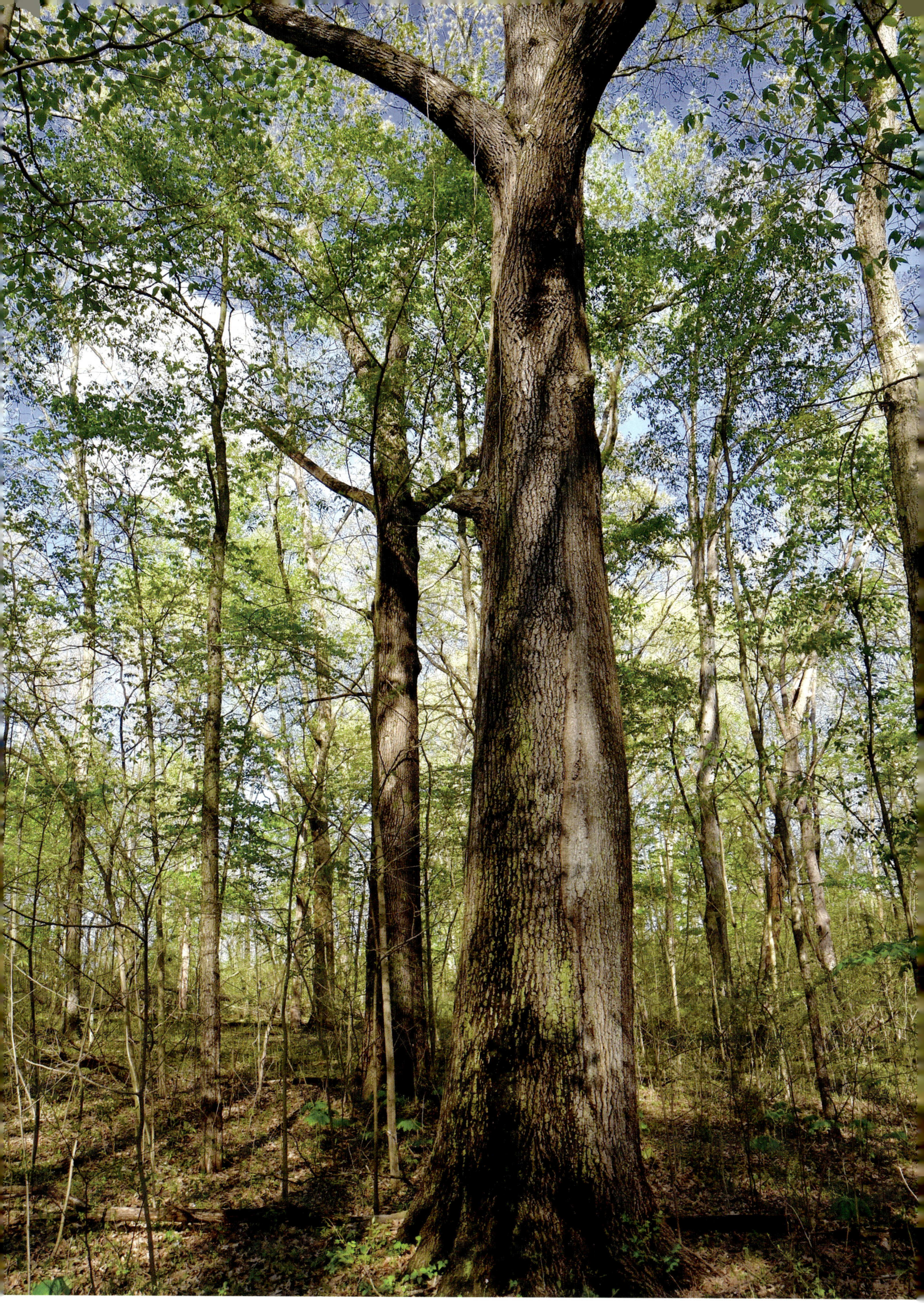

BLACK OAK

(*Quercus velutina*)

Also known as yellow oak, tanbark, or even quercitron (the latter deriving from early use as a yellow dye), the black oak has a long pedigree of use. Sometimes considered more of an unkempt member of the red oak group due to an often scraggly, irregular appearance, and its habitat upon rough and rocky locales, the black oak has not been prized in comparison to white oak and northern red oak. Nevertheless, some absolutely prime large, straight, fine specimens deserve much respect in the woodland. Open grown, of course the tree is expected to become limby and of poor appearance, as many others would do. But in a mature forest with other trees, the black oak may have a beautiful straight stem many feet to the first limb.

For identification, note the rather leather-like leaf, about 8 inches long and perhaps 6 inches wide, 5–9 lobes, but variable sinus depths. The lobes are bristle tipped. The leaf may have a pale-yellow color on the underside and an irregular base. Leaves themselves may not be reliable for absolute differentiation between other red oak members, thus further clues may help. The acorn is about ¾ inch long with a scaly cap covering about half of the nut, although some small acorns can be found almost enclosed. A twig can be scratched with a knife or fingernail to see the yellow layer of the inner bark.

The bark transitions from reddish-brown and smooth on young vigorous specimens, then upon maturity as a grand old patron of the forest, changes character to a black, rough, furrowed appearance. While some find the tree unattractive, especially in a savanna setting, they might venture into a mature forest to see this tall, stately tree, appreciating its longevity and distinguished countenance. A grove particularly stands out in ghostly form enshrined in fog on a March morning. With early low-angle light radiating in glorious beams through the outstretched limbs, quite a sight unfolds.

In years past, black oak was valued for its tannic acid, but also the presence in the inner bark of quercitron, producing the yellow dye used to color cloth in the weaving industry of mountain folk. Today, black oak is harvested along with red oak and used for some construction, railroad ties, barn siding, or flooring. The barns of yesteryear, constructed of timbers and planking from the local area, are fading away, replaced by pole structures with little character. A few Amish communities still erect wooden barns using a large group of men who can construct a barn in just a day or two.

Unfortunately, many oaks are highly impacted by oak decline, a serious problem from multiple stresses including droughts, cankers, moths, and root rot fungi. This decline appears as a large geographic impact across the eastern and central United States.[16] However, the state champion in Deming Park, Terre Haute, seemed in good shape at present. It was almost 6 feet across and 119 feet tall, an impressive specimen fully dominating the nicely manicured area.

Characteristics

- May be rather scraggly and a site companion to chestnut oak on rocky ridges, or nice timber tree in deep woods.
- May reach 60–90 feet, but the champion is nearly 120 feet in height and almost 6 feet across.
- Scratch test on twig for yellow color helps identify it.
- Leaves variable, alternate, in red oak group.
- Wood heavy, strong, close-grained.

Uses

- Rough lumber, ties, may be found in pallets or other low-grade uses.
- Acorn is pretty bitter, so probably selected after wildlife scavenges the sweeter nuts of other oaks.
- Can be a nice landscaping tree.

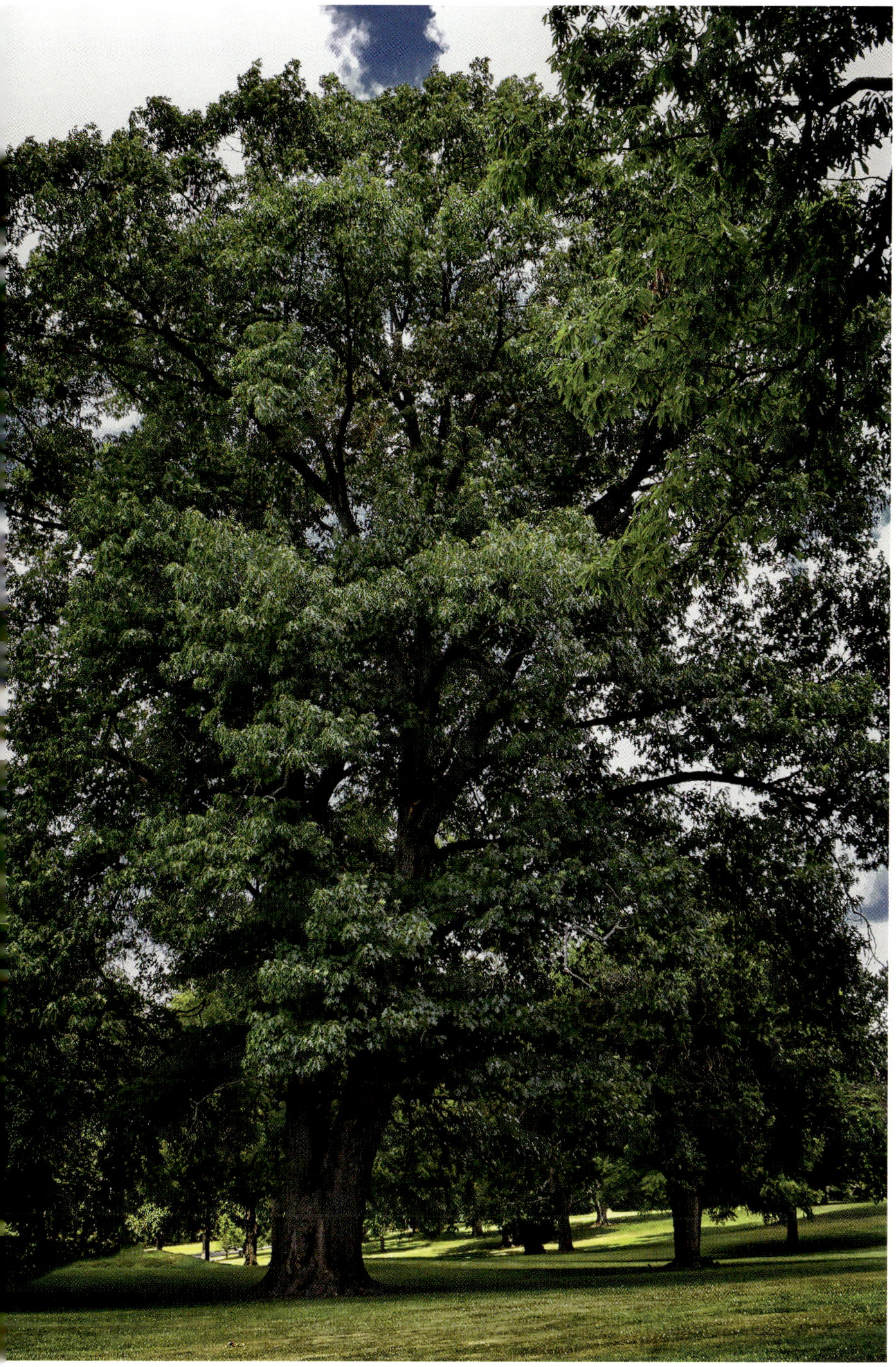

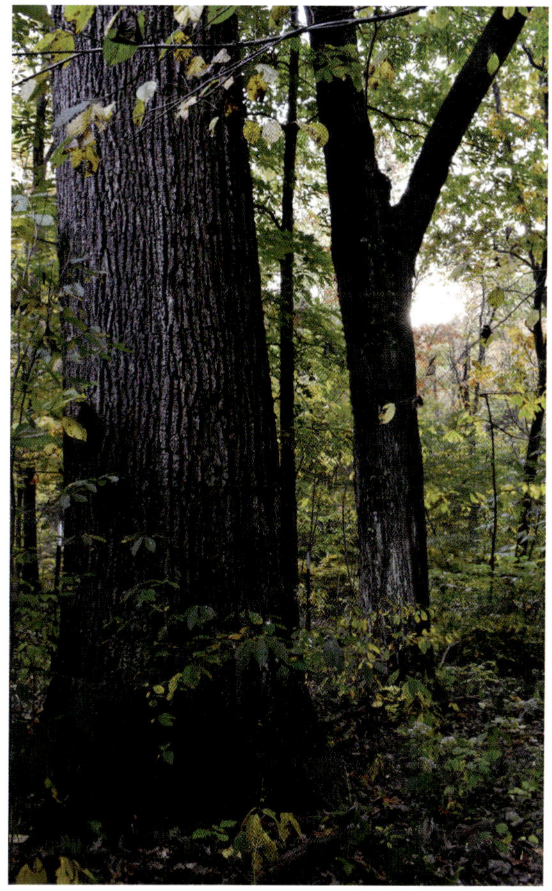

Left: State champion black oak, Terre Haute

Right: Exceptional black oak with companion pignut hickory

BUR OAK

(Quercus macrocarpa)

Shrader-Weaver Woods in Fayette County is one of Indiana's special places. (See Chapter 5 on old-growth trees, with photos.) Among other remarkable trees are several very large bur oaks, including one commanding utmost respect as an old-guard keeper of the property. How long had it been alive? Some estimates say around 300 years; perhaps it was a young tree during the American Revolution. It was certainly a monarch, king of the lowland.

Bur oaks had some historical significance in America's prairie ecosystems. Many are located upon historical sites, such as peace councils, surveyors' markers, Native American villages, and European-American towns. The largest old bur oak in the state (and national champion) is in Posey County in a remote area not accessible by the public. It is also the state champion, almost eight feet across. In presettlement Indiana this vast forested lowland of the Wabash contained huge tulip, cypress, sycamore, and other oak trees. Doubtless, this national specimen remains from that wondrous time of glorious woodlands.

Some bur oaks seem unkempt, for their branching is often wide, at right angles to the trunk, and on a very old tree the massive lateral limbs may almost reach the ground under their own weight. They prefer wet areas and in western regions of the United States may seek lowlands or riparian corridors. In prairie country they may be dispersed and in savanna areas may occur as scrubby shorter specimens. Originally common in northwest Indiana, this community type once covered thousands of acres. They are now rare, but one outstanding example may be seen at McCloskey's Burr Oak Savanna in Lake County.

When the tree does find the right location in our Midwest it can be impressive, presenting itself as a most grand specimen up to 100 feet in height with massive trunk and huge limbs. One of the most noticeable characteristics of the bur oak is its large acorn of up to two inches with a frilly cap that covers half the nut. This very distinguished attribute contributes to its use in fall craft displays.

Characteristics

- Sizes range depending on location, from scrubby to 100 feet.
- Spreading lateral branches.
- White oak–type leaf, leathery feel, up to 12 inches, lobes widest nearer top. Easy to identify. Scaly, fringed acorn cap to 1½ inches across.
- Alternate arrangement, may have corky twig.

Uses

- The wood is often cut as white oak and common uses are flooring, barrels, railroad ties, and cabinetry.
- It is also considered an ornamental and does well in urban areas.
- Old medicinal uses from the inner bark have included tonics for diarrhea and as an astringent for stopping bleeding. Native American tribes also roasted or boiled the acorns for food.

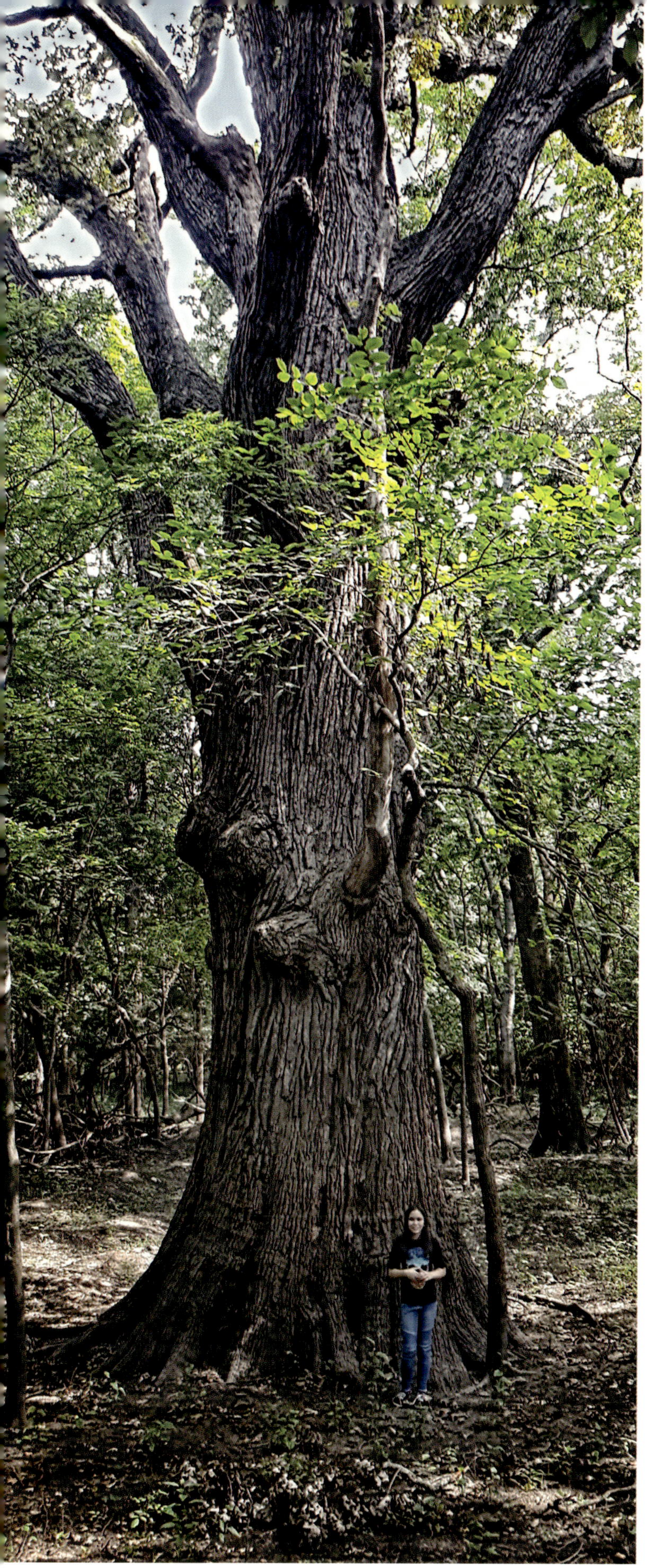

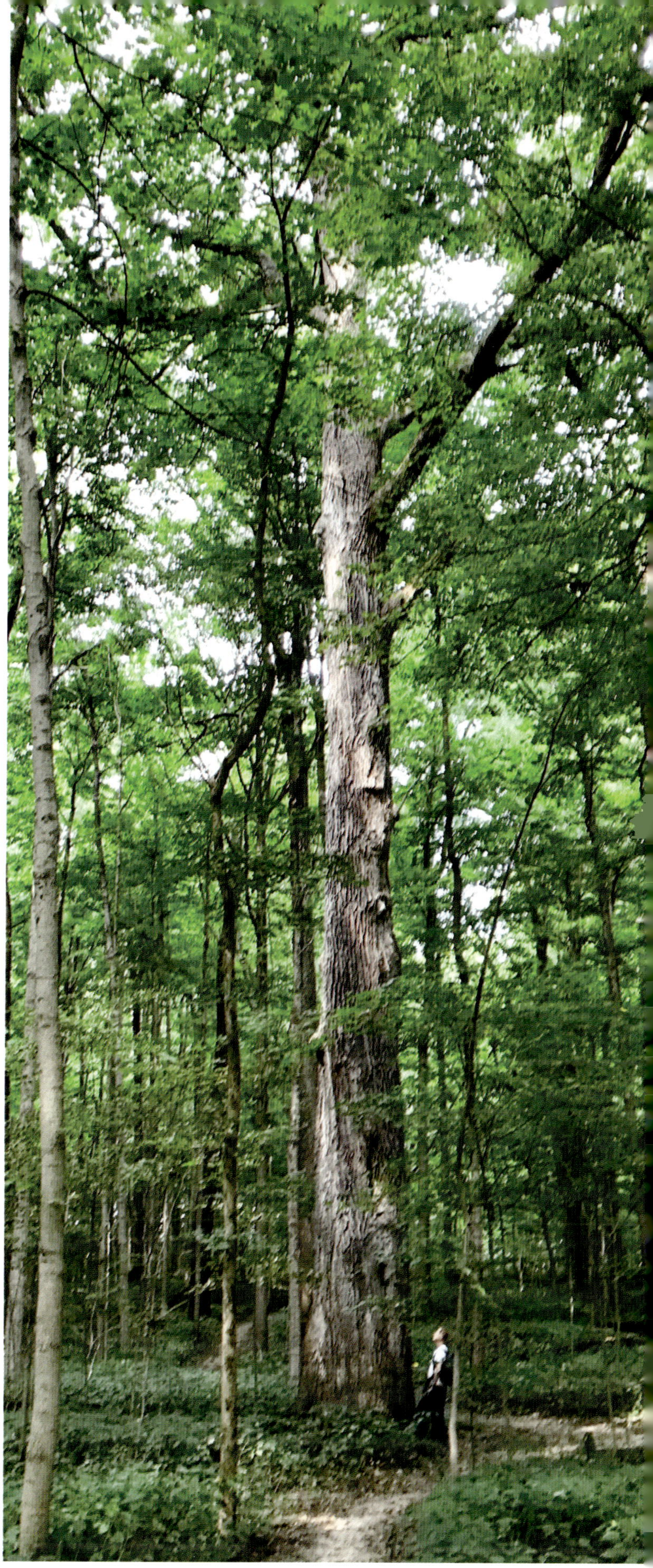

Left: Bur oak state and national champion, Posey County with Alicia Dickerson. *Courtesy of Shawn Dickerson*
Right: Stunning bur oak, Shrader-Weaver Nature Preserve, Fayette County

CHERRYBARK OAK

(*Quercus pagoda*)

This tree was certainly intriguing since it was not familiar and had an interesting name. Did the bark actually resemble that of a black cherry? There was a chance to see one of these, and the experience was rewarding. An absolutely huge one was indeed found on the expansive and well-kept grounds of the Evansville State Hospital. At almost 8 feet across and 97 feet high, with a limb spread of 93 feet, it must be the epitome of what a cherrybark is all about. And it is true—the bark does resemble black cherry, but in this particular old tree, it is even more rough, tough, and thicker, with fissures.

The natural range of cherrybark oak in Indiana is limited to the southwest corner of the state. The tree is often happiest in lowlands and swampy terrain, sharing ground with other friends such as overcup oak, post oak, swamp white, and sweet gum. Cherrybark oak has also been associated with southern red oak (*Quercus falcata*) and historically was called a variety of that (*pagodaefolia*). Now it stands as a distinct name unto itself. One of the most highly valued red oaks in the southern United States, it is larger and better formed than southern red oak and commonly grows on more moist sites. Strong wood and straight form make it an excellent timber tree. A faster growing oak than many, it reaches acorn production age in 25 years, with anywhere between 250 to 750 acorns per pound. The nut is a good food source for squirrels, deer, raccoons, turkeys, and wood ducks.

The leaf is distinguishable from *Q. falcata* with which it was grouped. The lobes of cherrybark are not always paired evenly on both sides of the midrib and project out at right angles to the centerline. There are 5–11 lobes and they are not recurved as seen in many red oaks, but resemble more of a saw blade tip form. The 7–9-inch-long leaf is dark green on top, paler underneath with a pubescent texture. When revisited in the fall some of the leaves were brilliant yellow and showed off the giant old tree with its finest décor. The dainty ½-inch hemispheric green-brown acorn with shallow bonnet was also an attraction.

From both reading about and visiting in person, the cherrybark oak is quite a grand *Quercus* indeed and we would concur that it would add splendor and great value to any locale in which it could be successfully grown. A Southerner by preference, how pleasing that it found favor in the southwest corner of our state.

Characteristics

- Strong, hardy, majestic tree to 100 feet or more and large diameter.
- Unique bark, but even variable in that character at times.
- Pleasing leaves, alternate on stems, darker above, paler below.
- Very attractive little acorns.

Uses

- Fine hardwood cabinetry, trim, interior finishing, and beautiful flooring
- As are most mast-bearing oaks, loved by many creatures.

Right page, top left: Cherrybark oak leaves in radiant beauty

Top right: Cherrybark oak, Twin Swamps Nature Preserve

Bottom: State champion cherrybark oak, State Hospital grounds, Evansville

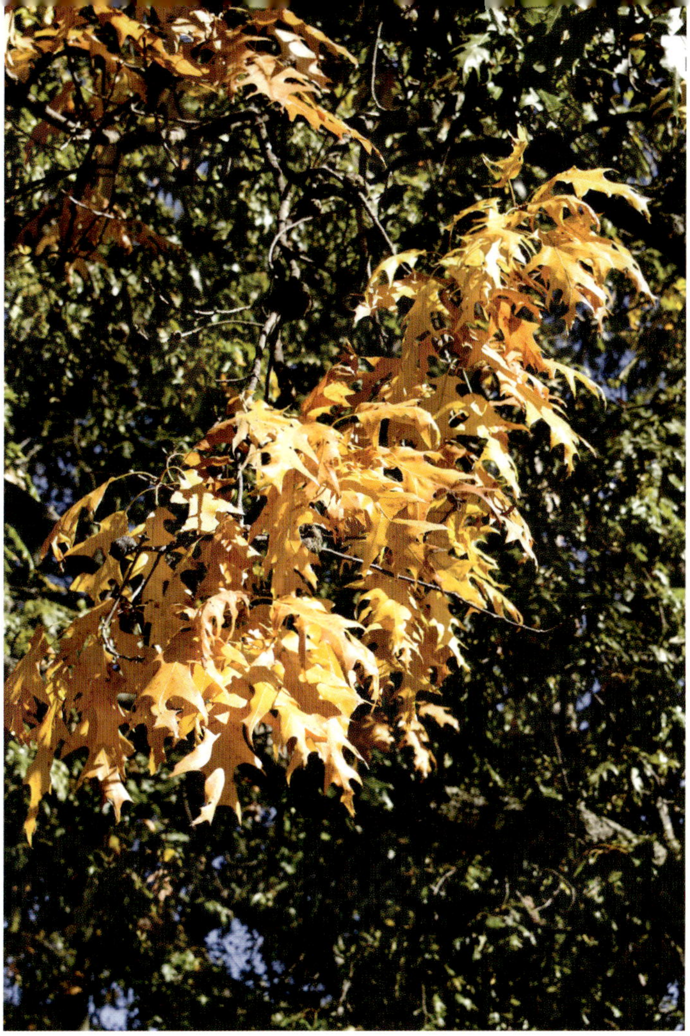
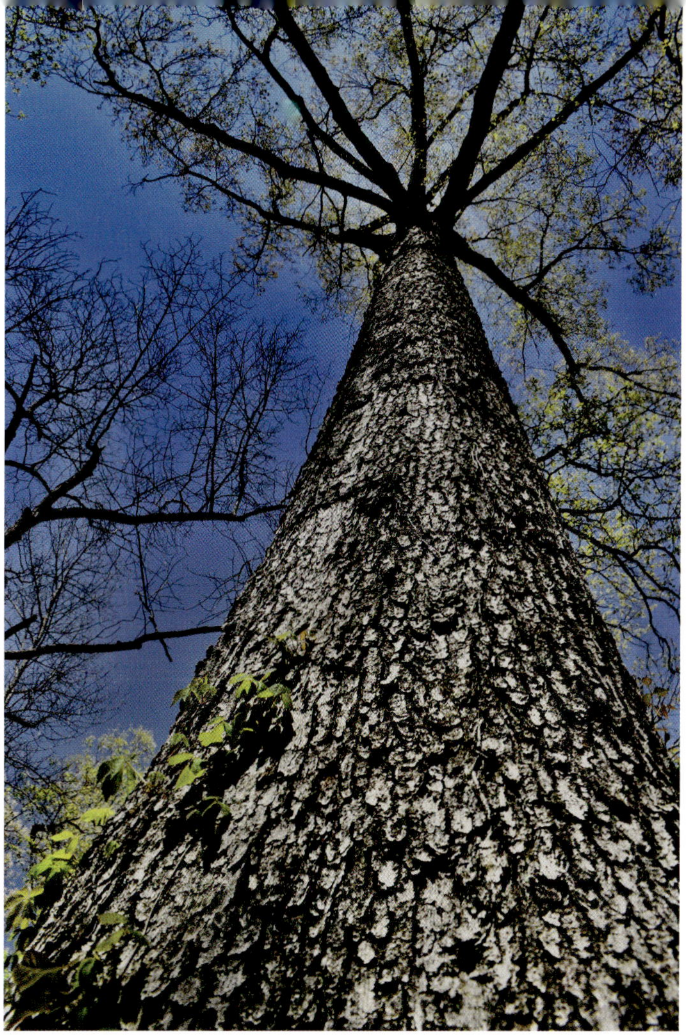
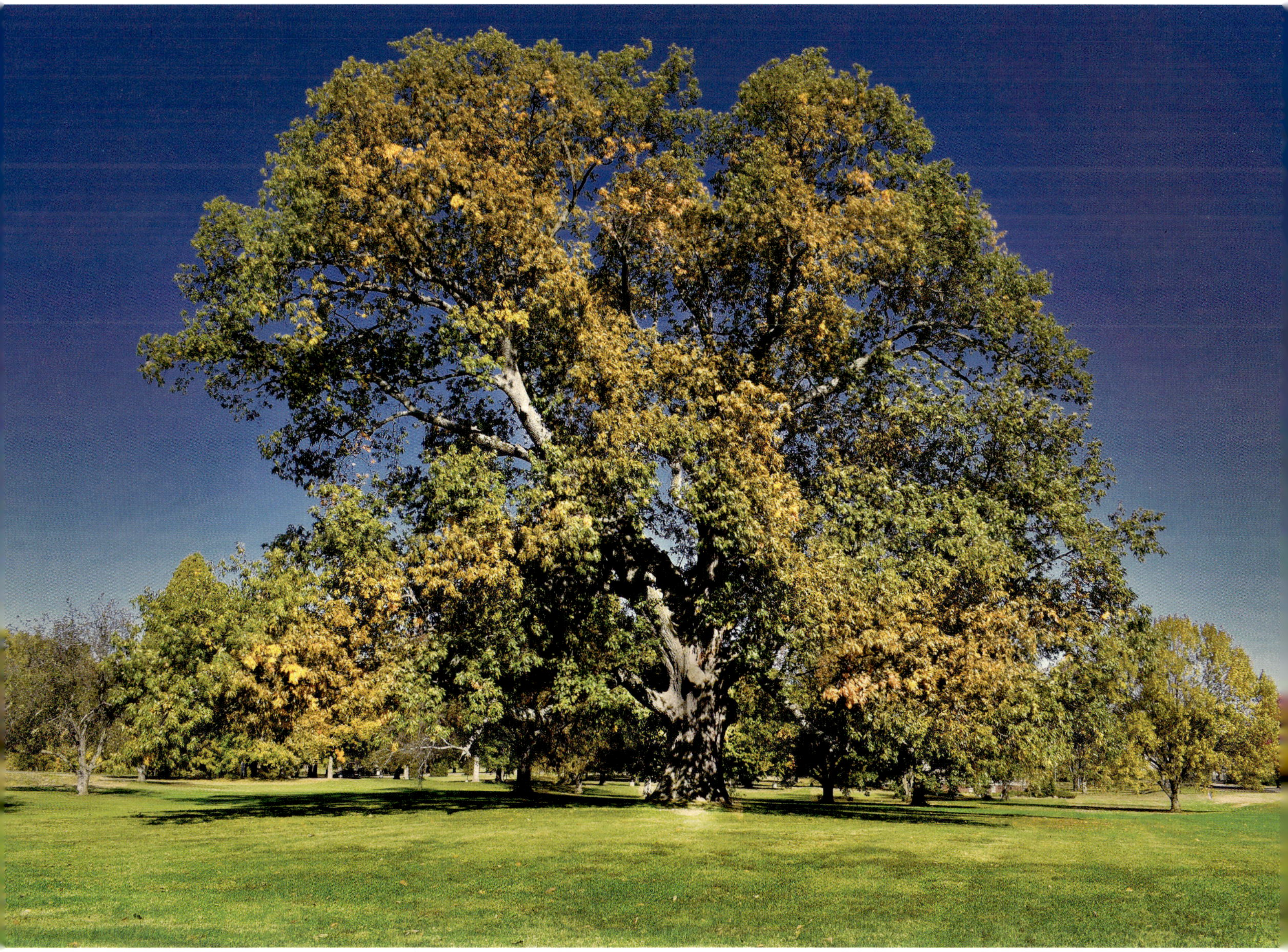

CHESTNUT OAK (OR MOUNTAIN CHESTNUT OAK)

(Quercus montana, formerly prinus)

Climbing rocky hills in southern Indiana leads one to find an intriguing oak that thrives in a rugged landscape of sandstone or siltstone outcrops. This species, also known as rock chestnut oak or rock oak, must smile at human efforts necessary to find and appreciate its tenacity. Found in several counties, it is at once charming and distinctive in both leaf and bark. Locations occur all the way from Monroe, Bartholomew, and Brown counties down to the Ohio River. Almost all settings favor trees that can tolerate such a rough domicile. Many do not reach great size, rather staying in the 40–50-foot height range and a foot or two in diameter. Nevertheless, they provide a wonderful variety to the woods. Anyone who is privileged to sit and contemplate the world in a grove of chestnut oaks gracing a ridge top overlooking a valley below is indeed fortunate. Often this terrain is almost barren-like, open, with sedges and even lowbush blueberry shrubs. Companions such as black oak and scarlet oak may dwell nearby, all sharing this special place.

Other creatures also see value here in this rocky domain, feasting upon the mast (acorns), which are large, rich, and somewhat sweet. It would not be uncommon to find evidence or sighting of deer, squirrels, and turkey that have found the delicacies beneath the gnarly trees. It was said that even black bears loved these acorns in the mountains back east, but might they not have also roamed our lovely hilltops two centuries ago as well?

Long ago, when the leather tanning industry was a prominent part of many towns and villages, tannic acid was produced from crushing the bark of the chestnut oak. This tree has a greater yield than most other oaks and was so desired that many trees were felled, stripped, and left lying to rot. Later, when the great forests of white oak were heavily cut out and supplies dwindled, lumbermen turned to the chestnut oak, since it was in the same group and produced similar products.

The featured champion chestnut oak pictured was found in Bartholomew County and only then with the help of IDNR forester Will Capello who had a GPS location for it. A quarter-mile hike through scrub, downfall, and briars finally allowed us to arrive at a ravine where the large old oak was located. It was a much taller and better specimen than many I have seen, even with a noticeable curvature near the base. That may have resulted early in its life or even due to some downslope creep of soil. At 4 feet in diameter and 138 feet in height, this one was truly impressive. Other locations visited in Brown, Monroe, and Bartholomew counties had some notable specimens as well, all in scenic spots.

Characteristics

- Medium to large tree with smooth bark in young trees but deeply ridged and blackish in old age.
- Leaves 6–9 inches, leathery, lighter green on top, hairy below. Coarsely toothed.
- Acorns to 1½ inches; cap covers ⅓ of nut, which is shiny, brown, and edible.
- Likes well-drained soils; can tolerate dry sites, rocky slopes, and ridge tops.

Uses

- Is in the white oak group and can be timbered and used as such.
- Source for tannins in the past.
- Good wildlife food.

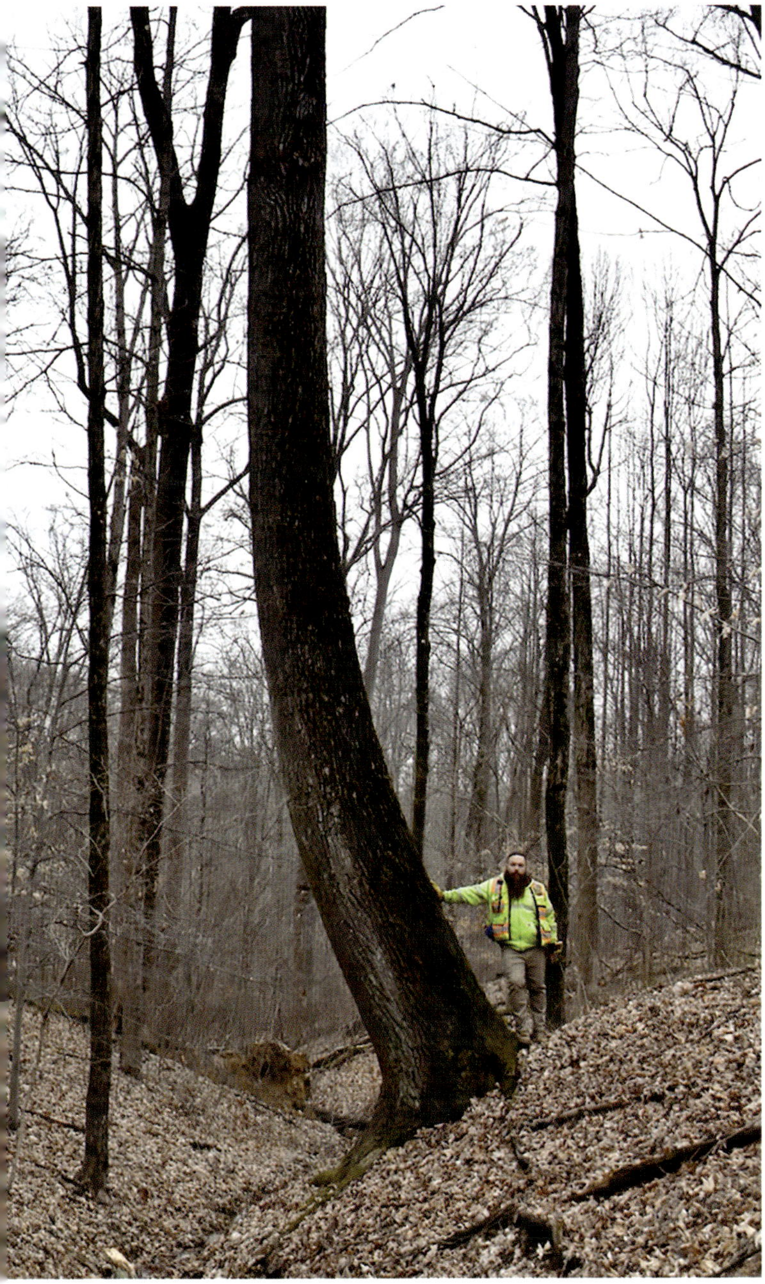
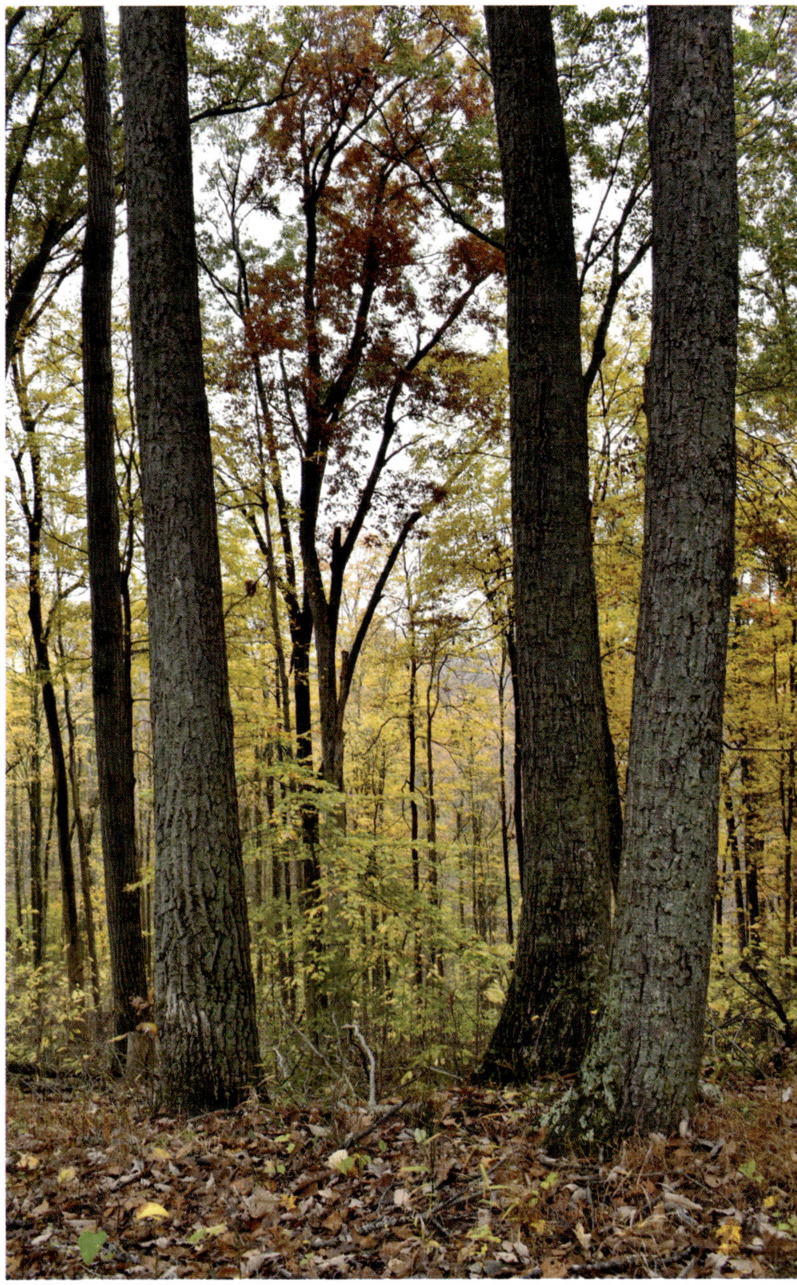

Left: State champion chestnut oak, Bartholomew County, with IDNR forester Will Capello
Right: Fine grove of chestnut oaks, Brown County

CHINQUAPIN OAK

(*Quercus muehlenbergii*)

Guardian of the woods' edge, mighty, and dominating its territory, the state champion chinquapin oak in Jackson County was truly impressive. Here it was, the sole giant left at the edge of the field, doubtless witness to over a century of observing changes in the world around it. What stories could be told of such a tree living as long ago as Abraham Lincoln's childhood. While writing this book, many grand chinquapins, or chinkapins as they may be called, have been found. These must have formed a pact agreeing to reign supreme in so many locations yet today.

Other great old chinquapins were photographed within Crane NSWC base, and another fabulous specimen in Monroe County. Investigation might show that almost every county has such a masterful tree.

There is another tree species called chinkapin, but it is in the chestnut genus *Castanea,* found regionally in the Appalachian country. Having two "chinkapins" seems confusing since even the leaf is toothed similarly. But with more experience and noting the blooms, seeds, and other features of the leaf and bark, it does become obvious these are two different trees. Our *Quercus* chinquapin was once considered a much-desired tree along with brethren oaks and hickories, for in pioneer days they were all superbly fitted for the task of making split rail fences, barrels, baskets, chairs, crossties, barn beams, and fuels for steam-powered trade along the Ohio River.

On a crisp fall day just before frost, the north wind may rattle the leaves into dances of merriment on big old chinquapins. This display of fluttering is characteristic of the tree along with the whitish-gray scaly bark and rather small, dainty frill-capped acorns. While potentially reaching 100 feet in height, open-grown field specimens often begin branching at 20 feet, resulting in burly giant side-limbs of massive size and weight.

Characteristics

- Up to 6 feet across and 103 feet in height (Indiana state champion).
- Massive appearance, often with huge limbs, imposing tree form.
- Likes well-drained soils but can be found in rugged terrain on cliff areas of limestone rock.
- Darker green leaf surface on top with paler or slightly hairy underside.
- Toothed margins, but in the white oak group, with rounded lobes and untipped.

Uses

- Mentioned above, many historical and current timber uses.
- Good for wildlife; look for turkey scratches in the soil and leaves under the tree, indicating a search for those sweet edible acorns.
- Impressive to leave an old giant as a reminder of the grandeur of Indiana history.

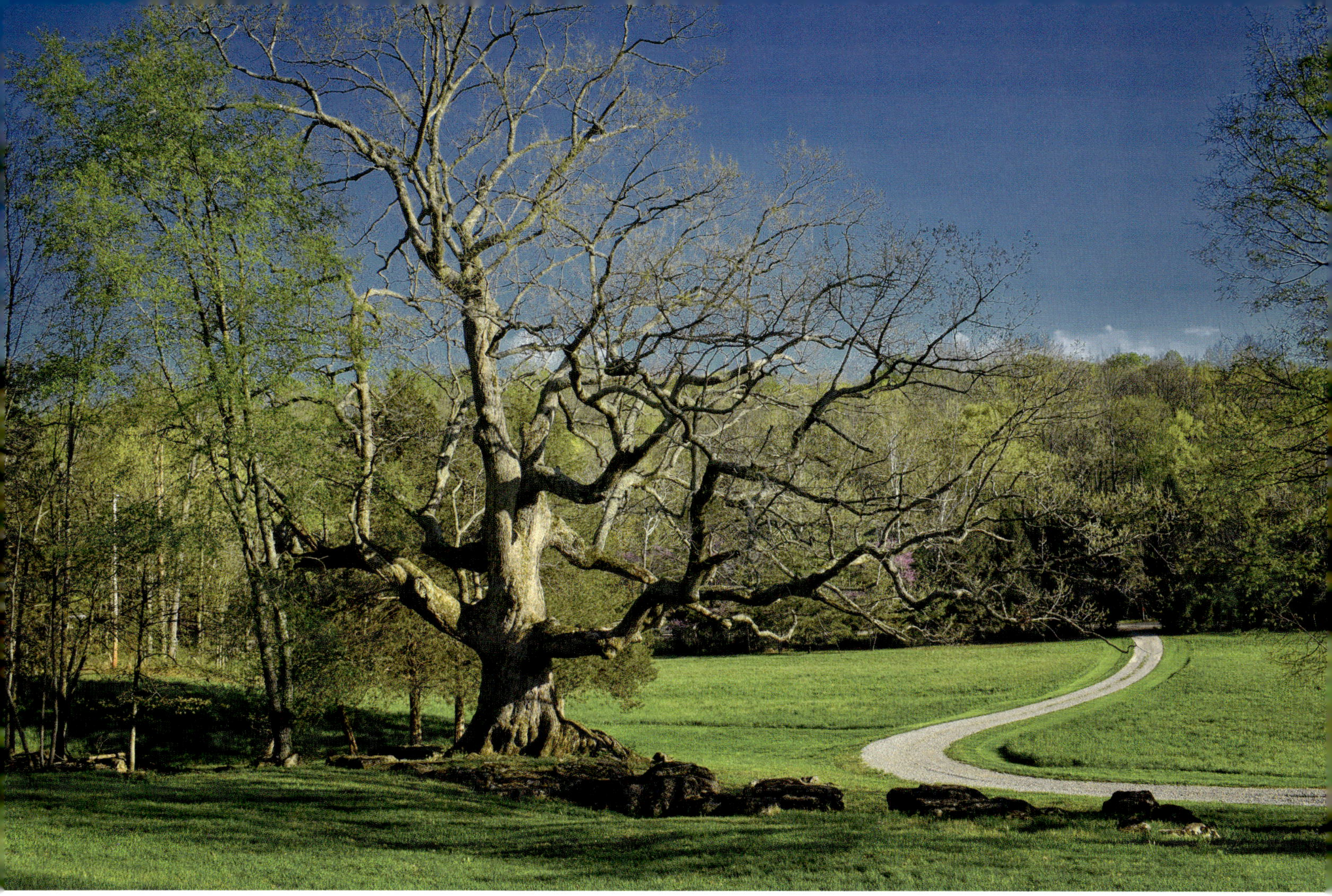

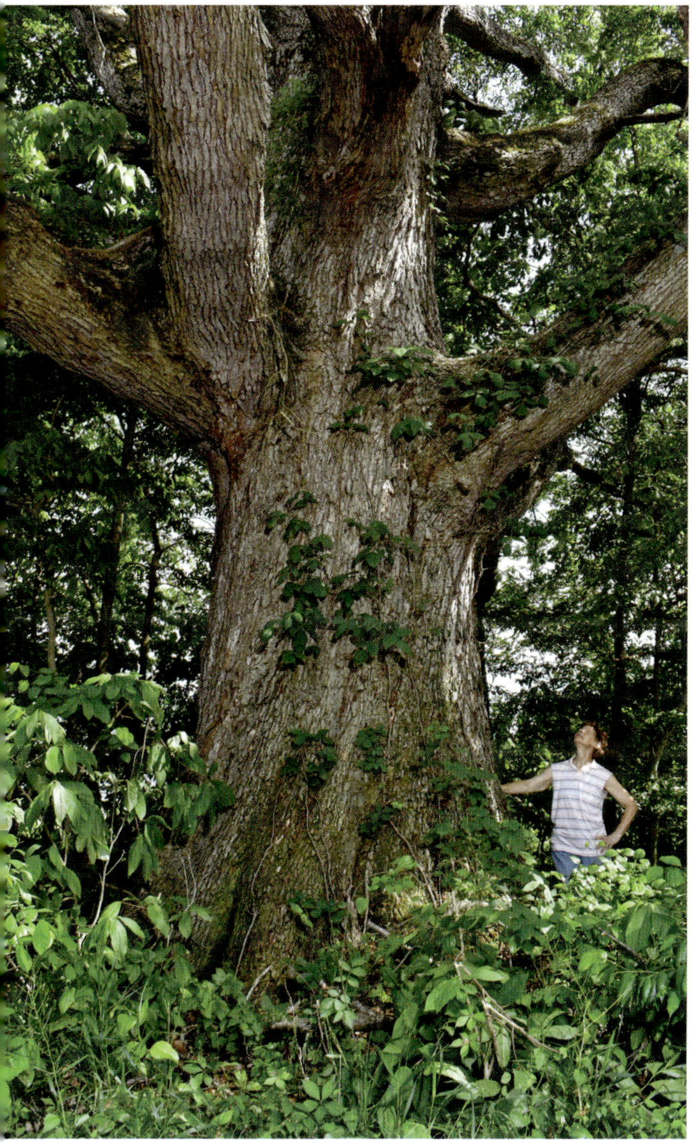

Above: Stunning Monroe County champion chinquapin oak

Left: State champion chinquapin oak, Jackson County

OVERCUP OAK

(*Quercus lyrata*)

Carefully watching every footstep on the verge of sinking into the muddy edges of Overcup Oak Swamp, a part of Twin Swamps Nature Preserve, was an adventure unto itself. In an area of dense vegetation including other oaks, maples, and shrubs that can tolerate very wet conditions, we could see the most likely candidates further out than we wanted to venture. One always hears about sinking out of sight, so we chose not to exercise that option.

Overcup oak is not familiar to most readers of this book, as its native range is in the southwest corner of the state. Here in Posey County, that is indeed as far as you can go. In this fascinating pocket of Indiana lay vast river floodplains, bottomland forests, sloughs, swamps, and the mighty Ohio River. A large variety of trees and shrubs include species that are at the northern end of their range. Overcup oak is more commonly found in southern states but is widely encountered from the southeast to Texas and Oklahoma. In Indiana, it is listed on the "watch list" as a species of concern.

If in a mixed forest with competition, it may reach to 100 feet in height and 3 feet across. The tree is handsome in its natural environment and quite impressive as a mature tree in urban landscapes. The scaly or platy gray bark with patches in old age reminds one of other white oak subgroup members. The graceful lyre-shaped leaf (hence the Latin "*lyrata*") has 5–7 rounded lobes and is very pleasing in appearance. The acorn is very distinctive with its scaly cap almost totally enclosing it, allowing only a small portion to peek outward and entice a gobbling turkey scratching in the soil.

In a timber harvest, overcup oak may be taken along with other white oaks, but it is not a prime choice for select-grade markets. The wood may show defects from fire damage if encountered during its growth and does not dry well due to extensive checking (end-cracking). It can be a valued tree for wildlife and is sometimes left for that purpose in a managed sale.

Two more remarkable overcup oaks were visited for their beauty and size. Both were in Evansville urban settings. At a stunning 5 feet in diameter, with great dignity, they graced their locale. One was at an apartment complex with curious children watching as we photographed. The other loomed on the corner of a private residence. With little traffic, the neighbors casually walked and bicycled beneath this well-loved focal point.

Characteristics

- May have short trunk and begin branching to a broad crown.
- Gray platy bark, some fissures in old age.
- Alternate leaf arrangement, each reaching 8–10 inches in size, hairy underside.
- A lyre-shaped leaf and the acorn really give it away in identification.

Uses

- Rough lumber, pallets, cants; inferior to white oak
- Ornamentally pleasing.
- Good wildlife tree in bottomland habitats.

Right page, top left: Co-champion overcup oak, Evansville

Top right: Co-champion overcup oak, Evansville

Bottom: Overcup Oak Swamp, Posey County

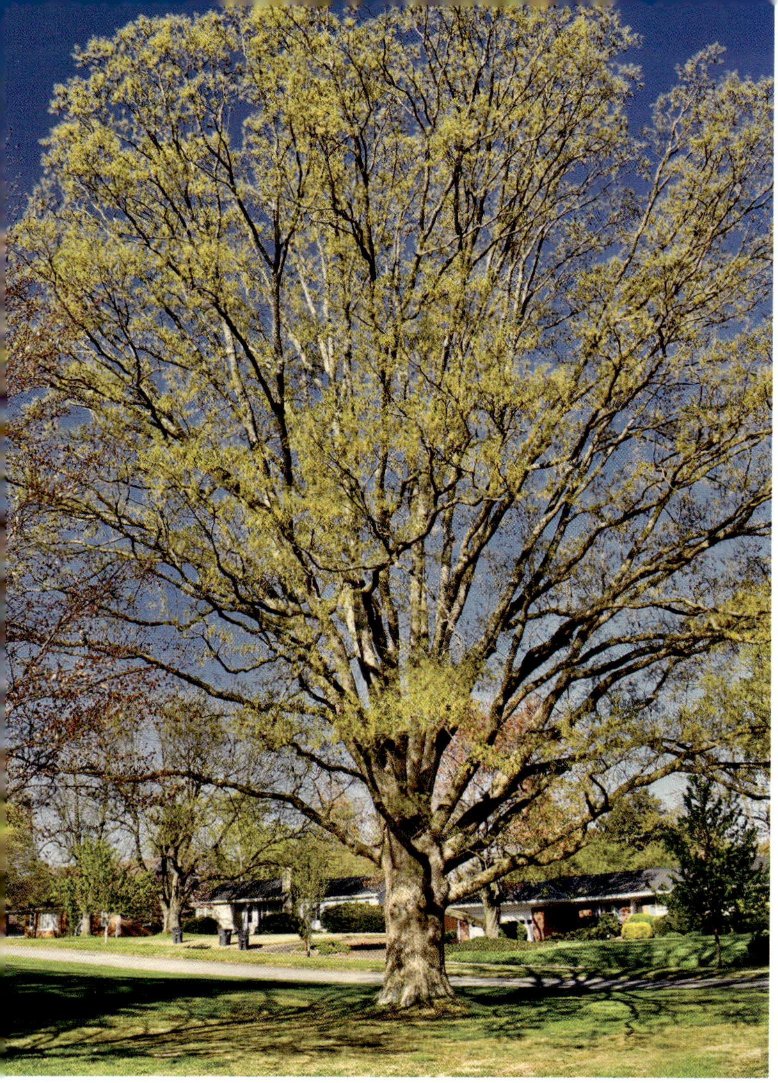
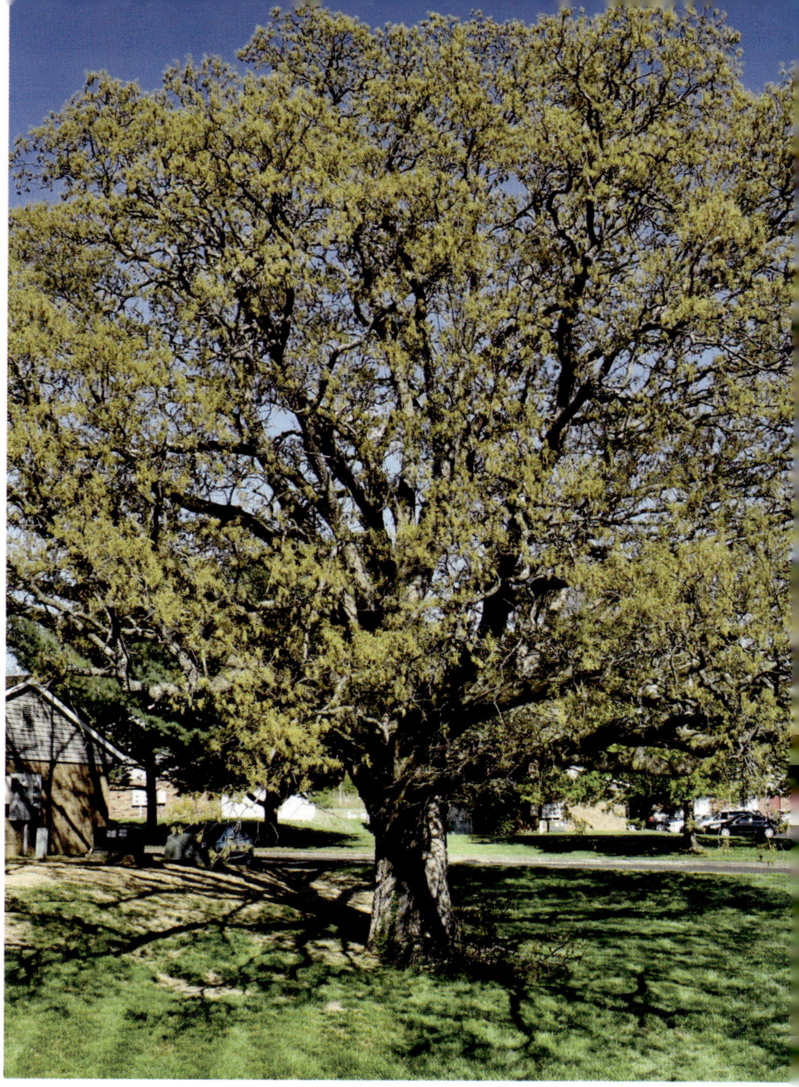
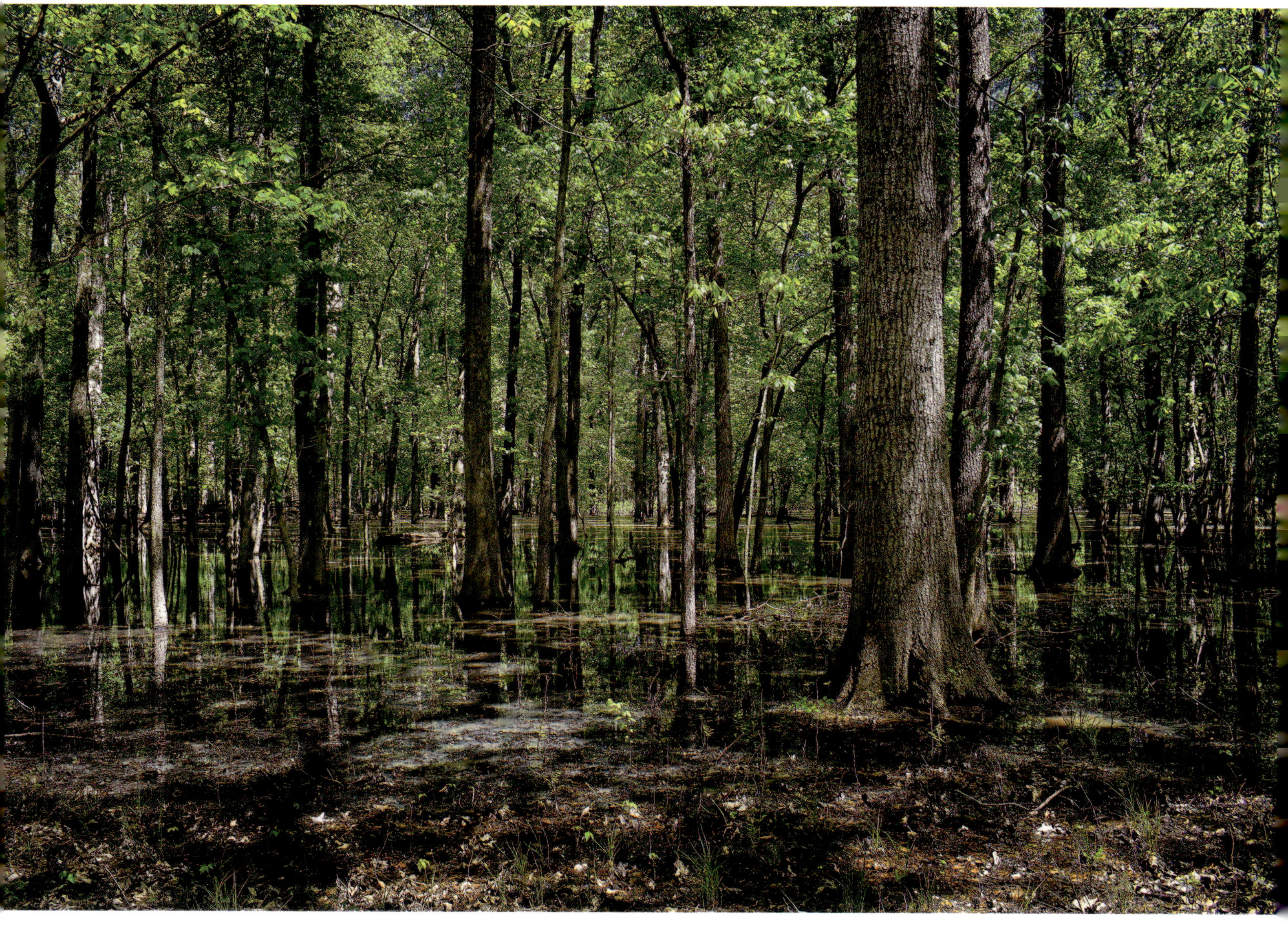

PIN OAK

(Quercus palustris)

The state champion pin oak was noticeable from a long distance. Walking back from the owner's home across a mowed field, I noticed the hulking tree standing in a small grove, ruling them all. It is a massive one indeed, larger than any I had seen, not in a swampy lowland, but here on a hillside in Greene County. The old giant was eight feet in diameter and 100 feet tall. Remarkably, this oak has been permitted to occupy its special place for most likely 300 years, a youngster when the Declaration of Independence was signed and already mature when Indiana attained statehood. It was very possibly left in later years as shade for livestock after the land was cleared and farmed.

Pin oaks are extraordinary trees: handsome, tall, and adaptable to many locations. Often seen when a person adventures into swampy bottomlands along streams with their muck boots on, these trees associate with other oaks such as swamp white, overcup, and swamp chestnut. Pushing upward with a fine vertical smooth gray spire, a relatively fast-growing specimen ascends into the canopy where it develops a rather pyramidal crown. In old age the bark becomes darker, somewhat furrowed, and scaly. The lower branches are maintained for a considerable time, droop into pleasing arch-like form, and finally die as their job has been completed. There are often many of these and an arborist seeking to prune them finds this a task indeed.

One may think that the word "pin" could be inferred from the very fine bristle tip of the deeply cut leaf. However, the name actually refers to the short branchlets on the main branches. The many lower limbs, which were attachments to the trunk, result in knotty wood upon sawing the tree into boards.

Of all the oaks, pin oak is perhaps the most often planted in yards and parks since it is indeed a fast grower, a fine looker, and relatively resistant to those lurking diseases and fungi. In the fall, after a fine display of color, the leaves are retained until deep winter when the entire tree is then unclothed and bares its many artistic branches against the harsh winter sky. The small delicate acorn is also notable with its shallow, thinly scaled cap. The greatest tribute to the pin oak is mostly ornamental since the wood itself is not valued, being weaker than its cousin northern red oak, and is also riddled with those many-branched "pins."

In northern Indiana counties, northern pin oak (*Quercus ellipsoidalis*) is found along with *palustris.* The low limbs may almost swoop to the ground. Consult an ID guide for the slight differences in the two species. Northern pin was considered by some as a northern expression variant of scarlet oak (*Quercus coccinea*), but Jackson and others have maintained it as a separate taxon. This shows the complexity of oaks, and when combined with possibilities of hybridization of pin and northern pin, separation and origins become difficult to "pin down."

Characteristics

- Normally 3–4 feet in diameter is the maximum, although the state champion is 8 feet.
- Heights vary up to 100 feet, but the champion was 110 feet.
- The leaves have 5–7 bristle-tipped lobes at right angles to the stem and these pleasantly diverge.
- Small acorn develops in second season, as do most red oaks.
- Found in wetlands as a preferred habitat, but so adaptable it is planted in many places.

Uses

- Cheap lumber uses since the wood cracks, warps, may not hold together, rots.
- Firewood use.
- Nuts consumed by wildlife; even wood ducks have a taste for them.
- Good for ornamental uses, and that may be the dominant use.

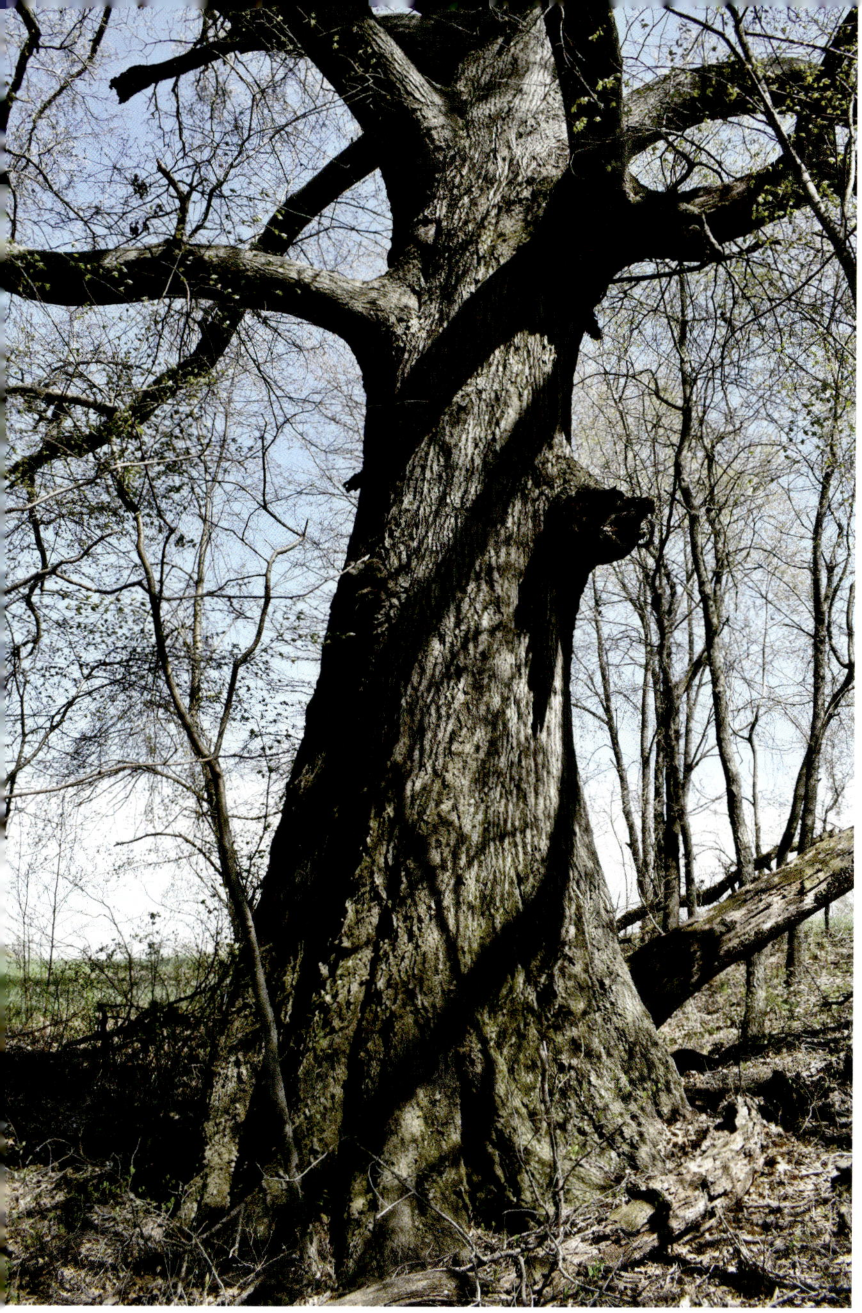

Left: Champion pin oak, Greene County

Bottom: Beauty of pin oak leaves in fall

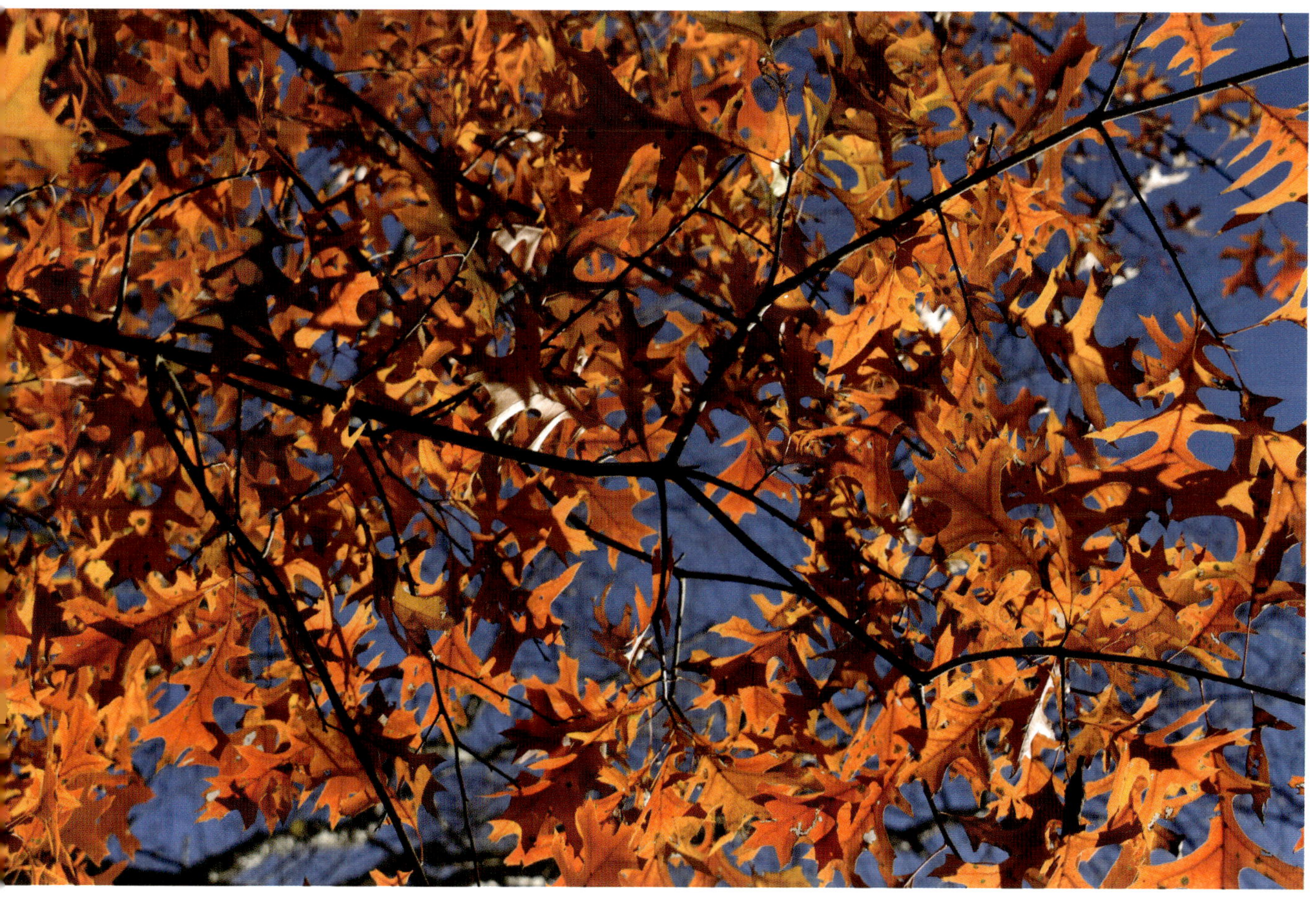

NORTHERN RED OAK

(Quercus rubra)

Grand, magnificent, and beautiful: few trees command such a stately presence in a mature woods. In an even-aged setting where other oaks and hickories abound and competition has urged the trees upward to the light, the entire cohort of oaks may grow tall and straight. Here is the inspiration of a cathedral presence—powerful, silent, humbling. As if the white oaks, red oaks, and black oaks all support and congratulate each other, wisdom of old age arrives after 100, 200, 300 years. If the saw has not felled them, and well it might, for these are all highly desired, stories may flow from their heartwood of all the historical events during their long lives.

Northern red oak is at once distinguishable from the others in its family, its trunk flowing upward with silver-streaked bark amid the blacker background. The lowest part of the base may be almost all dark and furrowed, while the very top branches are showing that scalier silver-gray. Oak flowers are both male and female on the tree, with the female flower diminutive and the male more conspicuous as a 4-inch pendant catkin, later to fall onto the ground where it is quite noticeable. Spring pollen production by oaks may be so prodigious that it coats car hoods and windshields, as well as additionally causing great misery as an allergen to us.

Variability of leaves in the red oak group pose difficulty in positive identification at times, thus other clues need to be ascertained, such as the bark, acorn, bud, twig, and flower. The acorn of red oak is pleasantly rotund with a shallow cap covering perhaps ¼ of the 1¼-inch-long nut.

Since early use of white oak in colonial times dramatically reduced its availability, the lumberman subsequently turned to red oak. Its properties are quite admirable: hard, heavy, strong, and in prime boards, exceptionally beautiful for trim and cabinetry. Being the fastest growing of our oaks, merchantable trees may be selected before the first hundred years, thus the rotation period is shorter. For ornamental plantings red oak is another great choice for its pace of growth, handsome canopy, longevity, and pleasing fall color.

Our grandest Indiana northern red oak is the state champion gracing a hillside in Gibson County with a stunning presence that overwhelms any observer. Measuring 6 feet across, 136 feet tall, and 106 feet in crown spread, it is a most majestic specimen, cared for by the exceptionally dedicated owners.

Another marvelous location to see stately red oaks is Highland Lawn Cemetery in Terre Haute. This grand 139-acre plot has many large trees of various species and its beauty was worthy of being placed on the National Register of Historic Places. There are several mature red oaks, all prominently overseeing the immaculate grounds.

Characteristics

- Up to 100 feet tall (state record is 136 feet as mentioned), and often 3–4 feet in diameter (may reach 6 feet).
- Bark is dark, shallow ridged, with silver streaks.
- Leaf has 7–11 lobes, sinuses extending halfway to midrib, bristle-tip end.
- Acorn develops in second year after flowering.

Uses

- If logs are of high quality, makes furniture, cabinets, and trim. Lower quality rough lumber for general uses.
- Ornamental tree or great companion to other trees in its forest home.
- Good wildlife value. While the sweeter acorn of white oak may be gobbled up first by wildlife, the red oak's bounty is not far behind.
- Red oak was extensively exported to China, although recent tariffs have impacted sales and the market price is low.

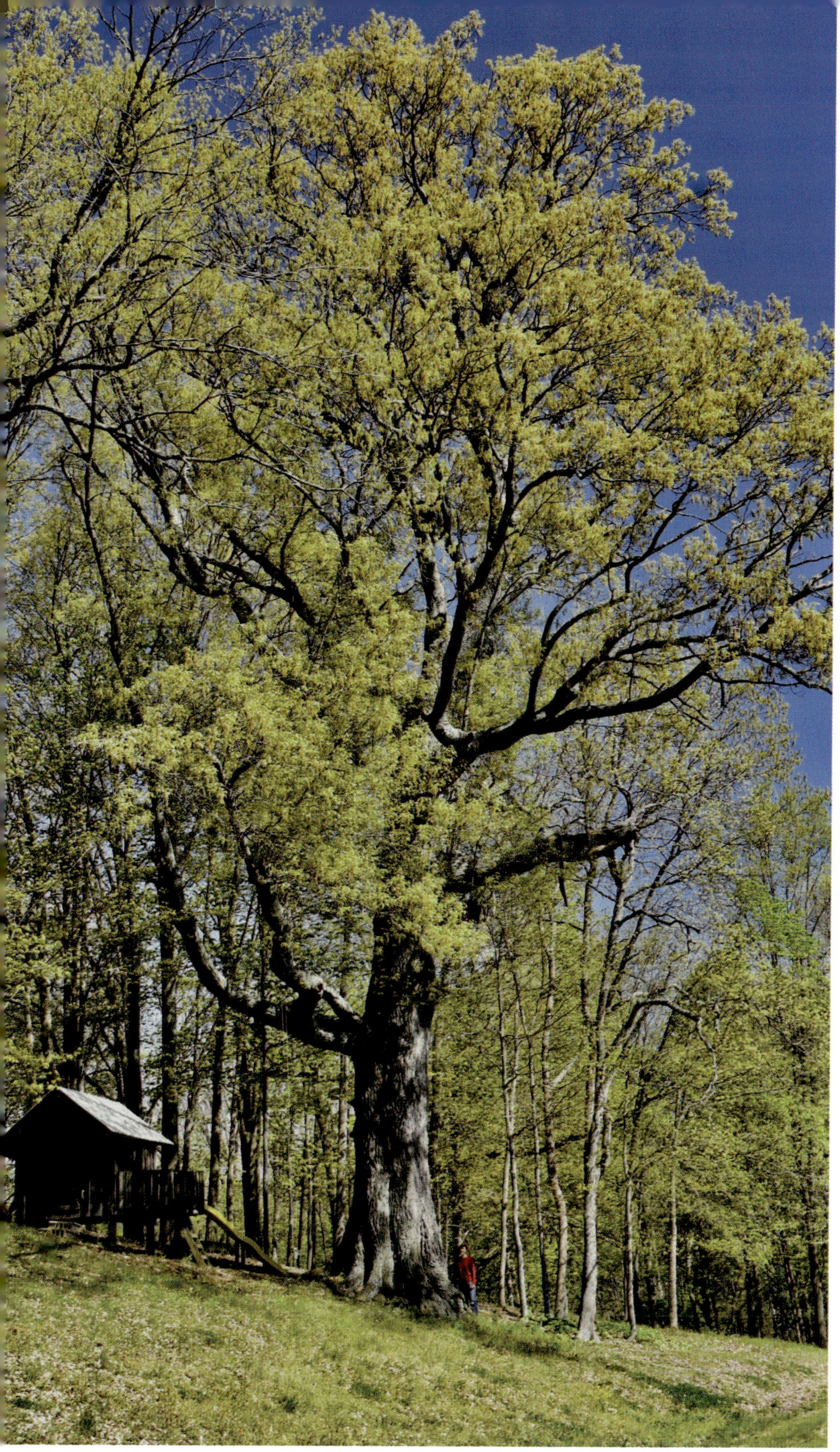
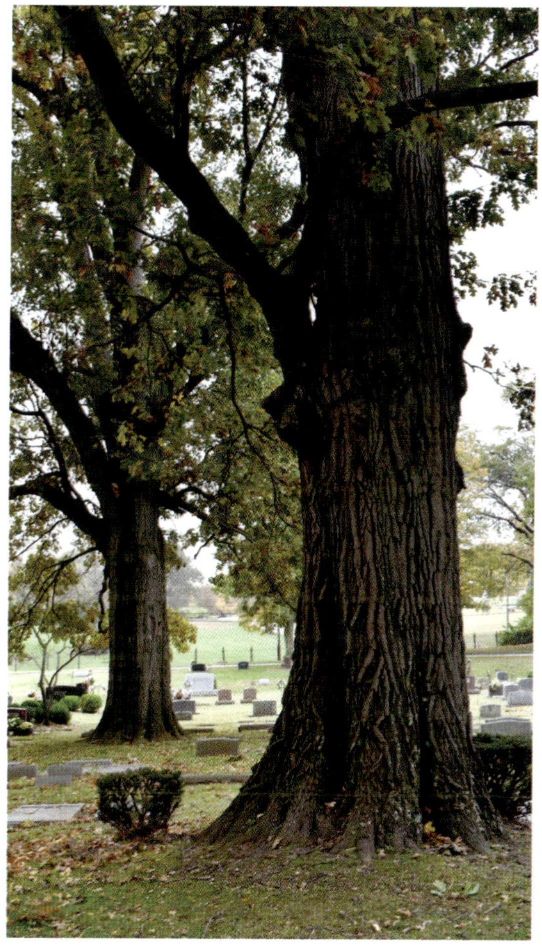

Left: Champion northern red oak, Gibson County. **Right:** Northern red oaks, Highland Lawn Cemetery, Terre Haute.

SHINGLE OAK

(*Quercus imbricaria*)

What an unusual oak: it has an elongated leaf but no lobes like most other oaks. It and willow oak both show this characteristic, and both are in the red oak group. With this shape, identification is made simpler, being assisted by inspecting the acorn and bark. The 4–6-inch leaf is glossy dark green while the underside is pale. The edges are smooth, although on very young trees may be slightly toothed. Acorns attach almost directly onto the twig, are generally small and bitter, only ½ to ¾ inch in size, dark brown, and with cap covering less than half the nut. Although the range occurs across the state, we have not found the tree very common except in southern Indiana. Some specimens were limby near the bottom and the tree form was not good for commercial purposes. One gnarly specimen was observed at Lincoln State Park, at first eluding identification. Outstanding trees in a few locations may reach 60–70 feet in height and some are fairly straight.

As you might guess, shingles are part of the story about its name. Although hard and heavy wood, it was split into shingles for pioneer cabin roofs. Peattie (1966) describes this very early use by French colonists. The site of their cabins near Kaskaskia, Illinois greeted the famous early French botanist André Michaux, who assigned the Latin *imbricaria* as the species.

Our Indiana champion was in Evansville, a stately tree almost six feet across and 80 feet tall, definitely larger than most run-of-the-mill shingle oaks. Note: As this book goes to press, it was learned that a freak accident caused the tree to split and fall into the road. We grieve with the owners for the loss of their precious, stately champion tree.

Characteristics

- Commonly 2–3 feet in diameter and up to 60 feet tall.
- Alternate arrangement of its dark green elongated leaves.
- Small, dark, bitter acorn, not edible except by some wildlife in hard winters.
- May have many low, gangly limbs.
- Prefers moist rich soil, can be found in sandy loams or even on limestone ridges.

Uses

- Shingles in olden days, more now for general uses as nonprime oak.
- Was used as fuel in early times and is still cut and split for firewood today.
- Originally for barn timbers and even mine posts or props.
- The attractiveness of the tree and its leaves does allow for ornamental use but it is susceptible to galls deemed unsightly to some folks, yet to others, an interesting oddity.

Right page: State champion shingle oak, Evansville

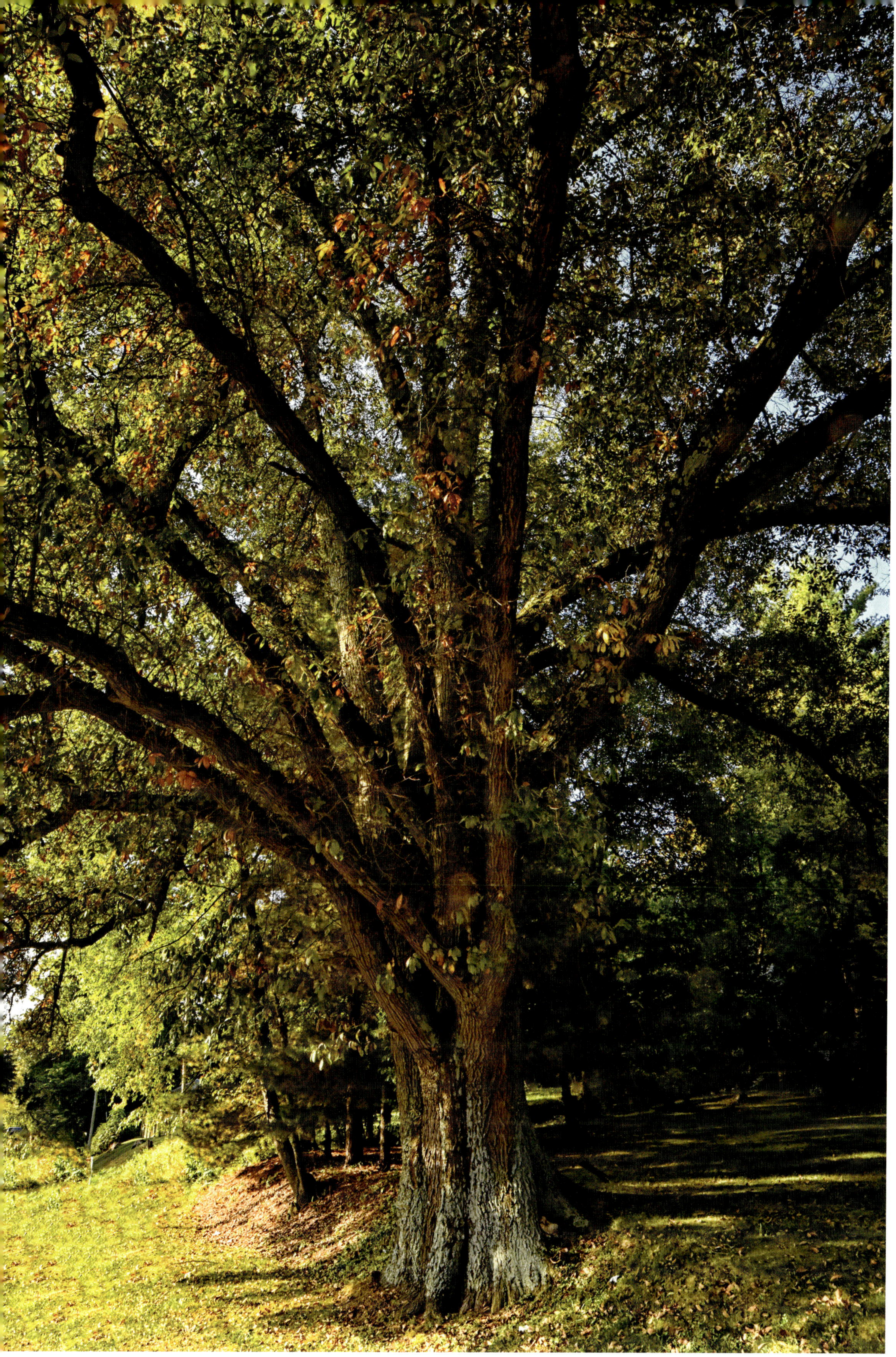

SHUMARD OAK

(Quercus shumardii)

One of the grandest of the former champion oaks in Indiana, a behemoth almost ten feet across recently lived in Floyd County. It had one of the highest total indexes of any tree in the state. But as with many of our old age giants, this one also succumbed and we will no longer be able to gasp at its dominance. A newer submission was found by Dave Coppert in the Muscatatuck National Wildlife Refuge, and it also is very large, albeit two trees joined as one as they grew up.

We hiked down an old road and then into a section of woods where this 6-foot-diameter champion was found along with other fine sweet gums, oaks, and beech. The ages of these trees would say they were present when the area had been settled 150 years ago and farmed up until the last 50 years.

Another location that features Shumards is Thousand Acre Woods in Daviess County, a huge wet bottomland hardwood forest and flatwoods. Even though drainage ditches from years ago affected the wetland regime, the protection now in place by the Nature Conservancy allows this rare forest to exist in the midst of farmland. It is here that Shumard oak can be found along with swamp white oak, pin oak, sweet gum, silver maple, and even elm. This species has also been known to hybridize with other *Quercus* species.

Named for Benjamin Franklin Shumard (1820–1869), state geologist of Texas, it is often grouped with northern red oak since it does resemble that species in many regards. But upon closer inspection shumard is definitely different in both leaf and acorn. In a fine old forest, they can tolerate drier upland conditions, reaching over 100 feet in height and 4 feet across. In their prime natural setting they are content with rich, wet bottomland soils. It is a species often raised by nurseries for landscaping. With tall straight trunks, broad open crown, and nice fall color, these fine trees are very desirable.

Characteristics

- Versatile growing sites, most at home in deep, moist soils in bottomlands.
- Can be a fine large straight tree to 100 feet, gray black to dark black bark, and fissures with age.
- The leaf has 7–9 lobes, deeply indented with those being a "C" shape.

Uses

- Often considered the same as northern red oak for products, prime wood is reddish brown and beautiful. Oak cabinets, furniture, and flooring are all desirable products.
- Beneficial wildlife tree.

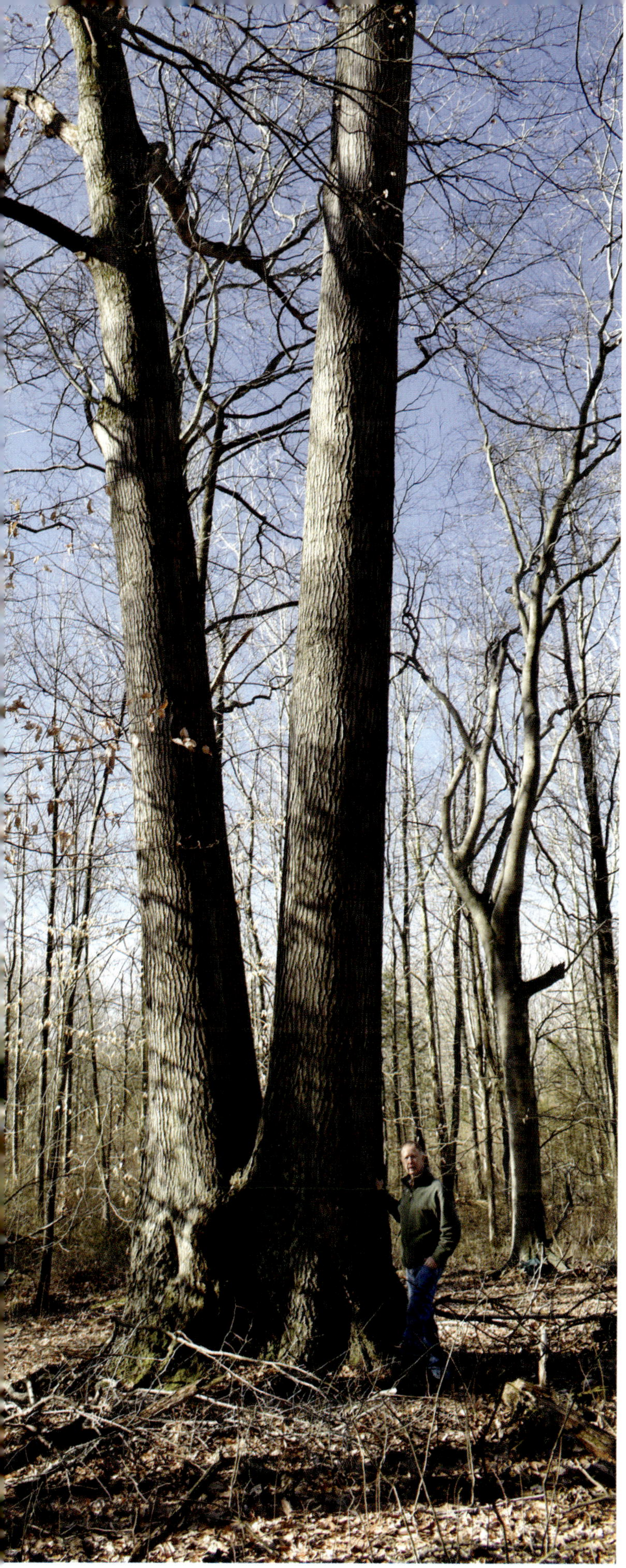

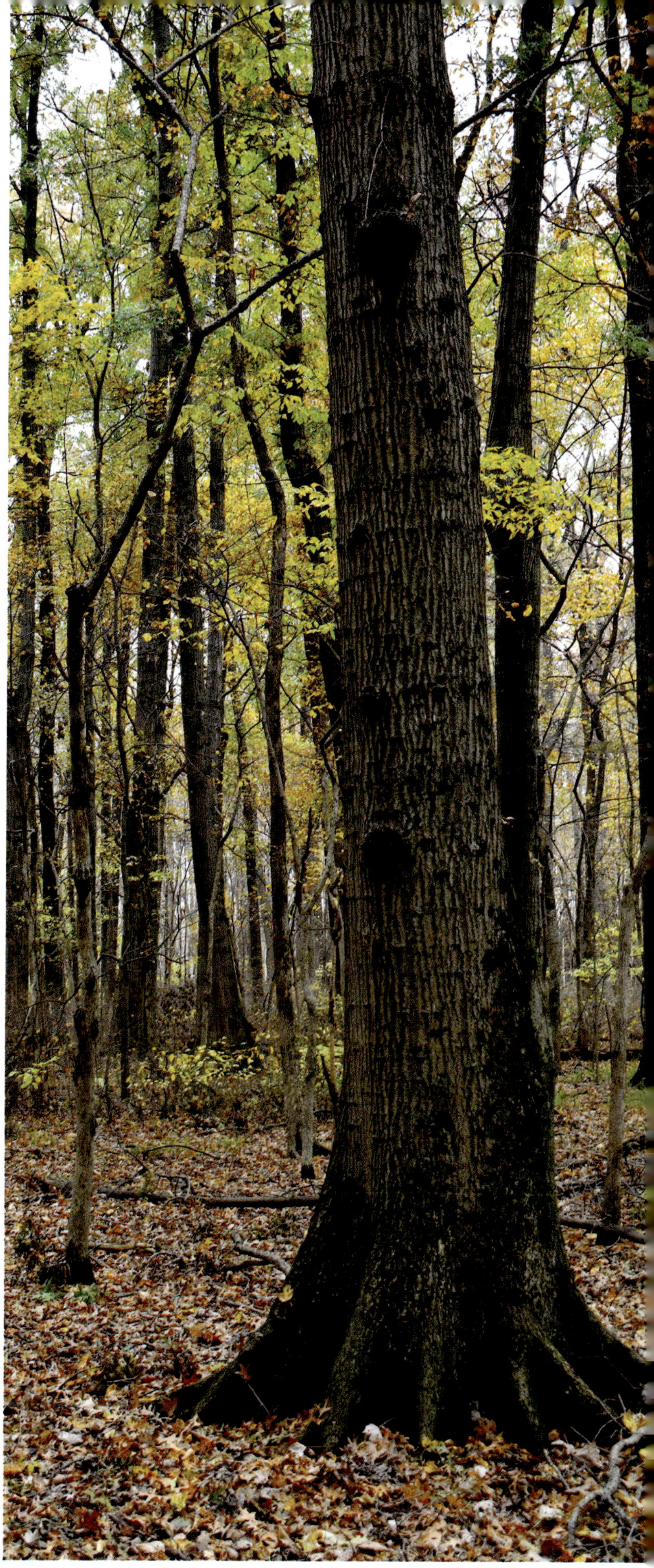

Left: State champion shumard oak, Muscatatuck NWR. **Right:** Shumard oaks, Thousand Acre Woods, Daviess County.

SOUTHERN RED OAK

(*Quercus falcata*)

There they are, on the ground, those verdant leaves in the shape of turkey tracks. Of course, leaves do vary, but these showed the deep sinuses, outstretched lobes, and narrow midrib. When this state champion tree in Vanderburgh County was visited, three identifiers were evident—those distinctive leaves; the rough, blackish, scaly bark; and dainty acorns with a delicately scaled little cap. Excellent photos of these features can be found in the previously cited *Native Trees of the Midwest* (Weeks et al.).

Southern red oak is related to northern red oak, but primarily found in the most southern Indiana counties. It is a highly desirable tree for the shade potential created by massive wide-ranging limbs, reaching out 55 feet on each side of the tree. The 6-foot-diameter, 82-feet-high champion in a residential yard provided superb ambiance and dignity. Imagine 200 years ago that this tree was on the original deeded parcel and was left as other companion trees were cleared. It has survived to this day, now a focal point for the current landowners. Several generations of happy squirrel families have been able to appreciate the productivity of this wondrous specimen.

This upland species tolerates some dryness as oaks often do, but not to the extreme. It can be found on slopes and ridges with poorer soils, or if given sites of richer alluvial soils in bottomland woods, it can express itself with much greater presence of tall, straight timber form.

Wildlife will be attracted to the small acorns produced every other year, and when the crop is abundant, the scratched soil under the tree will show evidence of turkey and deer rummaging for the starchy food supply. High up in the tree, a squirrel may sit and ponder where to find the next nut below. Whether as a food source, a beautiful yard tree, or just a great addition to the variety of our oak groups, southern red oak is a tree of earned respect.

Characteristics

- Distinctive leaves, variable from 3 to 7 lobes, turkey-track shape of some, but not necessarily of all leaves on the same tree. Underside of leaf lighter, soft whitish or reddish-hairy look.
- Acorn small, but desirable for wildlife feeding.
- Bark varies from deep gray to dark brownish-black, and may resemble that of black oak.

Uses

- Being an oak usually implies a valuable wood, but this one end-checks and warps and is not considered a prime species. It is used for rough lumber, pallets, crates, and firewood.
- Good yard tree when ample space is available.

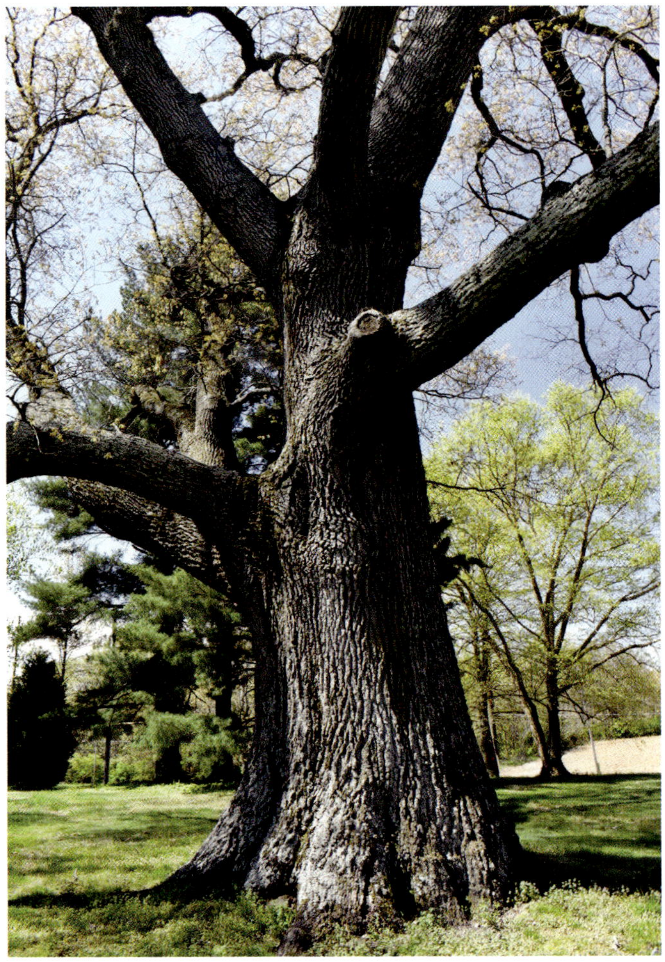

State champion southern red oak, closeup bark patterns

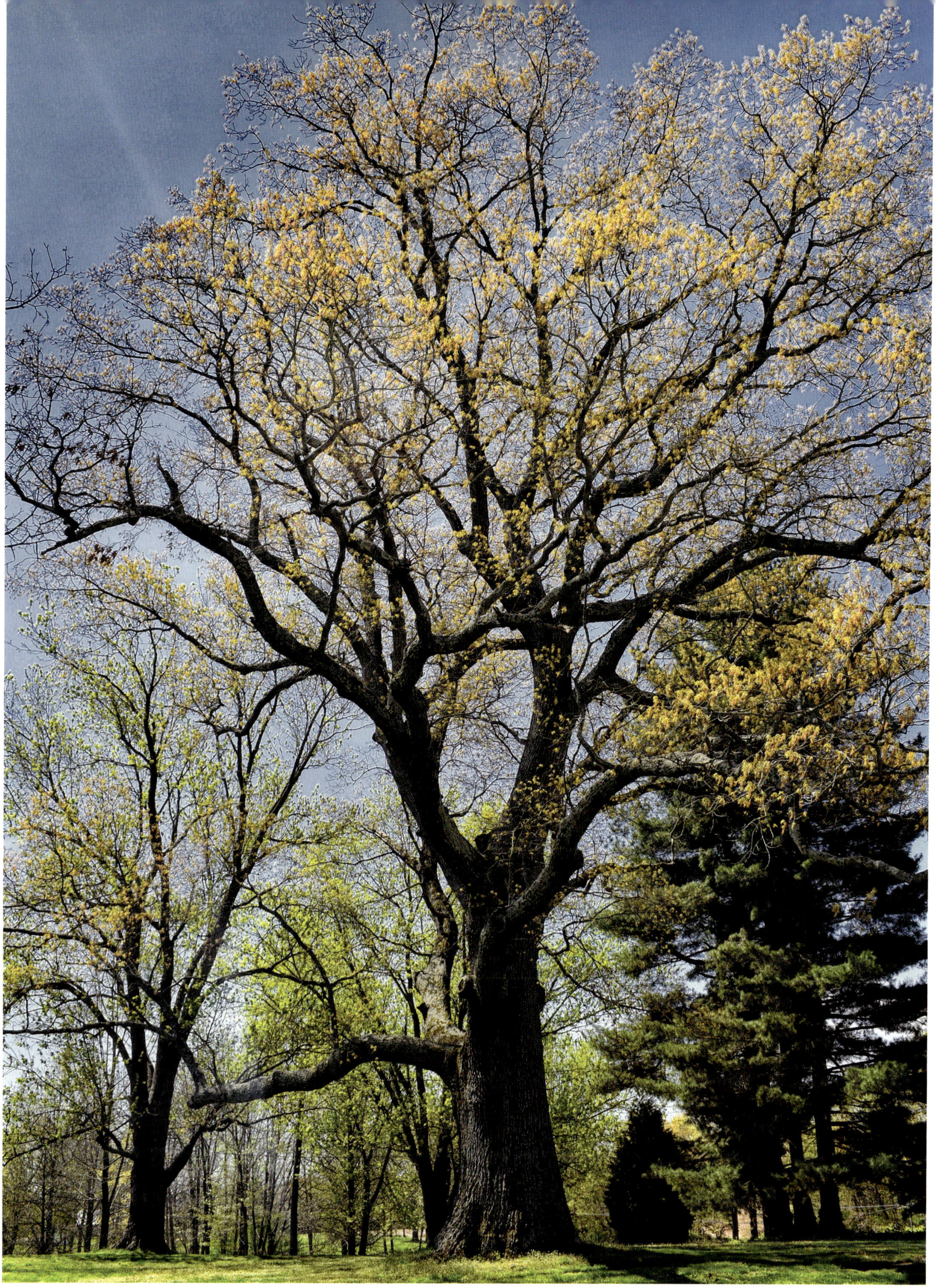

State champion southern red oak, Vanderburgh County

SWAMP CHESTNUT OAK

(Quercus michauxii)

This noted oak has a long history of names and uses. The Latin species *michauxii* honors that famed early French botanist who described many new trees of eastern North America in the late 1700s and early 1800s. The tree's acorns were so edible that upon falling to the ground, they quickly were eaten by cows grazing in the woodlots. Hence the common name "cow oak." The spring wood also split easily along planes with use of a wedge or drawknife. The strips produced could be interwoven into a crude basket. These baskets could carry farm items or be loaded up with cotton in the southern states. Hence another common name, "basket oak." In fact, that name is what Peattie uses for his descriptions, and carries back to when the species was grouped with *Q. prinus* (chestnut oak).

The range of swamp chestnut oak is expansive, from the eastern states, the deep South, westward to Texas and Oklahoma, and northward to the Ohio River valley, including Illinois and Indiana. In the Hoosier state, it seems more attuned to the southern third and is found in some of those slightly higher but moderately wet flatwoods communities.

If timbered, swamp chestnut oak is also taken in the white oak group. In an old wetland flatwood, you may notice fewer lower side limbs than a nearby swamp white oak might have.

Pictured is the champion swamp chestnut oak in Jennings County, a remarkable 24 feet around and 109 feet in height. It was formerly a national champion and may be submitted again for this honor. This great tree stands alone as a guardian giant and is most likely up to 300 years old, probably starting its life before Indiana achieved statehood in 1816.

Other remarkable locations for this species in Jennings County include Guthrie Woods, Wells Woods, and Tribbett's Woods. Swamp chestnut oak is also very common in the Muscatatuck National Wildlife Refuge, with many wonderful large specimens.

Characteristics

- White oak group, alternate arrangement of leaves, short stalk for acorn.
- Leaves of swamp chestnut have sort of a leathery feel and are hairier below on the silvered surface.
- Flowers also unisexual, on same tree.
- Bark gray, some narrower ridges, fissures in old age, scaly.
- Sweet acorn, consumed readily by deer and turkeys.
- Just a great tree overall, one of the author's favorites. The champion struck me with great emotion as I approached its majestic trunk.

Uses

- Typical oak uses: basket splints, barrel staves, and chair bottoms.
- Fine habitat tree, prodigious acorn gifts for browsing creatures below.

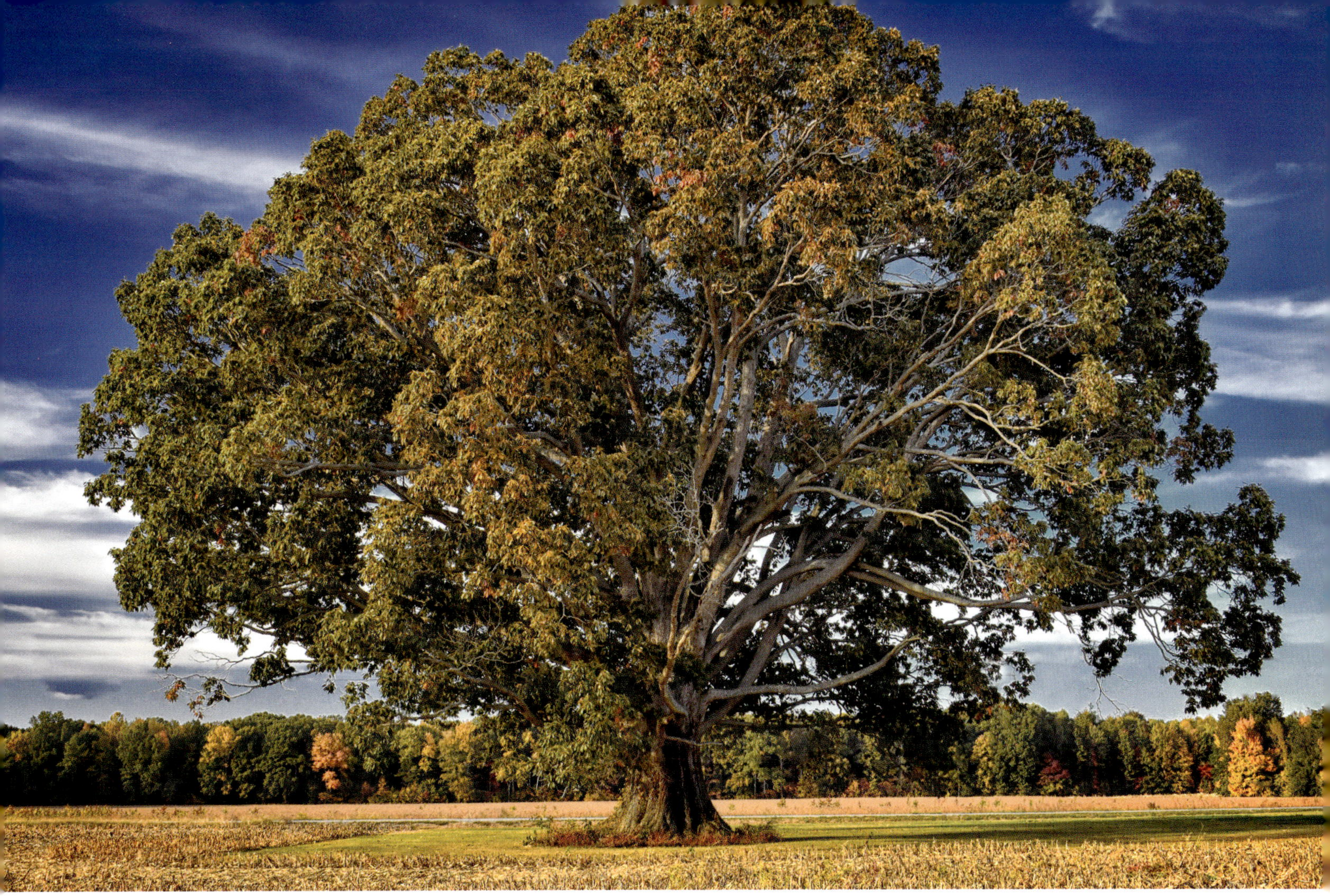

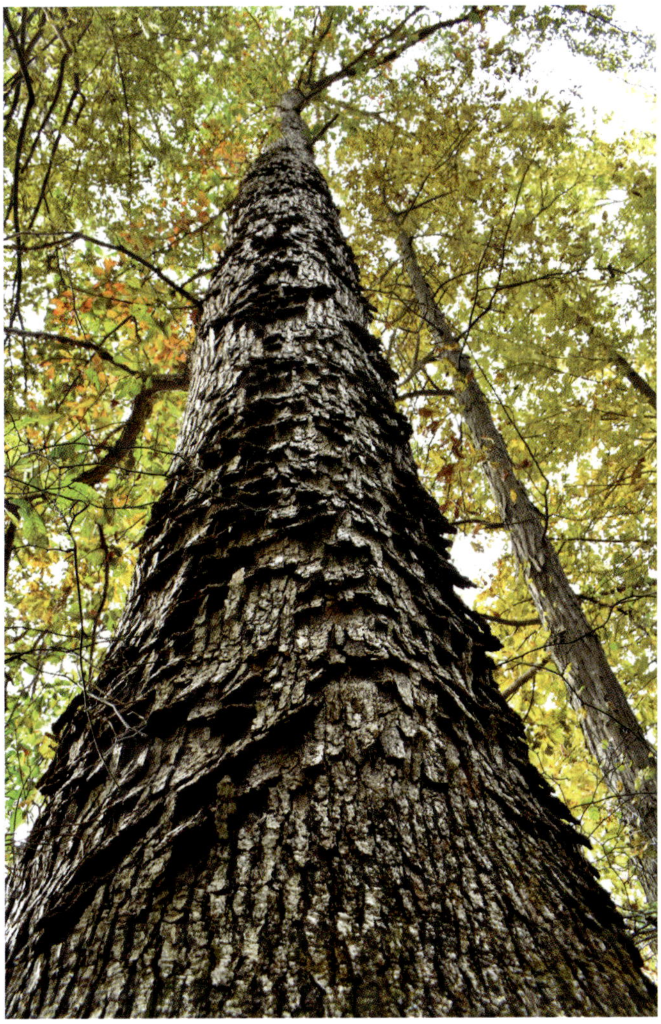

Above: State champion swamp chestnut oak, Jennings County

Left: Scaly bark on swamp chestnut oak, Guthrie Woods, Jennings County

SWAMP WHITE OAK

(*Quercus bicolor*)

The early morning fog was beginning to lift, permitting star-like rays of the sun to glance off the outstretched limbs of a most impressive oak. Here, in typical low-lying land, this Vigo County specimen seemed quite at home near Prairie Creek. The owners have long protected this aged resident of the farm. At 14½ feet in circumference and 85 feet in height, it was a dominant presence.

Swamp white oaks occur across the state in varying landscape types. Its preference might well be those soggy wetland soils, swamp margins, and creek banks. Yet it can be found on higher ground where good deep soils nurture the expansive root system. In central Indiana, on soils above the glacial till below, swamp white also does well. Such is the case for one very large specimen on the northside of Indianapolis. It shows the typical lower-level arching limbs, horizontal ones in the middle, and diverging limbs at the top. Surprisingly, this residential tree was never cut. It is now most likely over 150 years of age and has provided many years of distinguished service to the community.

The leaves are glossy green above but have a whitish hairy look below, hence its name "bicolor." It flagrantly shows off this light undercoat on any occasion of sweet breeze flowing through the woodland and rocking the leaf ever so slightly. The acorn on its long stem seems like a ruffian, more unrefined than the swamp chestnut acorn.

The wood from swamp white oak is often taken by the timber cutter as "white oak" but is often less desirable due to residual old lateral limbs persistent on lower areas. As with other oaks, the wood is quite heavy. The overall abundance of swamp white is nowhere near that of white oak, but the grandeur and self-declaration of its notable features speak for itself.

Right: Large open-grown swamp white oak, Broad Ripple, Indianapolis

Right page: Old swamp white oak on foggy morning, Vigo County

Characteristics

- Alternate arrangement of bicolored leaves.
- 2–3-inch-long stalk for acorn.
- Bark is platy, gray-brown, develops fissures in old age.
- Male and female flowers on same tree. Acorn develops first year.

Uses

- The wood is hard and heavy but of less value than white oak, due to many limbs.
- Good wildlife food source.

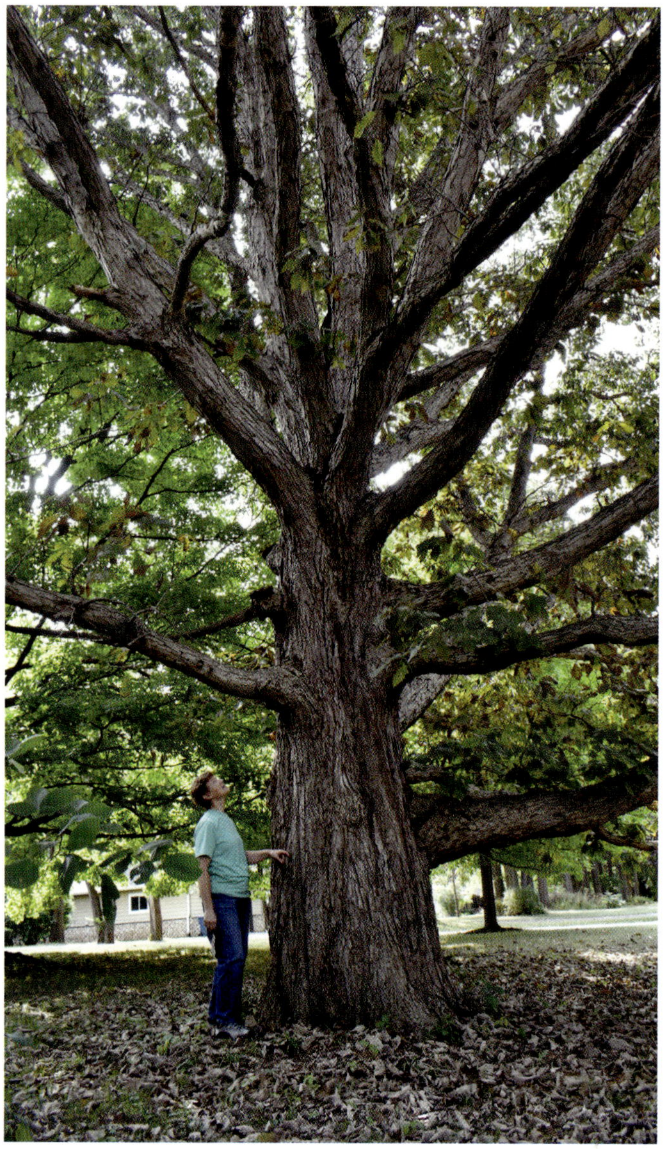

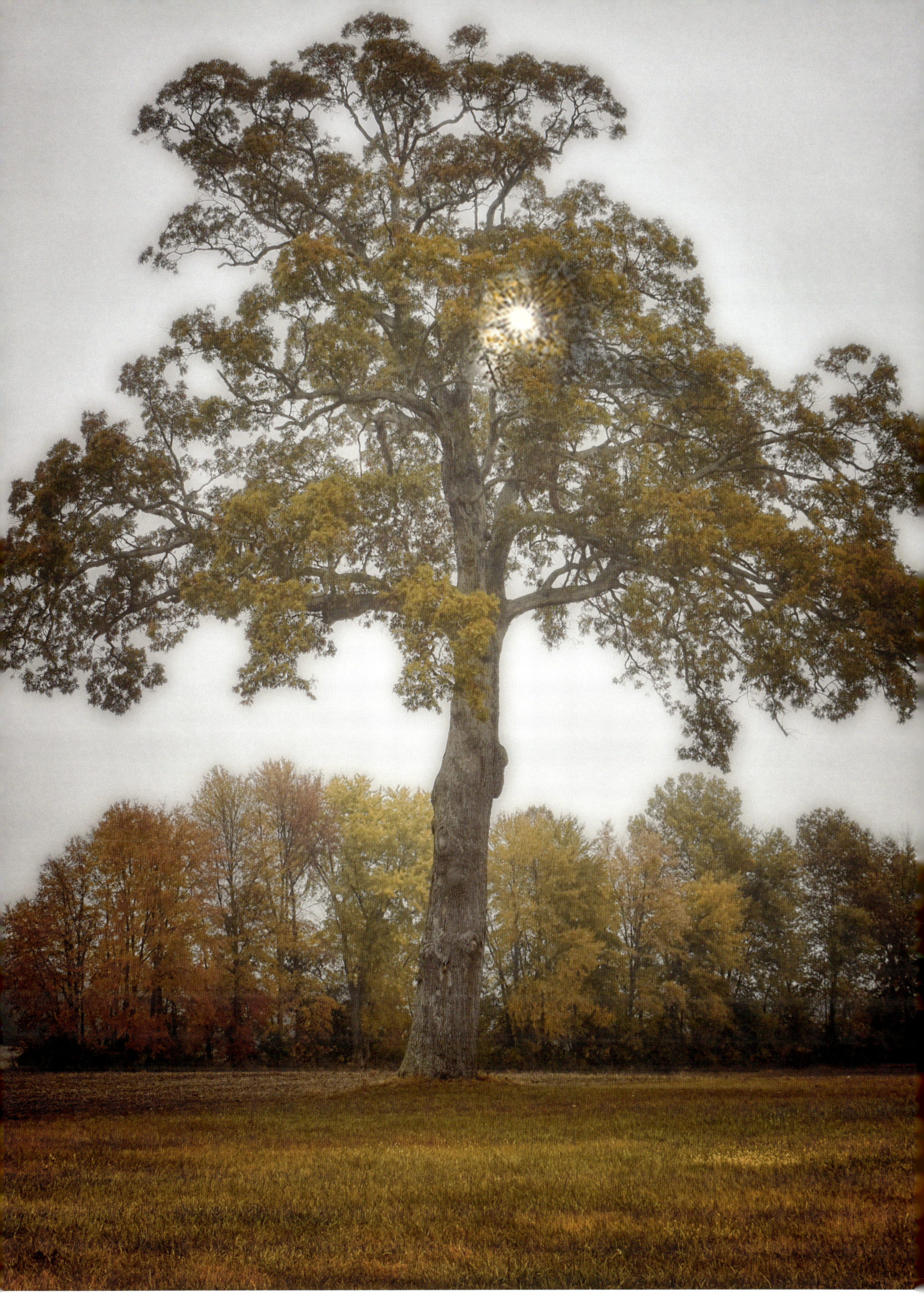

WHITE OAK (OR NORTHERN WHITE OAK)
(Quercus alba)

With such longstanding esteem, white oak rises to the top of the list of all-American, all-time deeply honored trees. Standing in the presence of an old giant, I was awed by the massive trunk, huge, outstretched arms, long, platy, furrowed bark, and verdant leaves gathering sunlight from the sky. We need no scale to rate it, for it sets the standards. The leaf alone says much as it is often used on logos for businesses or organizations, such as our Indiana chapter of the Nature Conservancy.

White oak has a large range from the eastern seaboard westward to Minnesota and south to Texas. In colonial times much fine timber was taken from the East for many demands, including shipbuilding. As settlement moved westward, white oak was found extensively, perhaps none finer than in Indiana forests. It was versatile for so many uses, from barns to flooring, paneling, cabinetry, and grandma's favorite rocking chair. In antique furniture, the era of "golden oak" found this highly varnished wood in vogue for decades. Many heirlooms have been passed from generation to generation and still grace homes today.

White oak is highly valued and in locations where veneer-grade oak is harvested, a single tree can be worth thousands of dollars. There is nothing quite like white oak for making those famous barrels holding bourbon whiskey. That use alone demands high quality for the cooperage process. From forming the staves to charring the barrel, each piece of oak is an important member of the cast.

The tree itself can be found as tall and straight to 60 feet before the first limb, or perhaps as a "wolf" tree: limby, wide, and dominant over subordinate species shaded out by the large spread. On my trips across the state, many white oaks stood out in yards, pastures, and parks. Each one was a special tree to the owners. In prime old forests like Tribbett Woods and Guthrie Woods in Jennings County, Donaldson's Woods in Spring Mill State Park, and other nature preserves, the most impressive white oaks can be found among giant beech, poplar, and other oak species.

The state champion is in northern Perry County, a huge tree with monstrous branches. It is quite hidden in this forested, rural area, but with guidance from the owner's nephews, we were able to marvel at the old giant.

Another remarkable white oak pictured was one of those in the famous Constitution Grove in Crane NSWC, Martin County. Forester Trent Osmon explained how these fine quality oaks are specifically managed as sources for repairing planking on the USS *Constitution*. That remarkable ship, also known as Old Ironsides, launched in 1797, can be visited in Boston Harbor.

In Chapter 5 on old-growth forests there are many examples of other extraordinary white oaks. With ages up to 400 years, the old monarchs are still alive today and stand as living memorials.

Characteristics

- Can be perfect 3-foot diameters and high grade, or 8-foot old, open-grown limby giants.
- Leaves to 9 inches, variable number of round lobes, from 5 up to 9. Indentations may be shallow or deep.
- Acorn to ¾ inch, greenish to light brown, cap covers ¼ of nut. Mature and set root in first season of falling, unlike the red oaks.

Uses

- Furniture, cabinets, trim, flooring, whiskey barrels.
- Veneer may be peeled from prime logs and then used over other woods.
- Lower grade oak may be used for ties, siding, cants, and pallets.
- Red and white oak species often exported.
- Landowners and Tree Farm members may plant nursery-grown oaks. Can be interspersed with chestnut in selected plantations.

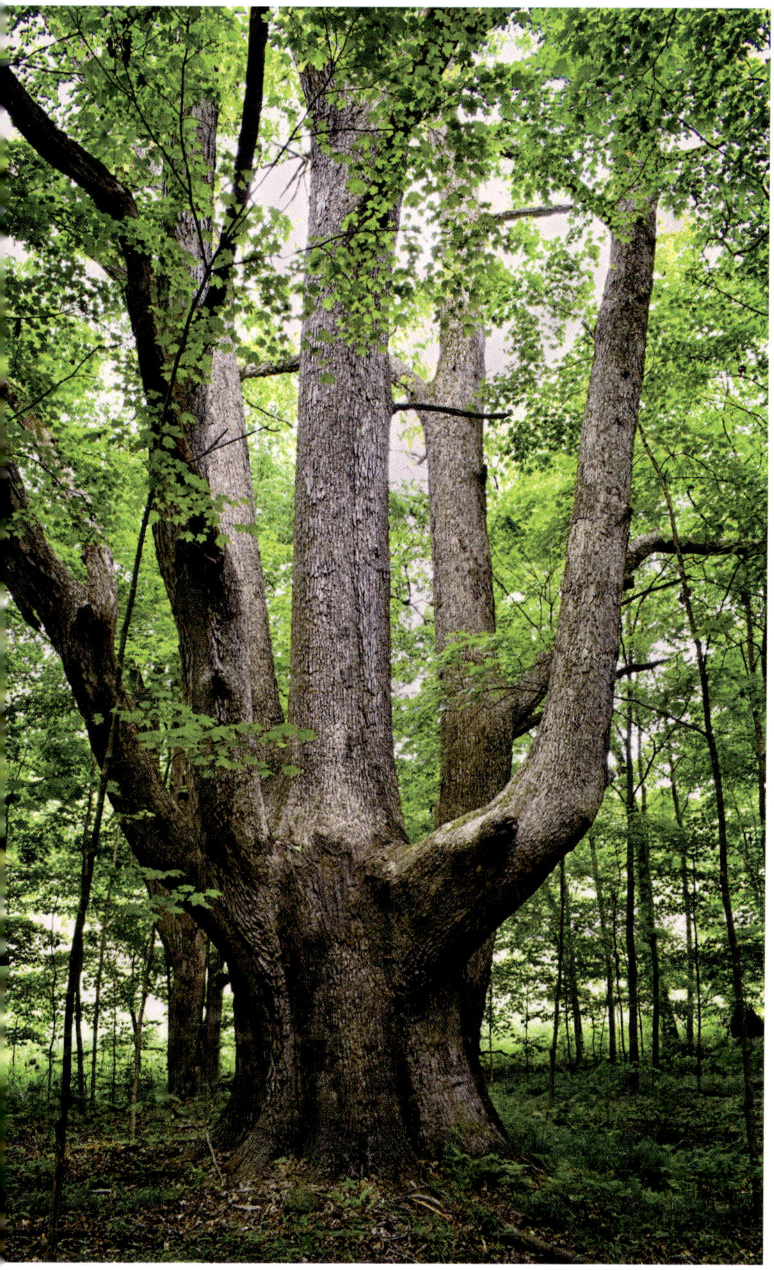

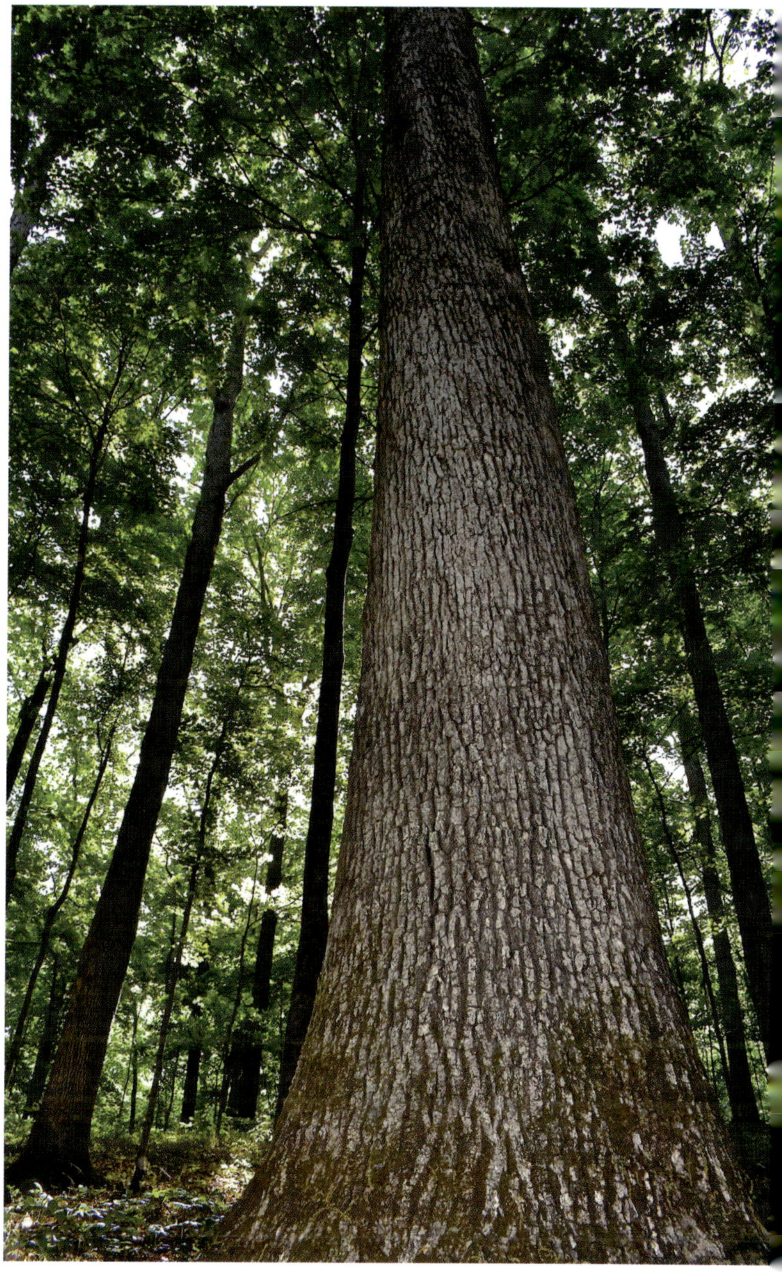

Left: State champion white oak, Perry County. **Right:** Fine white oak, Constitution Grove, Crane NSWC.

COMMON PERSIMMON

(*Diospyros virginiana*)

Truly delicious and celebrated, the ripe persimmon beckons consideration as one of the most-loved fall puddings, at least in Mitchell, Indiana, where contenders vie for the coveted "best pudding" prize during the highly popular annual Persimmon Festival. Close by at Spring Mill State Park, one can find this enticement on the dessert bar in the inn. The connotation of "pudding" is often a very soft substance like a mousse, but in our case the mix is baked in an oven and when done is a solid that is cut into squares and eaten with a fork. Adding a lemon sauce topping and whipped cream bonnet assures that this delicacy will be a gourmet's delight.

The search for the state champion led to New Harmony, not only an extraordinary place in Indiana's history, but also a location for many old or unique trees. On the south side of town is a wonderful old home now housing the Ferndale Education Center. On the beautifully manicured grounds are several large trees, among which is the big persimmon, its massive trunk rising with the dark, chunky, distinguished bark so typical of the species. This very impressive giant had no fruit when visited. A spring trip would tell whether it was a male tree or female, as the flowers help identification.

The *Diospyros* genus is represented by similar varieties of the fruit in Asia. In fact, according to Wikipedia, worldwide production of edible persimmons was over 7.9 million tons in 2018, with China alone producing over 6.3 million tons. Some fruits there are nonastringent, but our astringent variety must be fully ripe to avoid the bitterness puckering one's mouth. Ripening occurs in fall, usually after the first frost, producing fruit that is very sweet. A loaded tree will begin to drop persimmons shortly thereafter and 1-inch fruits must be retrieved quickly before the deer, opossums, and raccoons find them. They are a delicacy to people and critters alike. It is well accepted to cheat a little and knock some from the laden branches with a stick, but be sure to check that they are ripe. Locals often call the fruit a "simmon" or "possum apple." Persimmons are high in vitamin C and fiber. Producing the two cups of pulp necessary to make a pudding requires mashing the ripened fruit in a colander to remove the seeds within.

The wood is hard and has historically been used for billiard cues, utensils, mallets, drumsticks, and golf club heads. It is occasionally used in woodworking, more as a curiosity or unique touch, although the color and grain are not considered uniform or even pleasing unless prime boards are selected and sorted.

The tree itself is dioecious, meaning there are separate male and female trees. Male flowers are white/pink in groups of three, while the female flower is creamy white and single.

Old-timers say that inspecting the seeds will predict the winter, observing whether they are shaped as a spoon (lots of snow) or a knife (bitterly cold). At least, that's the old legend. One can cogitate on this while the delicious pudding is being finished in the oven.

Characteristics

- Height to 60–80 feet with usual diameter up to 2 feet. (Our state champion is 3 feet.)
- Limbs fairly perpendicular to trunk unless loaded with fruit, then may bend heavily or actually break.
- Alternate leaves, glossy green but showing nice color in fall.
- Bark is dark, blocky or chunky with perhaps a hint of orange between blocks.
- Fruit astringent until ripe, falls naturally from tree and may reach 2 inches in size.

Uses

- Items that need a hard wood as mentioned above.
- Some unique woodworking or even flooring.
- A delicious edible fruit.

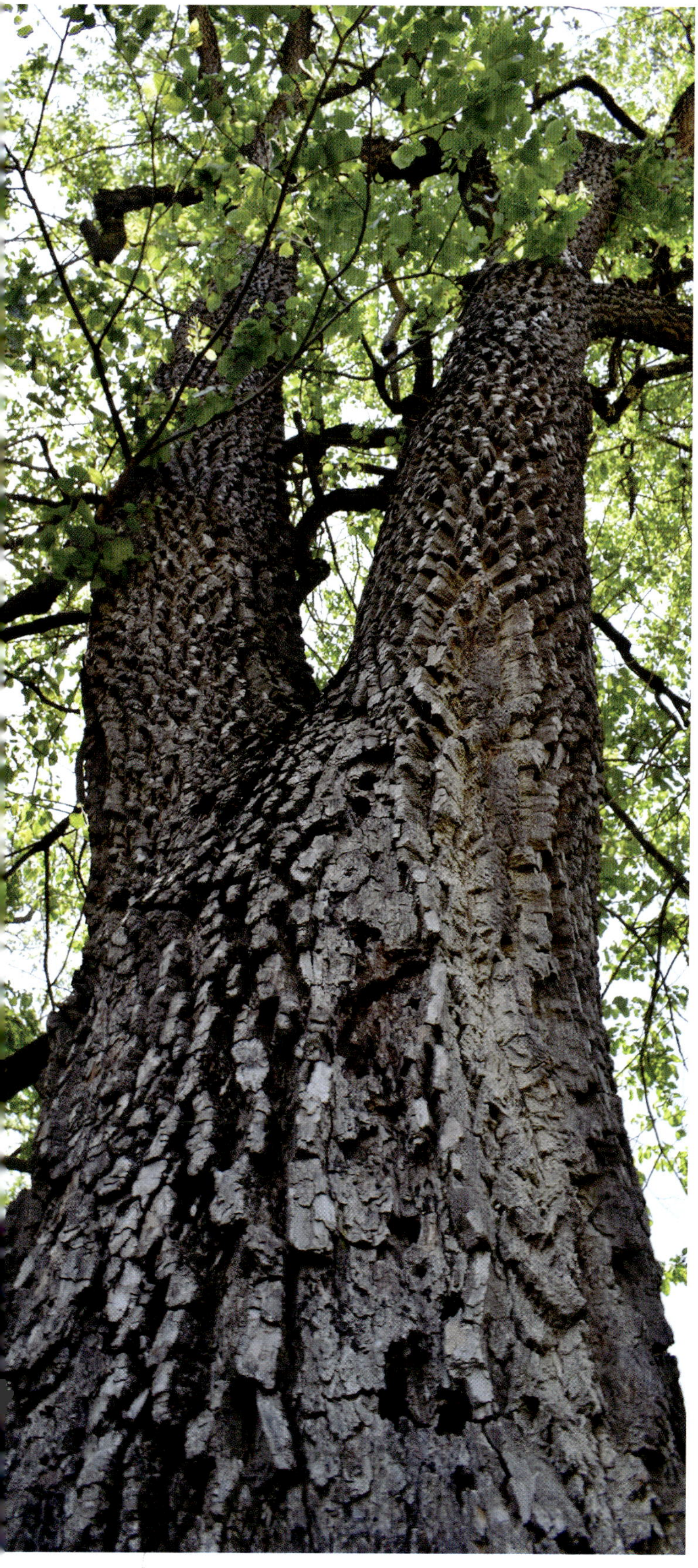

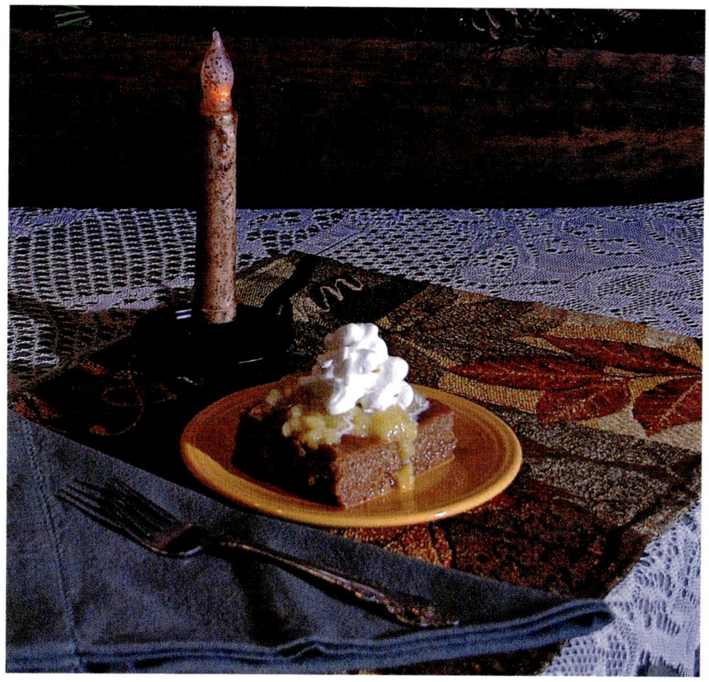

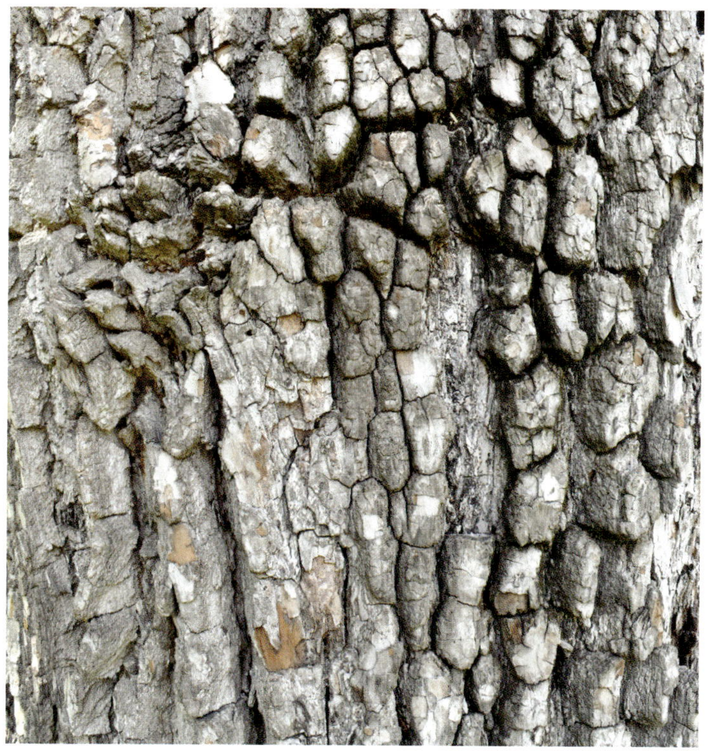

Left: State champion persimmon tree, New Harmony

Top right: Delicious persimmon pudding, a special Indiana treat

Bottom right: Persimmon bark close-up

BALD CYPRESS

(*Taxodium distichum,* var. *distichum*)

Those who speak of wading up to knee-deep in water are in good company with the spectacular bald cypress and its famous knees. To see them in their glory often requires hip boots or rowing in a boat, unless you are lucky enough to visit Twin Swamps in Posey County, where there is a boardwalk right to the middle of a great aggregation of these wondrous trees.

Twin Swamps Nature Preserve was set aside in 1987 to help save one of Indiana's last stands of state threatened bald cypress. These trees, which can live up to 1,000 years, are relatives of the ancient redwoods and sequoias of California. They are common in southern swamps along the Gulf Coast and the Lower Mississippi, reaching their northern limit here, not far from the Wabash River. In fact, southwestern Indiana has several other conservation parcels where the cypress is preserved. The Nature Conservancy protects Goose Pond Cypress Slough southeast of Mt. Vernon. Eagle Slough on the south side of Evansville is another great location for the species and is owned by Sycamore Land Trust. The largest old tree in southern Knox County, which reigned as the state champion for size, is in poor condition now and basically a stump remnant. A new nomination will be sought, and it is very possible one of these pictured trees may be it!

Southern Indiana once had tens of thousands of acres of bald cypress trees, but farming and dams on the Ohio have taken their toll. Seasonal backup from flooding has caused serious concern for survival of the species as well as other bottomland hardwoods such as overcup oak. This effect of high water is very evident at Hovey Lake Fish and Wildlife Area where the remaining stands are periodically flooded to higher levels than normal. In early days the scene would have presented a glorious realm of thousands of cypresses in the backwaters of the Ohio. Imagine floating down the river on flatboats carrying supplies and hearing Carolina paroquets (parakeets) chattering noisily from the trees and perhaps a pair of ivory-billed woodpeckers hammering away here at the far northern end of their geographic range. All along the Ohio it is also likely that thousands of passenger pigeons could be seen bending limbs to the breaking point, their group vocalizations heard for miles. Only old records and perhaps paintings of John James Audubon can remind us of those glorious days when nature was full of mystery and abundance.

The light gray-green emergence of needles in the spring signals awakening of life in the swamp and is accompanied by the joyous sounds of many varieties of birds such as the blue-gray gnatcatcher and the prothonotary warbler. In the heat of the summer, the humidity here is high, reminding one of the South, complete with mosquitoes. Fall is another magical time as the dainty pointed deciduous needles turn a golden color, then brown quickly before falling to the water's surface, temporarily floating, and covering it with a delicate carpet.

As interesting as the shredded appearance of the brown bark are those protruding knees, emerging with determination from the root system below the murky, dark, and somewhat weak tannic acid water. The knees may assist in additional support for the tree and perform other roles that have been proposed. Another notable feature is the spherical cone, about 1 inch in diameter and bearing two seeds. While borne by water in some cases, the seed does not germinate underwater and thus must be carried to a drier setting, especially if areas of the swamp dry out during seasonal cycles.

A very good reference on cypress, albeit focused on Louisiana stands, but with many similarities to our Hoosier specimens, is http://www.tulane.edu/~bfleury/envirobio/swamp.html

Right page: The grand cypress trees and their knees at Twin Swamps Nature Preserve, Posey County

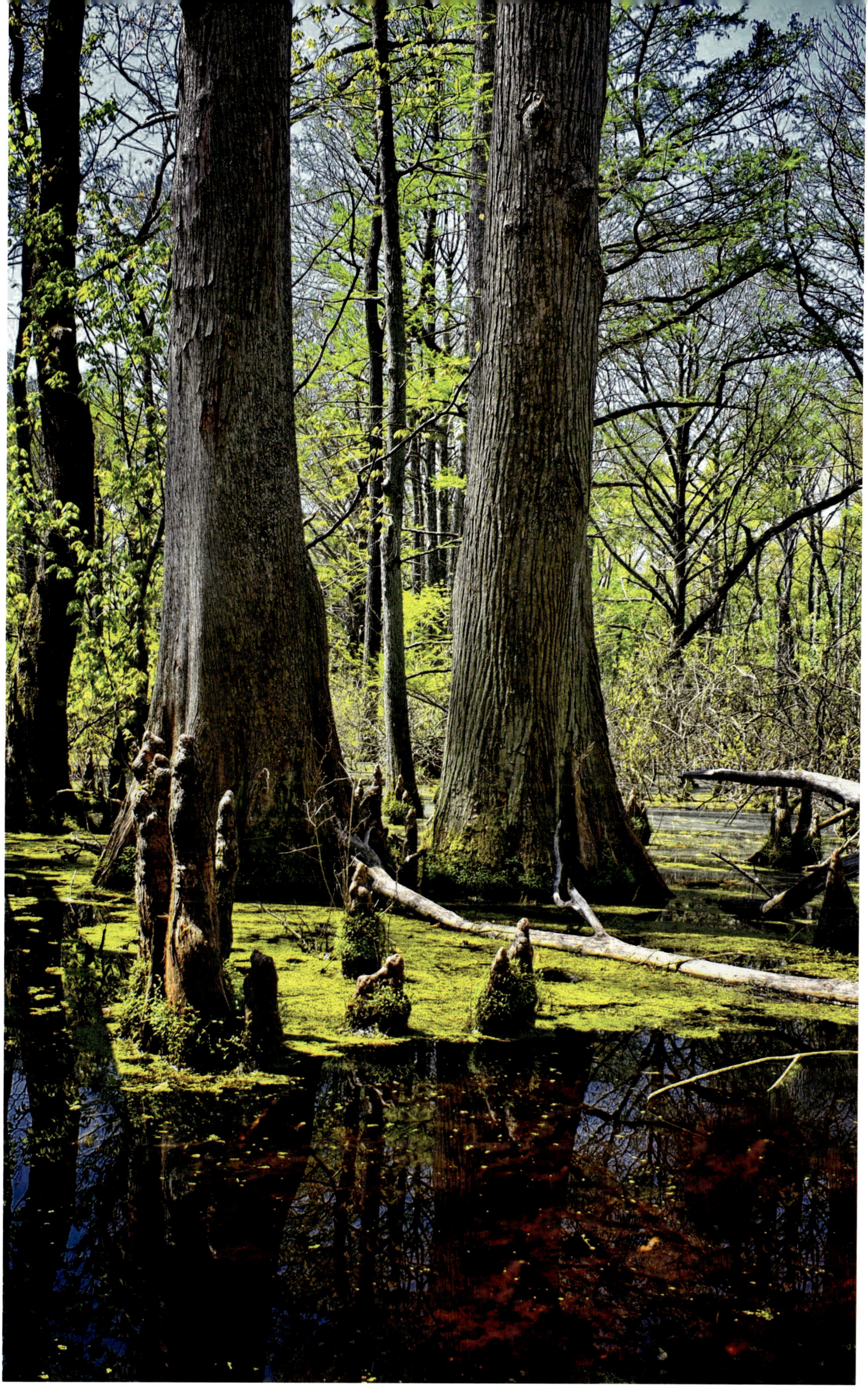

Characteristics

- Large tree, 100 feet in height, 4–10 feet in diameter.
- Delicate lacy ¾-inch needles, two-ranked, deciduous in fall.
- Swollen trunks are common in old trees, accompanied by "knees."
- Male flowers have a slender cone-like structure, female flower is globular, creates the rounded "fruit" cone. Both on same tree (unisexual).

Uses

- A very decay-resistant wood, it is mass produced in the South for siding, decks, nature preserve boardwalks, and many more uses.
- Ornamental and adaptable to dry sites for planting by almost anyone. Has been planted in wetlands such as Muscatatuck National Wildlife Refuge in Jackson/Jennings counties.
- Also used for strip-mined site remediation projects and pollution filtering.
- Tops of old trees open; provide nesting sites for bald eagles, ospreys, herons, and egrets.

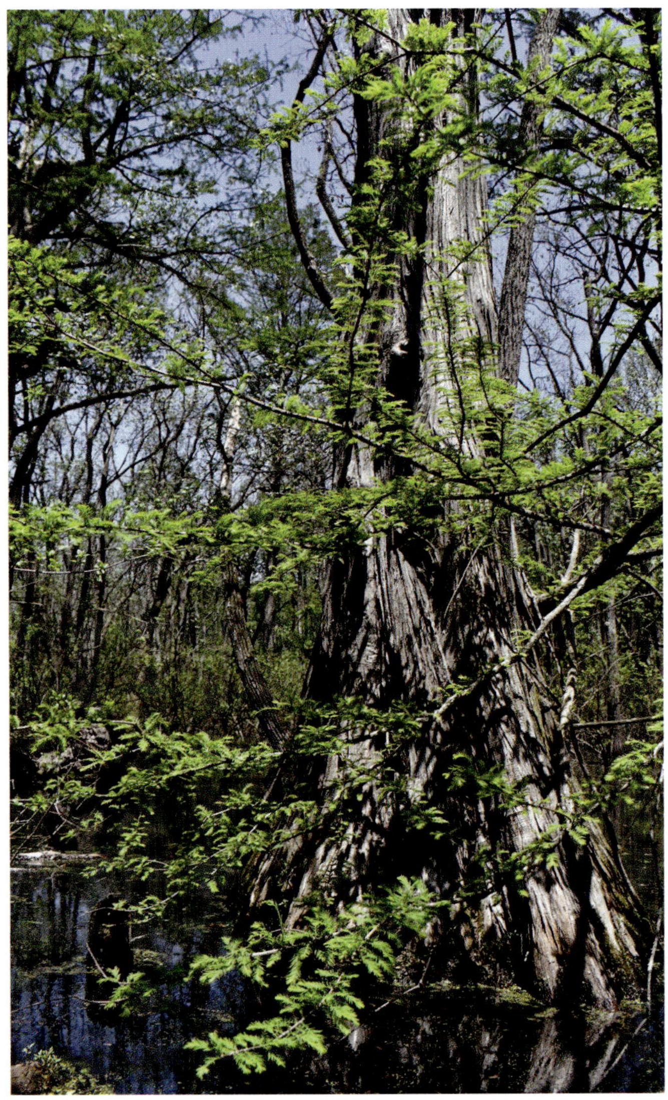

Right: Patriarch bald cypress, Twin Swamps Nature Preserve

Right page: Cypress swamp, Grays Estate Preserve, Posey County

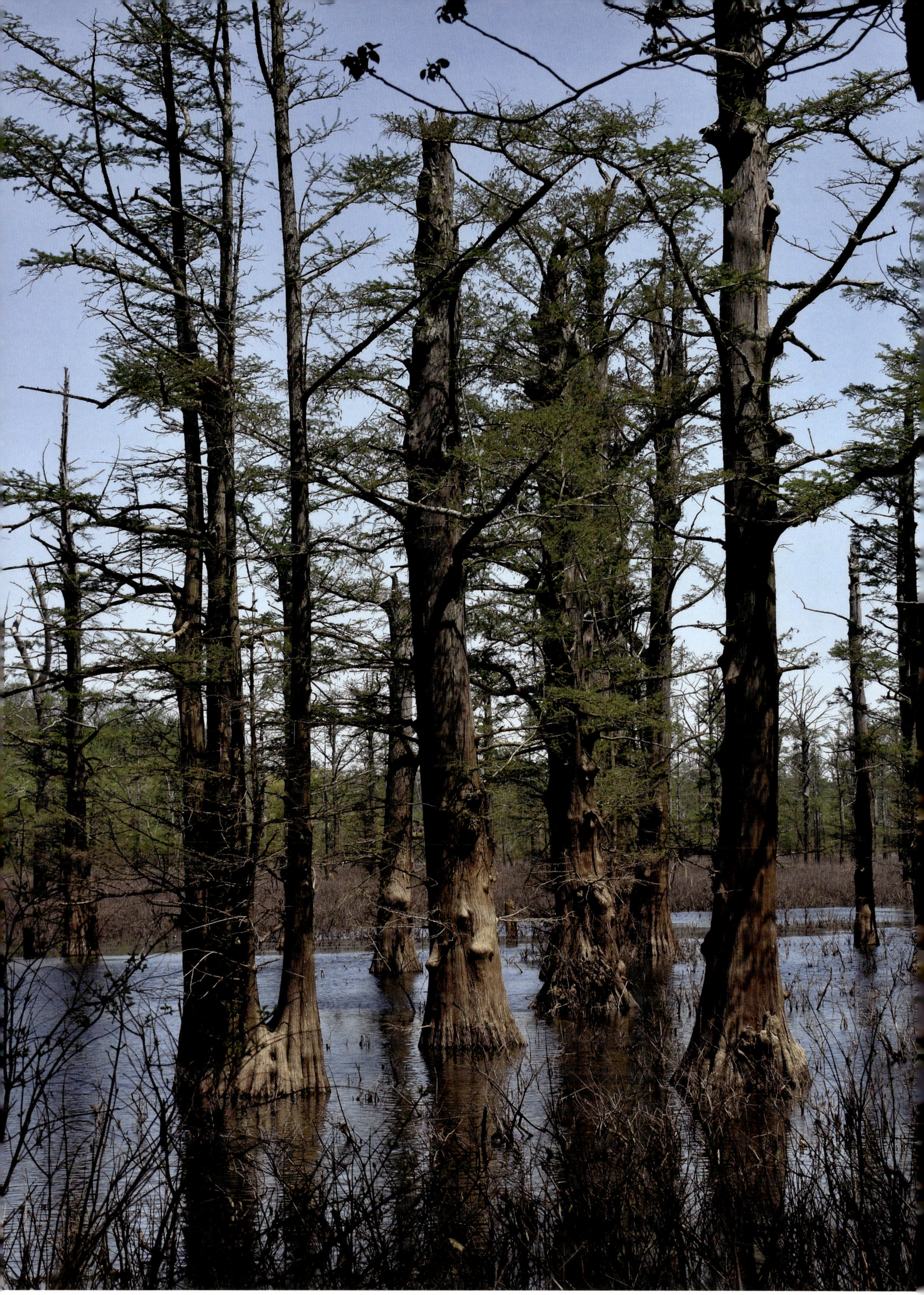

EASTERN HEMLOCK

(Tsuga canadensis)

Clinging to steep bluffs with stubborn determination, these noble descendants of the postglacial Pleistocene epoch rebuffed the heavy snowfall, shedding it from their drooping boughs. Here at Hemlock Bluff Nature Preserve in Jackson County, secretly nestled along Guthrie Creek, dwells a remnant of the past, preferring the north-facing steep slope of siltstone and shale. A steep gravel road leads down to an enchanting valley with the clear stream at the base of the 100-foot bluff. When it was dedicated as a bicentennial project in 1976 there were several outstanding old giants including a state champion 3 feet across. Some of the oldest trees are now gone but regeneration has maintained the overall population quite well.

There are several locations of relict hemlock in Indiana ranging from Jefferson, Crawford, and Perry counties all the way north to Fountain, Montgomery, Parke, and Putnam counties. Slow growing, quite happy with shade and cool temperatures, this tree may grow to 3 feet in diameter, 80 feet high, and mature in 200 years. Eastern hemlock has been estimated to live to 800 years, making it a Methuselah of conifers. The current state champion is in Vanderburgh County on private property and quite a nice specimen, almost 3 feet in diameter.

Content to wait, the germ of its tiny cones finally comes to life in rich humus soils among many kindred companions. Rising finally after decades of patience, it will compete with the surrounding beech and maple, punctuating the hardwood forest with royal green spires and sweeping arms touching and mingling with the competitors. Below them often flows a stream, gurgling or rushing over beds of sedimentary strata fallen from steep hillside exposures, or over marvelous pieces of fossil limestone abundant with crinoids and lampshells. Here in the peace of the natural world, with only the sounds of streams and soft wind, the wondrous hemlocks hold on to their niche in a changing climate, which may indeed contribute as much to their demise as humans have throughout their history. In addition, the arrival from Asia of the hemlock woolly adelgid insect has posed significant danger to the very survival of eastern hemlock, Carolina hemlock, and spruce species in the Appalachians. It has yet to infest our rather disjunct population in Indiana.

In earlier times great old hemlocks were felled, then stripped of their bark to yield the tannins so valued in tanning leather. Often, the remainder of the log, considered not as useful as white pine, was just left in the woods to decay. Today this wasteful practice would not be employed, as several by-product wood industries are available to utilize the residual materials. Hemlock wood is not especially valuable due to its brittle, soft nature and lacks resistance to decay. It is not harvested in Indiana; rather, any groves found are usually protected in preserves by the state, the Nature Conservancy, and land trusts. Other private tracts still occur and should be pursued for preservation or easement protection.

Characteristics

- Individual specimens may reach 3 feet in diameter and 80 feet in height.
- Very small cones to ¾ inch, small brown scales.
- Needles also small, dark green above, silver-green below with two lines.
- Mostly prefers north, cool, moist slopes but occasionally west-facing.
- Roots penetrate rocky soils and cling precariously to steep hillsides, even showing bending from decades of soil creep.

Uses

- Limited uses, lower value wood occasionally used for boxes, crates, rough lumber, pulpwood, or firewood.
- Important as a tannin source in earlier times.
- Great ornamental tree, often planted in Indiana.

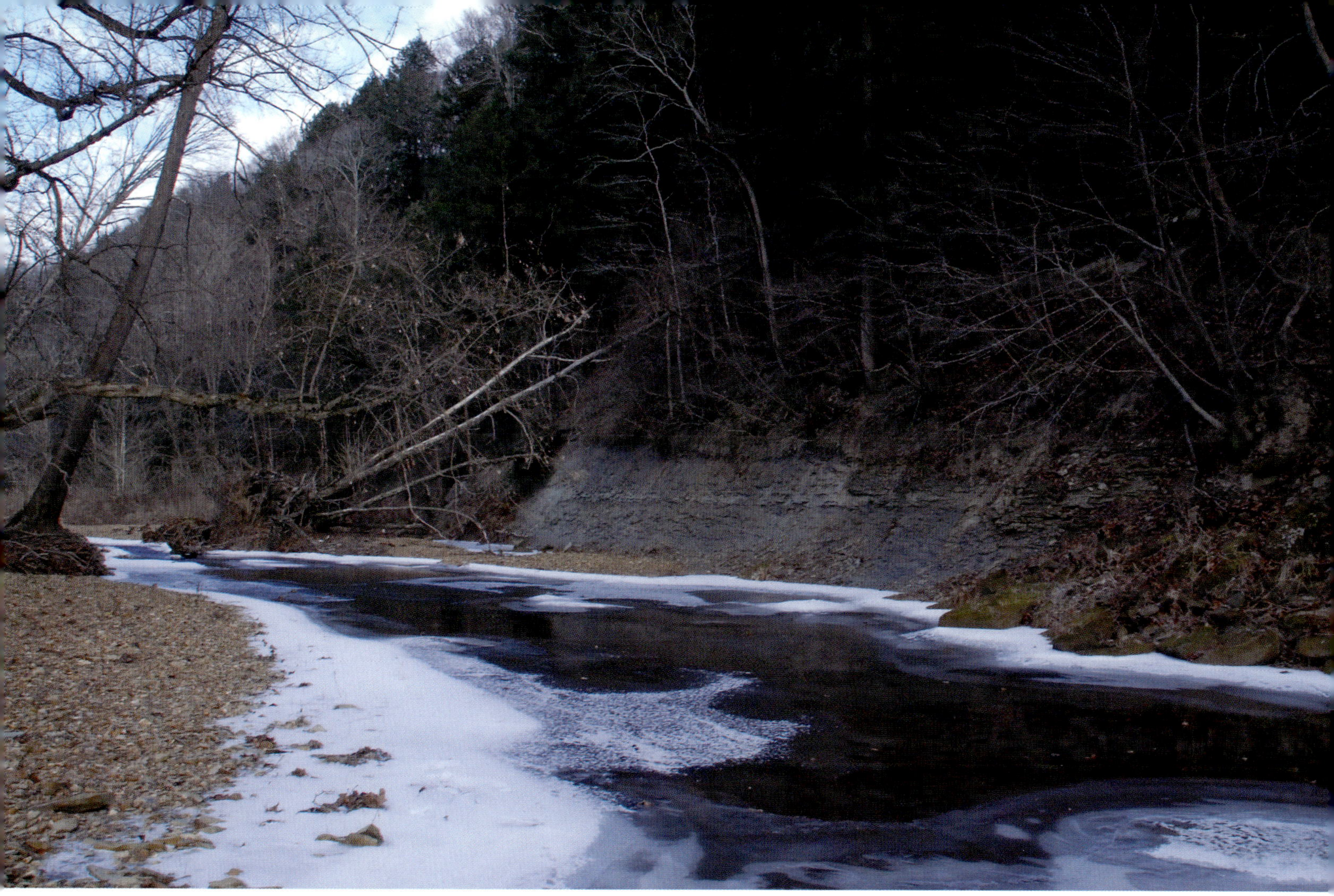

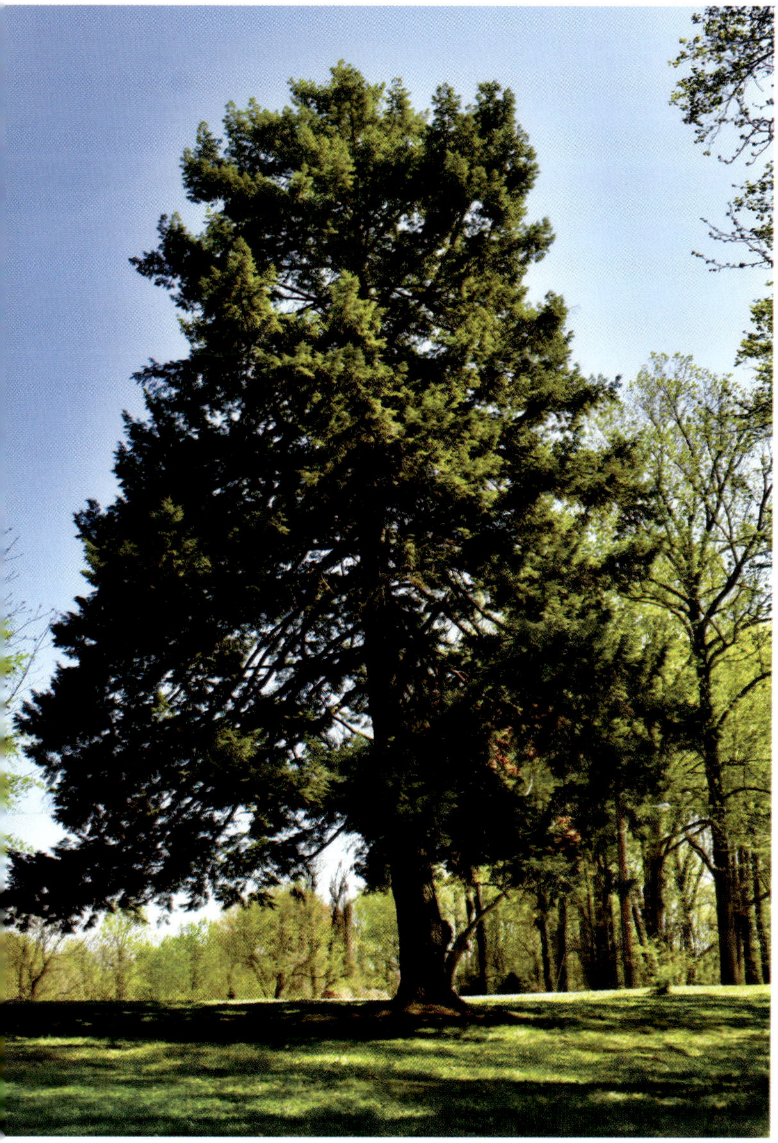

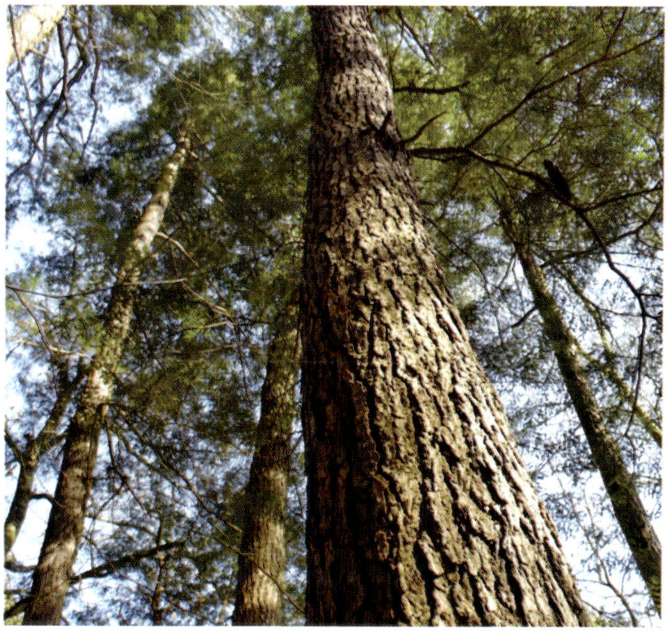

Top: Winter scene at Hemlock Bluff Nature Preserve, Jackson County

Left: State champion eastern hemlock, Evansville

Right: Fine hemlocks at Pine Hills Nature Preserve, Montgomery County

EASTERN REDCEDAR

(Juniperus virginiana)

The name of this evergreen sounds like a true cedar, but it actually belongs in the juniper genus. A long list of attributes comes with one of our most abundant trees. Notice the verdant green, delicate boughs, and feathery gray bark. Teeming with clusters of dainty little purple berries in winter, the snow-laden branches provide ideal food for the cedar waxwing.

Some may refer to this juniper as a lowly and worthless scrub tree. But its past uses were rather amazing—a source for pencils, often used as rough sawn lumber for cabins, for long-lasting fence posts, and of course a favorite for your grandmother's cedar chest, the source of that fragrant smell in her room. Many families fondly remember driving out to a farm field on a cold winter day and cutting down a beautiful cedar for their Christmas tree.

We would elevate this grand tree high up on the list for its shape, yearlong green punctuation of color, and overall uses it has nobly served. The accompanying photo taken in Spring Mill State Park shows a grand specimen, most likely present when the old village was established. Measuring 100 inches in circumference, this tree used to be the state champion, slightly surpassed more recently by another patriarch in Jackson County.

Redcedar occurs almost everywhere in southern Indiana and is a successional tree, not particular about occupying even red clay soil sites. Historically, this species was not as widespread as it is today. It may also be the oldest living tree in the state (Homoya, 2012, p. 127). Some of those aged specimens can be found along the precipitous cliffs of the Ohio River. Large gnarly ones can also be found in Muscatatuck National Wildlife Refuge along former forest roads and fence lines that have returned to nature.

Characteristics

- Up to 3 feet in diameter (rare) and 60 feet high.
- Leaves evergreen, may be braided or needle-like and thus sharp to the touch.
- Flowers unisexual (male and female on two different trees), tiny globe-like or cone shaped.
- Fruit a blue-purple fleshy cone-sphere with 1–4 tiny seeds inside. Lovely when hanging on a snow-covered branch in winter and a welcome morsel for birds.
- Host for cedar-apple rust, therefore affecting quality of nearby apple trees.

Uses

- Windbreaks: Plant eastern redcedar in the outer rows of multirow plantings where it will not be overtopped by taller trees. It can be used in single row windbreaks when a dense, medium height barrier is desired. Tolerates poorer site locations.
- Wildlife: This species provides food and cover for numerous birds and mammals. Nests may be well concealed and protected by the needles. Winter food and protection is particularly important for pheasant, mule deer, and whitetail deer. May provide a sheltered, snow-free bedding spot under the tree.
- Recreation and beautification: It is suitable for screen plantings. The yearlong coloration and attractiveness to wildlife adds variety to recreational sites

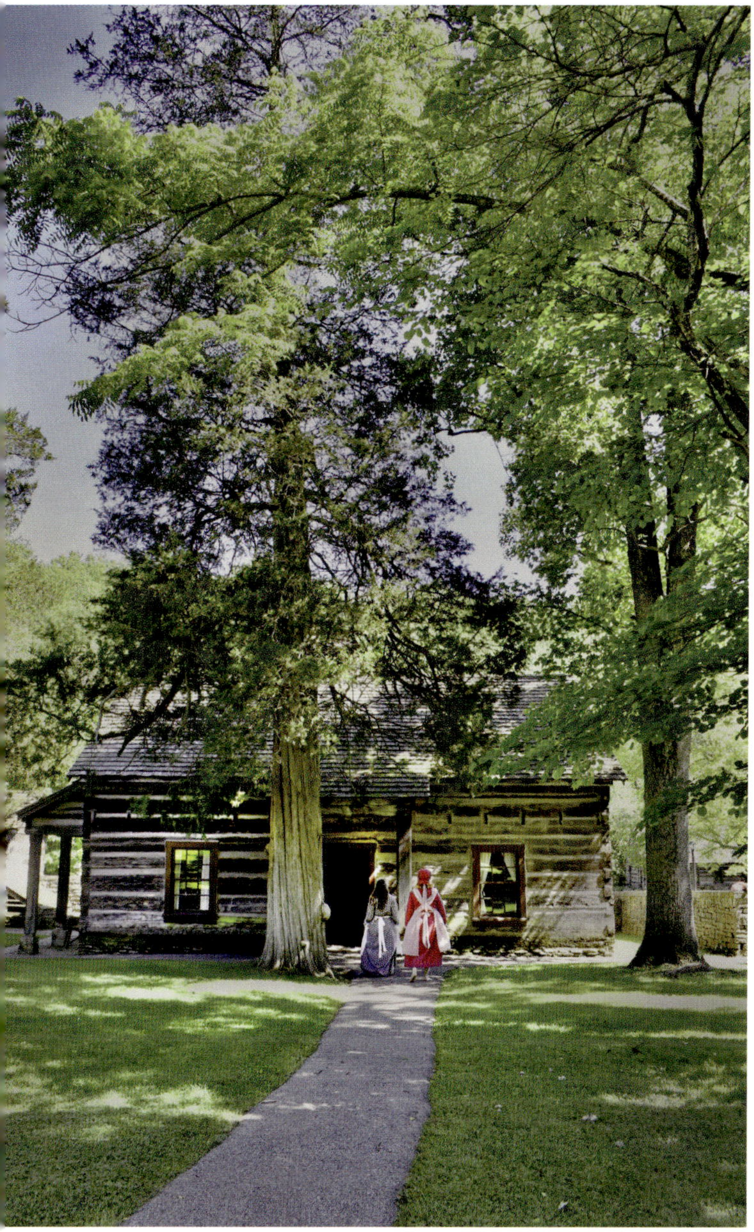

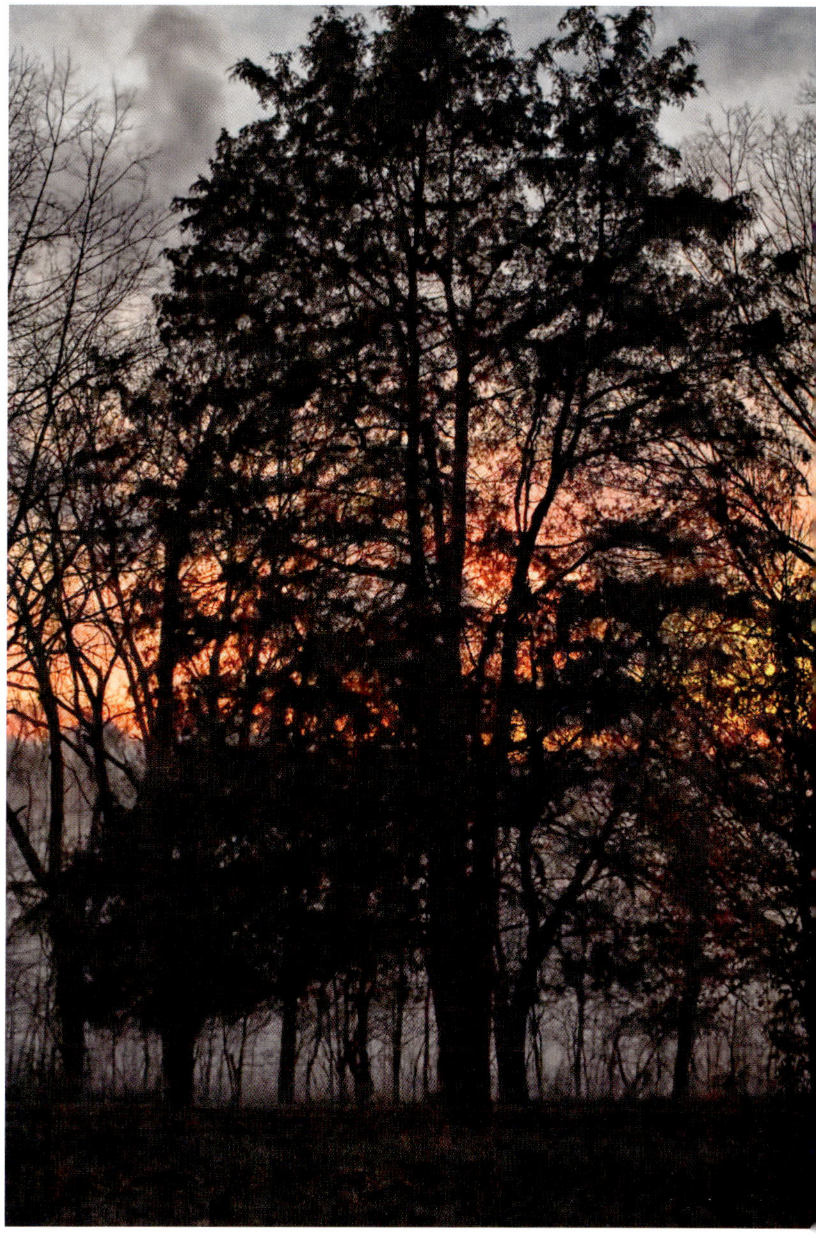

Left: Large eastern redcedar, Pioneer Village, Spring Mill State Park. **Right:** Cedars on foggy sunset, Lawrence County.

EASTERN TAMARACK

(*Larix laricina*)

This fascinating tree, also called eastern larch, is another one of Indiana's deciduous conifers. It is naturally found in the northern tier of counties in wetland bog settings. In an early morning fog in late October, serene lakes with alder, birch, and tamarack create a feel of the wild north country. Prime locations occur at Tamarack Bog Nature Preserve in LaGrange County and the surrounding Pigeon River Wildlife Area. This state threatened tree is generally rather small and often found in clusters around some of the northern Indiana lakes. However, like the bald cypress found in southwestern Indiana, it has been grown as an ornamental in drier settings and seems to adapt well. The state champion is a planted one at Sisters of Providence of Saint Mary-of-the-Woods near Terre Haute. At 3 feet in diameter and 75 feet tall, it is an impressive addition to the many other wonderful trees on campus.

Similar to our native bald cypress and the related western larch (*Larix occidentalis*), its glorious fall show of yellow needles is an impressive sight (see comparative picture). All display the grand color change before the needles turn brown and fall to the forest carpet for the winter. Both the eastern and western species are dwellers in often harsh winter conditions and range all the way to Labrador and Alaska. In some locales the tree goes by the old name "Hackmatack" of Algonquin origin. Tamarack is also unique in that its tiny leaves (needles) are delicate-appearing clusters on short spur branchlets. On close inspection they resemble little bottlebrushes and when touched feel fairly soft and flexible. Also of interest are small ovate cones only ¾ to 1½ inches long, with thin brown scales.

Characteristics

- Depending on latitude and environment may be short and limby or can range to 80 feet in height.
- Small delicate needles, bright pale green in summer, turn yellow in fall and drop.
- Likes open sun and no over-shading.
- Can be planted in wet sites out of its native range. Handsome addition to landscaping.
- Fairly resistant to animal browse.

Uses

- Hard, heavy, strong, durable, and like cypress, is resistant to decay.
- Used for telephone poles, rails, fence posts, and in olden days for shipbuilding.
- Can be a nice addition to ornamental selections.
- Host plant for larvae of several moths.
- Nesting site for several birds.
- Seeds eaten by pine siskins.

Right: Magnificent western larch, Alberta, Canada

Right page: State champion eastern tamarack, Vigo County

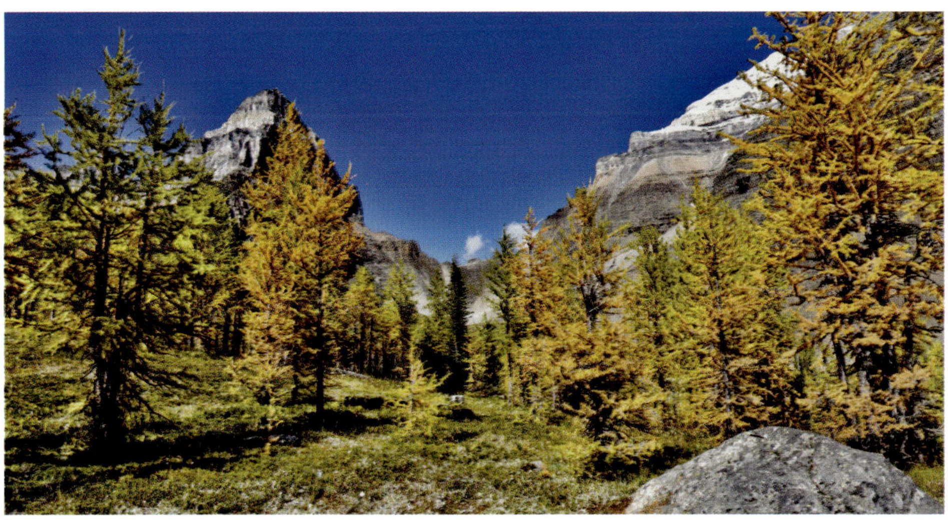

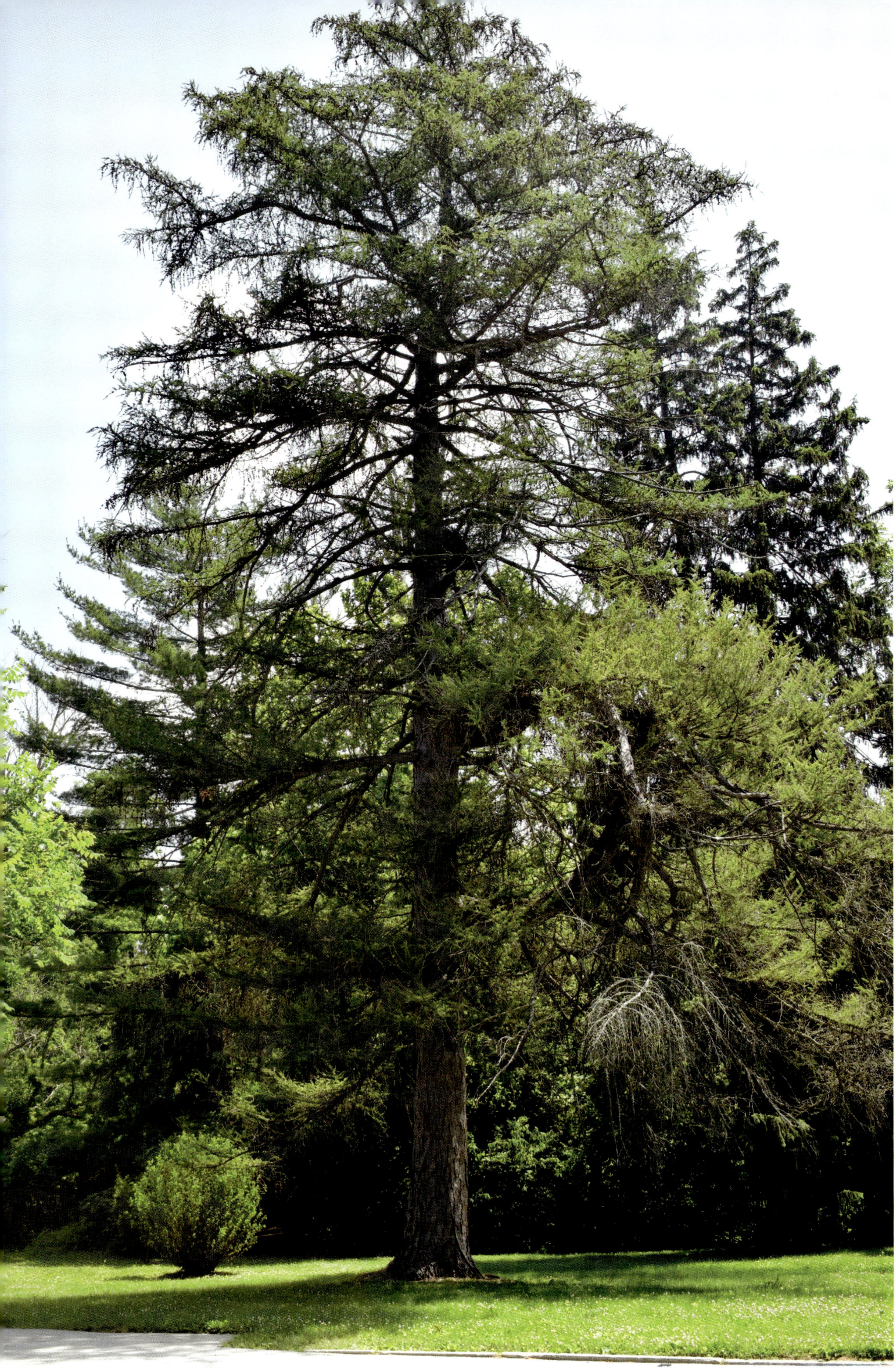

EASTERN WHITE PINE

(*Pinus strobus*)

In winter, verdant long, soft needles laden with fresh snow bending the boughs underneath bring out the beauty of this species. In groups of five per bundle, the needles are quite amenable to touch, unlike many other members of the genus *Pinus*. The bluish-green tint is most pleasing and coupled with a slight aromatic scent. In spring, the male flower of the tree, while not but ½ inch in length, produces a prodigious amount of yellow pollen, the grains of which can travel long distances in the wind. In days past when large stands of pine graced the hills, the yellow was cast in such profusion that it coated everything in the area. The cone develops from the separate female part of the tree, subsequently arriving at its gently curved 6–8-inch length and sometimes bearing a whitish resin coating. The branches, if broken, will certainly alert you to the tacky amber, and upon cutting a pine, you may well regret all the stickiness encountered. As the tree matures to old age, its smooth gray bark of youth becomes dark, somewhat ridged, and fissured, giving it the appearance of a weathered survivor of many years.

Upon arrival in North America, early frontiersmen encountered vast stands of pure white pine—extensive, large, and immediately available for use. Conflict developed quickly, as the lands belonging to the English Crown were considered their exclusive domain. Proclamations were issued that the finest pines be reserved for the Crown, as they were sorely needed to supply ship masts for the fleet. Restrictions did not sit well with colonists, who themselves wanted to control their own destiny, including uses of the virgin forests. This issue itself became one of the driving forces for impending separation from England. During the Revolutionary War, some of these great pines were turned into tall straight masts for colonial ships. Peattie (*A Natural History of Trees of Eastern and Central North America,* 1966) writes: "In three hundred years of its exploitation, white pine, more than any other tree in the country built this nation, literally and figuratively" (p. 11). He further writes eloquently much more about the fascinating history of this great species.

Within decades what was once an almost unlimited supply of majestic white pine in New England began to disappear. As expansion moved westward across Michigan, Wisconsin, and Minnesota, their great forests were also decimated. Today it is still present as second or third growth, none attaining those great heights of 150 feet and clear of limbs to 80 feet as encountered by the first lumbermen. Nonetheless, white pine is still in demand if found or grown, but other fast-growing pines in the south generally replace its traditional uses.

Found as a native in Indiana, its historic range is limited to a few western and northwestern counties, as noted by Deam and Shaw (*Trees of Indiana,* 1953). White pine is found in other county records in southern Indiana, including the Knobstone country. It is hard to establish the origin of seed for these locations since they are disjunct from the other Indiana sites. It is listed as a threatened species on Indiana's list.

Right page: State champion eastern white pine, Brown County

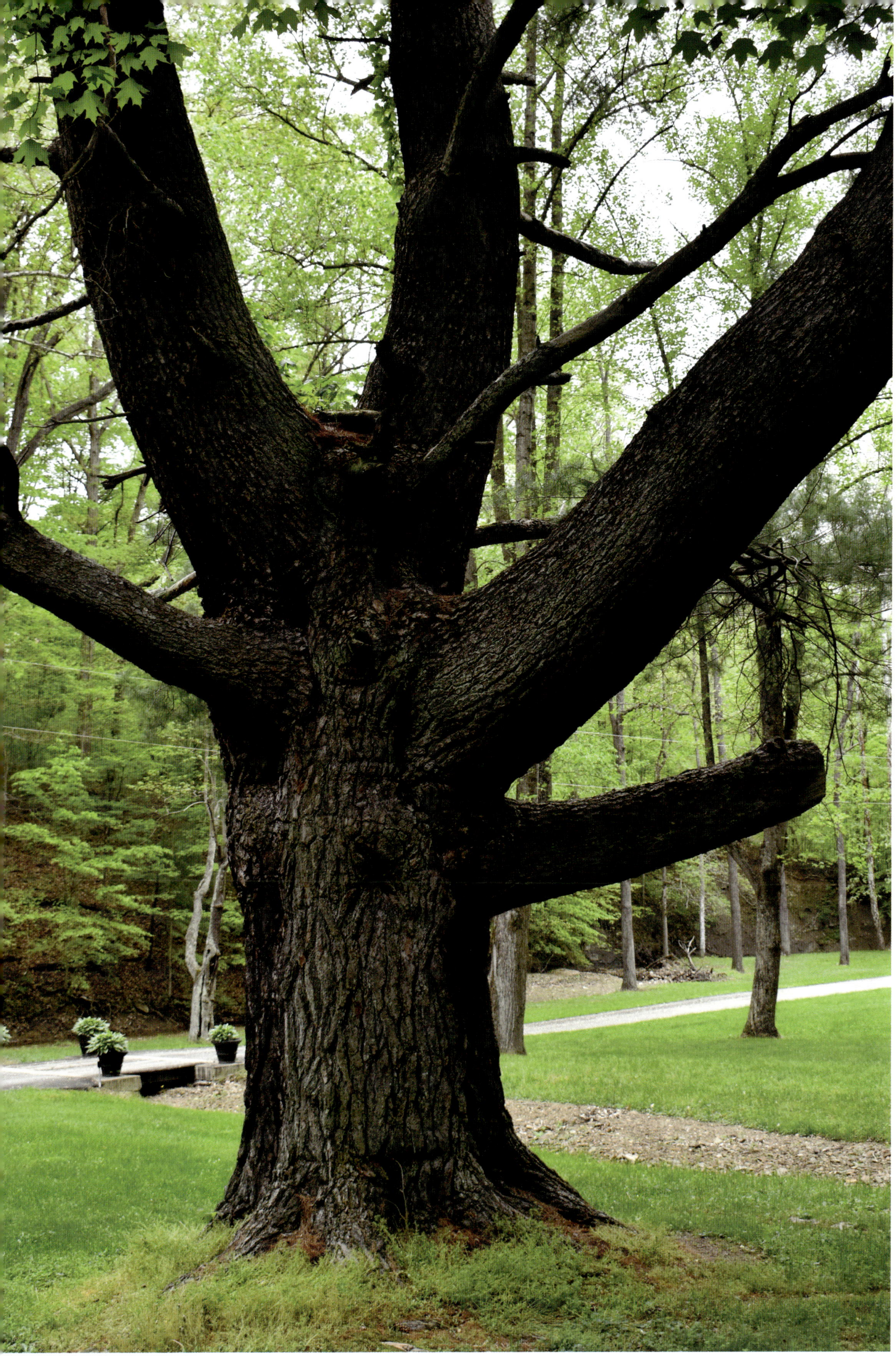

The current state champion is in Brown County and was a planted specimen. That large specimen was 4½ feet in diameter and 87 feet tall, impressive for Indiana. The other location visited was Pine Hills Nature Preserve in Shades State Park, Montgomery County. This remarkable area was the first nature preserve of the Indiana Chapter of the Nature Conservancy in 1960. These 600 acres are one of the most visited preserves and most spectacular. Pines there are native and recorded by Deam. Lindsey (1969 also writes about the great variety of old-growth species. The pine diameters approach 2½ feet with heights of 50 feet and occur with hemlock as a companion relict species. The mix of hardwoods, pine, and hemlock on cliffs, steep hillsides, and creek bottoms is a most rewarding scene that everyone should see.

Characteristics

- One of our largest native evergreens, to 100+ feet.
- Soft blue-green needles in bundles of five.
- In original forests, tall and straight but in plantings, may become limby and less attractive.

Uses

- Originally the most important tree east of the Mississippi.
- Uses were profound in ships, bridges, beams, early home construction, furniture, and interior trim.
- Planted as an erosion control tree in the 1930s and 1940s.
- Still handsome as an ornamental or windbreak.
- Good tree for bird nests of several species.

Right page: White pines were often planted at old homesteads, such as this one in eastern Lawrence County

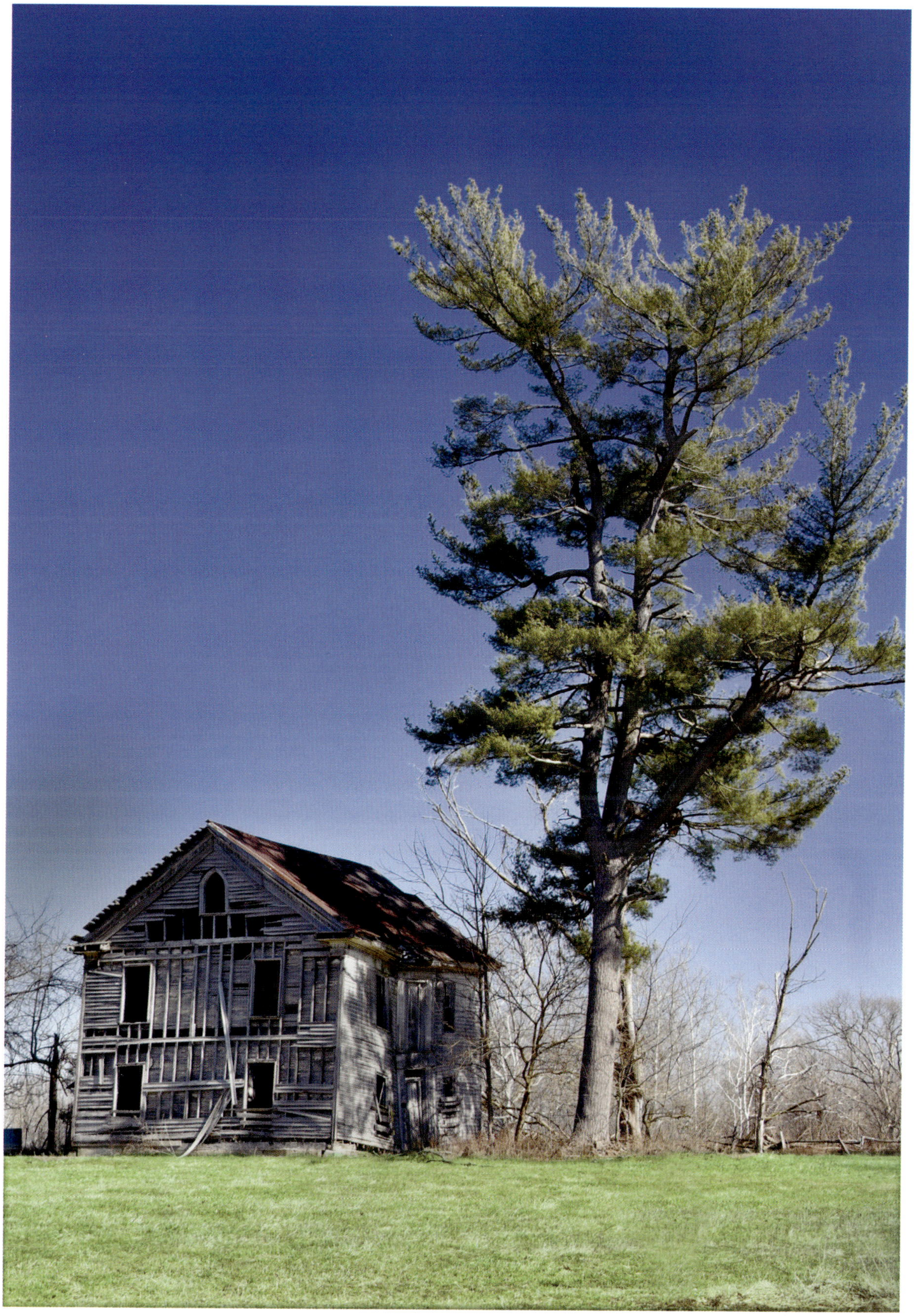

VIRGINIA PINE

(*Pinus virginiana*)

Passed over and mostly demoted to a low level of acclamation, this species is nevertheless quite important. Huge numbers of Virginia pine have been planted for years to control erosion. Also known as scrub pine, it is hardy and adaptable to poor sites, thus fitting right in when needed the most. These trees require little attention, and with a scraggly look, get but a furtive look from passers-by. Very common in the East, they may form almost pure stands. With rough bristle-tipped cones and slender twigs, these trees add a surrealistic art to winter-driven snow. Here in Indiana, Virginia pine may be found planted along with other pines more noble in appearance. It is often a selected choice for surface mine reclamation sites, where sheer tenacity, cheap cost, and determination make it useful.

The small 1½–2-inch slightly twisted needles occur in a bundle of two. Its cone has a sharp tip, which helps distinguish it from the jack pine (mostly in northern Indiana). Even after the cone opens and releases seeds scattered about, it remains on the tree for years.

Inspection of an old Virginia pine planting might show nests among the tangled limbs—those of squirrels, a crow, or perhaps a Cooper's hawk. Pecking into the cone hanging tightly on its limb might be a nuthatch, finch, or chickadee, going after that seed before it falls.

The champion specimen found in Floyd County was actually a fairly handsome tree attaining a height of 115 feet and diameter of 2 feet. Even though this tree was planted, Virginia pine does occur in the area naturally. One might occasionally find these old survivors upon the rough, rocky tops of the Knobstone Escarpment, predominantly on sandstone ridges.

Characteristics

- Typically growing to a height of 50 feet and a foot or two in diameter.
- Often considered scraggly and of poor form; assigned that status by humans, not necessarily by its own brethren.
- Needles in bundles of two, cones 1½ to 3 inches long, sharp-tipped.
- Bark scaly brown.

Uses

- Light, soft wood makes it relegated mostly to pulpwood or firewood.
- Does provide erosion control and suitable for poor terrain.
- Some wildlife values for nesting and seeds, low browse in harsh winters.

Right page: State champion Virginia pine, Floyd County

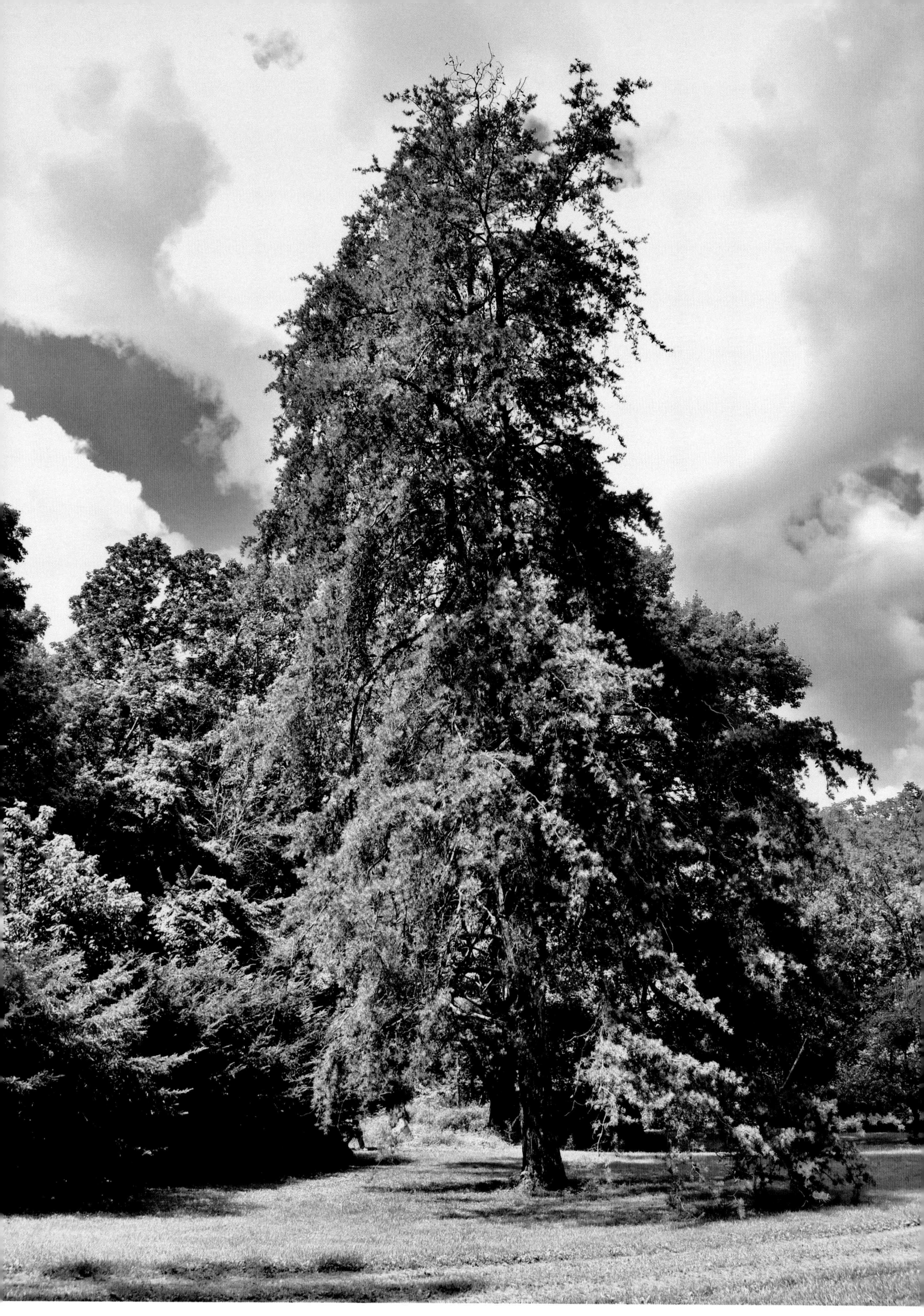

SASSAFRAS

(Sassafras albidum)

Sassafras is intriguing, both from word origin and from its lineage. First described by Spanish botanist Nicolas Monardes in 1569, the term comes from the Latin *saxifraga.* The genus *Sassafras* has three living species worldwide and one extinct, preserved in fossils from the Eocene period.[17] It is part of the Lauraceae family, which are generally aromatic evergreens. But sassafras varies from the norm and is deciduous.

Sassafras trees are one of those immediate occupiers of cleared fields or forests. They and tuliptrees act quickly as new homesteaders in company with dogwood, redbud, and occasionally black locust. Individuals may be of small stature, such as those growing in the sandy successional area of Indiana Dunes State Park, or may range to specimens such as our state champion at Harmonie State Park in Posey County. That imposing giant is almost 5 feet across and 70 feet tall.

Bark of old-age specimens is often very furrowed. The wood is rather light, soft, and weak, but has been valued for its interesting grain pattern, creating very beautiful cabinets and trim. Whereas the spring flowering blooms are rather inconspicuous, the new glossy leaves that burst forth are intriguing with oval, mitten, or occasionally three-lobed shapes. As emergent leaves were yet to show, the often-unnoticed blooms were on splendid display on the gorgeous Vanderburgh County champion tree.

Sassafras has an extraordinary history, fascinating in every detail and eloquently described by Peattie (pp. 291–297). Medicinal values ascribed to this tree reach far back to Native Americans who called it *Paumae* and passed the lore to the French and Spanish in the New World. They incorporated several parts of the tree into remedies for all sorts of conditions. Although it is not normally considered edible, it is said that chewing the leaves may increase one's saliva. The roots of sassafras have long been used for teas and root beer flavoring. However, safrole, its active ingredient, is used in the production of the street drug widely known as "ecstasy." Although sassafras oil was once widely used as a fragrance and flavoring agent, safrole is now recognized as a carcinogen, meaning that it is a cancer-causing agent.

The magnificence of sassafras in the fall comes about when the leaves turn shades of yellow, orange, red, or even nuanced pink. Contrasted with a deep azure October sky as a backdrop, and in juxtaposition with black gum or sumac, we have a most vivid display of sheer beauty.

Characteristics

- Young trees have green twigs and stems. Mature trunks are dark brown and fissured.
- Three leaf shapes possible on the same tree.
- The root is cinnamon colored or even yellow-red. It is very aromatic.
- Blue fruits are desired by birds and thus seeds are carried widely to new open areas.
- Old mature sassafras trees are often hollow and may serve as dens or bee trees.

Uses

- Less shrinking in drying than other hardwoods.
- Odor thought to drive away bugs; used in pioneer days for beds, floors, and even chicken coops.
- Flavorings and teas.
- Handsome color and grain, easy to work. Makes fine trim moldings and can be found in old antique furniture as well.

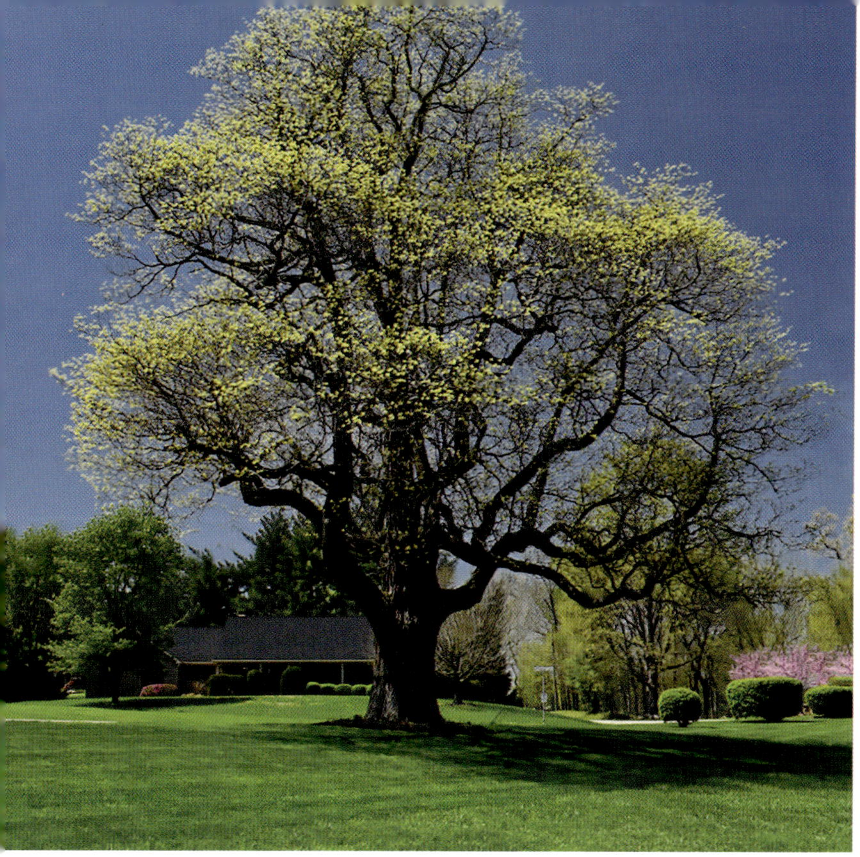

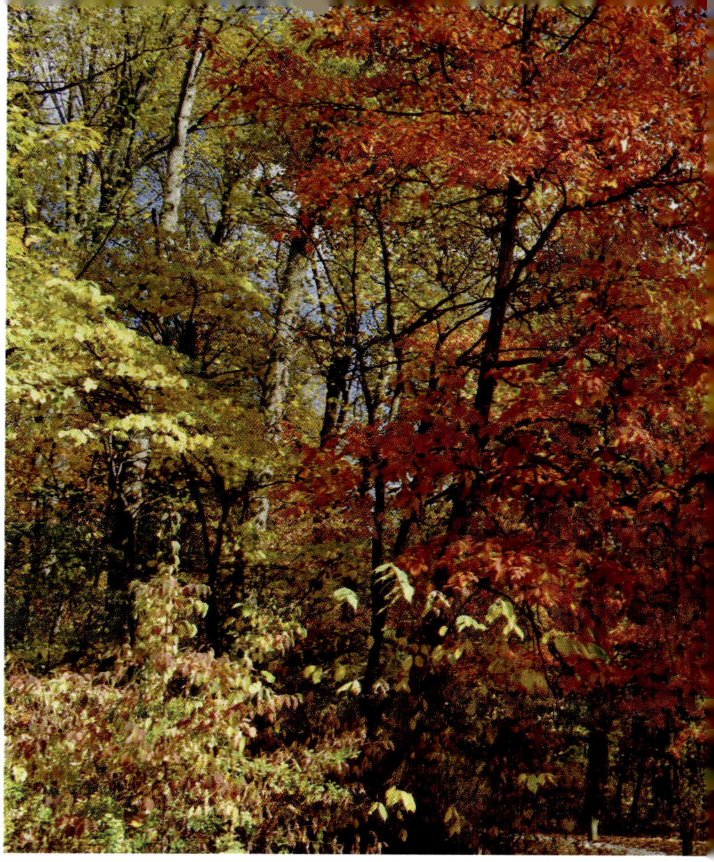

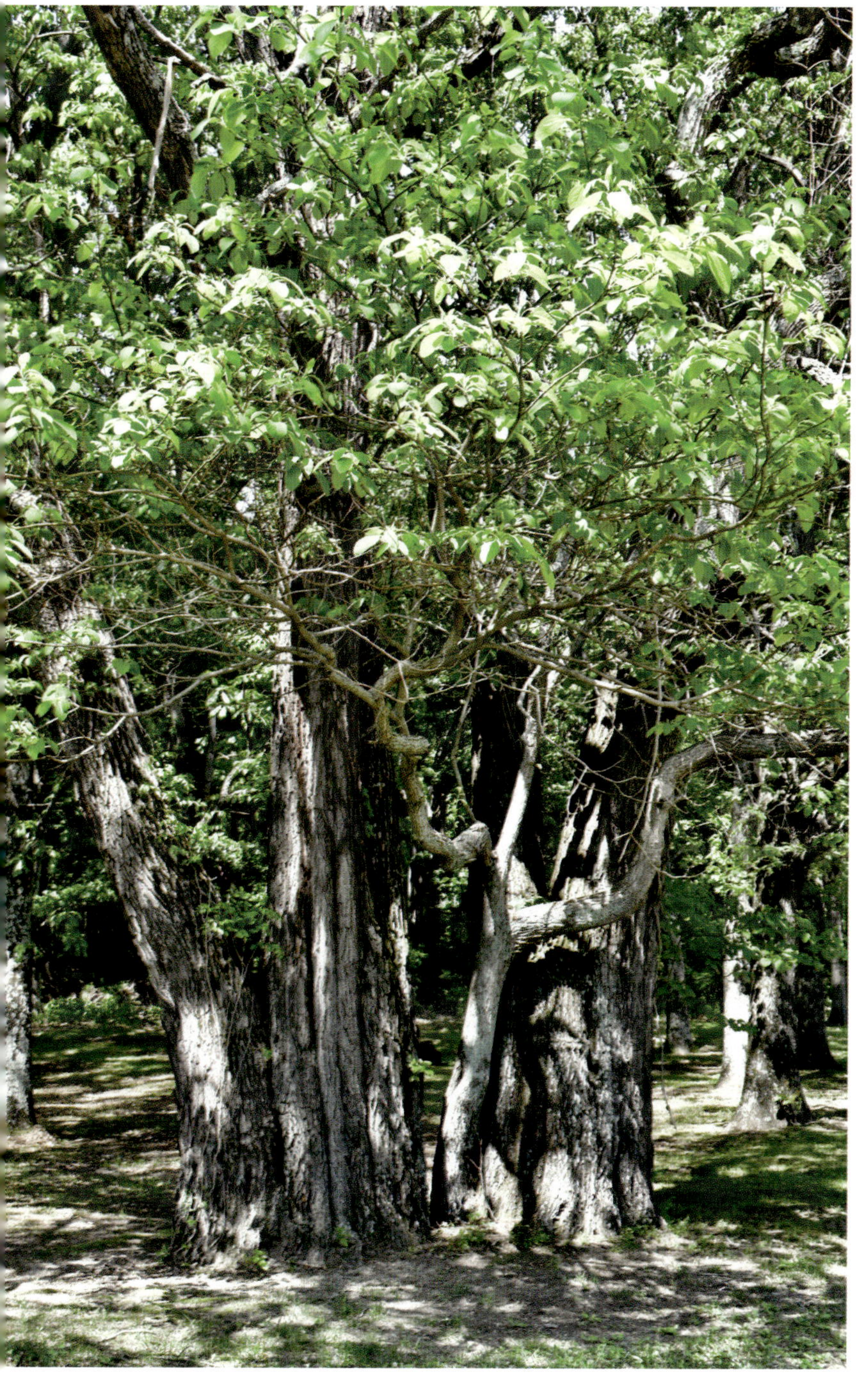

Top left: The perfect sassafras, Vanderburgh County champion

Top right: Sassafras in fall glory, McCormick's Creek State Park

Left: State champion sassafras, Harmonie State Park

SWEETGUM

(Liquidambar styraciflua)

Also known as redgum, star-leaved gum, and even alligator-wood, this most intriguing tree with its "fluid amber" is a well-known handsome presence in the woods and a chosen species for home landscaping. Tracking down the state record holder resulted in a trip to the grand Wesselman Park in Evansville. Led into the very impressive woods by the city's urban forester, Shawn Dickerson, we arrived at the huge tree standing among several others almost as large. The specimen was a fine one indeed, over 4 feet across, rough bark marching up the trunk to high limbs of smoother gray texture, and crowning out at 137 feet (fifth tallest of all Indiana champions in the Big Tree Register).

In southern Indiana lowlands and bottom hardwood forests, sweetgum also appears with companion species such as pin oak, red maple, overcup oak, and others that tolerate wet conditions.

Cabeza de Vaca apparently discovered the sweetgum in the mid-1600s during his expeditions into Florida. This new find established the gum tree in America, adding to similar known species in Asia. But sweetgum's origins are much further in the past, as fossil specimens have been found dating far back in geological time. Related species of gums evidently thrived throughout the world when continental positions were much different from today.

Extraction of the fluid amber resin from peeling back the bark of young trees or by tapping older ones yielded a sweet-smelling liquid that could be gently heated, strained, and canned. Many uses were made of this extracted exudate: treatment of sores and dysentery by doctors of the Confederate Army, as a primitive chewing gum, a soap additive, adhesive, and even mixed with tobacco for flavoring.

Gumwood has also been important for over a hundred years in making furniture, cabinets, boxes, and crates. When properly dried, some of the rosier colored heartwood can be rendered into fine-quality lumber resembling walnut. The lighter colored sapwood boards can be separated out and also make an admirable product.

As far as landscaping uses, the tree is hard to resist. The unique star-shaped leaf, light green on top, turns a wondrous yellow-red-scarlet in the fall and adds glory to any scene. In a deep forest, the leaf color in the high canopy is not so noticeable, but in an open setting it punches through with a great show.

In the open, sweetgum may not be more than 40 feet in height and have many side branches, although this is not a negative. What it does produce with proliferation is the unique spiny gumball, its fruiting body. This is a very distinguished adornment waiting to fall in profusion to the yard below. There it creates quite a messy clutter and can even roll when walked upon.

But all in all, the judgment of the sweetgum must leave us to conclude that this is a fine complement to a woods or parkland. Of special note is that sweetgum was one of two trees (the other being tuliptree) whose seeds were carried onboard the space shuttle in 1984 with Indiana's own Purdue aeronautical engineer Charlie Walker of Lawrence County. Those seeds returned to earth, were planted, and progeny survive to this day.

Characteristics

- Can become quite large in diameter and up to 100 feet tall, with spreading crown.
- Star-shaped beautiful leaves, alternate on sometimes corky twigs.
- Bark gray and relatively smooth on young trees, fissured, scaly, rough on large trees.
- Buds shiny, pointed, green-brown scales, may be sticky.
- Spiny gumball with many wind-dispersed seeds.

Uses

- Historically for pharmaceuticals, flavorings, even perfumes.
- Valuable wood for many uses as described above.

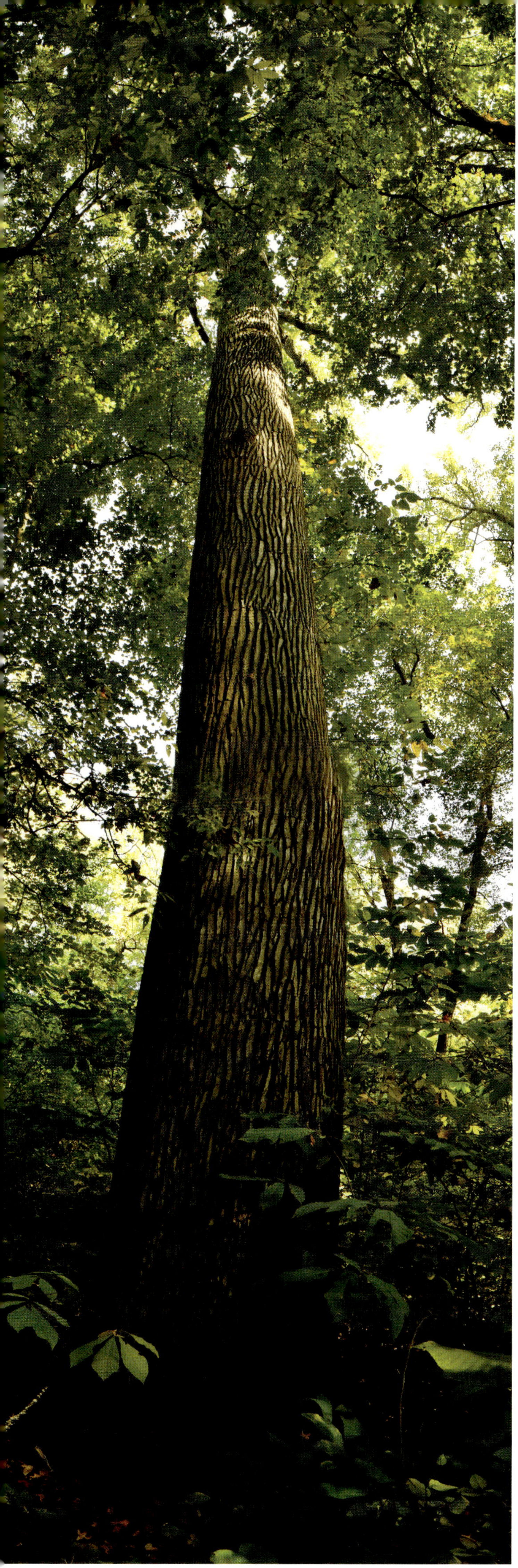

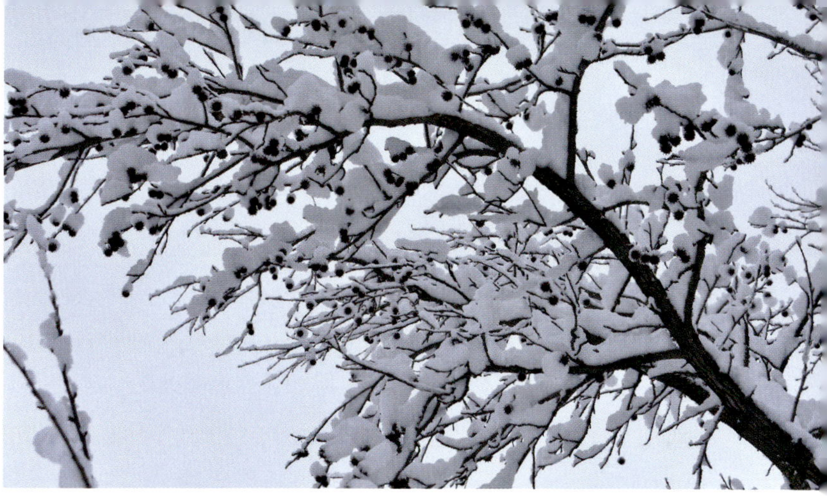

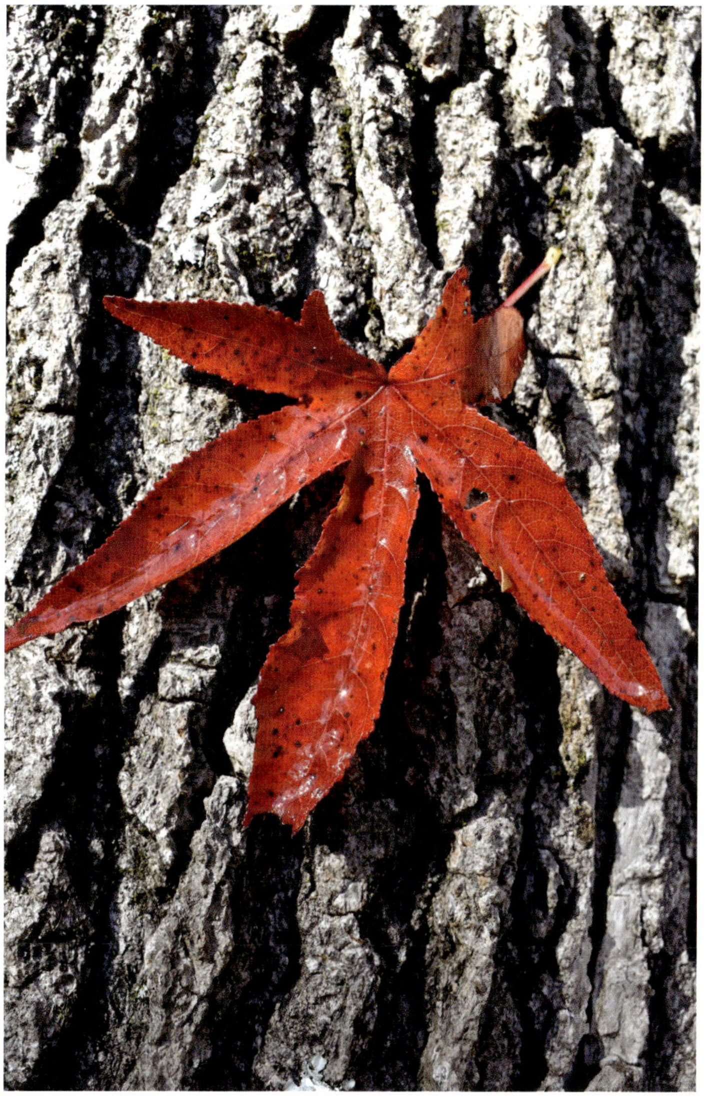

Left: State champion sweetgum, Wesselman Woods

Top right: Sweetgum balls hang on tight in winter

Bottom right: Sweetgum leaves show flaming reds or yellows in fall

AMERICAN SYCAMORE

(Platanus occidentalis)

Gracing wetlands, riverbanks, parks, and yards, this beautiful tree always stands out for its white peeling bark, sheer majestic form, and addition of variety to the landscape. No matter the season, sycamore demands the eye pay due recognition. With full large green leaf in summer, yellow-brown fall color, and sheer contrast of its white ghostly figure against azure skies in winter, sycamore is always admirable. It ranks as a high favorite in company with oak, maple, and beech as worthy of true appreciation.

Sycamore has long been part of Hoosier song, folklore, and history. Paul Dresser, in our state song, mentions it in "On the Banks of the Wabash, Far Away." Lyrics of Hanley and MacDonald's "Indiana," better known as "Back Home Again in Indiana," also feature the famous tree.

Early explorers and voyageurs wrote about the massive giants along river corridors upon which they plied, especially the mighty Ohio. Sycamore is the largest girth tree in the central and eastern United States. To realize the immensity of the largest ones from early times, take a string 47 feet long, bring it into the biggest room of your house, and make a circle from it. Here grows a tree of this size to 150 feet, as tall as a 15-story office building. Imagine in old age this tree now hollowed out at its base, providing a den for a mother bear and cubs. If not occupied, a pioneer family could "hole up" there until their log cabin could be constructed. Even James Audubon remarked upon a visit to an old giant that way above must have had an opening permitting hundreds of swifts to fly in at night and nest, creating a thunderous racket upon entering and then leaving again in the morning (Peattie, 1966, pp. 319–320).

An extraordinary sycamore (now gone) near Worthington, Indiana, should be mentioned. The historical information is on the Visit Greene County website.

> Located in the Worthington City Park just northwest of downtown Worthington on Worthington Street, a monument containing one of the surviving remnants of this tree, the western limb (23 ft. 2 in. in circumference) and smaller of the two, was moved to this location in 1925 after it succumbed to a storm. The Great Sycamore Tree was originally located on the Sloan-Dixon Farm about a ½ mile east of Worthington in the White River Bottoms of Highland Township. Estimated at 500 years old, the Oxford Journal of Heredity reported in September 1915 that the tree was the largest "Broad-Leaf Tree in the United States" measuring 42 feet 3 inches in circumference. In its heyday, the shady tree was a popular place [for] young lovers because the tree was so hollow one could have picnics inside the trunk and so large that a horse and buggy could easily be hidden behind it.[18]

Another memorable sycamore was located near Kokomo. The city's Highland Park brochure states: "The Sycamore Stump is one of Howard County's few remaining landmarks of the past. The old tree originally stood in the west end of Howard County about two miles north of New London. According to the description of those who remember the tree, it was a hundred feet high before storms broke it down to a huge, hollow stump. The trunk was more than 50 feet in circumference and one of its lower branches was reported to be eight feet in diameter. The tree was estimated to be 1,500 years old according to newspaper articles."

In 1916, the stump was moved where it could be preserved as a relic of the county's pioneer period. It is on display at the Visitors Center located in Highland Park.

Today, sycamore is still admired and adds interest wherever it is found. The state record tree in Johnson County is over 8 feet in diameter and 120 feet high, with a crown spread of over 100 feet. It is indeed a magnificent reminder of what was once a common occurrence. The phenomenon of peeling bark on the lower sections of tree exposes varying layers of white, tan, and gray, lending to its somewhat

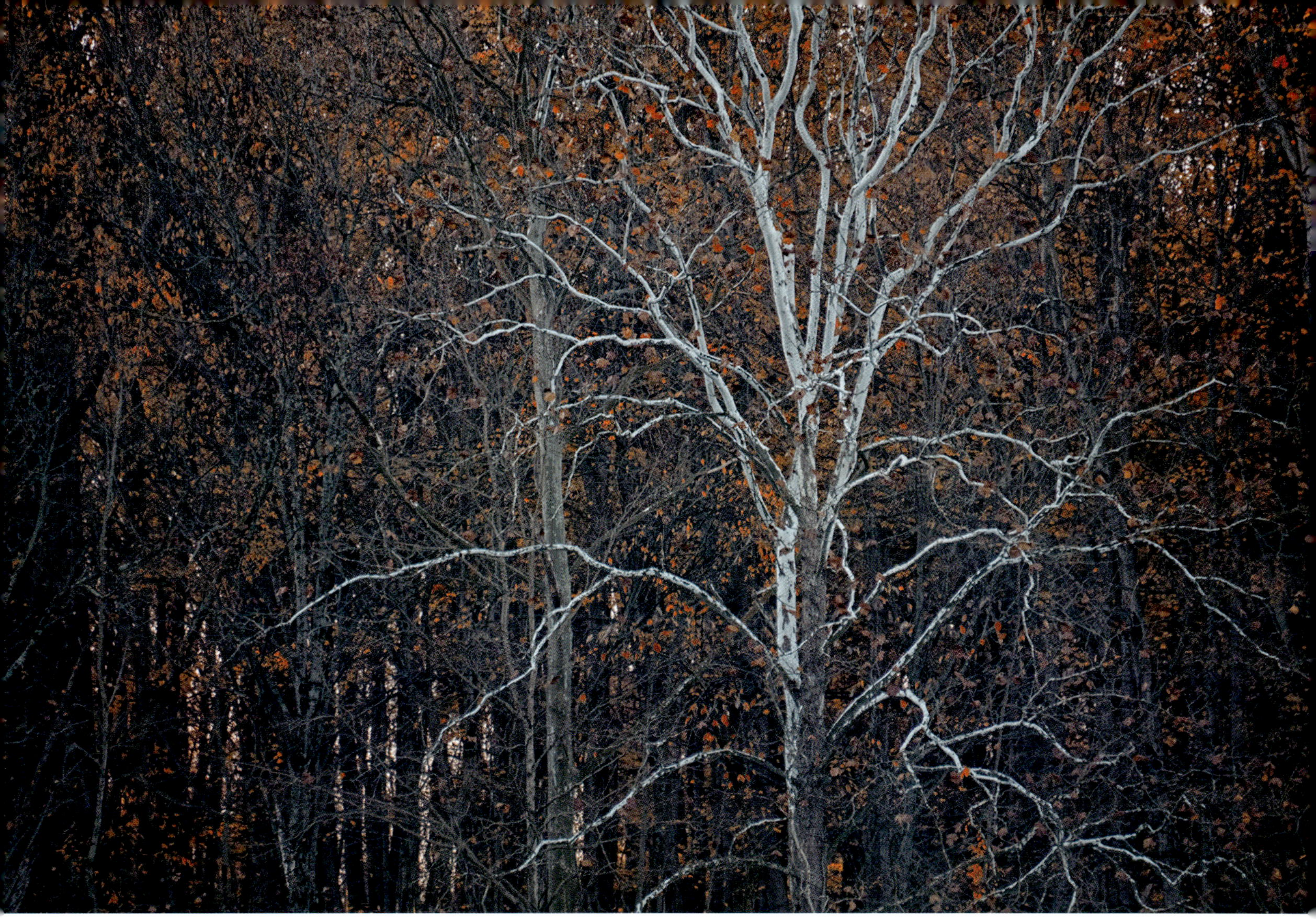

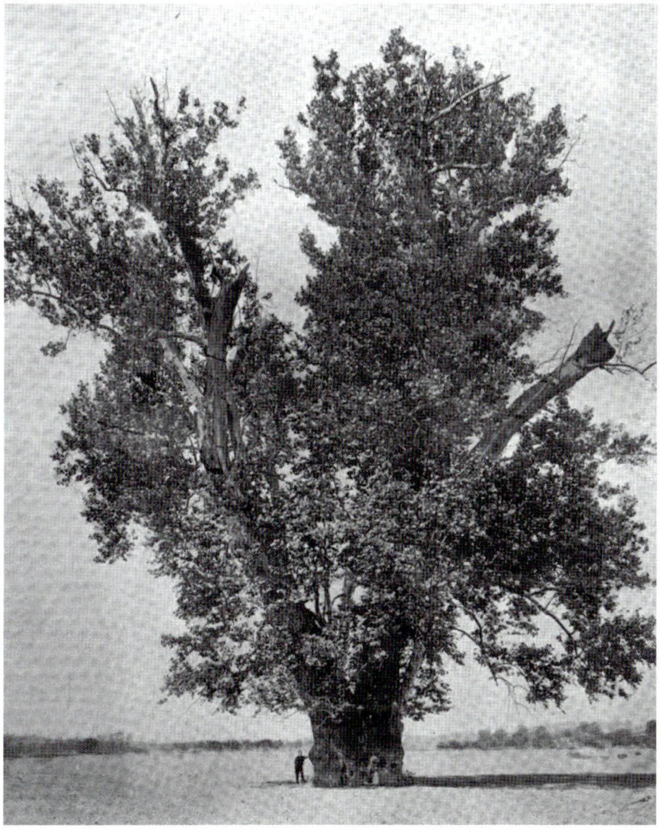

Above: Starkly beautiful sycamores at Eagle Creek Park, Indianapolis
Courtesy of Gary Potts

Left: Famous Worthington sycamore, courtesy of visitgc.com, where they cite origin from 1921. Also in *Trees of Indiana* by Charles Deam.

splotchy appearance. And when combined with moss or algae's green, the visual experience is quite intriguing.

Another old name for sycamore is "buttonwood." Production of the obvious "sycamore ball" or "button" fruit adds another interesting dimension. Of historical note is that the agreement on which the New York Stock Exchange was founded in 1793 is called the Buttonwood Agreement because it was signed under a sycamore tree located on Wall Street!

While highly attractive, sycamores do shed some of that scaly bark and drop twigs and branches. Monstrous leaves on some trees reach a foot across. Field trips with children should always include picking these up as reminders of their experience in nature. Large leaf litter increases raking if the tree is in a yard.

Mature trees do hollow out and in olden days those large old logs could be cut and used for primitive feeding troughs. Native Americans also used hollow logs to make dugout canoes.

For fuel use, sycamore can be tough to process even with a splitter due to its innate stubbornness and grain, making it difficult for working up a rick of wood. In the spring, a fungal anthracnose may cause leaf wilt and defoliation, forcing production of a second set of leaves. Sometimes the twig is also deformed and can be a detriment to growth. The sycamore leaf beetle is an obligate on the tree and can also be a stressor.[19]

Characteristics

- One of our most massive trees with huge and often forked trunks joined at the base.
- Flowers unisexual on same tree, bloom in May, forms the 1-inch spherical ball-like fruit laden with seeds clustered together. Balls ripen in October, may hang on during winter.
- Long-lived but in old age it hollows out.
- Good wildlife tree, especially for nesting in hollow cavities.

Uses

- In pioneer days, sections of solid rounds could be made into wheels for an ox cart.
- In the railroad era, sycamore paneling was used in Pullman cars.
- Saratoga trunks, piano and organ cases, stereoscopes, car dashes, and phonograph boxes also saw use of this light-colored, strong wood.
- Today, crates, boxes, pallet materials, butcher blocks, and some furniture are made from sycamore.

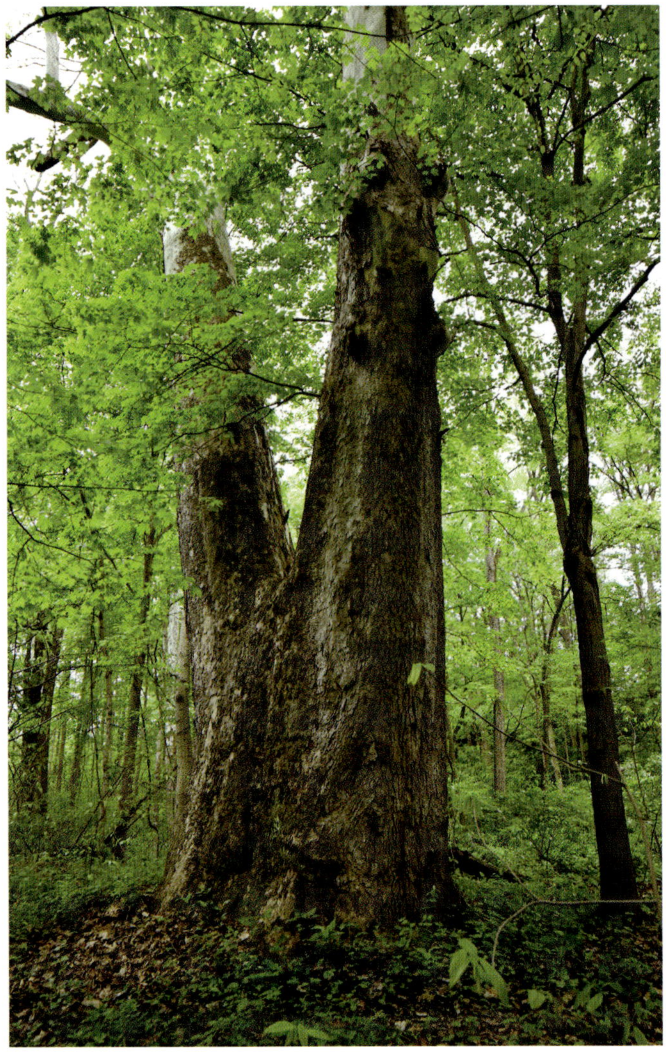

Top: State champion sycamore, Johnson County

Right page: Stately sycamores in Spring Mill State Park

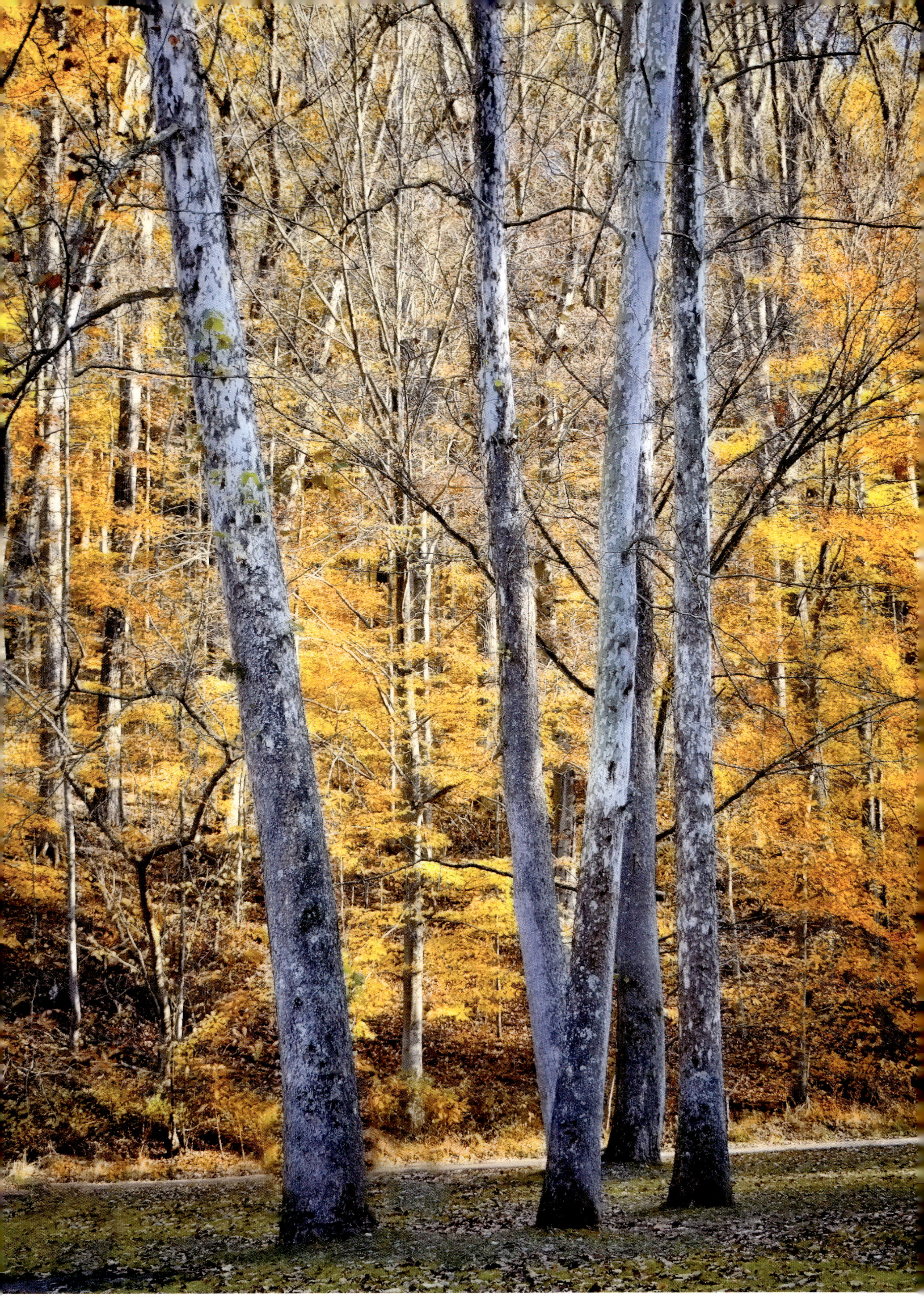

TULIPTREE OR YELLOW-POPLAR

(*Liriodendron tulipifera*)

Rising mightily to its 100 feet or more and with an immense trunk to inspire the viewer, behold Indiana's state tree. No other could be more fitting as its very magnificence of clear gray, rather smooth bark, stunning spring display of creamy white and orange flowers, and an artistically shaped leaf beckon all who observe it to be well pleased.

Native Americans in Indiana named what we now call the tuliptree *oonseentia*, but it is also known as American tuliptree, tulipwood, tulip-poplar, white wood, fiddle tree, and yellow-poplar. It was proclaimed as the state tree of Indiana and adopted by the General Assembly in 1931.

Tuliptree's uses have been profound for two centuries in this country. If one just counted the number of beams and sills this tree yielded from hand hewing alone, it would most likely be enormous. The author's 1878 Victorian country home rests on virgin timber poplar sills on hand-hewn sandstone blocks. Easily worked, fairly strong, resistant—what else could be asked of this honorable species?

Of course, the sheer joy of seeing those wonderful flowers in spring should bring out the canvas for all of us to paint or at least photograph up close. Remember, this species is not a poplar tree genus, but one of those splendid magnolia relatives.

The state champion tree in Daviess County is a sight to behold—old gnarly massive wide-spreading limbs radiating from a heavily furrowed trunk. Its circumference is almost 24 feet, with a height of over 100 feet.

In other settings within a closed forest, yellow-poplar may be found as exceptional specimens with diameters of 3–4 feet or more. As their clear trunks rise boldly to the very top of the forest canopy, they are truly awe-inspiring.

From Charles Deam's *Trees of Indiana* (1953), we find an interesting description of some of our early trees: "The tuliptree is the second largest tree of the state and the last colony of large trees can now be seen in the Turkey Run State Park. Concerning this colony, the following data may be found (Ann. Rept. Indiana Geol. Survey 6: 70. 1875): 'I measured four poplar trees that stood within a few feet of each other: the largest was thirty-eight feet in circumference three feet from the ground, one hundred and twenty feet high, and about sixty-five feet to the first limb. The others were, respectively, eighteen and a half, eighteen and seventeen feet in circumference at three feet from the ground'" (pp. 193–195).

Yellow-poplar makes a desirable street, shade, or ornamental tree but the large size may render it unsuited for many sites. Its good points for aesthetic use are: (1) rapid growth, (2) pyramidal form, (3) fair resistance to insect and disease damage, (4) handsome leaves and attractive flowers, (5) yellow autumnal color.

This great tree has some wildlife value. The fruits provide food for squirrels in the late fall and winter months, and white-tailed deer often browse on the twigs. Tulip is one of the first successional trees to pop up in a cleared woodland or field. It is sun loving and a vigorous young grower. Drought and tulip scale insects are extremely hard on these trees and limb-drop may be problematic in a yard.

Characteristics

- Up to 150 feet tall. Historic trees reached some 12 feet in diameter.
- May reach an age of up to 400 years.
- Alternate leaves on 2–4-inch stems with leaf smooth edged, up to 6 inches long.
- Buds greenish brown, resemble a duck's bill.
- Gorgeous blooms in May; seeds often dispersed by wind in fall. Seed pod body stays on in winter.
- Fast-growing tree, loves sunlight, and rapidly occupies cleared land.

Uses

- Great lumber tree: strong, workable, and abundant.
- Used in woodworking, cabinets, floors, trims, molding.
- Old poplar sills and beams still prized, often reused to build restored log cabins.

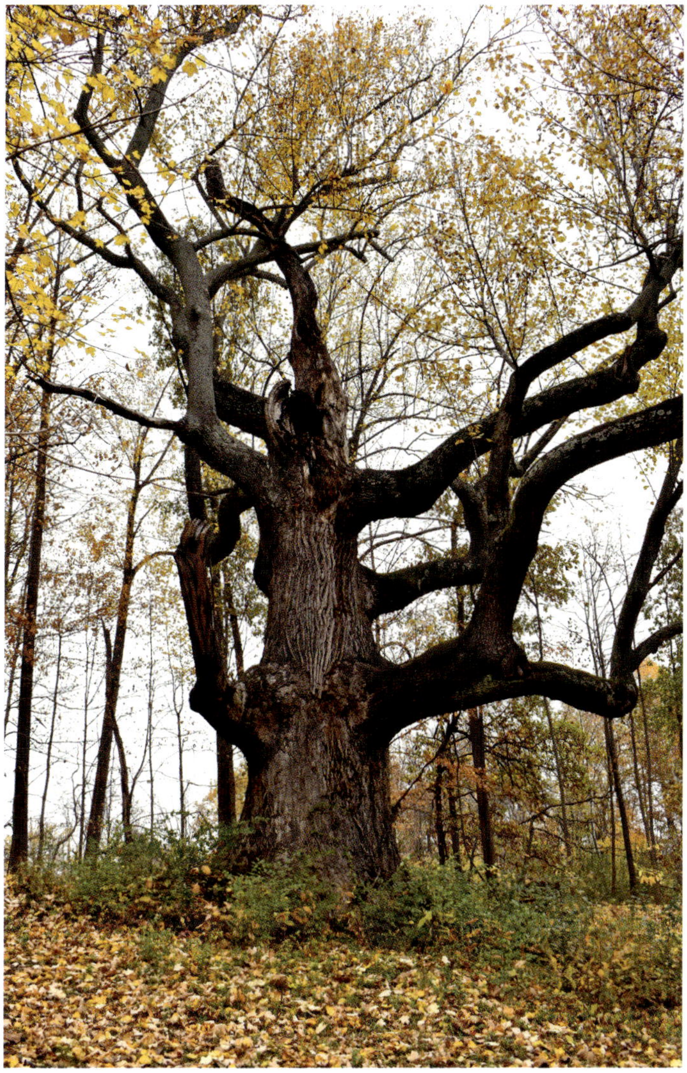

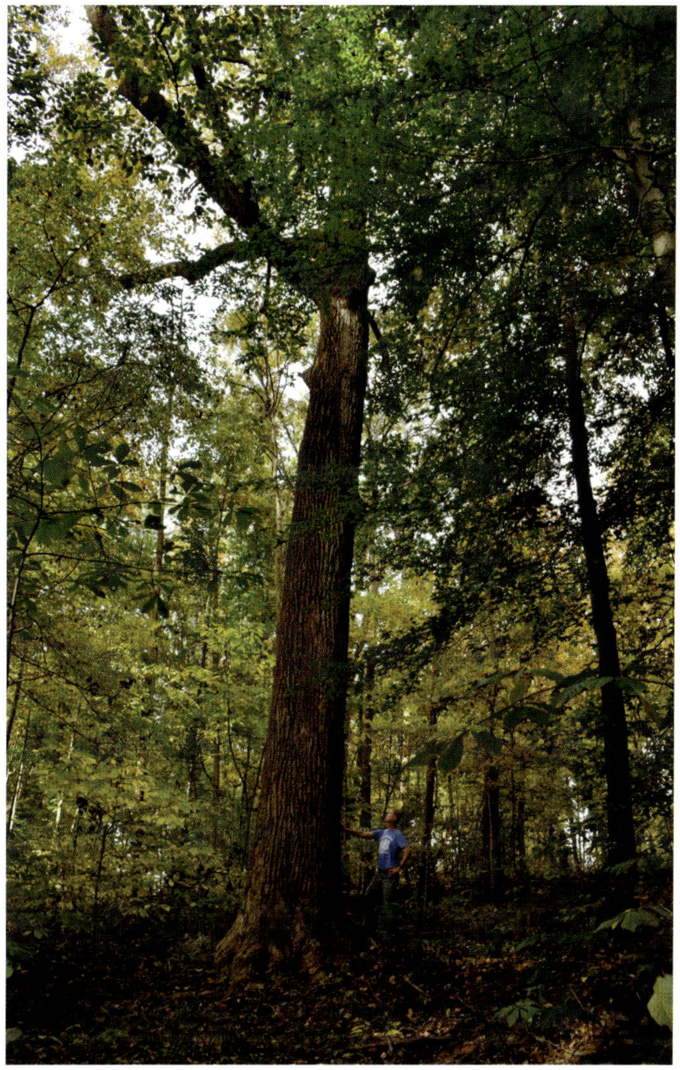

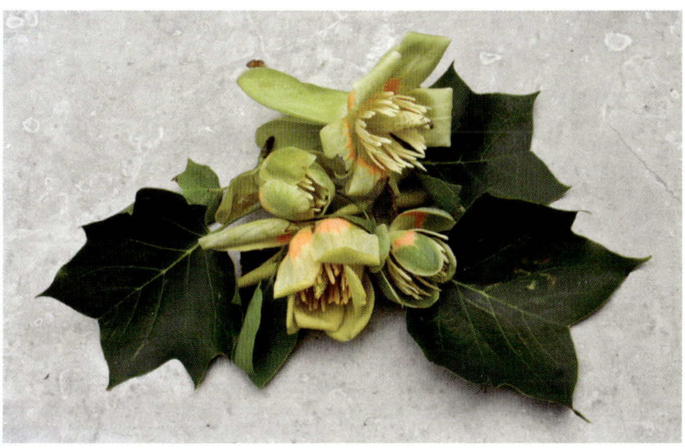

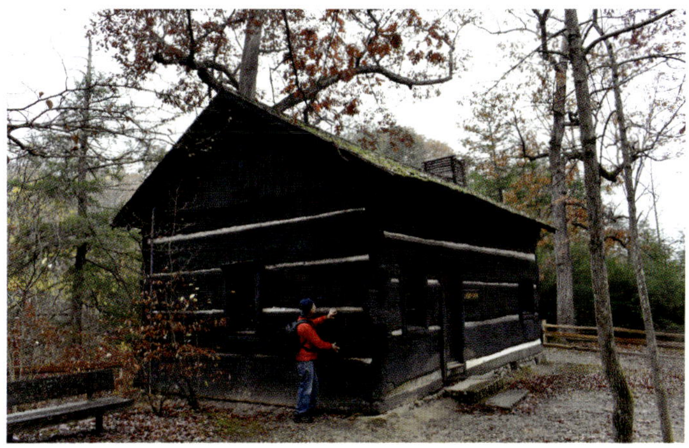

Top: State champion tuliptree, Daviess County

Bottom: Bloom and leaf of our state tree

Top: Fine, mature tuliptree, Lawrence County

Bottom: Lieber Cabin, built in 1848 from virgin tuliptrees, moved to Turkey Run in 1918 by Colonel Richard Lieber, creator of our state park system

KENTUCKY YELLOWWOOD

(Cladrastis kentukea)

Early explorer and botanist André Michaux was an important contributor to documenting new species in the wilderness country west of the Appalachians. While traveling in Tennessee on a rainy day in 1796, he noticed a curious unknown specimen. This new species was unique to America, a member of a genus only otherwise found in Japan and China.

Then and now, yellowwood was not common. The inner bark of the roots held something of value to early settlers. Yellow dye could be produced and colored homespun cloth. Further use of the tree came about once its hardness and ability to be polished lent it superbly to custom-made gunstocks or other wood-turned specialties.

Yellowwood is planted ornamentally and is quite attractive throughout the year. For many years, the champion was located on the campus of Indiana University. Another tree of slightly larger size was registered in Holcomb Gardens of Butler University for the 2015 Big Tree Registry. It has since died. A visit back to the IU tree was in order and it was still there in front of Rawles Hall. While suffering from decline in its old age, it may once again regain its champion status, at least for a few more years.

This elusive and endangered species occurs naturally only in Brown County in our state, which is the northern limit of its native range. Yellowwood is also found in limited locations from North Carolina to eastern Oklahoma and southward to Alabama. Civilian Conservation Corps workers first noted the odd tree in 1933 in Brown County State Park. Verifying that this find was indeed American yellowwood, state forester Charles Deam and T. E. Shaw of Purdue (Indiana's first extension forester) visited and recorded the locations. Later, populations of the tree were also found in adjacent Yellowwood State Forest.

Ten O'Clock Nature Preserve, Indiana's largest, contains specimens of this interesting tree. At 3,349 acres and a major part of the largest contiguous tract of intact forestland in Indiana, the habitat is conducive to preservation of yellowwoods and many other species of plants and animals that need large uninterrupted landscapes.

Since the occurrence of yellowwood seems to be confined to one localized area, it was originally hypothesized that perhaps early settlers had brought them in from locations outside of Indiana. Testing by Purdue's Hardwood Tree Improvement and Regeneration Center for TNC established that this disjunct occurrence is genetically unique from other populations in the United States. Today it is still very curious why only one Indiana county shows the species.

A pioneering effort to inventory the known yellowwoods was conducted in 1983 by Hank Huffman, then a naturalist with Brown County State Park. The survey documented 2,009 individuals within his study area of the park and part of Yellowwood State Forest. An inventory by IDNR in 2019 solely for YSF showed an increase from 261 individuals in 1983 to a current 819. The known population is now over 2,500 specimens. Because the yellowwood is so rare, the IDNR Division of Forestry has established HCVF status for 591 acres in Yellowwood State Forest. This high-priority conservation value designation assures management for its recovery. The regeneration strategy focuses on competition from both persistent shade-tolerant species and faster-growing shade-intolerant species, balancing enough sunlight for germination and growth with enough shade to keep sun-loving species at bay.

Throughout its greater range, established yellowwoods can be found growing in mixed or even moderately closed canopy, often as a mid-story tree with associated species including maple, oak, hickory, basswood, and others. In Indiana, current stewardship goals are driven to assure that yellowwoods will thrive and reproduce successfully here in Brown County.

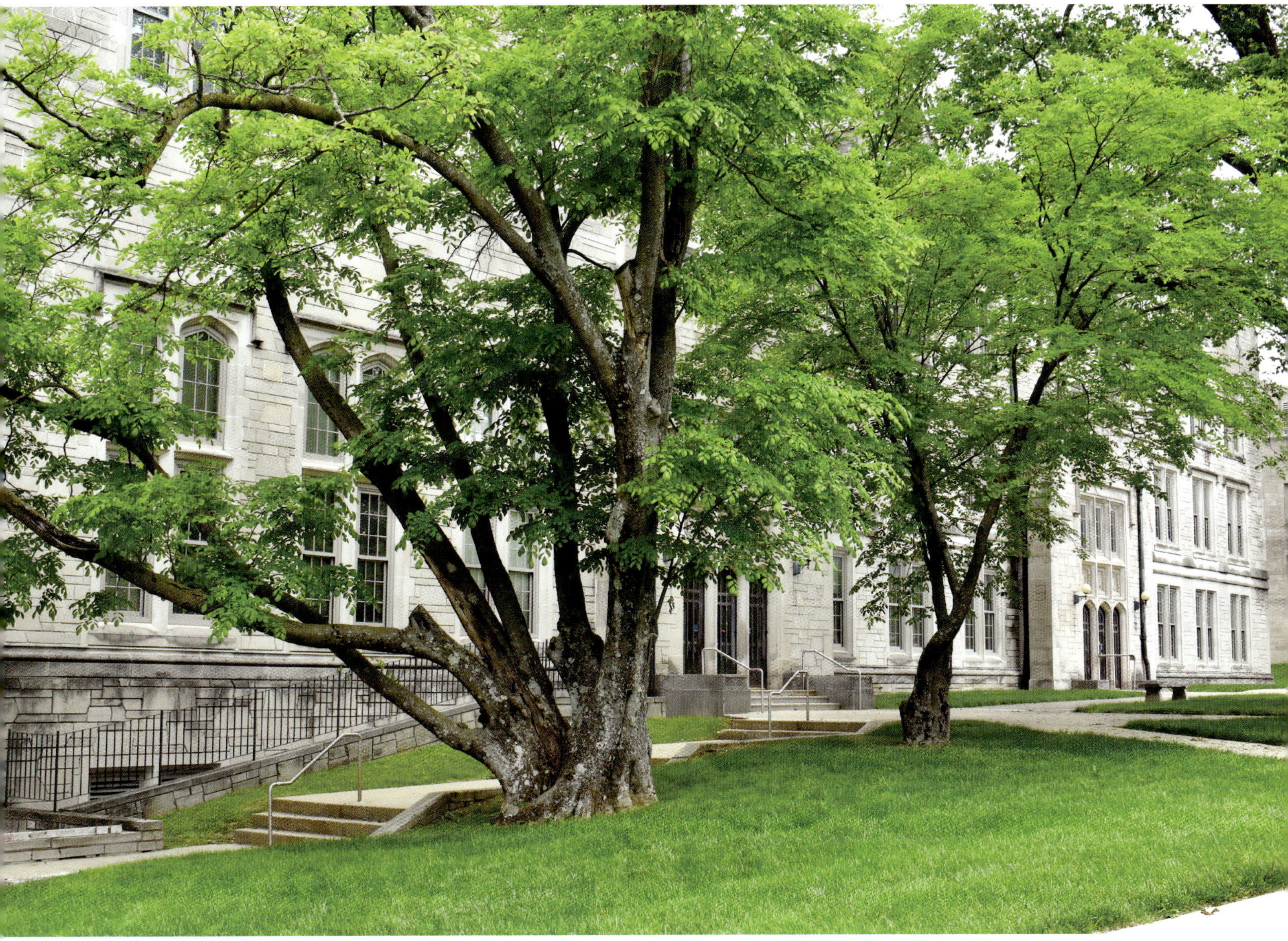

Original state champion yellowwood on the campus of Indiana University, with a companion nearby.

Characteristics

- In young to middle-aged trees, the bark resembles the gray smoothness of beech and has been confused with that species on several occasions, even being cut along with beech in a harvest.
- The tree's height often is 50 feet or less and diameter less than 2 feet.
- The leaves are alternate, pinnate, and compound.
- The bloom is exceptional with its gorgeous white clusters hanging delicately.
- The fruiting develops a bean pod, which places it in the legume group along with redbud and locust.
- Fall color is a pleasing yellow and commands attention in that season.

Uses

- The roots were chopped into small pieces and boiled, creating a yellow dye for homespun garments.
- The hardness of the wood and its color were desirable for pioneer gunstocks, often crafted individually by the settler.
- Today, yellowwood and its cultivars are handsome ornamentals, planted widely.

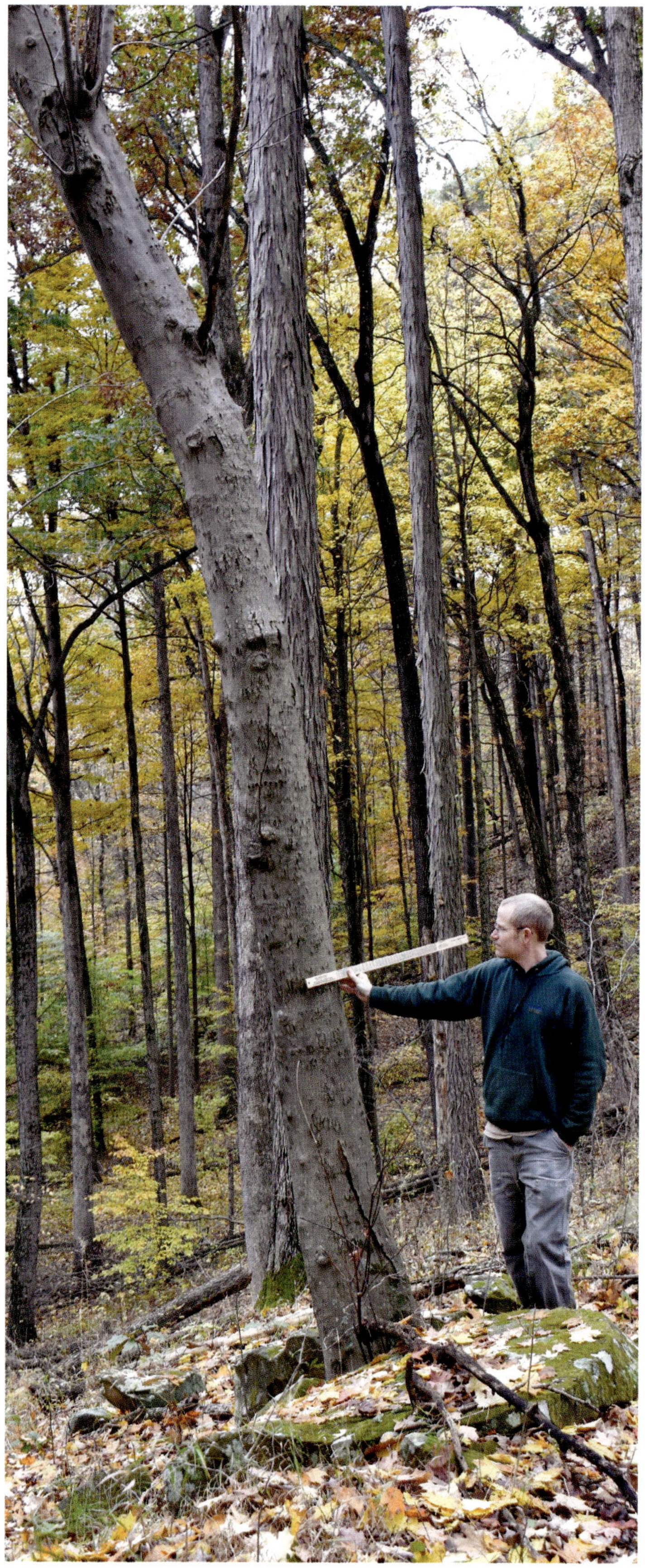

Michael Spalding, IDNR resource supervisor, Morgan-Monroe State Forest, with large Kentucky yellowwood tree

CHAPTER FIVE

Oldest of the Old: Indiana's Wondrous Old-Growth Woods

REMNANTS OF OLD-GROWTH FORESTS

The original landscape of Indiana with its magnificent forests, prairies, and wetlands was forever altered as westward expansion into the new state brought an increasing number of new settlers. For some, the journey was to extend on further west; to others, the productive landscape enticed them to choose this as a new home. The great presettlement forest of Indiana, while seemingly without end, quickly was transformed into homesteads and patchworks of woodland and fields. Even the largest of trees could finally be subdued, and they were. Rarely were any great old trees or sections spared. But a few remnants did indeed escape the axe and saw. Often, those were in inaccessible spots on steep hills or in swamps or flooded lowlands, which would not be suited for agriculture. There were a few untouched places, however, blessed by a stubborn curmudgeon who refused to have his great trees cut. Such tracts of land were often kept in the family for decades after his passing with the wish maintained. This is rather remarkable, considering, in some cases, the poverty during that period. In a few cases the land was owned by someone of wealth who would rather have the grand old woods stay intact rather than harvested for money. Many stories accompany those few protected woods, and their testimony lives today as remarkable windows into the past. This chapter explores several fascinating and inspiring locations.

The term "old-growth forest" will certainly create a certain perception in our mind, influenced by past experience or readings. For some, adventures in the redwoods and sequoias directly remind one of that overwhelming experience of being immersed in grandeur.

We often equate "old-growth forests" with very old age and size. That is our most common concept. But a tree's age is not always directly correlated to its size. Very old trees like bristlecone pines in the West may be 4,000 years old, but only 2–3 feet in diameter and less than 50 feet in height. Other krummholz-shaped trees in the Snowy Range of Wyoming or the Rockies grow slowly due to high elevation and long, harsh winters.

Closer to home, northern white cedar (*Thuja occidentalis*) is found in Indiana and does grow to medium size. But one specimen found in Ontario growing on a cliff side is reported to be 155 years old and only 4 inches in height.[1] Also, referenced in *The Natural Heritage of Indiana* (Jackson, 1997), Mike Homoya describes eastern redcedars up to 800 years of age along cliffs of the Ohio River. Trees in poorly drained flatwoods with standing waterlogged soils may not always produce exceptionally large specimens but do show very old age. Ginn Woods in Delaware County is an example of this occurrence.

Indiana is fortunate to have some marvelous pieces of the past left for us to see today. To walk in these woods is a humbling experience, in some ways sorrowful that only a few of these even exist, yet most exhilarating to allow escape into presettlement Indiana. We focus next on twenty wonderful locations that are labeled "old growth." While there are many suggestions for what the definition includes or excludes, we will refer to those offered by the Indiana Department of Natural Resources Division of Nature Preserves, other experts, and from long-term studies by Purdue, including the major contributions of Professor Emeritus George Parker in his important work over many years. We will say that the old-growth woods in this book generally have their oldest trees over 150 years of age, little or no harvesting for a very long period, several or many stems 4–5 feet across, often with heights over 100 feet, and overall showing the long-term tendency toward a beech-maple climax. The woods would also show mixed canopy, decayed logs, and open areas. There may also be some of the very aged oaks, walnuts, and tulips left as well. Most original elm and ash will have succumbed.

When looking closer at the dynamics within that forest, other observations occur. Over a very long period of time that forest has changed, and remnants today still undergo changes. It therefore is not static. The old forest has experienced events in its lifetime that have modified its age groups, species composition, and structure. Considering a 300-year-old woods, never cut, which we call "virgin forest," evidence can be found of events that happened over time. In fact, that woods continued much further back, before Europeans arrived. Many of the old trees reached their life span and have fallen. A severe windstorm toppled others. Fire from lightning or early humans modified the composition and favored species of resistance. Droughts inflict mortality on other species. Openings created in the canopy allow for release of young saplings aspiring to mature. Fungi, insects, and other biological factors may have played a role in the demise of trees. What we see today in our old-age woods is actually a mixture of ages, sizes, and species. There may be an understory of herbaceous plants, shrubs, and young trees. Another section of woods may have gone through this stage and now is in mid-level canopy, with perhaps mature companion trees. Close by may still be several old giants left and standing guard. But one of their kin, such as a huge old shumard oak, lays prostate upon the forest floor, providing a niche to insects and microbes busily at work. No matter the age of the "old" forest or the size of some of its giants, it is still a complex matrix. Inspiring? Yes, and more intriguing than we commonly thought.

THE MAGNIFICENT TWENTY

These remarkable places were selected from lists accessible to the public. Primary sources were the Indiana Department of Natural Resources Division of Nature Preserves, Indiana Division of Forestry, and *The Nature Conservancy's Guide to Indiana Preserves*. Other listings of old-growth sites were found in *Natural Areas of Indiana and Their Preservation* (Lindsey, Schmelz, and Nichols, 1969 edition), and research studies over time by Parker et al. at Purdue. Websites of Indiana's land trusts also mention old-growth locations of their properties. It is noted that most of the featured sites that follow do allow public visitation. When visiting, utmost respect should be paid to make no impact or leave any trace of your visit beyond footprints. Enter, absorb, and leave changed.

BENDIX WOODS
ST. JOSEPH COUNTY

Having an exquisite place all to yourself is rare and rewarding. On weekends, Bendix Woods is very busy, bustling with family activities or folks walking the many trails.

Our visit here was during the weekday and few visitors were seen. Following a picnic lunch, the goal was to hike into the old-growth woods. A little searching on the map led to the Runnels Shelter. Almost hidden behind was the Raccoon Trail, which shortly arrived at the junction for the nature preserve. This well-traveled trail proceeded uphill among larger and larger trees, first maple and then grand beech. There was a mystery to what must lie ahead in the gentle climb to the top, as if this were a discovery adventure.

At 770 feet above sea level, it was also intriguing to think of the geologic past of Indiana. Several glacial advances and retreats had influenced the rolling topography. Thick deposits of till and outwash overlay a series of shales deep below the surface. Here, among the current beautiful hardwoods, a look at the past might imagine ancient conifers, then succeeding birch and spruce, and now a more temperate beech-maple climax forest.

To have an old-growth woods preserved in this area of developed northern Indiana is truly worthy of admiration and appreciation. The impressive specimens of great character required pausing at each, allowing us to reflect on not only its longevity, but also the uniqueness of bark, limb structure, and leaf pattern. Some of the very stunning beeches were straight and reached almost to the clouds, it seemed. Unlike old, limby, gnarly beech in other places, these were almost perfect specimens. Adding interest to the forest composition were fine representations of basswood and red elm. Some old tree cavities provided homes to resident squirrels and owls. Rectangular holes indicated that pileated woodpeckers had been working diligently to find insects beneath the bark.

As the trail wound across the top and then began its descent, large open areas in the woods were noticed. These may be ones mentioned as resulting from a 1980 tornado that took out several trees. Wildflowers in these openings were spectacular, especially the blue cohosh and jewelweed. Early spring displays of large-flowered trillium and Solomon's seal must be quite a sight and would add a marvelous complement to the great trees overseeing the grandeur of nature here.

The generous 195-acre donation by the Bendix Corporation in 1966 created a most remarkable county park, the first for their county parks system and actually the first non-state-owned property dedicated by the Division of Nature Preserves. The property was an important part of the famous Studebaker history, complete with the huge oval track, which was the test site for those memorable cars of yesteryear. Many of those cars are now collectibles and bring high prices. Ironically, Studebaker produced electric cars from 1902 to 1912, a century ahead of our new look at this technology.

With the fascinating terrain, fine trees, wildlife habitat, and large wildflower meadows in the open valleys, the 27-acre Bendix Woods Nature Preserve is truly a gem. Proximity to South Bend and the Indiana Dunes to the west make this a highly recommended stop. Imagine yourself alone at the top, surrounded by glorious trees, with that 1963 Avanti speeding around the track at 100 mph, far below.

Location: 56960 Timothy Road, New Carlisle, IN 46552-9522

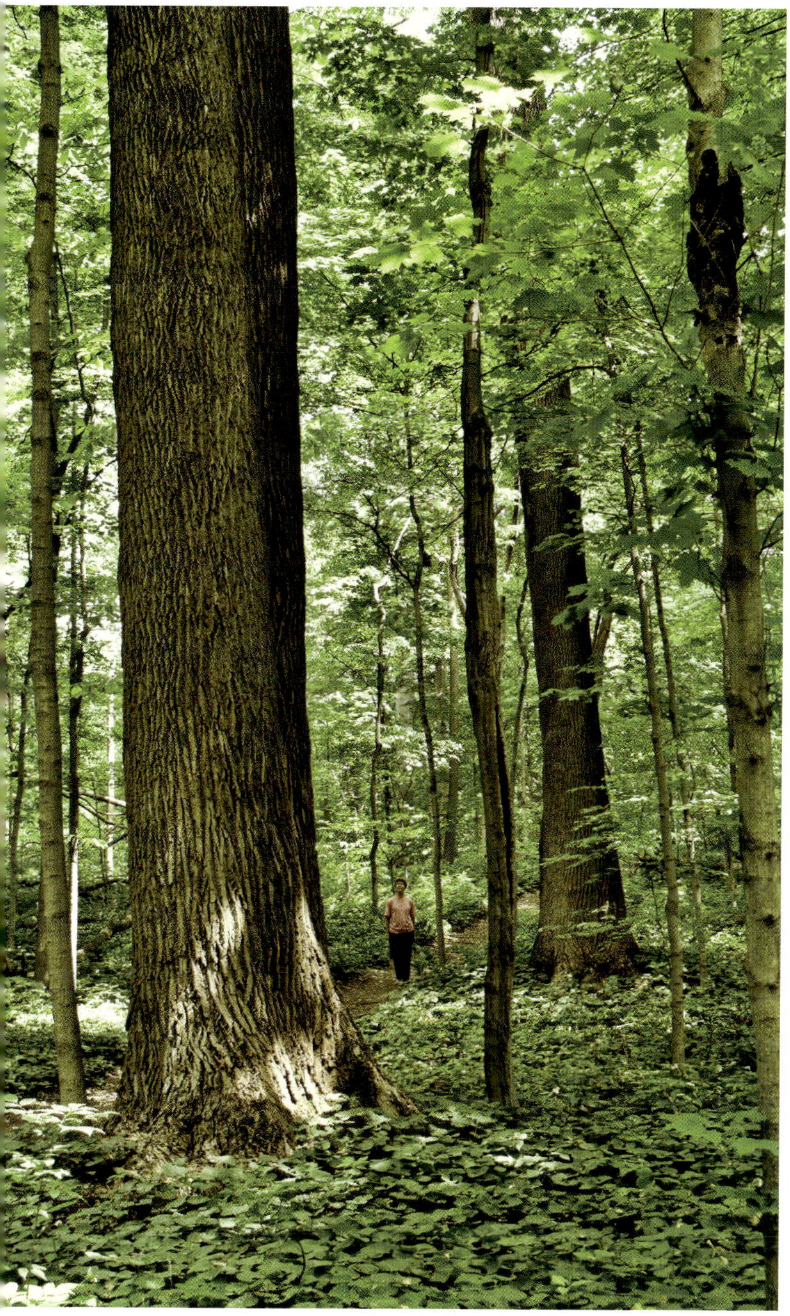

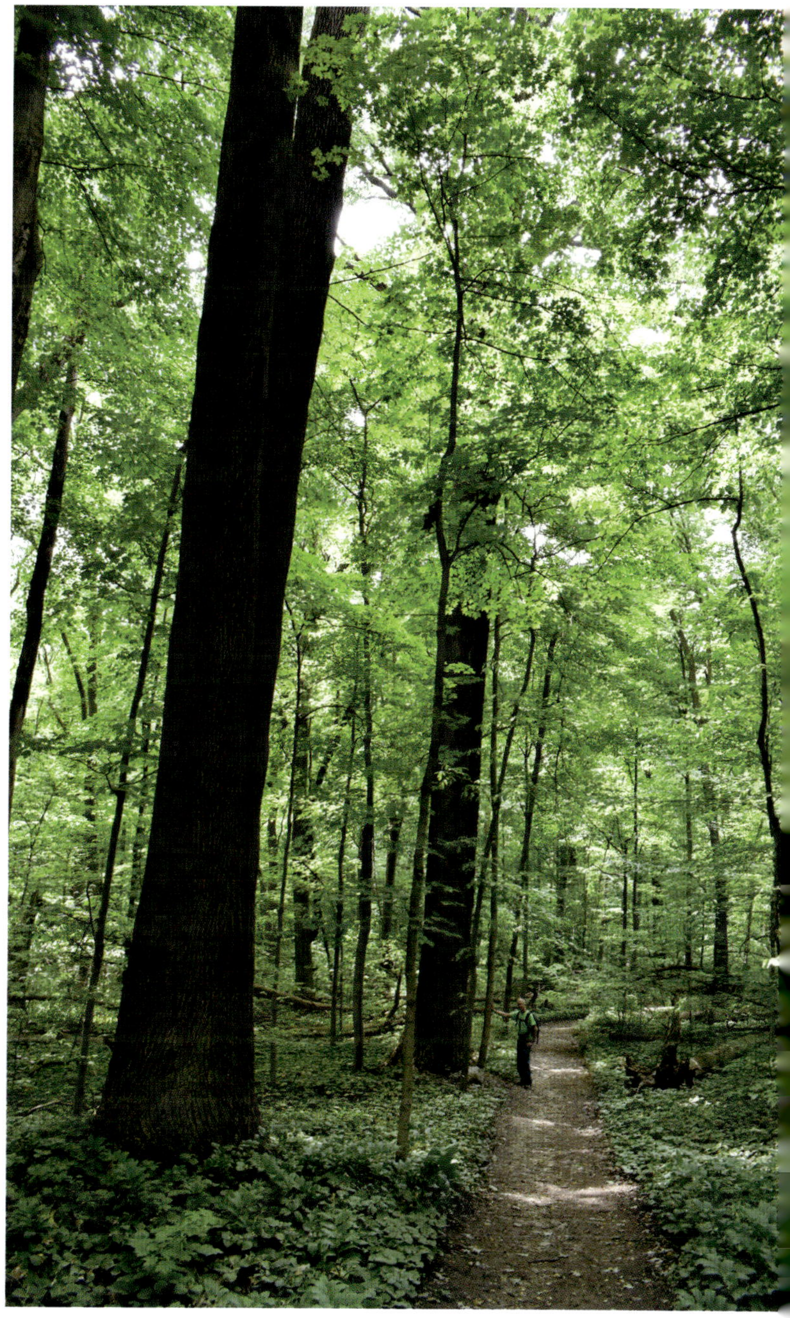

The allure of Bendix Woods Nature Preserve

CALVERT-PORTER WOODS
MONTGOMERY COUNTY

We like to think of our lives as having an ordered structure, often geometrically perfect, and all in sequence. Meticulously laid out rows were in perfect alignment and patterns were obvious as we hiked the ½ mile across the recently harvested cornfield. It had been planned well. Then, the wood line was in front of us and we entered. Immediately the world changed. Here was proof of nature's entropy—randomness seemed dominant, the physics of life now seen were not under our control. They, not us, determined tree spacing, species, and growth.

Calvert-Porter Nature Preserve is truly a place of special release from the hurried pace of life. Excitement and adventure lay here, the breeze beckoning the visitor inward to the kingdom of old growth, possessor of eternal spirit and infinite evolution.

The especially large husks and nuts from the shellbark hickory reminded us of the productivity of these valuable trees. Onward, the great swamp white oaks spoke of adaptation to this flatwoods, where drainage is poor and standing water occurs in heavy spring rains. Close by, the large leaning sycamore with verdant green algae crusting its flaky bark, leaned outward as if to defy gravity. Then came the splendid red maple, one of the largest in any preserve and possibly a new state champion. So high up in that glorious canopy, the flaming red of that distinctive three-lobed leaf was a magical contrast to the blue sky. Alas, as fall was fast approaching, those very leaves were gently drifting downward to create their own carpet on the forest floor.

Oaks, maples, sycamores, boxelder, and hickory, along with many fallen companions of yesteryear, all scattered in agreement that each needed its space to occupy, thrive, and reproduce.

For us finality to life means many possibilities, those ideas left to each individual to ponder. But in the old forest, there is life after life, contribution yet for the contributions already given. The old massive log lying on the forest floor now, seemingly silent and woefully useless, is anything but that. Still vital, its new role unfolds. In the return to the very earth that bore it, now the marvelous elements and compounds are source for new life to sprout forth. A small seedling finds a lush bed in which to spring forward and achieve the very same greatness as the old master. Scurrying within the rich decomposing humus are insects, which depend on the generosity of the progressing decay. Nutrients flow in the cycle of life here, enriching all that are interwoven in their journey. From the highest limb of an old ash, the crow's raucous call reminds us that all is well in this special place and will continue to be so.

Notes: Calvert-Porter Nature Preserve is not officially open to the public. Access is limited and no trail exists. The 40-acre old section lies a good distance from the nearest road. It is surrounded by farmland. Newer property acquisitions have added an additional buffer and will enhance the overall protection.

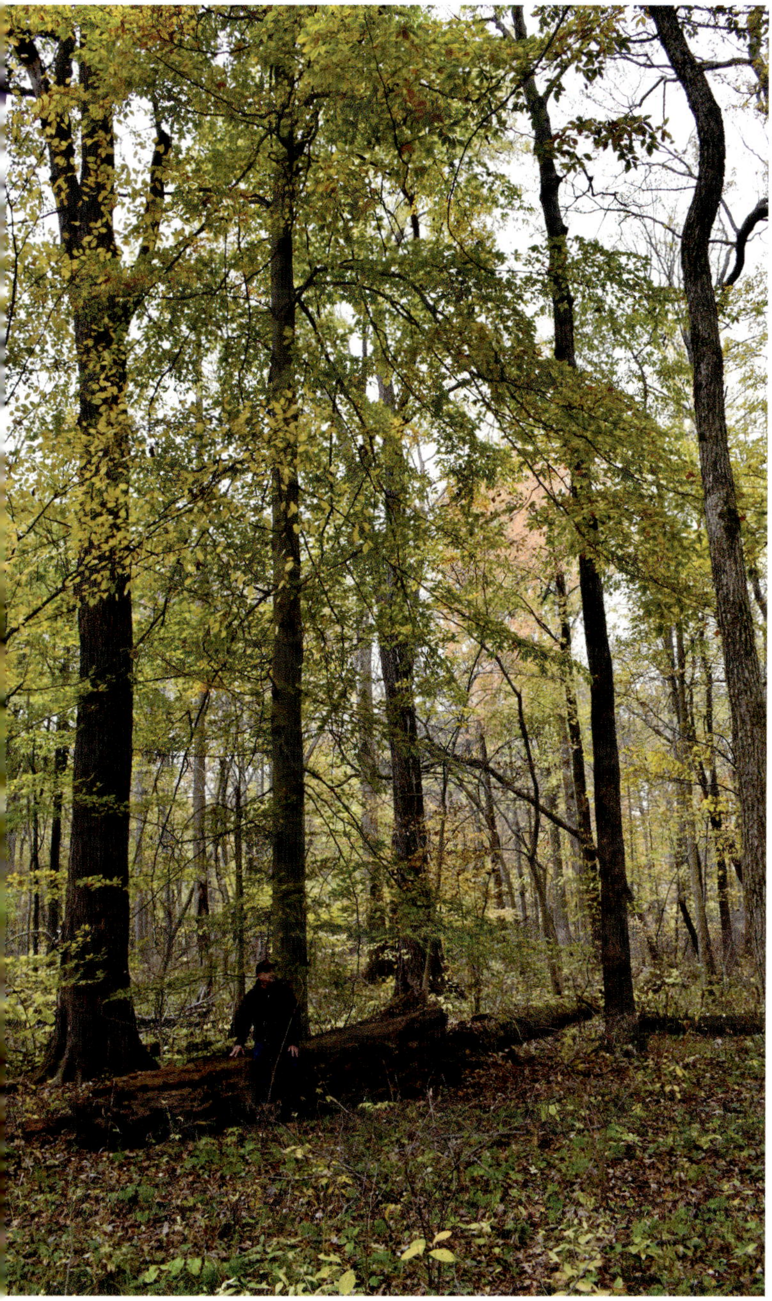

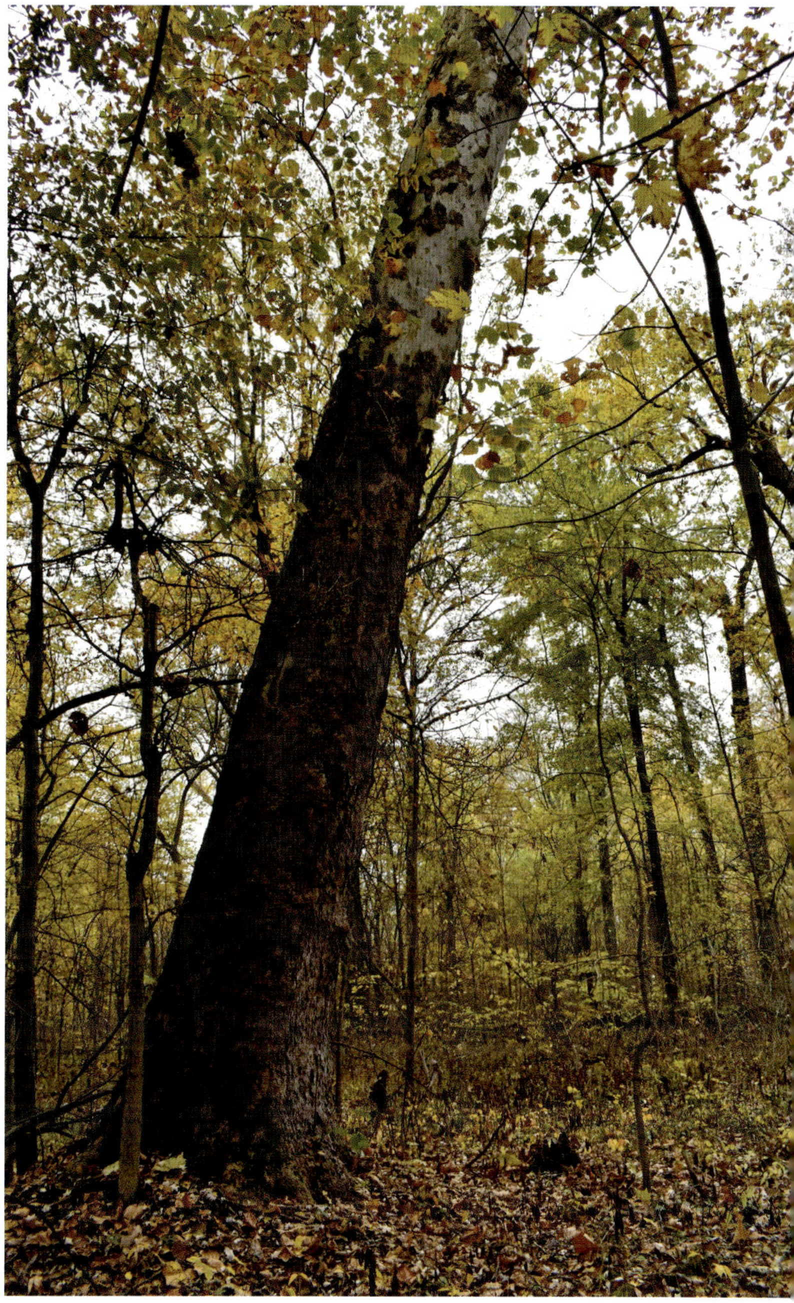

Left: Utter peace in Calvert-Porter Woods. **Right:** A giant overarching sycamore in Calvert-Porter Woods.

CHARLES MCCLUE NATURE RESERVE
STEUBEN COUNTY

This is a great spot to enjoy a morning hike after a cozy night at the nearby Potawatomi Inn on the shore of beautiful Lake James. The woods is quite an amazing parcel of preserved old-age trees and so unusual for northeastern Indiana. An avid naturalist and attorney, Maurice McClue, born in 1878, studied nature, loved birds, and began to keep a ledger he called his "Natural History Memoranda." Later in life he was able to set aside 80 acres of his family's original farm as a nature preserve. Named after his father, Charles McClue, the preserve was dedicated to the Steuben County Commissioners with expectations that it would be a great educational asset for children as well as adults. It has remained a wonderful gift to the community and is of significance to merit it becoming a state nature preserve in 1991. The property is maintained by a dedicated group of volunteers who have their own board and regularly report to the county commissioners.

A visit here was made in early June. Accompanying companions on the hike were numerous thirsty mosquitoes, thus repellent is in good order. The trail was easy to follow with quite an amazing array of large tuliptrees and many grand red and white oaks. Although some beech and maple are present, they are not the dominants. There had been wind damage in the recent past with lots of blowdowns, but it was still a nice remaining old forest. Downhill in a glacial depression was a swamp with large trees on the periphery. The quietude and peace were a highlight and only the sound of birds singing or communicating to each other about our human presence far below was evident.

A second loop trail takes one to a younger forest and old successional field, with a small pine plantation on the east side of the property. In the spring, dogwood and redbud punctuate the preserve with color. Although spring ephemerals are present, intrusion of garlic mustard poses a threat to the native vegetation. Another stop nearby should be made if you are in the area. Wing Haven Nature Preserve has a series of wetlands and lakes within the Seven Sisters Lakes region. Exceptional birding and wildflower profusion are high points of this great property owned by Acres, Inc. Land Trust. One great spring trip can catch the best of Pokagon, McClue, and Wing Haven, each with its own special attributes.

Directions: From Pokagon State Park, proceed east on county road 400 N for about 1 mile. The preserve is on the south side of the road with parking area, sign, and registration box.

Right page: Glacial basin wetland in Charles McClue Reserve

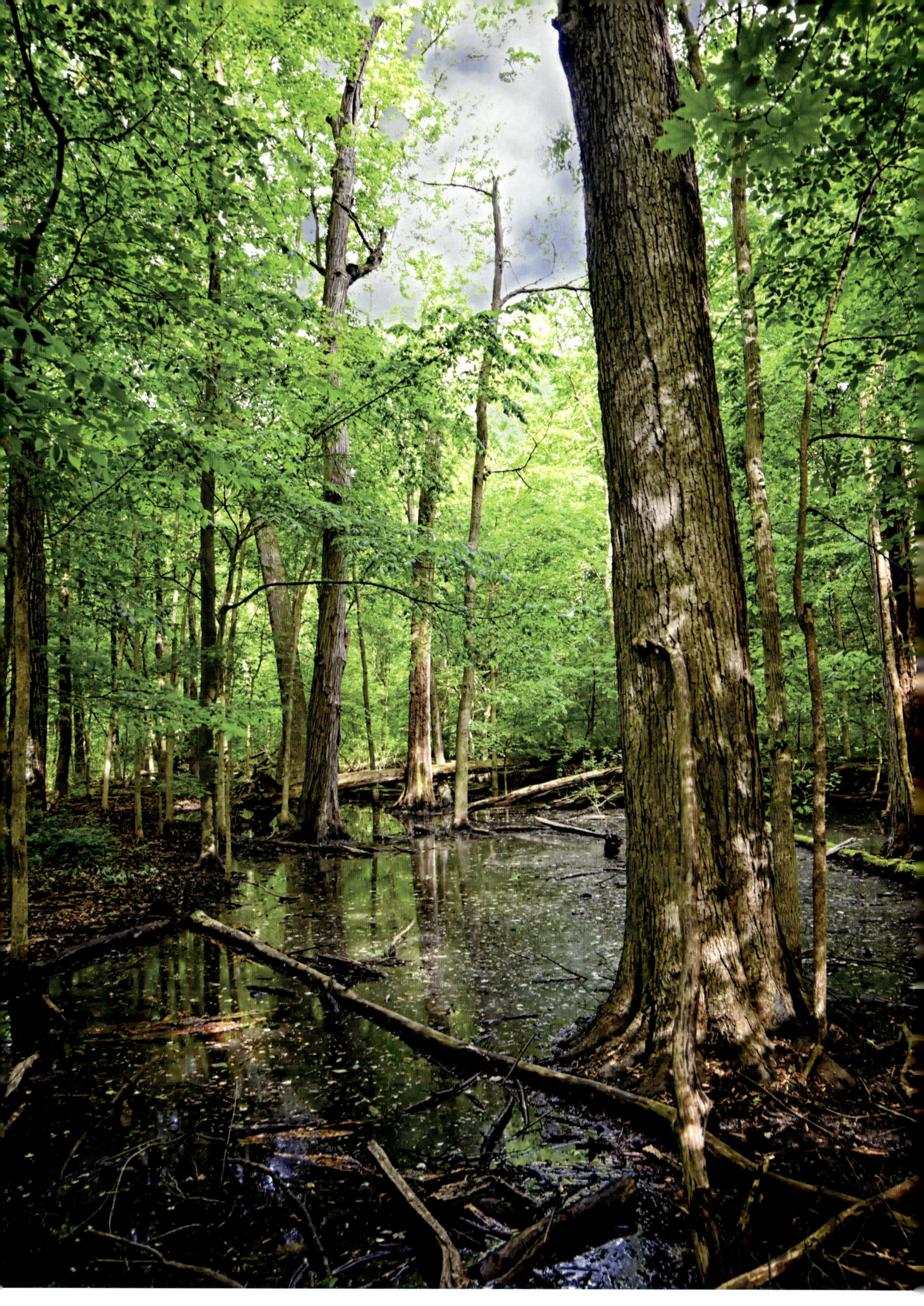

DAVIS WOODS
RANDOLPH COUNTY

Farmland, Indiana, is one of those fine representative small towns so typical of rural, friendly Hoosier country. As the name implies, there are hundreds of acres of productive farmland along State Road 1, which passes through this east-central Indiana community.

The Davis Purdue Agricultural Center is just a few miles north of town and plays a major role in Purdue's School of Agriculture research programs. Their focus on the 703 acres of agricultural land and 107 acres of managed forests is geared to state-of-the-art precision farming as well as sustainable forestry and research.

Our visit here was to view another remarkable component of this impressive facility. The property holds one of those rare old-growth woods pieces that remain intact from the very earliest times. In 1917, Martha Davis, widow of Dr. Lewis Davis, conveyed ownership of 385 acres known as the Herbert Davis Farm. In this tract, a 51-acre piece today known as Compartment 1 was so impressive and unusual that in 1975 it was recognized by the National Park Service as a National Natural Landmark. This is the oldest mapped and continuously researched temperate deciduous forest in North America. That research began in 1926 under Professor Burr N. Prentice and continues yet today, with both old original tags on big trees, and more recent tags over the past 50 years.

The plaque of dedication in memory of the Davises' son, Herbert, is first encountered on the woods edge, complete with a huge bur oak by its side. Entering the woods on the educational trail brings you quickly to another massive bur oak, then to the next, and then the chinquapin, and then a striking red oak. The pace slowed down from the very beginning tree, as each one called for its own special time to be admired and photographed. Here were champion survivors, stalwart manifestations of utmost dignity and perseverance: those that had stood against the roaring winds sweeping across the fertile flat landscape and those that had bent heavily under ice storms, their gnarly arms defying the frozen weight.

Among those distinguished denizens were big oaks with peeling bark, shaggy in age. Another old oak off in the distance had knobby stubs where large branches had been attached years ago, but given way, and healing tissue had closed in and sealed. A surprising specimen of a black gum 30 inches across rose majestically upward to 100 feet and added great interest to the forest composition. Other notable trees were sycamore, tulip, and many small blue beeches. On the forest floor, old logs were in the process of decay, returning nutrients to the soils and harboring insects, salamanders, and large fungi.

The woods was a place of solitude, with only the crickets providing a gentle hum in the background. Any car that passed in the distance was barely noticed and part of that other world we had left behind. The rain shower that had fallen was now finished. In this place, time and distractions were irrelevant—the moments of peace and the healing capacity of nature were brought forth, enriching the soul.

Location: 6230 IN-1, Farmland, IN 47340

Right page, left: Gnarly, old white oak, Davis Woods

Right: Davis Woods in fall splendor
Courtesy of Gary Potts

Bottom: Fine old white oak, Davis Woods

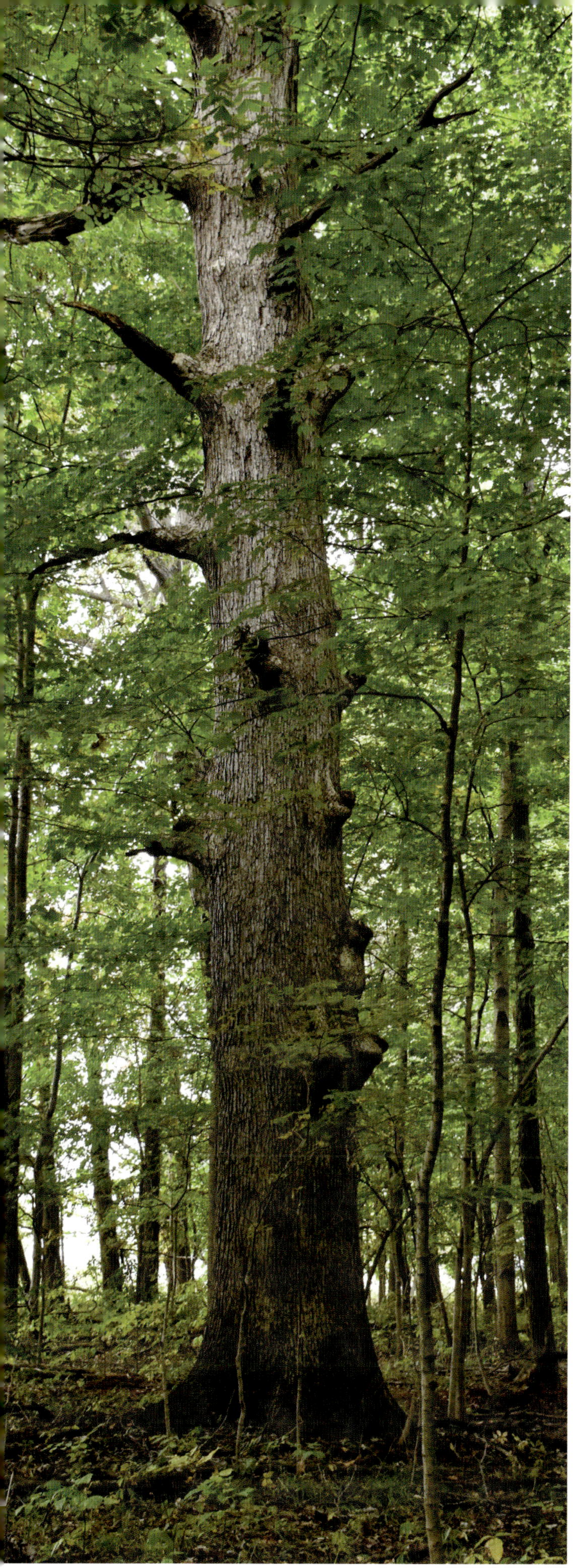

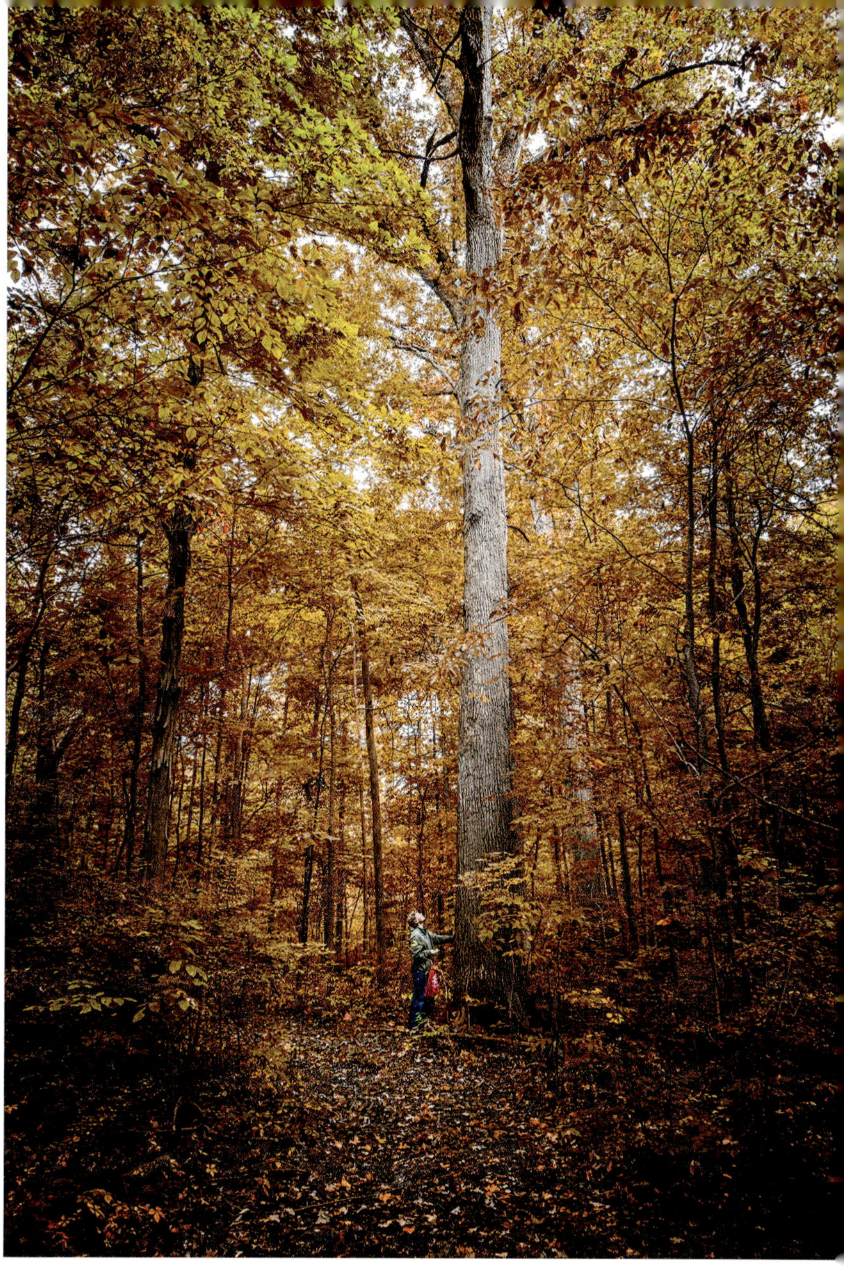

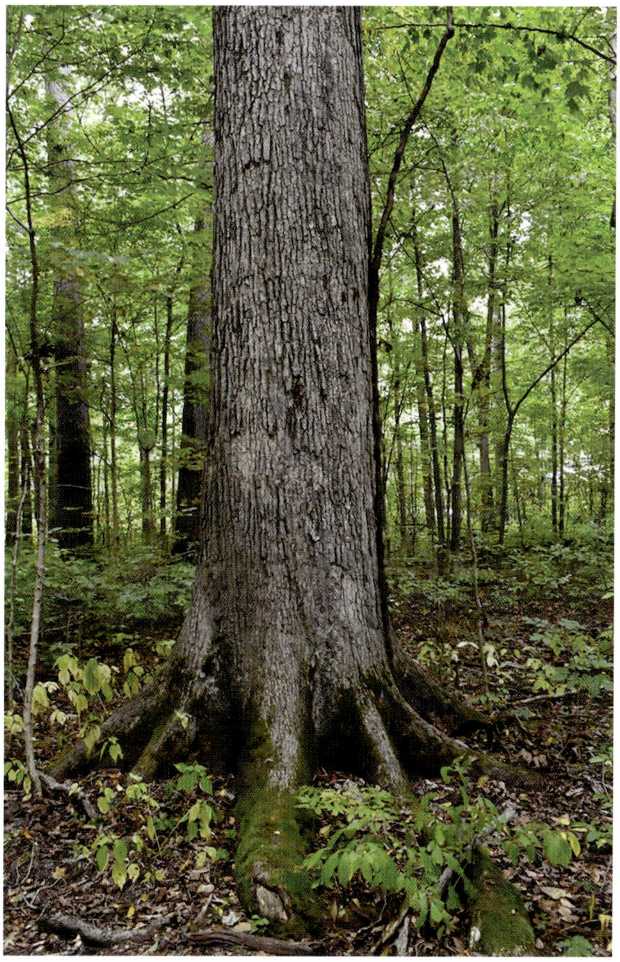

DOGWOOD NATURE PRESERVE
JENNINGS COUNTY

Tucked in at the south end of Versailles State Park, this seldom-visited preserve is not easily accessible or marked on the state park map. This 20-acre portion of the park includes old-growth beech-maple, with some oak and hickory as subdominants. Evidently, many years ago, dogwood was present in open areas, but little of that is now left except on the woods margin.

Finding this tract was somewhat difficult, as it was not well known or included any developed trails. Doubtless, Marion Jackson had ventured here in his youth, as he was raised not far from this special place.

Access must be made either through woods on state land, or around planted corn and soybean fields on private land. We chose the latter, with permission to walk the ½-mile field border to get to the back section. Halfway along it became unclear where to plunge into the woods to find these old trees. At that moment, the answer became much clearer. Deep within the woods a joyous and melodious song was our guide. This was the beautiful trill of the wood thrush, telling us we were close to his favored home of old forest. Following the sound and rounding the last field, we entered its sanctuary and found the old beech trees standing yet after 200 years, some intact, with others hollow but still regal. To confirm we were in the right place, an old Nature Preserves sign was still on its rusty post, somewhat askew but nevertheless an important marker. Nearby was a huge old beech lying on the ground, with a monstrous root ball and a water-filled basin where the tree had stood.

This upland woods contains slopes leading down to Turkey Creek and a bottomland of late successional growth. Outside the protected boundary of the park, timber had been removed over the years. But on the preserve the old intact forest from long ago was still present and a place of wonder and silence—only broken by the song of our little guide still celebrating his special world.

Location: South Cave Hill Road, Versailles, IN N-39.0376, W-85.2086

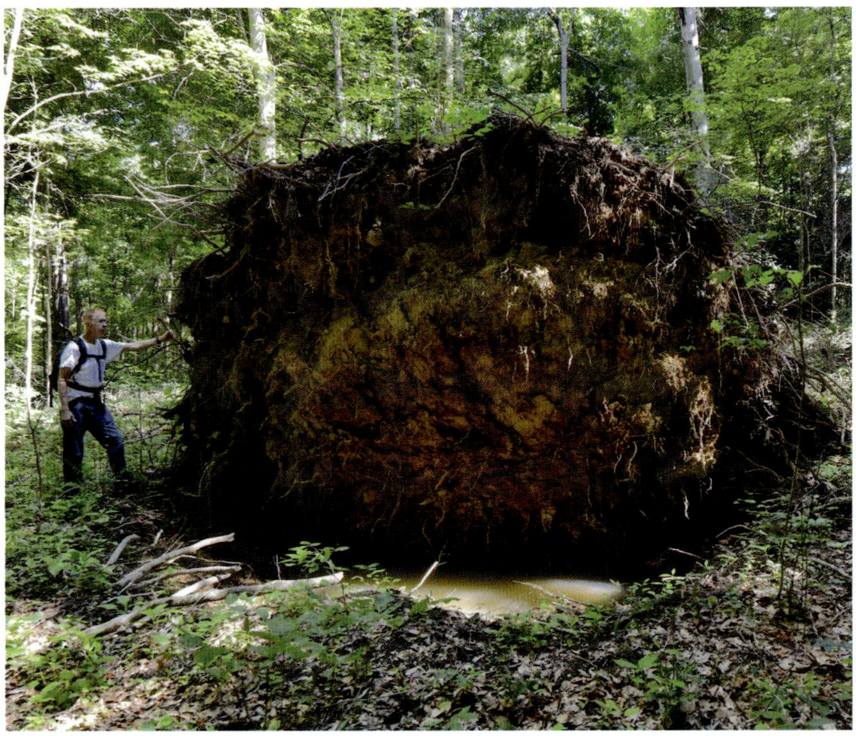

Right: Massive root wad from fallen old beech giant, Dogwood Nature Preserve, Ripley County

Right page: Intriguing old beech trees in Dogwood Nature Preserve, Ripley County

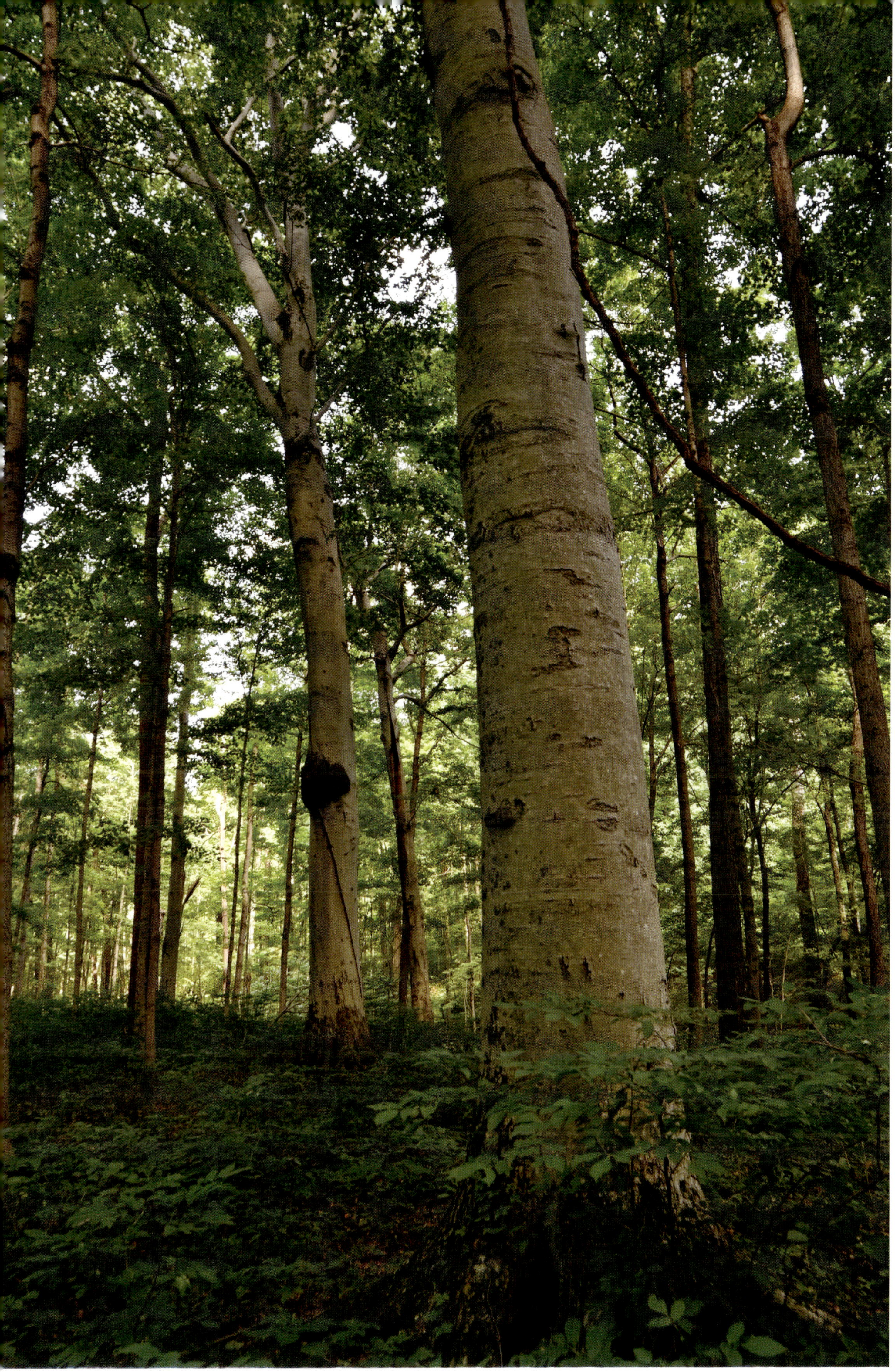

DONALDSON'S WOODS
LAWRENCE COUNTY

An outstanding woods that draws many appreciative hikers throughout the year, this Spring Mill State Park property has fine examples of an over-mature oak-hickory association, but with extraordinary tuliptrees making their grand statements as well. The ½-mile-long walk through this historical section ties together the whole Spring Mill story.

The village was established in the early 1800s, and with its distinguished mill, became an important source for grain and lumber. The tract that now includes the 67-acre old-growth forest was purchased in 1865 by a wealthy, eccentric Scotsman, George Donaldson. Although himself a big-game hunter, he reportedly never allowed hunting on his own property, nor did he ever allow timber to be cut. In the late 1800s, timber production had led Indiana to be a top producer, but Donaldson's refusal to cut his own trees proved our fortunate inheritance 150 years later. The woods are considered a remarkable example of a western mesophytic forest, meaning that it is a fine mix of oak-hickory and beech-maple. Today, as you walk through the splendid setting, it is obvious that many of the aged oaks are in decline, with some of the very oldest giants now but rich decayed humus, continuing to serve natural systems. One grand 6-foot-diameter white oak so fondly adored for generations by parents and children has been gone for many years but is firmly planted in our memory.

The well-traveled trail undulates as you pass outstanding 200-year-old citadels and younger trees taking up their future role. As windstorms and other events work on the old ones and bring them down, the next generation is willing to muster its troops for future grandeur. That the path goes up and down is another fascinating aspect of Donaldson's Woods. This is prime karst country—caves and sinkholes. The trail actually drops down into the large sinkholes and back up the other side. The ground on which visitors are walking lies directly above underground passages or collapses in the limestone. These features make Spring Mill a very special place in Indiana. In fact, spending a day in Spring Mill State Park allows all of us to step back in history and nature. Donaldson's Woods Nature Preserve is also linked to Donaldson's Cave Nature Preserve and Mitchell Sinkhole Plain Nature Preserve. Where else can one experience such a presentation of so many wonders?

Location: Three miles east of Mitchell on S.R. 60

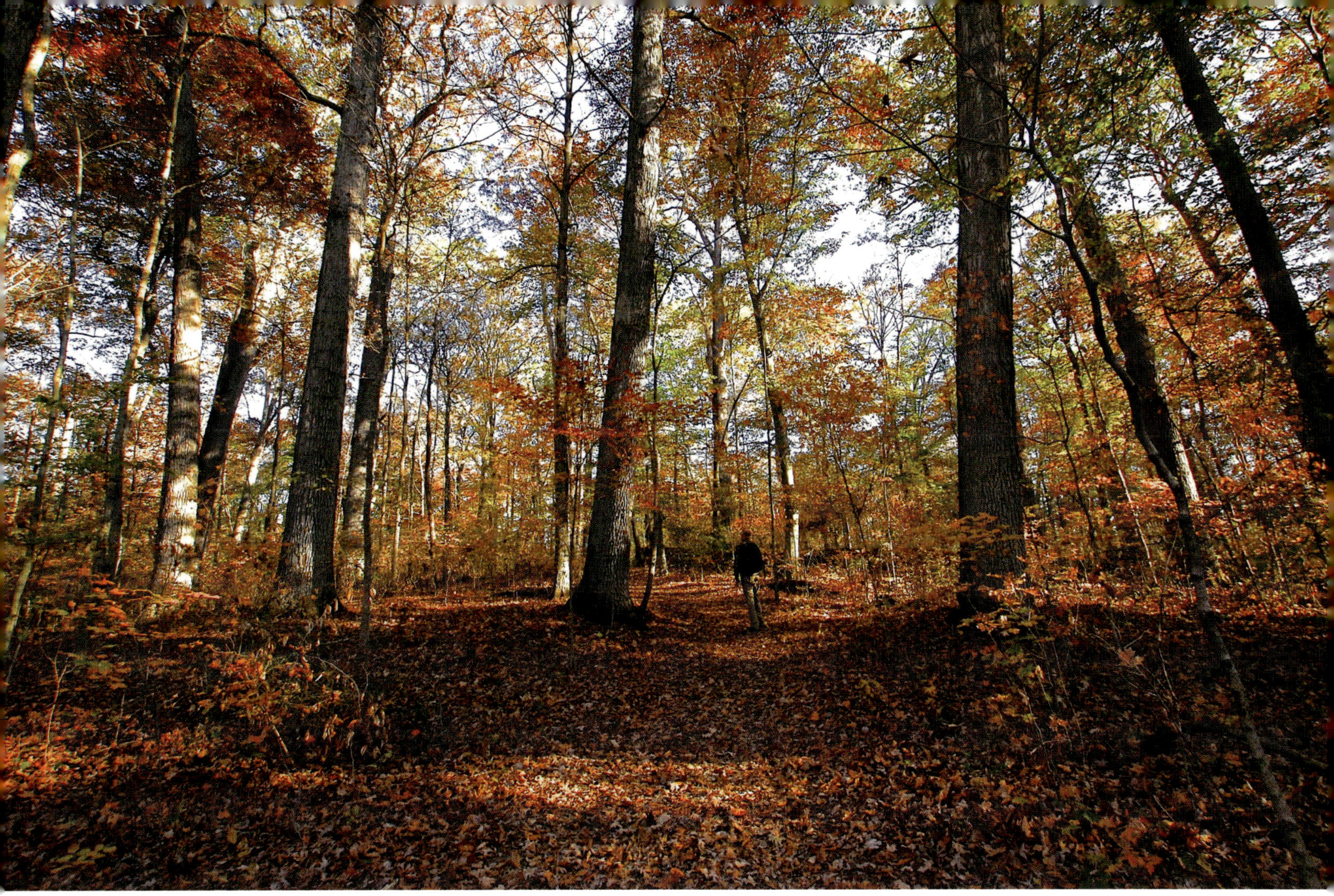

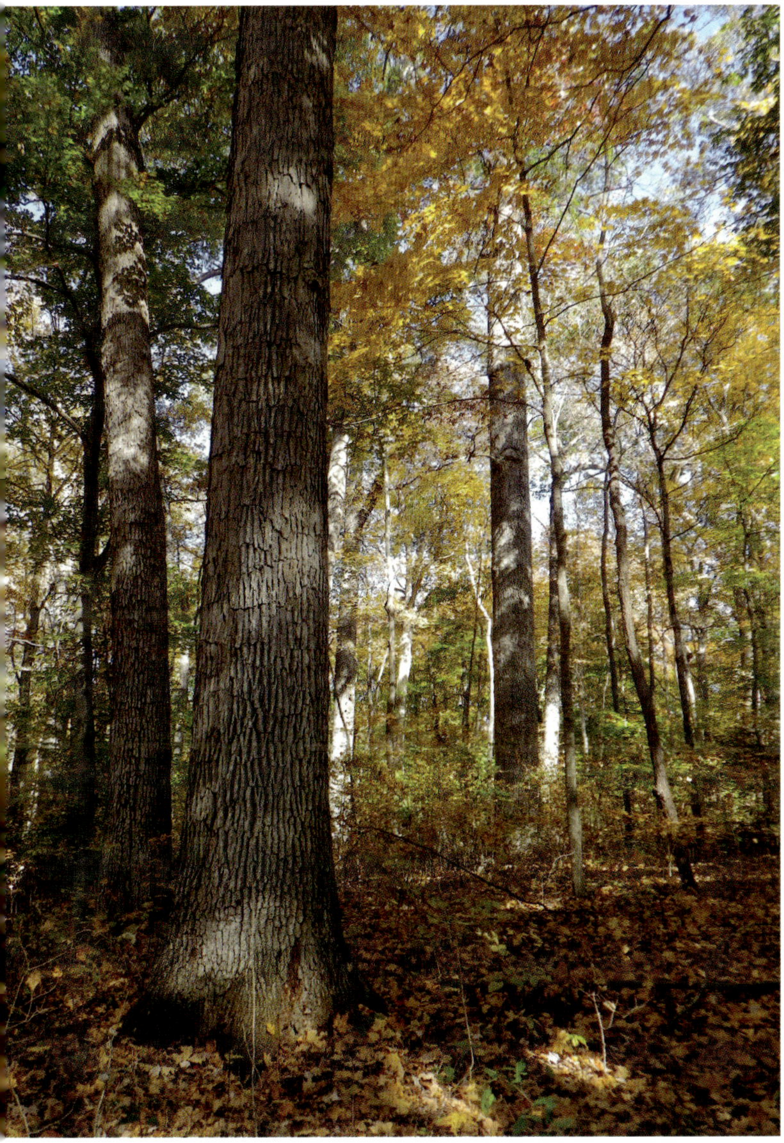

Above: An incomparable fall day in virgin timber of Donaldson's Woods, Spring Mill State Park

Left: Prime white oaks in Donaldson's Woods Nature Preserve

EFROYMSON WOODS (HAWK WOODS)
SHELBY COUNTY

The large, wooded tract known as Hawk Woods could be seen from U.S. 52 just west of Morristown. While several small wooded areas lay along county road 150E, this one stood out for its noticeable size among the large expanses of farm ground planted in soybeans. With fall colors just beginning to show, it was obvious that this woods might just be one of those great ones.

The entry sign of this nature preserve protected by the Nature Conservancy testified to the generosity of Robert and Shirley Efroymson in their wish to protect the intact old forest. Described as an old-growth woods, it was dedicated as a state nature preserve in 1987.

The 58-acre preserve has no trail but that is of benefit, as it allows wandering at heart's content through a splendid woodland among many trees, each enticing the visitor to examine its unique character. And what trees they were: beech, maple, tulip, oak, hackberry, and blue beech. The notoriety of this place is due to its classification as primarily beech-maple, one of only a few remaining tracts on the Tipton Till Plain. In fact, glacial till and erratics can be seen in the woods, linking back to the last Wisconsin glacial period. These transported granitic boulders resided here before the woods ever developed, but now add an intriguing component of interest to the old-growth setting. The understory has a good diversity of shrubs and spring ephemerals.

The wind was blowing steadily through the forest, as it most likely does much of the time across the vast flat farmscapes here in central Indiana. Fall was approaching and leaves were gradually drifting down to the forest floor. Great bounties of acorns had fallen from the oaks, and many had been consumed by the squirrel community. The pawpaws and spicebush, too, were yellowing, their photosynthesis closing down for the year. Beneath the great old red oak which had given its tremendous bounty of fancy acorns for the year, all was in order maintaining the role of this preserve as a place of refuge and beauty.

Location: 10560 N CR 150 E Morristown, IN 46161

Right page: A walk through the solitude of Efroymson Woods

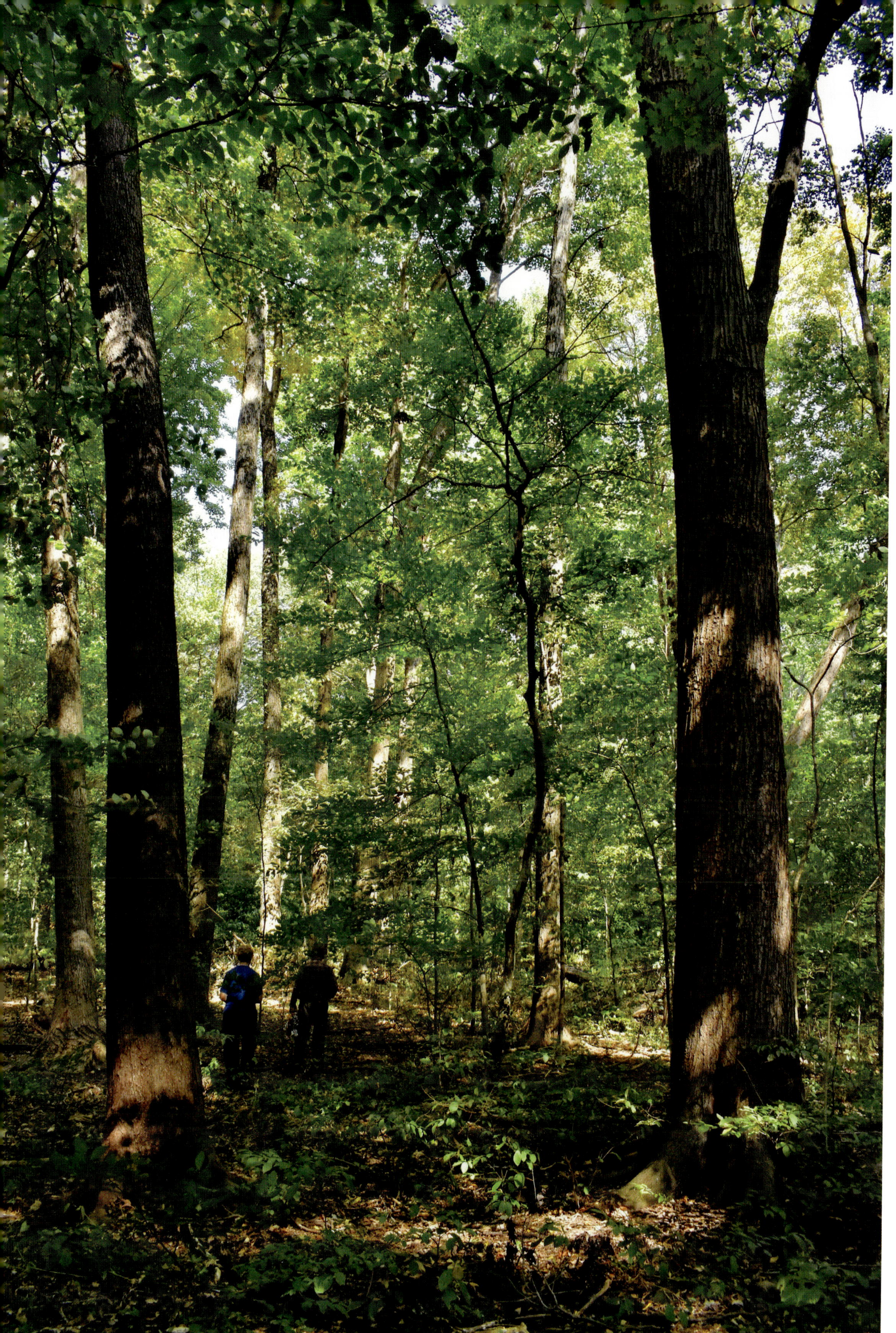

GINN WOODS
DELAWARE COUNTY

On a perfect early November day, with fall color still in show and warm sunlight penetrating the forest with halos through old beech limbs, the special allure of this woods began to take shape. Here, near the Mississinewa River, grows a 161-acre original tract of forest with little, if any, disturbance from humans. Any minimal impacts have been long erased. The original parcel was in the Ginn family from 1830 until 1970, when it was acquired by Ball State University. A total of four tracts now composes the greater Ginn Woods complex, giving it status as the second largest area of old-growth woods in the state.

The area is part of the Central Till Plain Natural Region (Homoya, 1985). This is a flatwoods, with soil types of poor drainage, fine texture, mottled subsoils, and lying above finely textured glacial till. Given the nature of the soils, croplands in the area require drainage channels. An old drainage ditch runs through part of the wooded property but does not appear to have affected the quality of the woods.

In our visit there, BSU lands manager John Taylor and biology professor Dave LeBlanc pointed out the plots being monitored, as well as showing us through the woods. One of the resident stewards of the property, a fine redheaded woodpecker, greeted us as we entered. Dry conditions made walking easy, and the nettles were gone. It was mentioned that in spring, the ephemerals are quite glorious, necessitating another visit.

Although this is noticeably a beech-maple forest, we also observed that there were many oaks spread throughout, including red, pin, shumard, white, and swamp white. Other species of interest this day were basswood, buckeye, tulip, cottonwood, elm, and hackberry. While most of the trees here are not massive giants, they are still impressive. Size does not always directly correlate with age due to several localized factors. Here, the fine old trees reach back to over 150 years in age, substantiating their classification as old growth. Ongoing research has utilized tools such as drones and aerial flights with LiDAR to determine canopy area, species abundance, tree heights, and mortality. Increment borer corings have also enabled aging to be determined, as well as assessments of past growth and climatic variations. The woods have been used for research and student projects for over 60 years and remain an important part of the university program.

The significance of Ginn Woods as one of the few old-growth forests left in Indiana has led to its recent designation as a dedicated state nature preserve. This recognition places it at high value for conservation and protection. The commitment of Ball State University to recognize these valuable assets and maintain them in their natural state is admirable.

Location: 15 miles NE of Muncie. Visitation here only through permission of BSU. Limited parking.

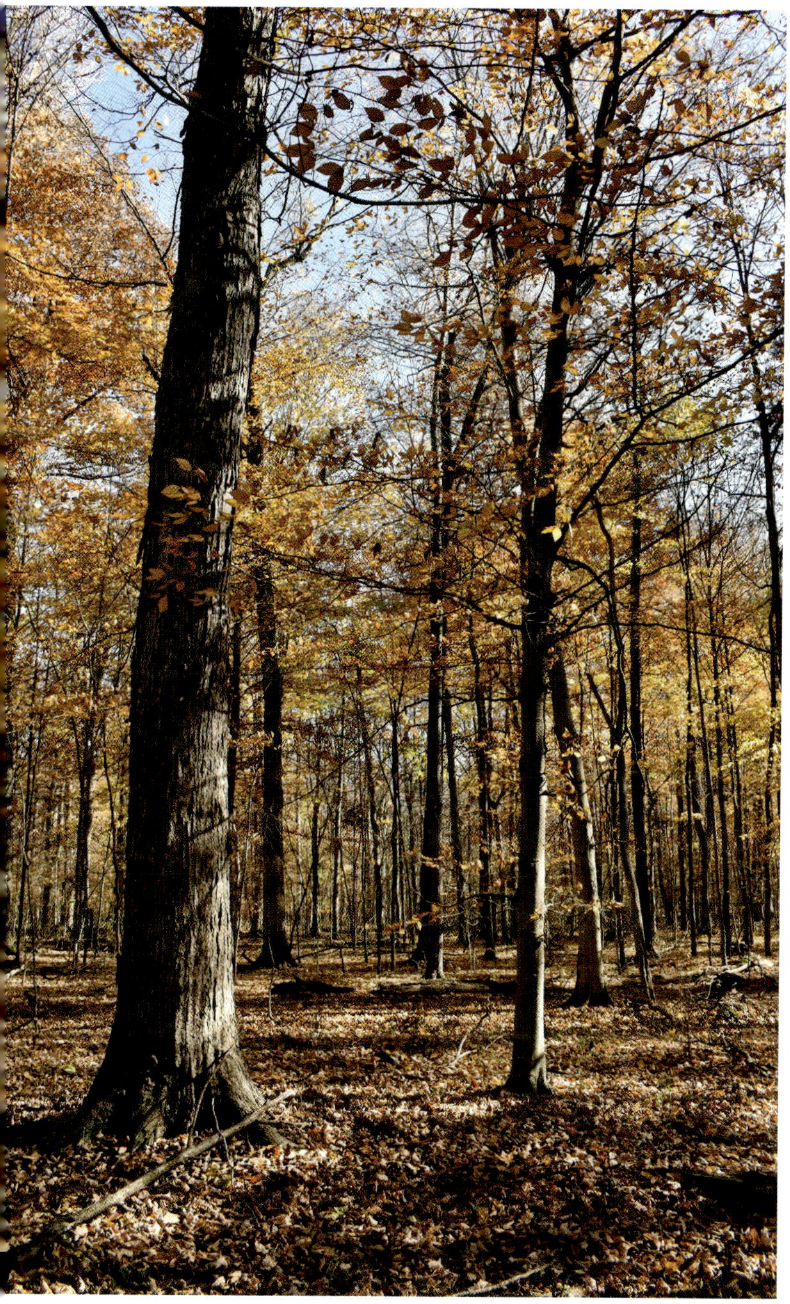

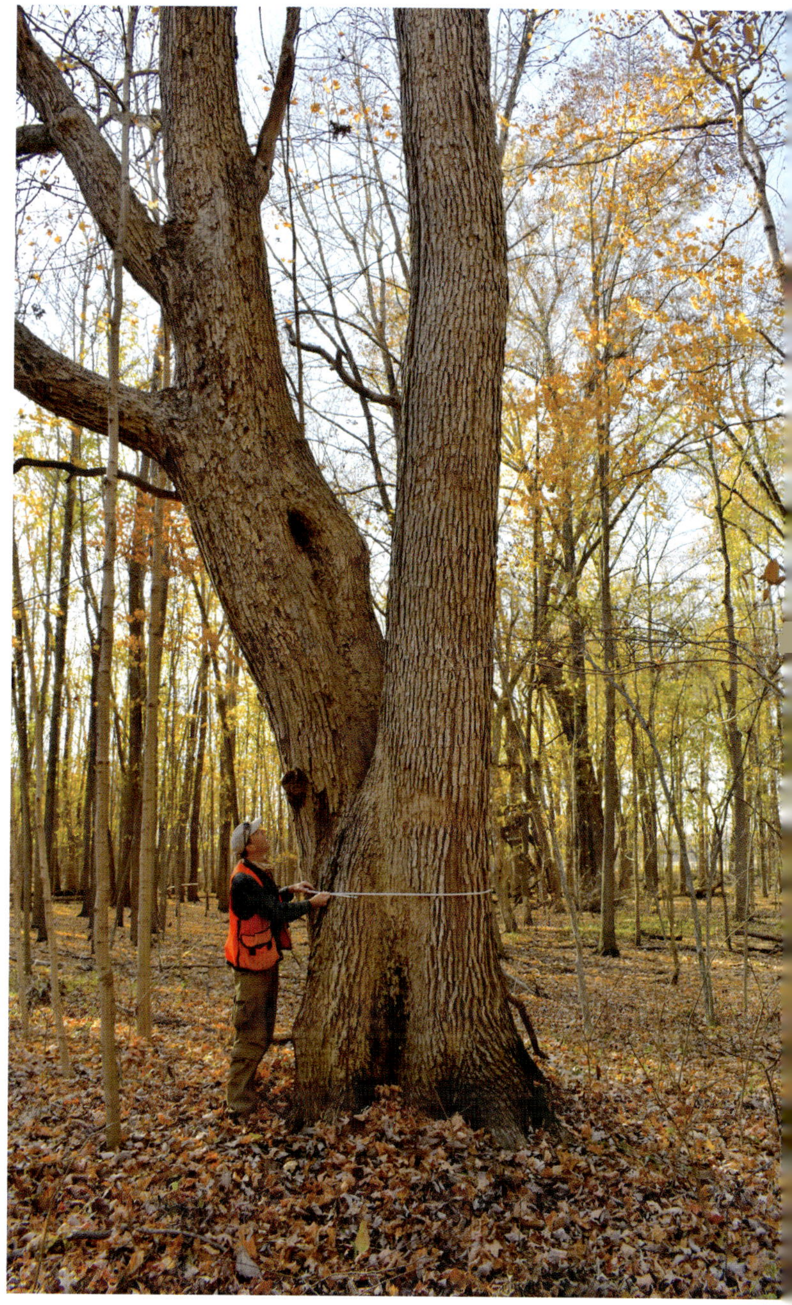

Left: Ginn Woods old growth. **Right:** John Taylor measures large chinquapin oak in Ginn Woods.

GUTHRIE, WELLS, AND TRIBBETT'S WOODS
JENNINGS COUNTY

This one county, named after our first governor, Jonathan Jennings, not only honors history, but also preserves some of the actual, original forest pieces that were present during his time. Perhaps he rode through this very area in 1817, when the county was formed, but did he admire the old giant trees, or were they so commonplace then that they were considered very normal? We may not know that, but upon entering each of these woods, we can step back over two hundred years to marvel at what is still here.

GUTHRIE WOODS NATURE PRESERVE

Another prime example of the Nature Conservancy's work along with the Nature Study Club of Indiana and the Indiana Division of Nature Preserves resulted in saving this fine old-growth woods. The Sarah Lewis Guthrie Memorial Woods officially protects one of the oldest remaining forests in the state. Originally donated to the Nature Study Club in 1927 by William Guthrie, the more recent coordination of partners resulted in its dedication as a state nature preserve in 1999. The stone marker in the southeast corner of the property reads: "This forest land is dedicated to Sarah Lewis Guthrie for a perpetual sanctuary as a living memorial to one who loved trees, flowers, and birds." The property was transferred to the Oak Heritage Conservancy, which now carries on the responsibility for protecting it in perpetuity.

Visiting here in 2019 and 2020 to photograph for this book was an inspiring experience. While it is brushy along the edge, upon entering the 63-acre woods it becomes quite obvious why visitors feel they are in a special place. Trees of mixed age classes constitute the southern half of the property, including beech, oak, and sweetgum. Many of these are already mature, with others rapidly coming into their own prominence. Very old specimens beckon one onward from tree to tree in the northern half. Here are some great swamp chestnut oaks, swamp white, and red oak. On the forest floor lie decaying remains of giants who have fallen in the battle of age, winds, and storms. Ever-present crayfish castles punctuate the loamy-clay soil, which allows very little percolation, resulting in standing pools during spring, later drying to cracked mud. The elevation change throughout is only 10 feet, certainly indicative of being called a "flatwoods." The gentle breeze whispering through the canopy allowed us to hear the woodpeckers at work, interrupted only by the flirting sound of chickadees.

Location: Just north of Dupont on road 500 S. See IDNR Nature Preserves or Oak Heritage Conservancy website.

WELLS WOODS NATURE PRESERVE

While at a rather small 20 acres, there is a lot of wondrous character packed into this splendid location. Known for many years in the little community of Commiskey, the property had been in the Wells family since the late 1800s. Eli and Jane had a fine brick home there and a school was later built on their property. We can imagine children running through this same old virgin timber woods over 100 years ago. The Wells family's legacy is perpetuated and the trees are never cut, as per their wish. Now a state nature preserve, the woods can be shared with all who love great trees.

The grand beech, oaks, and tulips in here are splendid—massive, dominating, towering. The "white clay flats," as they are called, create shallow standing water in the spring rains, but dry to hard pans in the late summer. Crayfish mounds dot the forest floor and woodpeckers spy down upon our presence before dismissing us and returning to work. Many old rotting logs from the ancient ones detour us around from tree to tree, and the abundance of pawpaws with tinges of gold remind all that fall is here.

Location: Southwest side of the town of Commiskey. Ownership: IDNR Division of Nature Preserves. See website. Parking along edge of road is difficult.

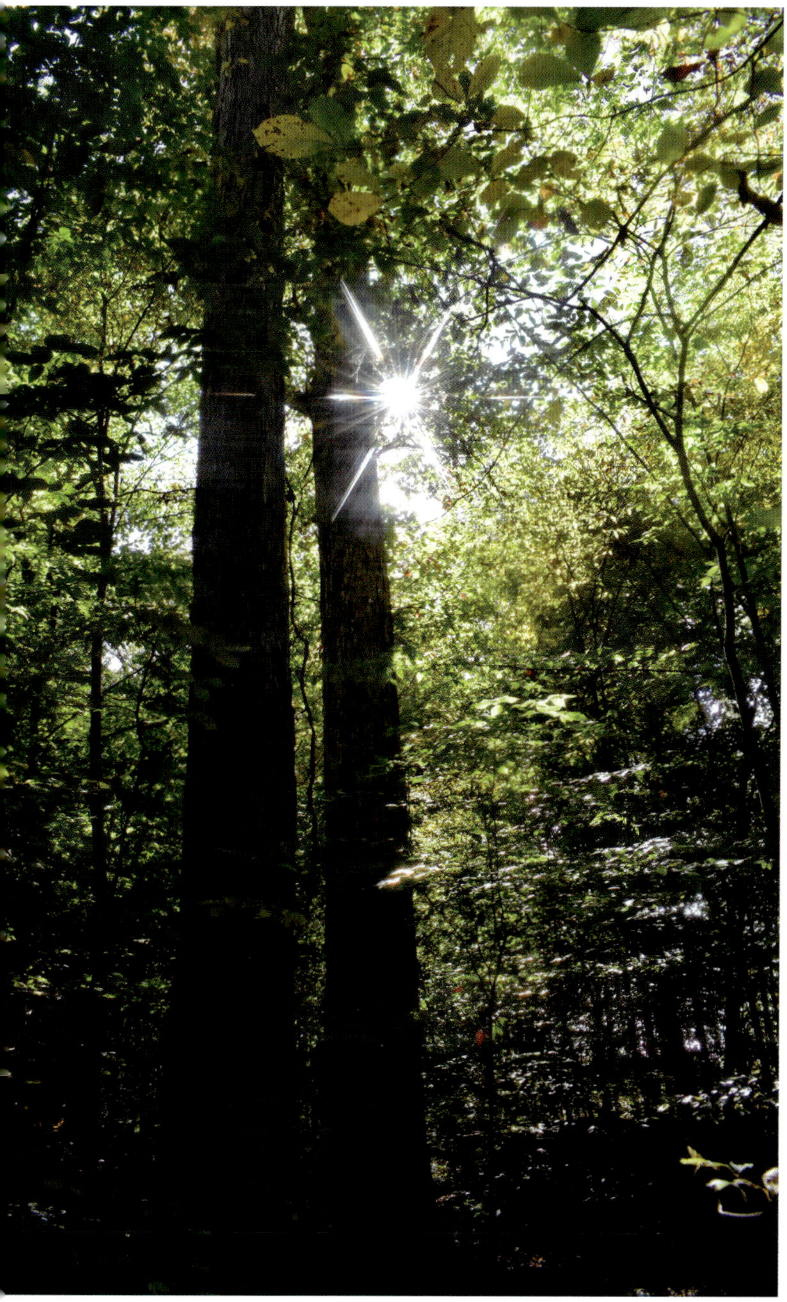

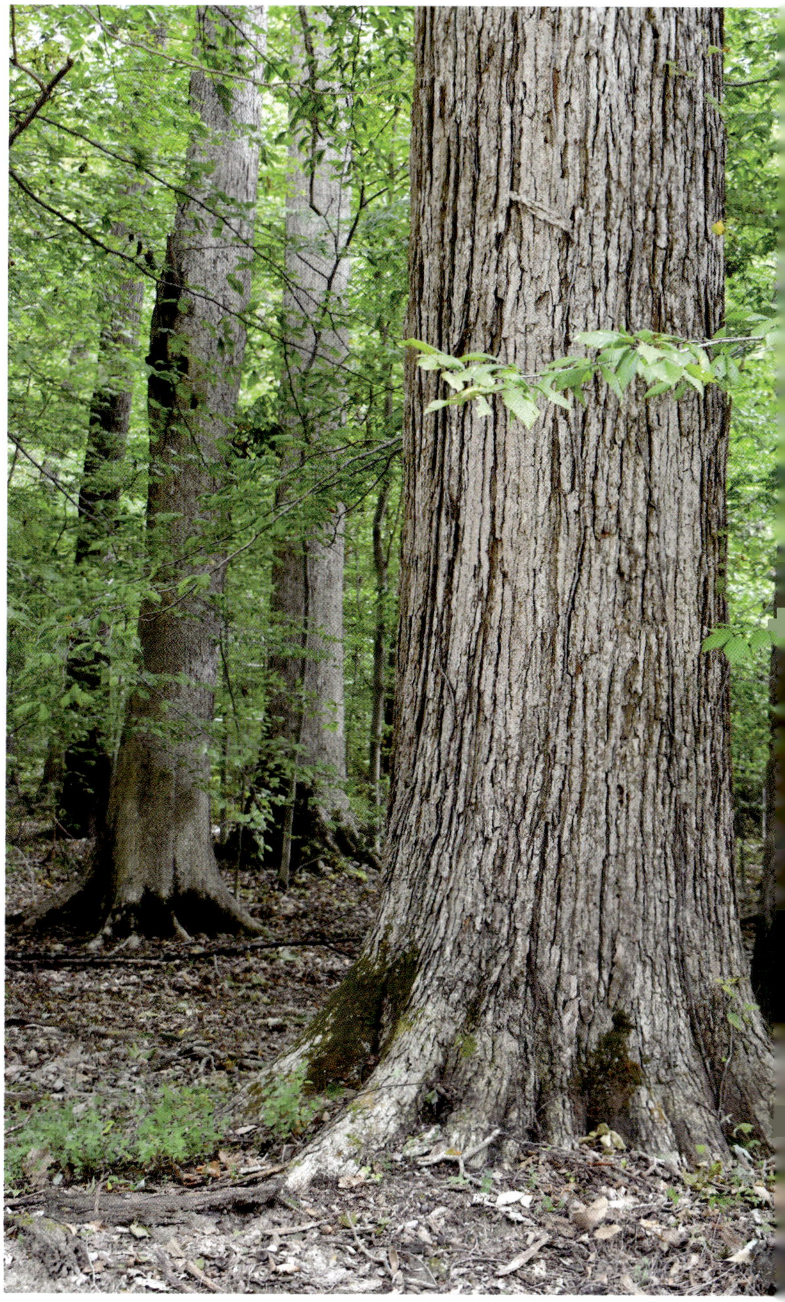

Left: Early morning in Guthrie Woods, Jennings County. **Right:** Grand old swamp chestnut oak, Guthrie Woods.

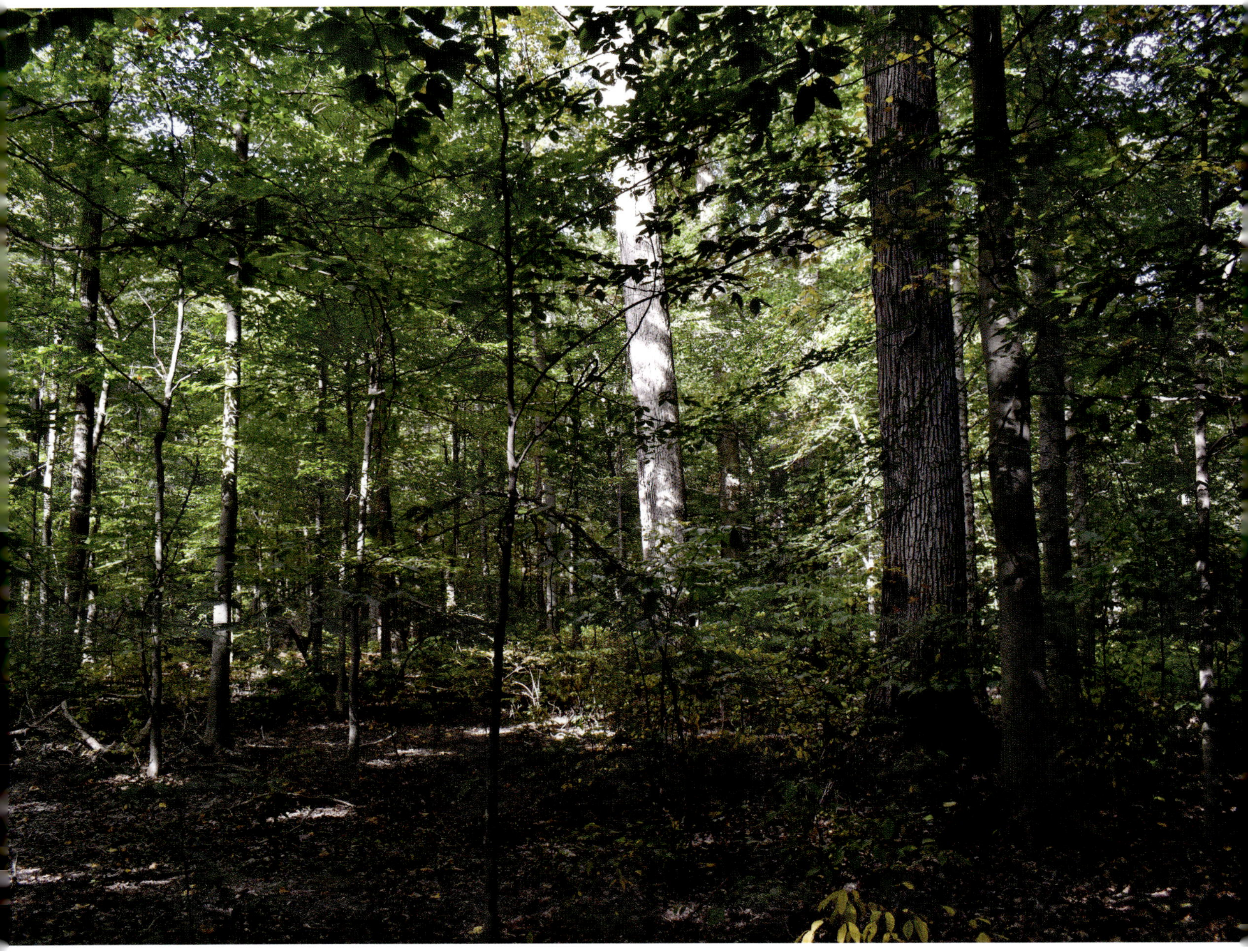

Sweeping panorama of old growth in Wells Woods

TRIBBETT'S WOODS NATURE PRESERVE

Clifford and Ida Tribbett would be proud today that their protective desire for this 33-acre tract is still honored and respected long after the original family purchase in 1887. Brother and sister, never married, born at the turn of 1900, they still owned the family farm in 1980. As Paul Carmony recounted in an essay for the Oak Heritage Conservancy, "In 1980 they were no longer farming, but Clifford still milked one cow and Ida churned the cream and made butter. She also kept a small flock of ducks and geese and raised a garden. An outhouse was still in use and a pendulum clock ticked off the minutes as we rocked and talked about their lives and the affairs of the world."[2] When Clifford passed on, Ida remained to see the woods protected by the Nature Conservancy. Transferred to Oak Heritage Conservancy in 2005, the guarantee is still there just as the Tribbetts wished.

As my wife and I entered the woods late in the afternoon in October 2020, weaving through greenbrier and colorful trees on the edge, we found an ideal spot on an old beech limb to have coffee from the thermos and sit quietly to observe. Large trees could be seen looming in the distance and barred owls began to call forth a welcome to their special domain. Further into the woods the call of a junco was heard, signaling early arrival in southern Indiana.

This property is another example of that "flatwoods" terrain encountered in the previous two locations. Poorly drained soils do suit some plant communities that are a little different from richer, well-drained soils. There were many old beech of great stature looking down upon smaller blue beech far below. The combination of the two smooth, grayish-barked tree types added an interesting mosaic. With an abundance of the parasitic plant called beech drops in the root flares, the symbiotic relationship was clearly seen. Not to be outdone, the powerful presence of mighty poplars, swamp chestnut oak, swamp white oak, and sweetgum completed the canvas. Here in this fairly remote and quiet area of farmlands resides a most worthy protected forest where the presence of Clifford and Ida Tribbett certainly remains forever.

Location: 4 miles northwest of Commiskey, Road 750S. See IDNR Nature Preserves website.

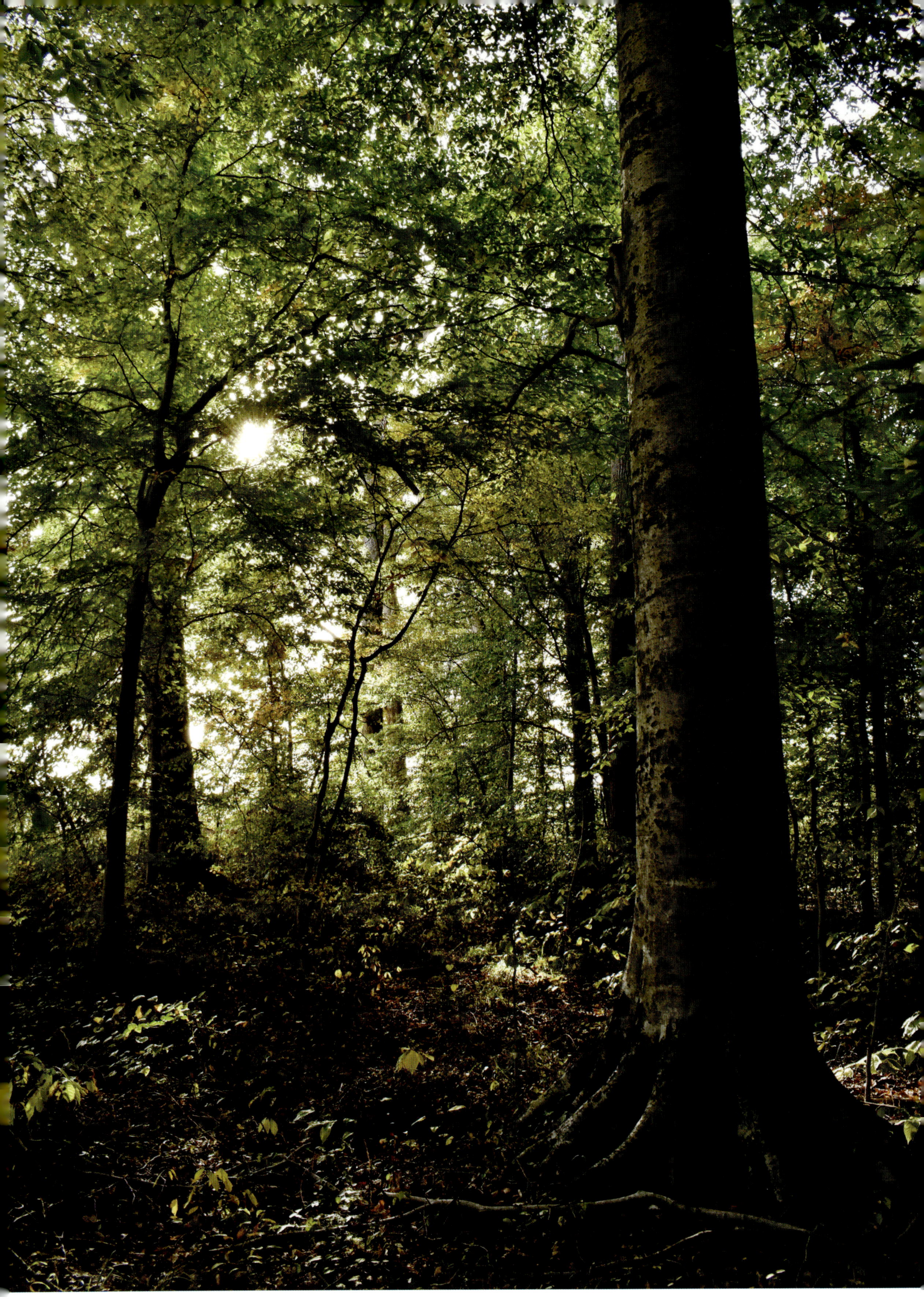

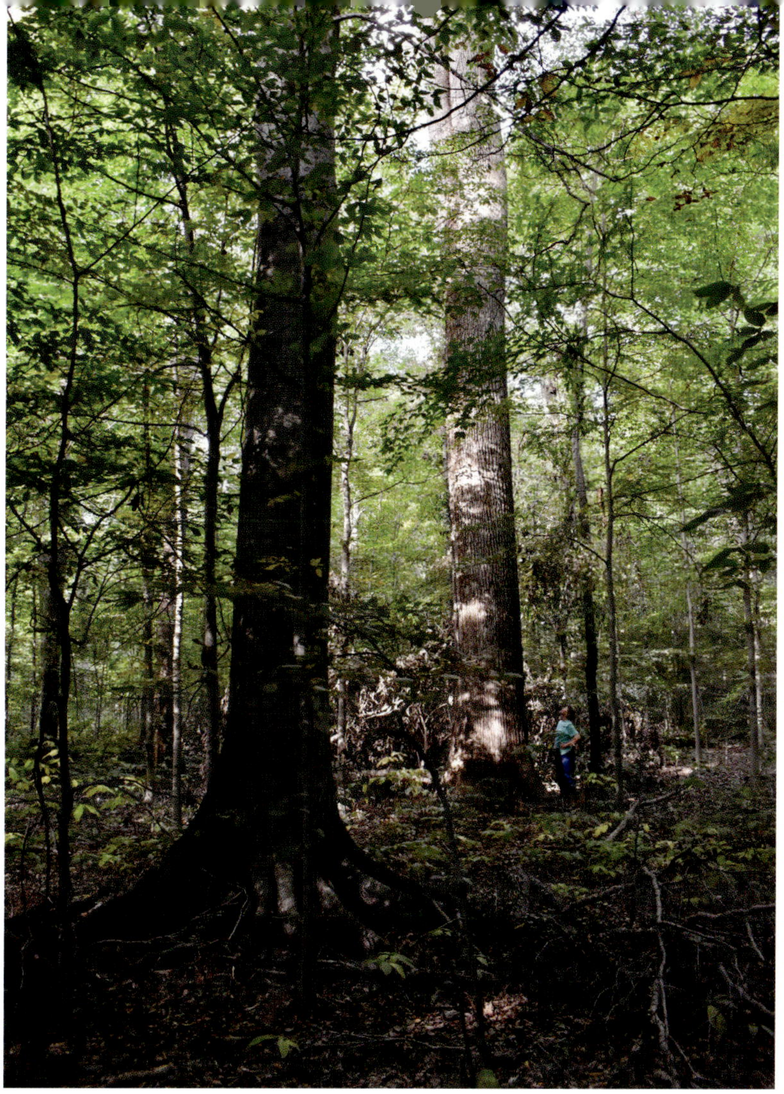

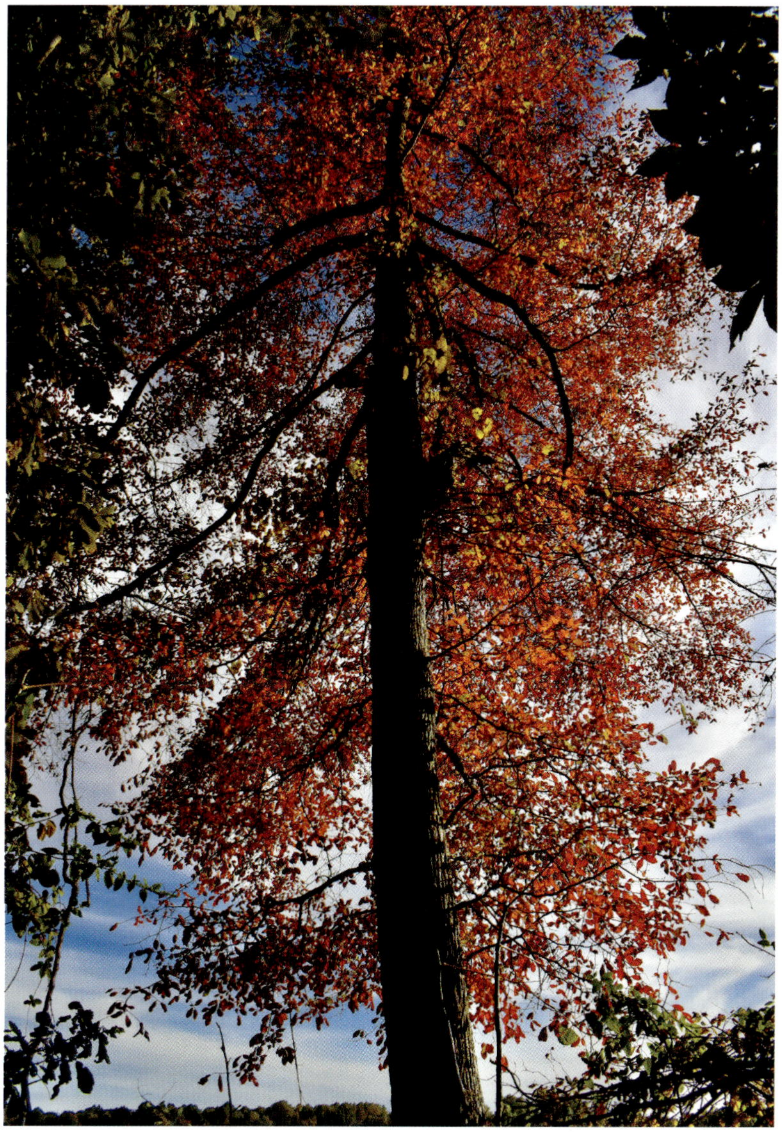

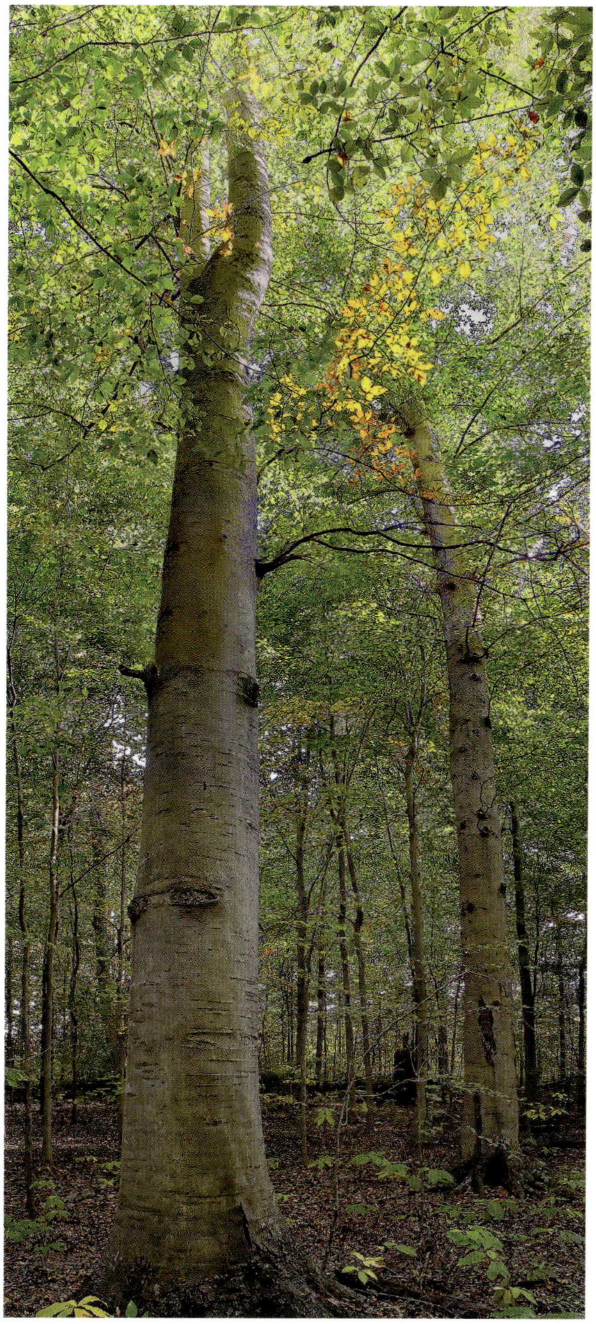

Left page: The awe of Tribbett's old woods inspires everyone

Right page, top left: The giants towering over all—Tribbett's Woods

Bottom left: Stunning black gum, Tribbett's Woods

Above: Tribbett's Woods beech panorama

HALL WOODS
PUTNAM COUNTY

The loud group of noisy grackles perched high in trees by the parking lot flew away in a great group swoop, as they do, leaving an abrupt pause before the cheery voices of songbirds regained prominence in the forest. A well-designed nature trail here at Hall Woods invites exploration immediately, and those who enter here will not be disappointed.

This property is part of the Big Walnut Valley Natural Area, a masterpiece of wondrous old trees, waters rushing over siltstone and glacial rocks, joyous bird life, and delightful hillsides and valley floors carpeted by lush wildflowers in spring. Over 3,000 acres are protected now in this corridor thanks to the Nature Conservancy and the Indiana Department of Natural Resources Division of Nature Preserves. The decades of assembling private parcels here was arduous and no mean feat, but the product—stunning.

As we proceeded down the trail, transition was made from successional forest to larger and larger trees. Oh, what trees these were. Gorgeous oaks everywhere, stately, massive, demanding the eye to move from flared trunk to heavenly top. White oak and red oak are signature trees on this commanding ridge, overlooking the valley floor down below. The trail begins its downhill slope a little further on, passing by an old, restored cabin that was probably a getaway in days past. Down the wooden stairs brings you to Big Walnut Creek, happily and teasingly flowing through rocks and the old dam structure. A startling flutter rising upward in a great rush drew our immediate attention. The great blue heron had been disturbed and had no intention of letting us watch him fish in the shallow waters. Away he flew down the creek corridor to another secret spot. We turned along the trail then, proceeding upstream among very fine old sycamores, boxelders, and silver maples. And then another great surprise as we lifted our head to a silent movement above. So graceful, calm, powerfully confident, inspiring in its very meaning, the bald eagle glided in the slightest breeze down the middle of the creek valley, not knowing, of course, that it had just touched the souls of these adventurous humans.

Following onward then, fully filled with excitement, we congratulated the big old leaning sycamore with moss-covered flaking bark, thanked the beautiful silver maples for just being there solely for us, then told the chunky-barked old cottonwood that we would return. Up the stairs brought us back onto the ridgetop, the loop now passing back through those same splendid oaks, allowing us to recapture the wonder of our first impressions.

Location: Half mile east of Bainbridge on U.S. 36, turn south on County Road 675N toward Baker's Camp, proceed half mile to parking on left.

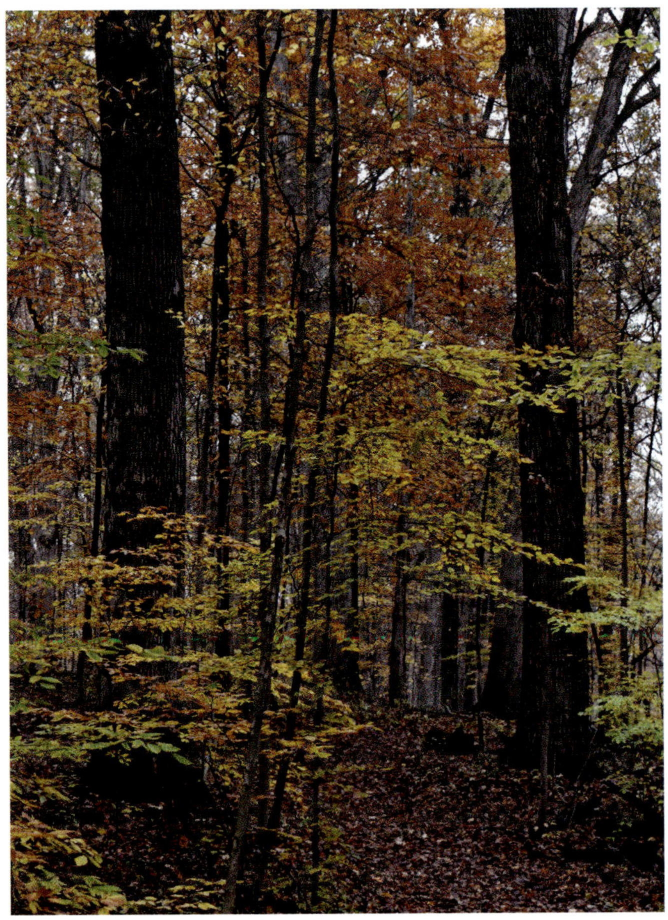

Fine old red oaks, Hall Woods Nature Preserve

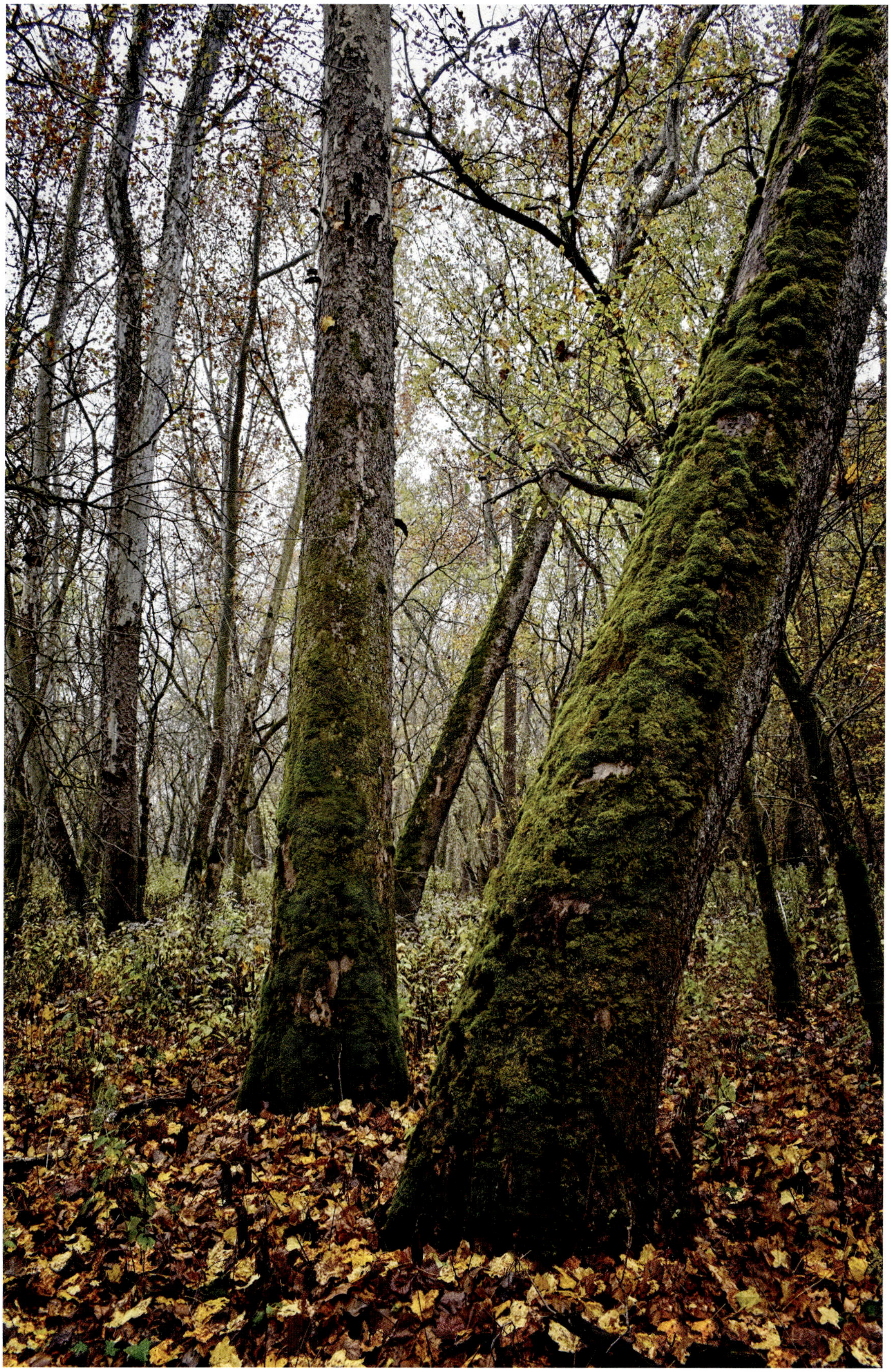

Stately green moss-laden sycamores, Hall Woods

HOOT WOODS
OWEN COUNTY

An April morning chill greeted us as we arrived at this rather remote location in rural Owen County. Walking along a creek and across a farm field brought us to the edge of the woods. Unless you knew about this place, you would never realize that it was there, basically untouched for hundreds of years. The peace and quiet were immediate rewards and prepared us for a memorable visit.

The low, swampy ground at the bottom had the typical species of blue beech, elm, and sycamore. On the other side of the drainage the obvious change in elevation was noticed, and since the vegetation was rather open, many large old trees could be seen awaiting investigation.

The hillside was a showplace of spring ephemerals, all vying for attention. Mayapple presented an almost universal carpet of green. Wild blue phlox was everywhere, with many patches and individuals on the rocky hillside, displaying a fine carpet below the distinguished beech. Squirrel corn was in prolific numbers as well, their pendant white blooms among the delicate basal green foliage. A full complement of blue and yellow violets and spring beauty added their importance to the mix.

It was obvious this was an old-growth setting from the very first moment. Many aged specimens were scattered all along the hillside, from lowland to top. Each beckoned a closer look, drawing us from one to the other. The spacing was prudently planned by nature, with the scatter of patriarchs, huge decaying logs, and medium-size trees ready to take future prominence.

The largest trees were mostly beech and tulip, with maple obviously striving to be among the future dominants. Of lesser importance were oak and hickory. One huge old chinquapin oak, although mostly dead, was an icon for the property and many visitors have been photographed by it. Beyond, and upslope, open areas at the top of the hill accommodated a great display of white dogwood.

Research here has continued for many years, with noted ecologists Robert Petty, Alton Lindsey, and Marion Jackson among those who documented changes over time. Some of the original survey points are still present. The woods was recognized as a National Natural Landmark in 1973. At that time, a conservation easement was granted to the Nature Conservancy, a milestone in steps to permanently recognize and protect this climax beech-maple forest complex.

Tribute must be given to the dedication of the Hoot family in preserving the presettlement character all these years. Emigrants from Germany in 1860, the family settled here on 160 acres. Very few trees were ever cut from this portion of the property and a family trust in 1975 helped assure lasting protection. In 2017, 80 acres of the woods were donated to Sycamore Land Trust.

As hawks glided silently overhead and songbirds cheerfully harmonized below, we departed quietly, leaving this memorable sanctuary to welcome the next visitor.

Location: Rural Owen County. Visitation conducted only through Sycamore Land Trust to protect the fragility and access easement.

Right page, top: A panoramic view of Hoot Woods

Left: The old denizens stand watch

Middle: If this old beech could speak . . .

Right: The ancient chinquapin oak awaits its finality

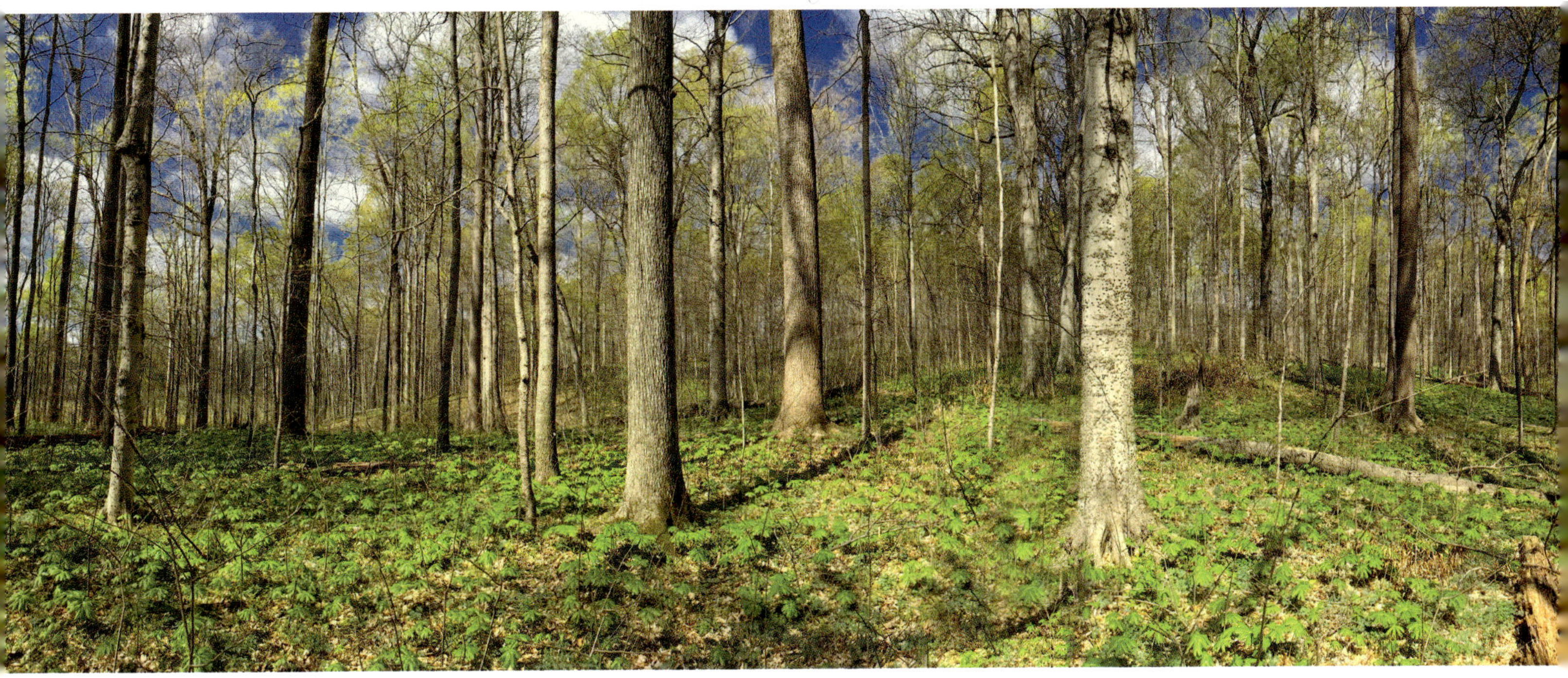
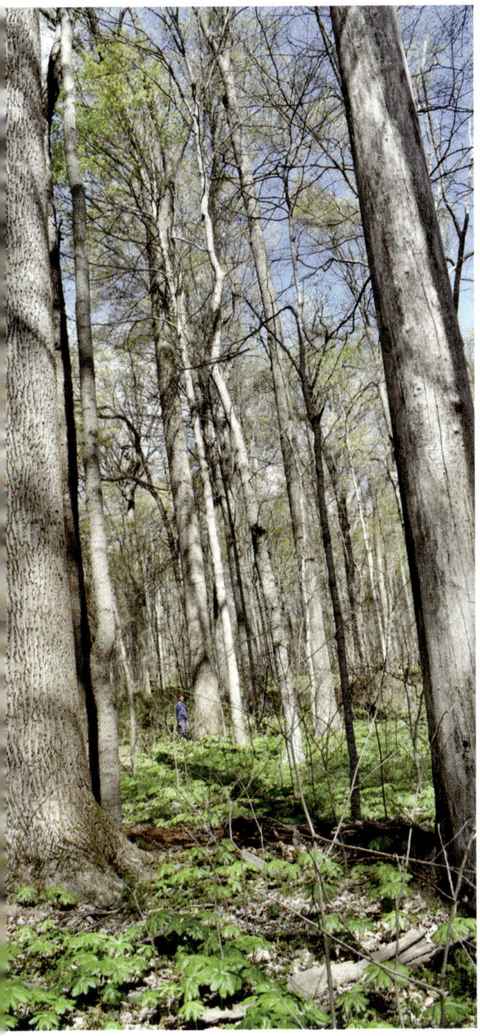
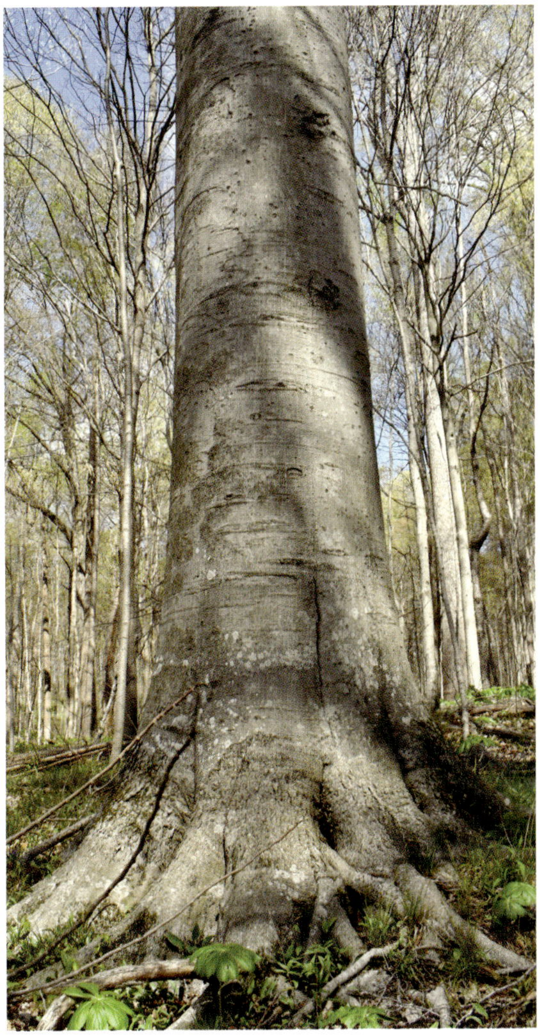
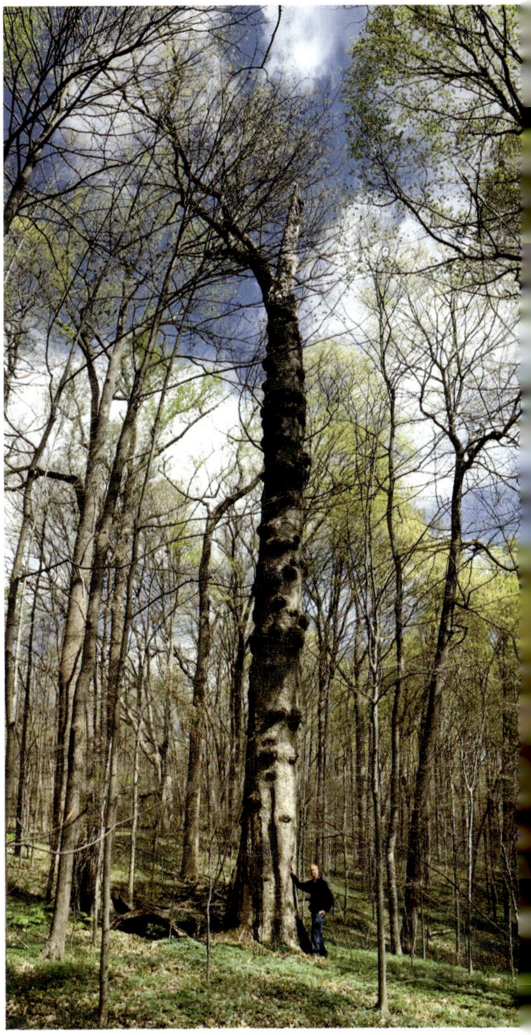

HENRY KRAMER ORIGINAL WOODS
SPENCER COUNTY

Many of the old bottomlands along the Ohio River were cleared over 100 years ago for farmland, leaving only scattered tracts considered too difficult to drain. There are a few locations where intact woods can be found, but this one is a top-quality, original, low wetland forest. When you are immersed within the great sentinels, it is no wonder that after Alton Lindsey's visit there in 1967, he, Father Damian Schmelz of St. Meinrad, and Stanley Nichols cited Kramer Woods as one of Indiana's finest potential natural areas.

This is another extraordinary story of how generations of a family passed on a remarkable original piece of Indiana. In 1854, Henry, then seven, was brought to this country from Prussia. The family settled in this area west of Rockport, eventually accumulating 2,000 acres. Henry became county treasurer, then state senator, and had a law office in Rockport. Even though he succumbed at the early age of 57, the family maintained the old intact woods. It is one of the state's earliest enrolled Classified Forests. Granddaughters Helen and Kathryn Hougland inherited the land, turning away timber buyers who thought the time might be ripe to get the valuable woods.

After Lindsey, Schmelz, and Nichols highly recommended protection, Helen and Kathryn began to pursue ways of honoring their grandfather's original wishes. Through many visits by the highly respected Father Damian, who gave wise counsel and, in fact, lived not far away at St. Meinrad Archabbey, discussions led to a grand solution. Helen bequeathed the property to the Nature Conservancy in 1998 at her death.

The property was transferred to the Division of Nature Preserves and dedicated as Indiana's 200th Nature Preserve in 2003. It is also a National Natural Landmark and remains a great tribute to Henry Kramer and his family.

The May visit guaranteed lots of vegetation and it was not surprising to find poison ivy, spicebush, and nettle. If an ecological study of "richness" were conducted, it would surely be composed mostly of these impediments to easy progress through the woods. However, disregarding these (not easily done), it is very inspiring to see absolutely huge and numerous trees everywhere. The composition of shumard oak, pin oak, hickory, and beech, in such numbers and sizes, makes this one of Indiana's most important remaining lowland forests. This and Wesselman Woods in Evansville are the most significant examples left in the state.

The total tract of 224 acres is quite large and bounded by Isaac Wright Drain and Hurricane Creek, both now quite grown up and not maintained. They have steep banks, can be dangerous if water-filled, and should not be crossed.

Prior to the emergence of understory vines, bushes, and nettles, we visited again in March 2021. In this season, we could really see through the woods. No matter where you looked or walked, very large trees invited inspection and admiration. Some standing water occupied a few spots, providing the perfect setting for a cacophony of spring peepers and green frogs. The old oaks really stood out, along with many sweetgums. Very grand swamp white oaks such as this one stood as guardians of their domain.

As is typical for old-growth woods, a mix of age classes was very evident. Several very large old decaying logs lay prostrate on the forest floor in various stages of decay. Young trees were beginning their march upward toward their chance at eventual supremacy.

This remarkable tract of virgin timber is a truly impressive place that really should be seen. Standing reverently here allows thoughts to be carried far away and back into time when Henry Kramer loved his old woods and did not cut it.

Location: From Rockport, take S.R. 66 west to S.R. 161, turn south, travel 3 miles to 300 S, turn west, and travel 2 miles. Park along the road, but off enough to allow farm machinery to pass. GPS coordinates: N 37.843932° W 87.137981°

Also see Division of Nature Preserves info sheet.

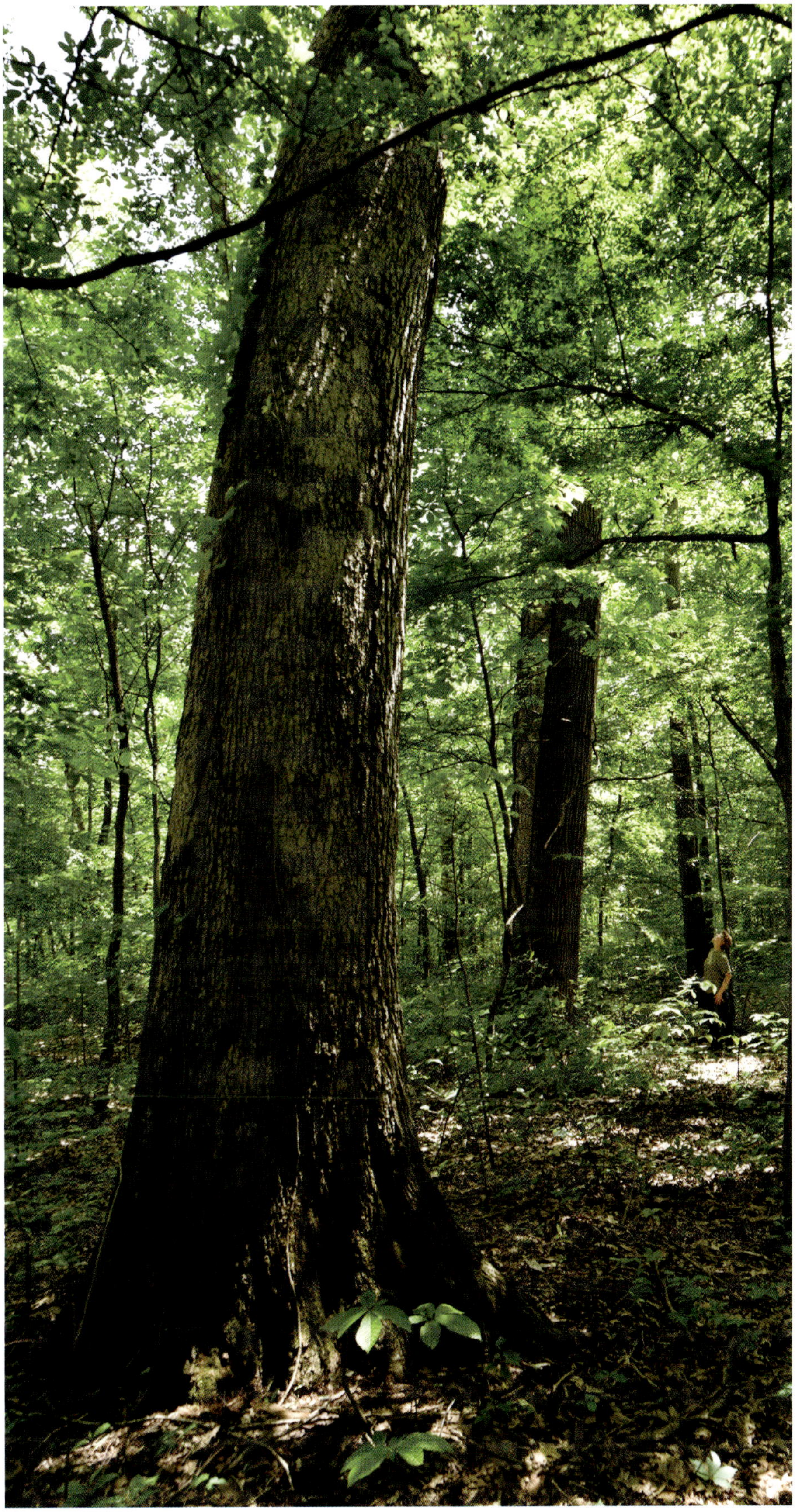

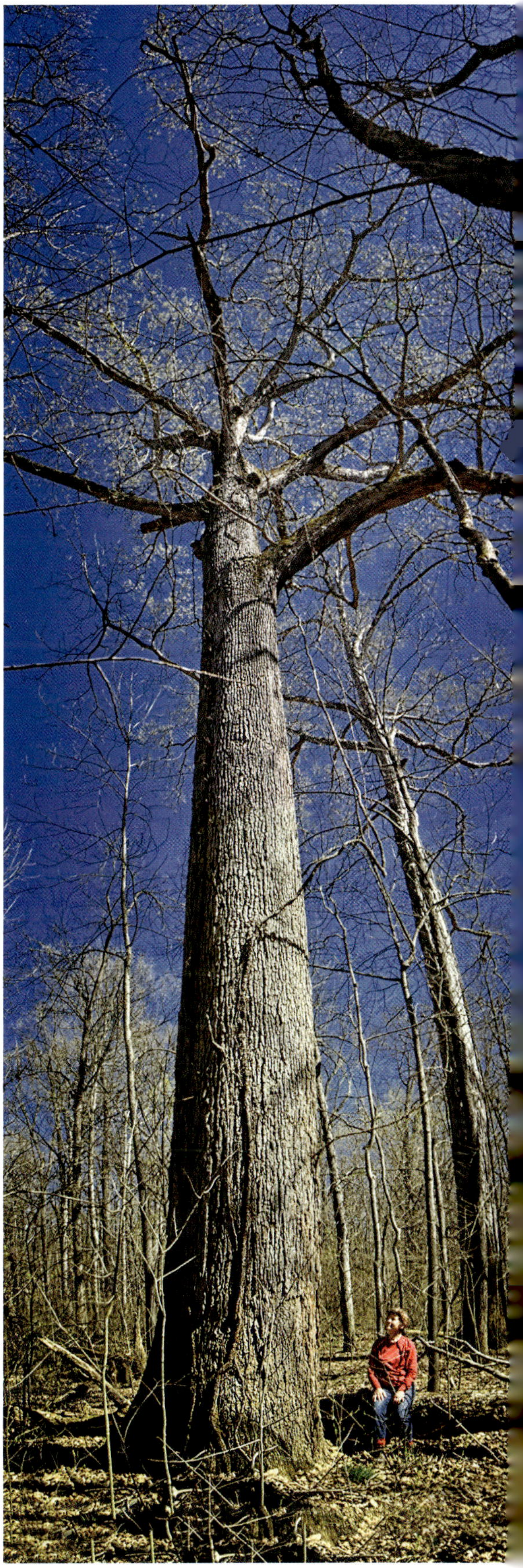

Left: The remarkable Kramer Original Woods, Spencer County
Right: Magnificent swamp white oak, Kramer Woods

MELTZER WOODS
SHELBY COUNTY

There are exceptional places, extraordinary places, and amazing places in Indiana. This preserve is all of them. When we were searching for old-growth locations, the descriptions of what was here were enticing and visitation became a must-see.

Immediately upon entering, a special world begins to unfold. Within minutes time stands still. You are beginning to be a viewer of what is, and what was. The old forest knows now, and has always known, the harmonious relationship of all natural elements in synchrony. While the activity of farming was heard on the outside of this captivating place and it was obvious that life was going on out there in the modern world, that was of no importance now. The old trees began to speak through their very majesty, kings of their domain, overseers of the intricate unfolding of time from 300 years in the past.

Huge old oaks, maples, beech, and tulip greet the hiker at every turn, always demanding a stop to admire, touch, and look far upward to the distant canopy, so high that binoculars are needed to see the leaf for identification.

The description of this place is so well stated by the Division of Nature Preserves fact sheet that we may quote from that:

> This nature preserve protects an example of high quality mixed mesophytic forest communities, the wetter forest dominated by Beech/Shumard Oak and the drier forest dominated by Beech/Maple. It is located within the Tipton Till Plain Section of the Central Till Plain Natural Region. Approximately 48 acres of the Meltzer property were never cleared. That old-growth stand was placed in the Indiana's Classified Forest Program in 1928. In 1973, this property was designated a National Natural Landmark. It is the last unprotected old growth forest in Indiana. In 2016, it was dedicated by the Division of Nature Preserves and partners.[3]

The forest had been part of the Meltzer family since 1857. It was sold through the family's generosity in 2016 by Phillip Meltzer and is now owned by the Central Indiana Land Trust. Mr. Meltzer passed away in 2020 and leaves a tremendous legacy for all Hoosiers.

The forest had a huge shumard oak—at one time the national champion. It fell in 2011 after 200 years of valiant service. Another huge tree is a swamp white oak, rated as the second tallest tree in Indiana. A third great find was the state champion black ash, which is also now gone, but is survived by another splendid one nearby and perhaps will be the new state record.

At the end of the mile-long nature trail, among the splendid poplars, passing the black ash and young beech, it can be said that reverence is truly in order and that the experience was one not to be forgotten.

Location: 1855 S 600 E. Shelbyville, IN 46176

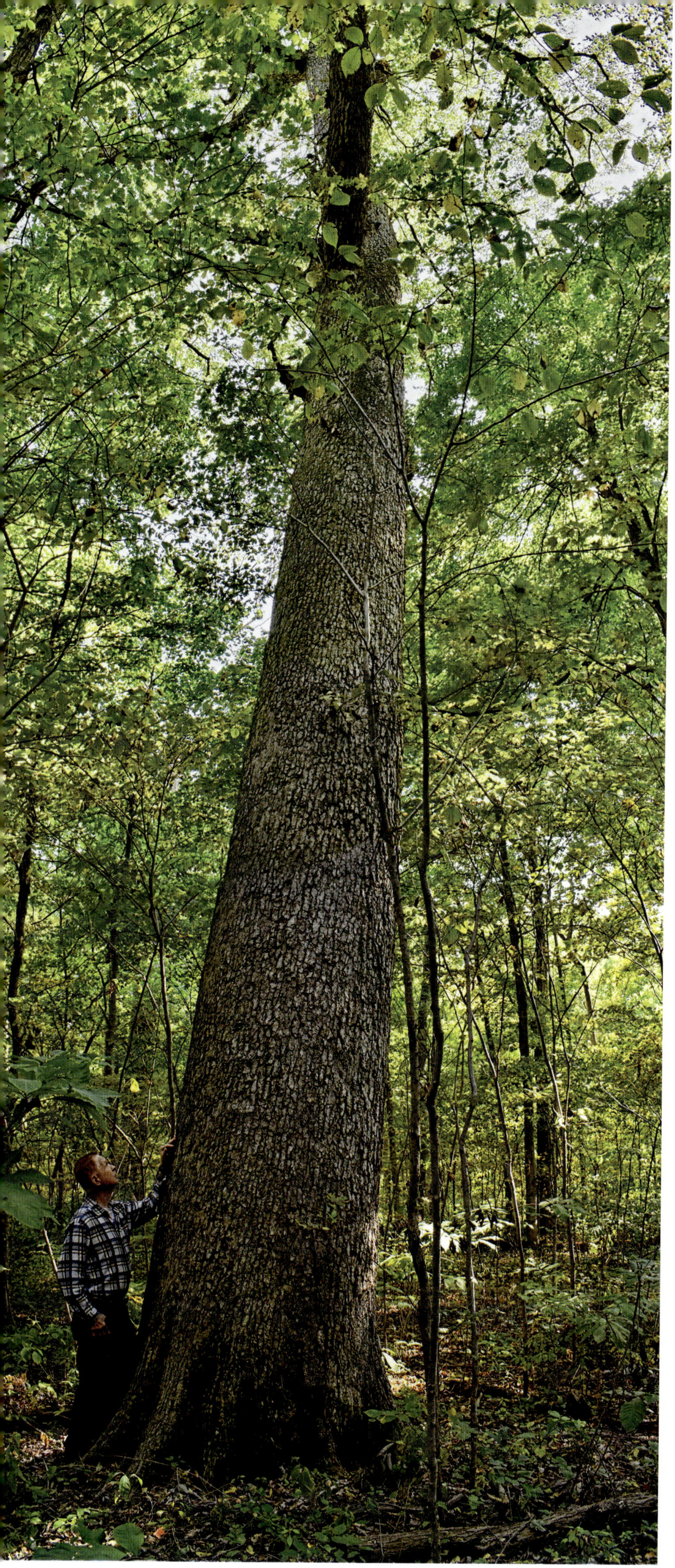

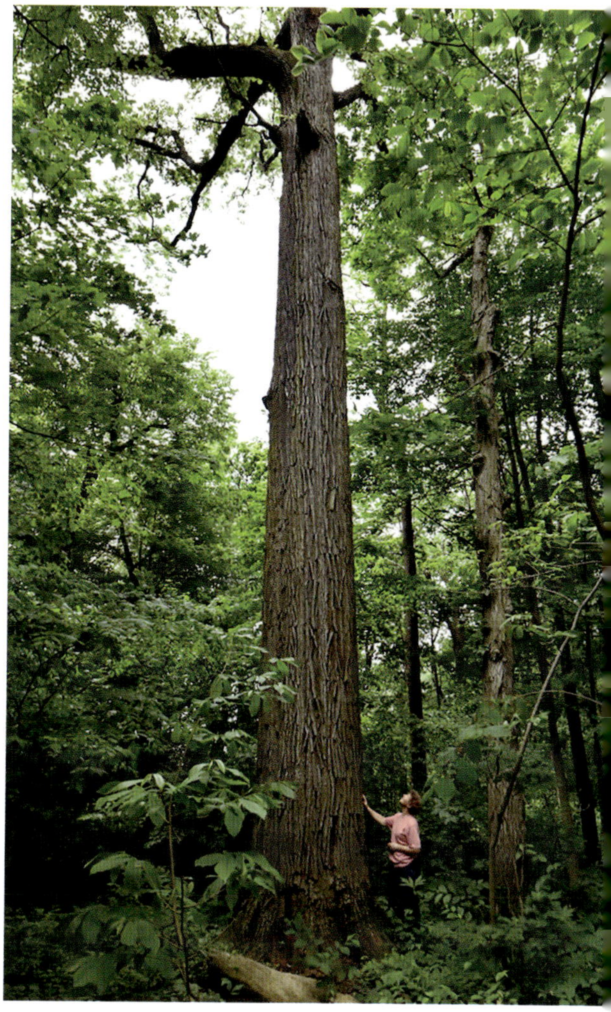

Left: Fantastic swamp white oak, Meltzer Woods

Above: One of Indiana's finest bur oaks, Meltzer Woods

PIONEER MOTHERS MEMORIAL FOREST
ORANGE COUNTY

The sheltered cove-like setting of these historic woods invited us to explore one of Indiana's original old-growth forests, a treasured place managed as a special area in the Hoosier National Forest. It has attracted those intrigued by very old trees for many years. Saved at the last minute from logging in 1940 by the Meridian Club of Paoli and the Pioneer Mothers Club, it is a tribute to the Joseph Cox family, which, even in poverty, refused to ever harvest it commercially. The family first settled on this hilly tract in 1816. The land was rough with very little flat area to farm, but close to Lick Creek, which at that time was most likely a wonderfully clear stream. The graceful, commanding sycamore shown here is close to an intriguing history story.

> Long before Joseph Cox arrived in 1811, Native Americans inhabited this area. One group is known as the Oliver Phase people. These prehistoric people are believed to have primarily lived in White River valleys between A.D. 1000 and 1500. They were a farming culture that lived in small groups (up to about 100 individuals). While most Oliver Phase villages have been found along the White River, at least one village was along Lick Creek in what is now the Pioneer Mothers Memorial Forest. This site was dated to A.D. 1380.[4]

We were looking for that well-known iconic black walnut, a giant among the other trees along the trail. It stands nobly on the left side of the pathway with fine companions of almost equal stature nearby. While not the state champion, it is still a magnificent long-lived specimen to be honored for holding this spot for over a century. No wonder this place was also called a Cathedral Grove—big walnuts, oaks, and tulips arching majestically overhead as if to create an atmosphere of reverence.

Years ago, the state champion giant white oak resided down the trail, a massive reminder of primeval Indiana. Many a group of schoolchildren, families, or friends would circle the tree with arms linked, posing for the perfect memory photo. No doubt some of those old photos still exist in treasured albums.

When visiting Pioneer Mothers, you will be treated to a mile-long trail passing among large sycamores near the creek and many fine old oaks, tulip, and walnut along the upland portion. The decayed remains of that beloved old oak lay just above the large impressive fieldstone Pioneer Mothers Memorial wall.

From its prehistoric occupants to the story of Joseph Cox, we cannot help but appreciate the cultural and natural history of this special place.

Location: 2 miles south of Paoli just off Highway 37. Second entrance on U.S. 150 one mile east of Paoli.

Ownership: U.S. Forest Service, 88 acres.

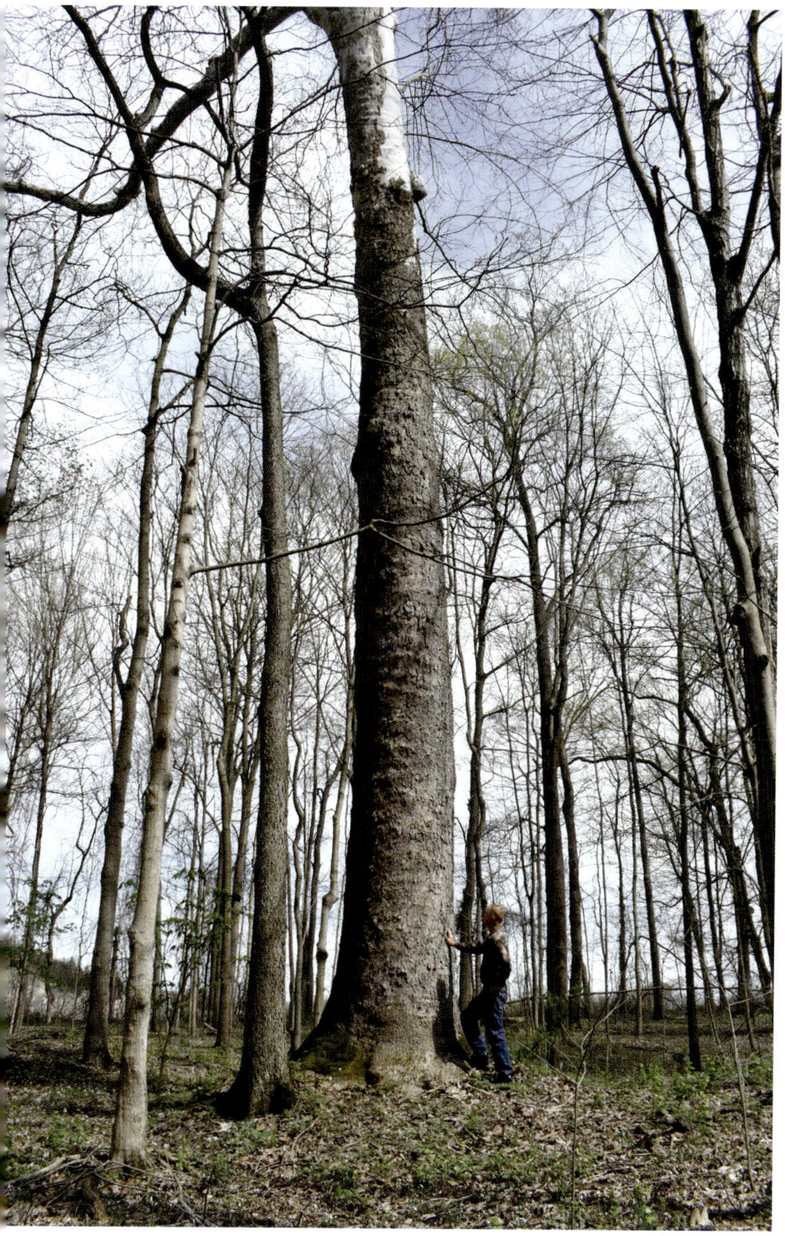

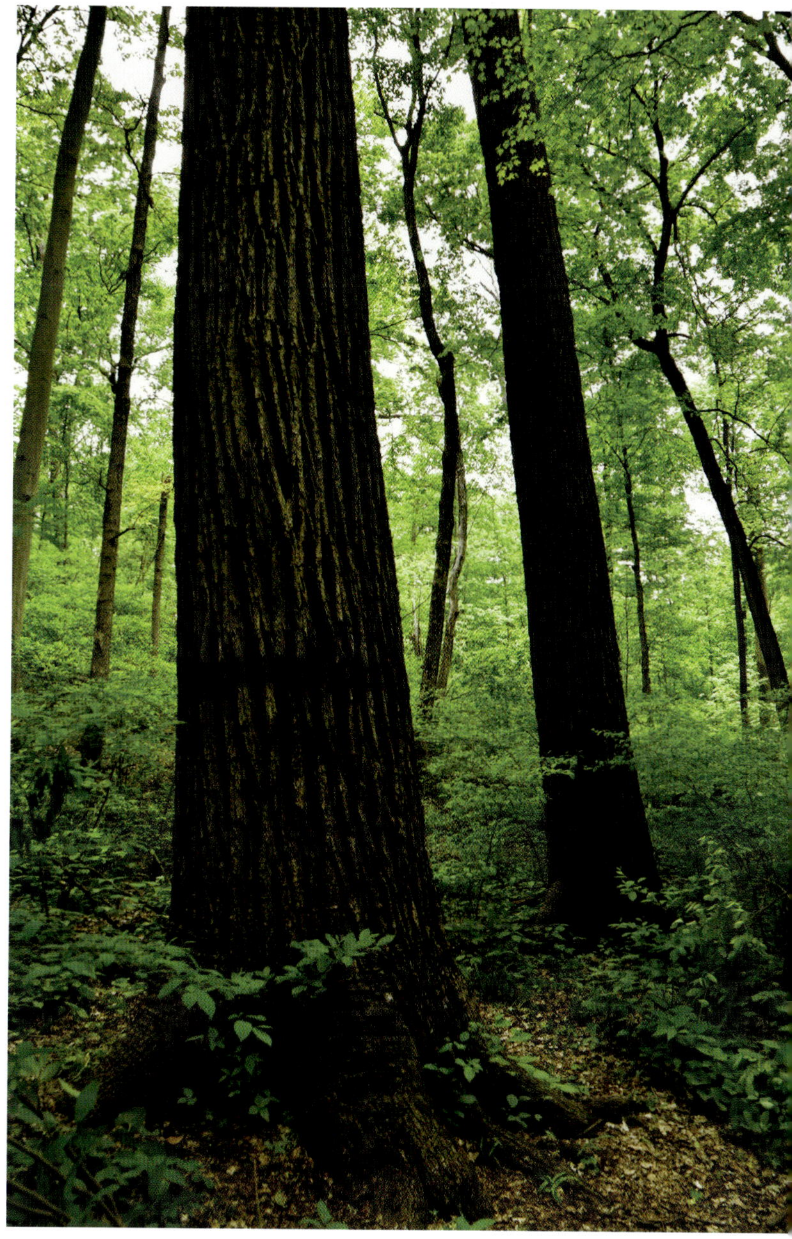

Left: Huge bottomland sycamore, Pioneer Mothers Forest. **Right:** Pioneer Mothers' finest walnuts.

ROCKY HOLLOW-FALLS CANYON NATURE PRESERVE TURKEY RUN STATE PARK

PARKE COUNTY

The early morning misty rain in late October brought a sheen to the stunning color of the canopy above. Raindrops pattered upon the leaves, which softened their journey to the earth below. With careful footsteps navigating the rocky trail weaving among sandstone walls and glacial boulders, wonder was around every corner. The day was a delightful escape into serene peace with nature at its best expression.

The park is one of Indiana's most popular, with the graceful Sugar Creek corridor, massive bluffs of Mansfield sandstone, and challenging terrain left from the last glacial age. Here are found those deeply cut canyons, boulder-scoured potholes, and fine lacy hemlocks adorning the precipitous cliffs and hillsides. On the floodplain below, massive sycamores ruled the rich bottoms.

Most do not know that 1,609 acres of this great park are set aside as the third-largest nature preserve in Indiana. Part of this was recognized in 1974 as a National Natural Landmark as well, and it is no wonder why the distinction was bestowed upon such a special area.

To see the best of the best, try trails 5 and 9. Trail 5 is less strenuous and leads up to some really great poplars and oaks. Trail 9 loops out to the west and then curls back around to meet trail 5. On this loop, there are some more difficult places to negotiate, but I must say there are true rewards to be gained. Very fine red oaks, white oaks, shagbark hickory, poplar, and beech can be seen. This area contains what is called virgin timber and shows no evidence of prior logging. While exertion is required, the views and magnificence make the experience very memorable. Groups of oaks and yellow-poplars rise upward to create the grandest natural cathedral. It was as if by consensus the massive poplars agreed to space themselves just right to claim their own dominating niche. These great old trees possess genetic material that has allowed them to survive for two or three human lifetimes. Below, the forest floor was carpeted with brown leaves, but the drapery behind all was a background of gold, green, and orange from the sugar maples.

Not to be overlooked, the plant communities on huge fallen rocks and in sandstone shelters showcase many ferns, hydrangeas, and mosses. The rather rare walking fern was a standout in the gorge, which also contained a slope of large glacially deposited boulders. From ground level to high canopy, this preserve is most highly recommended.

Location: Turkey Run State Park, 8121 East Park Rd., Marshall, IN 47859

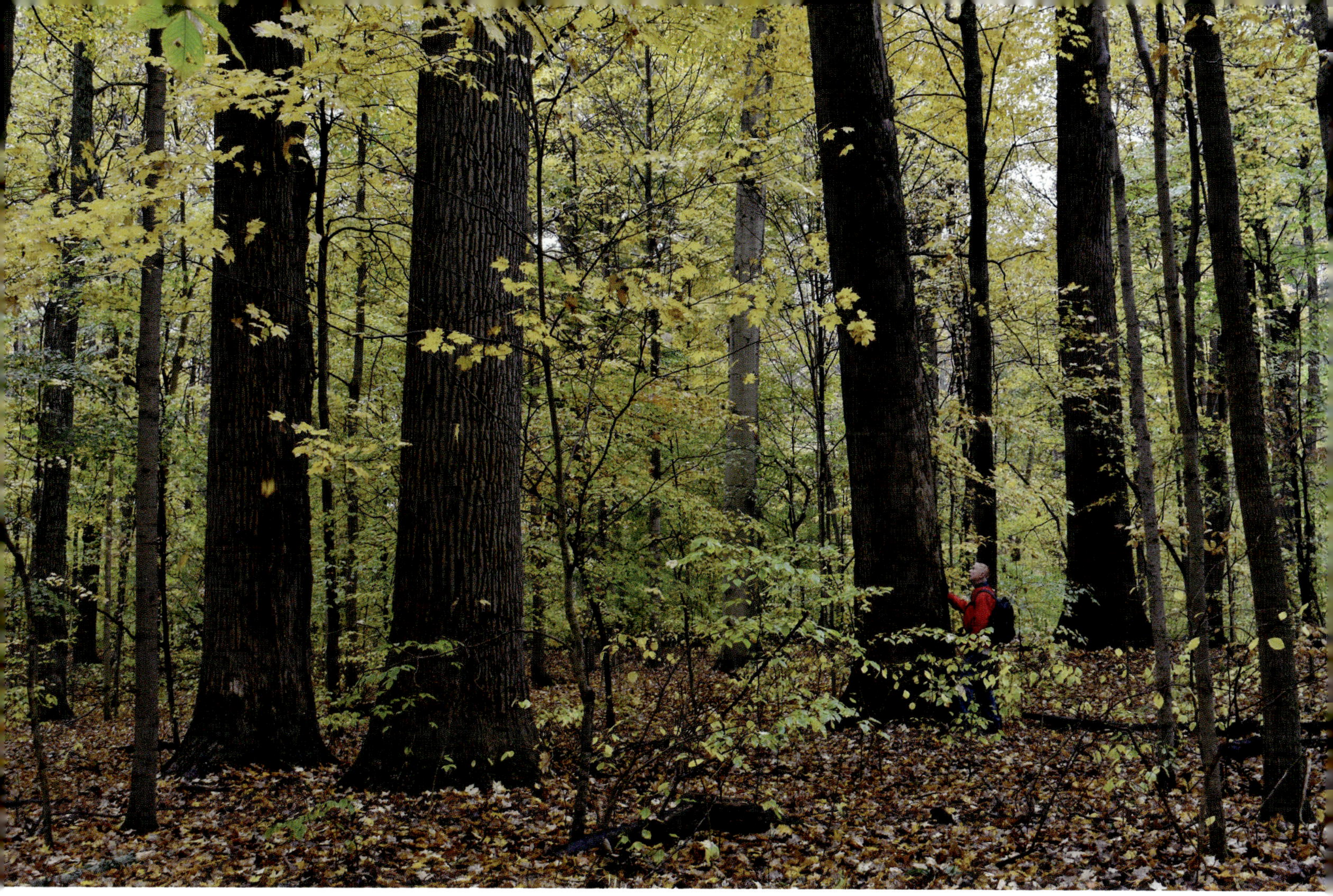

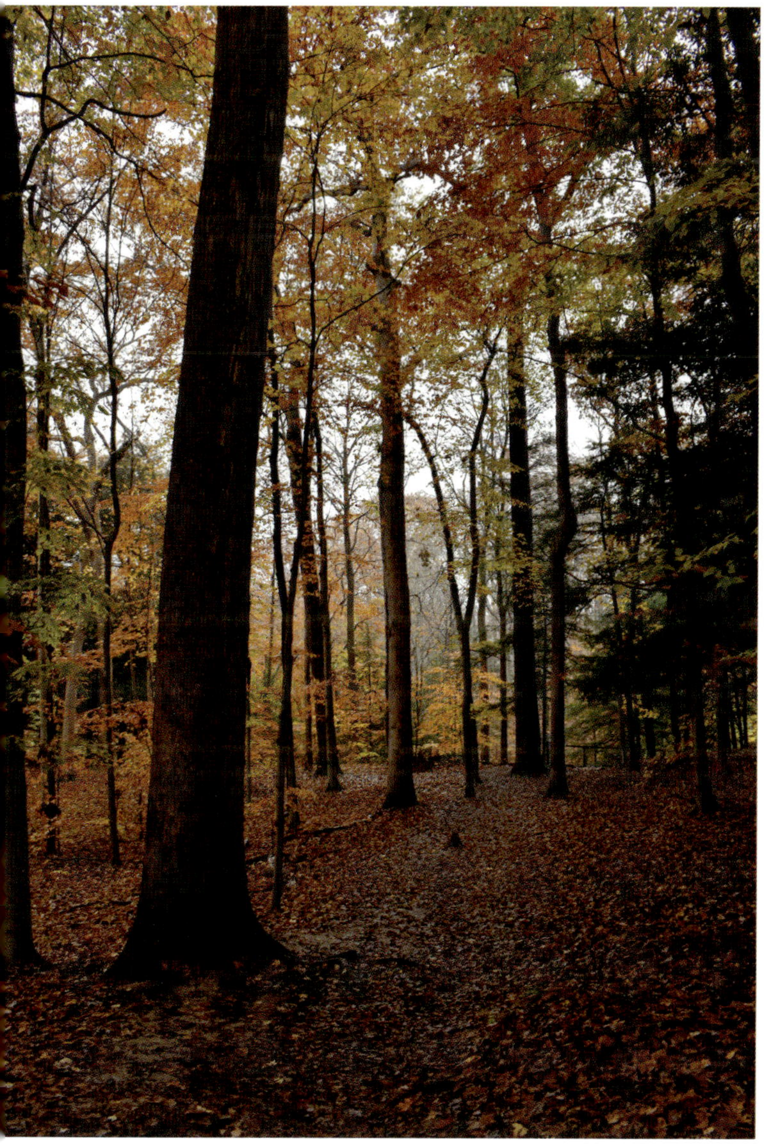

Above: Stunning tuliptrees grace the old-growth woods in Rocky Hollow–Falls Canyon Preserve

Left: Fabulous fall in Rocky Hollow–Falls Canyon Nature Preserve, Turkey Run State Park

SARAH LINCOLN'S WOODS
SPENCER COUNTY

So much history is wrapped into this area that I felt it deserved special attention. The woods and nature preserve are named in honor of the beloved older sister of Abraham Lincoln. Both were born in Kentucky, but their father, Thomas, brought them north to heavily wooded Spencer County, Indiana, in 1816. Abraham, then age seven, grew to manhood here. Abraham and Sarah's mother, Nancy Hanks Lincoln, died in 1818, leaving Sarah, only 11, to help raise young Abe and cousin Dennis Hanks. In 1826, at age 19, she married Aaron Grigsby, whose family lived nearby. Sarah died during childbirth in 1828. Upon hearing the news, Abraham, head in hands, wept profoundly at the great loss of his sister and her stillborn young son. Sarah and her son were buried together. Only three years later, Aaron also died. All are buried in Lincoln State Park in the Little Pigeon Baptist Church Cemetery.

How fitting to have a state nature preserve and trail named in her honor. It was a privilege to walk the trail into a woodland no doubt roamed by young Abraham Lincoln. This splendid spring afternoon, on top of the forested ridge, it was possible to imagine early life here in pioneer times. In this reverent place, with oaks, hickories, and patches we call barrens, the profuse white blooms of serviceberry created a most memorable scene. A gentle breeze made the loose leaves on the ground clatter. Woodpeckers called in the background, while a lone eastern bluebird announced that spring was in progress.

The 110 acres preserve a very dry upland forest with numerable blackjack, post, and black oaks, as well as hickory. The area is somewhat scrubby and open, with plant communities typical of barrens. The Division of Nature Preserves states that this area retains much of its presettlement character. Lower down, a more mixed woodland of second growth includes some large oaks, hickories, maples, sweetgum, black locust, and previously, ash.

To learn about those early days of Abraham Lincoln and family, Lincoln State Park and nearby Lincoln Boyhood National Memorial are well worth a day trip. A hike into Sarah Lincoln's Woods adds a special touch to your experience.

Location: Lincoln State Park, Lincoln City. Trail #3

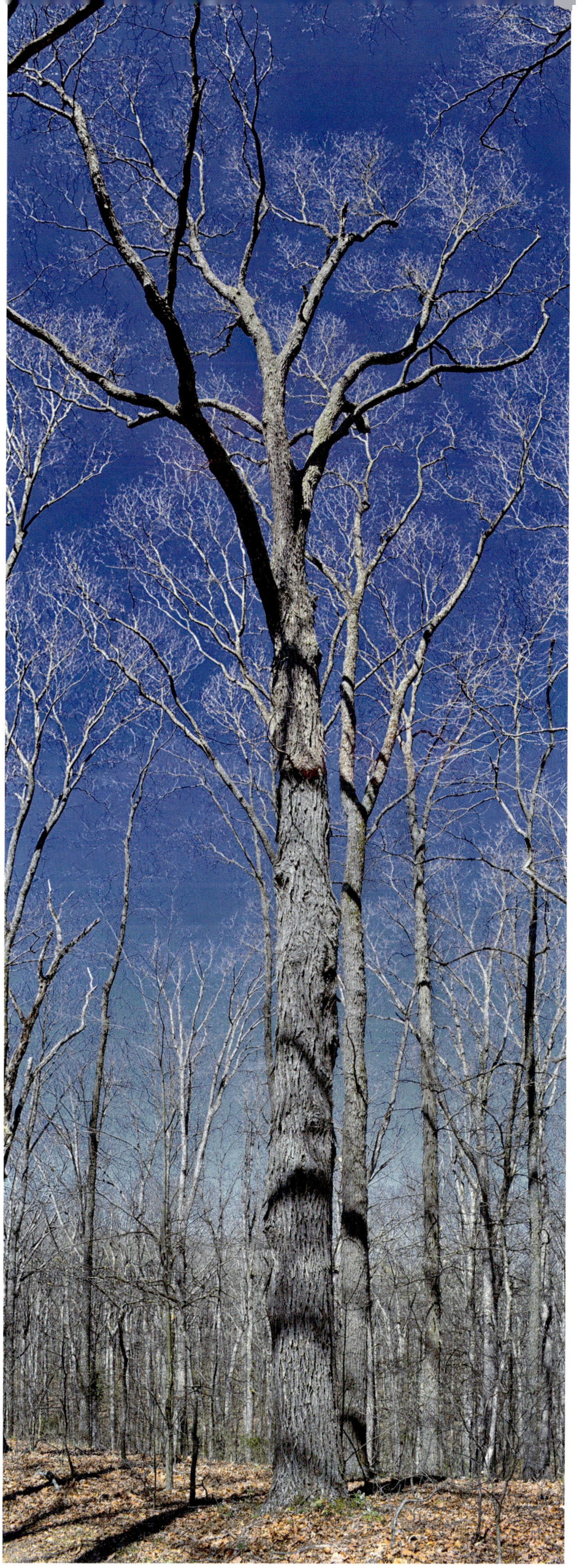

Shagbark hickory watches over the ridge of Sarah Lincoln Woods Nature Preserve

SHRADER-WEAVER WOODS
FAYETTE COUNTY

There are two remarkable things about this celebrated National Natural Landmark property. One, of course, is the splendid display of fine old trees. The second is the story of lineage leading to the preservation that enables this remnant to be protected in perpetuity for all of us.

Philip Shrader of Pennsylvania arrived in early Indiana in 1823, settling here in Fayette County, which then was most likely heavily forested. Other settlers were present on their own recently cleared tracts in this area, as it was attracting newcomers from the east. Shrader is considered one of the early pioneers in the county and lived on the homesite until his death in 1870. The old home built in 1830 still stands and is preserved as part of the 108-acre property. A daughter, Charlotte, was born here in 1831 and married James Weaver in 1859. James was also from one of the earliest lines of pioneers in Fayette County. One of their two sons, Frank, was born there in 1861 and his children Edith (1892–1987) and Laz (1894–1977), brother and sister, neither ever married, lived on the property and cared for the land until it was purchased by the Nature Conservancy in 1972. It was transferred to the Division of Nature Preserves and is now protected by the state of Indiana.

While researching background for this remarkable place, there serendipitously appeared a website that featured really great photos of the woods. The professional photographer was Robert Shrader, who is now living in Nashville, Tennessee. Bob is one of the descendants of the Shrader family. This provided a fine opportunity to use one of his photographs for the book. He readily assented to this idea, and the photo shows the depth of spirit present from the period of the Shrader family to present.

The second remarkable story is of course why people come here: serenity, peace, beauty, inspiration, and meditation. We arrived here on a September day, one of those glorious picture-perfect early fall occasions where everything is just right with the world.

Upon entering the preserve, the temperature immediately cooled, and the gentle breeze was refreshing. Venturing further along the trail and entering the canopy of large trees, the sound of the breeze took on a lower tone, almost as if to speak about the wonders unfolding. On left and right, close by and distant, were very fine old walnut, oak, beech, maple, and ash. As we paused to gaze, the yellowing walnut leaves softened the scene as they fluttered to the forest floor.

Of two trail systems, the old-woods one leads on to discovery of the perfect, spire-like tulips rising to 100 feet, clear of limbs to 60 feet and magnificent in stature. The striking, textured, interwoven furrows were especially attractive in the late afternoon sun. As the sound of falling walnuts occasionally punctuated the stillness, one realized the many years these old trees have been giving this bounty. Passing by a massive bur oak and then many large, smooth, gray beech also added to the realization of longevity here. An old fallen beech limb was the perfect place to ponder the meaning of life back then, as well as today. If these trees are 200 years of age, they were here when Philip bought the land. But they would have been very small. One can imagine the parents of these trees also present then, the extension backward into time of this continuing old-growth forest.

The lowland trail was also explored, that section being described as successional. This portion of the property had been cleared and probably grazed long ago. Yet there were some very stunning individual trees left from the old days, perhaps offering shade or marking a fence line or property boundary. Of most interest were many blue beech, some buckeyes, sycamores, and elms. But standing out were the monstrous old green ash and the "mega-size" bur oak five feet in diameter. The oak had finally given in to its ancient age and was dead. Final respects are due to it and the seedlings produced over the centuries.

The preserve is also noted for its abundant spring wildflowers and great fall color.

A winter hike must certainly be considered, enjoying a snow-covered trail among the old trees resting in utmost quiet and serenity.

Location: 5299 N County Rd 450 W, Connersville, IN 47331

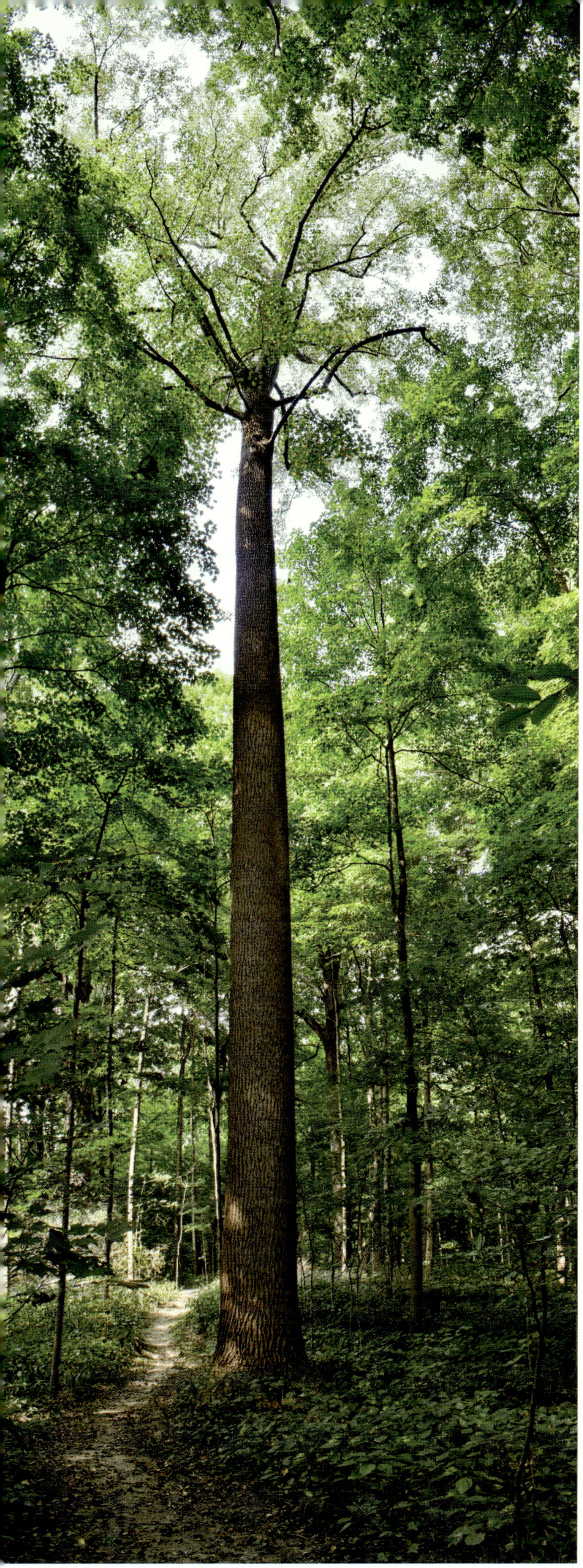

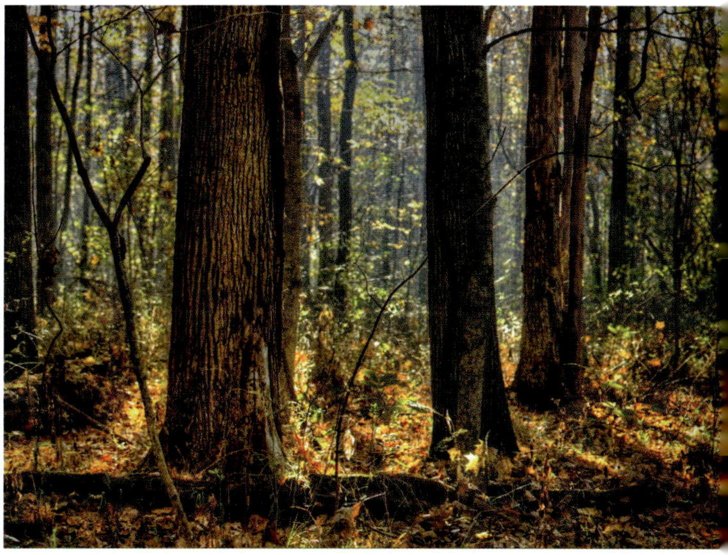

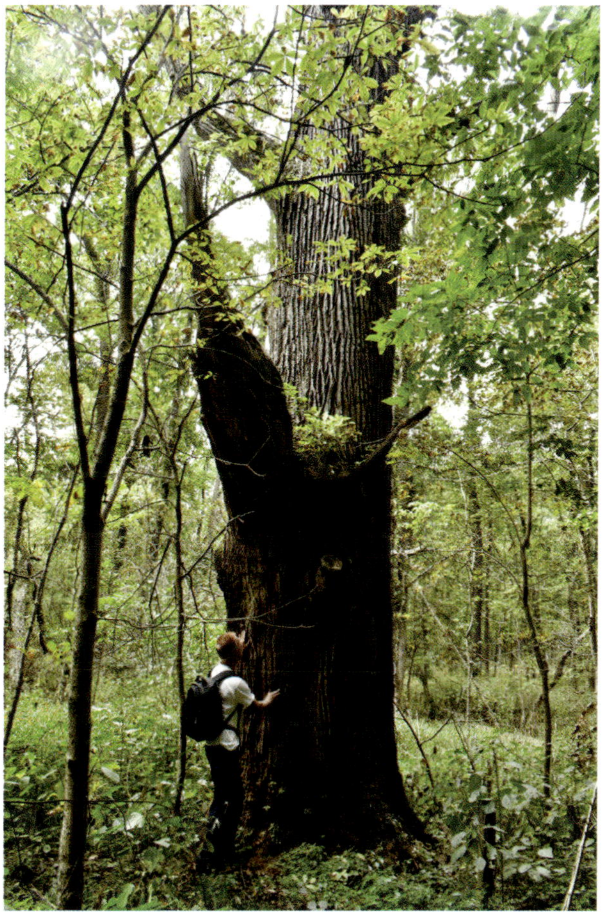

Left: Perfect yellow-poplar at Shrader-Weaver Preserve

Top right: Bob Shrader's rendition of the wondrous Shrader-Weaver Woods

Above: 300+-year-old bur oak in the bottomland of Shrader-Weaver Nature Preserve

WESSELMAN WOODS NATURE PRESERVE
VANDERBURGH COUNTY

The Nature Center at Wesselman Woods is a place of bustle, laughter, and joy. Children of all ages enjoy the grand outdoor setting loaded with education and activities oriented to enjoying nature. The Wesselman Nature Society summarizes it perfectly:

Wesselman Woods provides environmental education and outdoor recreation experiences designed to awaken the senses and enrich the lives of area residents and visitors. The mission of WNS is to create experiences which connect people with nature, motivate them to lead sustainable lives and take action to protect wildlife and wild places.

The day we visited here including photographing the state champion sweetgum across from the center in the other part of the woods not actually included in the preserve, but admirable as well. Naturalist Zach Garcia graciously pointed us out through the nature center onto the trail leading into the old-growth woods. Within one minute, the world changed. Gone were the distractions of the present—muted, dismissed as no longer of importance. Here, within a metropolitan area in the middle of development, was a huge tract of original woods, in fact the largest old, preserved forest within any U.S. city limits. This is truly remarkable, almost beyond comprehension how one city with foresight kept such a place preserved. The Wesselman Nature Society was able to purchase 200 acres of these virgin woods in 1972, adding more land later, and engaging in a plan to protect and preserve this rarity. There are some 4 miles of trails, which offer exceptional opportunities for hiking, bird watching, and witnessing some 300 species of wildflowers throughout the seasons. For the kids, there is the Nature Playscape, largest in the nation on three acres.

Through the years there have been many state champion trees here and within Vanderburgh County, many first recorded by urban forester Tom Westfall (deceased) and current forester Shawn Dickerson. Many species recorded include large sweetgum, tulip, red oak, pin oak, cherrybark oak, sugarberry, and maple. The trees are generally so big overall that they create the largest basal area of any Indiana woods. In addition, the absolute density of trees is also a record.

The day we visited with Shawn, no one else was in the immediate vicinity. The nature lecture back at the center was engaging the kids, but here we were able to absorb the spiritual feeling of the place, among many grand specimens of tulip and oak. No wonder this splendid retreat gets highest accreditation—a state nature preserve and National Natural Landmark.

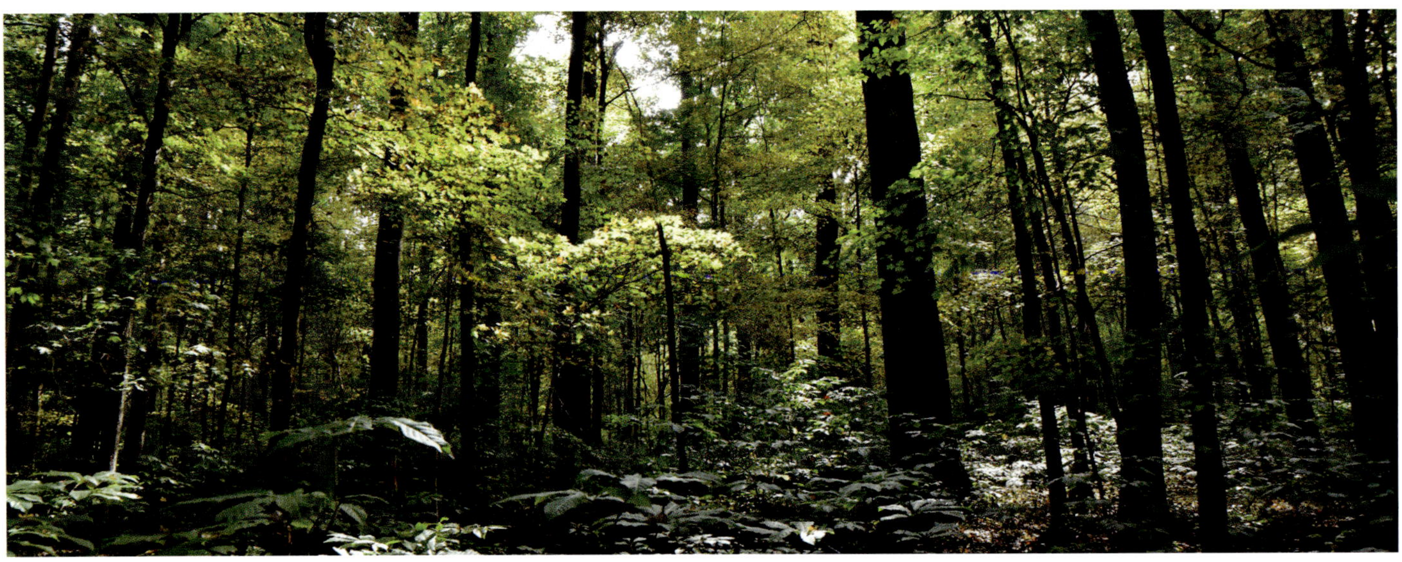

Above: Wesselman Nature Preserve's grandeur. **Right page:** Wesselman Nature Preserve in fall with large tuliptree and surrounding tree friends.

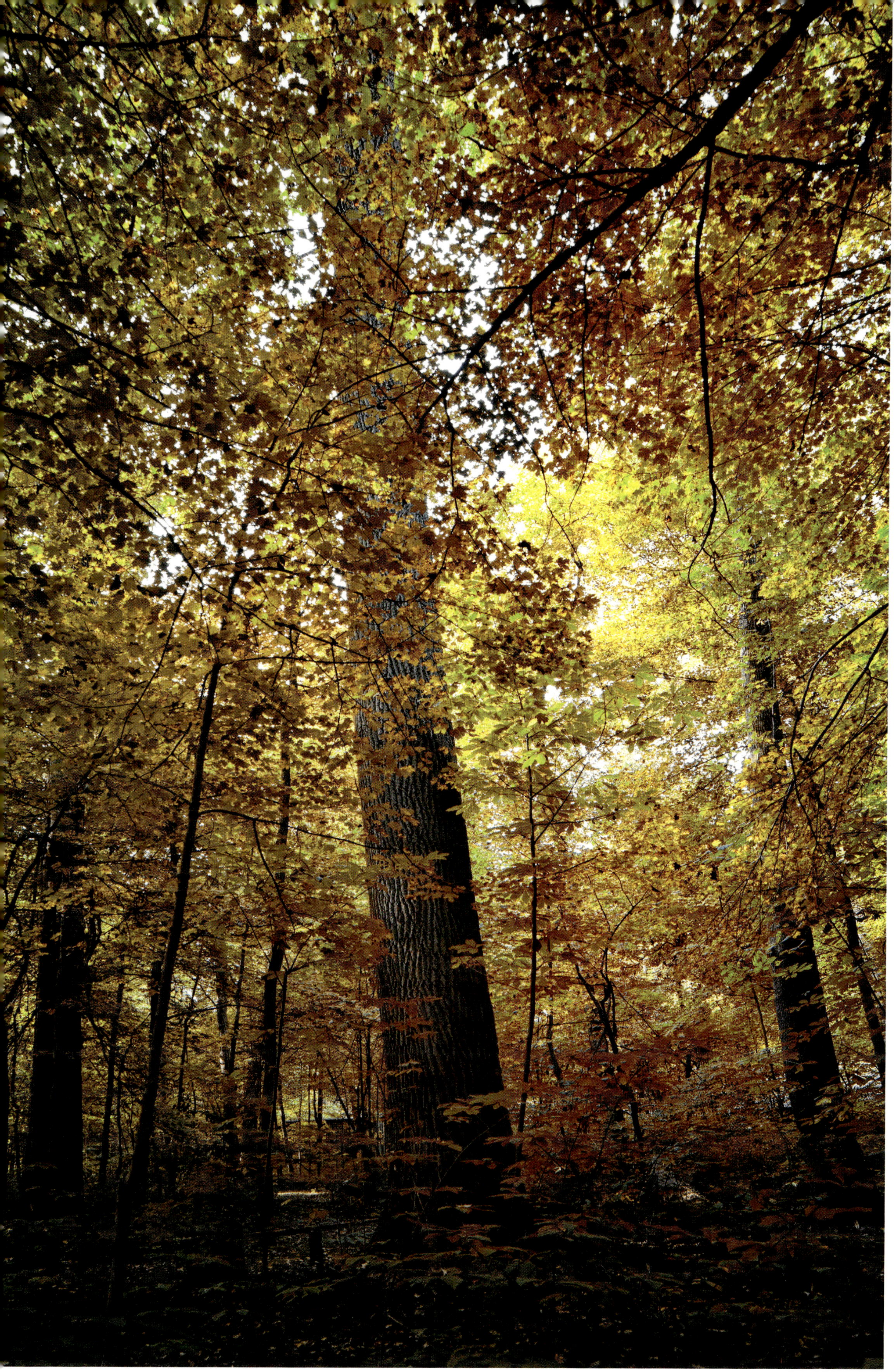

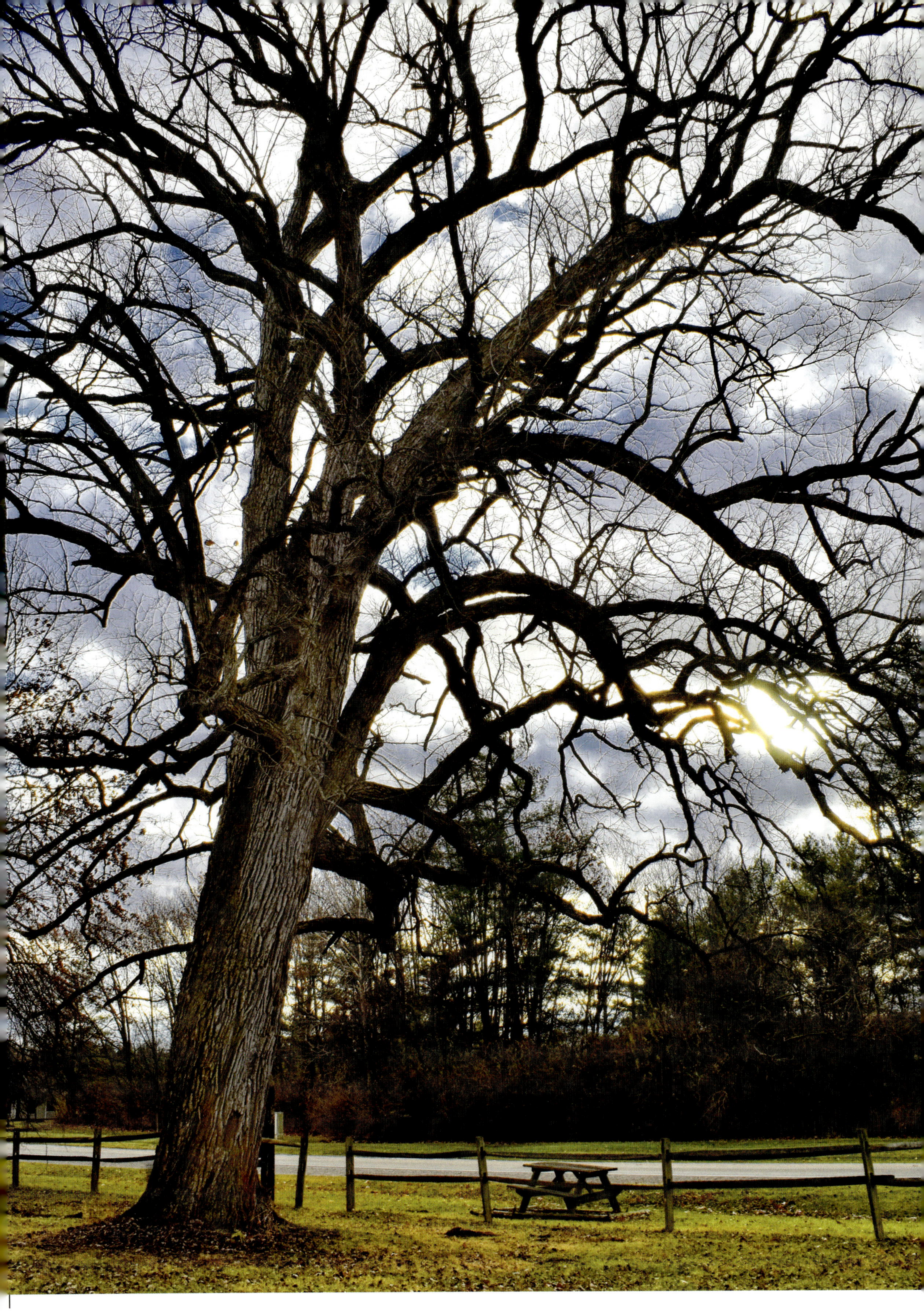

CHAPTER SIX

The Odd and Curious

While the primary focus of this book concentrates on species or specimens of well-known and loved icons, a diversion is entertained here by including trees found as oddities. These include strange forms, unusual settings, and species not normally recognized. It should be mentioned that landowners have planted many specialty trees in the past, such as callery pear, which were not native. Notwithstanding the intent of the nurseryman or the owner, we recognize that in many cases this introduction had long-term consequences that ended up being very undesirable.

CAUSES OF ODDITY IN TREES

A common question posed by the viewer is "What caused that odd tree shape?" There are many possibilities varying from credible to incredulous. Just as every small hillock is speculated to be "an Indian mound," some maintain that every bent tree is probably an "Indian marker tree." While true that the technique of bending a sapling might have

Left page: The famed Deam Oak, Wells County

been occasionally employed, it is also logical to speculate that Native Americans depended more on natural physiography and established game or foot paths. For other oddities of shape, many can be explained as resulting from physical deformation in storm events, during timber harvests, other natural factors, or even from pruning or attaching signs, wire, and so on. When we noticed a double trunk, a twinning joinery of two species, or one wrapping around another as both thrust upward for light, we were stimulated to think about such things. In woods with regeneration from decades ago, one may notice many two-stem trees or forks, both of which may now be quite large. This may have resulted from stump sprouts of cut trees.

Biological factors also play roles in odd physical expressions. Responses to fungi, viruses, insects, other pests, and genetic mutation cause odd shapes around the affected area. Large galls and burls may develop. Some of these growths, many on oaks, are actually sought after for woodworking specialties. On our state champion cherrybark oak, a profusion of oak twig galls was quite noticeable.

Another highly interesting phenomenon is soil creep on steep shale bluffs. Downward movement over time actually bends the tree as it tries to continue growing vertically. This is observable in some of the eastern hemlock sites where steep exposures exist.

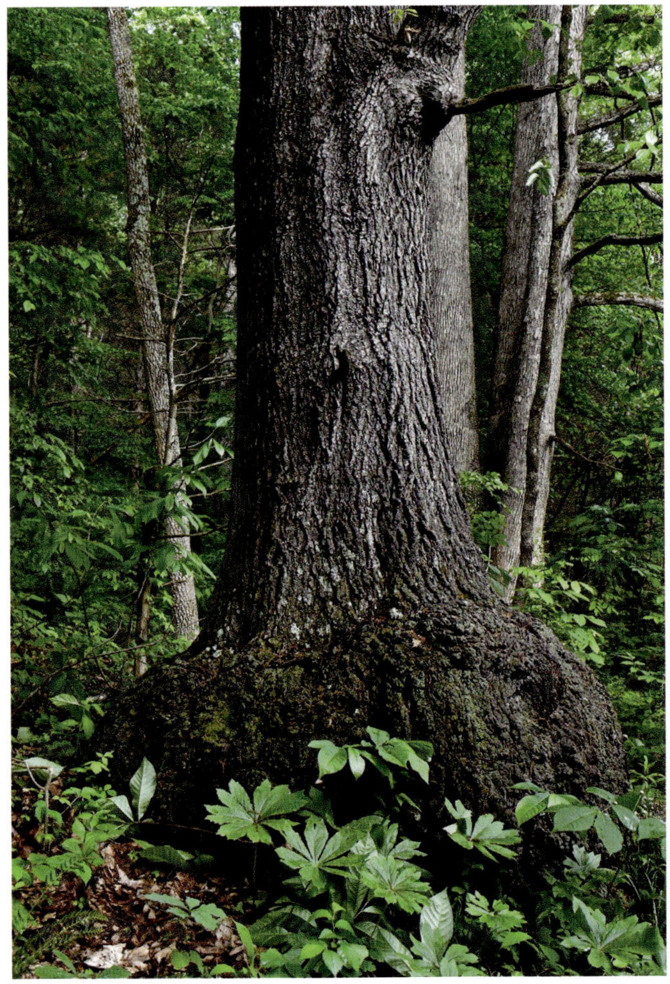

Large basal gall on black oak

HYBRIDIZATION

Hybridization is another possibility for a tree that just doesn't seem to match an ID key. It seems to have the character of two trees. These are mostly within the same group, such as crosses within the white oak group and crosses within the red oak group. The most noted example in Indiana is the Deam Oak, named of course after Charlie Deam. It is a cross between white oak and chinquapin oak. The Latin for the cross now reads *Quercus x deamii*. Discovered by Bruce Williamson and his father in 1904, its samples were sent to Deam, who forwarded them to Professor Trelease at the Missouri Botanical Garden. The tree was indeed a new hybrid. Misfortune was allayed just as the tree was going to be cut down. Deam was not successful in talking the owner out of this, so he did the next best thing—bought the one-fifth acre himself for $75. The tiny plot was then deeded to the State of Indiana and is protected in our smallest state nature preserve near Bluffton, where Deam resided. A great story about this can be found at arnoldia.arboretum.harvard.edu/pdf/articles/2012-69-4-charlie-deam-and-the-deam-oak-quercus-x-deamii.pdf.

Another example of an interesting hybrid is the Beadle's oak, a cross between swamp chestnut oak and

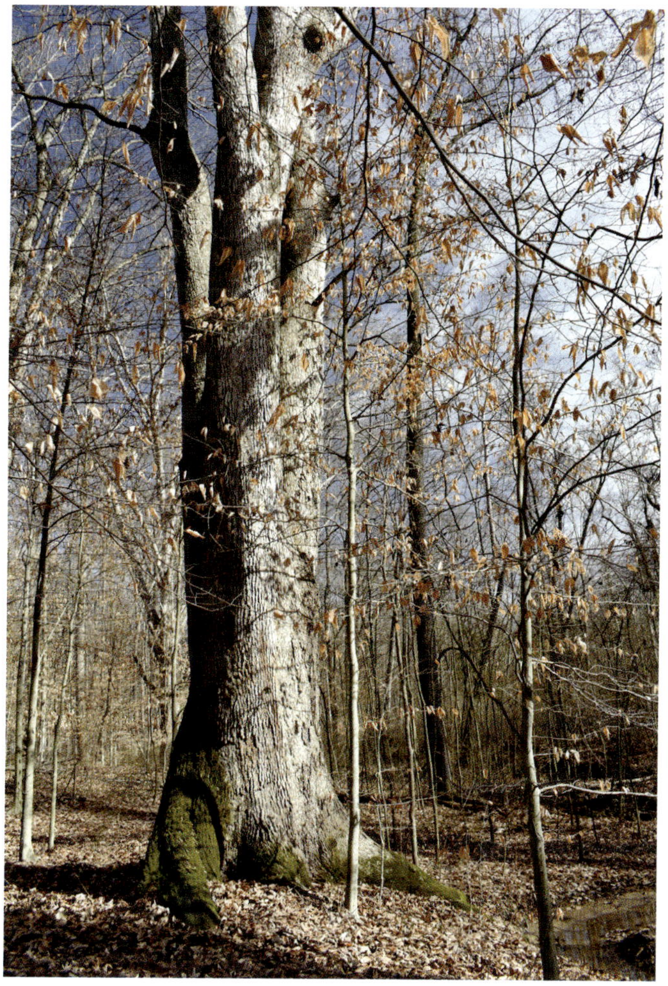

Hybrid Beadle's oak, Muscatatuck National Wildlife Refuge

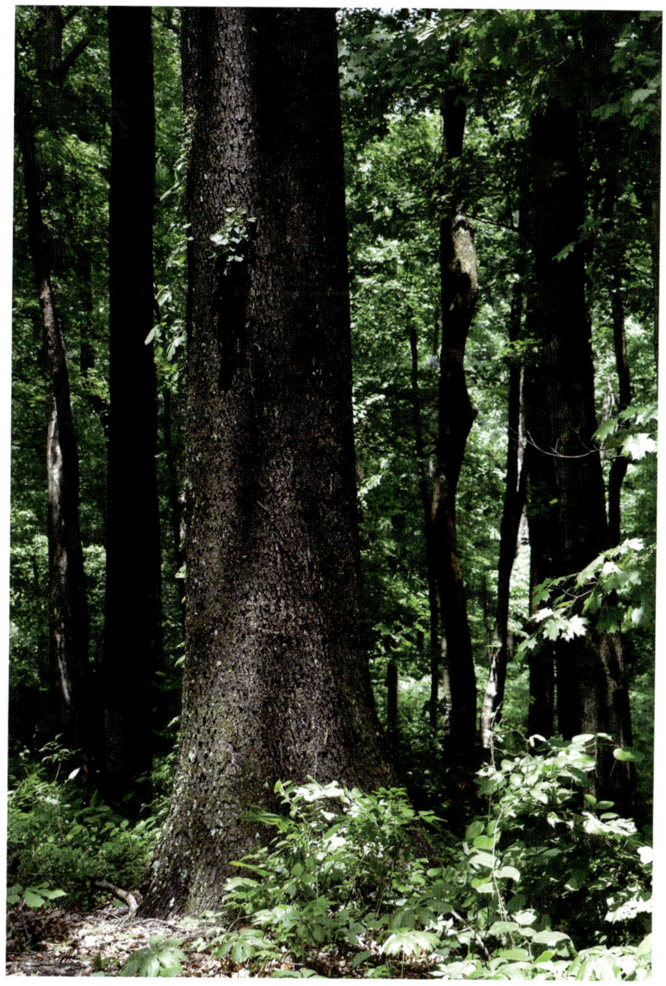

Hybrid oak, TNC Teeple Glade, Harrison County

white oak. Dave Coppert showed us this possible one he found in the depths of Muscatatuck National Wildlife Refuge, near Seymour. If this particular tree is verified, it may be the largest specimen in Indiana.

Another hybrid is on the Indiana University campus and identified as a cross between shingle oak and red oak. In Harrison County, a possible hybrid of white oak and chestnut oak was found in the Teeple Glade Nature Preserve.

Naturally occurring hybridization is quite common in oaks and hickories. There are many of these found across the United States, almost every combination of two different species. Most cross within their respective groups. Further, since backcrosses of the hybrid back to one of the primary species is common, the gradation of characteristics can become quite muddled. Factors influencing likelihood of hybridization include distances between species, density of species in a given area, pollen dispersion, receptivity, and other variables. One of the interesting discoveries of crosses is that the resultant characteristics may actually show some enhanced properties that one parent did not possess. In some cases, resistance to disease is increased. Hybridization is a practical tool in Purdue's work for hardwood tree improvement and regeneration. Commercial nurseries now carry hybrids as well, for disease resistance and attractive physical attributes.

Dwarf trees? One special little tree was shown by Allen Pursell of TNC at Buena Vista Glade in Harrison County: *Celtis pumila,* or dwarf hackberry. Totally natural, small, could be overlooked by anyone but a keen-eyed botanist. But on this rocky, sloped limestone outcrop, nestled in a crack, was a twisted specimen 12 inches tall, perhaps quite old. Its "poor form" might not attract attention, but then again, think "bonsai" and you might be enticed to learn more about this diminutive tree, which in good conditions can even grow to 25–30 feet! Great find at this special TNC nature preserve.

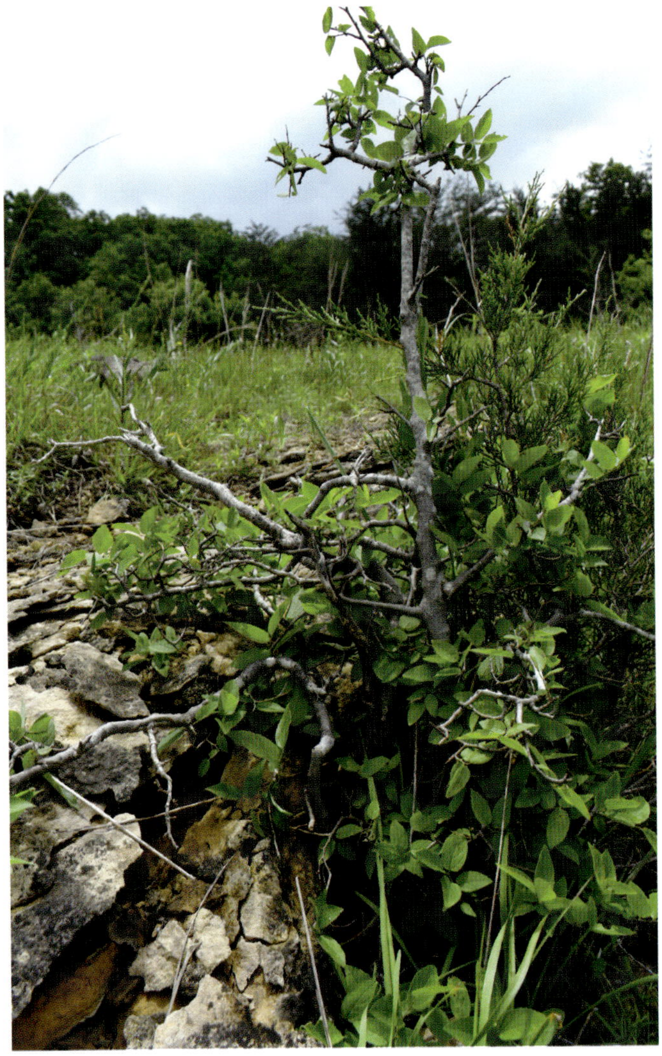

Dwarf hackberry, TNC Buena Vista Glade, Harrison County

The remainder of photos in this chapter illustrate many oddities found. They must be only a small representation of what a curious observer may find in a casual trip to the woods!

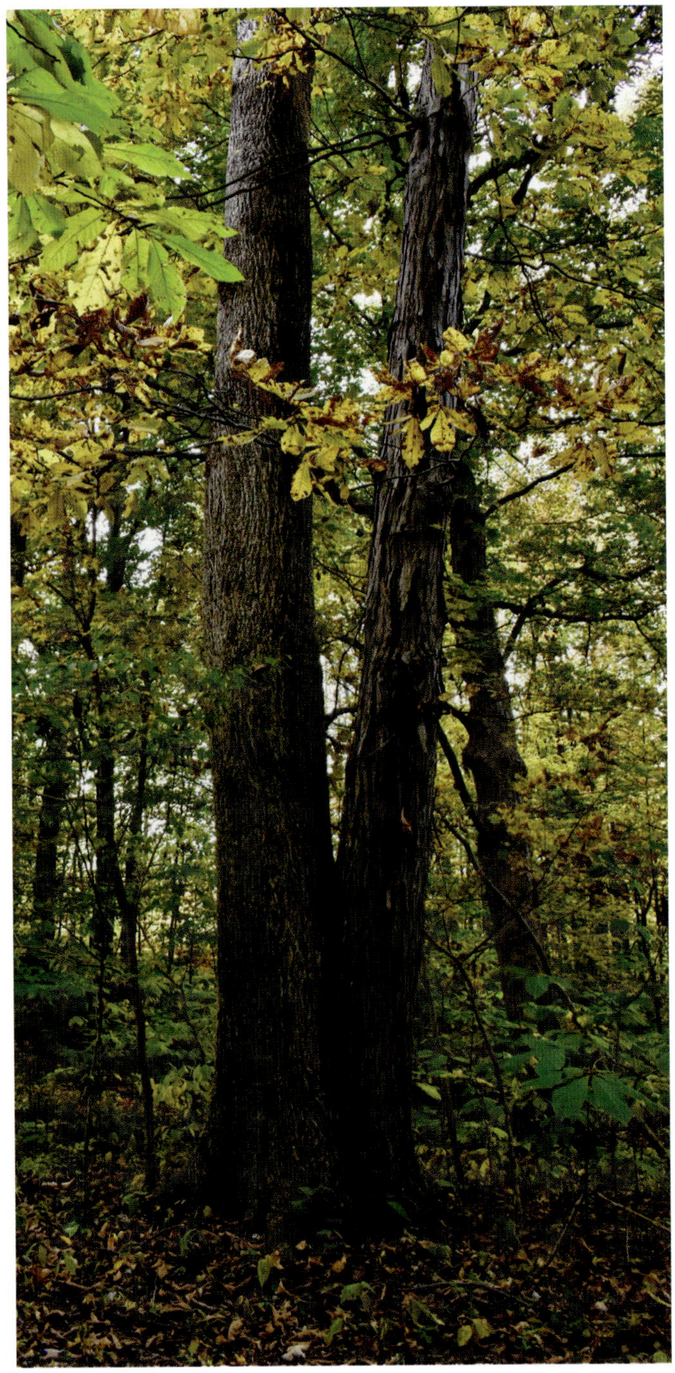

Bitternut and shagbark hickories twinned together

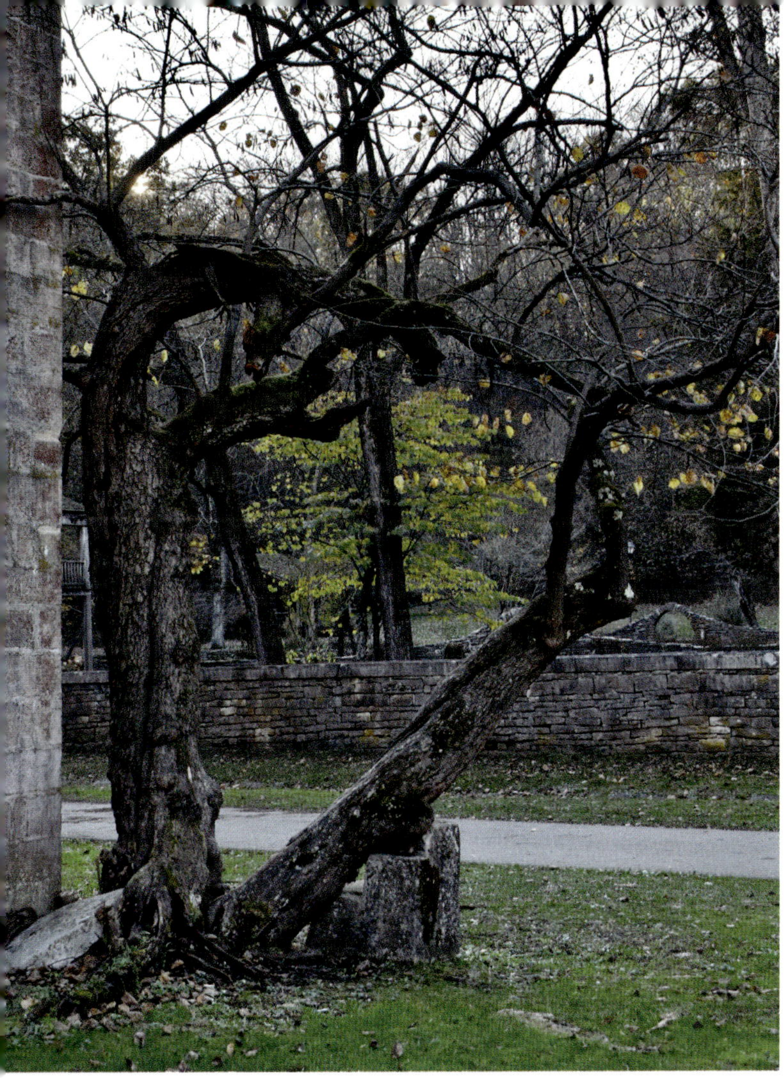

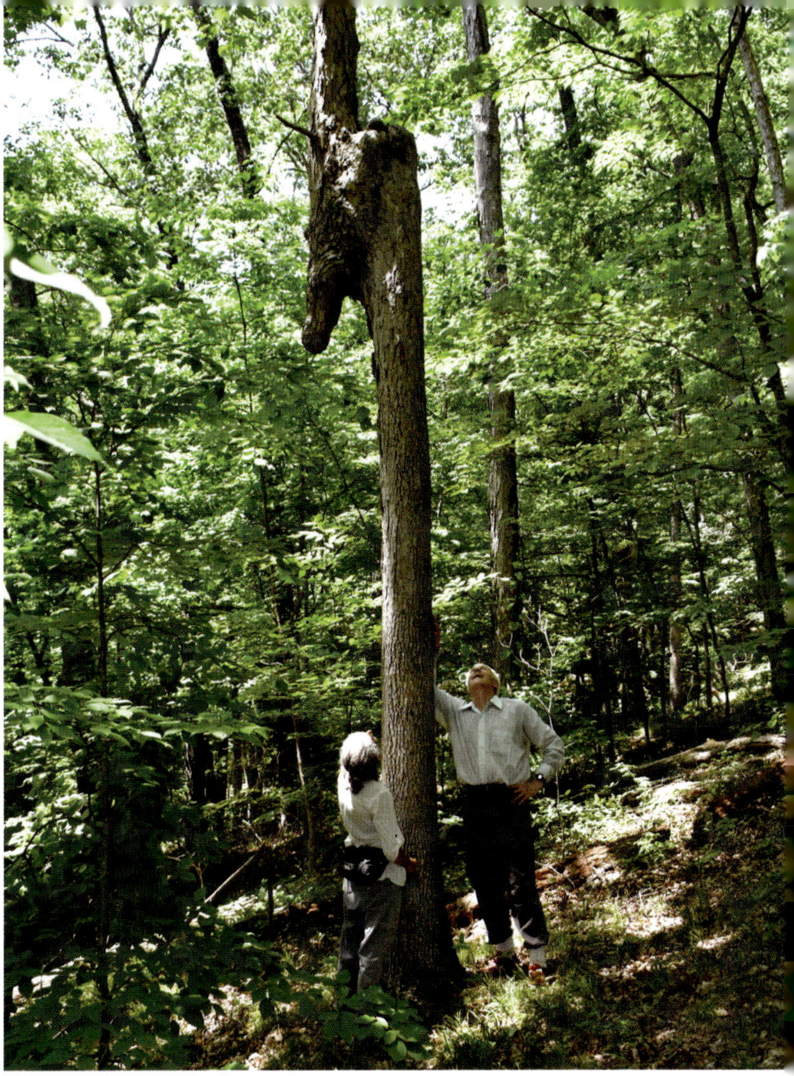

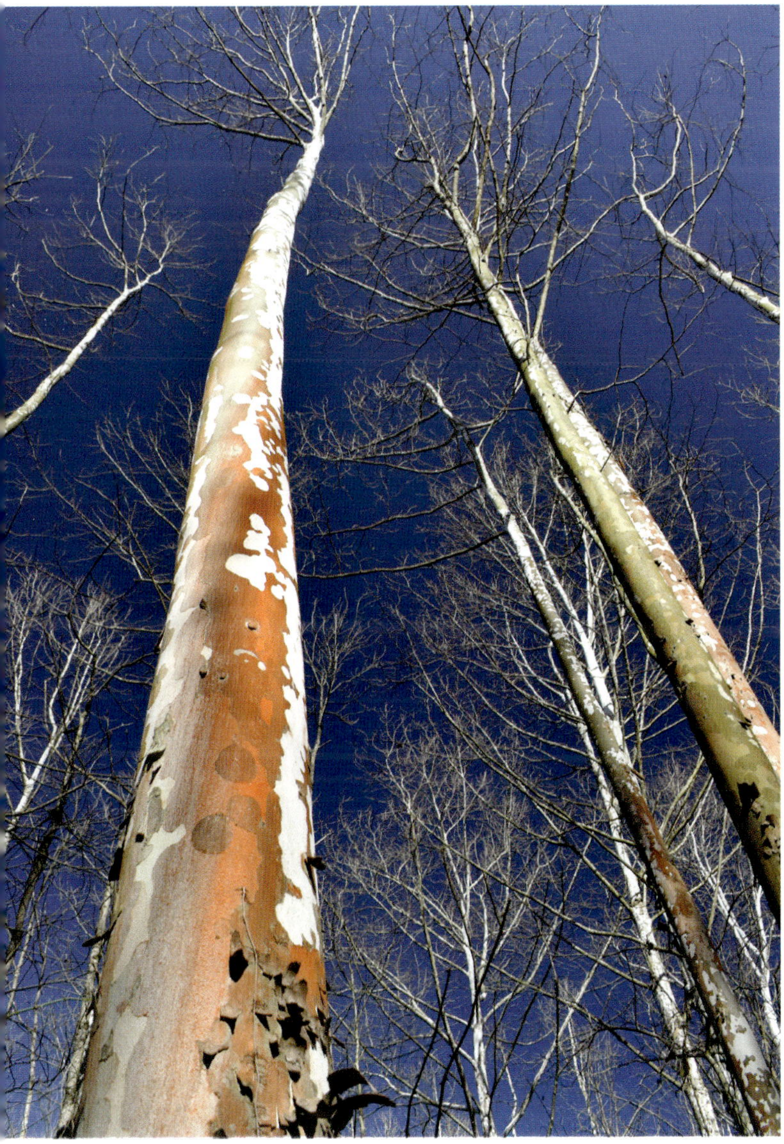

Top left: Old survivor—redbud at Spring Mill State Park

Top right: Pate Hollow Weird Tree, Monroe County

Bottom left: Sycamore with red bark syndrome, Muscatatuck National Wildlife Refuge

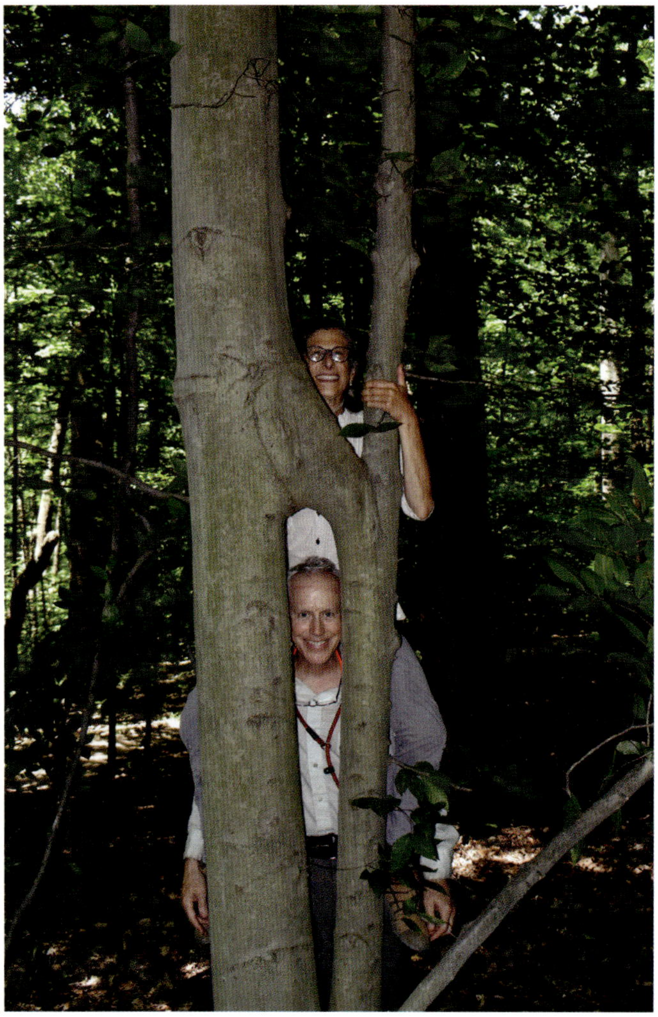
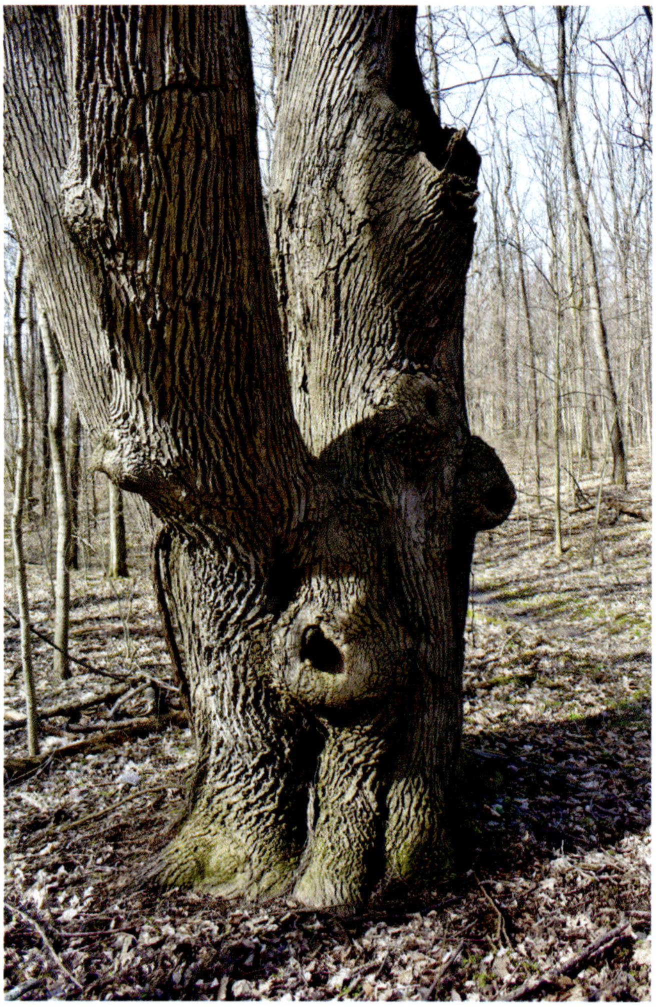
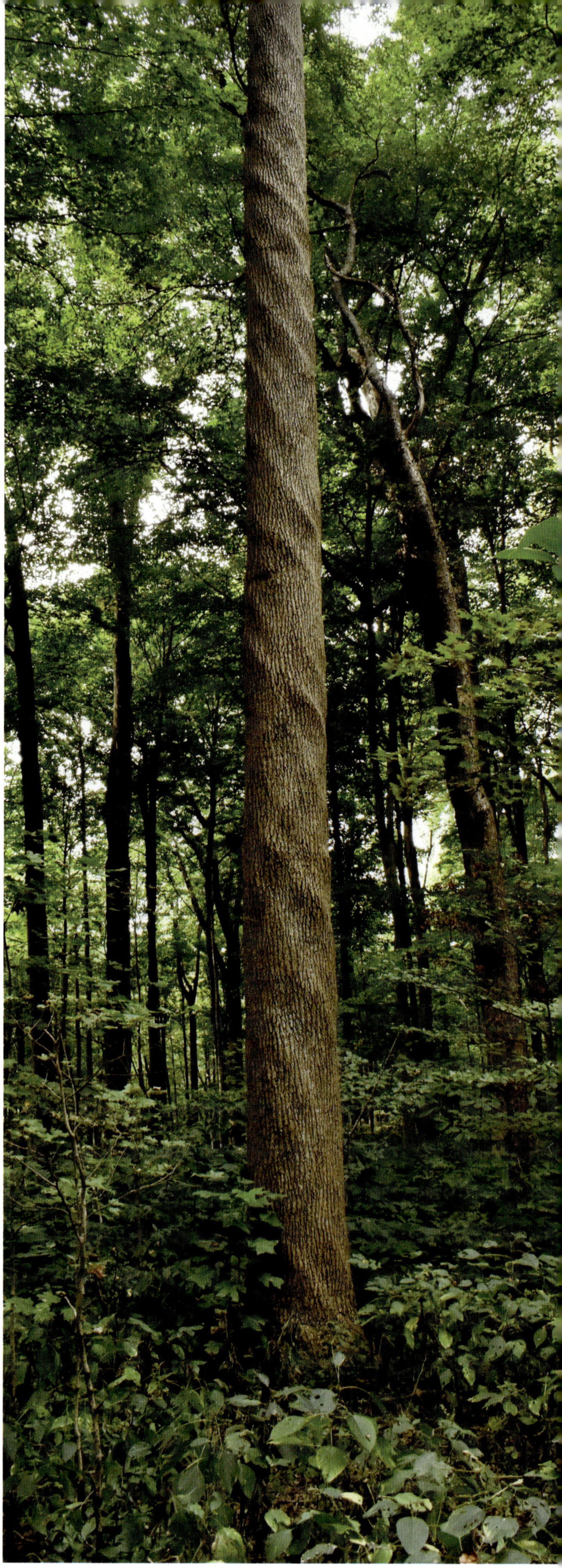

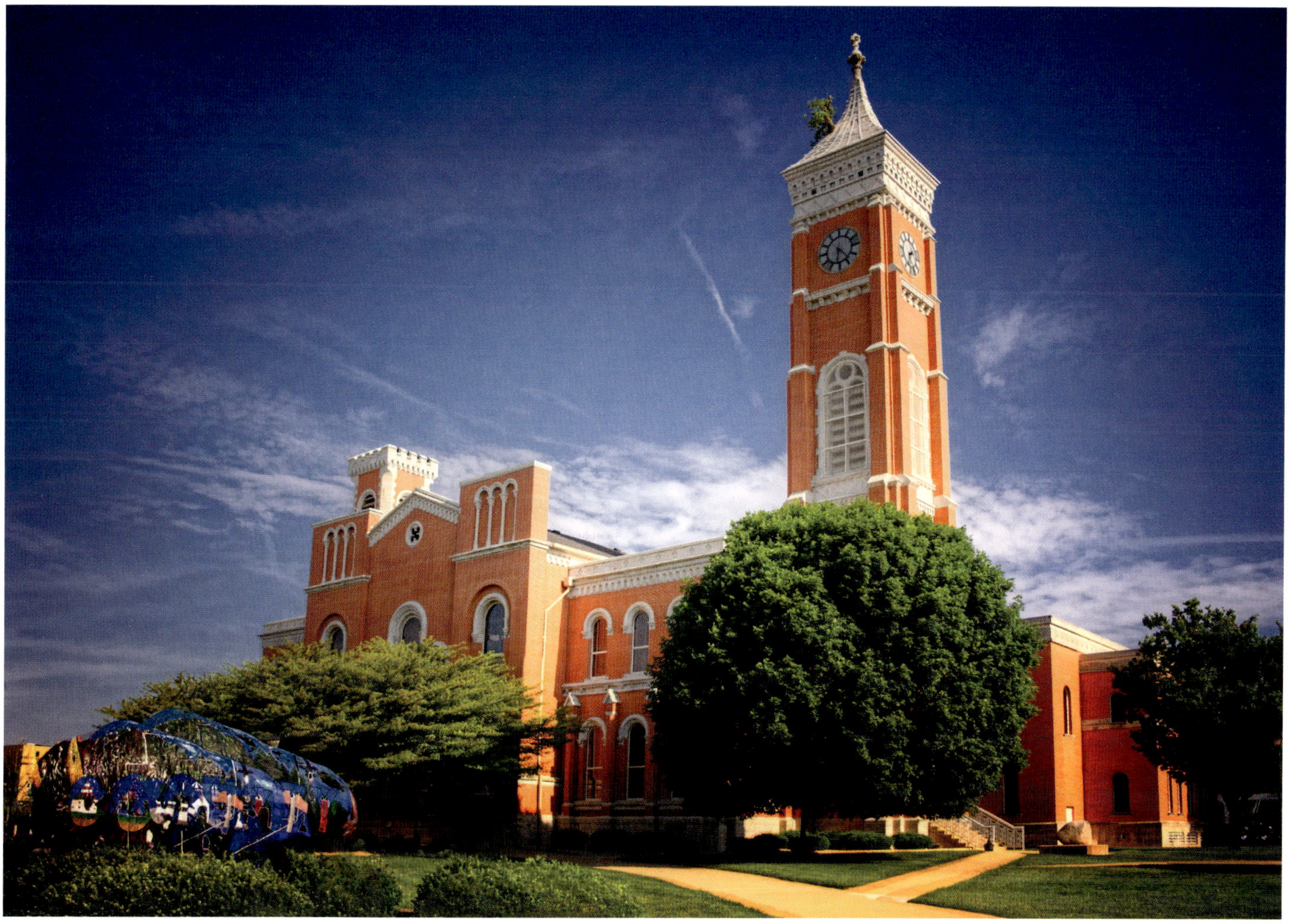

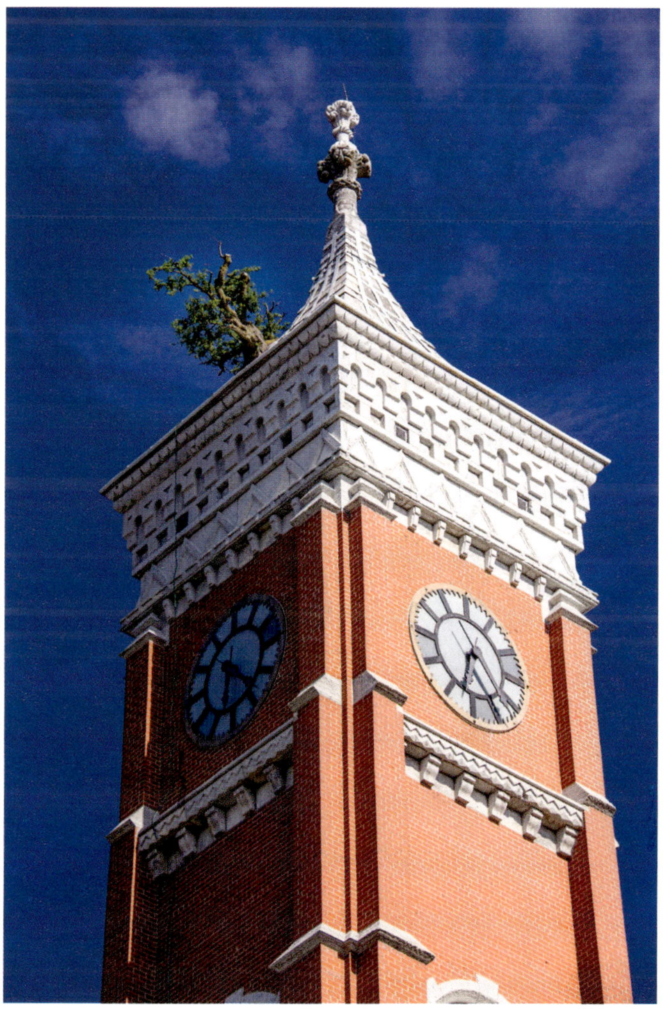

Left page, top left: Malcolm Dalglish and Judith Klein show off the "picture frame" on a beech at Griffy Nature Preserve, Monroe County

Left page, right: Marvelous, mysterious barber-pole tuliptree, Shrader-Weaver Woods

Left page, bottom left: Old ash after long, tough life. Shrader-Weaver Woods

Above: The famous mulberry tree in the courthouse tower, Greensburg
Courtesy of Gary Potts

Left: The Decatur County courthouse at Greensburg is famous for its "tower tree." While the original tree may have been an aspen, today's is a white mulberry.
Courtesy of Gary Potts

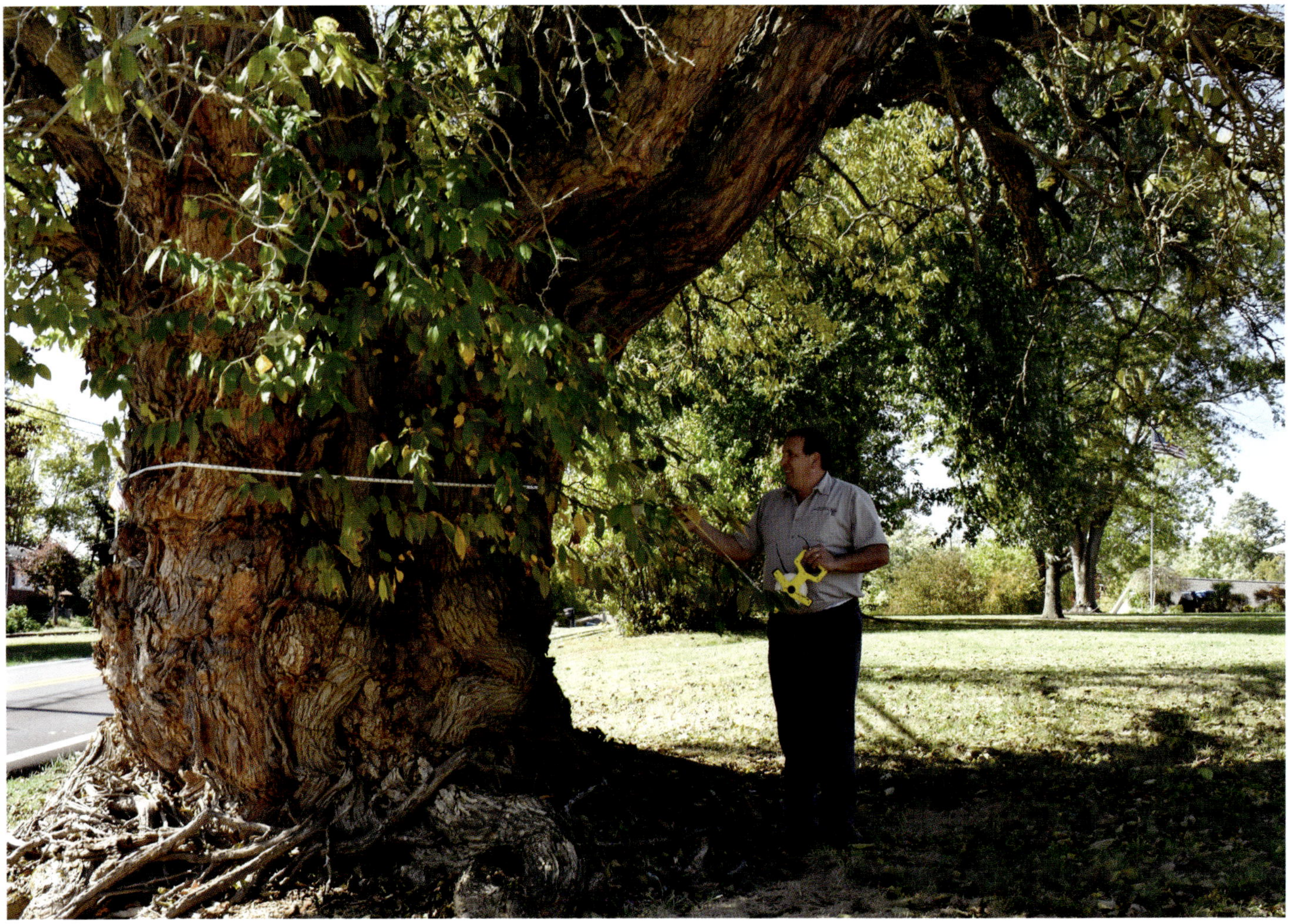

Above: Shawn Dickerson with huge Osage orange tree, Evansville

Right: IDNR district forester Ralph Unversaw with the oddest oak in Monroe County

Right page: Spooky Tree—old white oak, Camp Atterbury

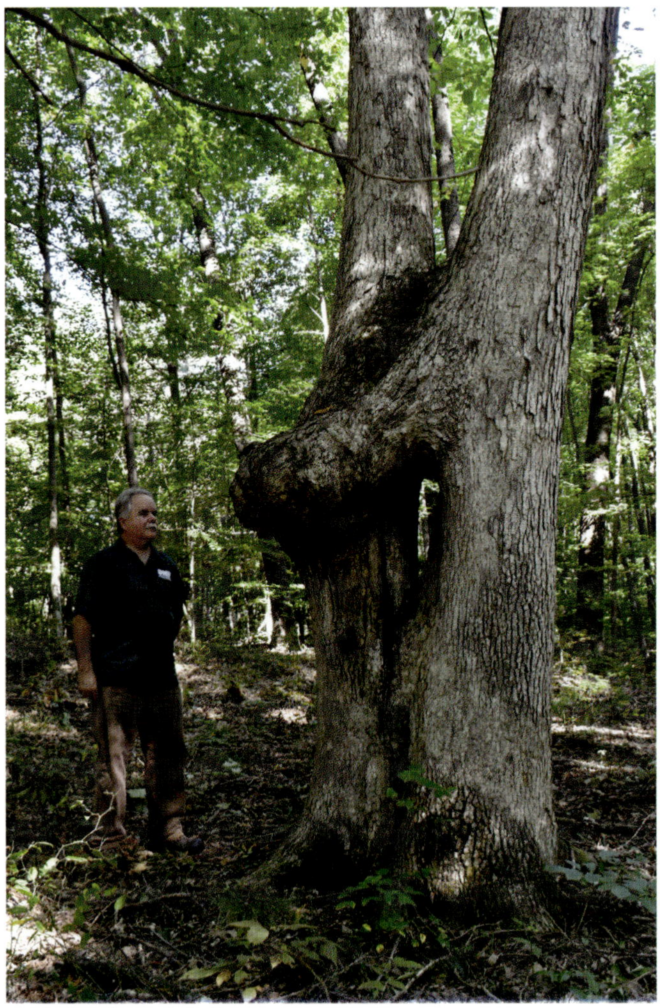

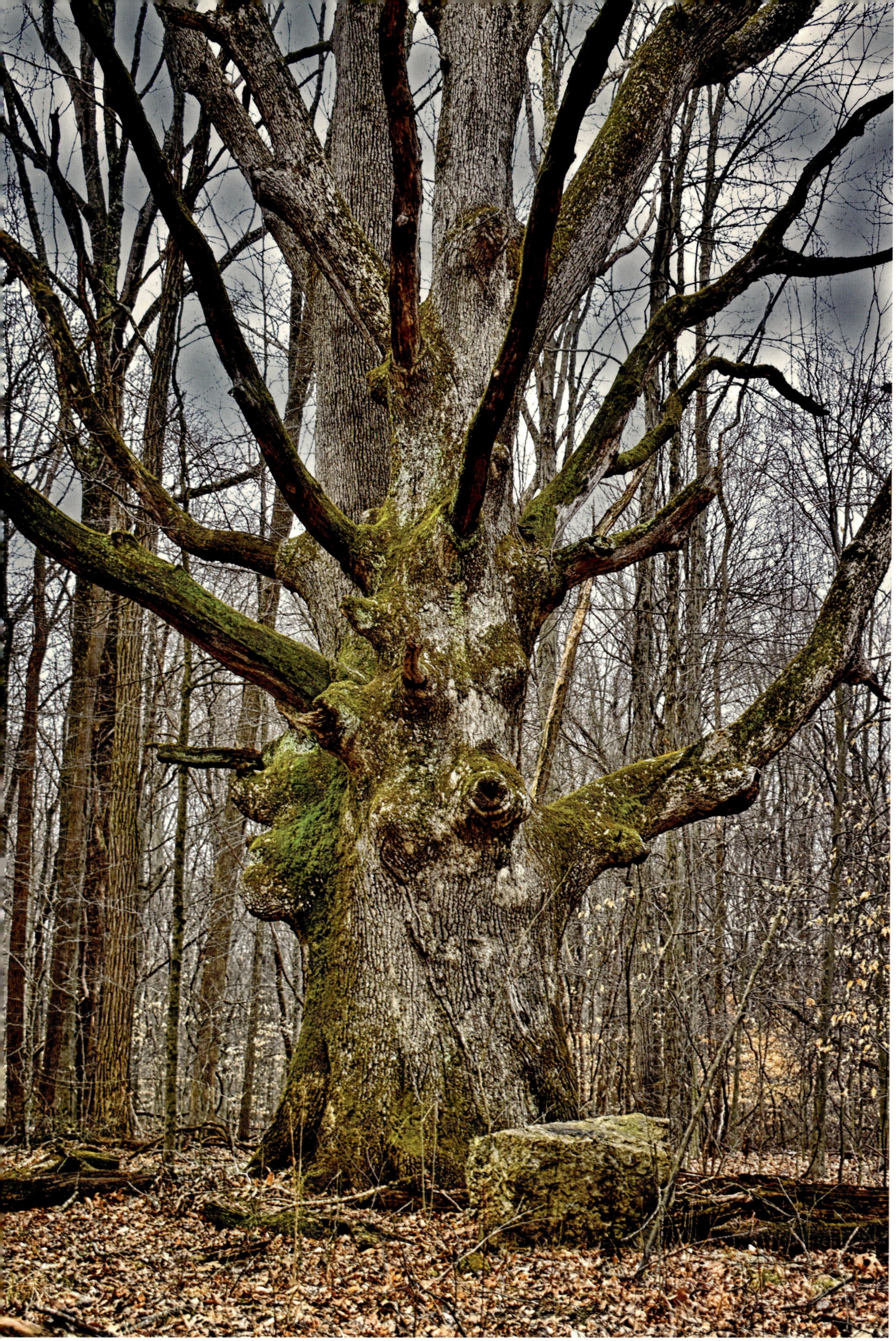

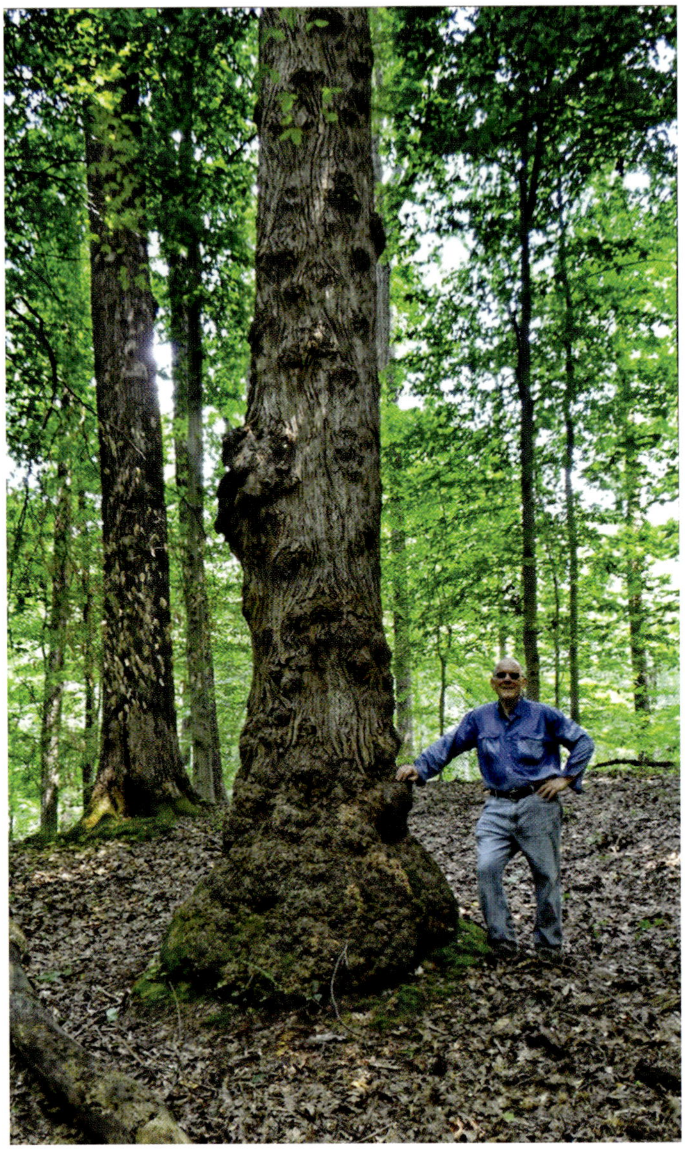

Yellow-poplar with exceptional disfiguring burls, Muscatatuck National Wildlife Refuge. *Courtesy Dave Coppert*

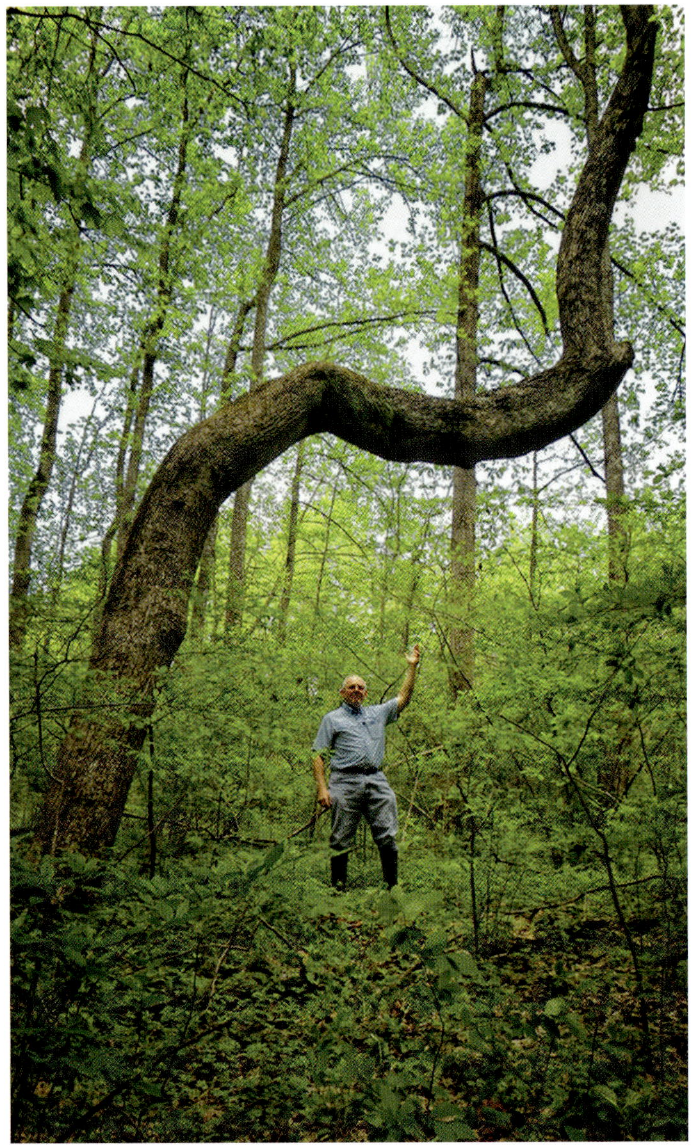

"Corkscrew" yellow-poplar, Muscatatuck National Wildlife Refuge. *Courtesy Dave Coppert*

Right page: Undecided old swamp white oak, Twin Swamps Nature Preserve

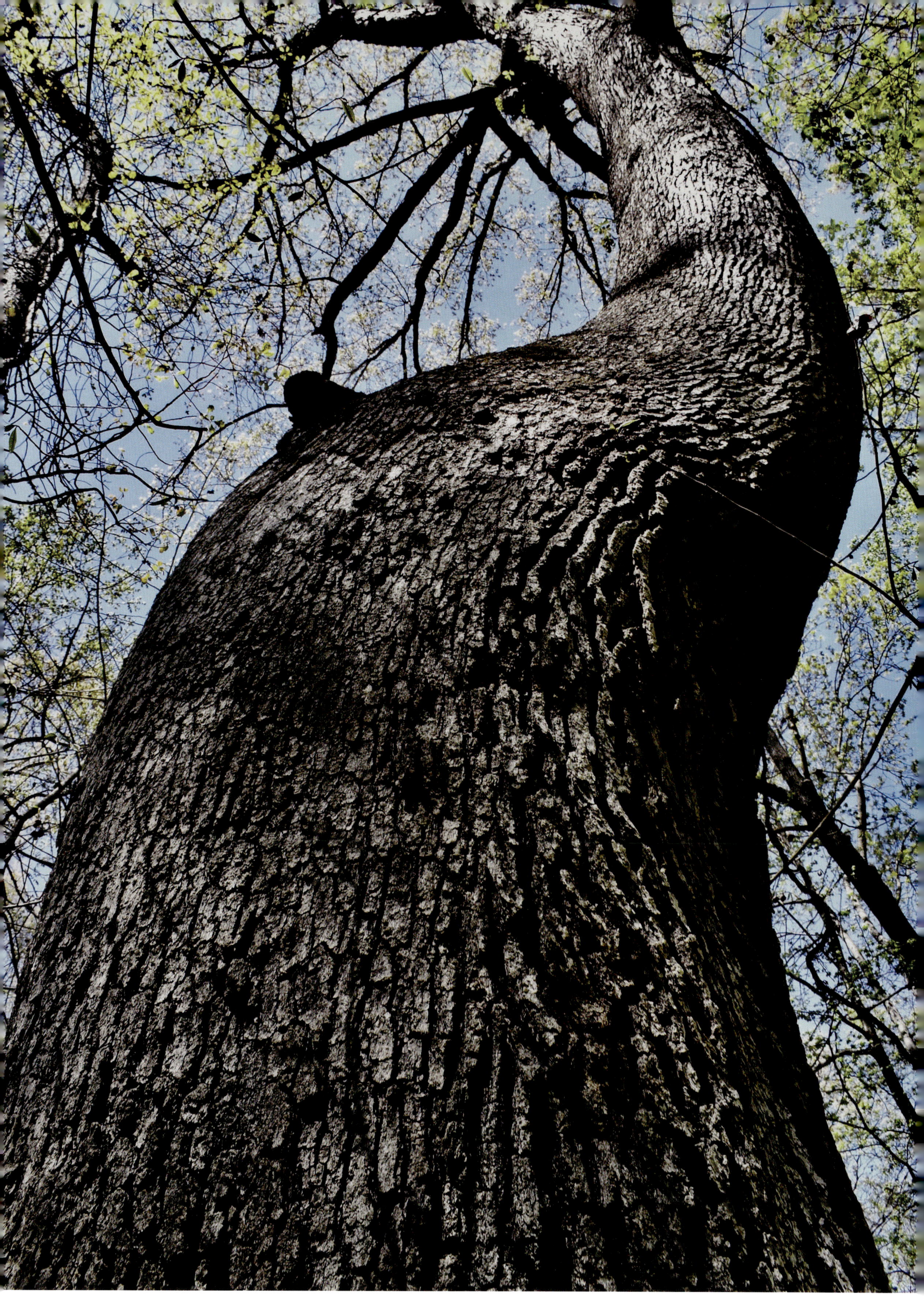

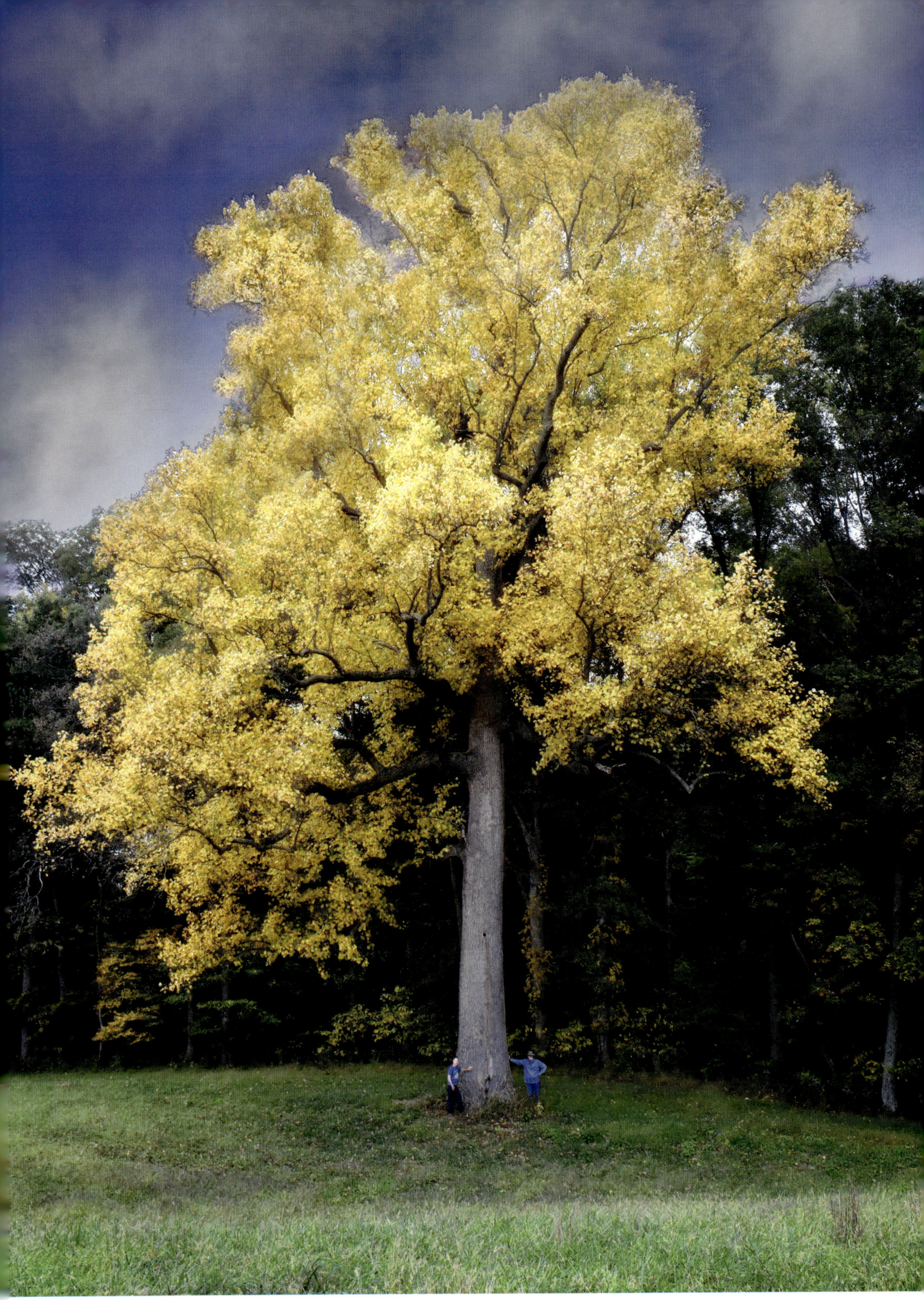

CHAPTER SEVEN

Sheer Beauty

In all seasons, trees have their own individual allure. Each is unique and worthy, but some seem to exhibit a little extra-special flair that attracts us. In some specimens the limb structure, bark, or root flare capture our attention. In others it may be the leaves, whether large and simple, or delicately double-compound. Color definitely adds a dimension of beauty in those fall days of transition from green to red, yellow, orange, and brown. With a backdrop of deep cobalt sky, the combination cannot be beat. This section features several that I deemed exceptional. From the hundreds of images, seventeen were chosen that appear here. They are a fine culmination of the creativity of nature, captured by me and great friend Gary Potts.

Left page: Superlative, majestic tuliptree, Lawrence County

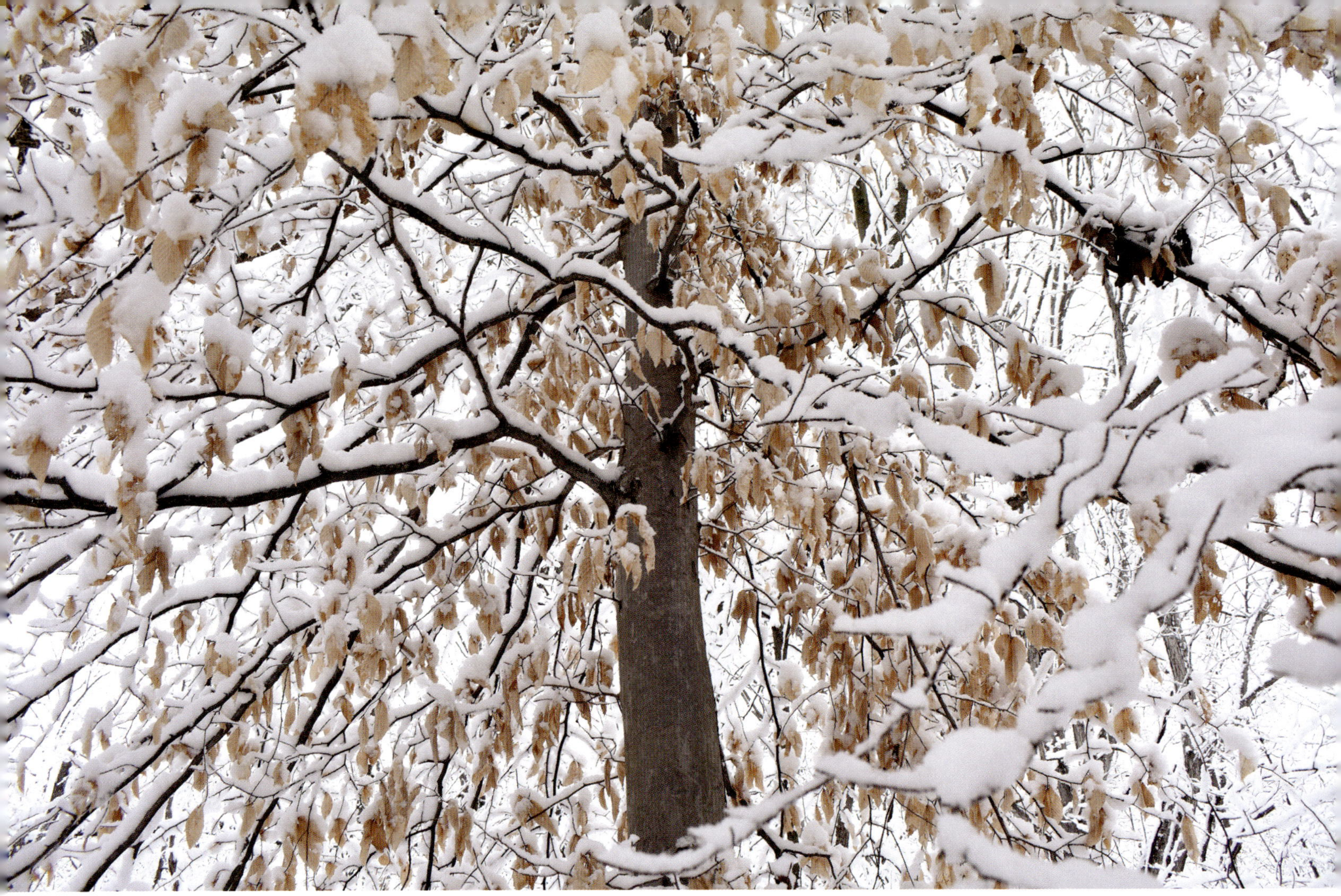

Above: Beech in winter

Right: Brilliant fall maple

Right page: A glorious fall day
Courtesy of Gary Potts

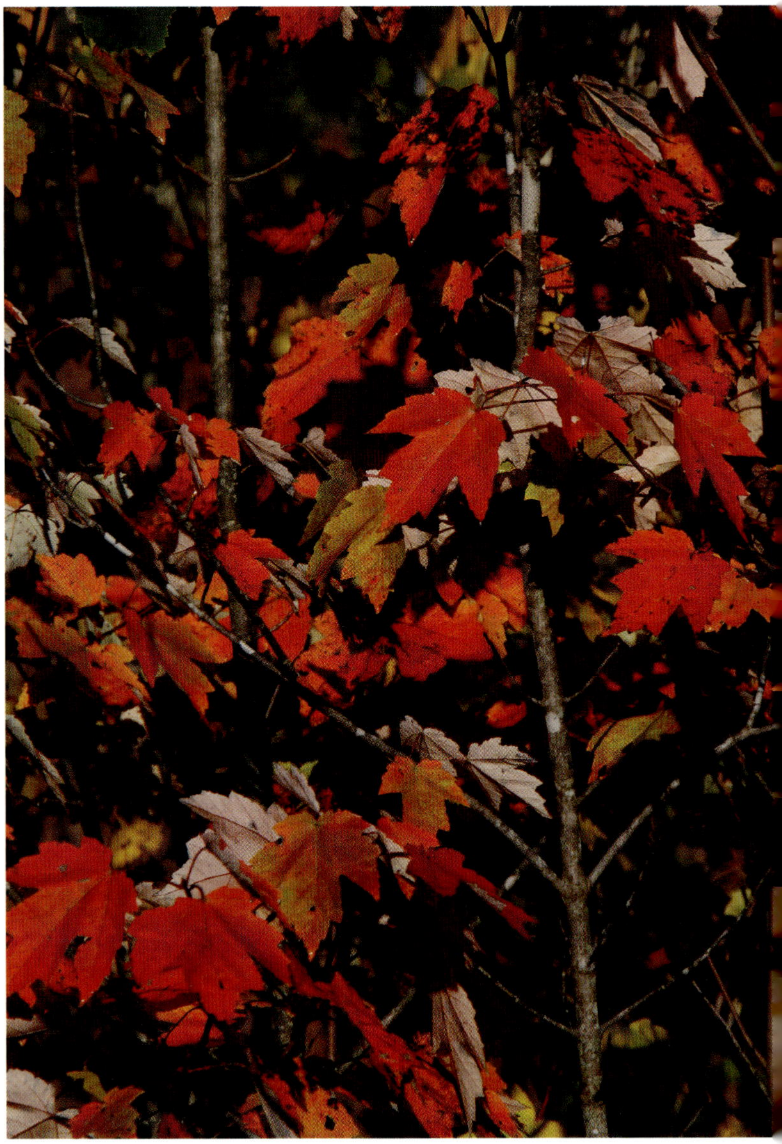

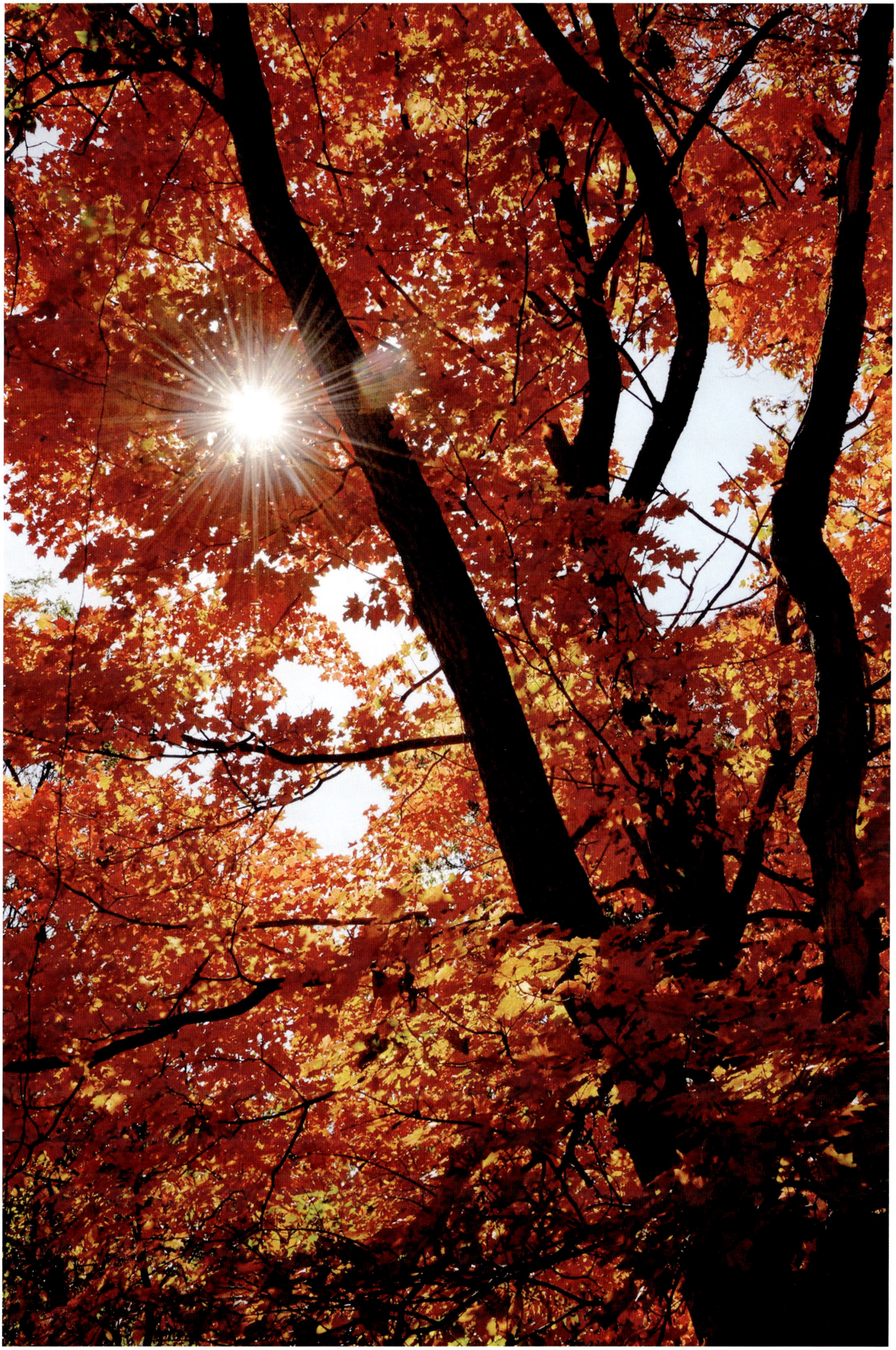

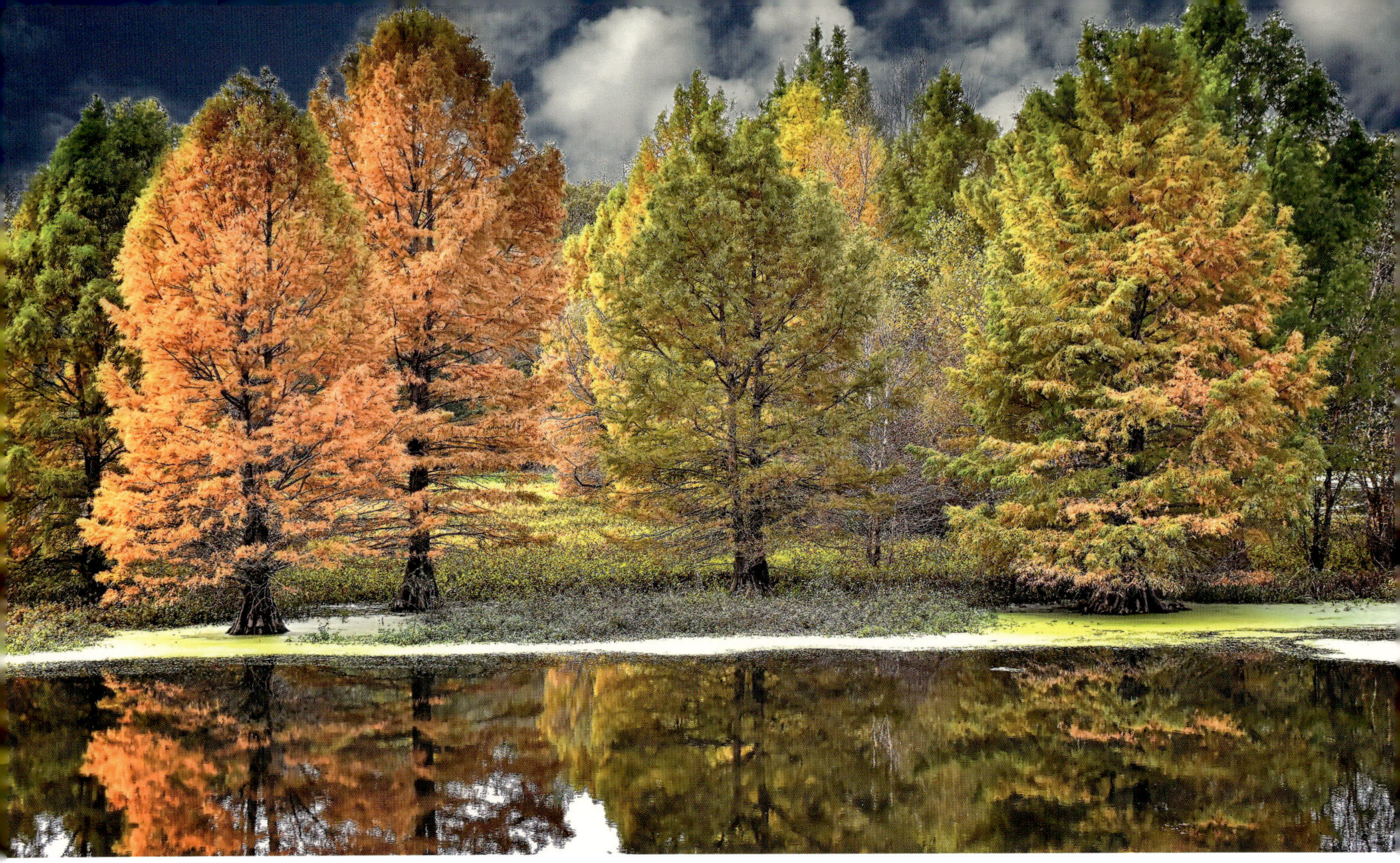

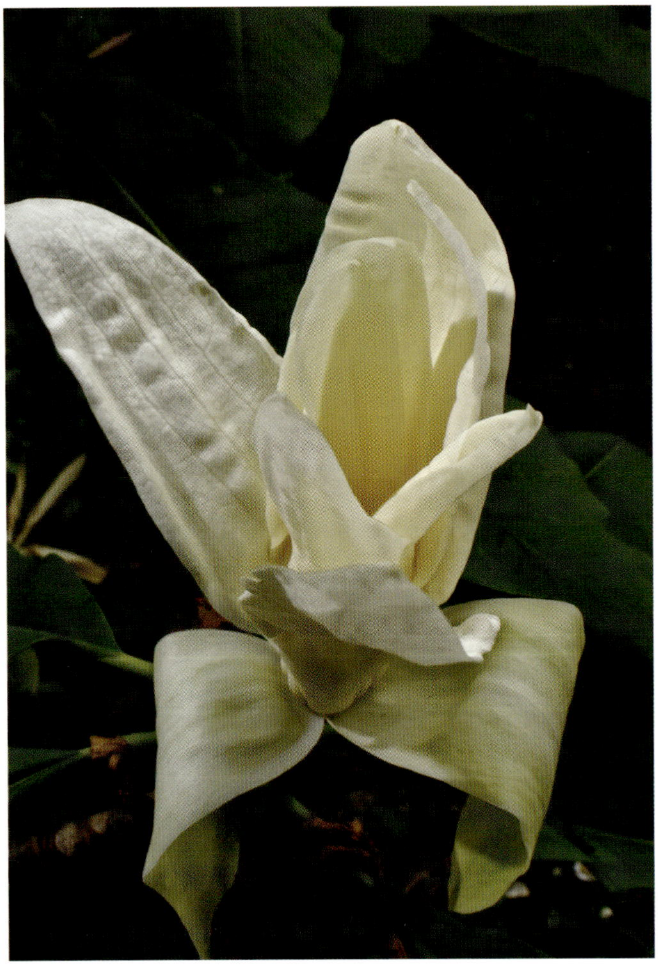

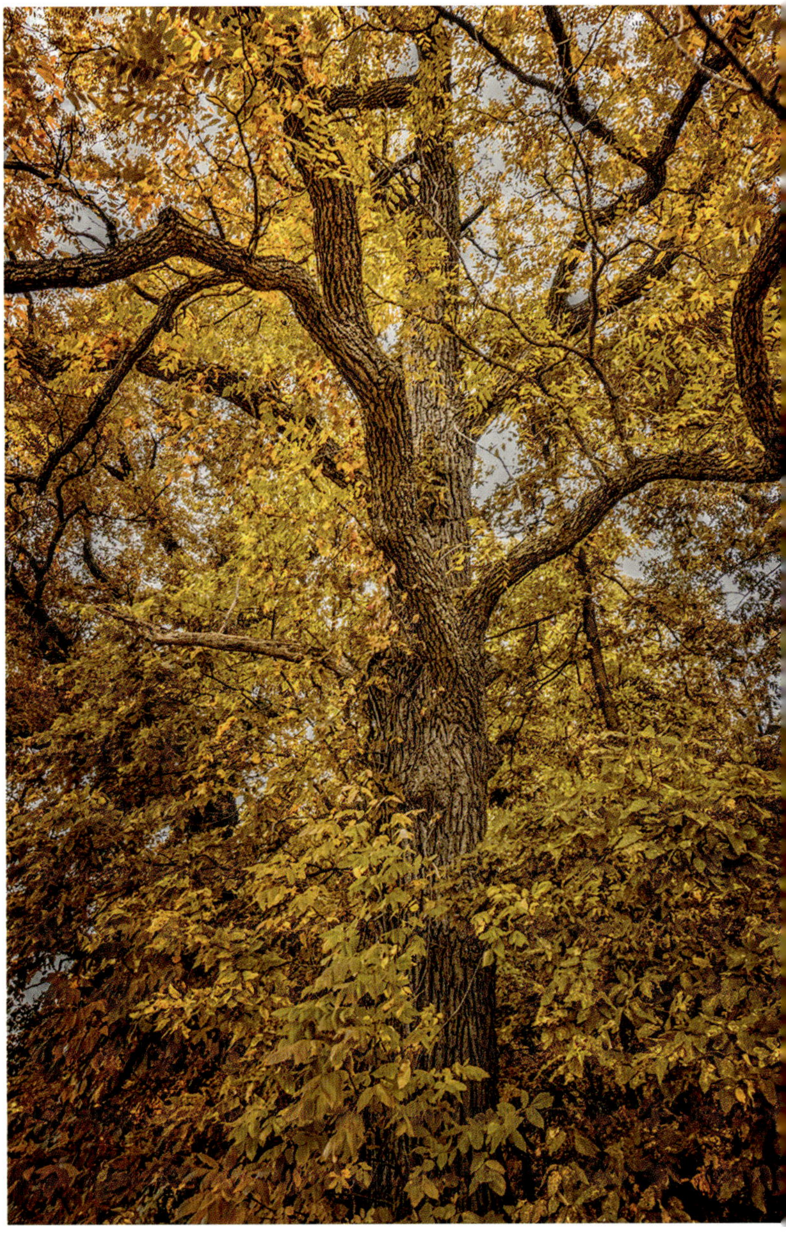

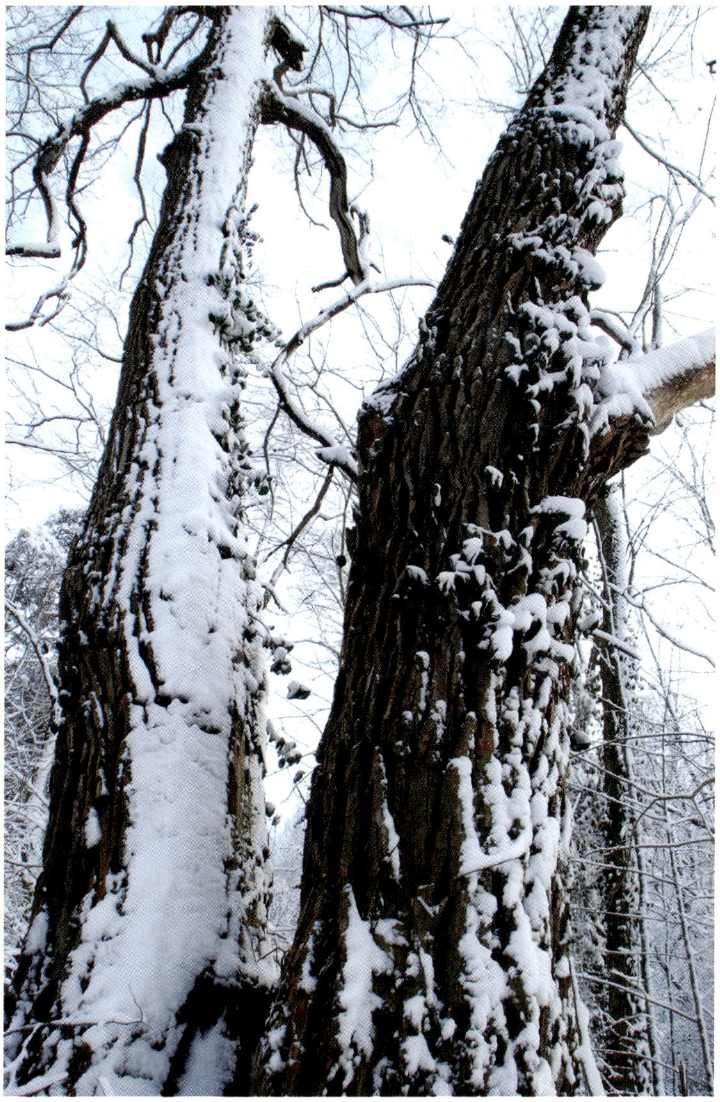

Left page, top: Cypress at Muscatatuck National Wildlife Refuge

Left page, bottom left: *Magnolia tripetala*'s perfect bloom

Left page, bottom right: Fall walnut lights up Purdue's Davis Woods
Courtesy of Gary Potts

Right page, left: Sassafras in snow

Right page, below: Sweetgum palette supreme

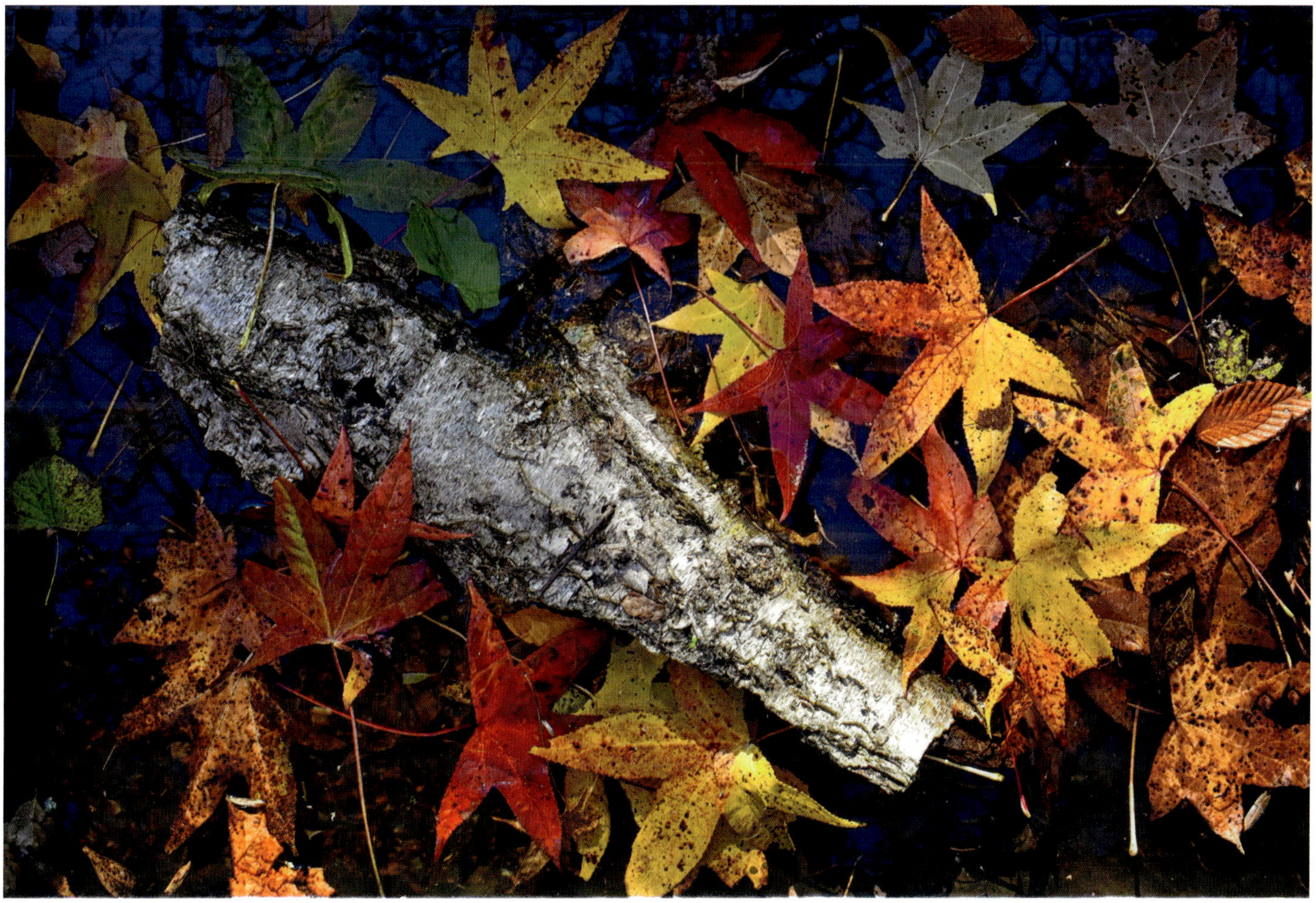

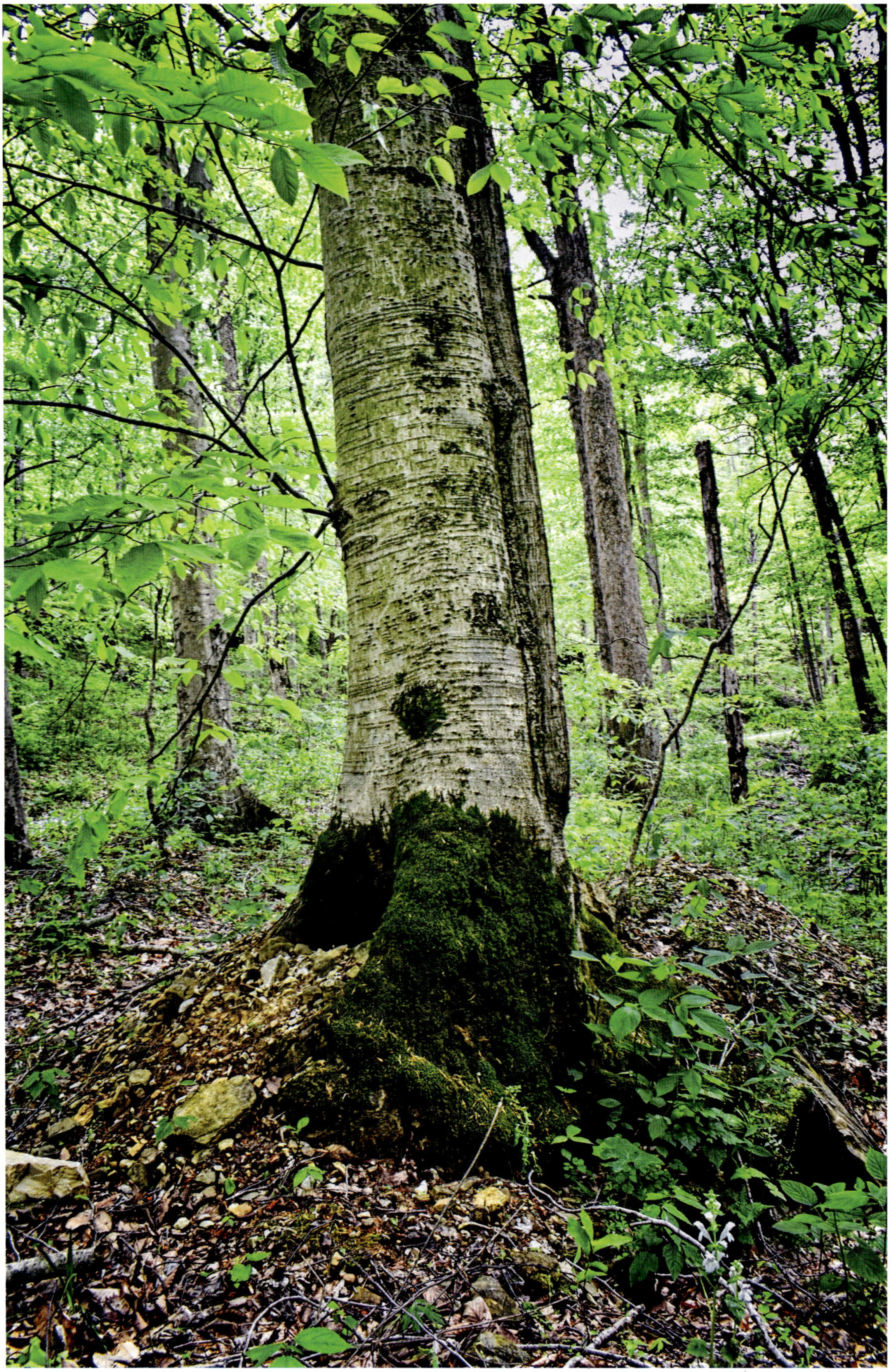

Above: Old beech with Irish-green frock, Crawford County. **Right page:** Fall beauty with large red oak.

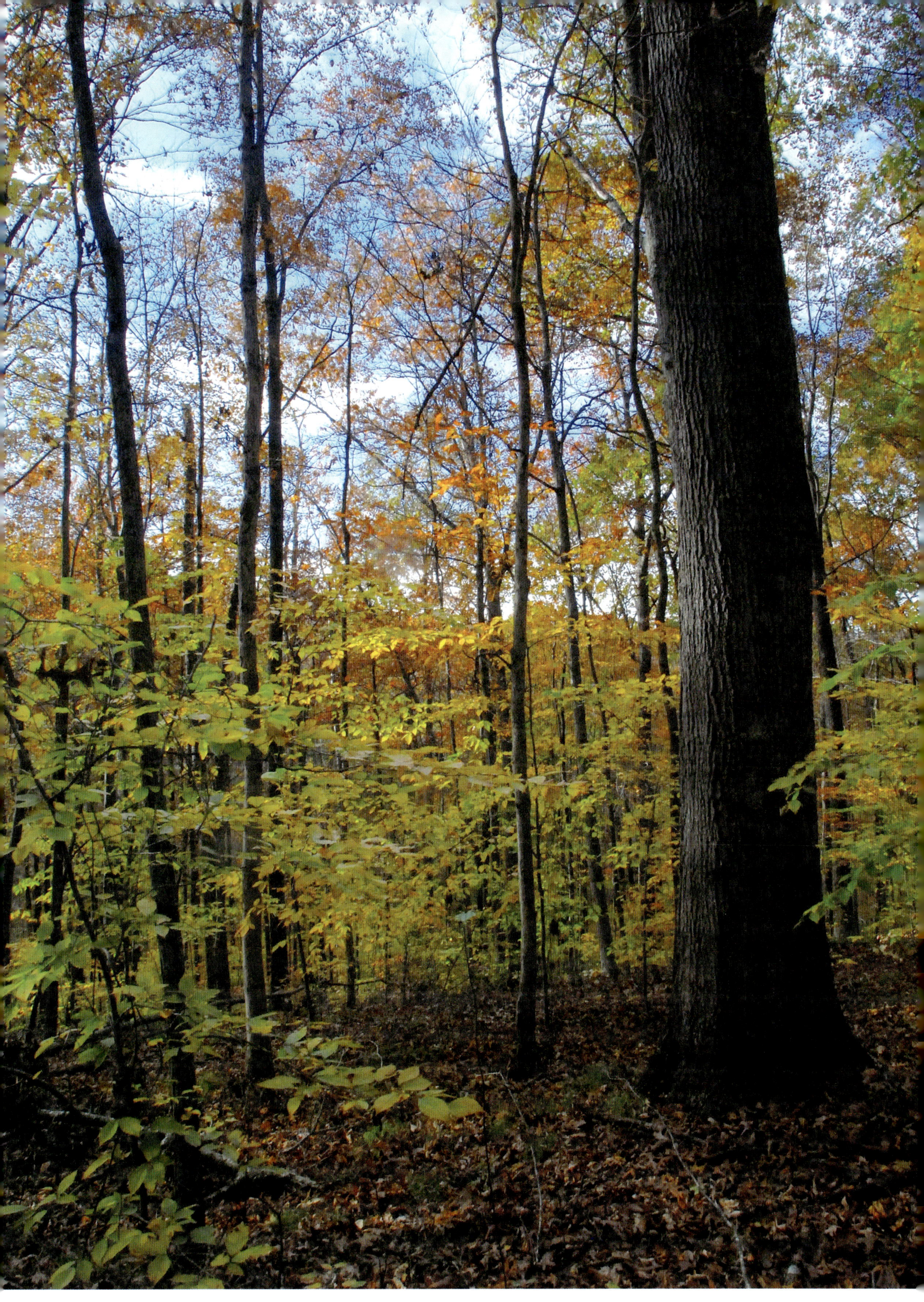

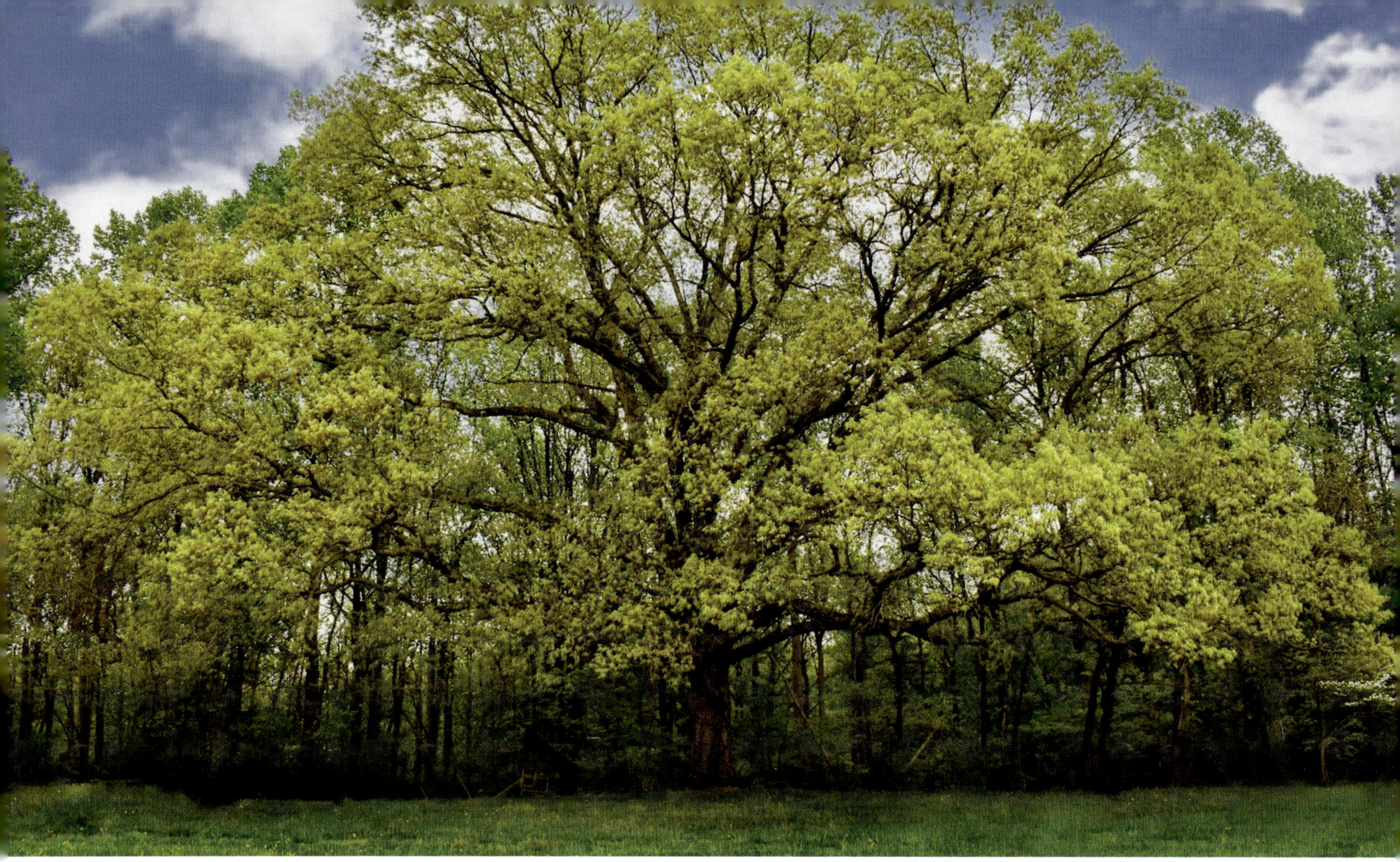

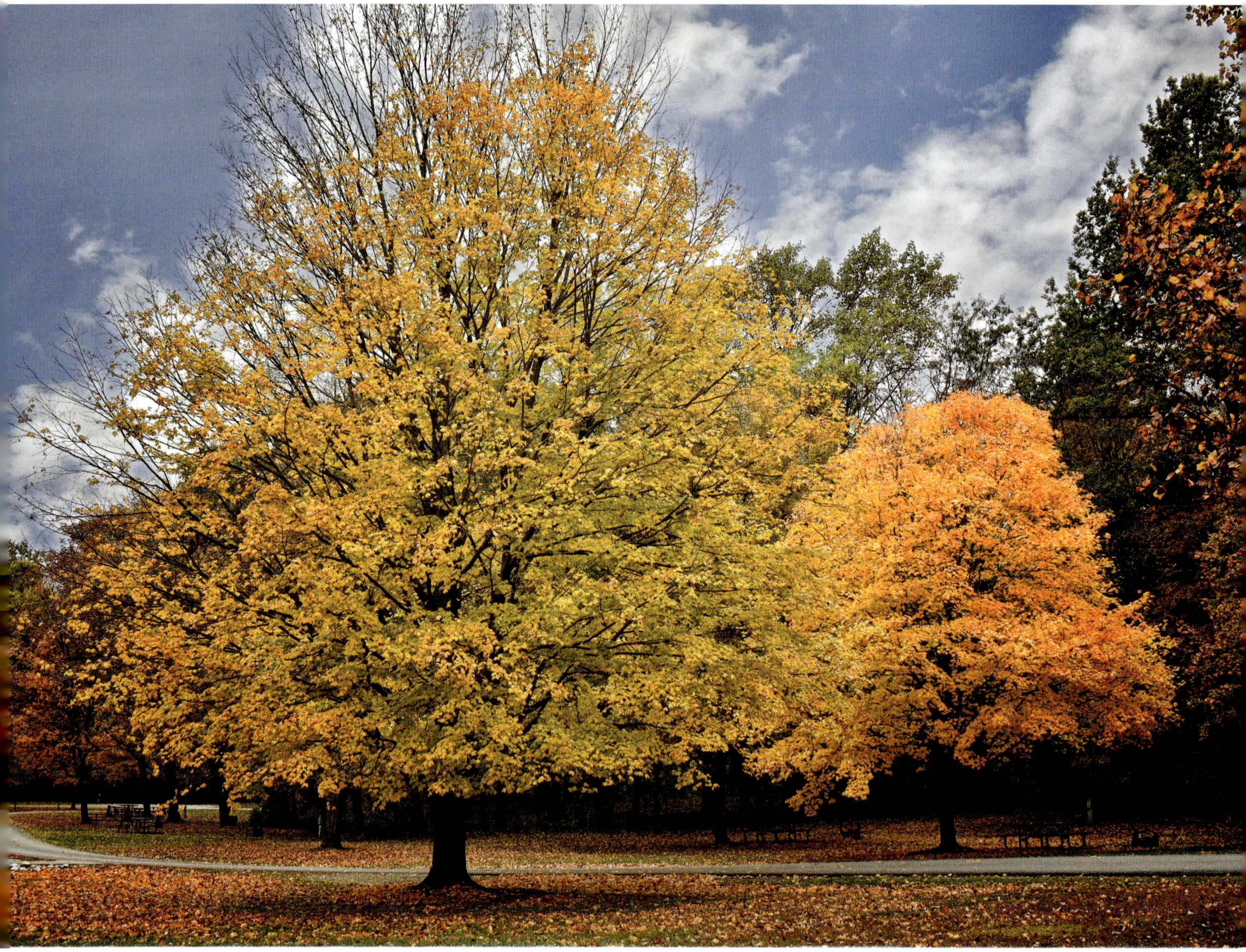

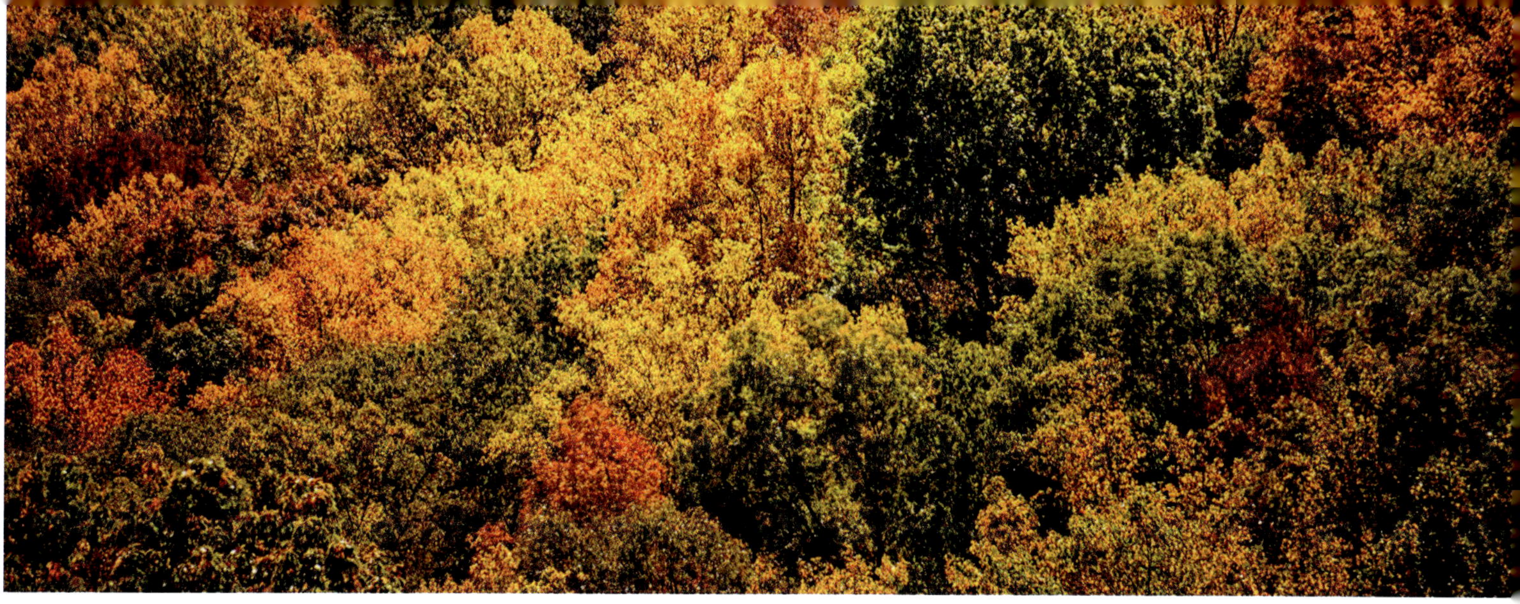

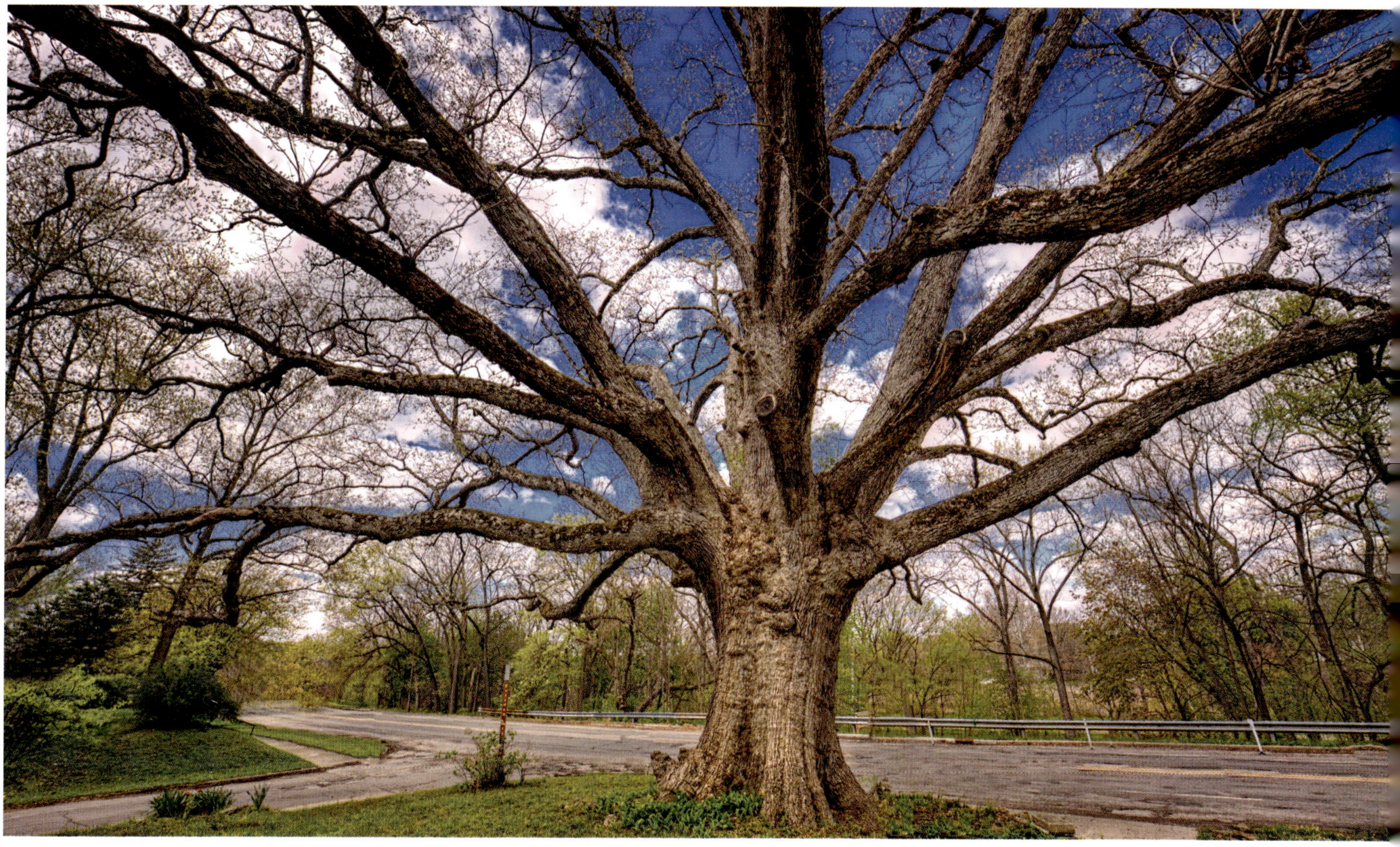

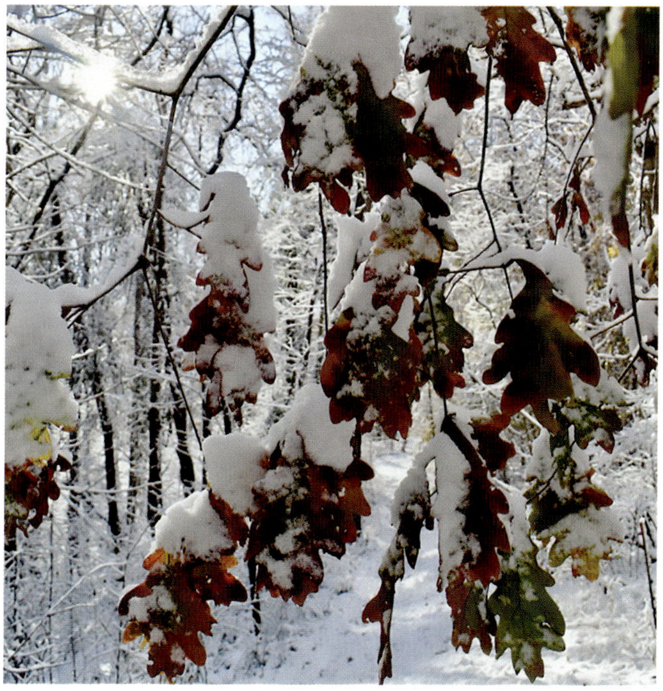

Left page, top: Sublime and perfect white oak, Orange County

Left page, bottom: Sugar maples, Prairie Creek Park, Vigo County

Right page, top: Unbeatable fall in Brown County
Courtesy of Gary Potts

Right page, middle: The much-loved Temple Oak in Indianapolis shows how much they add to urban neighborhoods.
Courtesy of Gary Potts

Right page, left: White oak leaves in snow

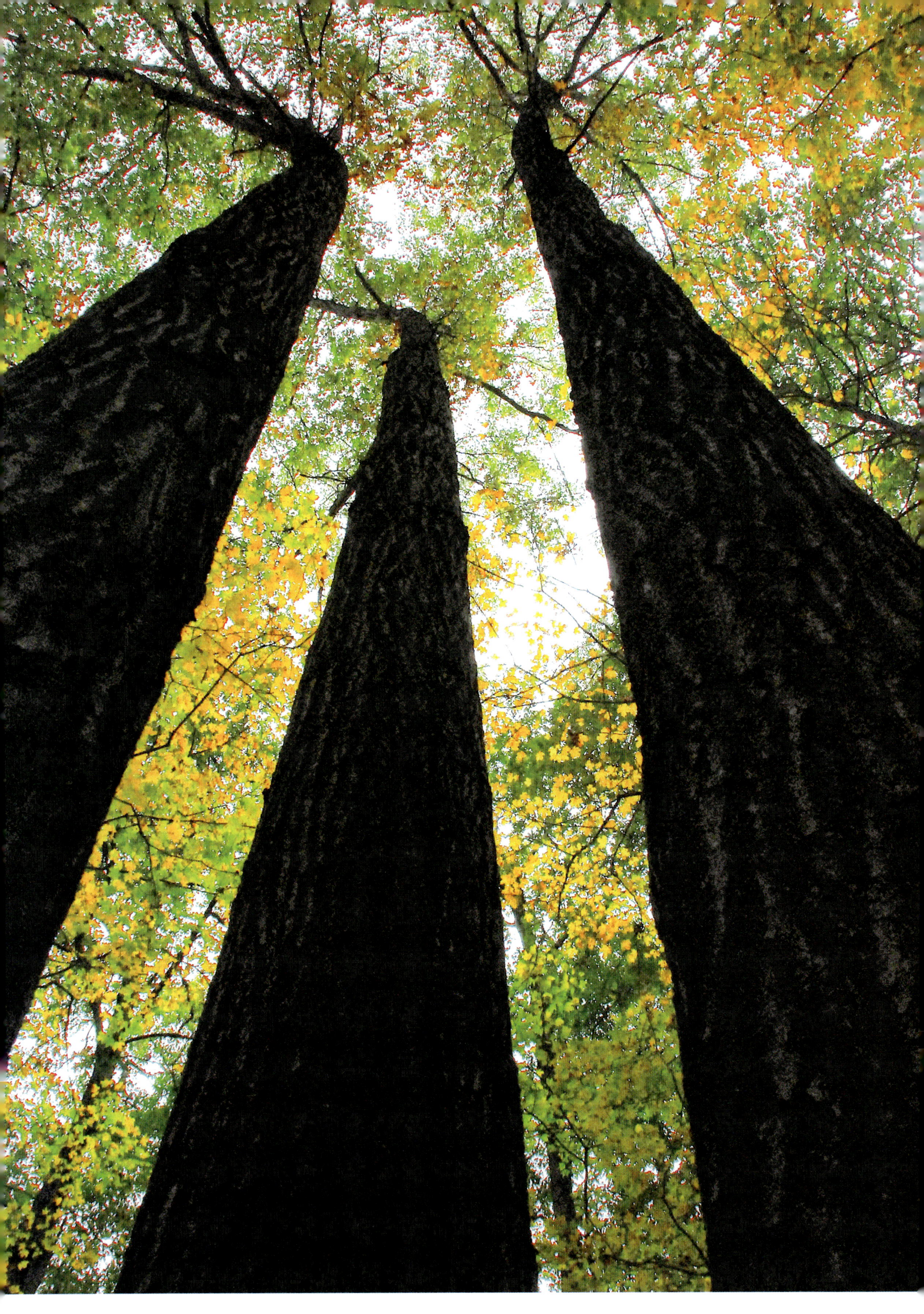

CHAPTER EIGHT

Woodland Values

Left page: Towering red oaks at SLT's Oakley Preserve, Lawrence County

HARDWOOD PRODUCTS, PAST TO PRESENT

Two men, two axes, wedges, an adze, and a froe. In pioneer times these were the basic tools for working the forest's bounty. One or two horses, mules, or oxen, harnessed up and standing nearby, were ready to drag out the log. Trees in the early 1800s were felled by axe and either bucked up (cut into shorter lengths) by axe or by a crosscut bucking saw, either one-man or two-man. Then they could use axe and wedge along the grain to split it. The crosscut saw was brought into even greater use by the late 1870s and 1880s for cutting down the tree itself.

Tulip and ash were most amenable to easy splitting and working up with an adze for shaping. If shingles were to be made with a froe (see Shingle Oak essay in Chapter 4), no doubt Abraham Lincoln was well attuned to the whole process as he grew up in Spencer County from 1816 to 1830.

When sawmills entered production, a rapid increase in the consumption of timber was possible. Local mills could be established near running water and powered directly by a rotating wheel or later by steam-powered boilers.

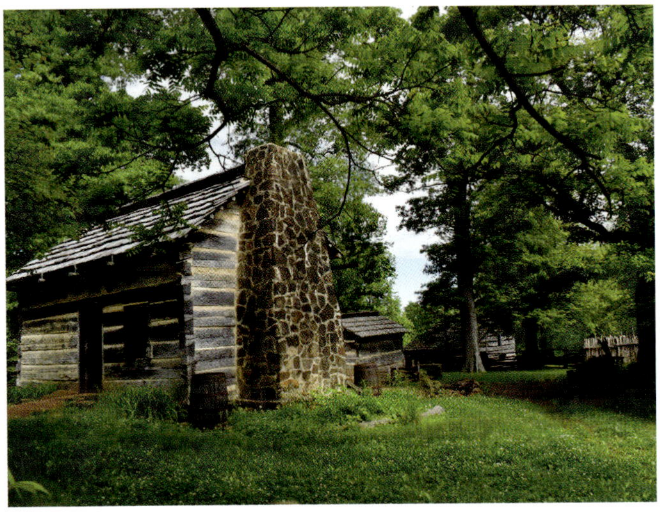

The Thomas Lincoln Homestead, Lincoln Boyhood National Memorial

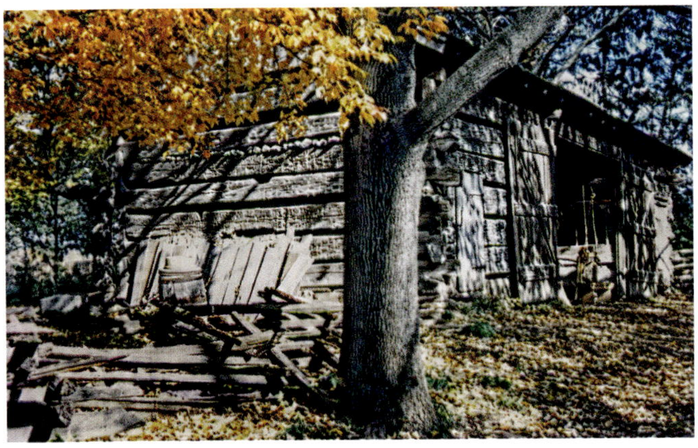

Old log barn from early homestead
Courtesy of Gary Potts

Imagine old log wagons pulled by horse or oxen, carrying or dragging fresh-cut trees downhill to the circular saw, powered by a chuffing steam boiler throwing hot plumes into the air. Here were gathered the farmers who brought the logs, along with groups of men and boys looking on. Then many hands threw the fresh-cut boards back onto the wagon for the trip home.

Beside large circular saws, pit saws could transition from a two-man operation of great physical labor to powered vertical or horizontal carriage machinery of wood

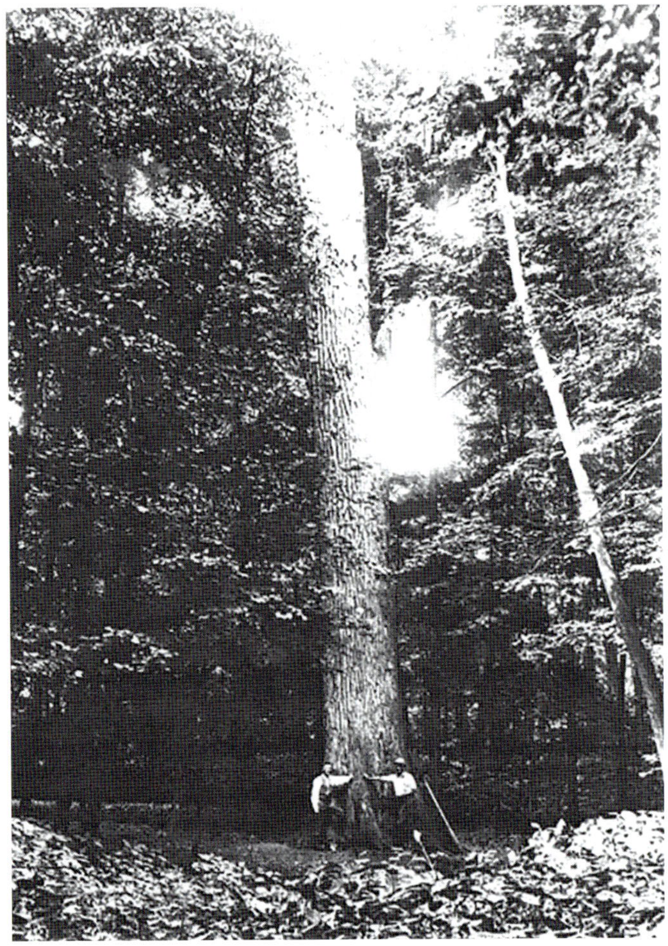

Early photo, old white oak
Courtesy of Indiana Department of Natural Resources

and iron. The original sawmill at Spring Mill State Park was built in 1824 by the Montgomery brothers. Powered by a water-turned wheel, it enabled logs to be cut more efficiently than the old methods by hand. The output was estimated to be 2,500 board-feet per day. The present structure pictured is a reconstruction of the old sawmill.

Products from timber became commonplace. As primitive roads became established, along with stream or canal boats, goods could be moved to distant locations. Note the many towns in Indiana with the suffix "port." These villages along rivers were strategically located to receive and ship out goods of commerce and industry. Local craftsmen in the community were able to acquire as much wood as

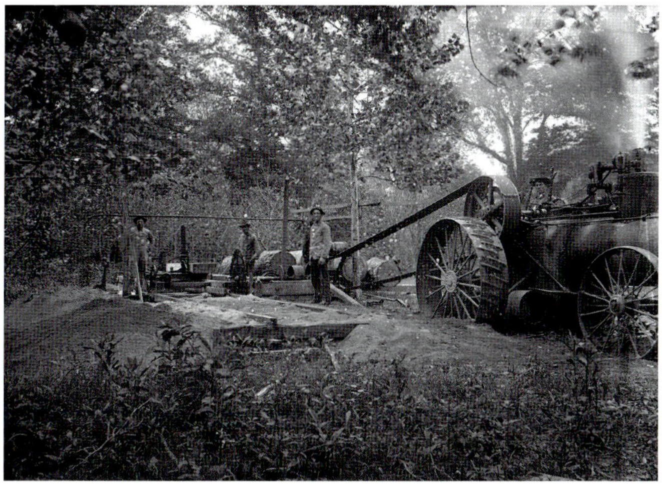

Historic steam-powered boiler sawmill, Floyd County
Courtesy of New Albany Public Library

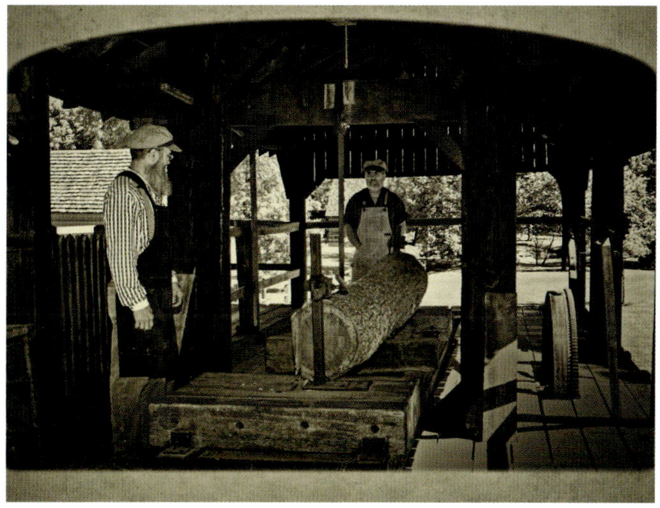

Replica of the old sawmill of the 1830s at Spring Mill State Park's pioneer village

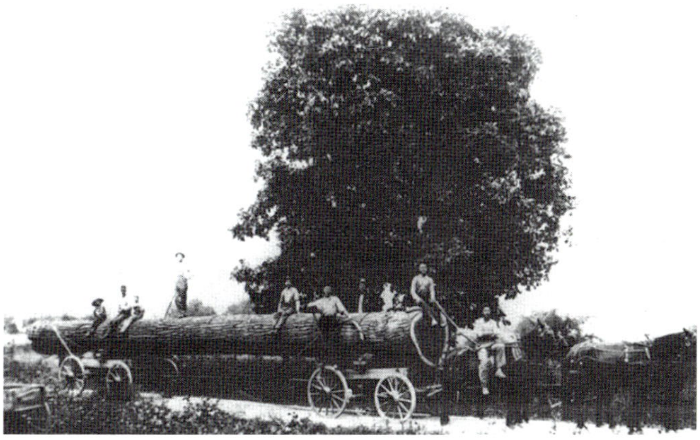

Old carriage with prime walnut log
Courtesy of Indiana Dept. of Natural Resources

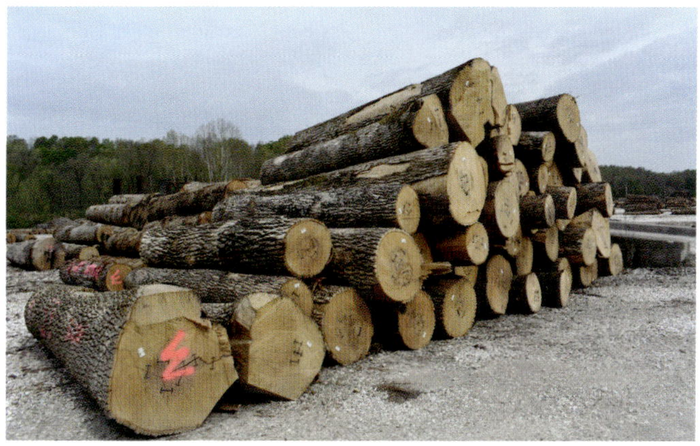

Stacked logs ready to move on to market—Orange County

necessary to expedite manufacturing of everything from sills, floors, framing, window frames, and cabinetry to whiskey barrels and many other items. Expanding population and urbanization began to change the face of early Indiana in the modern era.

Today, Indiana ranks first nationwide in production of wood office furniture and kitchen cabinet manufacturing. Our forests provide a high-quality sustainable resource for the hardwood products industry. It is estimated that forestry contributes over $10 billion to Indiana's economy through direct and related employment and products. Some 70,000 people are involved in the chain, all the way from logging up through manufacturing, distribution, and retail sales.[1]

Indiana's forestlands are among the most productive in the nation with regard to growing stock volumes per acre, up to twice the volume of other states in our region and somewhat larger than the national average.[2] Species of prime commercial value include red and white oak, hickory, yellow-poplar, walnut, and cherry. Before the emerald ash borer, ash was also an important tree but most of the good standing timber has been logged or just remains in the woods to naturally fall to the forest floor.

Trees that are harvested end up at several destinations. Primary mills will grade incoming logs for general lumber, veneer, pallets, mulch, pulp, or specialty uses. Some of the primary mill specialties will include manufactured veneer products, plywood, particleboard, or engineered wood products. Some saw logs are also exported. Secondary manufacturers then buy primary products and further render those into fine cabinetry, home and office furniture, windows, doors, and trim. Several very large operations in Indiana create nationally marketed fine furniture. Smaller and medium-sized operations also produce high-quality furniture and cabinetry, contributing to local economies and communities. Amish-made cabinets and custom furniture are also very much in demand.

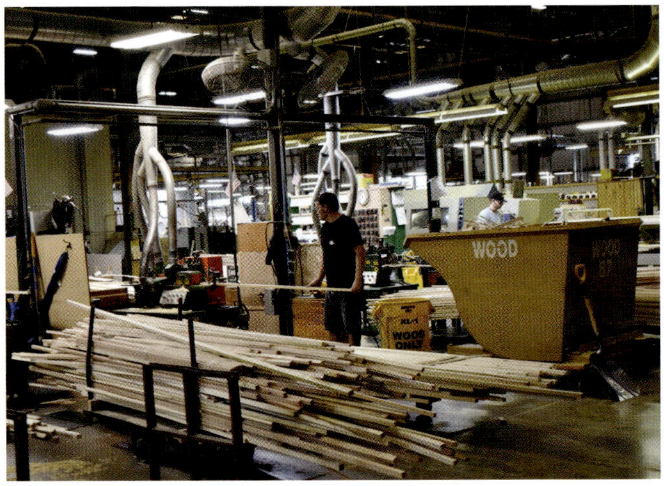

Koetter Woodworking, a large industry near Borden

TREE CROPS

Orchards around the state are extremely valuable and productive in supplying foods for local consumers as well as regional sales. Fruit trees contribute apples, peaches, plums, and cherries. According to Purdue, Indiana is the fifteenth largest producer of apples in the country, with 4,000 acres in trees and an annual production of 1.2 million bushels.[3] An orchard directory for the state lists a large number of producers, many small, but some fairly large. From fruit stands to local market stores, Hoosiers can enjoy a bag of fresh fruit, a caramel apple, and great apple cider.

Even persimmons are collected, processed, frozen, and shipped to make that delicious special pudding. Nut crops such as delicious pecans, hickory nuts, and walnuts are also derived from our trees, shared of course with those animal friends who are as eager to retrieve them as we are.

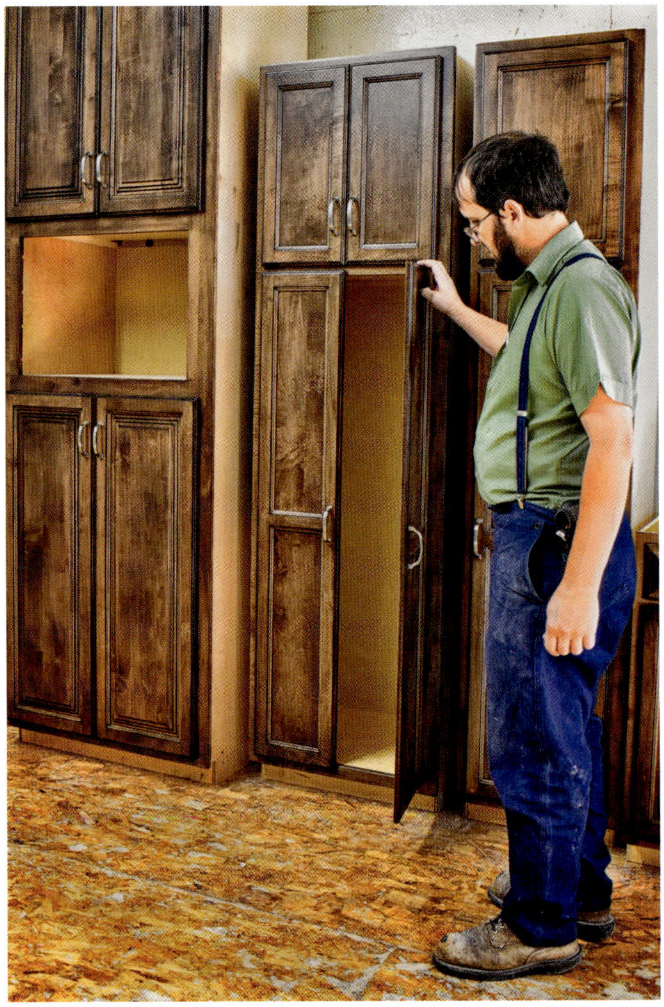

Larry Graber & Sons Cabinets, near Montgomery, exemplifies fine Amish craftsmanship

Further contributions derived directly or indirectly from Indiana's forestlands include products like maple

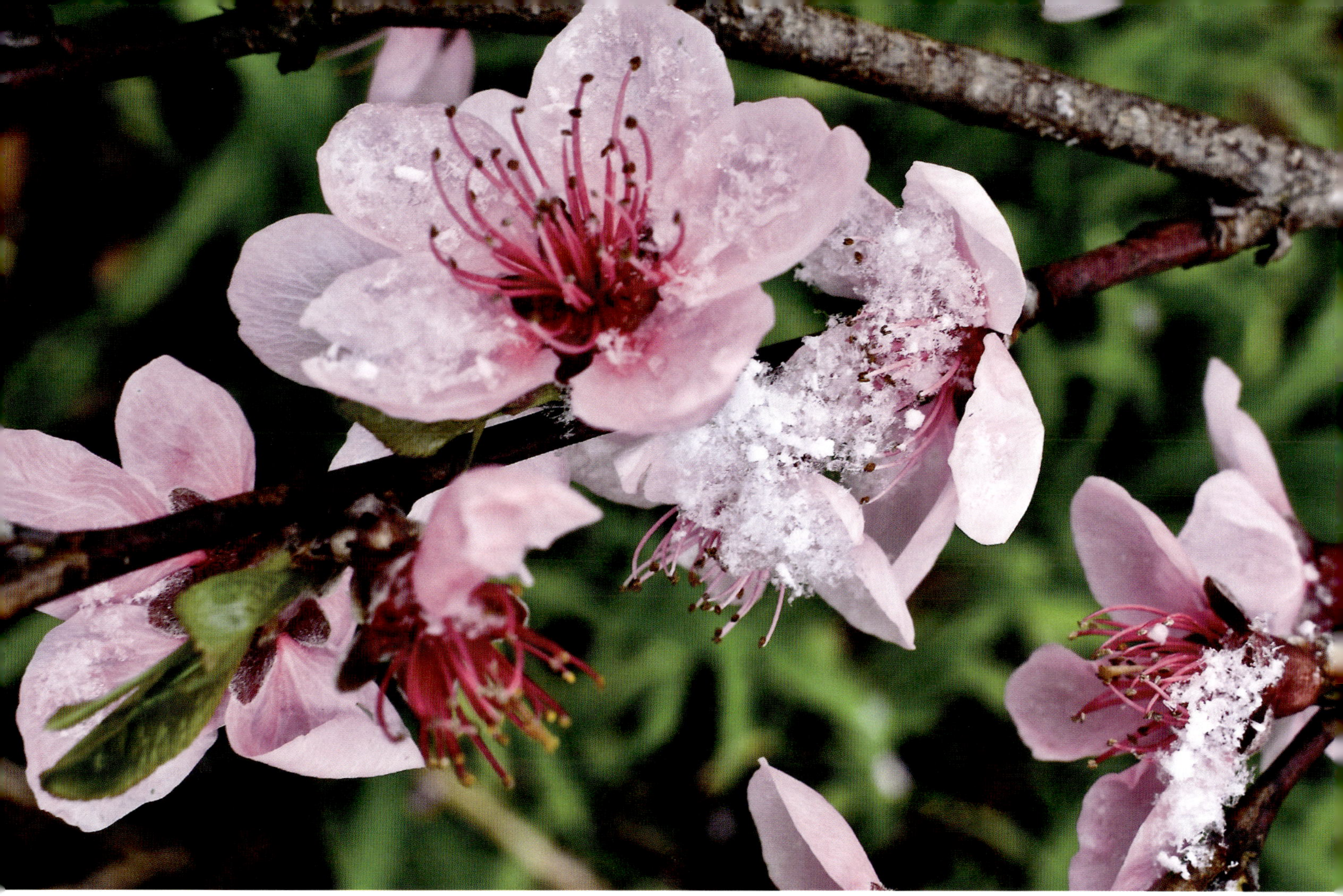

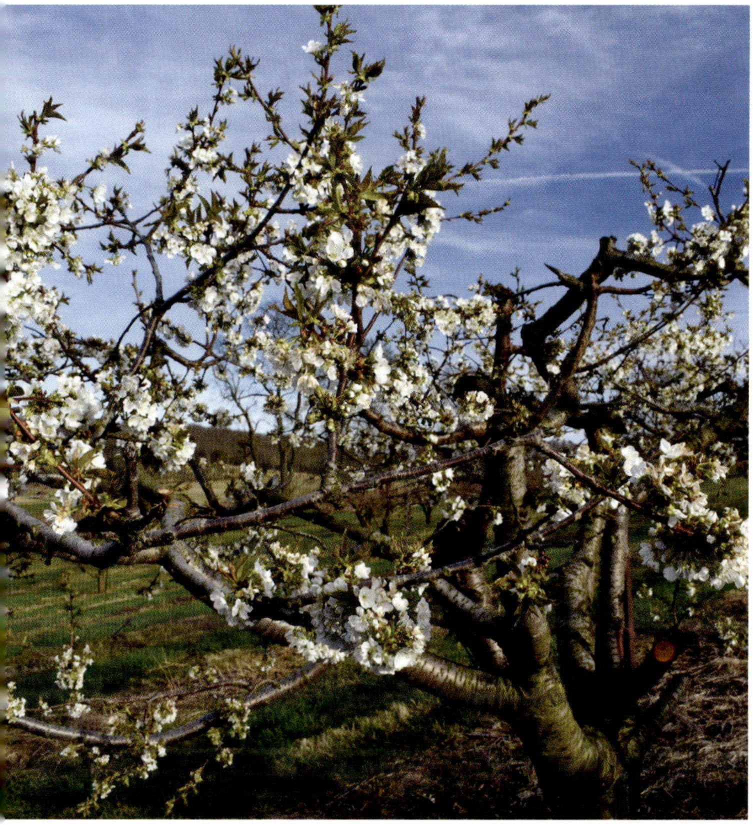

syrup, the "liquid gold" of the sugar maple. Many fond memories linger of the old sugar camp with buckets hanging on trees and steaming pans of cooking amber. Wood was fed to the fire all night long and sap added as necessary to get that one gallon of syrup for every 48 gallons of sugar water. The process often involved the whole family for those few nights in a narrow window of time when the sap was running.

The woods also provide other food items for both animals and humans. Acorns and other nuts, fruits, berries, and roots are nature's bounty throughout the seasons. The once immense number of chestnut trees alone provided tremendous wildlife and human benefits. Forest herbs and

Top: Peach blooms, Applacres Orchards, Bedford

Left: Spring blooms of Indiana's fine apple crop, Applacres orchard, Bedford

roots are collected for sale or direct use. Grapevines, cones, leaves, and boughs are used in many creative and decorative projects. Even locust pods, Osage orange slices, and bur oak caps, among many others, have found their way into wreaths and ornamental displays.

TREES AND WILDLIFE

It goes without saying that there are multiple, sometimes simple, but also complex relationships between flora and fauna. Through evolutionary history, species have in some cases become intricately tied through particular compounds created by one species and needed by another. In other cases, attachment surfaces, shelter, and moisture have been important and with fungal/algal symbiosis in lichens, we may see evidence directly on the tree trunk. Below ground, an entirely different world exists, driven by the cooperation of fungus and tree, sometimes beneficial and sometimes destructive. A perceptive description of this intriguing activity is offered by Wohlleben (2017). Beyond the myriad micro-web interrelationships, the most observable and poignant ties between flora and fauna go back to the simple facts of the food chain, those concepts taught in high school science and often played out in environmental education activities with youngsters. "Herbivore, carnivore, decomposer" become familiar terms. It is here that trees again play an important role, primarily that of producer, a source of plant materials needed for other parts of the chain of life. Leaves are, of course, vital as gatherers of sunlight and carbon dioxide in the photosynthetic realm, but also play host roles for various insects that may feed upon them. Some lay eggs on the leaf, which in turn becomes a food source in the larval stage of the insect. Other diseases of leaves such as spots and rusts are caused by fungi. Aphids and scale are a serious problem on yellow-poplar and if combined with other pests and in the middle of a drought year, cause serious stress on the tree.

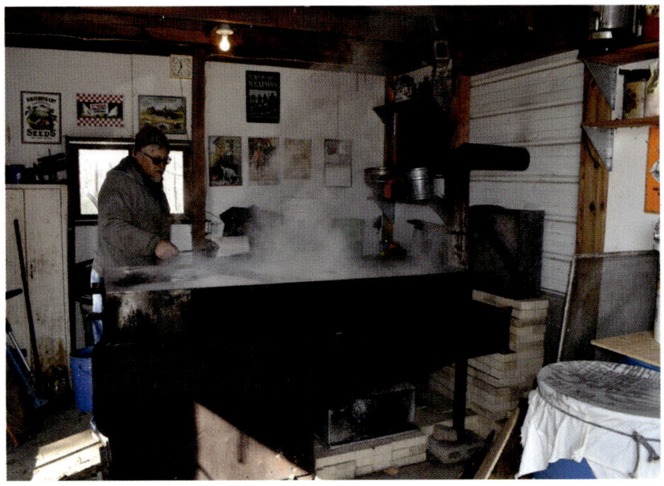

Boiling down the sap is a long process with a great final reward

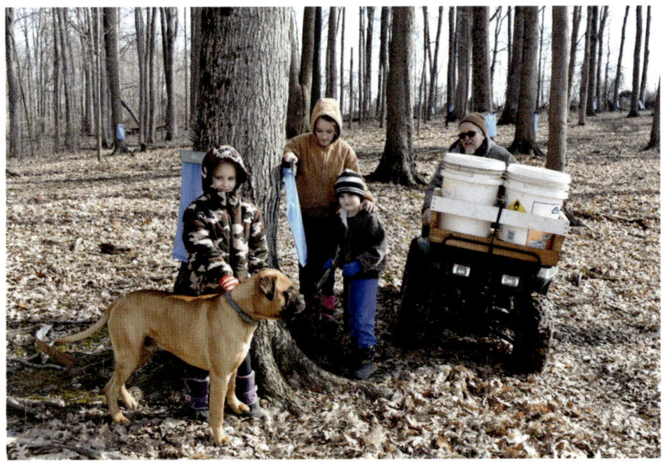

Sap collection is an important part of a family operation in Williams

Wildlife can be beneficial to the tree world, carrying nuts and seeds far and wide. But browsing on young seedlings, deer rubbing trunks to remove antler velvet, and birds pecking or boring holes into the cambium can be destructive. If deer overpopulate the woods, consume the majority of the acorns that year, then browse upon young shoots or tender twigs, oak reproduction is seriously jeopardized.

Animals have preferences in forest types; some depend upon conifers, some on hardwoods. Forest maturity also

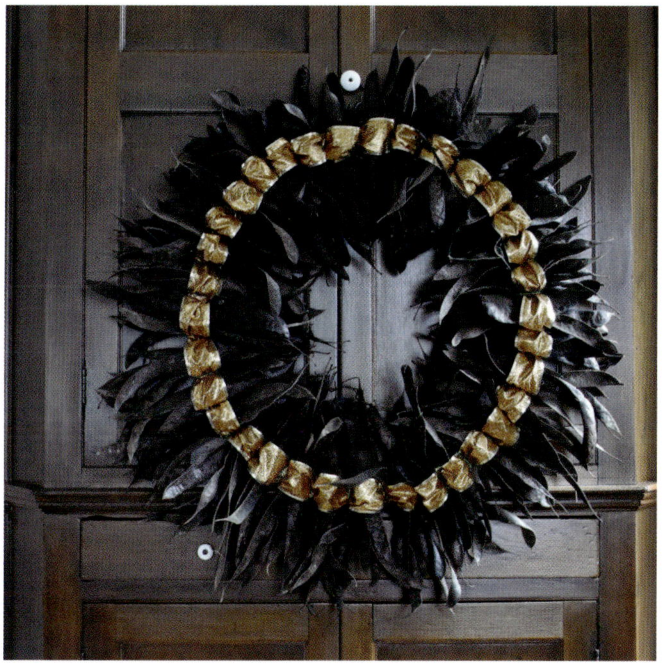

Craft use of honeylocust pods

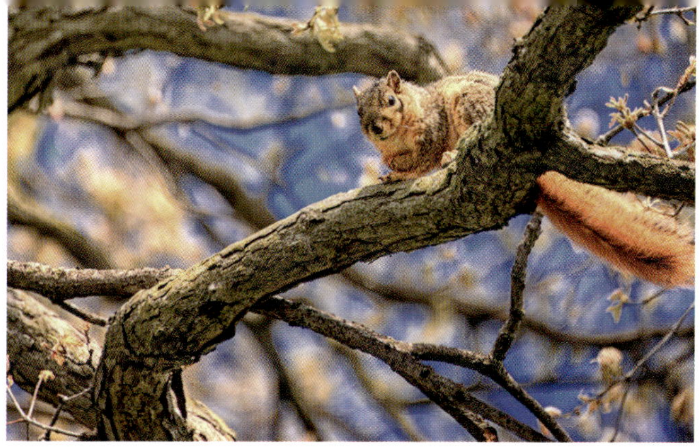

This red squirrel appreciates trees as much as we do
Courtesy of Gary Potts

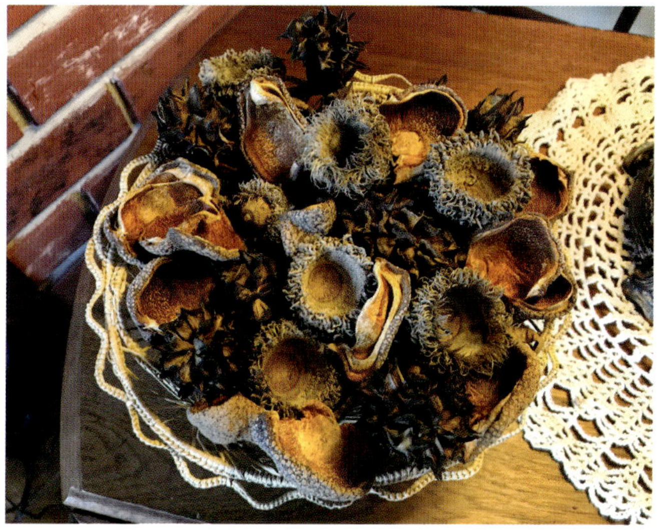

Bur oak caps provide interesting craft opportunities

highly affects many species with some preferring older mature growth but others dependent on an open or successional habitat. Certain birds need this early successional, brushy, small-tree environment, such as ruffed grouse and quail. In a timber harvest well planned and with distinct management objectives, some areas may have clearcuts or a few shelter trees left. This open environment is needed for successful habitat for these species. Specific management plans may also concentrate on bats, owls, or other endangered animals. Forestry is a science much deeper than the average person realizes, integrating the understanding of complex interrelationships across many fields of study.

OTHER TIES TO TREES

The tradition of going out to cut a Christmas tree is well remembered by many of us. Whether it was a redcedar out in the field or a pine or fir in a plantation, the memories are great ones. Sawing the tree, loading it onto the sled, pulling it across the snowy field, and strapping it on top of the car or in the bed of the pickup were all part of a memorable adventure with the family. Once home and the tree in its stand, warm hot chocolate ended the perfect day.

Trees are also the basic part of a landscaping business, with the added shrubs and flowers making up the design package. Native species were most desired originally, but then hybrids, grafts, and "new species" came along. Some of these were quite acceptable and beneficial, but other exotic ones turned out to be a problem a few years down the road. Once escaped from their original spot, a few haunt us now with their highly invasive nature—demanding attention and causing frustration and considerable cost. Arborists now are needed not only to shape, remove, and improve the native trees, but also to eliminate the unwanted ones such as callery pear, ailanthus, and corktree.

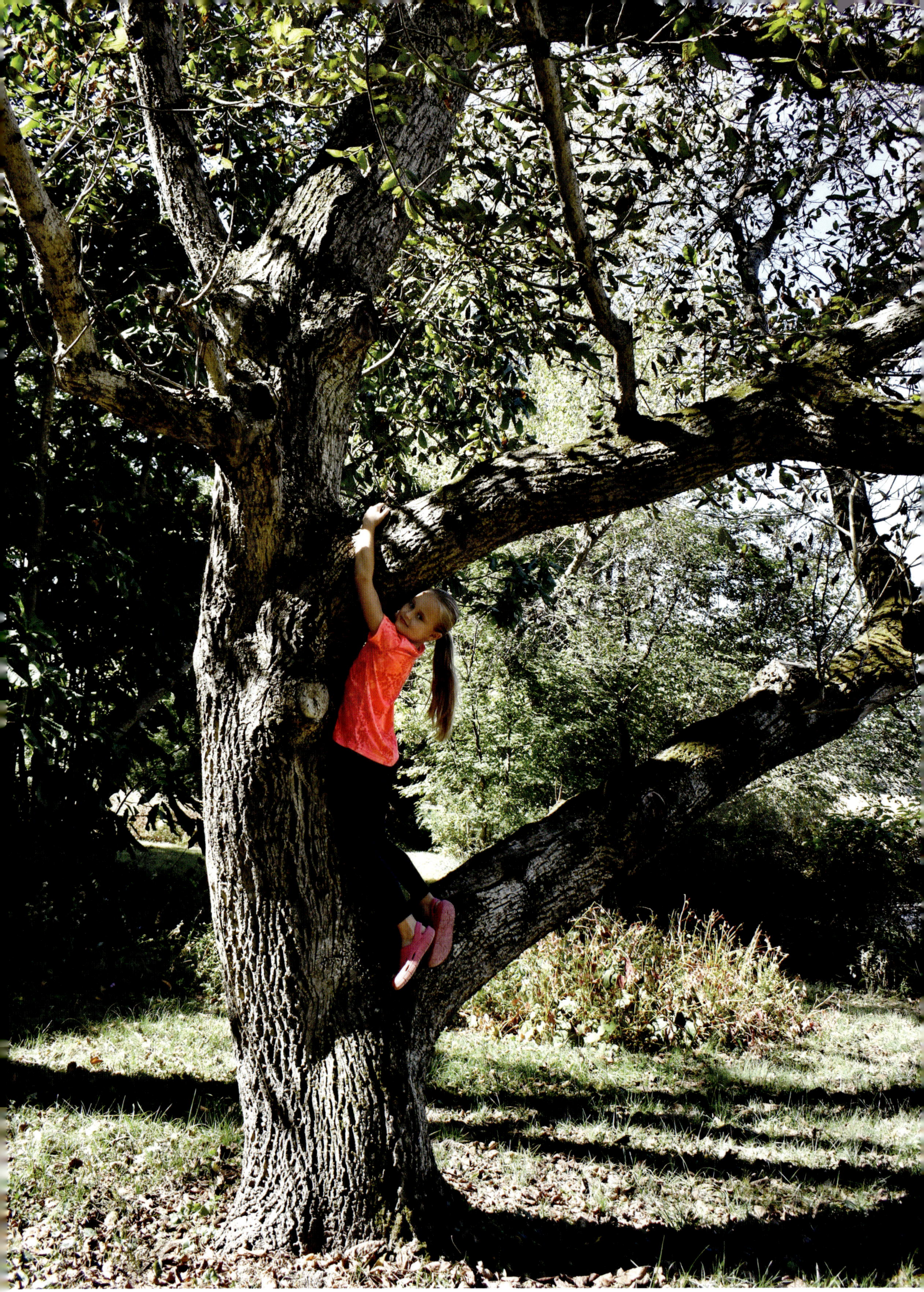

CHAPTER NINE

People and Trees

Left page: Climbing trees is just a natural fit for kids

Through the ages trees have been an important part of human needs, inspiration, and appreciation. They have borne heavy loads and responsibilities without the ability to voice objections. Carrying the burdens people placed upon them, they have served nobly and remarkably. Empires depended on great forests supplying wood for wagons, ships, fortresses, and homesteads. What was once considered an endless timber supply became more scarce, more costly, or unavailable to meet the demands of commerce, development, and even waste. Historical progression has in many ways enabled us in this modern age to consider wiser stewardship and more fully utilize multiple-use management concepts that began in Gifford Pinchot's time. He was the first chief of the U.S. Forest Service, appointed by Theodore Roosevelt in 1905.

For owls, raccoons, and hollow cavity dwellers, the tree is a home, but for us, it may take on other roles. A tree cabin created for his children by a resourceful father is a magical escape into a private space in nature. For a child swinging on a board seat suspended by long ropes from the branch of a giant white oak, there is pure enjoyment.

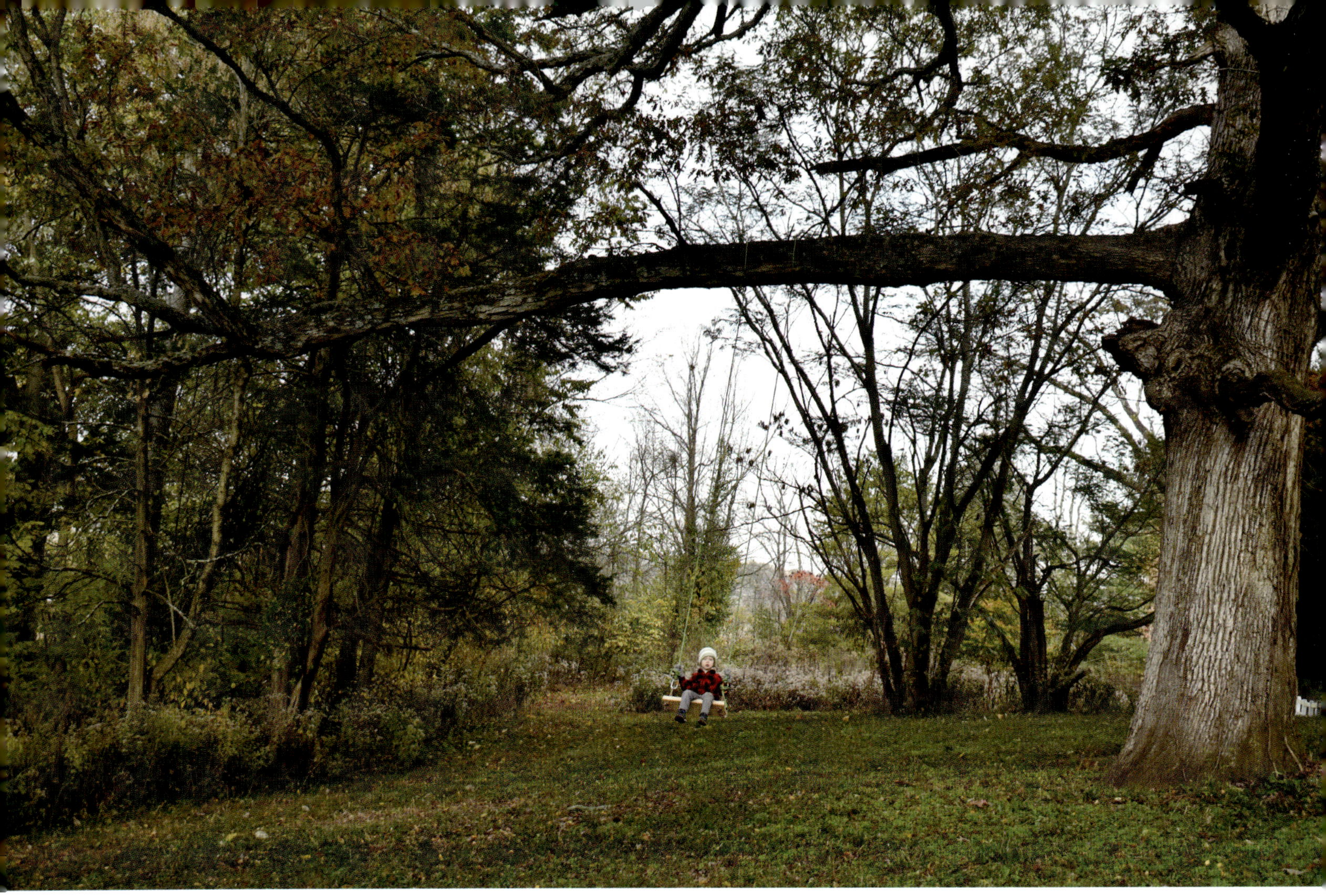

Swinging from a limb of a 150-year-old oak is hard to beat

Trees are subjects for painters who render their attributes into visual delights. The forest's abundant floral displays attract photographers to the subtle colors of spring and the flaming colors of fall. Trees are an integral part of design for most any campground and fond memories persist of their shade, protection, and beauty. An evening campfire with glowing wood embers followed by moonlight streaming through the trees prepares the camper for a most satisfying end to the day.

Indiana's establishment of state parks did not begin until 1916, one hundred years after statehood. Both McCormick's Creek and Turkey Run were dedicated that state centennial year and today remain as inspiring as they were then. We now have thirty-two state parks and many of our finest old trees exist within their boundaries. State forests also provide hiking trails as well as managed timber harvesting. Creation of the Charles C. Deam Wilderness in 1982 further set aside 13,000 acres to be preserved in perpetuity. Administered by the U.S. Forest Service, this large area permits hiking and horseback riding opportunities in a protected landscape. The 203,000 acres of the Hoosier National Forest also feature other opportunities to enjoy a forest environment at recreation sites, special areas, and geological wonders.

RECREATION, ENJOYMENT, AND EDUCATION

Recreational uses also make significant contributions to tourism and the state's economy. Hunting, fishing, birding, wildlife photography, hiking, and camping all depend on healthy and well-managed forests. According to IDNR's "Forests of Indiana: Their Economic Impor-

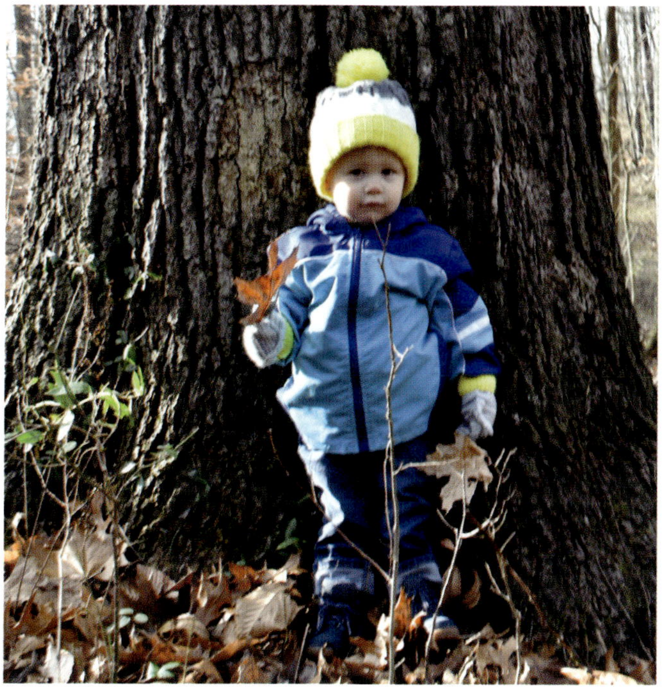

Learning early about trees

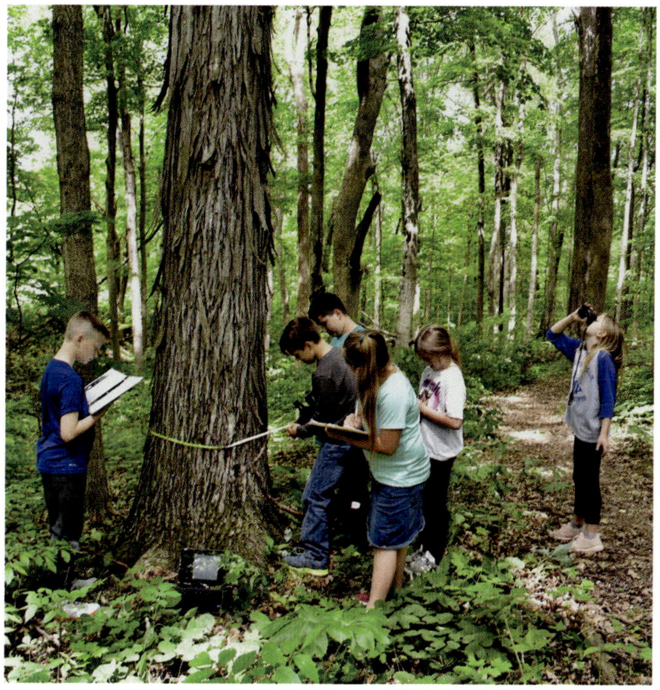

Students learn forestry measurements as part of outdoor educational experiences, while enriching their relationship with nature

tance," a conservative economic benefit to Indiana from all these sources was over $1 billion per year in 2004 and it is doubtless higher now. Destinations include state parks, wildlife refuges, state game areas, wilderness, trails like the Knobstone, nature preserves, the Hoosier National Forest, and privately leased lands.

Forest education takes many forms. State park nature centers and personnel provide interactive programs for all ages, which include tree identification, uses, and importance in the environment. Quality experiences can also be found at the Indiana Dunes federal and state facilities, and at the U.S. Department of the Interior's national wildlife refuges at Muscatatuck, Patoka, and Big Oaks, all in southern Indiana. Here, the visitor can see how forests, wetlands, replanting, and management all work together. Many other nature centers operated by county and city parks include forestry teaching in their programs. Wesselman Woods in Evansville has exceptional facilities and an old-growth woods, enabling them to conduct exemplary programs. A large facility, part of Goshen College, is the 1,100-acre Merry Lea Environmental Learning Center in Noble County. Ball State University has multiple sites that facilitate student research in natural settings, including old-growth Ginn Woods. Purdue's multiple wooded research areas such as McCormick Woods offer students and the public a chance to see natural systems. Stout Woods, a Purdue-owned dedicated state nature preserve, is another location for enjoyment. Bradford Woods, operated by Indiana University, has long provided outstanding programs for schools. Located in Morgan County, this 2,500-acre property specializes in outdoor learning of which tree studies is an important part.

It is well documented that people of all ages need exposure to nature for physical, emotional, and mental health. Children, especially, should have early and frequent exposure to the outdoors, stimulating the senses, mind, and creativity of the next generation. If there is no connection now, there may be little interest later in sustaining our forests and wetlands.

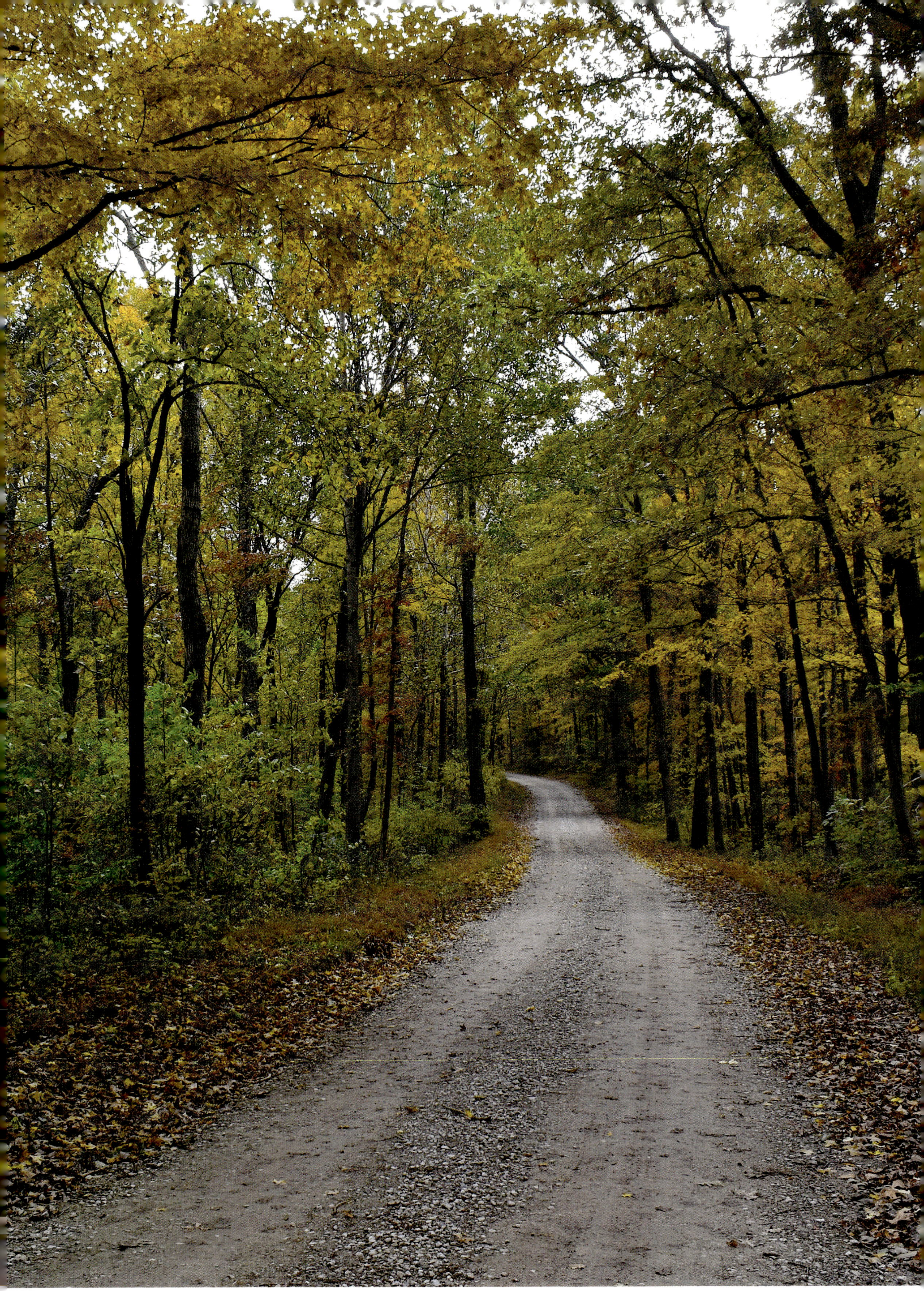

CHAPTER TEN

Protecting and Sustaining Our Forest Heritages

Many readers who do not own a woods still appreciate seeing or visiting them and understand the value of forested land. Since 87 percent of Indiana's 4.9 million acres of forest are privately owned, an emphasis on education and good forest stewardship is important for all. Readily available are resources like the state's Classified Forest and Wildlands Program with professional advice through district foresters, the Natural Resource Conservation Service's Environmental Quality Improvement Program, and its Conservation Stewardship Program. Experts in these areas work directly with landowners to provide valuable assistance including money to do self-management or to hire a consultant forester who can provide valuable recommendations on managing woodlands and preparing for any timber harvest.

For forests that are deemed to have great natural qualities worthy of permanent preservation, exceptionally valuable protection is possible through the Indiana Department of Natural Resources Division of Nature Preserves. Many of our finest examples of original Indi-

Left page: Scenic beauty in the Hoosier National Forest, Jackson County

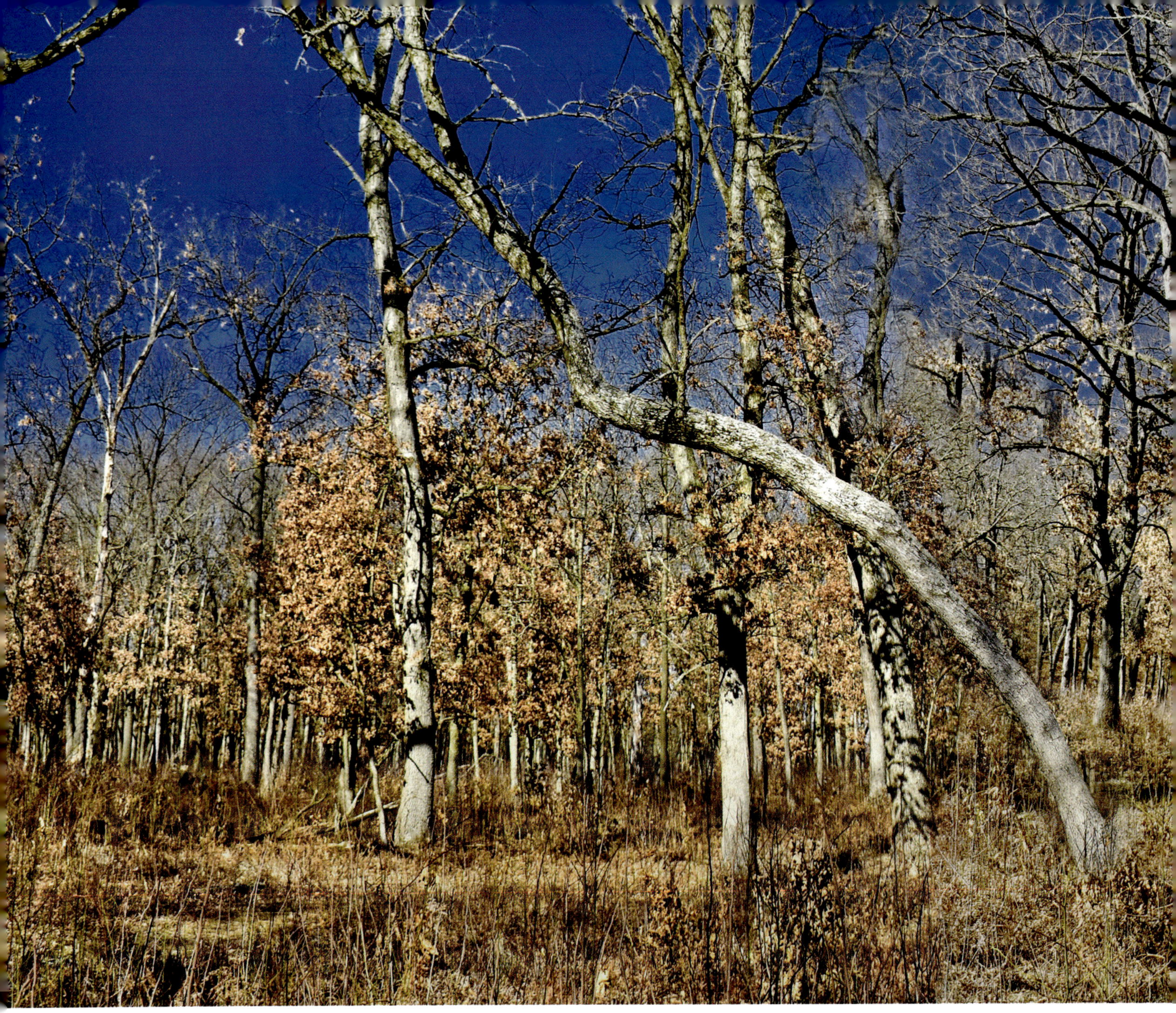

Intriguing Stoutsburg oak savanna, Jasper County

ana landscapes are due to their dedicated staff of professional botanists, foresters, ecologists, and land managers. From black oak savannas in the north to cypress swamps in the south, we can today see grand old trees and rare species.

The Hoosier National Forest has also designated special areas in some of our most rugged topography to protect rare plants and animals.

Nonprofit organizations become very valuable partners of private landholders, and also are nimble and flexible enough to be able to work quickly with corporate entities and governmental agencies. Combinations of expertise on high-priority projects thus allows for expediency in protecting an area of special quality. They further contribute to education, discussion, policy, advocacy, and protection. Indiana's land trusts are especially important for acquiring land from individuals and families who wish to protect their property from development. Hoot Woods in Owen County is a significant example of a magnificent setting now preserved in perpetuity by

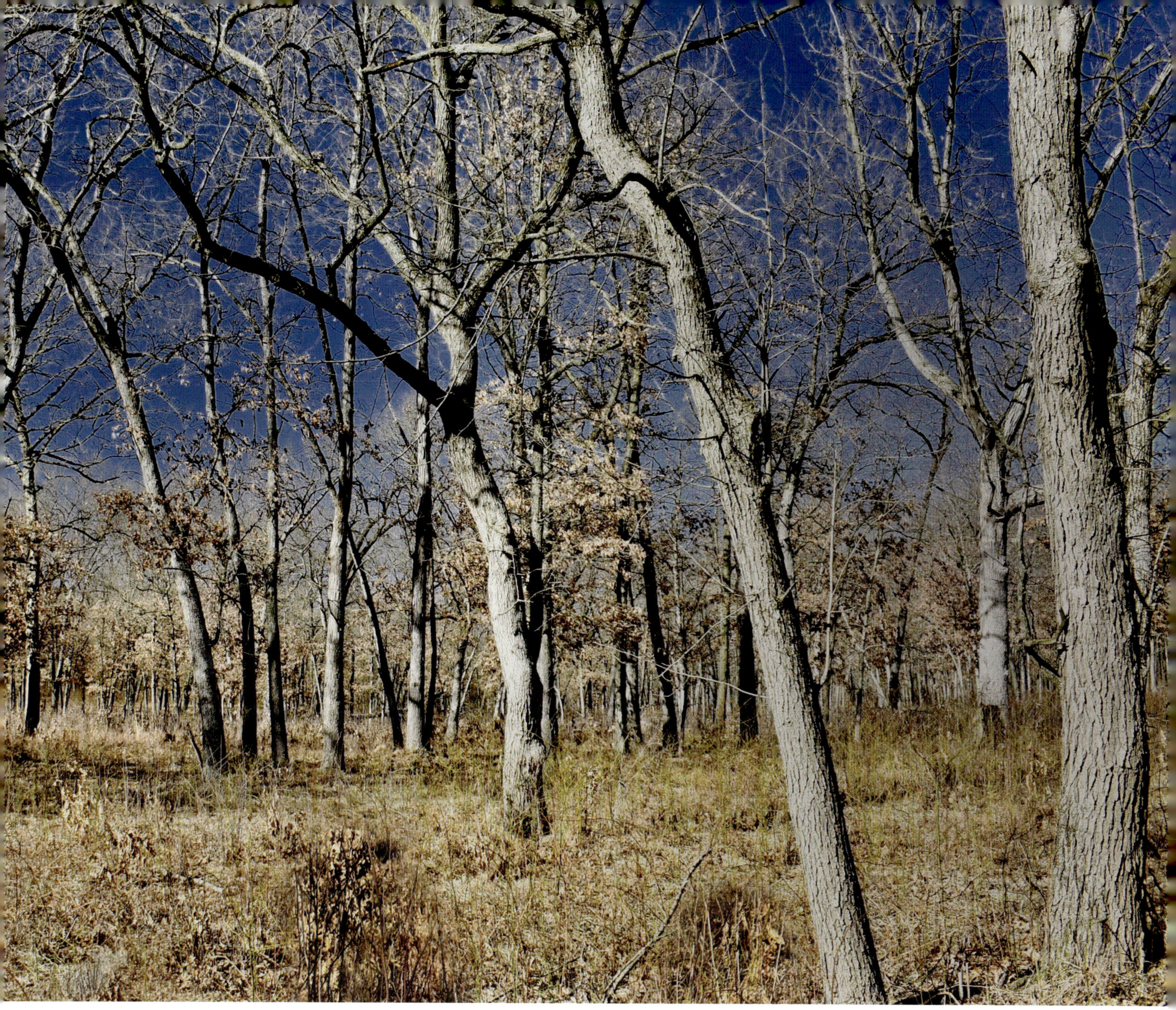

Sycamore Land Trust. Another major organization is the Nature Conservancy, active for sixty-three years in Indiana and dedicated to preserving the very best natural areas of the state. Pine Hills Nature Preserve in Montgomery County was their first Indiana Chapter project in 1968 and resulted in its dedication as the first state nature preserve. It is also a National Natural Landmark. Their many ecosystem-focused projects and acquisitions have contributed substantially to saving forest types and endangered species of plants and animals. Other grand areas saved by efforts of the Division of Nature Preserves, the Nature Conservancy, and local groups include the black oak savannas of northern Indiana. These intriguing barrens have much diversity on the sand ridges and swales between. The dry upland community favors scrubby black oaks with white oak, and even cherry. In low wet areas we also saw aspen and river birch. Intermixed with the widely spaced trees are plants characteristic of that open setting, including an abundance of spring, summer, and fall wildflowers and grasses.

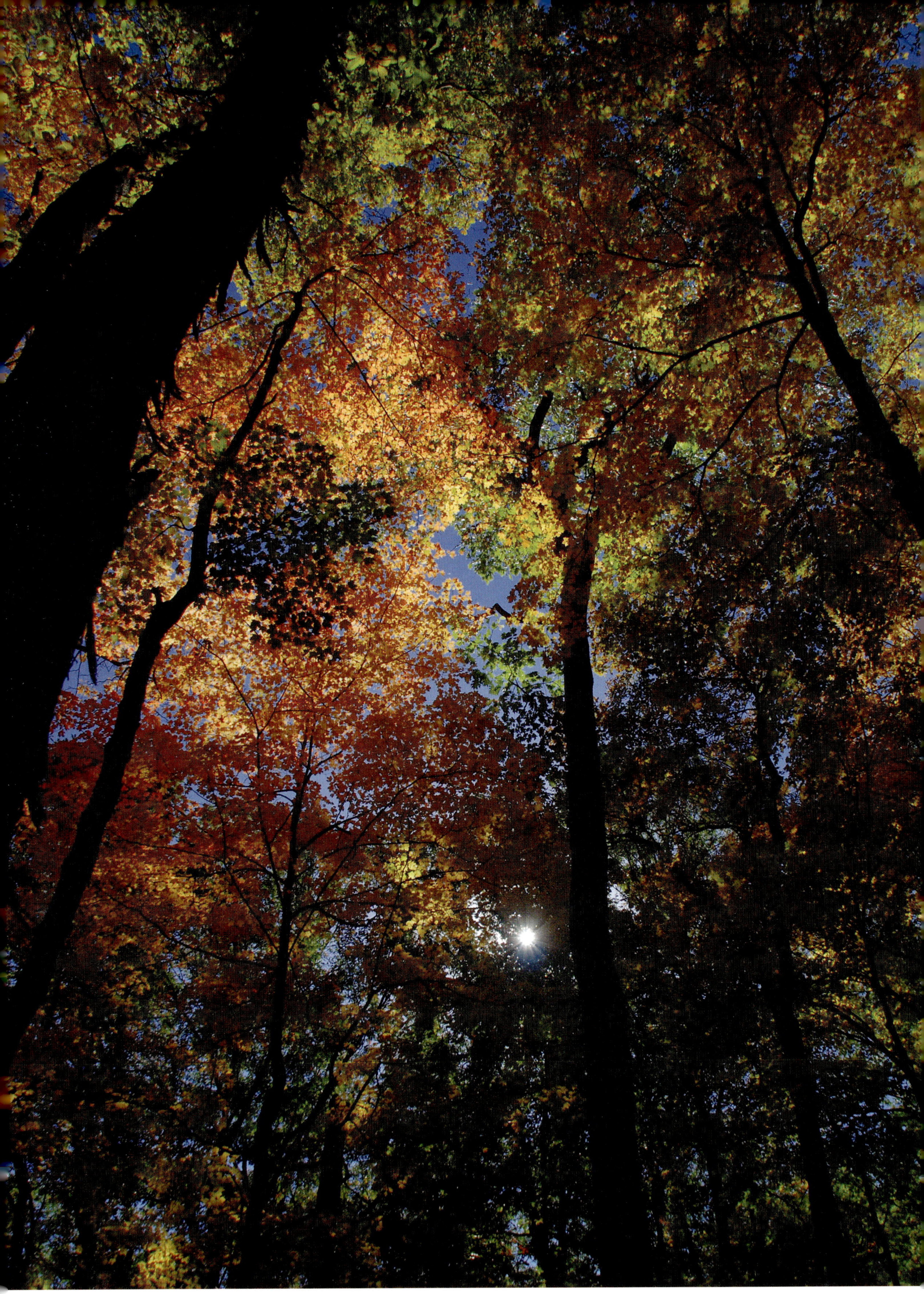

CHAPTER ELEVEN

Inspirations and Reflections

It was extraordinarily special to be immersed in deeply inspiring trees, old-growth forests, wetlands, savannas, swamps, and historic sites. Here are remnants of our past and promises of what grows for the future. Great folks were met, friendships formed, and optimism confirmed. There are programs to encourage landowners to plan for wise management of their properties and also consider passage to the next generation. State and federal agencies are committed to assuring forest health and diversity, while yet fulfilling multiple uses. The acreage of forestland in the state is actually increasing, a positive trend. We find a thriving wood products industry, which is so important to our economy. From the professional logger in the field to the highly skilled sawyer on computer-operated carriages in ultra-modern mills, to the small shop where a craftsman delicately fits the dovetail joinery from his jig into a walnut drawer, many are engaged in using Indiana's acclaimed hardwoods. The old cherry cut 150 years ago still lives today in the handcrafted three-corner cupboard in our family room.

Left page: The canopy of our magnificent trees

CLOSURE

And then there is silence in the old woods. The aged monstrous trees, the fallen mossy logs finding their way back into the lush deep soil, redheaded woodpeckers working their shift, squirrels cutting hickory nuts, and salamanders scurrying underneath the log on which you are sitting. Only the wind speaks through the far-up leafy canopy. Here is the place we meditate, that which has existed far before this day, but yet the place so dearly needed today. The Indiana of the past can still be with us and the Indiana of the future is yet to come. Our glorious trees, the silent workers. May we care for them as they have served us so long.

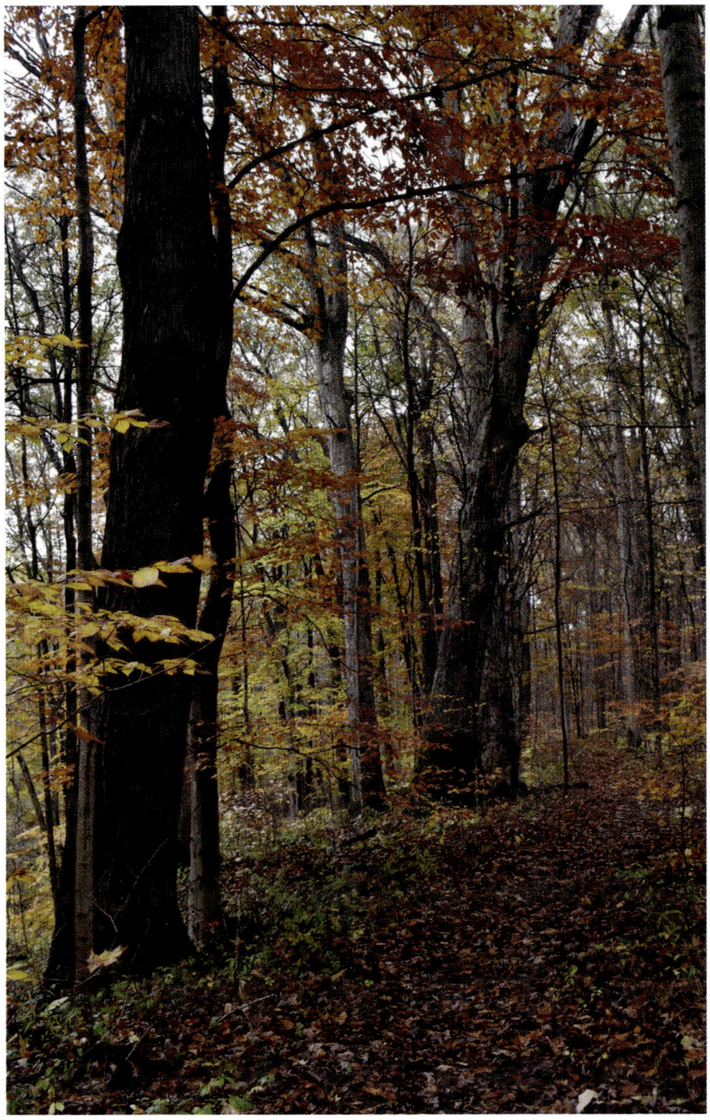

Notes

CHAPTER ONE

1. Pivot Point/Initial Point, Paoli, IN, 1805. U.S. Historic Survey Stones and Monuments, Waymarking.com, accessed 4/1/20, https://www.waymarking.com/waymarks/WMMCZF_Piviot_Point_Initial_Point_Paoli_IN_1805
2. Charles Pinckney, "Reminiscences of a Journey to Indianapolis in the Year 1836," Bowen-Merrill, 1883, accessed 4/3/20, http://ingenweb.org/ingibson/Cemeteries_wPhotos/Wabash%20Twp/Foote/Foote,%20Ziba%20reference%20materials.htm
3. J. H. Keith, "Presettlement Barrens of Harrison and Washington Counties, Indiana," *Proceedings of the Seventh North American Prairie Conference* (Springfield, MO: Southwest Missouri State University, 1980), 17–25.

CHAPTER FOUR

1. Donald Culross Peattie, *A Natural History of Trees of Eastern and Central North America* (Boston: Houghton-Mifflin, 1966), 184.
2. Portal.ct.gov/CAES/Fact-Sheets/Plant-Pathology. accessed 2/5/20.
3. Emerald Ash Borer Information Network, accessed 6.17.20, http://www.emeraldashborer.info.
4. USDA, *Betula alleghaniensis*, accessed 11/7/20, https://www.srs.fs.usda.gov/pubs/misc/ag_654/volume_2/betula/alleghaniensis%20.htm
5. Wikipedia, *Juglans Nigra*, accessed 8/20/20, https://en.wikipedia.org/wiki/Juglans_nigra
6. Purdue University, Forestry and Natural Resources, *Invasive Species Walnut Twig Beetle Detected in Indiana.* Posted April 2015, accessed 7/20/20, https://www.purdue.edu/fnr/extension/invasive-species-walnut-twig-beetle-detected-in-indiana
7. Walter F. Beineke, Purdue University Extension, Forestry and Natural Resources, *Black Walnut Plantation Management,* FNR-119, accessed 7/8/20, https://www.extension.purdue.edu/extmedia/FNR/FNR-119.html
8. https://en.wikipedia.org/wiki/Catalpa
9. *Garden and Forest,* vol. 9, no. 436, 18960701 (New York:

Garden and Forest Pub. Co., 1888–1897).
10. Personal communication email, 4/17/2020.
11. University of Georgia Extension—Topic Areas/Fruit, Vegetable & Ornamentals/Production/Pecans, accessed 10/23/20, https://extension.uga.edu/topic-areas/fruit-vegetable-ornamentals-production/pecans.html
12. Sally S. Weeks, Harmon P. Weeks, and George Parker, *Native Trees of the Midwest: Identification, Wildlife Values, & Landscaping Use* (West Lafayette: Purdue University Press, 2005).
13. University of Kentucky, College of Agriculture, Food, and Environment, "Kentucky Coffeetree," accessed 4//23/20, https://www.uky.edu/hort/Kentucky-Coffeetree
14. Wikipedia, "Kentucky Coffeetree," accessed 4/23/20, https://en.wikipedia.org/wiki/Kentucky_coffeetree
15. USDA, Plants Database, Spotlight/plant guide, accessed 4/23/20, https://plants.usda.gov/plantguide/pdf/cs_gydi.pdf
16. U.S. Dept. of Agriculture, Northern Research Station, Central Hardwoods Unit, "Oak Decline," accessed 1/23/20, https://www.nrs.fs.fwd.us/4154/focus/decline
17. Wikipedia, "Sassafras," accessed 12/20/20, https://en.wikipedia.org/wiki/Sassafras
18. Visit Greene County, Indiana, "Largest Sycamore Tree," accessed 10/30/20, https://visitgc.com/where-to-go/nature/largest-sycamore-tree/#.X5y5s1NKhcB
19. Bugwood Wiki, "Case Bearing Leaf Beetle," accessed 3/14/20, https://wiki.bugwood.org/Archive:Sycamore/Neochlamisus_platani

CHAPTER FIVE

1. Dean Brown, "Slowest Growing Tree," Arborist, 2006, accessed 7/21/2020, https://www.arboristsite.com/community/threads/slowest-growing-tree.35206
2. Paul Carmony, accessed 10/23/20, https://oakheritageconservancy.org/2015/09/09/tribbetts-woods
3. Indiana Department of Natural Resources, Division of Nature Preserves, "Meltzer Woods," https://www.in.gov/dnr/naturepreserve/files/np-meltzer_nature_preserve.pdf
4. Hoosier National Forest, "About the Forest—Pioneer Mothers Memorial Forest," https://www.fs.usda.gov/detailfull/hoosier/about-forest/?cid=fsbdev3_017499

CHAPTER EIGHT

1. Indiana State Dept. of Agriculture, "Indiana Hardwood Strategy," 2019 brochure.
2. Ibid.
3. Purdue University, College of Agriculture, "Fruit and Vegetable Connection," accessed 4/24/20, https://ag.purdue.edu/hla/fruitveg/Pages/apples.aspx

Bibliography

Allison, Harold. *Monarchs of the Forest: A Story of the Virgin Timber of Indiana*. Privately published, 1976.

Badger, Kemuel, and Marion T. Jackson. "A Study of the Natural History of Naturally Occurring Populations of Magnolia tripetala L. in Indiana." *Proceedings of the Indiana Academy of Science* 93 (1984): 309–312.

Badger, K. S., D. G. Ruch, A. Schoultz, J. E. Taylor, and B. E. Jones. "Structure and Composition of Ginn Woods, an Old-Growth Forest in East-Central Indiana." *Proceedings of the Indiana Academy of Science* 107 (1998): 1–15.

Bramble W. C., and H. H. Michaud. "Giants of the Original Forest of the Lower Wabash Valley." *Natural Resource Information for Indiana Forest Landowners, No. 3*. Purdue University, March 1971.

Bratkovich, Steven, Joey Gallion, Earl Leatherberry, William Hoover, William Reading, and Glenn Durham. *Forests of Indiana: Their Economic Importance*. U.S. Dept. of Agriculture, Forest Service. Technical Bulletin TP-02-04, 2004.

Brockman, C. Frank. *Trees of North America: A Guide to Field Identification.* Racine, WI: Western, 1968.

Butler, A. W. "Indiana: A Century of Changes in the Aspects of Nature." *Proceedings of the Indiana Academy of Science* 5 (1895): 31–42.

Crankshaw, W. B. "The Edaphology of Tree Species in Presettlement Indiana South of the Late Wisconsin Glacial Border." PhD dissertation, Purdue University, 1964.

Deam, Charles C., and Thomas F. Shaw. *Trees of Indiana*. 3rd ed. Indianapolis: Indiana Dept. of Conservation, 1953.

Den Uyl, Daniel. "Forests of the Lower Wabash Bottomlands During the Period 1870–1890." *Proceedings of the Indiana Academy of Science* 67 (1958): 244–248.

Den Uyl, Daniel. "Indiana's Old Growth Forests." *Proceedings of the Indiana Academy of Science* 63 (1953): 73–79.

Farlee, Lenny, et al. *Conservation and Management of Butternut Trees*. Purdue University Extension, FNR-421, n.d.

Grimm, William Carey. *The Book of Trees for Positive Identification.* New York: Hawthorn Books, 1962.

Hill, Steven R. *Conservation Assessment for Yellowwood*. Champaign, Illinois Division of Biodiversity and Ecological Entomology Biotic Surveys and Monitoring Section:

Prepared for the USDA Forest Service, Eastern Region (Region 9), Shawnee and Hoosier National Forests INHS Technical Report (28), 2007.

Hogue, Rolla M. "Life in Indiana 1800–1820." *Indiana Magazine of History* 9, no. 2 (June 1913). https://indianamemory.contentdm.oclc.org/digital/collection/p16066coll16/id/9946

Homoya, Michael A., D. Brian Abrell, James R. Aldrich, and Thomas W. Post. "The Natural Regions of Indiana." *Proc. Ind. Acad. Sci.* 94 (1985): 245–268.

Homoya, Michael. *Wildflowers and Ferns of Indiana Forests.* Bloomington and Indianapolis: Indiana University Press, 2012.

Huffman, Henry H. "A Field Survey of the Yellowwood, Cladrastis lutea, in Brown County, Indiana." *Proceedings of the Indiana Academy of Science* 95 (1986): 433–442.

Indiana Dept. of Natural Resources Division of Forestry. "2005, 2010, 2015 Indiana Big Tree Registers." Indianapolis.

Jackson, Marion T. "Forest Communities and Tree Species of the Lower Wabash River Basin." *Proceedings of the Indiana Academy of Science* 115, no. 2 (2006): 94.

Jackson, Marion T., ed. *The Natural Heritage of Indiana.* Bloomington: Indiana University Press, 1997.

Jackson, Marion T. *101 Trees of Indiana.* Bloomington: Indiana University Press, 2004.

Keith, J. H. "Presettlement Barrens of Harrison and Washington Counties, Indiana." *Proceedings of the Seventh North American Prairie Conference. Springfield, Missouri*, 17–25. Southwest Missouri State University, 1980.

Lindsey, Alton A., Damian V. Schmelz, and Stanley A. Nichols. *Natural Areas of Indiana and Their Preservation.* West Lafayette, IN: Purdue University, 1969.

Little, Elbert L., Jr. *Checklist of United States Trees (Native and Naturalized).* Agriculture Handbook 541. Forest Service. United States Dept. of Agriculture, 1979.

Louv, Richard. *Last Child in the Woods.* Chapel Hill, NC: Algonquin Books, 2005.

McPherson, Alan. *Nature Walks in Southern Indiana.* Indianapolis: Hoosier Chapter of the Sierra Club, 1991.

The Nature Conservancy. "Guide to Indiana Preserves." Bloomington: Indiana University Press, 2006.

Peattie, Donald Culross. *A Natural History of Trees of Eastern and Central North America.* Boston: Houghton Mifflin, 1966.

Purdue University. "Indiana's Future Forests: A Report from the Indiana Climate Change Impacts Assessment," 2018.

Rector, William. "1805 Survey of the Old Vincennes Trace." Indianapolis: Indiana State Archives. Unpublished manuscript.

Ridgway, R. "Notes on the Vegetation of the Lower Wabash Valley." *American Naturalist* 6 (1872): 658–665.

Ridgway, R. "Notes on the Native Trees of the Lower Wabash and White River Valleys in Illinois and Indiana." *Proceedings of the National Museum* 4 (1882): 49–88.

Rutkow, Eric. *American Canopy.* New York: Scribner, 2012.

Seiber, Ellen, and Cheryl Munson. *Looking at History: Indiana's National Forest Region, 1600 to 1950.* United States Dept. of Agriculture, Forest Service. U.S. Government Printing Office, Pub. 645-401, 1992.

Spetich, Martin A., George R. Parker, and Eric J Gustafson. "Spatial and Temporal Relationships of Old-Growth and Secondary Forests in Indiana, USA." *Natural Areas Journal* 17, no. 2 (1997).

Tekiela, Stan. *Trees of Indiana Field Guide.* Cambridge, MN: Adventure Publications, 2006.

Trees, Inc. "Champion Big Tree Registry, Vigo County, Indiana." Terre Haute, 2017.

Weeks, Sally S. *Indiana's Native Magnolias.* Purdue University Dept. of Forestry and Natural Resources, "Know Your Trees Series," FNR-238. West Lafayette, IN: 2015.

Weeks, Sally S., Harmon P. Weeks, Jr., and George R. Parker. *Native Trees of the Midwest, Identification, Wildlife Values, and Landscaping Use.* West Lafayette, IN: Purdue University Press, 2005.

Wilson, George R. "Early Indiana Trails and Surveys." Indianapolis: Indiana Historical Society Press, 1919.

Wilson, George R. *History of Dubois County: Its Primitive Days to 1910.* Jasper, IN: privately published, 1910.

Wohlleben, Peter. *The Hidden Life of Trees.* London: William Collins Books, 2017.

Index

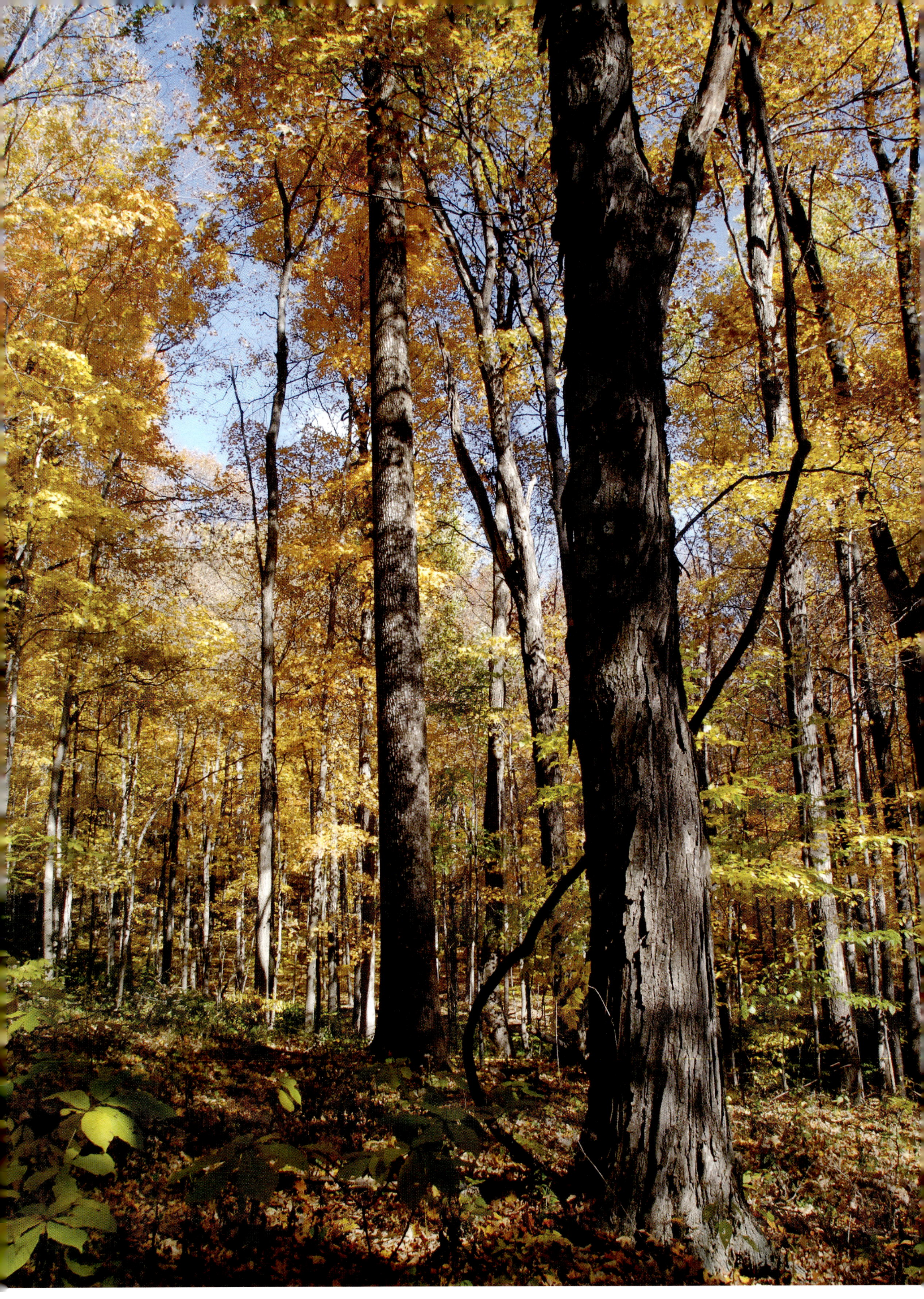

About the Author

Carroll D. Ritter is a retired science teacher with a lifelong interest in trees and wildflowers. His father took him to the woods when he was a child and those indelible memories fostered a deep appreciation for the beauty and splendor of nature. He attended Purdue University, received his master's degree from Indiana University, and did advanced coursework in field geology from Western Washington University. As a National Science Foundation Scholarship recipient, he designed programs for and instructed gifted and talented students in Bellingham, Washington. In Indiana, he provided quality teaching to high school students for 33 years. After retirement, he assisted Sycamore Land Trust, developing their first and very successful environmental education program working with children of all ages.

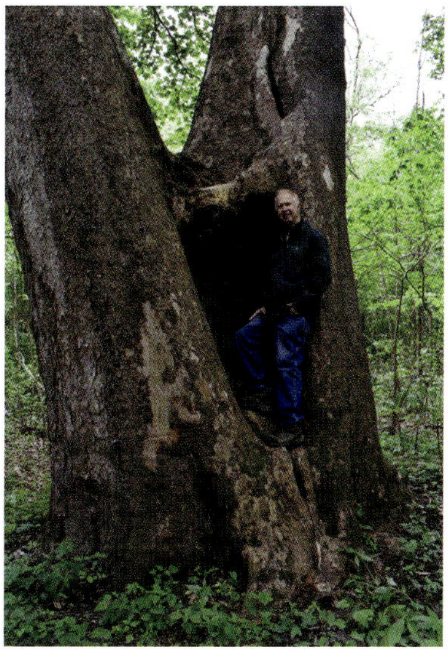

Past experiences also include environmental assessment and government committee roles. An avid mountain hiker, backpacker, and photographer, he has logged over 2,000 miles on trails in the United States and Canada. Taking his family to many adventures in the Rockies, Cascades, and Canada created a love for those great areas. Whether up to high alpine country with glacial lakes and cirques, to the extraordinary Banff and Jasper areas, or to marvelous old-growth forests in British Columbia, memories were glorious. Both his sons now live in the Pacific Northwest.

He has visited many of Indiana's nature preserves and has been keenly interested in the largest trees of our great state. This has resulted in nominations of seven state champion trees over the years including two new ones for the 2020 Indiana Big Trees Register. He practices forest conservation on his own land and still loves and admires his own trees.

Left page: Glorious fall in Porter Woods, Monroe County